Research and Development in
Intelligent Systems XXIII

Max Bramer, Frans Coenen and
Andrew Tuson (Eds)

Research and Development in Intelligent Systems XXIII

Proceedings of AI-2006, the Twenty-sixth SGAI International Conference on Innovative Techniques and Applications of Artificial Intelligence

 Springer

Professor Max Bramer, BSc, PhD, CEng, FBCS, FIEE, FRSA
Faculty of Technology, University of Portsmouth, Portsmouth, UK

Dr Frans Coenen, PhD
Department of Computer Science, University of Liverpool, Liverpool, UK

Dr Andrew Tuson, MA, MSc, PhD, MBCS
Department of Computing, City University, London

British Library Cataloguing in Publication Data
A catalogue record for this book is available from the British Library

ISBN-10: 1-84628-662-X   Printed on acid-free paper
ISBN-13: 978-1-84628-662-9

© Springer-Verlag London Limited 2007

Printed in the United Kingdom

9 8 7 6 5 4 3 2 1

Springer Science+Business Media
springer.com

TECHNICAL PROGRAMME CHAIR'S INTRODUCTION

M.A.BRAMER
University of Portsmouth, UK

This volume comprises the refereed technical papers presented at AI-2006, the Twenty-sixth SGAI International Conference on Innovative Techniques and Applications of Artificial Intelligence, held in Cambridge in December 2006. The conference was organised by SGAI, the British Computer Society Specialist Group on Artificial Intelligence.

The papers in this volume present new and innovative developments in the field, divided into sections on AI Techniques, Knowledge Discovery in Data, Argumentation, Dialogue Games and Optimisation, Knowledge Representation and Management, Semantic Web, and Model Based Systems and Simulation. For the first time the volume also includes the text of short papers presented as posters at the conference.

This year's prize for the best refereed technical paper was won by a paper entitled Combining Task Execution with Background Knowledge for the Verification of Medical Guidelines' written by a team comprising Arjen Hommersom, Perry Groot and Peter Lucas (University of Nijmegen, The Netherlands) and Michael Balser and Jonathan Schmitt (University of Augsburg, Germany). SGAI gratefully acknowledges the long-term sponsorship of Hewlett-Packard Laboratories (Bristol) for this prize, which goes back to the 1980s.

This is the twenty-third volume in the *Research and Development* series. The Application Stream papers are published as a companion volume under the title *Applications and Innovations in Intelligent Systems XIV*.

On behalf of the conference organising committee I should like to thank all those who contributed to the organisation of this year's technical programme, in particular the programme committee members, the executive programme committee and our administrator Mark Firman.

Max Bramer
Technical Programme Chair, AI-2006

ACKNOWLEDGEMENTS

AI-2006 CONFERENCE COMMITTEE

Dr. Andrew Tuson, City University	(Conference Chair)
Dr. Tony Allen, Nottingham Trent University	(Past Conference Chair and Deputy Application Program Chair)
Dr. Alun Preece, University of Aberdeen	(Deputy Conference Chair, Electronic Services)
Dr Frans Coenen, University of Liverpool	(Deputy Conference Chair, Local Arrangements and Deputy Technical Programme Chair)
Prof. Adrian Hopgood, Nottingham Trent University	(Workshop Organiser)
Rosemary Gilligan, University of Hertfordshire	(Treasurer)
Dr Nirmalie Wiratunga, The Robert Gordon University, Aberdeen	(Poster Session Organiser)
Richard Ellis, Stratum Management Ltd	(Application Programme Chair)
Professor Max Bramer, University of Portsmouth	(Technical Programme Chair)
Alice Kerly, University of Birmingham	(Research Student Liaison)
Dr. Miltos Petridis, University of Greenwich	(UK CBR Organiser)
Mark Firman, City University	(Conference Administrator)

TECHNICAL EXECUTIVE PROGRAMME COMMITTEE

Prof. Max Bramer, University of Portsmouth (Chair)
Dr. Frans Coenen, University of Liverpool (Vice-Chair)
Mr. John Kingston, University of Edinburgh
Dr. Peter Lucas, University of Nijmegen, The Netherlands
Dr. Alun Preece, University of Aberdeen
Dr. Nirmalie Wiratunga, The Robert Gordon University, Aberdeen

TECHNICAL PROGRAMME COMMITTEE

Alfonsas Misevicius (Kaunas University of Technology)

Emma-Claire Mullally (National University of Ireland)

David Muse (University of Sunderland)

Lars Nolle (Nottingham Trent University)

Tomas Eric Nordlander (University College Cork)

Dan O'Leary (University of Southern California)

Barry O'Sullivan (University College Cork)

Alun Preece (University of Aberdeen)

Juan Jose Rodriguez (University of Burgos)

Maria Dolores Rodriguez-Moreno (Universidad de Alcala)

Miguel A. Salido (Universidad Politécnica de Valencia)

Rainer Schmidt (University of Rostock, Germany)

Evgueni Smirnov (Maastricht University, The Netherlands)

Fernando Saenz Perez (Universidad Complutense de Madrid)

Fadi Thabtah (University of Huddersfield)

Jon Timmis (University of York)

Gianluca Torta (Università di Torino)

Andrew Tuson (City University)

M.R.C. van Dongen (University College Cork)

Marcel van Gerven (Radboud University, The Netherlands)

Graham Winstanley (University of Brighton)

Nirmalie Wiratunga (Robert Gordon University)

Fei Ling Woon (University of Greenwich

CONTENTS

SESSION 2b: ARGUMENTATION, DIALOGUE GAMES AND OPTIMISATION

SESSION 3: KNOWLEDGE REPRESENTATION AND MANAGEMENT

XIV

Note: × indicates SGAI recognition award

BEST TECHNICAL PAPER

Combining Task Execution and Background Knowledge for the Verification of Medical Guidelines

Arjen Hommersom, Perry Groot, and Peter Lucas

Institute for Computing and Information Sciences, Radboud University
Nijmegen, the Netherlands

Michael Balser and Jonathan Schmitt

Institut für Informatik, Universität Augsburg

Augsburg, Germany

Abstract

The use of a medical guideline can be seen as the execution of computational tasks, sequentially or in parallel, in the face of patient data. It has been shown that many of such guidelines can be represented as a 'network of tasks', i.e., as a number of steps that have a specific function or goal. To investigate the quality of such guidelines we propose a formalization of criteria for good practice medicine a guideline should comply to. We use this theory in conjunction with medical background knowledge to verify the quality of a guideline dealing with diabetes mellitus type 2 using the interactive theorem prover KIV. Verification using task execution and background knowledge is a novel approach to quality checking of medical guidelines.

1 Introduction

Computer-based decision support in health-care is a field with a long standing tradition, dealing with complex problems in medicine, such as diagnosing disease and prescribing treatment. The trend of the last decades has been to base clinical decision making more and more on sound scientific evidence, i.e., *evidence-based medicine* [15]. In practice this has led medical specialists to develop evidence-based medical guidelines, i.e., structured documents providing detailed steps to be taken by health-care professionals in managing the disease in a patient, for promoting standards of medical care.

Researchers in Artificial Intelligence have picked up on these developments and are working on providing computer-based support for guidelines by designing computer-oriented languages and developing tools for their deployment. In [4, 11] the emergence of a new paradigm is acknowledged for modelling complex clinical processes as a 'network of tasks', which model tasks as a number of steps that have a specific function or goal. Examples of languages that support task modelling are PRO*forma* [4] and Asbru [14], which have been evolving since the 1990s. Medical guidelines are considered to be good real-world examples of highly structured documents amenable to formalisation.

3

However, guidelines should not be considered *static* objects as new scientific knowledge becomes known on a continuous basis. Newly obtained evidence may result in a deterioration of guideline quality, because, for example, new patient management options invalidate the steps recommended by the guideline. Our aim, therefore, *is to provide support for verifying quality criteria of medical guidelines in light of scientific evidence.*

We approach this problem by applying formal methods to quality check medical guidelines. Here, we are mainly concerned with the meta-level approach [7], i.e., verifying general principles of good practice medicine as for example advocated by the General Medical Council [6]. For example, a guideline of good quality should preclude the prescription of redundant drugs, or advise against the prescription of treatment that is less effective than some alternative. For the verification of such quality criteria, the medical knowledge the guideline is based on, i.e., knowledge based on available evidence, is required. We will refer to this knowledge as *background knowledge.*

The structure of this paper is as follows. First, we model the background knowledge concerning the treatment of diabetes mellitus type 2. Then, the advises, given by the guideline as formalised as a 'network of tasks' using the language Asbru, are modelled. Finally, meta-level properties for this model are formalised and verified in KIV, an interactive theorem prover. To the best of our knowledge, verification of a fully formalised guideline, as a network of tasks, using medical background knowledge has not been done before.

2 Medical Guidelines

Clinical practice guidelines are systematically developed statements to assist practitioners and patients decisions about appropriate health care in specific clinical circumstances. A fragment of a guideline is shown in Figure 1, which is part of the guideline for general Dutch practitioners about the treatment of diabetes mellitus type 2 [13], and is used as a running example in this paper. The guideline contains recommendations for the clinical management in daily practice. Each of these recommendations is well-founded in terms of scientific evidence obtained from the literature, in conjunction with other considerations such as safety, availability, or cost effectiveness.

The diabetes mellitus type 2 guideline provides practitioners with a clear structure of recommended interventions to be used for the control of the glucose level. This kind of information is typically found in medical guidelines in the sense that medical knowledge is combined with information about order and time of treatment (e.g., a sulfonylurea drug at step 2), and about patients and their environment (e.g., quetelet index lower than or equal to 27).

Although diabetes mellitus type 2 is a complicated disease, the guideline fragment shown in Figure 1 is not. This indicates that much knowledge concerning diabetes mellitus type 2 is missing from the guideline and that additional knowledge is needed for verifying whether the guideline fulfils some property. The ideas that we use here for verifying quality requirements for

- Step 1: diet.

- Step 2: if quetelet index (QI) ≤ 27, prescribe a sulfonylurea (SU) drug; otherwise, prescribe a biguanide (BG) drug.

- Step 3: combine a sulfonylurea (SU) and biguanide (BG) drug (replace one of these by a α-glucosidase inhibitor if side-effects occur).

- Step 4: one of the following:
    • oral antidiabetic and insulin
    • only insulin

Figure 1: Guideline fragment on diabetes mellitus type 2 management. If one of the steps k is ineffective, the management moves to step $k + 1$.

medical guidelines are inspired by [7], where a distinction was made between the different types of knowledge that are involved in defining quality requirements. We assume that there are at least three types of knowledge involved in detecting the violation of good practice medicine:

1. Knowledge concerning the (patho)physiological mechanisms underlying the disease, and the way treatment influences these mechanisms (*background knowledge*).

2. Knowledge concerning the recommended treatment in each stage of the plan and how the execution of this plan is affected by the state of the patient (*order information from the guideline*).

3. Knowledge concerning good practice in treatment selection (*quality requirements*).

In the following sections we describe these three types of knowledge in more detail, give a formalisation of all three parts, and verify the requirements.

3 Formalisation of Medical Guidelines

It has been shown previously that the step-wise, possibly iterative, execution of a guideline can be described precisely by means of temporal logic [9]. In this paper we will use the variant of this logic supported by KIV [1], which is based on linear temporal logic. The language used is first-order logic, augmented with the usual modal operators □ and ◇. With □φ being true if φ is true in the current state and all future states, and ◇φ if φ holds in the current state or in some state in the future. We also use a special operator **last** which is true exactly if there does not exist a future point in time. Additional modal operators are supported by KIV, but they are not used in this article. Algebraic specifications are used in KIV to model the datatypes.

3.1 Background knowledge

In diabetes mellitus type 2 various metabolic control mechanisms are deranged and many different organ systems may be affected. Glucose level control, however, is the most important mechanism. At some stage in the natural history of diabetes mellitus type 2, the level of glucose in the blood is too high (hyperglycaemia) due to decreased production of insulin by the B cells. Oral anti-diabetics either stimulate the B cells in producing more insulin (sulfonylurea) or inhibit the release of glucose from the liver (biguanide). Effectiveness of these oral diabetics is dependent on the condition of the B cells. Finally, as a causal treatment, insulin can be prescribed. The mechanisms have been formalised in terms of a first-order predicate knowledge:

knowledge : patient × patient

where patient denotes an algebraic specification of all first-order formulas describing the patient state, e.g., *condition(hyperglycaemia)* represents those patients having a condition of hyperglycaemia. The postfix function [·] on patients selects the value for a certain variable from the state, e.g., *Patient['condition']* = *hyperglycaemia* if and only if *condition(hyperglycaemia)* holds for this patient. The predicate knowledge represents the state transitions that may occur between patient states, i.e., the first argument (denoted by pre below) represents the current patient state and the second argument (denoted by post below) represents the next patient state.

The predicate knowledge has been axiomatised with knowledge concerning the mechanism described above. The axiomatisation is a direct translation of an earlier formalisation in temporal logic [7] of which two examples are:

BDM2-1:
knowledge(pre, post) →
   (insulin ∈ pre['treatment'] →
   post['uptake(liver,glucose)'] = up ∧
   post['uptake(peripheral-tissue,glucose)'] = up)

BDM2-8:
knowledge(pre, post) →
   (post['uptake(liver,glucose)'] = up ∧
   post['uptake(peripheral-tissue,glucose)'] = up) ∧
   pre['capacity(B-cells,insulin)'] = exhausted ∧
   pre['condition'] = hyperglycaemia
   → post['condition'] = normoglycaemia)

The axiom BDM2-1 denotes the physiological effects of insulin treatment, i.e., administering insulin results in an increased uptake of glucose by the liver and peripheral tissues. Axiom BDM2-8 phrases under what conditions you may expect the patient to get cured, i.e., when the patient suffers from hyperglycaemia and insulin production of his B cells are exhausted, an increased uptake of glucose by the liver and peripheral tissues results in the patient condition changing to normoglycaemia.

3.2   Medical guidelines in Asbru

Much research has already been devoted to the development of representation languages for medical guidelines. Most of them consider guidelines as a composition of actions, controlled by conditions [10]. However, most of them are not formal enough for the purpose of our research as they often incorporate free-text elements which do not have a clear semantics. Exceptions to this are PRO*forma* [4] and Asbru [14]. The latter has been chosen in our research.

In Asbru, plans are hierarchically organised in which a plan refers to a number of sub-plans. The overall structure of the Asbru model of our running example (Figure 1), is shown in Figure 2. The top level plan Treatments_and_Control sequentially executes the four sub-plans Diet, SU_or_BG, SU_and_BG, and Insulin_Treatments, which correspond to the four steps of the guideline fragment in Figure 1. The sub-plan Insulin_Treatments is further refined by two sub-plans Insulin_and_Antidiabetics and Insulin, which can be executed in any order.

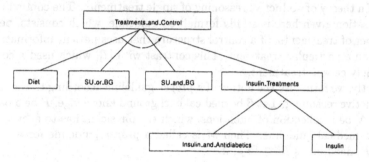

Figure 2: Asbru plan hierarchy of the diabetes mellitus type 2 guideline

The Asbru specifications of two plans in the hierarchy, namely SU_or_BG and Insulin_Treatments are defined as follows:

plan SU_or_BG
  effects
    $(QI \leq 27 \rightarrow SU \in Drugs) \wedge$
    $(QI > 27 \rightarrow BG \in Drugs)$
  abort condition
    condition = hyperglycaemia **confirmation required**
  complete condition
    condition = hypoglycaemia $\vee$
    condition = normoglycaemia

plan Insulin_Treatments
  body anyorder wait for one
    Insulin_and_Antidiabetics
    Insulin

In the case of SU_or_BG there is a relationship between the quetelet index

(QI) and the drug administered. If the quetelet index is less or equal than 27 then SU is administered, else BG is administered. The plan SU_or_BG corresponds to step 2 in the guideline fragment of Figure 1, which completes if the patient condition improves, i.e., the patient no longer has hyperglycaemia. This is represented by the **complete condition**. The plan SU_or_BG aborts when the condition of the patient does not improve, which is represented by the **abort condition**. It requires a manual confirmation to ensure that some time passes for the drugs to have an impact on the patient condition.

The plan Insulin_Treatments consists of two sub-plans, which correspond to the two options of step 4 in the guideline fragment of Figure 1, i.e., either insulin is administered or insulin and antidiabetics are administered.

3.3 Quality requirements

Here, we give a formalisation of good practice medicine of medical guidelines. This extends previous work [7], which formalised good practice medicine on the basis of a theory of abductive reasoning of single treatments. The context of the formalisation given here is a fully formalised guideline, which consists, besides a number of treatments, of a control structure that uses patient information to decide on a particular treatment. This contrast with [7], which used a context of a singly chosen treatment.

Firstly, we formalise the notion of a *proper* guideline according to the theory of abductive reasoning. Let B be medical background knowledge, P be a patient group, N be a collection of intentions, which the physician has to achieve, and M be a medical guideline. Then M is called a *proper* guideline for a patient group P, denoted as $M \in Pr_P$, if:

(M1) $B \cup M \cup P \not\models \bot$ (the guideline does not have contradictory effects), and

(M2) $B \cup M \cup P \models \Diamond N$ (the guideline eventually handles all the patient problems intended to be managed)

Secondly, we formalise good practice medicine of guidelines. Let $\preceq_\varphi$ be a reflexive and transitive order denoting a preference relation with $M \preceq_\varphi M'$ meaning that M' is *at least as preferred* to M given criterion φ. With $\prec_\varphi$ we denote the order such that $M \prec_\varphi M'$ if and only if $M \preceq_\varphi M'$ and $M' \not\preceq_\varphi M$. When both $M \preceq_\varphi M'$ and $M' \preceq_\varphi M$ hold or when M and M' are incomparable w.r.t. $\preceq_\varphi$ we say that M and M' are *indifferent*, which is denoted as $M \sim M'$. If in addition to (M1) and (M2) condition (M3) holds, with

(M3) $O_\varphi(M)$ holds, where O_φ is a meta-predicate standing for an optimality criterion or combination of optimality criteria φ defined as: $O_\varphi(M) \equiv \forall M' \in Pr_P : \neg(M \prec_\varphi M')$,

then the guideline is said to be *in accordance with good practice medicine* w.r.t. criterion φ and patient group P, which is denoted as $\mathsf{Good}_\varphi(M, P)$.

A typical example for O_φ is consistency of the recommended treatment order w.r.t. a preference relation $\preceq_\psi$ *over treatments*, i.e., $O_\varphi(M)$ holds if the guideline M recommends treatment T before treatment T' when $T' \prec_\psi T$ holds. For example, in diabetes mellitus type 2, a preference relation over treatments would be to minimise (1) the number of insulin injections, and (2) the number of drugs involved. This results, among others, in the following preferences: sulfonylurea drug $\sim$ biguanide drug, and insulin $\preceq_\psi$ insulin and antidiabetic $\preceq_\psi$ sulfonylurea and biguanide drug $\preceq_\psi$ sulfonylurea or biguanide drug $\preceq_\psi$ diet. A guideline M would then be in accordance with good practice medicine if it is consistent with this preference order $\preceq_\psi$, e.g., if M first recommends diet before a sulfonylurea or biguanide drug.

4   Verification using KIV

The formal verification was done with the interactive verification tool KIV [1]. A speciality of KIV is the use of primed and double-primed variables: a primed variable V' represents the value of this variable after a system transition, the double-primed variable V'' is interpreted as the value after an environment transition, where the environment transition models the communication of the system with its environment. System and environment transitions alternate, as shown in Figure 3, with V'' being equal to V in the successive state.

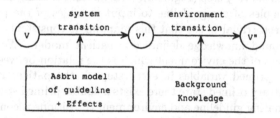

Figure 3: The relation between unprimed and primed variables as two transitions: the system transition (including the Asbru model and its effects) and the environment transition (including the background knowledge)

With the help of KIV, we have verified that the diabetes guideline is proper, i.e., that the guideline satisfies conditions (M1) and (M2), which is discussed in Subsections 4.1 and 4.2. Furthermore, with KIV we have verified various meta-level quality requirements of the diabetes mellitus type 2 guideline. Each meta-level quality requirement is verified using a sequent $\Gamma \vdash \Sigma$ where the succedent Σ is some instantiation of (M3) and the antecedent Γ consists of the initial state of a patient group, the initial state of the guideline, the medical guideline, effects of treatment plans, the background knowledge, and the environment assumptions, which is shown in Figure 4. The verification of two meta-level requirements are discussed in Subsections 4.3 and 4.4.

$$AS[\,'tc\,] = inactive, \ldots, \qquad\qquad /* \; Initial \; state \; of \; guideline \; */$$
$$[inactive\#(\,'tc',\,'st';AS,Patient)], \qquad /* \; Asbru \; plan \; */$$
$$\square(AS[\,'SU\_or\_BG\,] = activated \; \leftrightarrow \qquad /* \; Effects \; */$$
$$\quad BG \in Patient'[\,'treatment\,] \wedge \ldots),$$
$$\square knowledge(Patient',Patient'') \qquad\qquad /* \; Background \; knowledge \; */$$
$$\square(AS''[\,'tc\,] = AS'[\,'tc\,] \wedge \ldots) \qquad\qquad /* \; Environment \; assumption \; */$$

Figure 4: Antecedent of proof obligations with tc shorthand for Treatments_and_Control and AS an additional data structure of type asbru-state, which keeps track of all plan states over time, in which initially each plan is set to inactive.

4.1 Consistency of background knowledge

Property (M1) ensures that the formal model including the Asbru guideline and the background knowledge is consistent. The initial state is – in our case – described as a set of equations and it has been trivial to see that they are consistent. The guideline is given as an Asbru plan. The semantics of any Asbru plan is defined in a programming language where every program construct ensures that the resulting reactive system is consistent: in every step, the program either terminates or calculates a consistent output for arbitrary input values. The Asbru plan, thus, defines a total function between unprimed and primed variables in every step (Figure 3). The formula defining the effects maps the output variables of the guideline to input variables of the patient model. Again, it has been trivial to see that this mapping is consistent.

The background knowledge defines our patient model. We consider the patient to be part of the environment which is the relation between the primed and the double primed variables in every step. If the patient model ensures that for an arbitrary primed state there exists a double primed state, the overall system of alternating guideline and environment transitions is consistent: given an initial (unprimed) state, the guideline calculates an output (primed) state; the effects define a link between the variables of the guideline and the variables of the patient model; the patient model reacts to the (primed) output state and gives a (double primed) state which is again input to the Asbru guideline in the next step. In other words, the relation between the unprimed and the double primed state is the complete state transition. The additional environment assumptions referring to the Asbru environment do not destroy consistency as the set of restricted variables of the environment assumption is disjunct to the set of variables of the patient model.

It remains to ensure consistency of the background knowledge which we defined as a predicate knowledge. Consistency can be shown by proving the property

$$\forall pre. \; \exists post. \; knowledge(pre, post)$$

which ensures that the relation is total. In order to prove that this property holds an example patient has been constructed. Verifying that the example patient is a model of the background knowledge has been fully automatic.

4.2   Successful treatment

In order to verify property (M2), i.e., the guideline eventually manages to control the glucose level in the patient's blood, a proof has been constructed. The verification strategy in KIV is symbolic execution with induction [1]. The plan state model introduced in [2] defines the semantics of the different conditions of a plan and is implemented in KIV by a procedure called asbru, which is symbolically executed. Each plan can be in a certain state, modelled with a variable AS (i.e., inactive, considered, ready, activated, and aborted (or completed)) and a transition to another state depends on its conditions. In the initial state, the top level plan Treatments_and_Control (abbreviated tc) is in inactive state. After executing the first step, the plan is considered, after which execution continues as described in [2]. The execution is visualised in a proof tree (cf. Figure 5), where the bottom node is the start of the execution and splits if there is a case distinction.

Patients whose capacity of the B cells is normal are cured with diet, while for other patients diet will not be sufficient. In this case, we assume that the doctor eventually aborts the diet treatment. We use induction to reason about the unspecified time period in which diet is applied. As an invariant,

$$Patient[\,'capacity(B\text{-}cells,insulin)\,] \neq normal$$

is used. In the next step, the doctor has either aborted diet or diet is still active. In the second case, induction can be applied. When diet is aborted, tc sequentially executes the next plan, which is SU_or_BG (cf. Figure 2).

The second treatment SU_or_BG goes, as each Asbru plan, through a sequence of states, i.e., inactive, considered, ready, activated, and aborted, and thus becomes first considered and after some steps becomes activated (cf. Figure 5). In this case, either SU or BG is prescribed, depending on the quetelet index QI. For a patient whose B cell capacity is subnormal, the background knowledge ensures that the condition of the patient improves. Thus, for the rest of the proof we can additionally assume that

$$Patient[\,'capacity(B\text{-}cells,insulin)\,] \neq subnormal$$

After SU_or_BG aborts, the third treatment (SU_and_BG) is executed in similar fashion, where patients with nearly exhausted B cell capacity are cured. Thus, after aborting the first three treatments the precondition concerning the B cell capacity can be strengthened to

$$Patient[\,'capacity(B\text{-}cells,insulin)\,] \neq normal$$
$$\wedge\; Patient[\,'capacity(B\text{-}cells,insulin)\,] \neq subnormal$$
$$\wedge\; Patient[\,'capacity(B\text{-}cells,insulin)\,] \neq nearly\text{-}exhausted$$

12

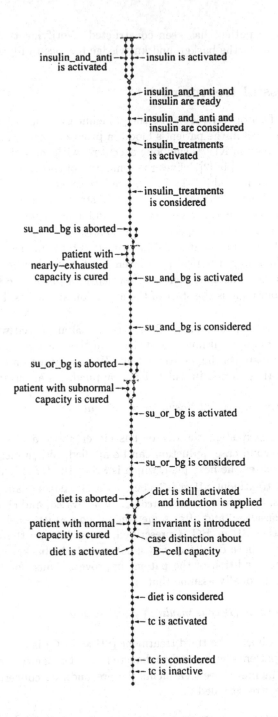

Figure 5: Overview of the proof that the guideline eventually manages all patient problems, which is explained in Section 4.2.

which, under the assumption that the only possible values of the capacity are normal, subnormal, nearly-exhausted, and exhausted, yields:

$$Patient[\text{'}capacity(B\text{-}cells, insulin)\text{'}] = exhausted$$

This statement together with the background knowledge ensures that the prescription of insulin, which is prescribed in both final treatments Insulin and Insulin_and_Antidiabetics, finally cures the patient.

4.3   Optimality of treatment

With respect to property (M3), an optimality criterion of the guideline is that no treatments are prescribed that are not in accordance with good practice medicine (Section 3.3), i.e., some preference relation $\preceq$ between treatments exists and the guideline never prescribes a treatment T such that $T \preceq T'$ and T' cures the patient group under consideration.

In our case study the preference for treatments is based on the minimisation of (1) the number of insulin injections, and (2) the number of drugs involved (cf. Section 3.3). We have defined this using a reflexive, transitive order $\leq$ such that for all treatments T, it holds that $insulin \leq T$ and $T \leq diet$. Furthermore, the treatments prescribing the oral anti-diabetics sulfonylurea and biguanide are incomparable. The proof obligation is then as follows:

$$\Box(\forall_T : Good_\leq(T, Patient) \rightarrow T \leq Patient[\text{'}treatment\text{'}])$$

where $Good_\leq(T, Patient)$ denotes that T is a treatment according to good practice medicine for $Patient$, as defined in [8]. To prove this, the following axiom was added to the system:

$$\Box Patient[\text{'}QI\text{'}] = Patient''[\text{'}QI\text{'}]$$

i.e., the quetelet index does not change during the run of the protocol. This axiom is needed, because the decision of prescribing a treatment is not exactly at the same time as the application of the treatment and therefore the decision of prescribing this treatment could be based on a patient with a different quetelet index than the patient that actually takes the drugs.

Proving this property in KIV was done in approximately 1 day using several heuristics for the straightforward parts. The theorem was proven using two lemmas for two specific patient groups. In total, it took approximately 500 steps, of which nearly 90% were done automatically, to verify this property.

4.4   Order of treatments

Finally, another instance of (M3) was proven. This property phrases that the order of any two treatments in the protocol is consistent with the order relation as we have defined in Subsection 3.3. In other words, in case a patient may receive multiple treatments, the less radical treatments are tried first. The formalisation of the property in KIV was done as follows:

$$\Box \forall_T (Tick \land T = Patient[\,'treatment\,']$$
$$\to \Box(\text{last} \lor (Tick \to \neg(T \leq Patient[\,'treatment\,']))))$$

At each time, the current treatment is bound to a static variable (i.e., unchanged by symbolic execution) T, which can be used to compare against subsequent steps in the protocol. For any future steps, we require that either the protocol completes (**last** holds) or that activated treatments are not more preferred than T. The additional Tick variable is needed in the formalisation to abstract from technical system steps.

This property also had a high degree of automation with roughly 800 steps in total. The reason for this slightly higher number of steps is due to nested temporal operators.

5   Discussion

As the interest in medical guidelines continues to grow, there is a need for criteria to asses the quality of medical guidelines. An important method for the appraisal of medical guidelines was introduced by the AGREE collaboration [3]. A solid foundation for the application of *formal methods* to the quality checking of medical guidelines, using simulation of the guideline [4, 12] and theorem proving techniques [9], can also be found in literature.

In [9], logical methods have been used to analyse properties of guidelines, formalised as task networks. In [8], it was shown that the theory of abductive diagnosis can be taken as a foundation for the formalisation of quality requirements of a medical guideline in temporal logic. This result has been used to verify quality requirements of good practice medicine of treatments [7]. However, in the latter work, the order between treatment depending on the condition of the patient and previous treatments was ignored. In this paper, we consider elements from both approaches by including medical background knowledge in the verification of complete networks of tasks. This required a major change to the previous work with respect to the formulation of quality criteria, because quality is now defined with respect to a complete network of tasks instead of individual treatments as presented in [8].

Compared to previous work concerning the verification of networks of tasks, the meta-level approach we have presented here has a number of advantages. In the meta-level approach, quality is defined independently of domain specific knowledge, and, consequently, proof obligations do not have to be extracted from external sources. One successful attempt of the latter was reported in [5], where quality criteria are formalised on the basis of instruments to monitor the quality of care in practice, i.e., medical indicators. Firstly, the question is whether these indicators, based on compliance with medical guidelines, coincide with the quality of the guideline itself. Secondly, it has been our experience that it is far from easy to find suitable properties in external sources, because these sources may not be completely applicable, e.g., typically, other guide-lines may address different problem in the management of the same disease. Thirdly, many useful quality criteria of guidelines are implicit, making this approach fundamentally limiting. In this sense, the meta-level approach provides a more systematic method for the formulation of proof obligations and, thus, verification of medical guidelines.

In summary, in this study we have setup a general framework for the verification of medical guidelines, consisting of a medical guideline, medical background knowledge, and quality requirements. A model for the background knowledge of glucose level control in diabetes mellitus type 2 patients was developed based on a general temporal logic formalisation of (patho)physiological mechanisms and treatment information. Furthermore, we developed a theory for quality requirements of good practice medicine based on the theory of abductive diagnosis. This model of background knowledge and theory of quality requirements were then used in a case study in which we verified several quality criteria of the diabetes mellitus type 2 guideline used by the Dutch general practitioners. In the case study we use Asbru to model the guideline as a network of tasks and KIV for the formal verification.

In the course of our study we have shown that the general framework that we have setup for the formal verification of medical guidelines with medical background knowledge is feasible and that the actual verification of quality criteria can be done with a high degree of automation. We believe both the inclusion of medical background knowledge and task networks to be necessary elements for adequately supporting the development and management of medical guidelines.

An important advantage of using theorem proving compared to alternative techniques such as model checking is that it provides insight in the proof structure. For each case, it is relatively easy to inspect the proof tree and to find out the reason that a certain quality criterion holds. On the other hand, KIV is a tool with a very expressive logic, which may result in an additional overhead when verifying quality criteria of medical guidelines. It is clear that tools for quality checking earlier on in the development process of a guideline, where such an additional overhead is not acceptable, would be useful. Therefore, also techniques such as model checking will be a topic for future research.

References

[1] M. Balser. *Verifying Concurrent System with Symbolic Execution – Temporal Reasoning is Symbolic Execution with a Little Induction.* PhD thesis, University of Augsburg, Augsburg, Germany, 2005.

[2] M. Balser, C. Duelli, and W. Reif. Formal semantics of asbru - an overview. In *Proceedings of the International Conference on Integrated Design and Process Technology*, Passadena, June 2002. Society for Design and Process Science.

[3] AGREE Collaboration. Development and validation of an international appraisal instrument for assessing the quality of clinical practice guidelines: the agree project. *Quality & Safety in Health Care*, 12:18–23, 2003.

[4] J. Fox and S. Das. *Safe and Sound: Artificial Intelligence in Hazardous Applications*. AAAI Press, 2000.

[5] M. van Gendt, A. van Teije, R. Serban, and F. van Harmelen. Formalising medical quality indicators to improve guidelines. In *AIME*, number 3581 in LNAI, pages 201–220. Springer Verlag, 2005.

[6] General Medical Counsil – Protecting patients, guiding doctors. Good medical practise. http://www.gmc-uk.org. Third edition, May 2001.

[7] A.J. Hommersom, P.J.F. Lucas, and M. Balser. Meta-level Verification of the Quality of Medical Guidelines Using Interactive Theorem Proving. In *JELIA'04*, volume 3229 of *LNCS*, pages 654–666. Springer-Verlag, 2004.

[8] P.J.F. Lucas. Quality checking of medical guidelines through logical abduction. In F. Coenen, A. Preece, and A.L. Mackintosh, editors, *Proc. of AI-2003*, volume XX, pages 309–321, London, 2003. Springer.

[9] M. Marcos, M. Balser, A. ten Teije, and F. van Harmelen. From informal knowledge to formal logic: A realistic case study in medical protocols. In *Proceedings of EKAW*, pages 49–64. Springer, 2002.

[10] S. Miksch. Plan management in the medical domain. *AI Communications*, 12(4):209–235, 1999.

[11] M. Peleg et al. Comparing computer-interpretable guideline models: a case-study approach. *Journal of the American Medical Informatics Association*, 10(1):52–68, 2003.

[12] S. Quaglini, M. Stefanelli, A. Cavallini, G Micieli, C. Fassino, and C. Mossa. Guideline-based careflow system. *Artificial Intelligence in Medicine*, 20(1):5–22, 2000.

[13] G.E.H.M. Rutten, S. Verhoeven, R.J. Heine, W.J.C. de Grauw, P.V.M. Cromme, and K. Reenders. NHG-standaard diabetes mellitus type 2 (eerste herziening). *Huisarts Wet*, 42:67–84, 1999.

[14] A. Seyfang, R. Kosara, and S. Miksch. Asbru's reference manual, asbru version 7.3. Technical Report Asgaard-TR-20002-1, Vienna University of Technology, Institute of Software Technology, 2002.

[15] S.H. Woolf. Evidence-based medicine and practice guidelines: an overview. *Cancer Control*, 7(4):362–367, 2000.

SESSION 1:

AI TECHNIQUES (GAs, BIO-MOTIVATED COMPUTING AND BAYES)

A Discrete Particle Swarm Optimization Algorithm for the Permutation Flowshop Sequencing Problem with Makespan Criterion

Quan-Ke Pan[1], M. Fatih Tasgetiren[2] and Yun-Chia Liang[3]

[1] College of Computer Science, Liaocheng University, Liaocheng, China
qkpan@lctu.edu.cn
[2] Department of Operations Management and Business Statistics, Sultan Qaboos University, P.O.Box 20, Al Khod 123, Muscat, Sultanate of Oman.
mfatih@squ.edu.om
[3] Department of Industrial Engineering and Management, Yuan Ze University, Taiwan
ycliang@saturn.yzu.edu.tw

Abstract. In this paper, a discrete particle swarm optimization ($DPSO$) algorithm is presented to solve the permutation flowshop sequencing problem with the makespan criterion. A new crossover operator, here we call it the PTL crossover operator, is presented. In addition, the $DPSO$ algorithm is hybridized with a simple local search algorithm based on an insert neighborhood to further improve the solution quality. The performance of the proposed $DPSO$ algorithm is tested on the well-known standard benchmark suite of Taillard with the best known upper bounds as of April 2004. The computational experiments show that the proposed $DPSO$ algorithm is either better or very competitive to all the existing approaches in the literature.

1 Introduction

The permutation flowshop sequencing problem ($PFSP$) is concerned with finding a permutation of jobs on machines to optimize certain performance measures when all of the jobs have the same machine sequence. Flowshop problems have attracted the attention of researchers since Johnson [1] first proposed the problem. Among these practical performance measures, the minimization of makespan is known to lead to the minimization of total production run, stable utilization of resources, rapid turn-around of jobs, and the minimization of work-in-process (WIP) inventory.

For the computational complexity of the $PFSP$ with the makespan criterion, Rinnooy Kan [2] proved that makespan minimization is NP-hard. Therefore, efforts have been devoted to finding high-quality solutions in a reasonable computational time by heuristic optimization techniques. Heuristics for the makespan minimization problem have been proposed by Palmer [3], Campbell et al. [4], Dannenbring [5], Nawaz et al. [6], Taillard [7], Framinan and Leisten [8], and

19

Framinan et al. [9]. To achieve a better solution quality, modern metaheuristics have been presented for the $PFSP$ with makespan minimization such as Simulated Annealing in [10, 11], Tabu Search in [12, 13, 14, 15], Genetic Algorithms in [16, 17, 18, 19, 20], Ant Colony Optimization in [21, 22], Iterated Local Search in [23], and Particle Swarm Optimization Algorithms in [24, 25, 26]. More recently, two new robust Genetic Algorithms are presented by Ruiz et al. [27] and a simple and effective iterated greedy algorithm is presented by Ruiz and Stutzle [28]. In order to test the performance of these heuristics, 120 benchmark instances presented by Taillard in [29] are generally used in these modern heuristic algorithms.

Here we can formulate the $PFSP$ as follows. Given the processing times p_{jk} for job j on machine k, and a job permutation $\pi = \{\pi_1, \pi_2, ..., \pi_n\}$ where n jobs $(j = 1, 2, ..., n)$ will be sequenced through m machines $(k = 1, 2, ..., m)$, then the problem is to find the best permutation of jobs to be valid for each machine. For $n/m/P/C_{max}$ problem, $C(\pi_j, m)$ denotes the completion time of job π_j on machine m. the calculation of completion time for the n-job m-machine problem is given as follows:

$$C(\pi_1, 1) = p_{\pi_1, 1} \tag{1}$$

$$C(\pi_j, 1) = C(\pi_{j-1}, 1) + p_{\pi_j, 1} \qquad j = 2, .., n \tag{2}$$

$$C(\pi_1, k) = C(\pi_1, k-1) + p_{\pi_1, k} \qquad k = 2, .., m \tag{3}$$

$$C(\pi_j, k) = max\{C(\pi_{j-1}, k), C(\pi_j, k-1)\} + p_{\pi_j, k} \; j = 2, .., n \; k = 2, .., m \tag{4}$$

Then the $PFSP$ is to find a permutation π^* in the set of all permutations Π such that

$$C_{max}(\pi^*) \le C(\pi_n, m) \quad \forall \pi \in \Pi \tag{5}$$

PSO was first introduced to optimize continuous nonlinear functions by Eberhart and Kennedy [30]. The comprehensive survey of the PSO algorithms and applications can be found in Kennedy et al. [31]. The major obstacle of successfully applying a PSO algorithm to combinatorial problems is due to its continuous nature. To remedy this drawback, recent attempts have been made in [24, 25, 26]. In addition, authors have successfully proposed a $DPSO$ algorithm to solve the no-wait flowshop scheduling problem in [32, 33] and the single-machine total earliness and tardiness problem with a common due date in [34, 35]. Based on the experience above, this study aims at solving the $PFSP$ with the makespan criterion by the $DPSO$ algorithm.

The paper is organized as follows. Section 2 introduces the details of the proposed $DPSO$ algorithm. Section 3 provides the computational results on benchmark problems. Finally, Section 4 summarizes the concluding remarks.

2   Discrete Particle Swarm Optimization Algorithm

In the standard PSO algorithm, each solution is called a "particle". All particles have their positions, velocities, and fitness values. Let NP denote the swarm size represented as $X^t = \lfloor X_1^t, X_2^t, .., X_{NP}^t \rfloor$ where X_i^t denotes the particle i. Then each particle in the swarm population has the following attributes: A current position represented as $X_i^t = \lfloor x_{i1}^t, x_{i2}^t, .., x_{in}^t \rfloor$; and a current velocity denoted by $V_i^t = \lfloor v_{i1}^t, v_{i2}^t, .., v_{in}^t \rfloor$. In addition, a current personal best position is represented as $P_i^t = \lfloor p_{i1}^t, p_{i2}^t, .., p_{in}^t \rfloor$; and a current global best position is defined by $G^t = \lfloor g_1^t, g_2^t, .., g_n^t \rfloor$. The current velocity of the jth dimension of the ith particle is updated as follows:

$$v_{ij}^t = \left(w^{t-1}v_{ij}^{t-1} + c_1 r_1 \left(p_{ij}^{t-1} - x_{ij}^{t-1}\right) + c_2 r_2 \left(g_j^{t-1} - x_{ij}^{t-1}\right)\right) \qquad (6)$$

where w^{t-1} is the inertia weight which is a parameter to control the impact of the previous velocities on the current velocity; c_1 and c_2 are acceleration coefficients and r_1 and r_2 denote uniform random numbers between (0,1).

The current position of the jth dimension of the tth particle is updated using the previous position and current velocity of the particle as follows:

$$x_{ij}^t = x_{ij}^{t-1} + v_{ij}^t \qquad (7)$$

Assuming that the function f is to be minimized, the personal best position of each particle is updated using

$$P_i^t = \begin{cases} P_i^{t-1} & \text{if } f(X_i^t) \geq f(P_i^{t-1}) \\ X_i^t & \text{if } f(X_i^t) < f(P_i^{t-1}) \end{cases} \qquad (8)$$

and the global best position found so far in the swarm population is obtained as

$$G^t = \begin{cases} argminf(P_i^t) & \text{if } f(P_i^t) < f(G^{t-1}) \quad 1 \leq i \leq NP \\ G^{t-1} & \text{else} \end{cases} \qquad (9)$$

It is obvious that standard PSO equations cannot be used to generate a discrete job permutation since positions of particles are real-valued. Instead, Pan, Tasgetiren and Liang [32, 33, 34, 35] proposed a newly designed method for updating the position of the particle based on the discrete job permutation. According to their method, the position of the ith particle at iteration t can be updated as follows:

$$X_i^t = c_2 \oplus F_3(c_1 \oplus F_2(w \oplus F_1(X_i^{t-1}), P_i^{t-1}), G^{t-1}). \qquad (10)$$

Given that λ_i^t and δ_i^t are temporary individuals, the update equation consists of three components. The first component is $\lambda_i^t = w \oplus F_1(X_i^{t-1})$, which represents the velocity of the particle. F_1 indicates the insert operator with the probability of w. In other words, a uniform random number r is generated between 0 and 1. If r is less than w, then the insert operator is applied to generate a perturbed permutation of the particle by $\lambda_i^t = F_1(X_i^{t-1})$, otherwise current permutation is kept as $\lambda_i^t = X_i^{t-1}$. The second component is $\delta_i^t = c_1 \oplus F_2(\lambda_i^t, P_i^{t-1})$ which is the "*cognition*" part of the particle representing the private thinking of the particle itself. F_2 represents the crossover operator with the probability of c_1. Note that λ_i^t and P_i^{t-1} will be the first and second parent for the crossover operator, respectively. It results either in $\delta_i^t = F_2(\lambda_i^t, P_i^{t-1})$ or in $\delta_i^t = \lambda_i^t$ depending on the choice of a uniform random number. The third component is $X_i^t = c_2 \oplus F_3(\delta_i^t, G^{t-1})$ which is the "*social*" part of the particle representing the collaboration among particles. F_3 denotes the crossover operator with the probability of c_2. Note that δ_i^t and G^{t-1} will be the first and second parent for the crossover operator, respectively. The outcome is either $X_i^t = F_3(\delta_i^t, G^{t-1})$ or $X_i^t = \delta_i^t$ depending on the choice of a uniform random number. For the *DPSO* algorithm, the *gbest* model of Kennedy et al. [30] was followed. The pseudo code of the *DPSO* algorithm is given in Fig.1.

```
Initialize parameters
Initialize population
Evaluate
Do{
    Find the personal best
    Find the global best
    Update position
    Evaluate
    Apply local search(optional)
}While (Not Termination)
```

Fig. 1. DPSO Algorithm with Local Search

In order to be employed in the position update equation for the *DPSO* algorithm, we propose a new crossover operator, called *PTL* crossover operator that always produces a pair of distinct permutations even from two identical parents. An illustration of the two-cut *PTL* crossover operator is shown in Table 1.

Table 1. An Example of the *PTL* Crossover Operator

Two-Cut *PTL* Crossover		Two-Cut *PTL* Crossover	
Parent1	5 1 4 2 3	Parent1	5 1 4 2 3
Parent2	3 5 4 2 1	Parent2	5 1 4 2 3
Offspring1	3 5 2 1 4	Offspring1	5 2 3 1 4
Offspring2	1 4 3 5 2	Offspring2	1 4 5 2 3

In the *PTL* crossover, a block of jobs from the first parent is determined by two cut points randomly. This block is either moved to the right or left corner of the offspring permutation. Then the offspring permutation is filled out with the remaining jobs from the second parent. This procedure will always produce two distinctive offspring even from the same two parents as shown in Table 1.

In this paper, one of these two unique offspring is chosen randomly with a flip probability of 0.5. To figure out how particle positions are updated, an example is illustrated in Table 2. Assume that the mutation and crossover probabilities are 1.0, two-cut *PTL* crossover operator and insert mutation operator are employed. Given the positions of a particle, its personal best and the global best, the update equation first mutates the particle. For example, in Table 2, the job 3 is inserted after the job 4, thus generating the individual λ_i. Then the individual λ_i is recombined with the personal best to generate the individual δ_i. Finaly, the individual δ_i is recombined with the global best to update the particle X_i.

Table 2. An Example of the Update Equation

$$X_i \ 3 \ 1 \ 4 \ 2 \ 5$$
$$P_i \ 2 \ 5 \ 4 \ 3 \ 1$$
$$G \ 1 \ 3 \ 2 \ 4 \ 5$$

Insert

$$X_i \ 3 \ 1 \ 4 \ 2 \ 5$$
$$\lambda_i \ 1 \ 4 \ 3 \ 2 \ 5$$

Crossover

$$\lambda_i \ 1 \ 4 \ 3 \ 2 \ 5$$
$$P_i \ 2 \ 5 \ 4 \ 3 \ 1$$
$$\delta_i \ 2 \ 5 \ 1 \ 4 \ 3$$

Crossover

$$\delta_i \ 2 \ 5 \ 1 \ 4 \ 3$$
$$G \ 1 \ 3 \ 2 \ 4 \ 5$$
$$X_i \ 3 \ 2 \ 4 \ 5 \ 1$$

For the initial population, we take advantage of the *NEH* heuristic of Nawaz et al. in [6]. The *NEH* heuristic has two phases. In the phase I, the jobs are ordered in descending sums of their processing times. In the phase II, a job sequence is established by evaluating the partial schedules based on the initial order of the first phase. Suppose a current sequence is already determined for the first k jobs, k+1 partial sequences are constructed by inserting job k+1 in k+1 possible slots of the current sequence. Among these k+1 sequences, the best one generating the minimum makespan is kept as the current sequence for the next iteration. Then job k+2 from phase I is considered and so on until all jobs have been sequenced. The swarm population is constructed as follows:

1. One particle is produced by the *NEH* algorithm. The rest of the population is constructed as follows: a permutation is produced randomly, then the first phase of the *NEH* heuristic is ignored by keeping the first two jobs (k) of the random permutation in the partial permutation. Then the second phase of the *NEH* heuristic is applied to the partial permutation with the remaining jobs from the random permutation to generate the permutation of the particle so as to be included in the initial swarm population.

2. The personal best of each particle is generated in a way that the best solution s_1 in the insert neighborhood of the particle is found, and then the best solution s_2 in the swap neighborhood of the solution s_1 is found. The personal best solution of particle i in the initial swarm population is determined such that

$$P_i^0 = min(s_1, s_2) \quad 1 \le i \le NP \tag{11}$$

At the end of each iteration t, a simple local search method based on the insert neighborhood with a simulated annealing type of acceptance criterion is applied to the global best solution to further improve the solution quality. The pseudo code of the local search procedure is given in Fig.2.

```
LS(Gᵗ){
s₀=Perturbation(Gᵗ)
flag = true
do{
    s₁=FindBest(s₀)
    if f(s₁) < f(s₀) then s₀ = s₁
    else {s₁ = s₀; flag = false}
}while(flag == true)
if f(s₁) < f(Gᵗ) then Gᵗ = s₁)
else if random < exp (−(f(s₁) − f(Gᵗ))/T) then Gᵗ = s₁
```

Fig. 2. Local Search Procedure

The constant temperature is used in the simulated annealing type of acceptance criterion as suggested by Osman and Potts [10]:

$$T = \frac{\sum_{j=1}^{n} \sum_{k=1}^{m} p_{jk}}{10 * n * m} * h \tag{12}$$

where $h = 0.5$.

In this way, the global best solution in the swarm population is diversified by giving chances to some inferior solutions during the search process. In the local search algorithm above, the perturbation strength was four insertions to the global best solution to avoid getting trapped at the local minima. In the $FindBest()$ routine, it is obvious that the size of the insert neighborhood is $(n-1)^2$. However, it causes to a significant amount of computation times for larger instances. In order to reduce the CPU time requirements, the speed-up method presented in Taillard [7] is employed for the insert neighborhood in the $FindBest()$ routine. The $DPSO$ algorithm with the local search is denoted as $DPSO_{LS}$ from now on throughout the paper.

3 Computational Results

The proposed $DPSO$ and $DPSO_{LS}$ algorithms were coded in Visual C++ and run on an Intel PIV 2.4 GHz PC with 256MB memory. Regarding the parameters of the $DPSO$ and $DPSO_{LS}$ algorithms, two-cut crossover probabilities were set to $c_1 = c_2 = 0.8$, respectively. The mutation (insert) probability was fixed to 0.95 and the swarm population size was 20. The proposed $DPSO$ and $DPSO_{LS}$ algorithms were applied to the well known benchmark suite of Taillard [29] with the best known upper bounds as of April 2004 in [36]. There are 120 instances ranging from 20 jobs with 5 machines to 500 jobs with 20 machines. For each given size of n and m, 10 instances are provided. Some of the instances in this benchmark set are known to be extremely difficult to solve.

Very recently in 2006, Ruiz and Stutzle [28] developed an iterative greedy algorithm without and with a local search denoted by IG_RS and IG_RS_{LS}, respectively. To compare the performance of the IG algorithms to well-known techniques from the literature, Ruiz and Stutzle [28] have re-implemented 12 classical or recent, well performing algorithms. The algorithms that they have re-implemented are as follows: NEH heuristic of Nawaz et al. [6] with the improvements of Taillard [7] denoted as $NEHT$; the simulated annealing algorithm of Osman and Potts [10] denoted as SA_OP; the tabu search algorithm of Widmer and Hertz [12] denoted as $SPIRIT$; the pure genetic algorithm of Chen et al. [18] and Revees and Yamada [17] denoted as GA_CHEN and GA_REEV, respectively; the hybrid genetic algorithm with local search of Murata et al. [20] denoted as GA_MIT; two recent genetic algorithms of Ruiz et al. [27] denoted as GA_RMA and HGA_RMA; the genetic algorithm of Aldowasian and Allahverdi [19] denoted as GA_AA; the iterated local search of Stutzle [23] denoted as ILS; and two recent ant colony algorithms of Rajendran and Ziegler [21] denoted as M_MMAS and $PACO$, respectively. In Ruiz and Stutzle [28], all 14 algorithms were implemented in Delphi 7.0 with a stopping criterion of a computational time limit of $n.(m/2).60$ milliseconds on a PC with an Athlon XP 1600++ processor (1400 MHz) with 512 MB of main memory. For each algorithm, $R=5$ independent runs were carried out, except for the deterministic $NEHT$ algorithm for which only a single run was conducted, for each problem instance to report the statistics based on the percentage relative deviations from the best known upper bounds of Taillard's instances as of April 2004 in [36].

Since we use a machine with 2.4 GHz which is approximately 70% (2400/1400= 1.7) faster than the one used in Ruiz and Stutzle [28], the maximum CPU time in our runs is, exactly to the half of the CPU time of Ruiz and Stutzle [28], fixed to $n.(m/2).30$ milliseconds to have a fair comparison with respect to the results of $n.(m/2).60$ milliseconds in Ruiz and Stutzle [28]. $R=5$ independent runs are conducted to collect the statistics to be consistent with Ruiz and Stutzle [28]. To be more specific, average relative percent deviation was computed as follows:

$$\Delta_{avg} = \sum_{i=1}^{R} \left(\frac{(F_i - F_{ref}) \times 100}{F_{ref}} \right) / R \tag{13}$$

where F_i , F_{ref} , and R were the fitness function value (makespan) generated by the $DPSO$ and $DPSO_{LS}$ algorithms in each run, the reference makespan values either optimal or the lowest known upper bound for Taillard's instances as of April 2004, and the number of runs, respectively. For convenience, Δ_{min} , Δ_{max} and Δ_{std} denote the minimum, maximum, and standard deviation of relative percent deviation R runs, respectively. For the computational effort considera- tion, t denotes the time to reach the best objective function value in each run averaged over R runs in seconds, i.e., the time that the best-so-far solution did not change after that point of time.

Computational results of the $DPSO$ and $DPSO_{LS}$ algorithms are given in Table 3 and Table 4. The pure $DPSO$ algorithm was able to find results on overall average no worse than 1.47% from the best known upper bounds or optimal solutions. It was also so robust that the standard deviation of relative percent deviation was 0.08. It was also very efficient given the overall average CPU time of 13.8 seconds. However, the inclusion of the local search algorithm in the $DPSO$ algorithm has significantly improved all the solution quality measures of the pure $DPSO$ algorithm such that the average relative percent deviation was decreased from 1.47% to 0.44%, which is one of the best results reported so far in the literature.

Table 3. Computational Results of the Pure $DPSO$ Algorithm

n	Δ_{avg}	Δ_{min}	Δ_{max}	Δ_{std}	t_{avg}	t_{min}	t_{max}	t_{std}
20 × 5	0.34	0.08	0.61	0.07	0.22	0.00	0.72	0.09
20 × 10	0.93	0.55	1.44	0.18	1.14	0.11	2.34	0.22
20 × 20	0.81	0.37	1.20	0.12	1.15	0.02	3.48	0.50
50 × 5	0.08	0.02	0.13	0.02	0.25	0.04	0.96	0.08
50 × 10	2.37	1.91	2.77	0.13	2.62	0.16	6.76	0.98
50 × 20	3.75	3.44	4.03	0.12	1.10	0.36	3.39	0.32
100 × 5	0.06	0.01	0.14	0.02	0.44	0.17	0.92	0.09
100 × 10	0.87	0.66	1.07	0.05	3.73	0.84	8.65	0.77
100 × 20	3.55	3.26	3.81	0.09	4.37	2.09	10.70	0.90
200 × 10	0.52	0.42	0.64	0.03	7.49	3.77	12.84	1.52
200 × 20	2.89	2.71	3.04	0.05	14.74	11.68	26.23	1.15
500 × 20	1.47	1.38	1.56	0.02	128.36	124.40	140.7	1.52
Mean	1.47	1.24	1.70	0.08	13.8	11.97	18.14	0.68

In order to compare the performance of the $DPSO$ and $DPSO_{LS}$ algorithms with the best algorithms in the literature, the results of the re-implementations in Ruiz and Stutzle [28] have been adopted since the maximum CPU time is restricted to the half of their CPU time in the $DPSO$ and $DPSO_{LS}$ algorithms. Table 5 and 6 show the results of all 16 algorithms appeared to be the best performing in the literature.

Table 4. Computational Results of the $DPSO_{LS}$ Algorithm

n	Δ_{avg}	Δ_{min}	Δ_{max}	Δ_{std}	t_{avg}	t_{min}	t_{max}	t_{std}
20 × 5	0.04	0.04	0.04	0.00	0.04	0.01	0.11	0.01
20 × 10	0.03	0.00	0.07	0.02	0.63	0.25	1.30	0.31
20 × 20	0.03	0.00	0.07	0.02	1.59	0.13	3.90	0.56
50 × 5	0.00	0.00	0.01	0.00	0.43	0.08	0.75	0.13
50 × 10	0.58	0.40	0.72	0.03	3.89	1.77	6.11	0.78
50 × 20	0.89	0.67	1.15	0.07	9.91	5.61	13.74	1.43
100 × 5	0.01	0.00	0.01	0.00	0.74	0.12	1.85	0.17
100 × 10	0.25	0.12	0.39	0.04	5.80	1.46	11.46	1.10
100 × 20	1.28	0.95	1.48	0.10	21.03	13.22	26.74	2.89
200 × 10	0.17	0.07	0.30	0.05	11.94	3.92	21.31	2.71
200 × 20	1.30	1.04	1.50	0.09	39.99	23.39	55.54	6.04
500 × 20	0.74	0.65	0.86	0.04	124.47	104.77	145.03	6.28
Mean	0.44	0.33	0.55	0.04	18.37	12.89	23.99	1.87

It should be noted that Tasgetiren et. al. [25] first developed a *PSO* algorithm for the *PFSP* with a variable neighborhood search (*VNS*). Their overall average percentage relative deviation was 0.46, which was very competitive to the best results in the literature. However, it was computationally very expensive due to the nature of the *VNS* local search hybridized with the *PSO* algorithm. For this reason, it was not included in the following comparisons.

As seen in Table 5 and 6, the pure *DPSO* algorithm has generated much better average relative percent deviation than *NEHT*, *SA_OP*, *SPIRIT*, *GA_CHEN*, *GA_REEV*, *GA_MIT* and *GA_AA*. It was slightly better than *GA_REEV* and also competitive to *GA_ RMA*. Among all the algorithms compared, the best performing algorithm without a local search is *IG_RS*. However, the inclusion of a local search in *DPSO* algorithm led to generate the same results as in the one generated by the IG_RS_{LS} algorithm. That is the $DPSO_{LS}$ algorithms produced the average relative percent deviation of 0.44% too. It should be noted that *HGA_RMA*, *M_MMAS* and *PACO* algorithms are also very competitive to the IG_RS_{LS} algorithm. Among all 16 algorithms compared, the IG_RS_{LS} and $DPSO_{LS}$ algorithms outperformed other competing algorithms in the literature since they both generated the same average relative percent deviation of 0.44%.

As indicated in Ruiz and Stutzle [28], the experimental comparison of known algorithms for the *PFSP* does not include some of the most effective metaheuristics from the literature such as the *TSAB* algorithm of Nowicki and Smutnicki [15], the *RY* genetic algorithm with path relinking by Revees and Yamada [17], and the recent *TSGW* algorithm of Grabowski and Wodecki [14]. Ruiz and Stutzle [28] were unable to obtain the source code of those algorithms to reimplement. That is why they are not included in our comparison too. However, it should be noted that the *TSAB*, *RY* and *TSGW* algorithms are very sophisticated and efficient algorithms for the *PFSP* even though they have some disadvantages such as difficulty in coding and not applicable to some extensions of the *PFSP* with sequence dependent set-up times or with other objectives than makespan.

Table 5. Comparison of Results

$n \times m$	NEHT	GA_RMA	HGA_RMA	SA_OP	SPIRIT	GA_CHEN	GA_REEV	GA_MIT
20×5	3.35	0.26	0.04	1.09	4.33	4.15	0.62	0.80
20×10	5.02	0.73	0.13	2.63	6.07	5.18	2.04	2.14
20×20	3.73	0.43	0.09	2.38	4.44	4.26	1.32	1.75
50×5	0.84	0.07	0.02	0.52	2.19	2.03	0.21	0.30
50×10	5.12	1.71	0.72	3.51	6.04	6.54	2.06	3.55
50×20	6.26	2.74	1.28	4.52	7.63	7.74	3.56	5.09
100×5	0.46	0.07	0.02	0.30	1.06	1.35	0.17	0.27
100×10	2.13	0.62	0.29	1.48	3.01	3.80	0.85	1.63
100×20	5.23	2.75	1.66	4.63	6.74	8.15	3.41	4.87
200×10	1.43	0.43	0.20	1.01	2.07	2.76	0.55	1.14
200×20	4.41	2.31	1.48	3.81	4.97	7.24	2.84	4.18
500×20	2.24	1.40	0.96	2.52	12.58	4.72	1.66	3.34
Mean	3.35	1.13	0.57	2.37	5.09	4.83	1.61	2.42

4 Conclusions

A discrete version of the *PSO* algorithm is presented in this paper. Unlike the standard *PSO*, the *DPSO* and *DPSO$_{LS}$* algorithms employ permutation representation and work on the discrete domain. As in [32, 33, 34, 35], the main contribution of this paper is due to the fact that a new position update method for particles is developed to be applied to all classes of combinatorial optimization problems in the literature. In addition, the *DPSO* algorithm is hybridized with a simple local search based on the insert neighborhood to further improve the solution quality. The proposed *DPSO* and *DPSO$_{LS}$* algorithms were applied to the benchmark suite of Taillard with the best known upper bounds as of April 2004 in [36]. The computational results show that the pure *DPSO* algorithm generated either better or very competitive results to the best algorithms in the literature. In fact, the *IG_RS$_{LS}$* and *DPSO$_{LS}$* algorithms generated the best results among 16 algorithms compared. In addition, a new *PTL* crossover operator is developed. The *PTL* crossover generates two unique offspring even from the identical two parents. The advantage of the *PTL* operator is owing to the fact that when the population converges, the individuals in the population

Table 6. Comparison of Results

$n x m$	ILS	GA_AA	M_MMAS	PACO	IG_RS	IG_RS$_{LS}$	DPSO	DPSO$_{LS}$
20 × 5	0.49	0.94	0.04	0.21	0.04	0.04	0.34	0.04
20 × 10	0.59	1.54	0.15	0.37	0.25	0.06	0.93	0.03
20 × 20	0.36	1.43	0.06	0.24	0.21	0.03	0.81	0.03
50 × 5	0.20	0.36	0.03	0.01	0.04	0.00	0.08	0.00
50 × 10	1.48	3.72	1.40	0.85	1.06	0.56	2.37	0.58
50 × 20	2.20	4.69	2.18	1.59	1.82	0.94	3.75	0.89
100 × 5	0.18	0.32	0.04	0.03	0.05	0.01	0.06	0.01
100 × 10	0.68	1.72	0.47	0.27	0.39	0.20	0.87	0.25
100 × 20	2.55	4.91	2.59	2.09	2.04	1.30	3.55	1.28
200 × 10	0.56	1.27	0.23	0.27	0.34	0.12	0.52	0.17
200 × 20	2.24	4.21	2.26	1.92	1.99	1.26	2.89	1.30
500 × 20	1.25	2.23	1.15	1.09	1.13	0.78	1.47	0.74
Mean	1.06	2.28	0.88	0.75	0.78	0.44	1.47	0.44

resemble each other and parents chosen from the converged population generates almost identical child as their parents. Of course, we did not investigate the effect of the *PTL* crossover operator in comparison to the others in the literature. This is a future research direction of this paper too. As for the future work besides the impact of the *PTL* crossover operator, the authors have already solved the *PFSP* with the total flowtime criterion. They have also developed a discrete version of the differential evolution (*DDE*) algorithm. A detailed analysis of both *DPSO* and *DDE* with a variety of local search algorithms for the *PFSP* will be presented in the literature in the near future.

References

1. S.M. Johnson, Optimal two-and three-stage production schedules, Naval Research Logistics Quarterly 1 (1954) 61-68.
2. A.H.G. Rinnooy Kan, Machine Scheduling Problems: Classification, Complexity, and Computations, Nijhoff, The Hague, (1976).
3. D.S. Palmer, Sequencing jobs through a multistage process in the minimum total time: A quick method of obtaining a near-optimum, Operational Research Quarterly 16 (1965) 101-107.
4. H.G. Campbell, R.A. Dudek, M.L. Smith, A heuristic algorithm for the n job, m machine sequencing problem, Management Science 16(10) (1970) B630-B637.
5. D.G. Dannenbring, An evaluation of flow shop sequencing heuristics, Management Science 23(11) (1977) 1174-1182.
6. M. Nawaz, E.E. Enscore Jr., I. Ham, A heuristic algorithm for the m-machine, n-job flow shop sequencing problem, OMEGA 11(1) (1983) 91-95.
7. E. Taillard, Some efficient heuristic methods for the flowshop sequencing problems, European Journal of Operational Research 47 (1990) 65-74.

30

8. J.M. Framinan, R. Leisten, An efficient constructive heuristic for flowtime minimisation in permutation flow shops, OMEGA 31 (2003) 311-317.

9. J.M. Framinan, R. Leisten, R. Ruiz-Usano, Efficient heuristics for flowshop sequencing with the objectives of makespan and flowtime minimisation, European Journal of Operational Research 141 (2002) 559-569.

10. I. Osman, C. Potts, Simulated annealing for permutation flow shop scheduling, OMEGA 17(6) (1989) 551-557.

11. F. Ogbu, D. Smith, The application of the simulated annealing algorithm to the solution of the n/m/Cmax flowshop problem, Computers and Operations Research 17(3) (1990) 243-253.

12. M. Widmer, A. Hertz., A new heuristic method for the flow shop sequencing problem, European Journal of Operational Research 20(7) (1989) 707-722.

13. C. Reeves, Improving the efficiency of tabu search for machine sequencing problem, Journal of the Operational Research Society 44(4) (1993) 375-382.

14. J.Grabowski, M. Wodecki, A very fast tabu search algorithm for the permutation flowshop problem with makespan criterion, Computers and Operations Research, 31(11) (2004) 1891-1909.

15. E.Nowicki, C. Smutnicki, A fast tabu search algorithm for the permutation flowshop problem, European Journal of Operational Research 91 (1996) 160-175.

16. C. Reeves, A genetic algorithm for flowshop sequencing, Computers and Operations Research 22(1) (1995) 5-13.

17. C. Reeves, T. Yamada, Genetic algorithms, path relinking and the flowshop sequencing problem, Evolutionary Computation 6 (1998) 45-60.

18. C. L. Chen, V. S. Vempati, N. Aljaber, An application of Genetic algorithms for flow shop problems, European Journal of Operational Research 80(2) (1995) 389-396.

19. T. Aldowaisan, A. Allahverdi, New heuristics for no-wait flowshops to minimize makespan, Computers and Operations Research 30(8) (2003) 1219-1231.

20. T. Murata, H. Ishibuchi, H. Tanaka, Genetic algorithms for flowshop scheduling problems, Computers and Industrial Engineering 30(4) (1996) 1601-1071.

21. C. Rajendran, H. Ziegler, Ant-colony algorithms for permutation flowshop scheduling to minimize makespan/total flowtime of jobs, European Journal of Operational Research 155(2) (2004) 426-438.

22. T. Stutzle, An ant approach to the flowshop problem, In: Proceedings of the 6th European Congress on Intelligent Techniques and Soft Cmputing (EUFIT'98), Verlag Mainz, Aachen, Germany, (1998) 1560-1564.

23. T. Stutzle, Applying iterated local search to the permutation flowshop problem, Technical Report, AIDA-98-04, Darmstad University of Technology, Computer Science Department, Intellctics Group, Darmstad, Germany, (1998).

24. M.F. Tasgetiren, M. Sevkli, Y.C. Liang, and G. Gencyilmaz, Particle swarm optimization algorithm for permutation flowshop sequencing problem, In: Proceedings of the 4th International Workshop on Ant Colony Optimization and Swarm Intelligence (ANTS2004), LNCS 3172, Brussels, Belgium, (2004) 382-390.

25. M.F.Tasgetiren, Y.C. Liang, M. Sevkli, G. Gencyilmaz, Particle swarm optimization algorithm for makespan and total flowtime minimization in the permutation flowshop sequencing problem, European Journal of Operational Research, in press (2006).

26. C.-J. Liao, C.-T. Tseng, P. Luarn, A discrete version of particle swarm optimization for flowshop scheduling problems, Computers and Operations Research, in press.

27. R. Ruiz, C. Maroto, J. Alcaraz, Two new robust genetic algorithms for the flowshop scheduling problems, OMEGA 34 (2006) 461-476.

28. R. Ruiz, T. Stutzle, A simple and effective iterated greedy algorithm for the permutation flowshop scheduling problem, European Journal of Operational Research, in press (2006).

29. E. Taillard, Benchmarks for basic scheduling problems, European Journal of Operational Research 64 (1993) 278-285.

30. R.C. Eberhart and J. Kennedy, A new optimizer using particle swarm theory, In: Proceed-ings of the Sixth International Symposium on Micro Machine and Human Science, Nagoya, Japan, (1995) 39-43.

31. J. Kennedy, R.C. Eberhart, and Y. Shi, Swarm Intelligence, San Mateo, Morgan Kaufmann, CA, USA, (2001).

32. Q.K. Pan, M.F. Tasgetiren, and Y.C. Liang, A discrete particle swarm optimization algorithm for the no-wait flowshop scheduling problem with makespan criterion, In: Proceedings of the International Workshop on UK Planning and Scheduling Special Interest Group (PLANSIG2005), City University, London, UK, (2005) 34-43.

33. Q.K. Pan, M.F. Tasgetiren, and Y.C. Liang, A discrete particle swarm optimization algorithm for the no-wait flowshop scheduling problem with makespan and total flowtime criteria, (Under review by Computers and Operations Research).

34. Q.K. Pan, M.F. Tasgetiren, and Y.C. Liang, A discrete particle swarm optimization algorithm for the single-machine total weighted earliness and tardiness penalties with a com-mon due date, In: Proceeding of the World Congress on Evolutionary Computation (CEC06), accepted (2006).

35. Q.K. Pan, M.F. Tasgetiren, and Y.C. Liang, Minimizing total earliness and tardiness penalties with a common due date on single machine using a discrete particle swarm optimization algorithm, In: Proceedings of the 5th International Workshop on Ant Colony Optimization and Swarm Intelligence (ANTS2006), Accepted (2006).

36. E. Taillard, Summary of best known lower and upper bounds of Taillard's instances. Available in http:// ina2.eivd.ch/ collaborateurs/ etd/ problemes.dir/ ordonnance-ment.dir/ ordonnancement.html

Initialization Method for Grammar-Guided Genetic Programming

M. García-Arnau, D. Manrique, J. Ríos, A. Rodríguez-Patón
Artificial Intelligence Department, U. Politécnica de Madrid
dmanrique@fi.upm.es

Abstract

This paper proposes a new tree-generation algorithm for grammar-guided genetic programming that includes a parameter to control the maximum size of the trees to be generated. An important feature of this algorithm is that the initial populations generated are adequately distributed in terms of tree size and distribution within the search space. Consequently, genetic programming systems starting from the initial populations generated by the proposed method have a higher convergence speed. Two different problems have been chosen to carry out the experiments: a laboratory test involving searching for arithmetical equalities and the real-world task of breast cancer prognosis. In both problems, comparisons have been made to another five important initialization methods.

1. Introduction

Genetic programming (GP) is a means of automatically generating computer programs by employing operations inspired by biological evolution [1]. First, the initial population is randomly generated, and then genetic operators, such as selection, crossover, mutation and replacement, are executed to breed a population of trial solutions that improves over time [2].

All genetic programming algorithms start with the random generation of the initial population, which is composed of individuals (computer programs) that represent possible solutions to the search problem at hand. The main disadvantage of this process is that, being completely random, it causes the generation of invalid individuals: programs that too large or that do not belong to the search space because they do not represent possible solutions to the problem. One way to overcome this drawback is to keep on generating individuals, discarding the invalid ones, until the initial population is complete. However, the computational cost of this approach is extremely high for problems requiring large population sizes [3].

Grammar-guided genetic programming (GGGP) is an extension of traditional GP systems whose goal is to solve the closure problem [4]. This problem involves always generating valid individuals (points or possible solutions that belong to the search space), which directly affects the initial population-generating algorithm. To solve the closure problem, GGGP employs a context-free grammar (CFG), which establishes a formal definition of the syntactical restrictions of the problem to be solved and its possible solutions. Each of the individuals handled by GGGP is a derivation tree that generates and represents a sentence (solution) belonging to the language defined by the CFG [5].

The issue of population initialization has received surprisingly little attention in the genetic programming literature. Since the Grow, Full and Ramped Half-and-half algorithms [6], only a few papers have appeared on the subject [7], and one simple and commonly used approach to generating the initial population in GGGP is to randomly execute the grammar productions that output sentences belonging to the language defined by the CFG. This is what is known as Basic procedure and starts with the axiom of the grammar and continues with the non-terminal symbols of the consequents of the productions executed until no more non-terminal symbols are obtained. These approaches assure the generation of valid sentences, but they cannot control the size of the trees generated (size is equivalent to depth, defined as the maximum number of connected nodes existing from the root to the leaves of a derivation tree).

Random Branch [8] is another interesting tree-generation algorithm that takes a requested size and guarantees the generation of trees of that or a smaller size. The disadvantage here is that there are many trees that this algorithm cannot produce. So, the populations generated are not well distributed within the search space, what has a negative impact on the convergence speed of the genetic programming system [9]. Uniform is the name usually given to the Exact Uniform Tree Generation algorithm [10]. This approach also takes a requested tree size and guarantees that it will create a tree chosen uniformly from the full set of all possible trees of that size. Uniform is too complex, as it must first compute a number of tables offline, including a table of numbers of trees for all sizes up to a maximum permitted depth. PTC1 and PTC2 modify the Grow algorithm to guarantee that generated trees will be around an expected size [3].

This paper proposes a new tree-generation algorithm to initialize grammar-guided genetic programming systems that is called GBIM: grammar-based initialization method. GBIM is able to generate valid individuals, not larger than a predefined size, to build a random initial population. This algorithm has been compared to the five tree generation algorithms described above: Ramped Half-and-Half, Basic, Random Branch, Uniform and PTC2, which have been chosen because of their widely differing approaches and importance in literature. The results show that GBIM has an important feature: the populations generated are well distributed in terms of tree size and within the search space. According to recent research pointing out that the method for initializing the population is very important in the convergence speed of GGGP [9], the experiments show that the same genetic programming system converges faster when the initial population is generated by GBIM.

Two problems have been used to carry out the experiments. The first involves the genetic programming of a laboratory problem involving searching for arithmetical equalities. The second problem consists of analyzing masses in breast tissue suspected of being carcinomas. The training and test patterns have been extracted from a database of real patients stored at a university hospital in Madrid.

1.1 Theoretical Background

A context-free grammar G is defined as a string-rewiring system comprising a 4-tuple $G=(\Sigma_N, \Sigma_T, S, P) / \Sigma_N \cap \Sigma_T = \emptyset$, where Σ_N is the alphabet of non-terminal symbols, Σ_T is the alphabet of terminal symbols, S represents the start symbol or axiom of the grammar, and P is the set of production rules, written in BNF (Backus-Naur Form).

Based on this grammar, the individuals that are part of the genetic population are defined as derivation trees, where the root is the axiom S, the internal nodes contain only non-terminal symbols and the external nodes (leaves) contain only terminal symbols. A derivation tree represents the series of derivation steps that generate a sentence that is a possible solution to the problem. Therefore, an individual codifies a sentence of the language generated by the grammar as a derivation tree.

By way of an example, which will be used throughout this paper for the sake of clarity, a CFG is defined in (1). This CFG represents arithmetic equalities with sums and subtractions of one-digit integer numbers on the left side of the equality and a one-digit integer number on the right side.

$G=(\Sigma_N, \Sigma_T, S, P)$ with:

$\Sigma_N = \{S, E, F, N\}$

$\Sigma_T = \{0, 1, 2, 3, 4, 5, 6, 7, 8, 9, +, -, =\}$

$P = \{ \quad S ::= E = N;$

$\qquad E ::= E + E \mid E\text{-}E \mid F + E \mid F - E \mid N;$

$\qquad F ::= N$

$\qquad N ::= 0 \mid 1 \mid 2 \mid 3 \mid 5 \mid 6 \mid 7 \mid 8 \mid 9 \quad \}.$

$\hfill (1)$

A sentence is ambiguous if it can be obtained by different derivation trees. A grammar G is ambiguous if any sentence that belongs to the language defined by the grammar is ambiguous. The grammar defined in (1) is ambiguous because there are sentences for which more than one derivation tree can be found. Figure 1 shows that sentence $3 + 4 = 7$ can be obtained from two different derivation trees. Ambiguous grammars will be used in the experiments to employ the grammar-based crossover operator [11] in the genetic programming system that evolves the populations initialized by GBIM and the other approaches to be compared.

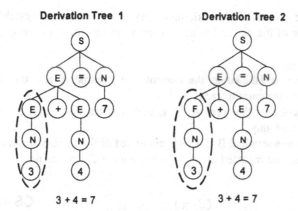

Figure 1 Representation of two different derivations for the sentence (3 + 4 = 7)

2.   The Grammar-Based Initialization Method

The algorithm for randomly generating populations (GBIM, Grammar-Based Initialization Method) aims to output the initial population of any GGGP system. This algorithm's key feature is that, when generating individuals, their productions are not selected totally at random, but are chosen especially because they assure that the individual belongs to the language generated by the grammar and that the size of its derivation tree does not surpass a preset value. This leads to a significant computational saving in terms of time and memory, especially in large populations, since all the individuals generated are valid for the population, and none are discarded on the grounds of syntactic disqualification or for being oversized. Also, as shown in the results section, the trees generated by GBIM are uniformly distributed in terms of size and throughout the search space, which helps to increase the convergence speed of GGGP.

GBIM has two parameters: the target number of individuals for the population (N) and the maximum permitted size (D). Given a CFG G=(Σ_N, Σ_T, S, P), GBIM consists of three steps:

1. Calculate the length for each production rule of the grammar A::=α $\in$ P, A$\in\Sigma$N, $\alpha$$\in\Sigma$* : Σ = ΣN U ΣT. To do this, the following definitions are given:
   Definition 1. The length of a terminal symbol a$\in\Sigma_T$ is 0. It is denoted by L(a) = 0.
   Definition 2. The length of a production rule that only derives terminal symbols is 1. It is denoted by L (A ::=a) = 1, $\forall$A $\in$ ΣN and $\forall$a $\in$ ΣT*.
   Definition 3. The length of a production rule A::= α is the result of adding one to the maximum of the symbol lengths constituting the consequent. It is denoted by L(A::=α).
   Definition 4. The length of a non-terminal symbol A is the minimum of the lengths of all its productions. It is denoted by L (A).

2. Calculate the length of the axiom, L (S) = d. This length establishes the minimum size of the derivation tree of the valid sentences of the grammar, so that d ≤ D.
3. Repeat N times:
    3.1 The axiom is labeled as the current non-terminal A and the value 0 is assigned to the current size (CS).
    3.2 A production of the form A ::= α that satisfies CS + L(A ::= α) ≤ D is selected randomly.
    3.3 For each non-terminal B ∈ α, B is annotated as the current non-terminal and 3.2 and 3.3 are repeated increasing the value of CS by one unit.

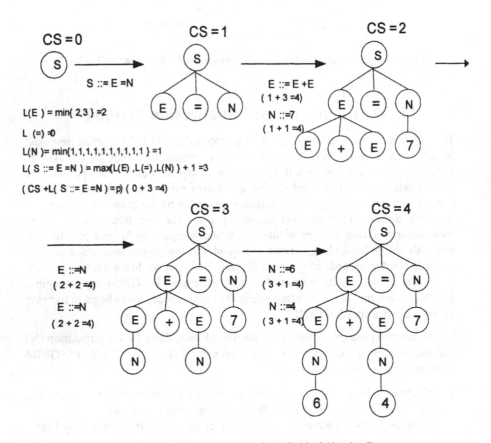

Figure 2 Using GBIM to generate the individual (6 + 4 = 7)

Figure 2 shows the generation process of the individual 6 + 4 = 7, which belongs to the grammar proposed as an example in (1) and taking D=5. First, the length of each grammar production is calculated by applying definitions 1, 2, 3 and 4, as shown in Table 1. Since L(S)=3, then d=3; therefore, it is possible to generate individuals with a size lower than D=5.

Then, CS = 0 is assigned and the only production holding for the axiom is selected: S::=E=N, which satisfies CS+ L(S::=E=N)≤ 5. For each non-terminal B Є {E=N}, a production that meets the condition of 3.2 is randomly selected and then CS is incremented by 1.

Table 1 Production rules p defined in (1) and their lengths L(p), which have been calculated following definitions 1, 2, 3 and 4

Production p	L (p)
S::= E = N	3
E::= E + E	3
E::= E - E	3
E::= F + E	3
E::= F - E	3
E::= N	2
F::= N	2
N::= 0|1|2|3|4|5|6|7|8|9	1

3.   Results

The results yielded by the proposed initialization method (GBIM) and their comparison with Ramped Half-and-Half, Basic, Random Branch, Uniform and PTC2 are presented and discussed in terms of distribution of the generated tree sizes, the computational cost needed to generate initial populations and the convergence speed exhibited by a GGGP when using each of these approaches. In all experiments, sample size was 100.

To do so, two problems have been employed: the search of arithmetical equalities (the example used throughout this paper), whose possible solutions are expressed by means of the grammar defined in (1); and a complex real-world classification problem that consists of providing a prognosis (benign or malignant) from the morphological characteristics of one of the most frequent types of oncological lesions: abnormal masses found in breast tissue.

The GGGP system used in the experiments employs the genetic operators (selection, crossover, mutation and replacement) to search for the optimal solution from populations initialized with the six generation algorithms to be compared. Tournament selection has been used. The chosen crossover is the Grammar-Based Crossover operator [11] to exploit its capabilities working with ambiguous grammars like the one defined in (1). The subtree generated in mutation from an established node uses GBIM to restrict the size of the new mutated tree, and SSGA is employed for replacement. For each test, a set of 100 independent runs was performed to give averaged results. After some tuning runs, we decided on the following settings. The operator rates were: 80% crossover, 15% straight reproduction and 5% mutation. Tournament with a size of 7.

3.1 Search for Arithmetical Equalities

To give an idea of the importance of approaches that can control the size of the individuals (derivation trees) that are being generated, we first show the results yielded by the algorithm called Basic when generating the initial population. This approach does not check whether the randomly generated individuals exceed the maximum permitted size and, therefore, whether they are valid. The parameters for this algorithm are the maximum permitted size of the individuals to be generated (D) and the number of trees of which the population is composed (population size). Table 2 shows the invalid individuals generated and the average size of the individuals of the population according to the two input parameters, as well as their standard deviations (SD) in brackets.

Table 2 Invalid individuals generated by the Basic initialization method. Values achieved after 100 independent runs. Standard deviations are represented are shown within brackets

Size (D)	Population size	Avg. tree size		Invalid individuals	
3	10	3.00	(0.0)	85.03	(12.38)
3	20	3.00	(0.0)	121.15	(14.10)
3	50	3.00	(0.0)	390.85	(34.87)
3	100	3.00	(0.0)	844.09	(66.52)
12	10	5.40	(2.27)	2.62	(0.69)
12	20	5.15	(2.21)	3.14	(0.88)
12	50	4.90	(2.15)	3.23	(0.86)
12	100	5.66	(2.34)	12.04	(2.26)

The minimum size for an individual in this problem is 3. Logically, the closer D is to this value the more invalid individuals are generated using the Basic approach, because there are few possibilities of selecting productions in the grammar that generate small-sized individuals. For example, an average of 112 individuals are generated to yield 100 with a size less than or equal to 12 (last row of Table 2: 100 + 12.04 ≈ 112). However, when D = 3, the Basic approach generates a total of 944 individuals (100 + 844.09) to yield 100 valid individuals. From these results, we can conclude that the larger the population size to be generated and the smaller the maximum permitted size are, the more efficient GBIM, Ramped Half-and-Half, Random Branch, Uniform and PTC2 are, because none of them generate invalid individuals.

The next experiment compares the average tree sizes, the efficiency of the six tree generation algorithms under study and the convergence speed achieved by the same GGGP system starting from initial populations generated by Ramped Half-and-Half, Basic, Random Branch, Uniform, PTC2 and GBIM.

Table 3 shows the results of this experiment taking a maximum tree size of 12 (D = 12) in all cases. The number of individuals to be generated for the initial population (population size) ranged from 10 to 100, although Table 3 only shows the results for generating 10 and 100 individuals, because they are the most representative. The second column of this table indicates the algorithm used to initialize the population, then the average tree size of the individuals of the population generated is shown for each algorithm and population size. Computational cost expresses the mean number of operations (in thousands) needed to generate an initial population, and, finally, the last column shows the average number of generations needed to reach convergence. The fitness of an individual for the GGGP system in this experiment is calculated as the absolute value of the difference between the left- and right-hand sides of the equality within the arithmetical expression. So, this is a minimization problem and is assumed to converge when at least half of the individuals of the population represent a true arithmetical expression (fitness = 0).

Table 3 Comparison of the tree generation algorithms: average tree size, operations needed to initialize the population and the convergence speed of the GGGP system that employs each initialization method for D = 12. Values achieved after 100 independent runs. Standard deviations are represented in brackets

Population size	Algorithm	Avg. tree size		Computational Cost (thousands)		Generations	
10	Basic	5.40	(1.18)	62.8	(8.36)	19.7	(2.34)
100	Basic	5.66	(1.21)	644.6	(78.34)	78.3	(6.12)
10	Ramped	5.95	(1.96)	63.2	(8.38)	14.8	(2.15)
100	Ramped	6.12	(1.94)	664.9	(80.24)	55.1	(5.43)
10	Random B.	6.21	(2.10)	64.3	(8.42)	16.0	(2.22)
100	Random B.	6.02	(2.08)	883.0	(85.36)	58.3	(5.75)
10	Uniform	11.86	(0.36)	87.2	(9.79)	17.4	(2.29)
100	Uniform	11.91	(0.29)	901.3	(94.77)	64.9	(5.92)
10	PCT2	6.43	(2.39)	65.9	(8.39)	13.5	(2.16)
100	PCT2	6.95	(2.44)	678.2	(81.56)	52.6	(5.40)
10	GBIM	7.20	(3.02)	66.3	(8.35)	12.7	(2.13)
100	GBIM	7.68	(3.32)	685.7	(82.56)	45.8	(5.38)

Looking at the results, we find from the average tree size column that the Basic algorithm generates individuals that tend to be small, which indicates that the populations generated by this algorithm are not adequately distributed in the search space. This behaviour is because the generation of larger trees increases the probability of invalid (oversized) individuals being output. The Uniform algorithm, evidently, generates uniformly distributed individuals, but all of them very close to the maximum permitted size. Therefore, a well distributed population is not generated because it does not include trees of all possible sizes. The remainder of algorithms generate populations that can be considered suitably distributed, with an average tree size ranging from 6 to 8 and high standard deviation (not shown in Table 3), which indicates a wide range of different tree sizes.

Following on with the analysis of the results reported in Table 3, the average number of generations needed by the GGGP system to reach convergence confirms that the convergence speed of GGGP depends on the exploratory capability of the initialization algorithm employed [12]. GBIM and PCT2 get the best results. It should be stressed that the Uniform and Basic algorithms yield the worst results because they cannot generate initial populations formed by individuals that are well distributed in size and, therefore, throughout the search space. Random Branch also gets poor results because it cannot create well distributed populations in the search space either. The reason, in this case, however, is because this method cannot produce all possible individuals.

The computational cost of generating the initial populations column of Table 3 reports that the Basic algorithm is less costly than the others, because it does not run any checks at the time of generating the individuals. Another important point in this respect is the high computational cost of generating larger populations exhibited by Uniform. The reason is that this is a more complex algorithm because it has to place a limit on the size of the trees created of about 12. GBIM, PCT2 and Ramped Half-and-Half achieve similar and intermediate results.

From the results of this table, it can be concluded that the GGGP system employing GBIM as an initialization algorithm achieves the best results in terms of convergence speed. This is because GBIM outputs initial populations that are adequately distributed in size and, therefore, throughout the search space, with an intermediate computational cost as compared with the other approaches studied.

3.2 Breast Cancer Prognosis: Suspect Masses

The second experiment involved searching a knowledge base of fuzzy rules [13] that could give a prognosis of masses present in breast tissue suspected of being carcinomas. A total of 315 mass-type lesions are stored in a database of real patients aged from 25 to 79 years at a Madrid university hospital. From these 315 lesions, 265 were selected randomly to train the genetic programming system, and the remaining 50 were used to perform tests. For each lesion, the database stores the hospital expert radiologists' prognosis, the actual prognosis after carrying out a biopsy and the following morphological characteristics:

- Size. This represents the size of the mass, measured as the widest diameter in millimeters.
- Morphology of the mass. This has five possible values: architectural distortions, lobulated, oval, round and irregular.
- Margins. This characteristic describes the external limits of the mass. It has five possible values: circumscribed, ill-defined, microlobulated, spiculated and obscured.
- Density. This represents the texture of the tissue inside the mass. The possible values are: high, equal, low and fatty.

It took a CFG containing 16 non-terminal symbols, 51 terminals and 55 production rules to set up a fuzzy knowledge base to solve this problem. Figure 3 shows, by way of an example, part of a valid individual (derivation tree) that represents a fuzzy rule included in the knowledge base that best solves the masses prognosis problem. The fitness value of an individual corresponds to the number of lesions in which the prognosis inferred by the fuzzy knowledge base represented by this individual is different from the prognosis made after the biopsy.

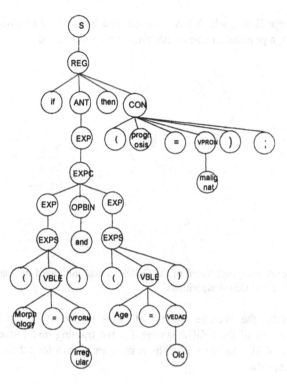

Figure 3 An individual representing the fuzzy rule: if (Morphology = Irregular) and (Age = Old) then (Prognosis = Malignant)

Experimentation has been done to show the number of invalid individuals that can be generated if there is no control over the tree sizes as occurs with the Basic initialization algorithm. An average of 434.37 invalid individuals is generated to get a population of 100 individuals of a maximum tree size (D) of 7, which is the minimum size that the individuals can have in this problem. If D is raised to 20, then 256.62 oversized trees are obtained to generate a population of 100 individuals. This value is higher than the number output in the same experiment on the previous problem for D = 12 (see Table 2). This is explained by the higher complexity of the grammar used to define the syntactical rules of this problem, which indicates that individuals tend to be larger.

The findings for this experiment are similar to the results shown in Table 3. Taking D = 20, the average tree size generated by GBIM to build an initial population is 13.60. Values ranging from 10 to 14 are achieved by PCT2, Random Branch and Ramped Half-and-Half. On the other hand, Basic generates individuals with an average size of 7.47, and, logically, the size of the individuals created by Uniform is close to 20. Again, GBIM and PCT2 get the best results in terms of the convergence speed of the GGGP system starting from the populations generated by these two algorithms. Figure 4 shows the evolution process (200 generations) for the average fitness of the populations generated by all the tree generation algorithms except Basic, which has been omitted because of its poor results. For this experiment, a population size of 100 and D = 20 were used.

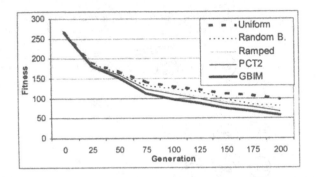

Figure 4 Average convergence speed of the GGGP system initialized by Ramped, Random B., Uniform, PCT2 and GBIM algorithms

Table 4 illustrates the average number of cases incorrectly classified after 200 training generations of the GGGP system for the training and test cases, using a population size of 100 and D = 20. The results are shown for all the initialization algorithms except Basic.

Table 4. Average number of masses incorrectly classified after 200 generations for the training and test cases by the same GGGP system using different initialization algorithms. Population size is 100 and D = 20

Initialization Algorithm	Misclassified cases. Training	Misclassified cases. Testing
Uniform	99/265 (37.36 %)	19/50 (38 %)
Random B.	83/265 (31.32 %)	16/50 (32 %)
Ramped	75/265 (28.30 %)	14/50 (28 %)
PCT2	68/265 (25.66 %)	13/50 (26 %)
GBIM	58/265 (21.89 %)	11/50 (22%)

PCT2 and GBIM get better results than the Ramped, Random Branch and Uniform initialization methods. Again, this is because these two algorithms distribute the individuals of the population throughout the search space better, and therefore puts the GGGP system at an advantage for achieving the best solutions. The GGGP system with PCT2 correctly classifies 74.34% (197/265) of the training lesions and 74% (37/50) of the test lesions. The GGGP system working with GBIM yields the best results and the swiftest convergence speed: 78.11 % (207/265) of correct results in training lesions and 78% (39/50) in test lesions.

4. Conclusion

This paper proposes a new tree generation algorithm, called Grammar-Based Initialization Method (GBIM), for grammar-based genetic programming. This approach can establish a parameter indicating the maximum size of the trees generated for the initial population of a GGGP system. GBIM is able to generate trees that are well distributed in terms of size. This is a very important feature because, according to recent research results, we have experimentally shown that the initialization strategy is very important in GGGP.

The overall results of GGGP are strongly affected by the initialization method used. The results section reported that GBIM can lead the GGGP system employed to the highest convergence speed with an intermediate computational cost. We suggest that the high convergence speed is because GBIM provides an adequate size distribution of the individuals in the initial population, which creates more structural diversity. Good structural diversity in the initial population implies a good distribution of its individuals throughout the search space. This leads to very good initial exploratory capabilities, enabling the GGGP to arrive very rapidly at the optimum solution.

As future research work, we intend to explore the breadth of these conclusions by extending the investigation to a wider sample of problems. We are also researching the design of a new GGGP system by developing new crossover and mutation operators that can take advantage of the features provided by GBIM to improve the overall performance of GGGP.

Acknowledgements

This research is being funded by the Spanish Ministry of Science and Education under project Ref. DEP2005-00232-C03-03.

References

1. Koza JR. Genetically Breeding Populations of Computer Programs to Solve Problems in Artificial Intelligence. Tech. Rep. CS-TR-90-1314, Department of Computer Science, Stanford University, 1990
2. Langdon WB, Poli R. Foundations of Genetic Programming. Springer-Verlag, London, UK, 2001
3. Luke S. Two Fast Tree-Creation Algorithms for Genetic Programming. IEEE Trans. on Evolutionary Computation 2000; 4, 3: 274-283
4. Koza JR, Keane MA, Streeter MJ, et al. Genetic Programming IV: Routine Human-Competitive Machine Intelligence. Kluwer Academic Publishers, Norwell, MA, 2005
5. Whigham PA. Grammatically-Based Genetic Programming. In: Rosca JP (ed) Proceedings of the Workshop on Genetic Programming: From Theory to Real-World Applications. Tahoe City, California, USA, 1995, pp 33-41
6. Koza JR. Genetic Programming: On the Programming of Computers by Means of Natural Selection. MIT Press, Cambridge, MA, USA, 1992

44

7. Luke S, Panait L. A Survey and Comparison of Tree Generation Algorithms. In: Proceedings of the Genetic and Evolutionary Computation Conference, San Francisco, CA, USA, 2001, pp 81-88
8. Chellapilla K. Evolving Computer Programs without Subtree Crossover. IEEE Transactions on Evolutionary Computation 1997; 1, 3: 209-216
9. Hao HT, Hoai NX, McKay RB. Does This Matter Where to Start in Grammar Guided Genetic Programming?. In: Proceedings of the 2nd Pacific Asian Workshop in Genetic Programming, Cairns, Australia, 2004 (Electronic)
10. Bohm W, Geyer-Schulz A. Exact Uniform Initialization for Genetic Programming. In: Belew RK, Bose M (ed) Foundations of Genetic Algorithms IV, Morgan Kaufmann, University of San Diego, CA, USA, 1996, pp 379-407
11. Manrique D, Márquez F, Ríos J, Rodríguez-Patón A. Grammar Based Crossover Operator in Genetic Programming. In: Mira J, Alvarez JR (ed): Artificial Intelligence and Knowledge Engineering Applications: A Bioinspired Approach. Springer-Verlag, New York, 2005, pp 252-261 (Lecture notes in computer science no. 3562)
12. Barrios D, Carrascal A, Manrique D, Ríos J. Optimization with Real-Coded Genetic Algorithms Based on Mathematical Morphology. Intern J Computer Math 2003; 8, 3: 275-293
13. Geyer-Schulz A. Fuzzy Rule-Based Expert Systems and Genetic Machine Learning, vol 3. Springer-Verlag, New York, 1996

Improving the Gradient Based Search Direction to Enhance Training Efficiency of Back Propagation Based Neural Network Algorithms

Nazri Mohd Nawi, Meghana R. Ransing and Rajesh S. Ransing
Civil and Computational Engineering Centre, University of Wales
Swansea, United Kingdom
R.S.Ransing@swan.ac.uk
www.swan.ac.uk/c2ec

Abstract

Most of the gradient based optimisation algorithms employed during training process of back propagation networks use negative gradient of error as a gradient based search direction. A novel approach is presented in this paper for improving the training efficiency of back propagation neural network algorithms by adaptively modifying this gradient based search direction. The proposed algorithm uses the value of gain parameter in the activation function to modify the gradient based search direction. It has been shown that this modification can significantly enhance the computational efficiency of training process. The proposed algorithm is generic and can be implemented in almost all gradient based optimisation processes. The robustness of the proposed algorithm is shown by comparing convergence rates for gradient descent, conjugate gradient and quasi-Newton methods on many benchmark examples.

1. Introduction

Improving training efficiency of neural network based algorithm is an active area of research and numerous papers have been proposed in the literature. Early research on back propagation algorithms saw improvements on: (i) selection of better error functions [1-8]; (ii) different choices for activation functions [3, 9] and, (iii) selection of dynamic learning rate and momentum [10-12].

Later, as summarised by Bishop [13], various optimisation techniques were suggested for improving efficiency of the error minimisation process or in other words the training efficiency. Among these are methods of Fletcher and Powel [14] and the Fletcher-Reeves [15] that improve the conjugate gradient method of Hestenes and Stiefel [16] and the family of Quasi-Newton algorithms proposed by Huang [17].

This paper suggests that a simple modification to the gradient based search direction used by almost all optimisation method that has been summarised by Bishop[13] can substantially improve the training efficiency. The gradient based search direction is locally modified by a gain value used in the activation function

45

of the corresponding node to improve the convergence rates respective of the optimisation algorithm used.

The remaining of the paper is organised as follows: Section two illustrates the proposed method. In the following section, Section three, the implementation issues of the proposed method in other gradient based optimisation process are discussed. In Section four, the robustness of proposed algorithm is shown by comparing convergence rates for gradient descent, conjugate gradient and quasi Newton methods on many bench mark examples. The paper is concluded in the final section along with short discussion on further research.

2.   The Proposed method

The following iterative algorithm has been proposed for changing the gradient based search direction using a gain value.

Initialise the initial weight vector with random values and the vector of gain values with unit values. Repeat the following steps 1 and 2 on an epoch-by-epoch basis until the given error minimisation criteria are satisfied.

Step 1   *By introducing gain value into activation function, calculate the gradient of error with respect to weights by using Equation (5), and gradient of error with respect to the gain parameter by using Equation (7)*

Step 2   *Use the gradient weight vector and gradient of gain vector calculated in step 1 to calculate the new weight vector and vector of new gain values for use in the next epoch.*

2.1   Derivation of the expression to calculate gain value:

Consider a multilayer feed-forward network, as used in standard back propagation algorithm[18]. Suppose that for a particular input pattern o^0, the desired output is the teacher pattern $t = [t_1...t_n]^T$, and the actual output is o_k^L, where L denotes the output layer. The error function on that pattern is defined as,

$$E = \frac{1}{2}\sum_k (t_k - o_k^L)^2 \tag{1}$$

Let o_k^s be the activation values for the kth node of layer s, and let $o^s = [o_1^s...o_n^s]^T$ be the column vector of activation values in the layer s and the input layer as layer 0. Let w_{ij}^s be the weight values for the connecting link between the ith node in layer $s-1$ and the jth node in layer s, and let $w_j^s = [w_{1j}^s...w_{nj}^s]^T$ be the column vector of weights from layer $s-1$ to the jth node of layer s. The net input to the jth node of layer s is defined as $net_j^s = (w_j^s, o^{s-1}) = \sum_k w_{j,k}^s o_k^{s-1}$, and let $net^s = [net_1^s \dots net_n^s]^T$ be the column vector of the net input values in layer s. The activation value for a node is given by a function of its net inputs and the gain parameter c_j^s;

$$o_j^s = f(c_j^s net_j^s) \tag{2}$$

where f is any function with bounded derivative. This information is now used to derive an expression for modifying gain values for the next epoch. Most of gradient based optimisation methods use the following gradient descent rule:

$$\Delta w_{ij}^{(n)} = -\eta^{(n)} \frac{\partial E}{\partial w_{ij}^{(n)}} \tag{3}$$

where $\eta^{(n)}$ is the learning rate value at step n and the gradient based search direction at step n is $d^{(n)} = -\frac{\partial E}{\partial w_{ij}^{(n)}} = g^{(n)}$.

In the proposed method the gradient based search direction is modified by including the variation of gain value to yield

$$d^{(n)} = -\frac{\partial E}{\partial w_{ij}^{(n)}}(c_j^{(n)}) = g^{(n)}(c_j^{(n)}) \tag{4}$$

The derivation of the procedure for calculating the gain value is based on the gradient descent algorithm. The error function as defined in Equation (1) is differentiated with respect to the weight value w_{ij}^s. The chain rule yields,

$$\frac{\partial E}{\partial w_{ij}^s} = \frac{\partial E}{\partial net^{s+1}} \cdot \frac{\partial net^{s+1}}{\partial o_j^s} \cdot \frac{\partial o_j^s}{\partial net_j^s} \cdot \frac{\partial net_j^s}{\partial w_{ij}^s}$$

$$= [-\delta_1^{s+1} \dots -\delta_n^{s+1}] \cdot \begin{bmatrix} w_{1j}^{s+1} \\ \vdots \\ w_{nj}^{s+1} \end{bmatrix} \cdot f'(c_j^s net_j^s) c_j^s . o_j^{s-1} \tag{5}$$

where $\delta_j^s = -\frac{\partial E}{\partial net_j^s}$. In particular, the first three factors of Equation (5) indicate that the following equation holds:

$$\delta_1^s = (\sum_k \delta_k^{s+1} w_{k,j}^{s+1}) f'(c_j^s net_j^s) c_j^s \tag{6}$$

It should be noted that, the iterative formula as described in Equation (6) to calculate δ_1^s is the same as used in the standard back propagation algorithms [19] except for the appearance of the gain value in the expression. The learning rule for calculating weight values as given in Equation (3) is derived by combining (5) and (6).

In this approach, the gradient of error with respect to the gain parameter can also be calculated by using the chain rule as previously described; it is easy to compute as

$$\frac{\partial E}{\partial c_j^s} = (\sum_k \delta_k^{s+1} w_{k,j}^{s+1}) f'(c_j^s net_j^s) net_j^s \tag{7}$$

Then the gradient descent rule for the gain value becomes,

$$\Delta c_j^s = \eta \delta_j^s \frac{net_j^s}{c_j^s} \tag{8}$$

At the end of every epoch the new gain value is updated using a simple gradient based method as given by the following formula,

$$c_j^{new} = c_j^{old} + \Delta c_j^s \tag{9}$$

3. Implementation of the proposed method with various optimisation techniques:

3.1 Gradient Descent Method with Adaptive Gain Variation (GD/AG)

In gradient descent method, the search direction at each step is given by the local negative gradient of the error function, and the step size is determined by a learning rate parameter. Suppose at step n in gradient descent algorithm, the current weight vector is w^n, and a particular gradient based search direction is d^n. The weight vector at step n+1 is computed by the following expression:

$$w^{(n+1)} = w^n + \eta^n d^n \tag{10}$$

where, η^n is the learning rate value at step n. By using the proposed method, the gradient based search direction is calculated at each step by using Equation (4).

3.2 Conjugate Gradient with Adaptive Gain Variation (CGFR/AG)

Most widely used conjugate gradient algorithms are given by Fletcher and Powel [14] and Fletcher-Reeves [15]. Both procedures generate conjugate directions for search and therefore aim to minimize a positive definite quadratic function of n variables in n steps.

The proposed algorithm known as CGFR/AG begins the minimization process with an initial estimate w_0 and as initial gradient based search direction as:

$$d_0 = -\nabla E(w_0) = -g_0 \tag{11}$$

Then, for every epoch by using our proposed method in Equation (4) the search direction at $(n+1)^{th}$ iteration is calculated as:

$$d_{n+1} = -\frac{\partial E}{\partial w_{n+1}}(c_{i,n+1}) + \beta_n(c_{i,n})d_n(c_{i,n}) \tag{12}$$

where the scalar β_n is to be determined by the requirement that d_n and d_{n+1} must fulfil the conjugacy property[13]. There are many formulae for the parameter β_n. In this paper we used the formula introduced by Fletcher and Reeves [15] and is given as:

$$\beta_n = \frac{g_{n+1}^T g_{n+1}}{g_n^T g_n} \tag{13}$$

The complete CGFR/AG algorithm works as follows;

Step 1 Initialize the weight vector randomly, the gradient vector g_0 to zero and gain vector to unit values. Let the first search direction d_0 be g_0. Set $\beta_0 = 0$, $epoch = 1$ and $n = 1$. Let Nt be the total number of weight values. Select a convergence tolerance value as CT.

Step 2 At step n, evaluate the gradient vector $g_n(c_n)$.

Step 3 Evaluate $E(w_n)$. If $E(w_n) < CT$ then STOP training ELSE go to step 4.

Step 4 Calculate a new gradient based search direction which is a function of gain parameter: $d_n = -g_n(c_n) + \beta_{n-1}d_{n-1}$

Step 5 If $n > 1$ THEN,

update $\beta_{n+1} = \frac{g_{n+1}^T(c_{n+1})g_{n+1}(c_{n+1})}{g_n^T(c_n)g_n(c_n)}$ ELSE go to step 6.

Step 6 If $[(epoch+1)/Nt] = 0$ THEN 'restart' the gradient vector with $d_n = -g_{n-1}(c_{n-1})$ ELSE go to step 7.

Step 7 Calculate the optimal value for learning rate η_n^* by using line search technique such as: $E(w_n + \eta_n^* d_n) = \min_{\lambda \geq 0} E(w_n + \eta_n d_n)$

Step 8 Update w_n: $w_{n+1} = w_n - \eta_n^* d_n$

Step 9 Evaluate the new gradient vector $g_{n+1}(c_{n+1})$ with respect to gain value c_{n+1}.

Step 10 Calculate the new gradient based search direction:
$$d_{n+1} = -g_{n+1}(c_{n+1}) + \beta_n(c_n)d_n$$
Step 11 Set $n = n+1$ and go to step 2.

3.3 Quasi-Newton method with Adaptive Gain Variation (BFGS/AG)

The Broyden-Fletcher-Goldfarb-Shanno (BFGS) algorithm [20, 21] is an approximation to Newton's method that is briefly explained below. Suppose that we have an error function $E(w)$ which we want to minimize with respect to the parameter vector W, then the search direction d for Newton's method is found by solving the system of equations

$$d = -[\nabla^2 E(w)]^{-1}\nabla E(w) \qquad (14)$$

where $\nabla^2 E(w) = H$ is the Hessian matrix and $\nabla E(w) = g$.

With the proposed approach, particularly using the gradient vector that is a function of the gain parameter $(g_n(c_n))$ as described in Equation (4), the modification can also be easily implemented in the BFGS algorithm. The modified BFGS algorithm (BFGS/AG) is described as follows:

Step 1 Initialize the initial weight vector $w(0)$ to random values and undertake a positive definite initialization of the Hessian matrix $H(0)$. Select a convergence tolerance CT.

Step 2 Compute the gradient based search direction d_n at step n by taking into account the gain variation $d_n = -H_n g_n(c_n)$

Step 3 Search the optimal value for η_n^* by using line search technique such as:
$$E(w_n + \eta_n^* d_n) = \min_{\lambda \geq 0} E(w_n + \eta_n d_n)$$

Step 4 Update w_n: $w_{n+1} = w_n - \eta_n^* d_n$

Step 5 Compute:
$$s_n = w_{n+1} - w_n$$

$$y_n = g_{n+1}(c_{n+1}) - g_n(c_n)$$

$$\nabla_n = \left(1 + \frac{y_n^T H_n y_n}{s_n^T y_n}\right)\frac{s_n s_n^T}{s_n^T y_n} - \frac{s_n y_n^T H_n}{s_n^T y_n}$$

Step 6 Update the inverse matrix H_n: $H_{n+1} = H_n + \nabla_n$

Step 7 Compute the error function value $E(w_n)$

Step 8 If $E(w_n) > CT$ go to step 2, else stop training

4 Results and Discussions

4.1 Preliminaries

The performance criteria used to asses the result of proposed method focuses on the speed of convergence, measured in number of iterations as well as the corresponding CPU time. The benchmark problems used for verification process are taken from the open literature[22].

Four classification problems have been tested including Thyroid, Wisconsin breast cancer, Diabetes and IRIS classification problem. The simulations have been carried out on a Pentium IV with 3 GHz PC, 1 GB RAM and using MATLAB version 6.5.0 (R13).

On each problem, the following nine algorithms were analysed and simulated.

1) The standard gradient descent with momentum (*traingdm*) from 'Matlab Neural Network Toolbox version 4.0.1'.
2) The standard Gradient descent with momentum (GDM)
3) The Gradient descent with momentum and Adaptive Gain (GDM/AG)
4) The standard Conjugate gradient-Fletcher-Reeves (*traincgf*) from 'Matlab Neural Network Toolbox version 4.0.1'.
5) The standard Conjugate gradient-Fletcher-Reeves (CGFR)
6) The Conjugate gradient-Fletcher-Reeves method with Adaptive Gain (CGFR/AG)
7) The standard Broyden-Fletcher-Goldfarb-Shanno (*trainbfg*) from 'Matlab Neural Network Toolbox version 4.0.1'.
8) The standard Broyden-Fletcher-Goldfarb-Shanno (BFGS).
9) The Broyden-Fletcher-Goldfarb-Shanno method with Adaptive Gain (BFGS/AG).

To compare the performance of the proposed algorithm with respect to other standard optimization algorithms from the MATLAB neural network toolbox, network parameters such as network size and architecture (number of nodes, hidden layers etc), values for the initial weights and gain parameters were kept same. For all problems the neural network had one hidden layer with five hidden nodes and sigmoid activation function was used for all nodes. All algorithms were tested using the same initial weights that were initialized randomly from range [0, 1] and received the input patterns for training in the same sequence.

For gradient descent algorithm, the learning rate value was 0.3 and the momentum term value was 0.7. The initial value used for the gain parameter was one. The values were used for comparison purpose only and hence there were no particular reason for their choice.

For each run, the numerical data is stored in two files:- the results file, and the summary file. The result file lists data about each network. The number of iterations until convergence is accumulated for each algorithm from which the mean, the standard deviation and the number of failures are calculated. The cases

52

that failed to converge are obviously excluded from the calculations of the mean and standard deviation but are reported as failures.

4.2 Verification on Bench Mark problems

For each problem, 100 different trials were run, each with different values for weights. For each run, the number of iterations required for convergence is reported. For an experiment of 100 runs, the mean of the number of iterations, the standard deviation, and the number of failures are collected. A failure occurs when the network exceeds the maximum iteration limit; each experiment is run to one thousand iterations except for back propagation which is run to ten thousand iterations as it took nine to ten thousands iterations for back propagation to reach the target error; otherwise, it is halted and the run is reported as a failure. Such a large limit for back propagation algorithm was acceptable because it is inherently inefficient as compared to other optimization algorithm. Convergence is achieved when the outputs of the network confirm to the error criterion as compared to the desired outputs.

Figure 1 displays a summary of the Thyroid classification problem. The 2D plot shows the mean, the standard deviation, and the number of failures out of 100 runs. The plot is sorted by the values of the mean. In figure 1 (a) both of the proposed algorithms show better results because they converge in smaller number of epochs as suggested by the low value of the mean. However, CGFR/AG had 3 failures as compared to the BFGS/AG algorithm. This makes the BFGS/AG algorithm a better choice for this problem since it had only 1 failure for the 100 different runs.

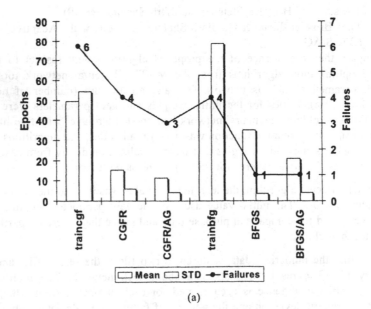

(a)

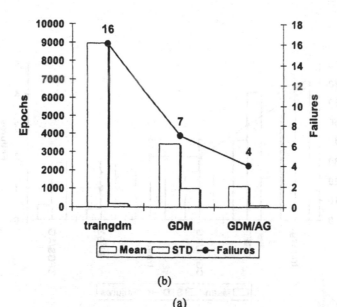

(b)

(a)

Figure 1 Thyroid summary Chart using optimisation methods (a), and gradient descent method
(b)

Figure 1 (b) also shows that training with neural network toolbox (*traingdm*) took 9000 iteration to reach the target error with 16 failures. The proposed method reduces the number of iteration for almost 9 times with only 4 failures and clearly shows that the proposed method outperforms the neural network toolbox.

Figure 2 below, shows the 2D plot for the results of the Cancer classification problem. As it can be seen from Figure 2(a) both of the proposed algorithms still outperform other algorithms as shown by the low mean value for epochs that were required for convergence. Yet for this problem BFGS/AG outperform CGFR/AG with a mean of 29, a standard deviation of 7.66 iterations and 1 failure. As for the case of gradient descent based method training, the proposed method was 8 times faster as compared to neural network toolbox (*traingdm*) in reaching the target error. Furthermore the number of failures also indicated that the training efficiency of the gradient descent method improved drastically by using the proposed method.

In Figure 3(a) the Diabetes problem required longer learning times than other previous two problems. The mean convergence ranged from 40 to 100 iterations. Even though both of the proposed methods outperform other algorithms, for this problem CGFR/AG produced the best results with 40 iterations. The neural network algorithm (*traincgf*) took twice as long to learn than the proposed method (CGFR/AG). As for gradient descent training in Figure 3(b) the neural network toolbox (*traingdm*) took almost twice longer iteration to reach the target error as compared to the proposed method. Nevertheless with only 4 failures as compared to 13 failures for the neural network toolbox, the proposed method clearly outperformed both other methods.

54

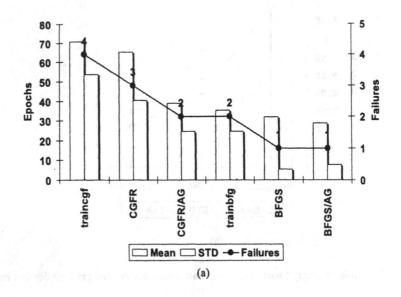

(a)

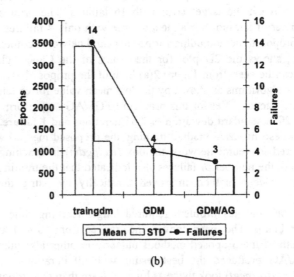

(b)

Figure 2 Cancer summary Chart using optimisation methods (a), and gradient descent method (b)

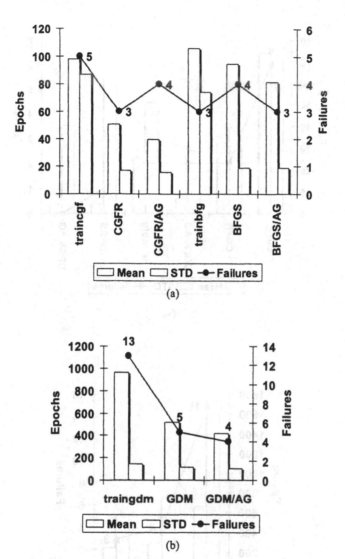

Figure 3 Diabetes summary Chart using optimisation methods (a), and gradient descent method (b)

Figure 4 below, shows the 2D plot for the results of the IRIS classification problem. Both of the proposed algorithms in Figure 4(a) showed better results as compared to other algorithms. Yet BFGS/AG had no failures compared to CGFR/AG with 2 failures. This makes BFGS/AG algorithm a better choice for this problem. In Figure 4(b) the proposed method clearly shows a better result in term of number of iterations required to converge. The proposed method is three times faster as compared to the neural network toolbox (*traingdm*).

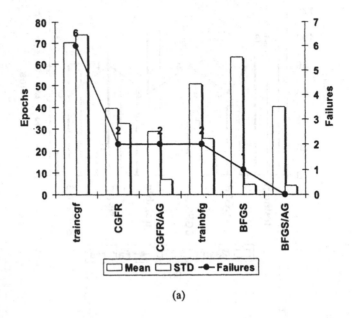

(a)

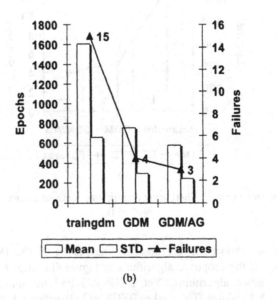

(b)

Figure 4 IRIS summary Chart using optimisation methods (a), and gradient descent
method (b)

5. Conclusion

A novel approach is presented this paper for improving the training efficiency of back propagation neural network algorithms by adaptively modifying the gradient based search direction. The proposed algorithm uses the gain value to modify the gradient based search direction. The proposed algorithm is generic and has been implemented in all commonly used gradient based optimisation processes. The results showed that the proposed algorithm is robust and has a potential to significantly enhance the training efficiency of feed forward neural networks.

Acknowledgements

Financial support for this research was provided by Kolej Universiti Teknologi Tun Hussen Onn (KUiTTHO) Malaysia. This support is gratefully acknowledged.

References

1. A. van Ooyen and B. Nienhuis, *Improving the convergence of the back-propagation algorithm.* Neural Networks, 1992. 5: p. 465-471.
2. M. Ahmad and F.M.A. Salam, *Supervised learning using the cauchy energy function.* International Conference on Fuzzy Logic and Neural Networks, 1992.
3. Pravin Chandra and Yogesh Singh, *An activation function adapting training algorithm for sigmoidal feedforward networks.* Neurocomputing, 2004. 61: p. 429-437.
4. Krzyzak A., Dai W., and Suen C. Y., *Classification of large set of handwritten characters using modified back propagation model.* Proceedings of the International Joint Conference on Neural Networks, 1990. 3: p. 225-232.
5. Sang Hoon Oh, *Improving the Error Backpropagation Algorithm with a Modified Error Function.* IEEE TRANSACTIONS ON NEURAL NETWORKS, 1997. 8(3): p. 799-803.
6. Hahn-Ming Lee, Tzong-Ching Huang, and Chih-Ming Chen, *Learning Efficiency Improvement of Back Propagation Algorithm by Error Saturation Prevention Method.* IJCNN '99, 1999. 3: p. 1737-1742.
7. Sang-Hoon Oh and Youngjik Lee, *A Modified Error Function to Improve the Error Back-Propagation Algorithm for Multi-Layer Perceptrons.* ETRI Journal, 1995. 17(1): p. 11-22.
8. S. M. Shamsuddin, M. Darus, and M. N. Sulaiman, *Classification of Reduction Invariants with Improved Back Ppropagation.* IJMMS, 2002. 30(4): p. 239-247.
9. S. C. Ng, et al., *Fast convergence for back propagation network with magnified gradient function.* Proceedings of the International Joint Conference on Neural Networks 2003, 2003. 3: p. 1903-1908.
10. R.A. Jacobs, *Increased rates of convergence through learning rate adaptation.* Neural Networks, 1988. 1: p. 295–307.

58

11. M.K. Weir, *A method for self-determination of adaptive learning rates in back propagation.* Neural Networks, 1991. 4: p. 371-379.

12. X.H. Yu, G.A. Chen, and S.X. Cheng, *Acceleration of backpropagation learning using optimized learning rate and momentum.* Electronics Letters, 1993. 29(14): p. 1288-1289.

13. Bishop C. M., *Neural Networks for Pattern Recognition.* 1995: Oxford University Press.

14. R. Fletcher and M. J. D. Powell, *A rapidly convergent descent method for nlinimization.* British Computer J., 1963: p. 163-168.

15. Fletcher R. and Reeves R. M., *Function minimization by conjugate gradients.* Comput. J., 1964. 7(2): p. 149-160.

16. M. R. Hestenes and E. Stiefel, *Methods of conjugate gradients for solving linear systerns.* J. Research NBS, 1952. 49: p. 409.

17. HUANG H.Y., *A unified approach to quadratically convergent algorithms for function minimization.* J. Optim. Theory Appl., 1970. 5: p. 405-423.

18. D.E. Rumelhart, G.E. Hinton, and R.J. Williams, *Learning internal representations by error propagation.* in D.E. Rumelhart and J.L. McClelland (eds), Parallel Distributed Processing, 1986. 1: p. 318-362.

19. Rumelhart D. E., Hinton G. E., and Williams R. J., *Learning internal representations by back-propagation errors.* Parallel Distributed Processing, 1986. 1 (Rumelhart D.E. et al. Eds.): p. 318-362.

20. Adrian J. Sheperd, *Second Order Methods for Neural Networks-Fast and Reliable Training Methods for Multi-layer Perceptrons*, ed. J.G. Taylor. 1997: Springer. 143.

21. Byatt D., Coope I. D., and PriceC. J., *Effect of limited precision on the BFGS quasi-Newton algorithm.* ANZIAM J, 2004. 45: p. 283-295.

22. Lutz Prechelt, *ftp://ftp.ira.uka.de/pub/neuron/proben1.tar.gz.* 1994.

A Decision Tree-Based Attribute Weighting Filter for Naive Bayes

Mark Hall

Department of Computer Science, University of Waikato

Hamilton, New Zealand

Abstract

The naive Bayes classifier continues to be a popular learning algorithm for data mining applications due to its simplicity and linear run-time. Many enhancements to the basic algorithm have been proposed to help mitigate its primary weakness—the assumption that attributes are independent given the class. All of them improve the performance of naive Bayes at the expense (to a greater or lesser degree) of execution time and/or simplicity of the final model. In this paper we present a simple filter method for setting attribute weights for use with naive Bayes. Experimental results show that naive Bayes with attribute weights rarely degrades the quality of the model compared to standard naive Bayes and, in many cases, improves it dramatically. The main advantages of this method compared to other approaches for improving naive Bayes is its run-time complexity and the fact that it maintains the simplicity of the final model.

1 Introduction

All practical learning algorithms based on Bayes' theorem make some independence assumptions. The naive Bayes method takes this to the extreme by assuming that the attributes are statistically independent given the class. This leads to a simple algorithm where training time is linear in both the number of instances and attributes. Although the independence assumption is grossly violated in practice, naive Bayes performs surprisingly well on many classification problems [7]. However, because of this assumption, the posterior probabilities estimated by naive Bayes are typically poor. For example, in an extreme case where a single redundant attribute (i.e., an attribute that is perfectly correlated with another) is present in the data, that attribute effectively has twice as much influence as the other attributes.

Many techniques have been developed to reduce the 'naiveity' of the naive Bayes algorithm. Zheng and Webb [28] provide a comprehensive overview of work in this area. One simple approach that often works well is to combine naive Bayes with a preprocessing step that attempts to remove redundant attributes from the training data. Various methods from the attribute selection community have been applied to naive Bayes for just this purpose. However, one related area that has received little attention with regards to naive Bayes is the use of attribute weights[1].

---

[1]Attribute selection can be viewed as a special case of attribute weighting where the weights are restricted to zero or one.

This paper presents a filter method that sets attribute weights for use with naive Bayes. The assumption made is that the weight assigned to a predictive attribute should be inversely related to the degree of dependency it has on other attributes. Our method estimates the degree of attribute dependency by constructing unpruned decision trees and looking at the depth at which attributes are tested in the tree. A bagging procedure is used to stabilize the estimates. Attributes that do not appear in the decision trees receive a weight of zero. Our experimental results show that using attribute weights with naive Bayes improves the quality of the model compared to standard naive Bayes in terms of probability estimation and area under the ROC curve.

This paper is structured as follows. In Section 2 we present our approach for enhancing naive Bayes by learning attribute weights. Section 3 contains experimental results for a collection of benchmark data sets and shows that the performance of naive Bayes can be improved by using attribute weights. Section 4 discusses related work on enhancing the performance of naive Bayes. Section 5 summarizes the contributions made in this paper.

2 Using attribute weights with naive Bayes

Naive Bayes computes the posterior probability of class c_l for a test instance with attribute values $a_1, a_2, ..., a_m$ as follows:

$$p(c_l|a_1, a_2, ..., a_m) = \frac{p(c_l) \prod_{i=1}^{m} p(a_i|c_l)}{\sum_{q=1}^{o} [p(c_q) \prod_{i=1}^{m} p(a_i|c_q)]}, \tag{1}$$

where o is the total number of classes. The term in the denominator of the the right-hand side of Equation 1 can be omitted as it is a normalizing factor. The individual probabilities on the right-hand side of this equation are estimated from the training data. In the case of discrete attributes they are computed from frequency counts. If a numeric attribute is present, we make the normality assumption and estimate its mean and variance. Incorporating attribute weights into the formula gives:

$$p(c_l|a_1, a_2, ..., a_m) = p(c_l) \prod_{i=1}^{m} p(a_i|c_l)^{w_i}, \tag{2}$$

where w_i is the weight of attribute A_i.

Our method for enhancing naive Bayes aims to weight predictive features according to the degree to which they depend on the values of other attributes. Since naive Bayes makes the independence assumption we want to assign lower weights to those attributes that have many dependencies. To estimate the degree to which an attribute depends on others, we first construct an unpruned decision tree from the training data and then note the minimum depth[2] at which the attribute is tested in the tree. The weight for an attribute is set

---

[2]The root node of the tree has depth 1.

```
1. Repeat i times:
2.      Randomly sample (with replacement) j% of the training data.
3.      Learn an unpruned decision tree from the resampled data.
4.      FOR each attribute in the training data DO:
5.       IF the attribute is NOT tested in the tree THEN
6.          Record a weight of 0.
7.       ELSE
8.          Let d be the minimum depth that the attribute is tested at.
9.          Record a weight of 1/√d.
10. FOR each attribute in the training data DO:
11.     Set the final weight equal to the average of the i weights.
12. Optionally remove from the data all attributes with zero weight.
13. Learn a naive Bayes model using the final attribute weights.
```

Figure 1: Attribute weighted Bayesian classifier algorithm

to $1/\sqrt{d}$, where d is the minimum depth at which the attribute is tested in the tree. Attributes that do not appear in the tree receive a weight of zero. Since decision tree learners are inherently unstable, we stabilize the estimated weights by building multiple decision trees using bagging and then average the weights across the ensemble. The method has two parameters—i the number of bagging iterations, and j the percentage of the training data to use for learning a tree in each iteration. Our experimental results show that the method is relatively insensitive to the value of j. Figure 1 shows the algorithm for the attribute weighted Bayesian classifier.

3 Experimental results

This section evaluates the performance of attribute weighted naive Bayes (AWNB) using our tree-based weighting scheme on a collection of 28 benchmark data sets from UCI repository [2]. The properties of these data sets are shown in Table 1.

We ran two sets of experiments. The first compares attribute weighted naive Bayes (using 10 bagging iterations and subsamples of the training data of size 50% for weight estimation) with standard naive Bayes. In this experiment we also evaluate the effect of using weights versus feature selection (i.e. zero/one weights) and the effect of varying the size of the random subsamples used to build the trees. Finally, we include results for bagged unpruned decision trees, so that the reader can compare AWNB with the performance of just using the source of our weight estimation procedure for prediction. The second experiment compares our tree-based method for setting attribute weights to a simple weighting scheme based on gain ratio, a weighting scheme based on the ReliefF attribute ranking algorithm [14, 22], the CFS attribute selection algorithm [10], a decision tree-based attribute selection scheme [21], the wrapper-based selective Bayes algorithm [18] and the NBTree decision tree/naive Bayes hybrid [15]. The latter is included as an example of an enhanced naive Bayes variant—with

Table 1: Datasets used for the experiments

Dataset	Instances	% Missing	Numeric	Nominal	Class
annl	898	0.0	6	32	5
aust	690	0.6	6	9	2
autos	205	1.1	15	10	6
bal-s	625	0.0	4	0	3
brst-c	286	0.3	0	9	2
brst-w	699	0.3	9	0	2
diab	768	0.0	8	0	2
ecoli	336	0.0	7	0	8
crd-g	1000	0.0	7	13	2
glass	214	0.0	9	0	6
hrt-c	303	0.2	6	7	2
hrt-h	294	20.4	6	7	2
hrt-s	270	0.0	13	0	2
hep	155	5.6	6	13	2
colic	368	23.8	7	15	2
hypo	3772	6.0	23	6	4
iono	351	0.0	34	0	2
iris	150	0.0	4	0	3
kr	3196	0.0	0	36	2
labor	57	3.9	8	8	2
lymph	148	0.0	3	15	4
sick	3772	6.0	23	6	2
sonar	208	0.0	60	0	2
splice	3190	0.0	0	61	3
vehic	846	0.0	18	0	4
vote	435	5.6	0	16	2
wave	5000	0.0	40	0	3
zoo	101	0.0	1	15	7

a richer representational structure than naive Bayes with or without feature selection/weighting—that still maintains a single interpretable model.

In our experiments we calibrated the probability estimates produced by each learning algorithm by fitting a linear logistic regression function to the outputs of the learner generated during an internal run of 10 fold cross-validation on the training data. For each data set/classifier combination we performed five separate runs of 10 fold cross-validation and computed the average root relative squared error (RRSE) of the probability estimates produced over all 50 folds. For a single train/test split the RRSE is given by the square root of the quadratic loss [26] of the learning algorithm normalized by the quadratic loss of simply predicting the most common class present in the training data. We also computed the area under the ROC curve (AUC) for the 16 two-class datasets. Throughout we speak of two results for a data set as being "significantly different" if the difference is statistically significant at the 5% level according to the corrected resampled t-test [19], which has acceptable Type I error.

Table 2 shows the RRSE results for the first experiment. Compared to standard naive Bayes, attribute weighted naive Bayes ($i = 10, j = 50$) has significantly lower RRSE on 12 data sets and significantly higher RRSE on only two data sets. In many cases our method improves the performance of naive Bayes considerably. For example, on the kr data RRSE decreases from 59.5% to 39%. Similar levels of improvement can be seen on vote, iono, aust and colic.

Table 2: Experimental results for attribute weighted naive Bayes (AWNB) versus naive Bayes (NB), AWNB using zero/one weights (ASNB) and bagged unpruned decision trees: mean root relative squared error (RRSE) and standard deviation.

Data	AWNB i = 10 j = 50	NB	AWNB i = 1 j = 100	AWNB i = 10 j = 25	AWNB i = 10 j = 75	AWNB i = 10 j = 100	ASNB i = 10 j = 50	Bagging i = 10 j = 100
annl	50.38± 8.7	53.64± 7.3	54.43± 9.3	49.14±11.1	51.57± 9.0	51.52± 8.9	54.38± 6.5 o	20.03±12.8 •
aust	70.03± 7.0	79.27± 5.8 o	72.46± 7.0	67.43± 6.7 •	71.72± 6.9 o	72.07± 7.0 o	79.57± 5.9 o	66.33± 8.2
autos	80.36± 9.3	85.73± 8.8 o	81.39± 8.9	81.14± 9.5	80.71± 9.5	80.80± 9.2	85.57± 8.8 o	54.59±14.9 •
bal-s	46.55± 6.1	41.18± 6.1 •	58.79± 6.0 o	46.21± 5.6	47.82± 5.8	48.41± 6.5	41.18± 6.1 •	58.97± 6.2 o
brst-c	94.84± 6.2	94.40± 6.3	94.99± 6.0	95.20± 5.9	94.76± 6.2	94.72± 6.1	94.40± 6.3	97.61± 5.1
brst-w	37.60±11.5	39.29±10.4	37.39±12.0	38.43±11.6	38.14±11.4	38.35±11.0	39.11±10.6	37.54± 9.4
diab	84.72± 6.9	86.28± 6.3 o	84.90± 6.9	84.63± 7.0	84.78± 6.9	84.86± 6.9	86.28± 6.3 o	85.31± 5.6
ecoli	56.18±10.8	57.72±11.4	56.90±11.2	57.31±10.9	56.35±11.0	57.22±10.9	57.40±11.0	59.91±10.1
crd-g	89.54± 4.4	89.80± 4.3	89.73± 4.3	89.42± 4.5	89.70± 4.5	89.64± 4.4	89.80± 4.3	93.05± 3.4 o
glass	86.07± 5.5	85.98± 5.5	86.74± 5.5	85.90± 5.5	85.89± 5.5	85.93± 5.3	85.98± 5.5	73.91± 8.3 •
hrt-c	68.80±13.8	69.37±14.3	69.42±13.6	69.46±13.2	68.68±14.3	68.66±14.2	69.37±14.3	75.00± 9.5
hrt-h	72.91±13.7	71.16±13.2	72.63±13.9	73.83±13.0	72.38±13.9	72.16±13.8	71.20±13.2	75.56±11.5
hrt-s	70.76±10.1	69.86±10.7	71.08± 9.5	70.73±10.0	70.65±10.2	70.53±10.0	69.86±10.7	74.78± 9.7
hep	83.43±18.3	79.84±18.9	85.74±16.6	84.74±16.9	83.97±17.7	83.89±16.5	79.78±19.5	88.38±14.0
colic	71.35±10.8	79.58± 8.6 o	72.31±10.2	70.60±11.1	71.79±10.4	72.09±10.3	79.35± 8.8 o	70.62±11.2
hypo	76.45± 5.6	71.87± 5.4 •	75.79± 5.6 •	77.09± 5.6 o	76.18± 5.6 •	76.01± 5.5 •	71.35± 5.5 •	18.57± 9.6 •
iono	57.17± 14.8	72.63±10.8 o	58.23±14.8	57.71±14.3	56.04±14.2	55.77±15.7	63.07±13.4	50.03±13.9
iris	26.23±20.5	27.77±20.1	26.23±20.7	25.69±20.8	26.23±20.4	26.32±20.4	26.34±20.0	31.67±20.3
kr	38.98± 3.7	59.53± 4.1 o	40.72± 3.8	38.79± 3.9	39.54± 3.5 o	40.19± 3.6 o	53.65± 3.9 o	12.01± 5.9 •
labor	58.65±30.3	36.50±31.3	64.45±32.9	67.72±28.7	57.08±30.6	54.93±31.6	45.46±31.0	66.22±28.2
lymph	75.18±15.7	72.40±17.2	77.75±15.1	75.31±15.6	74.46±16.5	74.26±16.5	73.78±16.7	77.56±16.3
sick	64.88± 7.7	76.60± 5.4 o	66.03± 7.5	65.06± 8.0	64.98± 7.5	65.14± 7.5	75.73± 5.6 o	37.57±10.8 •
sonar	86.94±10.8	91.10± 7.9 o	90.48± 9.5	86.73±10.5	87.16±11.6	86.99±11.1	91.82± 8.5 o	75.40±11.9 •
splice	30.76± 3.5	34.66± 3.9 o	31.21± 3.7	31.65± 3.4 o	30.41± 3.4	30.26± 3.7	34.36± 3.8 o	38.64± 4.1 o
vehic	88.00± 2.4	91.18± 1.8 o	88.36± 2.3	87.45± 2.4	88.37± 2.3 o	88.41± 2.2 o	91.18± 1.8 o	64.04± 4.5 •
vote	39.67±12.5	58.04±12.1 o	42.00±12.4	38.23±12.8	40.73±12.3	41.46±12.3	54.90±12.5 o	32.98±14.9 •
wave	59.72± 2.3	63.52± 2.3 o	59.94± 2.2	59.50± 2.4	59.77± 2.2	59.79± 2.2	63.52± 2.3 o	62.50± 2.6 o
zoo	39.32±29.7	25.15±25.2	56.19±25.7	51.33±28.9	40.99±29.7	33.87±29.2	34.97±26.3	38.62±23.6

•, o statistically significant improvement or degradation over AWNB with $i = 10, j = 50$.

In order to determine whether the improvement over standard naive Bayes is due to the attribute weights or just feature selection (recall that attributes that do not appear in the tree(s) receive zero weight) we ran AWNB and set all non-zero weights to 1. This scheme is referred to as ASNB in Table 2. From the results it is clear that the attribute weights do help in improving the quality of the probability estimates produced by naive Bayes. Using attribute weights, as opposed to just eliminating those attributes that do not appear in the trees, results in significant improvements on 12 data sets and significant degradation on two. We also investigated the effect of varying the size of the samples used to build the trees for AWNB. Setting j to 25, 75 and 100 resulted in similar performance to using $j = 50$. $j = 50$ is significantly worse than the other two settings of j on one data set, and significantly better on two data sets ($j = 25$) and three data sets ($j = 75$, $j = 100$). Instead of using 10 bagging iterations to construct 10 trees, we also tried building just one tree ($i = 1$) using all the training data. Although there are only three significant differences compared to building 10 trees, it can be seen from Table 2 that on all but two data sets this results in either a higher RRSE or larger standard deviation. Finally, we compared AWNB to bagged unpruned decision trees using 10 bagging iterations ($i = 10$) and randomly sampled training sets of the same size as the original training data ($j = 100$). With nine significant wins and four significant losses in favour of bagged trees it is clear that AWNB is inferior to this ensemble method. However, AWNB's single model has the advantage of being interpretable.

Table 3 shows the area under the curve results on the two class data sets

Table 3: Experimental results for attribute weighted naive Bayes (AWNB) versus naive Bayes (NB), AWNB using zero/one weights (ASNB) and bagged unpruned decision trees: area under the ROC curve and standard deviation.

Data	AWNB i = 10 j = 50	NB	AWNB i = 1 j = 100	AWNB i = 10 j = 25	AWNB i = 10 j = 75	AWNB i = 10 j = 100	ASNB i = 10 j = 50	Bagging i = 10 j = 100
aust	90.67± 3.2	89.53± 3.4 o	90.13± 3.4	91.21± 3.1	90.30± 3.3	90.25± 3.4	89.50± 3.4 o	91.91± 3.3
brst-c	69.87±10.3	70.38±10.0	70.08±10.4	69.77±10.1	70.08±10.3	70.15±10.4	70.38±10.0	63.66±11.5
brst-w	98.67± 1.2	98.33± 1.2	98.78± 1.1	98.63± 1.2	98.62± 1.3	98.60± 1.2	98.35± 1.2	98.78± 1.0
diab	82.37± 5.6	81.42± 5.4	82.26± 5.4	82.31± 5.7	82.34± 5.5	82.27± 5.5	81.42± 5.4	81.25± 5.0
crd-g	78.84± 4.7	78.66± 4.6	78.66± 4.7	78.91± 4.9	78.74± 4.8	78.81± 4.8	78.66± 4.6	73.15± 4.8 o
hrt-c	90.60± 6.1	90.70± 6.4	90.49± 6.2	90.31± 6.1	90.57± 6.5	90.63± 6.3	90.70± 6.4	87.98± 5.7
hrt-h	90.50± 5.9	90.74± 5.5	90.24± 6.2	90.17± 5.5	90.61± 5.7	90.47± 5.8	90.70± 5.5	88.49± 6.7
hrt-s	89.19± 5.9	90.20± 5.5	89.83± 5.4	89.41± 5.9	89.58± 5.9	89.76± 5.8	90.20± 5.5	88.37± 5.9
hep	84.53±13.6	85.26±12.9	85.89±11.2	85.60±12.0	85.29±12.8	84.96±12.8	85.26±13.0	81.72±12.7
colic	88.16± 6.0	84.34± 6.2 o	87.68± 6.1	88.67± 6.0	87.72± 6.0	87.70± 6.1	84.42± 6.2 o	88.93± 5.2
iono	94.79± 4.1	93.81± 3.6	93.78± 4.7	94.60± 4.4	95.04± 3.8	94.99± 4.0	94.82± 3.6	96.48± 3.7
kr	98.93± 0.4	95.21± 1.2 o	98.68± 0.5 o	98.96± 0.4	98.85± 0.4 o	98.76± 0.5 o	96.76± 0.9 o	99.95± 0.1 •
labor	95.08±11.4	97.38± 6.4	90.25±19.1	91.58±13.3	95.17±11.1	95.58±11.1	96.67± 8.8	92.08±15.8
sick	93.26± 4.4	92.59± 3.7	93.26± 4.4	93.26± 4.4	93.25± 4.3	93.24± 4.4	92.56± 3.8	99.28± 1.3 •
sonar	79.33±10.4	78.94±10.2	77.18±10.3	79.39±11.1	79.02±10.9	79.38±11.0	78.82±10.5	87.36± 7.4 •
vote	98.97± 1.0	97.39± 1.8 o	98.66± 1.4	99.04± 1.0	98.93± 1.0	98.89± 0.9	97.75± 1.6 o	98.33± 2.4

•, o statistically significant improvement or degradation over AWNB with i = 10, j = 50.

for the first experiment. Compared to standard naive Bayes, AWNB ($i = 10, j = 50$) is significantly better on four data sets and significantly worse on none. Varying the percentage of data used to build the trees and the number of bagging iterations has minimal effect. The other settings of i and j are significantly worse on only one data set. Compared to simply eliminating those attributes that do not appear in the trees (ASNB), AWNB is significantly better on four data sets and significantly worse on none. Compared to bagged unpruned decision trees, AWNB is significantly better on one data set and significantly worse on three.

Table 4 shows the RRSE results for the second experiment. In this experiment we compared AWNB against two other attribute weighting schemes for naive Bayes, three feature selection methods and naive Bayes trees. The first of the weighting methods (GRW) assigns weights to attributes proportional to their gain ratio score [27]:

$$w_i = \frac{GainRatio(A_i) \times m}{\sum_{i=1}^{m} GainRatio(A_i)}, \tag{3}$$

where m is the number of attributes. For the purpose of computing these weights, all numeric attributes are discretized in a copy of each train/test split using the supervised discretization method of Fayyad and Irani [8]. Compared to GRW, we can see from Table 4 that our tree-based method for determining weights results in significantly lower RRSE on 13 data sets and significantly higher RRSE error on only one. This suggests that information about attribute dependencies captured in the tree structure is useful when setting weights for naive Bayes. The second weighting scheme (RW) applies the ReliefF attribute selection [14, 22] algorithm and uses the resulting attribute relevance scores as weights. Any relevance scores less than zero are set to zero. Compared to AWNB, RW is significantly worse on seven data sets and significantly better on one. The ReliefF algorithm can identify relevant attributes that depend on

Table 4: Experimental results for attribute weighted naive Bayes (AWNB) versus naive Bayes with gain ratio based weighting (GRW), naive Bayes with ReliefF based weighting (RW), naive Bayes with correlation-based feature selection (CFS), Selective Bayes (SB), the Selective Bayesian classifier (SBC) and NBTree: mean root relative squared error (RRSE) and standard deviation.

Data	AWNB	GRW	RW	CFS	SB	SBC	NBTree
annl	50.38± 8.7	57.21± 7.0 o	49.89± 6.5	60.58± 7.3 o	60.46±12.3	69.12± 8.2 o	26.18±11.8 •
aust	70.03± 7.0	72.89± 7.6 o	68.62± 7.8	77.95± 7.8 o	66.22± 7.6	76.58± 7.6 o	68.69± 7.4
autos	80.36± 9.3	86.31± 8.1 o	81.29± 8.9	84.82± 7.2	88.12±18.1	85.15± 8.2 o	71.05±12.9 •
bal-s	46.55± 6.1	47.65± 5.8	48.62± 6.5	41.52± 5.9 •	41.18± 6.1 •	41.18± 6.1 •	78.03± 5.6 o
brst-c	94.84± 6.2	94.58± 5.6	94.91± 5.8	94.52± 6.2	95.61± 5.3	94.92± 6.2	95.21± 5.5
brst-w	37.60±11.5	39.50±10.5	37.91±10.1	39.29±10.4	39.48±11.2	39.38±12.1	34.85±11.5
diab	84.72± 6.9	86.09± 7.0 o	85.35± 7.2	85.17± 6.3	85.41± 6.1	86.60± 6.5 o	85.99± 6.4
ecoli	56.18±10.8	57.70±10.1	58.46±10.1	57.39±11.5	58.38±10.9	58.79±12.5	66.03±10.7 o
crd-g	89.54± 4.4	90.59± 4.2	90.85± 4.0	91.92± 3.7 o	91.26± 3.5	90.61± 4.0	91.12± 4.1
glass	86.07± 5.5	86.06± 5.3	86.35± 5.3	85.96± 6.0	89.31± 6.2	87.64± 5.7	80.32±10.4
hrt-c	68.80±13.8	71.12±14.6	71.66±12.2	70.39±14.8	72.95±12.5	75.11±19.0	73.77±12.8
hrt-h	72.91±13.7	77.43±13.1 o	80.77±10.4	72.24±13.1	74.91±13.0	79.41±19.0	73.80±12.8
hrt-s	70.76±10.1	71.21±10.1	72.09±11.0	71.39±10.4	72.85±10.3	72.03±11.5	76.72±11.0
hep	83.43±18.3	85.33±17.0	81.88±15.6	82.77±18.8	89.93±13.5	88.74±15.6	88.24±15.7
hrss-c	71.35±10.8	77.56± 9.5 o	76.87±10.3 o	74.97± 9.0	74.26±10.2	76.40±10.0 o	76.52± 9.6
hypo	76.45± 5.6	70.20± 6.0 •	72.62± 4.7 •	78.64± 5.3 o	71.89± 5.6 •	73.36± 6.1 •	20.16±12.2 •
iono	57.17±14.8	65.43±12.9	70.03±11.3 o	59.70±15.6	57.01±13.2	59.40±14.4	60.84±12.1
iris	26.23±20.5	26.87±20.3	27.20±20.5	24.95±20.2	28.39±21.0	26.46±19.8	34.88±21.3
kr	38.98± 3.7	50.34± 4.4 o	52.55± 5.0 o	48.67± 4.0 o	40.86± 5.0	54.91± 5.6 o	23.27± 9.1 •
labor	58.65±30.3	62.77±33.0	54.80±33.1	58.95±32.8	51.87±34.0	79.46±28.0 o	42.92±33.7
lymph	75.18±15.7	77.68±15.4	78.39±17.5	76.81±15.9	74.35±14.3	78.61±17.6	75.30±19.4
sick	64.88± 7.7	81.91± 3.4 o	93.46± 1.8 o	72.42± 6.6 o	66.71± 7.1	72.34± 8.1 o	56.45± 7.8 •
sonar	86.94±10.8	93.70± 7.7 o	90.08±11.1	92.05± 8.7 o	88.35± 9.5	89.73± 9.6	82.34±11.5
splice	30.76± 3.5	40.23± 3.7 o	36.75± 3.9 o	32.62± 3.6 o	35.98± 3.8 o	36.38± 4.4 o	34.80± 3.9 o
vehic	88.00± 2.4	92.17± 1.6 o	93.33± 1.5 o	88.75± 2.4	89.86± 2.9	90.65± 3.0 o	70.84± 4.1 •
vote	39.67±12.5	47.50±14.2 o	41.12±14.3	40.81±13.0	39.19±12.8	40.17±14.7	39.87±14.3
wave	59.72± 2.3	67.15± 2.0 o	63.73± 2.4 o	62.86± 2.3 o	62.53± 2.4 o	63.38± 2.8 o	67.84± 3.5 o
zoo	39.32±29.7	31.60±25.2	39.80±24.7	38.19±23.3	28.00±25.9	73.09±21.1 o	29.58±27.6

•, o statistically significant improvement or degradation over AWNB with $i = 10, j = 50$.

the values of other attributes. However, for the purposes of naive Bayes this can result in scores that are too high for attributes with many dependencies.

Columns five through seven of Table 4 show the results for naive Bayes when combined with the three feature selection algorithms. Correlation-based feature selection (CFS) [10] is particularly well suited for use with naive Bayes as its evaluation heuristic prefers subsets of attributes with low levels of redundancy. From the results we can see that AWNB is significantly better than CFS on nine data sets and significantly worse on one. Selective Bayes (SB) is a wrapper-based feature selection method developed by Langley and Sage [18]. AWNB achieves results comparable to SB—each significantly outperforms the other on two data sets. The Selective Bayesian Classifier (SBC) is a bagged decision-tree based attribute selection filter for naive Bayes [21]. From Table 4 we can see that SBC is significantly better than AWNB on two data sets and significantly worse on 12. The last column in the table shows the results for naive Bayes Trees (NBTree) [15]. NBTree builds a decision tree with local naive Bayes models at each leaf. NBTree's superior representational power is reflected in six significant wins versus four significant losses against AWNB. However, these gains in predictive performance come at the cost of increased running time over our method.

Table 5 shows the area under the curve results on the two class data sets for the second experiment. It is interesting to note that AWNB is significantly outperformed in terms of AUC in only one case—on the kr-vs-kp data by NBTree. Looking at the two weighting schemes (GR and RW), we can see

Table 5: Experimental results for attribute weighted naive Bayes (AWNB) versus naive Bayes with gain ratio based weighting (GRW), naive Bayes with ReliefF based weighting (RW), naive Bayes with correlation-based feature selection (CFS), Selective Bayes (SB), the Selective Bayesian classifier (SBC) and NBTree: area under the ROC curve and standard deviation.

Data	AWNB	GRW	RW	CFS	SB	SBC	NBTree
aust	90.67± 3.2	90.51± 3.3	91.74± 2.9	90.12± 3.4	90.96± 3.3	89.88± 3.8	91.33± 3.5
brst-c	69.87±10.3	70.95±10.0	69.28±10.7	69.87±11.0	67.92±11.0	69.57±10.5	68.45±10.3
brst-w	98.67± 1.2	98.33± 1.2	98.42± 1.2	98.33± 1.2	98.94± 1.0	98.67± 1.3	98.75± 1.3
diab	82.37± 5.6	81.99± 5.7	82.53± 5.9	82.03± 5.6	82.14± 5.6	81.04± 5.4	80.89± 5.8
crd-g	78.84± 4.7	77.29± 5.1 o	77.52± 4.8	75.27± 4.9 o	78.39± 4.5	77.57± 4.7	76.23± 5.8
hrt-c	90.60± 6.1	89.99± 7.0	90.57± 5.5	89.32± 7.4	88.99± 5.4	87.16±12.2	88.21± 6.7
hrt-h	90.50± 5.9	89.11± 6.4	89.37± 5.7	90.76± 5.1	91.01± 5.8	87.22±10.4	89.22± 7.4
hrt-st	89.19± 5.9	89.47± 6.2	89.72± 5.7	88.78± 6.2	88.97± 5.7	88.78± 6.1	85.47± 7.7
hep	84.53±13.6	86.95±12.4	86.52±12.3	85.63±14.5	82.71±13.6	80.48±16.0	81.34±12.6
colic	88.16± 6.0	87.90± 6.3	88.45± 5.9	86.11± 6.2	87.20± 5.5	85.32± 6.2 o	85.96± 6.2
iono	94.79± 4.1	94.64± 3.7	94.37± 3.6	94.32± 4.3	95.99± 3.8	93.21± 5.6	93.19± 4.3
kr	98.93± 0.4	98.11± 0.6 o	98.50± 0.6 o	96.86± 0.8 o	98.62± 0.6	94.31± 1.4 o	99.54± 0.5
labor	95.08±11.4	94.25± 9.4	94.87± 9.8	94.25±12.0	96.79± 6.4	81.21±22.2	95.92±10.6
sick	93.26± 4.4	93.55± 4.0	90.86± 3.0 o	93.68± 3.3	94.41± 2.7	92.85± 4.3	93.74± 4.0
sonar	79.33±10.4	79.02±10.9	81.82±10.7	79.49±10.9	83.62± 9.7	76.81±11.4	83.11± 9.2
vote	98.97± 1.0	98.24± 1.4 o	98.82± 1.1	98.88± 1.3	98.92± 1.4	98.36± 1.5	98.77± 1.5

, o statistically significant improvement or degradation over AWNB with $i = 10, j = 50$.

that AWNB is significantly better that GR on three data sets and significantly better than RW on two data sets. AWNB has two significant wins against both CFS and SBC. For this experiment we modified the wrapper-based SB to optimize AUC rather than accuracy. From Table 5 we can see that AWNB is comparable to SB in terms of AUC as there are no significant differences on any of the data sets. However, AWNB is much faster than SB because it has running time that is still linear in the number of attributes (log-linear in the number of instances) while SB's running time is at least quadratic in the number of attributes.

4   Related work

A fair amount of work has been done in investigating attribute weighting schemes in the context of nearest neighbor learning. The primary goal of these methods is to mitigate the "curse of dimensionality", where the number of training cases needed to maintain a given error rate grows rapidly with the number of attributes. Methods can be roughly divided into two groups: wrapper approaches, i.e. those that use performance feedback from the nearest neighbor method to adjust the values of the weights, and filter methods, i.e. those that incorporate another model's fixed bias in a preprocessing step to set the weights. Examples of the former include Salzberg's EACH system [23], Aha's IB4 [1], The Relief system and its extensions [14, 22] and the DIET scheme [16] (which, unlike the other methods, restricts the weight space to a small user-selectable set of discrete values). Examples of the latter include using information theoretic-based measures such as mutual information and gain ratio to assign feature weights [25], setting weights based on class conditional probabilities [5] and Stanfill and Waltz's value-difference metric [24]. Weighting schemes for nearest neighbor can also be separated into those methods that find one globally applicable set of weights (all the previously mentioned methods fall into this category) and those that find locally applicable weights—either local to training instances or specifically tailored to the test instance. Examples of local weighting schemes include those by Cardie and Howe [4, 11] and the RC algorithm of Domingos [6]. For a good survey of attribute weighting methods for nearest neighbor algorithms see Wettschereck et al. [25].

There is comparatively less work on using attribute weights in conjunction with naive Bayes. Zhang and Sheng [27] investigate a gain ratio-based weighting scheme and several wrapper-based methods for finding attribute weights in order to improve AUC performance for naive Bayes. In a text classification setting Kim et al. [13] explore information gain and chi-square statistics to set attribute weights for a Poisson naive Bayes model. Ferreira et al. [9] discretize numeric attributes and then compute a weight for each attribute that is proportional to how predictive of the class it is. Classification accuracy for a weighted version of naive Bayes is compared to standard naive Bayes and C4.5 on a small selection of UCI data sets. Unfortunately, comparison based on accuracy is unfair if calibration or threshold selection is not used (which would be necessary to maximize the accuracy of each classifier).

Using information captured in decision trees to improve the performance of other learning algorithms was first explored by Cardie [3] and Kubat et al. [17]. Cardie used only those features appearing in a C4.5 [20] tree as input to a nearest neighbor learner, while Kubat et al. did the same for naive Bayes. In an approach very similar to these two, Ratanamahatana and Gunopulos' [21] Selective Bayesian classifier (SBC) uses attributes that appear in only the top three levels of a decision tree to improve the performance of naive Bayes. Similar to our method, SBC uses a bagging procedure to generate multiple trees; unlike our method bagging is used primarily to speed up the tree growing process and so only a small percentage (10%) of the training data is sampled in each iteration. In an approach related to the one presented in this paper, Cardie [4] used an information gain metric based on the position of an attribute in a decision tree to derive feature weights for a nearest neighbor algorithm. This method differs from ours in that it is a local weighting scheme (i.e. weights are derived for each test instance according to the path it takes through the tree), it derives weights directly from information gain scores, it uses a single pruned decision tree and it is aimed at improving the prediction of minority classes.

The literature on feature selection in machine learning is too extensive to review in detail here, so we will mention just a few articles relevant to the investigation reported in this paper. John et al. [12] are credited with coining the terms "wrapper" and "filter" to describe those methods that use performance feedback from a learning algorithm to guide the search for good features versus those that incorporate another model's fixed bias to select features. An example of the wrapper approach specifically tailored to naive Bayes is Langley and Sage's selective Bayesian classifier [18]. This method uses the accuracy of naive Bayes on the training data to evaluate feature subsets and a conservative forward selection search that continues to add attributes as long as the predictive performance does not decrease. CFS (correlation-based feature selection) [10] is an example of a filter approach that is well suited to naive Bayes. CFS uses a heuristic that is biased towards subsets of features that are highly correlated with the class attribute and have low levels of redundancy.

5 Conclusions

This paper has investigated a decision tree-based filter method for setting attribute weights for use with naive Bayes. Empirically, our attribute weighting method for naive Bayes outperforms both standard naive Bayes and weighting methods based on information gain and the ReliefF algorithm. Furthermore, it has performance that is comparable with a more computationally intensive wrapper-based feature subset selection for naive Bayes.

In terms of computational complexity, our weighting method increases naive Bayes' runtime from linear in the number of attributes and examples to linear in the number of attributes and log-linear in the number of instances. This compares favourably with other enhanced versions of naive Bayes that maintain a single interpretable model such as naive Bayes trees [15] and selective Bayes, both of which are quadratic in the number of attributes.

References

[1] D. W. Aha. Tolerating noisy, irrelevant, and novel attributes in instance-based learning algorithms. *Int. Journal of Man-Machine Studies*, 36:267–287, 1992.

[2] C.L. Blake and C.J. Merz. UCI repository of machine learning databases. University of California, Irvine, Dept. of Information and Computer Science, 1998. [www.ics.uci.edu/~mlearn/MLRepository.html].

[3] C. Cardie. Using decision trees to improve case-based learning. In *Proc. of the 10th Int. Conf. on Machine Learning*, pages 25–32. Morgan Kaufmann, 1993.

[4] C. Cardie and N. Howe. Improving minority class prediction using case-specific feature weights. In *Proc. of the 14th Int. Conf. on Machine Learning*, pages 57–65. Morgan Kaufmann, 1997.

[5] R. H. Creecy, B. M. Masand, S. J. Smith, and D. L. Waltz. Trading MIPS and memory for knowledge engineering. *Communications of the ACM*, 35:48–64, 1992.

[6] P. Domingos. Context-sensitive feature selection for lazy learners. *Artificial Intelligence Review*, 11(227–253), 1997.

[7] P. Domingos and M. J. Pazzani. On the optimality of the simple Bayesian classifier under zero-one loss. *Mach. Learning*, 29(2-3):103–130, 1997.

[8] U. M. Fayyad and K. B. Irani. Multi-interval discretization of continuous-valued attributes for classification learning. In *Proc. of the 13th Int. Joint Conf. on AI*, pages 1022–1027. Morgan Kaufmann, 1993.

[9] J. T. A. S. Ferreira, D. G. T Denison, and D. J. Hand. Data mining with products of trees. In *Proc. of the 4th Int. Conf. on Advances in Intelligent Data Analysis*, pages 167–176. Springer, 2001.

[10] M. Hall. Correlation-based feature selection for discrete and numeric c lass machine learning. In *Proc. of the 17th Int. Conf. on Machine Learning*, pages 359–366, 2000.

[11] N. Howe and C. Cardie. Examining locally varying weights for nearest neighbor algorithms. In *Case-Based Reasoning Research and Development: 2nd Int. Conf. on Case-Based Reasoning*, pages 455–466. Springer, 1997.

[12] G. John, R. Kohavi, and K. Pfleger. Irrelevant features and the subset selection problem. In *Proc. of the 11th Int. Conf. on Machine Learning*, pages 121–129. Morgan Kaufmann, 1994.

[13] S. Kim, H. Seo, and H. Rim. Poisson naive Bayes for text classification with feature weighting. In *Proc. of the 6th Int. Workshop on Information Retrieval with Asian Languages*, pages 33–40, 2003.

[14] K. Kira and L. Rendell. A practical approach to feature selection. In *Proc. of the Ninth Int. Conf. on Machine L earning*, pages 249–256. Morgan Kaufmann, 1992.

[15] R. Kohavi. Scaling up the accuracy of naive-Bayes classifiers: a decision tree hybrid. In *Proc. of the 2nd Int. Conf. on Knowledge Discovery and Data Mining*, pages 202–207, 1996.

[16] R. Kohavi, P. Langley, and Y. Yun. The utility of feature weighting in nearest-neighbor algorithms. In M. van Someren and G. Widmer, editors, *Poster Papers: Ninth European Conf. on Machine Learning*, Prague, Czech Republic, 1997. Unpublished.

[17] M. Kubat, D. Flotzinger, and G. Pfurtscheller. Discovering patterns in EEG signals: Comparative study of a few methods. In *Proc. of the 1993 Europ. Conf. on Mach. Learn.*, pages 367–371. Springer-Verlag, 1993.

[18] P. Langley and S. Sage. Induction of selective Bayesian classifiers. In *Proc.. of the 10th Conf. on Uncertainty in Artificial Intelligence*, pages 399–406. Morgan Kaufmann, 1994.

[19] C. Nadeau and Yoshua Bengio. Inference for the generalization error. In *Advances in Neural Information Processing Systems 12*, pages 307–313. MIT Press, 1999.

[20] R. Quinlan. *C4.5: Programs for Machine Learning*. Morgan Kaufmann, 1993.

[21] C. A. Ratanamahatana and D. Gunopulos. Feature selection for the naive Bayesian classifier using decision trees. *Applied Artificial Intelligence*, 17(5-6):475–487, 2003.

[22] M. Robnik-Sikonja and I. Kononenko. Theoretical and empirical analysis of Relieff and RRelieff. *Mach. Learning*, 53(1-2):23–69, 2003.

[23] S. L. Salzberg. A nearest hyperrectangle learning method. *Machine Learning*, 6:251–276, 1991.

[24] C. Stanfill and D. Waltz. Toward memory-based reasoning. *Communications of the Assoc. for Computing Machinery*, 29:1213–1228, 1986.

[25] D. Wettschereck, D. W. Aha, and T. Mohri. A review and empirical comparison of feature weighting methods for a class of lazy learning algorithms. *Artificial Intelligence Review*, 11:273–314, 1997.

[26] Ian H. Witten and Eibe Frank. *Data Mining: Practical Machine Learning Tools and Techniques with Java Implementations*. Morgan Kaufmann, 2000.

[27] H. Zhang and S. Sheng. Learning weighted naive Bayes with accurate ranking. In *Proc. of the 4th IEEE Int. Conf. on Data Mining*, pages 567–570, 2004.

[28] Zijian Zheng and Geoffrey I. Webb. Lazy learning of Bayesian rules. *Machine Learning*, 41(1):53–84, 2000.

Graphical Reasoning with Bayesian Networks

Ildikó Flesch and Peter Lucas
Department of Information and Knowledge Systems
Institute for Computing and Information Sciences
Radboud University Nijmegen, The Netherlands
Email: {ildiko,peterl}@cs.ru.nl

Abstract

Nowadays, Bayesian networks are seen by many researchers as standard tools for reasoning with uncertainty. Despite the fact that Bayesian networks are graphical representations, representing dependence and independence information, normally the emphasis of the visualisation of the reasoning process is on showing changes in the associated marginal probability distributions due to entering observations, rather than on changes in the associated graph structure. In this paper, we argue that it is possible and relevant to look at Bayesian network reasoning as reasoning with a graph structure, depicting changes in the dependence and independence information. We propose a new method that is able to modify the graphical part of a Bayesian network to bring it in accordance with available observations. In this way, Bayesian network reasoning is seen as reasoning about changing dependences and independences as reflected by changes in the graph structure.

1 Introduction

Bayesian networks are examples of probabilistic graphical models that are powerful tools for data analysis and problem solving in areas involving uncertainty, such as medicine [2]. A Bayesian network consists of two parts: (1) an acyclic directed graph that represents the dependences and independences in a domain of concern, and (2) a joint probability distribution of a set of random variables that is associated with the vertices. It is a very convenient formalism for specifying probabilistic information; by taking into account the independences represented by the graph, usually much less probabilistic information needs to be specified than would be required otherwise.

Bayesian networks are used in problem solving. This is normally accomplished by instantiating the random variables that have been observed; subsequently, the probability distributions of the individual random variables that have not been observed are computed, taking into account the influence of the observations. The results of the computation are visualised by plots. As we only consider discrete probability distributions, the plots are then bar-graphs.

While the bar-graphs are informative to the user, the entered observation may, under certain conditions, change the dependences and independences in a Bayesian network. The surprising fact, however, is that normally the graph structure is kept unchanged in the reasoning process. One may wonder why the changes are not clearly indicated to the user, thus supporting the user's understanding of how dependences and independences change in the face of observed evidence. The authors of this paper believe that without the possibility of displaying the changes in the graphical part of a Bayesian network, reasoning with Bayesian networks is incomplete. In this paper, we propose a new method for graphical reasoning with Bayesian networks. It is expected that a user's understanding of the graphical part of the reasoning process endorses the exploitation of Bayesian networks as problem solvers.

The results obtained by the research discussed in this paper are two-fold. Firstly, we develop a method of graphical reasoning with Bayesian networks that is mathematically sound; secondly, we show that this form of reasoning can be looked upon as reasoning with a class of acyclic directed graphs, rather than reasoning with a single graph. As far as we know, it is the first time that reasoning in Bayesian networks is looked upon in this particular fashion.

The paper is organised as follows. In the next section, the ideas underlying this research are motivated further. The basic concepts used in this paper are next reviewed in Section 3. Subsequently, in Section 4, a new equivalence relation on Bayesian networks is developed, taking into account random variables that have been observed. In Section 5, work that is related to the research presented in this paper is reviewed and compared to our work. Finally, in Section 6, we summarise what has been achieved and consider further research.

2 Motivating Example

Before going into the details of Bayesian networks and their representation of (in)dependence information, we demonstrate that it is to some extent possible to draw conclusion about dependence and independence of random variables, or variables for short, in Bayesian networks using conventional Bayesian network reasoning, just by looking at probability distributions. The method used is straightforward: by looking at changes in the marginal probability distributions visualised for individual variables, and instantiating some of the other variables, it is possible to conclude that two or more variables are dependent of one another. However, dependences and independences can also be read off from a graph by using particular subgraph structure rules, to be reviewed in the next section. Readers not familiar with these rules, should for the moment simply try to develop some intuition of reasoning in Bayesian networks.

Consider the specification of a Bayesian network shown in Figure 1; it consists of an acyclic directed graph and a joint probability distribution, factorised in terms of local probability distributions of the form

$$P(X_v \mid X_{\pi(v)})$$

where v is a vertex, $\pi(v)$ the set of parents of vertex v, and X_v is the random variable associated with the vertex v. For the sake of simplicity, we assume here that vertices and variables have the same name.

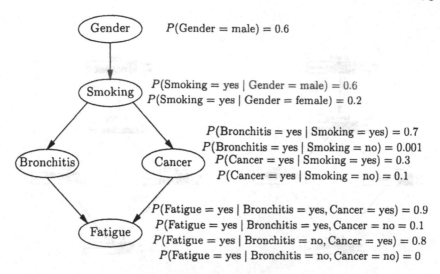

Figure 1: Acyclic directed graph (left) and associated joint probability distribution (right) of a fictitious Bayesian network concerning causes and consequences of bronchitis and cancer; only half of the probabilistic information is given: the complementary probabilities can be obtained by use of the axiom $P(X = \text{no}) = 1 - P(X = \text{yes})$.

The marginal probability distributions $P(X_v)$, for each vertex v in the graph, are shown in Figure 2(a); these have been computed by probabilistic inference. Using the rules for extracting (in)dependence information from acyclic directed graphs, the variables 'Bronchitis' and 'Cancer' in Figure 2(a) are dependent, as they are connected via the variables 'Smoking'. However, in Figure 2(b) the variables 'Bronchitis' and 'Cancer' have become *in*dependent, as their common cause (Smoking) has been observed. This should be interpreted as saying that once we know that somebody smokes, also knowing that somebody has cancer does not change our beliefs about whether or not the person has bronchitis; 'Smoking' is the variable that completely explains the dependence that exists between 'Cancer' and 'Bronchitis'. Figure 2(c) proves that this is indeed a correct interpretation of this reasoning process, as the probability distributions of 'Bronchitis' in Figure 2(b) and Figure 2(c) are exactly the same, even though in Figure 2(c) we know, in addition to the fact that the person smokes, that the person has cancer. In contrast, in Figure 2(d) both probability distributions of the random variables 'Bronchitis' and 'Cancer' have changed in comparison to Figure 2(b), despite the fact that 'Smoking' was observed as well. The reason for this is that observing that the person has fatigue, which is a common consequence of bronchitis and cancer, has again made these two random variables dependent of each other.

Clearly, it is possible to reason about changes in dependences and independences in Bayesian networks by looking at changes in the underlying probabil-

74

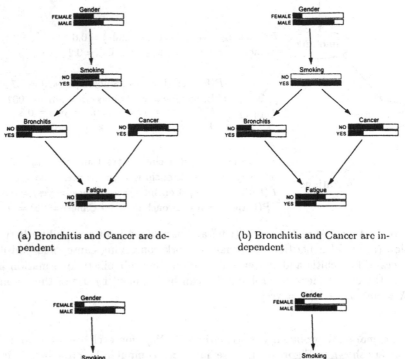

(a) Bronchitis and Cancer are dependent

(b) Bronchitis and Cancer are independent

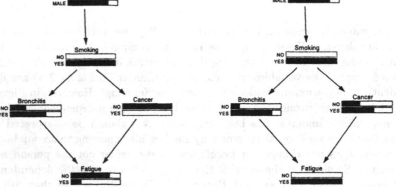

(c) Proof that Bronchitis and Cancer are independent

(d) Bronchitis and Cancer are dependent

Figure 2: Bayesian networks with associated marginal probability distributions obtained from the specification given in Figure 1; marginal probability distributions (a) and distributions obtained after entering observations concerning smoking (b), smoking and cancer (c) and smoking and fatigue (d).

ity distributions. However, it would have been much more convenient if these changes had been visualised by changing the graphical part of the Bayesian network, e.g., by the addition or deletion of arcs. Current Bayesian network packages, however, do not offer this capability. In fact, as we will see, things are not as easy as simply adding and deleting arcs, because by reasoning with an acyclic directed graph we may move beyond this class of probabilistic graphical models, i.e., the result may no longer be an acyclic directed graph. In the remainder of the paper, we will develop the necessary theory to be able to offer this kind of support.

3 Mathematical Preliminaries

Even though the graphical part of a Bayesian network is an acyclic directed graph, we need other graphical representations as well in order to develop our theory of graphical reasoning. In particular, we sometimes need to replace arcs by lines. We first summarise some bits and pieces of graph theory required in the remainder of the paper and some of the theory of statistical independence, which this paper has taken as a starting point.

3.1 Some Elements of Graph Theory

We assume the reader has some familiarity with notions from graph theory (cf. [2, 3]), such as graph, undirected graph, acyclic directed graph, also called ADG[1] for short in the following, vertex, arc (a directed edge $u \to v$ between two vertices u and v), line (an undirected edge $u - v$ between two vertices u and v). Here, if $u \to v$, then u is called the parent of v. The set of parents of a vertex $v \in V$ is denoted by $\pi(v)$. A graph G is denoted by $G = (V, E)$, where V is the set of vertices and E is the set of edges, i.e., arcs, lines, or both arcs and lines.

A *path* in a graph $G = (V, E)$ is a sequence of unique vertices $v_1, v_2, \ldots, v_n$, with possible exception of v_1, v_n, where either $v_i \to v_{i+1}$ or $v_i - v_{i+1} \in E$ for each i, $1 \leq i \leq n - 1$. If all arcs on a path have the same direction, and the path consists of at least *one* arc it is called a *directed path*. A *directed cycle* is a directed path with $v_1 = v_n$. A *trail* τ is a sequence of vertices, where either $v_i \to v_{i+1}$ or $v_{i+1} \to v_i$, or $v_i - v_{i+1}$ are unique edges in graph G for each i. The set of descendants of a vertex $v \in V$, denoted by $\delta(v)$, is the largest set of vertices $U \subseteq V \setminus \{v\}$, where v is connected to each $u \in U$ by a directed path. Let $G = (V, E)$ be an ADG, then if for $W \subseteq V$ it holds that $\pi(v) \subseteq W$ for all $v \in W$, then W is called an *ancestral set*. By $an(W)$ is denoted the *smallest* ancestral set containing W.

In addition to undirected graphs and ADGs we need the concepts of *mixed graph*, which is a graph that contains arcs and lines, and *chain graph*, which is a mixed graph without directed cycles. The notion of chain graph is essential to the remainder of the paper.

---

[1]The abbreviation DAG is also frequently used.

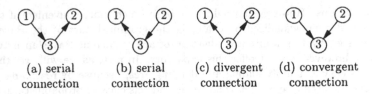

| (a) serial | (b) serial | (c) divergent | (d) convergent |
| connection | connection | connection | connection |

Figure 3: Connections as representations of conditional (in)dependences.

3.2 Independence Information

Let $U, W, S \subseteq V$ be disjoint sets of vertices. Let $G = (V, E)$ be an undirected graph. Then, if *each* path between each vertex in U and each vertex in W contains a vertex in S, then U and W are said to be *u-separated* by S; otherwise, they are said to be *u-connected*.

Let $u, w \in (V \setminus S)$ be distinct vertices in the ADG $G = (V, E)$, connected to each other by the trail τ. Then τ is said to be *blocked* by $S \subseteq V$ in G if one of the following conditions is satisfied: (i) $s \in S$ appears on the trail τ, and the arcs of τ meeting at vertex s constitute a serial or divergent connection (See Figure 3); (ii) $s \notin S$ and $\delta(s) \cap S = \varnothing$, i.e., if s appears on the trail τ then neither s nor any of its descendants occurs in S, and the arcs meeting at s on τ constitute a convergent connection as shown in Figure 3, where vertex 3 is called a *collider* or common child. Then, if *each* trail τ in G between each $u \in U$ and each $w \in W$ is blocked by S, sets U and W are said to be *d-separated* by S; otherwise, U and W are *d-connected* by S.

From an ADG G we can derive its associated undirected *moral graph* G^m that allows reading off all conditional dependences in G, and is constructed by the *moralisation* procedure: (i) add lines to all non-connected vertices, which have a common child, and (ii) replace each arc with a line in the resulting graph. The correspondence between d-separation and moralisation is established by the following proposition:

Proposition 1 *Let $G = (V, E)$ be an ADG and let $U, W, S \subseteq V$ be disjoint sets of vertices. Then, U and W are d-separated by S iff U and W are u-separated in the moral graph of the set of vertices $an(U \cup W \cup S)$, i.e., $G^m_{an(U \cup W \cup S)}$.*
Proof: See Ref. [2], page 72. □

This means that we can choose between two different methods for determining whether two sets of vertices are dependent or independent given a third, possibly empty, set of vertices. By the d-separation method we consider trails between two vertices, look subsequently at the form of the connections at vertices based on Figure 3, and then decide whether the vertices are dependent or not. In the moralisation procedure, the relevant part of the ADG is transformed into an undirected graph. We can then use u-separation, which is simpler than d-separation, to find out whether two sets of vertices are (in)dependent given a third set of vertices.

Finally, for chain graphs we have the notion of *c-separation*, which is closely related to the notion of d-separation (cf. [3, 6] for details). For example, the vertices v_1 and v_4 in the trail $v_1 \rightarrow v_2 - v_3 \leftarrow v_4$ become c-connected by $S = \{v_2\}$, whereas, if it is the only trail, v_1 and v_4 are c-separated by $S = \varnothing$.

All the graph separation notions (u-, d- and c-separation), can be used to define independence relations $\perp\!\!\!\perp_G$, where the presence of lines or arcs represent dependences and the absence of lines or arcs independences. For example, for an ADG G we say that

$$U \perp\!\!\!\perp_G W \mid Z,$$

holds if U and W are d-separated by Z. Complementary to the independence relation $\perp\!\!\!\perp_G$, there is the dependence relation $\not\perp\!\!\!\perp_G$ (as sets of vertices are either dependent or independent given a third set of vertices).

Let P be a *joint probability distribution*, or JPD for short, of the set of discrete random variables X. Instead of random variables we will write variables, for short. Let $U, W, Z \subseteq V$ be disjoint sets of vertices corresponding to sets of variables in the set X, then X_U is said to be *conditionally independent* of X_W given X_Z relative to P, denoted by $U \perp\!\!\!\perp_P W \mid Z$, if

$$P(X_U \mid X_W, X_Z) = P(X_U \mid X_Z), \text{ with } P(X_W, X_Z) > 0 . \tag{1}$$

An ADG G that is a graphical representation associated with a joint probability distribution P, is called a directed *independence map*, *I-map* for short, if it respects all the dependences in P, i.e.,

$$U \perp\!\!\!\perp_G W \mid Z \Rightarrow U \perp\!\!\!\perp_P W \mid Z,$$

for all disjoint sets $U, W, Z \subseteq V$. It is said that P obeys the *global directed Markov property* relative to G [2].

A *Bayesian network*, BN for short, is a pair $\mathcal{B} = (G, P)$, where G is an I-map of P. The I-map relation means that the joint probability distribution P obeys all independence statements relative to G. Hence, the graphical part of a Bayesian network can never contain an independence that does not hold for the associated JPD, but it may contain a dependence that does not hold for the JPD.

As an example, consider the Bayesian network from Figure 1 again; some of the dependence and independence statements that hold for the graphical part G of the Bayesian network are:

$\{$Bronchitis$\}$ $\not\perp\!\!\!\perp_G$ $\{$Cancer$\}$ $\mid \varnothing$
$\{$Bronchitis$\}$ $\perp\!\!\!\perp_G$ $\{$Cancer$\}$ $\mid \{$Smoking$\}$
$\{$Bronchitis$\}$ $\not\perp\!\!\!\perp_G$ $\{$Cancer$\}$ $\mid \{$Smoking, Fatigue$\}$
$\{$Smoking$\}$ $\not\perp\!\!\!\perp_G$ $\{$Fatigue$\}$ $\mid \{$Bronchitis$\}$
$\{$Smoking$\}$ $\not\perp\!\!\!\perp_G$ $\{$Fatigue$\}$ $\mid \{$Cancer$\}$
$\{$Smoking$\}$ $\perp\!\!\!\perp_G$ $\{$Fatigue$\}$ $\mid \{$Bronchitis, Cancer$\}$

The first three (in)dependence statements are interesting. The first statement says that 'Bronchitis' and 'Cancer' are dependent; the reason for this is that there is a common course, smoking, which renders these vertices dependent. As soon as we know the common course 'Smoking', all dependence between 'Bronchitis' and 'Cancer' is explained, and thus, 'Bronchitis' and 'Cancer' become independent, as signified by the second statement. The third statement says that if in addition to 'Smoking' 'Fatigue' is observed, 'Bronchitis' and 'Cancer' have again become dependent through the common consequence 'Fatigue'. Note that the independence relation $\perp\!\!\!\perp_P$ shows a similar behaviour, as can be verified by looking at Figure 2; G is an I-map of P.

We have seen that independence information can be represented in different form, e.g., in graphical form or hidden within a probability distribution. However, usually these representations are not unique. We, therefore, need to take into account that different ADGs may encode the same independence information. We only consider equivalence of ADGs:

Definition 1 *(independence equivalence [6]) Let G, G' be two ADGs and let $\perp\!\!\!\perp_G$ and $\perp\!\!\!\perp_{G'}$ be their independence relations, defined by the d-separation criterion. If $\perp\!\!\!\perp_G = \perp\!\!\!\perp_{G'}$, then the two graphs are said to be* independent equivalent *to one another.*

Independence equivalence of ADGs can also be defined in an other way. The undirected version of G is called the *skeleton* of G. A subgraph $G' = (V', E')$ of an ADG $G = (V, E)$, with $V' = \{u, w, z\} \subseteq V$, $E' = E \cap (V' \times V')$, is called an *immorality* if $u \rightarrow z, w \rightarrow z \in E'$ and $u \rightarrow w, u \leftarrow w \notin E'$. We now have the following theorem by Verma and Pearl [7]:

Theorem 1 *Two ADGs are independence equivalent with each other iff they have the same skeleton and the same set of immoralities.*

It now appears that classes of independence equivalent ADGs can be uniquely described by means of chain graphs, called essential graphs, which thus act as class representatives [1]; they are defined as follows:

Definition 2 *(essential graph) Let E denote an equivalence class of acyclic directed graphs that are independence equivalent. The* essential graph G^* *is then the smallest graph larger than any of the acyclic directed graphs G in the equivalence class E; formally*

$$G^* := \bigcup \{G \mid G \in E\}, \tag{2}$$

where the union of graphs, denoted by $\bigcup$, is obtained by taking the union of their vertex sets and their sets of arcs, where arcs connecting the same vertices, but pointing in different directions, are replaced by a line.

Note that G^* is the least upper bound of all the graphs that it represents.

4 Taking into Account Observations

Problem solving using a Bayesian network involves instantiating variables, and computing the new probability distribution. We also consider the consequences for the (in)dependence information in this section.

4.1 Probability Updating

In using a Bayesian network when solving a problem at a certain instance, variables are instantiated to values, that have been observed. Thus, the following mutually disjoint sets are distinguished:

- O, *observed vertices* (shown as shaded circles or ellipses in diagrams), and

- U, *unobserved vertices* (shown as non-shaded circles or ellipses in diagrams).

Likewise, we also distinguish between observed variables X_O (e.g., whether or not the person smokes) and *unobserved variables*, X_U. A variable cannot be both observed and unobserved.

The JPD obtained by incorporating observed variables, called the *observed joint probability distribution P_O*, is defined as follows:

$$P_O(X_V) := P(X_V \mid X_O = x_O). \tag{3}$$

The definition of observed joint probability distribution gives rise to the introduction of independences; in the following proposition the consequences with respect to the independence relationships between observed and unobserved variables are explored.

Proposition 2 *Let V be a set of vertices with associated set of variables X_V. Furthermore, let $O' \subseteq O$, $V' \subseteq V \setminus O'$, then, it holds that $X_{O'}$ and $X_{V'}$ are independent with respect to P_O, i.e., for all possible values $x_{O'}$ and $x_{V'}$ it holds that $P_O(X_{O'} = x_{O'}, X_{V'} = x_{V'}) = P_O(X_{O'} = x_{O'})P_O(X_{V'} = x_{V'})$.*

The following specific properties with respect to P_O are a consequence of the proposition above: (1) sets of observed variables are independent of the unobserved variables, and (2) sets of observed variables are mutually independent.

4.2 Transformation due to Observations

If the observation of a variable gives rise to the creation of a new dependence, then it appears that one proper way in which the new dependence can be represented is by inserting lines into the graph. Let $G = (V, E)$ be an ADG, and let $O \subseteq V$ be the set of observed vertices. Furthermore, let $u, w \in U$, $u \neq w$, be two unobserved vertices and let $o \in O$ be either the common child or a descendant of the common child of an immorality with u and w as parents. Then, the line (u, w), which is inserted into graph G, is called a *moral line*. The set of moral lines of graph G is denoted by $M_G(O)$; e.g., $3 - 4$ in Figure 4(b) is a moral line with $O = \{2\}$. Clearly, it holds that $M_G(\varnothing) = \varnothing$.

Moral lines play a crucial role in the context of the observation of variables, since they depict the new dependences created by the observations. However, by inserting a line into an ADG, the result is no longer an ADG. Sometimes, the result is not even a chain graph, but rather a mixed graph that is cyclic. However, even though moral lines can be inserted into a graph, we still want to keep the chain graph property. This would allow us to apply c-separation to the graphical model, which enables us to uncover the independence relation from the graph. The following transformation essentially repairs these 'side effects' of moral line insertion.

Let $G = (V, E)$ be an ADG with observed vertices $O \subseteq V$. Then, the *arc–line transformation*, denoted by T_A is defined as

$$T_A : G = (V, E) \mapsto G_A = (V, E_T),$$

where E_T denotes the smallest set of edges defined as follows. For each $(u, v) \in E$:

- if $u \in an(\{v\} \cup O)$, $v \in an(\{u\} \cup O)$ and $u, v \notin O$, then $u - v \in E_T$;

- otherwise, $u \to v \in E_T$.

Proposition 3 *Let G be an ADG with set of observed vertices O. Then, the resulting graph G_A obtained by the arc-line transformation is a chain graph.*

Proof: Suppose that G_A consists of the directed cycle $v_1 \to v_2 \to \cdots \to v_m - v_1$, and, thus, is not a chain graph. This can happen because of one of the following two reasons: (i) arc (v_1, v_m) in G and there is a path from vertex v_m to an observed vertex $o \in O$, or (ii) arc (v_m, v_1) in G and there is a path from vertex v_1 to vertex $o \in O$. But then, all arcs in the directed cycle also satisfy the first condition of the arc–line transformation and should have been replaced by a line as well; contradiction. Thus, graph G_A does not include directed cycles, and, hence, is a chain graph. □

To determine the set of independence statements following specific properties of P_O, we need to take into account that (1) observed variables are independent of the remaining, unobserved variables, and (2) that sets of observed variables are independent. Based on these properties, these created independences are depicted by labelling arcs as *semi-observed arcs*, which connect an unobserved and an observed vertex, and as *observed arcs*, which connect two observed vertices. The sets of semi-observed and observed arcs are denoted by E_S and E_O, respectively. The conditional independence set mirrored by the graph G_O, denoted by $\perp\!\!\!\perp_{G_O}$, is then defined by *observed c-separation*, explained below.

An ADG $G = (V, E)$ can be transformed into a chain graph $G_O = T_O(G)$ by an *observation transformation*, denoted by T_O, which includes the additional (in)dependences obtained by observational knowledge, as follows:

$$T_O : G = (V, E) \mapsto G_O = (V, (E_T \cup M_G(O)) \setminus (E_S \cup E_O)),$$

where E_T, E_S and E_O are defined as above. Thus, (semi)observed arcs are removed; observed c-separation is then nothing else then c-separation applied to G_O.

Proposition 4 *Let $B = (G, P)$ be a BN with observed variables X_O. Then, $G_O = T_O(G)$ is a chain graph, which is an I-map of P_O.*

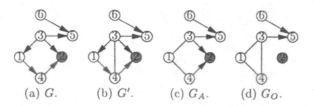

(a) G.   (b) G'.   (c) G_A.   (d) G_O.

Figure 4: Example of arc–line and observation transformation.

Proof: The I-map property implies that each dependence in P_O should also be represented in the graph G_O. As (semi)observed arcs mirror independences created in P_O, the I-map property could only be lost because of two reasons: (i) the insertion of moral lines into the graph, (ii) the replacement of arcs by lines by the arc–line transformation. (i) Note that moral lines depict additional dependence between parents, reflecting dependence because of an *observed* collider. (ii) Replacing arcs by lines, we do not change arcs involved in an immorality into a line by the arc–line transformation. We conclude that any dependence added to the graph is valid; moreover, no valid dependences are removed. □

Consider the ADG shown in Figure 4(a), with $O = \{2\}$. Here, the moral line $3 - 4$ needs to be inserted into the graph; however, the resulting graph would contain a directed cycle, see (b). Therefore, we first apply the arc–line transformation to the graph G to remove this potential directed cycle, by transforming the arcs $3 \rightarrow 1$ and $1 \rightarrow 4$ into lines, as is shown in (c). The resulting chain graph $G_O = T_O(G)$ obtained by applying the observation transformation is shown in (d).

4.3 Observed Equivalence Classes

An interesting question is whether it is possible that two different ADGs that are independence equivalent are again independence equivalent after entering observations. Related to this question is the issue whether two ADGs that are not independence equivalent can become independence equivalent after taking into account observations. These questions will be briefly explored in this section.

Let G and G' be two ADGs, then they are said to be *observed independence equivalent* with each other with respect to the set of observed vertices O, if it holds that $\perp\!\!\!\perp_{G_O} = \perp\!\!\!\perp_{G'_O}$. Chain graphs obtained by the observation transformation are used as a basis to establish equivalence, using observed c-separation.

As an example, consider Figure 5 with the graphs G^a and G^b as the two left-hand side graphs, which are *not* independence equivalent. However, when taking the observed variables $X_O = \{X_1, X_5, X_6\}$, the graphs G_O^a and G_O^b do become observed independence equivalent; both graphs are now represented by the graph in Figure 5(c).

Independence equivalence between graphs implies observed independence equivalence:

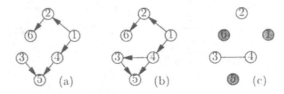

Figure 5: Example of observed equivalence graphs.

Proposition 5 *Let G and G' be two independence equivalent ADGs, then $G_O = T_O(G)$ and $G'_O = T_O(G')$ are again independence equivalent.*

An observed independence equivalent class can be uniquely represented by an *observed essential graph*, which simply is an essential graph taking into account the special nature of observed vertices.

Thus, independence equivalent ADGs remain equivalent, possibly as a chain graph that is not an ADG, after taking into account observations; in addition, ADGs that originally were not equivalent, can become independence equivalent after the processing of observations.

4.4 Graphical Reasoning Illustrated

We illustrate the theory developed above by considering the Bayesian network shown in Figure 6(a), which is an extension of the network of Figure 1.

As a result of the observation of indolence, the variables 'Bronchitis' and 'Cancer' become directly dependent, indicated by a line connecting the corresponding vertices shown in Figure 6(b). This dependence cannot be changed, except when observing either or both of these variables. In addition, most of the arcs have been changed into lines, with the exception of the arc pointing towards 'Weightloss', which has not changed as observing indolence has not changed the dependence information concerning this variable. Note that it still holds that {Smoking} $\perp\!\!\!\perp_{G_O}$ {Fatigue} | {Bronchitis, Cancer}, as the observation of indolence is unable to create a direct dependence between smoking and fatigue.

After observing fatigue, the variables 'Bronchitis' and 'Cancer' become directly dependent, as indicated in graph (c). Furthermore, similar to graph (b), some arcs will be replaced by lines. Three arcs that are related to this observed variable are removed from the graph. The resulting graph, (c), expresses the information that smoking still depends on gender and affects the occurrence of bronchitis and cancer. If smoking *is* observed, bronchitis and cancer are still dependent of each other.

Graph (d) represents the effects of observation of the variable 'Smoking'. In this case, the lower part of the graph remains unchanged, since the joint probability distribution of bronchitis and cancer already incorporates the observation of smoking. Therefore, we are also able to remove some arcs from the original graph related to smoking. We conclude that the graph transformations are consistent with our intuition.

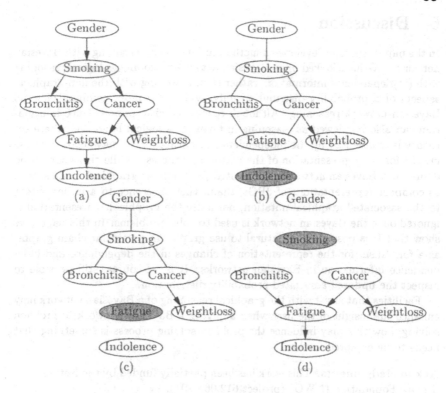

Figure 6: Example transformations due to various observations.

5 Related Work

Richardson and Spirtes have investigates the properties of maximal ancestral graphs (MAGs), which are hybrid graphs containing directed and undirected edges as well as double directed edges, under variable selection and marginalisation [5]. They have shown that MAGs are closed under these two operations. Variable selection is related to the concept of observed variables introduced in this paper. However, the work by Richardson and Spirtes does not focus on reasoning with a Bayesian network, but, instead, considers the representation of selection effects in probabilistic graphical models. In addition, the work does not consider the changes in the relationships between equivalence classes when taking into account observed variables.

Van der Gaag has studied the effects on the efficiency of probabilistic inference when taking into account observed variables [4]. The transformation proposed in the paper by Van der Gaag is different from the one proposed in our paper, as it was necessary to keep some of the semi-observed arcs, as dependences created by the observation of variables were not represented by the insertion of extra lines, as in our paper. In addition, Van der Gaag's work neither considers chain graphs, nor independence equivalence.

6 Discussion

In the paper, we have developed a method for graphical reasoning with Bayesian networks. We have looked upon Bayesian network reasoning as logical reasoning with (in)dependence information, rather than reasoning with the non-graphical aspects of a probability distribution only, which is a more common view on Bayesian-network reasoning. Although reasoning with independence information can also be viewed as reasoning in terms of a logical language, where set theory is augmented by the independence predicate ⊥⊥, we have chosen to use graphs for the representation of the reasoning process. While there can be no doubt that Bayesian networks and related probabilistic graphical models, seen as compact representations of JPDs, thank their existence to a major extent to the associated graphical notation, normally the graphical representation is ignored once the Bayesian network is used to solve problems. In this paper, we show that it is possible and natural to use graphs, in particular chain graphs, as a formalism for the representation of changes in the dependence and independence information in Bayesian networks. It is, of course, still possible to inspect the updated associated probability distribution.

Facilities that assist with the graphical reasoning of a Bayesian network may enhance the insight of the user when applying a Bayesian network to problem solving; how this may influence the problem-solving process is something that needs to be explored further.

Acknowledgements. This work has been partially funded by the Netherlands Science Foundation (NWO) (project 612.066.201).

References

[1] Andersson, S. A., Madigan, D., and Perlman, M. D. A Characterization of Markov Equivalence Classes for Acyclic Digraphs. *Annals of Statistic 25* (1997), 505–541.

[2] Cowell, R. G., Dawid, A. P., Lauritzen, S. L., and Spiegelhalter, D. J. *Probabilistic Networks and Expert Systems*. Springer-Verlag New York, 1999.

[3] Flesch, I., and Lucas, P.J.F. Markov Equivalence in Bayesian Networks. Technical Report, Radboud University Nijmegen, NIII-R0436, 2004.

[4] Gaag, L. C. van der. *Evidence Absorption for Belief Networks*. Technical Report RUU-CS-93-35, Utrecht University, 1993.

[5] Richardson, T., and Spirtes, P. Ancestral graph Markov models. *Annals of Statistics 30* (2002), 962–1030.

[6] Studený, M. *Probabilistic Conditional Independence Structures*. Springer-Verlag London, 2005.

[7] Verma, T., and Pearl, J. Equivalence and synthesis of causal models. In UAI'90 (San Francisco, CA, 1990), Morgan Kaufmann, pp. 220–227.

SESSION 2a:

KNOWLEDGE DISCOVERY IN DATA

RANKED MULTI-LABEL RULES
ASSOCIATIVE CLASSIFIER

Fadi Thabtah
Department of Computing and Engineering
University of Huddersfield, HD1 3DH, UK
F.Thabtah@hud.ac.uk

Abstract

Associative classification is a promising approach in data mining, which integrates association rule discovery and classification. In this paper, we present a novel associative classification technique called Ranked Multilabel Rule (RMR) that derives rules with multiple class labels. Rules derived by current associative classification algorithms overlap in their training data records, resulting in many redundant and useless rules. However, RMR removes the overlapping between rules using a pruning heuristic and ensures that rules in the final classifier do not share training records, resulting in more accurate classifiers. Experimental results obtained on twenty data sets show that the classifiers produced by RMR are highly competitive if compared with those generated by decision trees and other popular associative techniques such as CBA, with respect to prediction accuracy.

1. INTRODUCTION

Classification is an important task in data mining, which aims to predict the classes of future data objects. In classification, one builds a model (set of rules) from a group of classified training data records in order to forecast the classes of previously unseen data records as accurately as possible. Association rule discovery is another central task in data mining, which aims to discover the correlations among items in a transactional database [1]. The main difference between association rule discovery and classification is that there is no class to predict in the former, whereas in the latter, the ultimate goal is to predict the class labels of test data objects. In the last few years a new hybrid approach that uses association rule discovery methods to build classifiers called associative classification (AC), has been proposed [2, 6 & 7]. AC is a promising classification approach, which has been shown to build more accurate set of rules than traditional classification approaches such as decision trees and rule induction [6, 7, 11 & 14].

Association rule discovery approaches consider the correlation among all possible items in a transactional database and therefore, rules generated share transactional training records. In other words, a single transactional data record is allowed to be used in the production of multiple association rules. Since AC approach uses association rule discovery methods to find the rules, rules in it's classifier share training data objects as well. This may result in a problem where some of the classes associated with many rules learned during the training phase are not the most accurate ones.

To explain such a problem, consider Table 1, which represents a partial training data set where "Att1" and "Att2" columns are attributes and the last column is the class attribute. Assume that there are two potential rules extracted from Table 1, e.g. $r_1 : a \wedge b \rightarrow c_1$ and $r_2 : b \rightarrow c_1$, and assume that r_1 precedes r_2. Now, once r_1 is evaluated and inserted into the classifier using an AC technique such as CBA [7] or CMAR [6], all training data associated with r_1 are removed, i.e. rows (1, 2, 3) using the database coverage pruning [7]. The database coverage heuristic removes training objects covered by every evaluated rule and ensures that each rule must cover at least one training object to be part of the final classifier. In cases where the evaluated rule covers no training objects, it will be then discarded.

This paper argues that the removal of the training objects associated with $r1$ may influence other potential rules that share training objects with r_1 such as r_2. Consequently, after inserting r_1 into the classifier, the "statistically fittest" class c_1 of rule r_2 that was learned during the training phase would not be the fittest class any more; rather a new class at that point becomes the fittest class, c_2, because it has the largest representation among the remaining r_2 rows in the training data. We call this problem, which has resulted from rule pruning, the "fittest class problem". To the best of the author's knowledge, there are no AC methods which take the fittest class problem into consideration. This paper investigates the impact of removing the training data objects associated with each evaluated rule during pruning on other candidate rules that share training data. This may involve applying new class labels for some of the rules during the prediction phase rather than the class labels learned for these rules during the training phase. More specifically, in the example demonstrated above, unlike current AC algorithms [2, 6, 7, 11& 14] which consider class c_1 for r_2, the proposed algorithm considers class c_2 instead since rows(1,2,3) are already used in the training phase for a higher precedence rule, i.e. r_1.

Table 1. Partial training data

Row Id	Att1	Att2	Class
1	a	b	c_1
2	a	b	c_1
3	a	b	c_1
4	e	b	c_1
5	d	b	c_1
6	-	b	c_2
7	-	b	c_2
8	-	b	c_2
9	e	f	c_3
.	-	-	-

In the training phase, rules generated by AC methods are associated with the largest frequency classes, however, the influence of the deleted training data records for each evaluated rule during pruning is not considered on other potential rules that use these deleted records, thus, there could be many redundant rules in the final classifier. A post- pruning method like [6], which discards detailed specific rules with lower confidence values than general rules can be applied to reduce rules redundancy. But, in the example demonstrated above, the specific rule (r_1) has occurred only with class c_1 in the training data, i.e. (3/3)100% confidence, whereas the general rule (r_2) has (5/8) 62.50% confidence and therefore, this pruning method can not do much in this case. If the effect of removal of training records for the evaluated rules during pruning is considered on other candidate rules in the training phase, then a more realistic classifier that assigns the true class fitness to each rule will result.

A new AC algorithm called Ranked Multilabel Rule (RMR), which uses the fittest class associated with a rule in the prediction step rather than the largest frequency class learned for that rule, is presented. The fittest class is assigned to each rule by a pruning heuristic, which ensures training data records cannot be shared by rules. This pruning heuristic discards the training data records for each selected rule and these discarded records become unavailable for the remaining lower ranked candidate rules. This means even though a training record has been used in learning multiple rules, the pruning method proposed ensures that the final rules in the classifier do not share training records similar to rule induction approaches [3 & 9] (Section 3.2 gives further detail). The pruning heuristic may change the class for some of the impacted rules due to removing the overlapping among rules training data records.

Basic concepts in AC and demonstrated example are presented in Section 2. The proposed algorithm and experimental results are discussed in depth in Sections 3 and 4, respectively. Finally, conclusions are presented in Section 5.

2. ASSOCIATIVE CLASSIFICATION

In AC, the training data set T has m distinct attributes $A_1, A_2, \ldots , A_m$ and C is a list of classes. The number of rows in T is denoted $|T|$. An attribute may be categorical (where each attribute takes a value from a finite set of possible values) or continuous where each attribute takes a value from an infinite set, e.g. (reals or integers). For categorical attributes, all possible values are mapped to a set of positive integers. In the case of continuous attributes, a discretisation method such as [5] can be used.

Definition 1: An *item* can be described as an attribute name A_i and its value a_i, denoted (A_i, a_i).

Definition 2: The j_{th} *row* or a *training object* in T can be described as a list of items $(A_{j1}, a_{j1}), \ldots, (A_{jk}, a_{jk})$, plus a class denoted by c_j.

Definition 3: An *itemset* can be described as a set of disjoint attribute values contained in a training object, denoted $< (A_{i1}, a_{i1}), \ldots, (A_{ik}, a_{ik})>$.

Definition 4: A *ruleitem r* is of the form *<cond, c>*, where condition *cond* is an itemset and *c∈C* is a class.

Definition 5: The actual occurrence (*actoccr*) of a *ruleitem r in T* is the number of rows in *T* that match *r's* itemset.

Definition 6: The support count (*suppcount*) of *ruleitem r* = *<cond, c>* is the number of rows in *T* that matches *r's* itemset, and belongs to a class *c*.

Definition 7: The occurrence (*occitm*) of an itemset *I* in *T* is the number of rows in *T* that match *I*.

Definition 8: An itemset *i* passes the minimum support (*minsupp*) threshold if (*occitm(i)/|T|*) ≥ *minsupp*. Such an itemset is called a *frequent* itemset.

Definition 9: A *ruleitem r* passes the *minsupp* threshold if, *suppcount(r)/ |T|* ≥ *minsupp*. Such a *ruleitem* is said to be a *frequent ruleitem*.

Definition 10: A *ruleitem r* passes the minimum confidence (*minconf*) threshold if *suppcount(r) / actoccr(r)* ≥ *minconf*.

Definition 11: A rule in the RMR rule based system is represented in the form: $cond \rightarrow c_1 \vee c_2 \vee ... \vee c_j$, where the left-hand-side of the rule (antecedent) is an itemset and the right-hand-side of the rule (consequent) is a ranked list of class labels.

In general, most AC algorithms work in two phases, phase one involves the discovery of frequent *ruleitems* (attribute values that occur with a class label above the user specified support threshold). In the second phase, a classifier is built from the frequent *ruleitems* found in phase one. To explain the discovery of rules and building the classifier in AC, consider the training data set shown in Table 2, which represents whether or not a person is likely to buy a new car. Assume that *minsupp* = 2 and *minconf* = 50%. Frequent *ruleitems* discovered in phase one along with their relevant support and confidence values are shown in Table 3. In phase two and before constructing the classifier, most AC algorithms including [2, 6, 7, 11 & 14] sort the rules discovered in phase one according to their confidence and support values and then apply pruning heuristics to discard redundant and useless rules. *Ruleitems* in bold inside Table 3 cover all the training data records of Table 2 and represent the classifier after applying the database coverage pruning.

A recently proposed associative algorithm, called MMAC [12] has introduced a new class of methods, which generate rules with multiple classes from data sets where each of their data records is associated with just a single class. This provides

Table 2: Car sales training data

Age	Income	has a car	Buy/class
senior	middle	n	yes
youth	low	y	no
junior	high	y	yes
youth	middle	y	yes
senior	high	n	yes
junior	low	n	no
senior	middle	n	no

Table 3: Possible Ruleitems from Table 2

Itemset	AC Ruleitem		
	Class	Support	Confidence
{low}	no	2/7	2/2
{high}	yes	2/7	2/2
{senior, no}	yes	2/7	2/3
{middle}	yes	2/7	2/3
{senior}	yes	2/7	2/3
{y}	yes	2/7	2/3
{n}	yes	2/7	2/4
{n}	no	2/7	2/4

decision makers with useful knowledge discarded by other current AC algorithms. The proposed algorithm produces multi-label classifiers similar to MMAC, however, the class labels applied for most of RMR rules in the classification step are different than that of MMAC due to the pruning heuristic employed by RMR algorithm to eliminate the overlapping among rules training data records (Section 3.2 provides further details).

3. The RMR ALGORITHM

The algorithm presented in this paper consists of three main phases: Rules discovery, repeated learning and classification. Pseudocode for the algorithm is given in Figures 1 and 2, which we will explain in depth in Sections 3.1, 3.2 and 3.3, respectively.

3.1 FREQUENT RULEITEMS DISCOVERY

The frequent *ruleitems* discovery method employed by RMR has been adapted from a recently developed AC algorithm called MCAR [11], where during the first training data scan, frequent one-itemsets are determined, and their occurrences in the training data (rowIDs) are stored inside an array. Also, classes and their frequencies are stored in an array. Any itemset that fails to pass the support threshold is discarded. We use the (produce function) shown in Figure 2 to find frequent itemsets of size k by appending disjoint frequent itemsets of size k-1 and intersecting their rowIDs. The result of a simple intersection between rowIDs of two itemsets gives a set, which holds the rowIDs where both itemsets occur together in the training data. This set along with the class array, which holds the class labels frequencies can be used to compute the support and confidence of the new *ruleitem* resulted from the intersection. The rowIDs of itemsets used in this paper is similar to the tid-list (transaction identifier list) of itemsets concept in vertical association rule mining [15].

We briefly explain how support and confidence for *ruleitems* are found. To find the support for a *ruleitem*, we use the rowIDs of its condition (itemset) to locate classes associated with it in the class array and select the class with the largest

Input: Training data T, *minsupp* and *minconf* thresholds
Output: A classifier R and a list Tp of the covered rows
A rule r in R has the following properties: Items, class, rowIDs (tid-list)
Step 1: Rule Discovery

Scan T for the set S_1 of frequent one-itemset

$$R \leftarrow S_1$$
$$i \leftarrow 1$$
while $(S_i \neq 0)$
{

$\quad S_{i+1} \leftarrow produce(S_i)$ $\qquad$ //see Figure 2 for produce function

$\quad R \leftarrow R \cup S_{i+1}$

$\quad i \leftarrow i + 1$

}
Step2: Evaluation Step (Pruning) for each candidate rules produced during an iteration:

$$R' = \{r_1\}$$
$$Tp = \{r_1.rowIDs\}$$
For i=2 to $|R|$

$\quad Temp = (r_i.rowIDs - Tp)$

$\quad$ if $(|Temp| > 0)$

$\qquad$ Update r_i class by considering only rowIDs which are in *Temp*

$$R' \leftarrow R' \cup r_i$$
$$Tp \leftarrow Tp \cup Temp$$

$\quad$ end if
end for
end
return R', Tp
Step 3: Multi-label rules Step:
Do

$\quad i \leftarrow 1$

$\quad T' \leftarrow T$

$\quad R \leftarrow \phi \text{ (or \{\})}$

$\quad T' \leftarrow T' - Tp$

$\quad (R', Tp) = RMRScan(T', MinSupp, MinConf)$ // Repeat step 1 on T'

until no further frequent *ruleitem* is found

$\quad R \leftarrow R \cup R'$

While $(R' \neq \phi)$

$\quad$ return R

Figure 1 The RMR algorithm

Function produce
Input: A set of itemsets S
Output: set of S' produced ruleitems

$S' \leftarrow 0$
Do
    For each pair of disjoint items I_1, I_2 in S Do
      If ($<I_1 \cup I_2>$, c) passes the *minsupp* threshold
        if ($<I_1 \cup I_2>$, c) passes the *minconf* threshold

$$S' \leftarrow S' \cup (<I_1 \cup I_2>, c)$$

        end if
      en if
    end
end
Return S'

Figure 2 Rule discovery algorithm of RMR

frequency. Then by taking the cardinality of the set of the rowIDs where the itemset and its largest class occur and dividing it by the size of the training data set, one can obtain the *ruleitem* support. The calculation of the confidence is done similarly except that the denominator of the fraction is the size of the set of the rowIDs of the *ruleitem* condition instead of the size of the whole training data set. It should be noted that every time a frequent *ruleitem* is found, only the rule with the largest confidence is considered. In the case that a *ruleitem* is associated with two classes with identical confidence, the choice of the rule is arbitrary.

3.2 CLASSIFIER BUILDER and PRUNING

The RMR algorithm shown in Figure 1 derives a set of potential rules during each iteration and stores them in a descending order based on the ranking procedure shown in Figure 3 (Step 1). Then a pruning step is performed to measure the effectiveness of each rule and allow the removal of training records shared by rules. In the rule pruning as shown in Figure 1, the highest ranked potential rule is inserted into the classifier and its associated rowIDs are put into a temporary array, Tp. For each other potential lower ranked rule r_i, one can check if it covers any training objects by performing simple set difference operation between r_i rowIDs set and Tp. The resulting set will represent training objects row numbers of r_i, excluding the training objects row numbers used by any higher ranked rules than r_i (rules that already have been evaluated and inserted into the classifier). This set (*Temp*) will be used by the RMR algorithm as the new rowIDs set of r_i where class labels in this set are the only ones to be considered for rule r_i in the learning step. Consequently, after ignoring all training row numbers used by any higher ranked rules that share some training objects with r_i, the statistically fittest class associated with r_i may not be the fittest class learned during the training phase any more.

The RMR algorithm checks if rule r_i covers any training objects, if so r_i is then inserted into the classifier as well as its updated set of rowIDs (*Temp*) into Tp and continuously repeats the same process on the remaining potential rules. It should be noted that methods such as CBA, CMAR and MCAR consider all data records for the largest frequency class associated with r_i in the training phase regardless if a higher precedence rule, which may use some of r_i training data records, is already inserted into the classifier. On the other hand, RMR ignores any data records for r_i if these records have been used in the generation of a higher ranked rule and this explains why RMR may end up with a different class for r_i.

The proposed algorithm learns all possible classes associated with each candidate itemset in the training data set to extract the multi-label classifier. For a given multi-class training data T, existing AC algorithms learn and derive a single label rule set and form a default class for the remaining unclassified objects in T. On the other hand, RMR utilises a recursive learning phase similar to MMAC algorithm [12] in order to derive more than one rule set and merges them to form a multi-label classifier. The main difference between the proposed algorithm and the MMAC is that MMAC does not employ the pruning step described above and thus rules produced do overlap in their training data records similar to regular AC algorithms. The proposed algorithm produces a first-pass rule set in which each rule is associated with the most obvious class. Once this initial rule set is generated, all training objects associated with it are discarded and the remaining unclassified objects become a new training data set, T'.

The process of discarding the training data objects of the first rule set is performed using the rowIDs of the rules conditions. According to Figure 1, the highest ranked potential rule rowIDs are inserted in a temporary array, Tp, and we iterate over the remaining potential rules. For each lower ranked rule, one can perform a simple difference operation between the rowIDs set of such rule and Tp, if the result of the difference is an empty set, meaning, the current rule training data objects are already covered by other higher ranked rules, the rule is discarded. If the resulting set contains values, those values are inserted into Tp and the rule is put into the classifier. The same process is repeated on the remaining rules. Once all rules are tested, the resulting Tp holds all training objects row numbers for rules that have been inserted into the classifier in a pass.

Data set T', is generated from the difference between T and Tp. The RMR algorithm checks whether there are still more frequent *ruleitems* remaining undiscovered in T' (rules derived from T which may be associated with more than one class). If so, a new set of rules will be generated from T', and the remaining unclassified data objects in T' will form new training data, and so on. The algorithm proceeds with learning until no more frequent *ruleitems* are discovered in a pass. At that stage, any remaining unclassified objects will form a default class. This process results in learning from several subsets of the original training data and generating a number of rule sets. It should be noted that frequent *ruleitems* discovered during all iterations that come after the initial iteration pass the *minsupp* over all the training data objects. This means all frequent *ruleitems* discovered by the RMR algorithm during all iterations are globally frequent. In other words, potential rules derived after the first iteration must pass the *minsupp* and *minconf* thresholds over the original training data and not on the subset of data, which they have been generated from.

3.3 RULE RANKING PROCEDURE

Rule ranking in AC is an important step that helps in choosing the most effective rules for prediction. For instance, CBA and CMAR algorithms use the database coverage pruning to build their classifiers, where using this pruning, rules are tested according to their ranks. Generally, rule ranking is based on support, confidence and length/cardinality of the rule's antecedent. This sequence of parameters was introduced in [7] and later utilised by other techniques, including [2 & 6]. When several rules have identical confidence, support and cardinality, these techniques choose one of the rules randomly, which possibly in some cases may degrade accuracy. This random selection happens frequently in mining classification data sets where certain attribute values occur frequently. In order to ensure a subset of effective rules form the classifier, RMR uses a sorting method shown in Figure 3 that considers the class distribution frequency parameter after confidence, support and rule antecedent cardinality to distinguish among rules with similar confidence and/or support in the rule ranking process. This parameter proved to be effective in reducing rule random selection for dense data sets according to [12]. The RMR algorithm invokes the above rule ranking method during each iteration on the potential generated rules set in order to ensure that only high confidence rules are kept for prediction.

Given two rules, r_a and r_b, r_a precedes r_b $(r_a \rangle r_b)$ if:

1. The confidence of r_a is greater than that of r_b.
2. The confidence values of r_a and r_b are the same, but the support of r_a is greater than that of r_b.
3. Confidence and support values of r_a and r_b are the same, but r_a has fewer conditions in its left hand side than of r_b.
4. The confidence, support and conditions cardinality values of r_a and r_b are the same but r_a is associated with more frequently occurring class than that of r_b
5. All above criteria are identical for r_a and r_b, but r_a was generated from items that occur earlier in the training data than that of r_b.

Figure 3 Rule ranking method used by RMR

3.4 PREDICTION PROCEDURE

In classification, let R be the set of generated rules and Ts be the set of test data objects. The basic idea of the classification procedure used by the proposed algorithm as shown in Figure 4 is to choose the best rule among a set of high confidence, representative and general rules in R to predict Ts. In classifying a test object (line 1), the classification procedure uses a simple approach, which states that the first rule in the set of ranked rules that matches the test object condition classifies it (line 5). In a case where no rule fully matching the test object condition, the RMR prediction procedure seeks for the highest precedence rule that matches part of the test object and applies it (line 7). This is the first rule in Tr, which its body matches any attribute value of the test object and not necessarily the one which matches the maximum number of attribute values in the test object condition. In cases where no rule matches the test object condition, the default class will be assigned to the test data object (line 8). This classification process ensures that only the highest ranked rules classify test data objects. It should be noted that the top ranked class of a rule is assigned to the test data object by RMR during the classification process.

Input: Classifier (R), test data set (Ts), array Tr
Output: Prediction error rate Pe
Given a test data set (Ts), the classification process works as follow:
1 For each test instance ts in Ts Do
2 For each rule r in the set of ranked rules R Do
3   Find all applicable rules that match ts body and store them in Tr
4   If Tr is not empty Do
5   If there exists a rule r that fully matches ts's condition
6   assign r's class to ts
7   else assign the highest precedence rule class from Tr to ts
       end if
8   else assign the default class to ts
9 end if
10 empty Tr
11 end for
12 end for
13 compute the classification accuracy

Figure 4 RMR prediction algorithm

4.   EXPERIMENTAL RESULTS

Experiments have been performed on twenty data sets from the *Weka* data collection [17] and real world optimisation data [4]. Three popular classification techniques have been compared to RMR in terms of classification accuracy and the number of rules derived on the ten binary and multi-class data sets (C4.5 [8], RIPPER [3], CBA [7]) in order to evaluate the predictive power of the proposed method. We also compared RMR with CBA on a real world multi-label data.

To run the experiments, stratified ten-fold cross-validation [13] was used. The experiments of C4.5 and RIPPER algorithms were conducted using the *Weka* software system [17]. CBA experiments were conducted using a VC++ implementation version provided by [16] and RMR was implemented in Java. The *minsupp* has been set to 2% in CBA and RMR experiments since more extensive experiments reported in [2, 7 & 11] suggested that it is one of the rates that achieve a good balance between accuracy and the size of the classifiers. The confidence threshold, on the other hand, has a smaller impact on the behaviour of any AC method and it has been set to 30%.

The classification accuracy and the number of rules produced using stratified ten-fold cross-validation of C4.5, RIPPER, CBA and RMR against ten classification data sets from *Weka* are shown in Table 5. Since RMR produces rules with multiple labels, only the top ranked class for each rule is considered to obtain the accuracy for fair comparison. RMR achieved higher classification accuracy than C4.5 on seven out of ten benchmark problems. RMR also achieved higher accuracy

Table 5. Classification accuracy and classifier sizes of C4.5, RIIPER, CBA and RMR algorithms

Data-set	Size	Class No	Accuracy (%)				Num. Of Rules			
			C4.5	RIPPER	CBA	RMR	C4.5	RIPPER	CBA	RMR
Glass	214	7	66.82	68.69	69.89	71.07	30	8	36	31
iris	150	3	96.00	94.66	93.25	93.87	5	4	18	15
tic-tac	958	2	83.71	96.97	100.00	100.00	95	9	25	26
breast	699	2	94.66	95.42	98.84	95.92	14	6	45	60
zoo	101	7	93.06	88.14	95.96	95.15	10	6	7	8
heart	270	2	86.67	78.98	83.32	84.74	18	5	52	75
Diabetes	768	2	85.82	76.04	75.34	78.79	20	4	36	65
Pima	768	2	72.78	73.30	75.49	78.05	26	3	36	65
vote	435	2	88.27	87.35	86.91	88.70	4	4	40	84
balance-scale	625	3	64.32	74.56	67.24	77.00	33	17	15	17
Average			83.21	83.41	84.62	86.32				

than CBA on seven benchmark problems with one further tied result. On average, the RMR algorithm achieved +3.11%, +2.91% and +1.70% above C4.5, RIPPER and CBA learning methods with respect to accuracy, respectively. The accuracy figures provide evidence for the hypothesis that in general AC techniques are more accurate than traditional classification ones such as rule induction and decision trees. This supports other research findings conducted in AC such as [6, 7 & 14].

The number of rules generated by the proposed method and CBA are often larger than those derived by C4.5 and RIPPER for the majority of the data sets. This is not surprising, since traditional methods (RIPPER, C4.5) use extensive pruning such as global optimisation [3] and pessimistic error [8] to cut down the number of rules. Moreover, the heuristic method employed by RIPPER to discover the rules produces its classifiers locally and in a greedy fashion, which explains its limited sized classifiers. The derived rules for RIPPER are local because when a rule is discovered, all training data objects associated with it are discarded and the process continues until the rule found has unacceptable error rate. This means rules are discovered from partitions of the training data and not from the whole training data once. The search process for the rules is greedy since RIPPER looks for the rule condition that maximises a statistical measure called Foil-gain [9]. On the other hand, AC algorithms such as CBA and RMR utilise association rule discovery strategies to find the rules. These strategies normally explore all possible associations between attribute values in the training data which explains the exponential growth of rules.

Data from several runs generated by a Peckish hyperheuristic for a personnel-scheduling problem were provided by the authors of [4]. Data from ten solution runs in separate text files were used. Each row in the data represents an effective local search neighbourhood (low-level heuristic) for a set of ten possible local search neighbourhoods developed for a personnel-scheduling problem. Each file consists of data from five thousand local search applications. The term Hyperheuristic is a general method that manages the choice of which neighbourhood search technique to apply during the construction process of a solution for optimisation problems. The main difference between hyperheuristic and metaheuristic approaches such as tabu search and simulated annealing is that hyperheuristic requires limited knowledge about the domain of the problem under investigation and does not search directly for the solution, and thus it can be applied to different problem without making any significant changes. The peckish hyperheuristic, which has been used to produce the data used in the experiments, selects and applies the low-level heuristic that leads to the largest improvement on the objective function (if one exists), and this is the class we want to find.

Table 6 represents part of a solution run (data) generated by Peckish hyperheuristic where columns **LLH_2** and **LLH_1** represent the low-level heuristics applied at the previous two iterations. Column **LLH** represents the current low-level heuristic that improved the objective function and column **Imp** represents the improvement on the objective function value. Finally column **Apply** represents whether or not the selected low-level heuristic has been applied by the hyperheuristic. The data generated by the hyperheuristic have multiple labels, since at each iteration there could be more than one low-level heuristic that improves the objective function. For example, at the first iteration in Table 6, there are three low-level heuristics (LLH 2, LLH 43, LLH 74) that improve the objective function. Thus, there are three class labels associated with the instance <(LLH_2, 1), (LLH_1, 1)>. Generally, each training instance in the optimisation data may associate with more than one class.

Figure 5 shows the relative prediction accuracy of RMR with respect to that CBA. In other words, how much better or worse RMR performs in term of accuracy with respect to CBA learning algorithm. The relative prediction accuracy numbers shown in the figures are estimated using the formula $\dfrac{(Accuracy_{RMR} - Accuracy_{CBA})}{Accuracy_{CBA}}$.

The accuracy RMR has been derived using the label-weight evaluation measure [12] for the multi-label data sets. This evaluation method enables each class for a rule to play a role in classifying a test data object based on its ranking, therefore this method assigns a weight for each class in a rule according to its number of occurrences in the training data with that rule. To clarify, consider for example a

Table 6. Sample of optimisation data

Iteration	LLH_2	LLH_1	LLH	Imp	Apply
1	1	1	2	987	1
1	1	1	43	2	0
1	1	1	74	2	0
2	1	2	1	92	1
3	2	1	2	981	1
3	2	1	58	8	0

rule, $r: (x \wedge y) \rightarrow c_1 \vee c_2 \vee c_3$, the standard error-rate evaluation method [13] considers only class c_1 as a correct classification in the prediction stage. All other applicable test data objects having either c_2 or c_3 are considered a misclassification. However, classes c_2 and c_3 can contribute to the final decision because they pass support and confidence requirements. The label-weight method gives a value for each test data object that contains item (x, y) in its body and has either class c_1, c_2 or c_3 based on the class labels frequencies in the training data set. The summation of class labels weights for a rule is equal to one. This method reflects the true distribution frequency for each class when associated with a particular itemset.

Figure 5 shows that the proposed algorithm consistently produces more accurate classifiers than that of CBA methods for most data sets. Since RMR beats CBA with regards to accuracy, the effectiveness of removing the training objects for evaluated rules from other potential rules on accuracy is relatively high. The Figure also reveals that using rules with non-overlapping training data records is a more accurate approach when compared to AC approaches that use overlapping rules. Particularly, the proposed algorithm outperformed CBA on seven out of ten scheduling data sets.

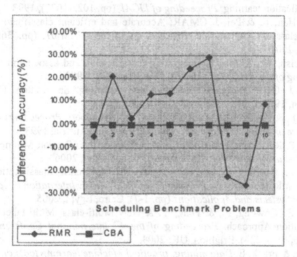

Figure 5 Difference of accuracy between RMR and CBA algorithm

5. CONCLUSIONS

In this paper, a new classification based on association rule mining algorithm that generates rules with multiple labels was proposed. Unlike current associative algorithms, which allow each training data record to be used for the generation of multiple rules in the training phase, the proposed algorithm ensures that rules in the final classifiers do not overlap in their training data records. This has been accomplished using a pruning heuristic that removes the training records for each evaluated rule from any lower ranked rules that share these records with it and thus results in updating the rank of class labels associated with some of the rules. Experiments on twenty data sets indicated that the proposed method is highly competitive when compared with the state-of-the-art AC and traditional techniques in term of classification accuracy. The results on the real data revealed that RMR extracts more accurate classification systems if compared with popular associative algorithms such as CBA. In near future, we intend to investigate the utilisation of new prediction methods for multi-label associative classification algorithms.

References

1. Agrawal, R., & Srikant, R. Fast algorithms for mining association rule. *Proceedings of the 20th International Conference on Very Large Data Bases*, (pp. 487-499), 1994.
2. Baralis, E., & Torino, P. A lazy approach to pruning classification rules. *Proceedings of the 2002 IEEE International Conference on Data Mining*, (pp. 35), 2002.
3. Cohen, W. Fast effective rule induction. *Proceedings of the 12th International Conference on Machine Learning*, (pp. 115-123). Morgan Kaufmann, CA, 1995.
4. Cowling P., & Chakhlevitch, K. Hyperheuristics for Managing a Large Collection of Low Level Heuristics to Schedule Personnel. *Proceedings of 2003 IEEE conference on Evolutionary Computation*, Canberra, Australia, 8-12 Dec, (pp. 1214-1221), 2003.
5. Fayyad, U., & Irani, K. Multi—interval discretisation of continues-valued attributes for classification learning. *Proceeding of IJCAI*, (pp. 1022-1027), 1993.
6. Li , W., Han, J., & Pei, J. CMAR: Accurate and efficient classification based on multiple-class association rule. *Proceedings of the ICDM'01*, (pp. 369-376). San Jose, CA, 2001.
7. Liu, B., Hsu, W., & Ma, Y. Integrating classification and association rule mining. *Proceeding of the KDD*, (pp. 80-86). New York, NY, 1998.
8. Quinlan, J. C4.5: *Programs for Machine Learning*. San Mateo, CA: Morgan Kaufmann, 1993.
9. Quinlan, J., & Cameron-Jones, R. FOIL: A midterm report. *Proceedings of European Conference on Machine Learning*, (pp. 3-20). Vienna, Austria, 1993.
10. Thabtah, F. Rule Preference Effect in Associative Classification Mining. *Journal of Information and Knowledge Management*, Vol 5(1):1-7, 2006.
11. Thabtah, F., Cowling, P., & Peng, Y. MCAR: Multi-class Classification based on Association Rule Approach. *Proceeding of the 3rd IEEE International Conference on Computer Systems and Applications* (pp. 1-7). Cairo, Egypt, 2005.
12. Thabtah, F., Cowling, P., & Peng, Y. A New Multi-class, Multi-label Associative Classification Approach. *Proceeding of the 4th International Conference on Data Mining* (pp. 217-224). Brighton, UK, 2004.
13. Witten, I., & Frank, E. *Data mining: practical Machine learning tools and techniques with Java implementations*. San Francisco: Morgan Kaufmann, 2000.
14. Yin, X., & Han, J. CPAR: Classification based on predictive association rule. *Proceedings of the SDM* (pp. 369-376). San Francisco, CA, 2003.
15. Zaki, M. & Gouda K. Fast Vertical Mining using Diffsets. Proceedings *of the ninth ACM SIGKDD international conference on Knowledge discovery and data mining*, (pp. 326-335). Washington, D.C., 2003.
16. CBA. http://www.comp.nus.edu.sg/~dm2/p_download.html, 1998.
17. WEKA. Data Mining Software in Java: http://www.cs.waikato.ac.nz/ml/weka, 2001.

Two Different Approaches to Automated Mark Up of Emotions in Text

Virginia Francisco, Raquel Hervás, Pablo Gervás

Dep. Sistemas Informáticos y Programación

Universidad Complutense de Madrid

Madrid, Spain

email: {virginia, raquelhb}@fdi.ucm.es, pgervas@sip.ucm.es

Abstract

This paper presents two different approaches to automated marking up of texts with emotional labels. For the first approach a corpus of example texts previously annotated by human evaluators is mined for an initial assignment of emotional features to words. This results in a List of Emotional Words (LEW) which becomes a useful resource for later automated mark up. The mark up algorithm in this first approach mirrors closely the steps taken during feature extraction, employing for the actual assignment of emotional features a combination of the LEW resource and WordNet for knowledge-based expansion of words not occurring in LEW. The algorithm for automated mark up is tested against new text samples to test its coverage. The second approach mark up texts during their generation. We have a knowledge base which contains the necessary information for marking up the text. This information is related to actions and characters. The algorithm in this case employ the information of the knowledge database and decides the correct emotion for every sentence. The algorithm for automated mark up is tested against four different texts. The results of the two approaches are compared and discussed with respect to three main issues: relative adequacy of each one of the representations used, correctness and coverage of the proposed algorithms, and additional techniques and solutions that may be employed to improve the results.

1   Introduction

The task of annotating text with specific labels indicating its emotional content or inclination is fundamental for any attempt to make computer interfaces respond in some way to the affective nature of the content they are handling. This is particularly true for research attempts to produce synthesised voice with different emotional states, but it may also be applicable in other contexts, such as multimodal presentation, where colors, typography or similar means can be used to convey emotion.

A comprehensive definition of emotion must take into account the conscious feeling of the emotion, the processes that appear in the nervous system and in the brain and the expressive models of the emotion [6]. Two issues must be addressed when experimenting in this field: to obtain a corpus of emotionally annotated texts to act as reference data, and to decide on a particular representation of emotion. For the study of emotional texts we need to decide which emotions we are going to model, and how we are going to represent them. There are different methods for representing emotions [2]:

- Emotional categories: The most common description of emotions is the use of emotion-denoting words, or category labels. Human languages have produced extremely powerful labels for emotional states.

- Descriptions based on psychology: The appraisal of a stimulus determines the significance of stimulus for the individual, and triggers and emotion as an appropriate response [1].

- Descriptions based on evaluation: These theories describe the emotions from the point of view of the evaluations involved.

- Circumflex models: Emotional concepts are represented by means of a circular structure [10] such that two emotional categories being close in the circle represents the conceptual similarity of these two categories.

- Emotional dimensions: Emotional dimensions represent the essential aspects of emotion concepts. Evaluation (positive/negative) and activation (active/passive) are the main dimensions; sometimes they are augmented with the power dimension (dominant/submissive). This approach is very useful because it allows measurement of the similarity between different emotional states. Another important property of this method is the relative arbitrarily in naming the dimensions.

For the particular purpose contemplated in this paper we have chosen emotional categories. One of the issues we want to discuss is how large a number of emotions is needed for adequate coverage. Too large a set of emotions makes the task very complex. Several approaches have been proposed in the literature for reducing the number of emotion-denoting adjectives:

- Basic emotions: There is general agreement that some full-blown emotions are more basic than others. From this point of view, the basic emotions appears in every person. The number of basic emotions is usually small (in early studies 10, in more recent ones between 10 and 20), so it is possible to characterize each emotional category in terms of its intrinsic properties [2].

- Super ordinate emotional categories: Some emotional categories have been proposed as more fundamental than others on the grounds that they include the others. Scherer [11] and Ortony suggest that an emotion A is more fundamental than other emotion B if the set of evaluation components of the emotion A are a subset of the evaluation components of the emotion B. An example that may clarify the idea: five prototypes are proposed as underlying all emotional categories: anger, love, joy, fear and sadness. Joy, for example, would be subdivided into pride, contentment, and zest. Cowie and Cornellius [2] give a short overview of recent proposals of such lists.

- Essential everyday emotion terms: A pragmatic approach is to ask for the emotion terms that play an important role in everyday life. The approach is exemplified by the work of Cowie [3], who proposed a Basic English Emotion Vocabulary. Starting from lists of emotion terms from the literature, subjects were asked to select a subset which appropriately represents the emotions relevant in everyday life. A subset of 16 emotion terms emerged.

The aim of this work is to present two different approaches to emotional tagging and compare the results obtained with them when marking up texts of a particular domain - simple versions of children fairy tales. The last section discusses some ideas we are working on to improve these results.

2 Annotating Text with Labels for Emotional Content

This section presents a brief review of previous work on the labeling of texts with emotions. An important decision when annotating text with emotions is which particular approach should be used to relate emotions and textual elements.

Existing approaches can be grouped in four main categories [5]: keyword spotting - text is marked up with emotions based on the presence of affective words - , lexical affinity - not only detects affective words but also assigns arbitrary words a probability of indicating different emotions -, statistical natural language processing - involves feeding a machine learning algorithm a large training corpus of text marked-up with emotions - , approaches based on large-scale real-world knowledge - this method evaluates the affective qualities of the underlying semantic content of text - and hand-crafted methods - involves modeling emotional states in terms of hand-crafted models of affect based on psychological theories about human needs, goals, and desires -. The two approaches presented in this paper are based on lexical affinity and hand-crafted methods:

- Lexical affinity: This method not only detects affective words, as keyword spotting, but also assigns words a probability, obtained from a corpus, of indicating different emotions. The weaknesses of this approach are mainly two: it operates only at the word-level, so it can easily have problems when emotional words appear within the scope of negation; and lexical affinity is obtained from a corpus, which makes it difficult to develop a reusable, domain-independent model.

- Hand-Crafted method: This method involves modeling emotional states in terms of hand-crafted models of affect based on psychological theories about human needs, goals, and desires. This requires a deep understanding and analysis of the text. The difficulty with this approach is that it is very difficult to generalize.

On deciding the parts of the text which are going to be marked with emotions there are different options [5]: word, phrase, paragraph, chapter ... One of the simplest approaches is to have sentences as emotional structures. Another solution is to combine the sentences into large units using an algorithm to summarise the affect of text over multi-sentence regions (winner-take-all scheme, Bayesian networks ...). Our approaches mark up emotions at the sentence level.

3   EmoTag

The first method for annotating text relies on a dictionary of word to emotion assignments. This is obtained from a corpus of human evaluated texts by applying language analysis techniques. Similar techniques are later applied to assign emotions to sentences from the assignments for the words that compose them.

3.1   Construction of the Dictionary

This section deals with the process of building two basic resources for emotional mark up: a corpus of fairy tale sentences annotated with emotional information, and a list of emotional words (LEW). Both the corpus and the list of emotional words are annotated with emotional categories (happy, sad, angry ...). In this first approach all the emotional categories are available, we have not used any of the approaches for reducing the number of labels.

The method we are going to use for the mark up follows an approach based on lexical affinity. Based on a large corpus of marked up emotional text we have obtained a list of words and their relation with emotions (LEW). When we mark up a text we look for every word in this first list. If the word is not in our list we try to obtain from an ontology (WordNet) a word related to it which is in one of our emotional word lists. In the following sections we describe in detail how we have obtained the list of emotional words (LEW) and how our approach works.

3.1.1   How to Annotate the Corpus

If we want to obtain a program that marks up texts with emotions, as a human would, we first need a corpus of marked-up texts in order to analyze and obtain a set of key words which we will use in the mark up process. These texts must be marked up by different people. Each of the texts which forms part of the corpus may be marked by more than one person because assignment of emotions is a subjective task so we have to avoid "subjective extremes". In order to do that we obtain the emotion assigned to a phrase as the average of the mark-up provided by fifteen evaluators. Therefore the process of obtaining the list of emotional words involves two different phases:

- Evaluation method: Several people mark up some texts from our corpus.

- Extraction method: From the mark-up texts of the previous phase we obtain the list of emotional words.

First we had to decide which texts are going to be part of our corpus. We decided to focus the effort on a very specific domain: fairy tales. This decision was taken mainly because generally fairy tales are intended to help children understand better their feelings, and they usually involve instances of the emotions that most children experiment on their way to maturity: happiness, sadness, anger, fear ... The emotions in tales have mainly three functions: to communicate to the listener the personality of a given character to induce a certain emotional response in the listener and to communicate to the listener the emotions which given characters feels at given moments in the tale

Once the domain of the corpus' texts is established, the set of specific tales that we are going to work with must be selected. We have selected eight tales, every one of them popular tales with different lengths(altogether they result in 10.331 words and 1.084 sentences), in English. The eight tales are marked up with emotional categories: happy, sad, anger, surprise... In order to help the evaluators in the assignment of emotional categories we provide a list of different emotions. This list is only a guide, and they can add every category they need.

3.1.2 How to Extract the List of Emotional Words

Based on the tales marked up by the evaluators we obtain a data base of words and their relation to emotional categories.

Firstly we split the text into phrases and we obtain for every phrase the emotion assigned to it by most of the people, that is if one phrase has been marked as sad by 1 evaluator and as happy by 10 evaluators we considered that the phrase is happy. Phrases are processed with the qtag part-of-speech(POS) tagger, qtag [1], which assigns a part-of-speech tag (e.g. noun, verb, punctuation, etc.) to each word in a text. Every phrase is divided into words and with every word and its label we carry out the following process:

- Check if the label is in the list of stop POS tags, if it is we leave it out. Our stop list is composed of the following labels: verbs *"to be"*, *"to do"*, *"to have"* and all their conjugations, conjunctions, numbers, determiners, existential there, prepositions, modal auxiliary (*might, will*), possessive particles, pronouns, infinitive marker (*to*), interjections, adverbs, negative markers (*not, n't*), quotation mark, apostrophe...

---

[1]http://www.english.bham.ac.uk/staff/omason/software/qtag.html

- If the label is not in the stop list we proceed to extract the stem of the word. In order to do that we employ the Porter stemming algorithm with some changes. The Porter stemming algorithm (or "Porter stemmer") is a process for removing the most common morphological and inflexional endings from words in English [9].

- Once we have the stem of the word it is inserted into our word data base with the value 1 in the field of the emotion assigned to the phrase in which the word was; if the word was already in our list we add 1 to the field of the phrase's emotion.

- Once we have all the words in our list we carry out a normalization. We divide the numeric value we have for each of the emotions, by the number of appearances of the word in the text. In this way we have the probability of the presence of the word in a text indicating the emotions we are studying.

- Once all the tales have been processed we carry out an expansion process of our list of words. We extend our list with synonyms and antonyms. Synonyms and antonyms of every word are looked up in WordNet [7]. This process looks up all the synonyms and antonyms for every word in the list, and all of them are inserted into our data base. For inserting related words into the database, the same probabilities of the original word are used in the case of synonyms and the opposite probability is used in the case of antonyms (1- original probability).

3.2   A Method for Automated Mark Up of Emotions

Our process classifies sentences into emotions, the first step is to perform sentence detection and tokenization in order to carry out our process based in the relation between words and different emotions. In the following sections we describe how we carry out this process.

- By means of the tagger qtag, mentioned in the previous section, we obtain the POS tag for every word in the sentence. Based on these tags and words we decide the emotion of the sentence.

- If the tag associated with the word is in our label stop list we leave it out.

- If the tag is not in our stop list we get the stem of the word by means of the modified Porter stemming algorithm mentioned before.

- Once we have the stem of the word that we want to classify, we look it up in the lists of emotional words (LEW). If the word is present we assign to it the probability of carrying the emotions we are studying. Based on these probabilities of the words we obtain the final emotion of the sentence.

- If the word is not in the list we look up the hypernyms of the word in WordNet, and look them up in the LEW list. The first appearance of a hypernym is taken and the emotional content associated to our original word and the new word is inserted in the LEW list for subsequent occurrences of these words in our tales.

- If none of the hypernyms appear in the LEW list we leave out the word and it does not take part in the mark up process.

- Once all the words of the sentences have been evaluated, we add up the probability of each emotion of the different words and assign to the sentence the emotion which has a bigger probability.

A sample part of a marked tale:

...

<anxiety> The knight faced the lioness. </anxiety>
<neutral> He fought she. </neutral>
<neutral> The knight threw the spear. </neutral>
<sad> It killed the fierce lioness. </sad>
<neutral> The knight drew the knife. </neutral>
<neutral> The knight opened the lioness. </neutral>
<happy> The knight resurrected the pretty blonde princess. </happy>
<delight> She returned to the strong castle. </delight>
<happy> The knight and the princess lived happy ever afterward. </happy>

4 cFROGS Tagger

The cFROGS Tagger marks up text using emotional categories as does EmoTag, but not all the possible categories are used. This tagger uses one of the existing approaches for reducing the number of categories seen in Section 1: Basic Emotions. The following five basic emotions have been selected for this tagging: "happy", "sad", "angry", "fear" and "surprise". The emotion "neutral" is also used in the absence of any other emotion.

With cFROGS Tagger texts are marked up while they are being generated. In order to get tales tagged at the same time as we generate them, an existing module for automatic story generation [4] has been modified. This module generated a conceptual representation of fairy tales and its corresponding text by means of natural language generation techniques. The input of the module are the actions which take part in the story plot and the semantic information about characters, locations, attributes and relations involved in the actions. From this input the story is generated automatically.

The semantic information about the elements involved in the story is stored in a knowledge base of conceptual information about the discourse elements that appear in the input [8]. It is organized as a tree, including individuals, locations, objects, relations between them and their attributes. An extract of the knowledge base is given in Table 1.

```
character:
    human:
        no-magical:
            character(ch0,prince)
            character(ch23,hunter)
            [...]
    animal:
        can-fly:
            character(ch17,dragon)
            [...]
        cannot-fly:
            character(ch55,snake)
            character(ch28,lion)
            [...]
location:
    natural:
        location(17,cave)
        location(115,forest)
        [...]
    artificial:
        location(11,palace)
        [...]
```

Table 1: Partial view of the knowledge base

The marking up of tales in our generator is carried out in the *lexicalization* stage of the natural language generation process, where it is decided which specific words and phrases should be chosen to express the domain concepts and relations which appear in the messages. Given the basic linguistic structures used by the generation module, the mark up is done by phrases. The result of the *lexicalization* stage is a list of messages with their correspondent lexical forms and the emotion they are going to be marked up with. A final stage of *surface realization* assembles all the relevant pieces into linguistically and typographically correct text.

Two elements of the tales are taken into account when deciding the emotion associated to each sentence:

- Characters.

- Actions in which the characters are involved.

4.1   Emotions Associated to Characters

Using the traditional distinction between good and evil, the characters in our stories are supposed to be involved in good, bad or neutral situations. For each case, one of the basic emotions is associated to the character. For the tale "Cinderella" the emotions in Table 2 have been considered for the main characters.

As they are the villains of the tale, for the "stepmother" and "stepsisters" the emotion assigned for the good situations is angry. For the hero and victim, the assigment is just the opposite.

	Good	Bad	Neutral
Cinderella	Happy	Sad	Neutral
prince	Happy	Sad	Neutral
father	Neutral	Neutral	Neutral
mother	Neutral	Neutral	Neutral
stepmother	Angry	Happy	Neutral
stepsisters	Angry	Happy	Neutral

Table 2: Emotions associated to characters

4.2 Emotions Associated to Actions

The actions are considered as good, bad or neutral situations. When choosing the emotion associated to the message representing the action, the characters involved in it are taken into account. There is a type of action that must be treated in a special way. These are the surprising actions, that are always assigned the surprise emotion, not taking into account its arguments. The information about the type of action is specified in the story plan received by the generation module as input.

4.3 An Example

An example of the resulting mark up with the emotions in Table 2 is:

...
<sad>Cinderella lost her mother.</sad>
<angry>The father married a stepmother.</angry>
<sad>The stern stepmother made Cinderella work very hard.</sad>
<angry>The stepmother let the stepsisters do no work. </angry>
...
<surprised>The prince recognized Cinderella. </surprised>
<happy>The handsome prince married Cinderella. </happy>

In this example the action "marry" stands out. Being considered a happy situation, it is associated with different emotions angry or happy depending on the characters involved.

5 Evaluation

Both taggers are evaluated separately, and then they are both compared in a back-to-back test for the same two stories.

5.1 EmoTag

In order to evaluate our work we carried out a test. In this test four tales are going to take part, two of them had been in our original corpus, the corpus we used to obtain our LEW list and the other two are new tales, which did not take part in our extraction method. In this way we will measure on the one hand how our process marks the tales from which we have obtained our LEW list and on the other hand how our approach works with tales that have not been involved in our extraction process. The tales which take part in this test are English popular tales with different number of words (from 153 words and 20 lines to 1404 words and 136 lines).

Each of our four tales will be marked with the emotional categories by different evaluators. Two aspects must be discussed: the results of the tagging by the human evaluators and the results of tagging by EmoTag. The results obtained are explained below.

- Evaluator's results: We have noticed that the percentage of sentences on which the majority of the human evaluators - half of their number plus one - agrees on the assignment of an emotion is very low, around 45%. This is an important data when it comes to interpreting the results obtained by our tagger. A reference value for the emotion of each phrase is obtained by choosing the emotion most often assigned to that sentence by the human evaluators.

- EmoTag's results: The reference value obtained in the evaluator's tales is used to compare with the results generated by EmoTag. The graph in Figure 1 shows the percentages of success obtained for each tale. Each sentence has been considered successfully tagged if the emotion assigned by the tagger matched the reference value.

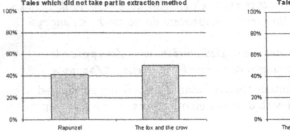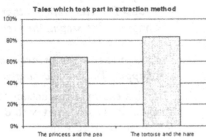

Figure 1: Percentage of success with EmoTag

Figure 2 shows the relationship between the percentage of success and the percentage of sentences whose reference value is supported by one more than half the number of evaluators.

With respect to the percentage of success we can conclude that the best results are obtained with the tales which took part in our extraction method ("The tortoise and the hare" and "The princess and the pea").

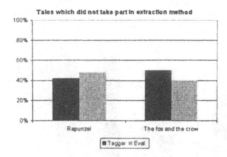 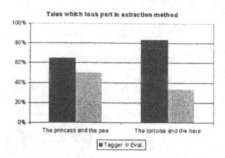

Figure 2: Success percentage and majority-supported evaluators with EmoTag

Analysis of the sentences that were tagged incorrectly indicates that most of them are either very long, include negations, or correspond to situations where human evaluators do not agree. These correspond to sentences where the reference value is not supported by at least one more than half the number of evaluators.

5.2   cFROGS Tagger

In order to evaluate our work we carried out a test with ten evaluators, in this test two tales are going to take part. These tales have been produced by cFROGS. Evaluators are asked to mark up the two tales with the six different emotions which we considered in this tagger: happy, sad, anger, surprise, fear and neutral. The results of this tests are the two tales marked with the basic emotional categories by different evaluators. Then we will obtain how we mark up every tale with our process.

- Evaluator's results: We have noticed that the percentage of sentences on which the majority of the human evaluators - half of their number plus one - agrees on the assignment of an emotion are higher than in the previous tagger, around 65%. This is an important data when it comes to comparing the results obtained by this tagger with the ones obtained in the previous tagger. A reference value for the emotion of each phrase is obtained by choosing the emotion most often assigned to that sentence by the human evaluators.

- cFROGS Tagger's results: The reference value obtained in the evaluator's tales is used to compare with the results generated by our tagger. The graph in Figure 3 shows the percentages of success obtained for each tale and the percentage of sentences whose reference value is supported by one more than half the number of evaluators. Each sentence has been considered successfully tagged if the emotion assigned by the tagger matched the reference value.

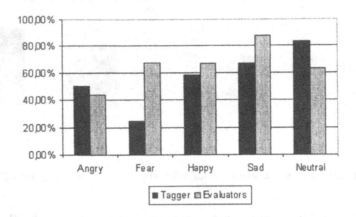

Figure 3: Success percentage and majority-supported evaluators with cFROGSTagger

Figure 4 shows the relationship between the percentage of success and the percentage of sentences whose reference value is supported by one more than half the number of evaluators in each of the tales studied.

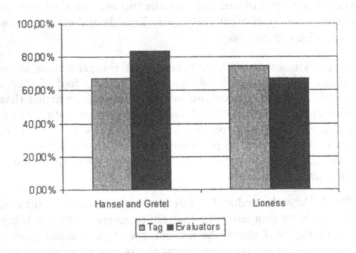

Figure 4: Percentage of success and majority-supported evaluators for the different tales with cFROGSTagger

5.3 Evaluation conclusions

With respect to the percentage of success we can conclude that in the case of EmoTag the best results are obtained with the tales which took part in our extraction method ("The princess and the pea" and "The tortoise and the hare"). If we compare the results of the two approaches we can see that if all the results are includes the best results are obtained with the cFROGS Tagger. If we compare the results of cFROGS Tagger with the subset of the results of EmoTag which correspond to tales used in the extraction method, EmoTag has a higher success rate.

Figure 5 shows the percentage of sentences in which EmoTag and cFROGS Tagger have selected the same emotion in order to mark up a sentence.

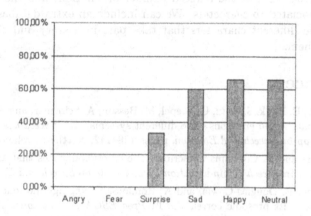

Figure 5: Percentage of sentences in which EmoTag and cFROGS Tagger mark up sentences with the same emotion

6 Conclusions

EmoTag reduced one of the disadvantages of methods based on lexical affinity. We have reduced the dependency on a given corpus by complementing our data base of emotional words with synonyms, antonyms, and hypernyms. Nonetheless, we still get better results for the tales used to obtain the LEW corpus than for new tales, so we consider necessary to continue exploring better solutions for this problem. Some issues related to context still need further work. Negation, for instance, may have the effect of inverting the polarity of the emotional content of words under its scope. We are considering the use of shallow parsing techniques to determine the scope of negations appearing in the sentences, in order to take their effect into account, both when computing word emotion from sentence emotion and viceversa.

Aside from these issues requiring improvement, we have observed that very long sentences lead to confusion when assigning emotions. In future versions we will consider a finer granularity for representing sentences.

Another problem was the large observable disagreement between human evaluators. This disagreement is lower in the cFROGS Tagger which indicates that the lower the number of emotions is, the lower the disagreement between evaluators is. We are considering reducing the number of emotions in EmoTag using one of the existing approaches mentioned in the introduction. The one which is better suited to our goal is the essential everyday emotion terms.

cFROGS Tagger obtains the better results in sentences marked by evaluators as *neutral, sad, happy* and *fear*. It is necessary to improve the results in the case of sentences marked as *angry* and *surprise*.

In future versions we will consider including some aspects of cFROGS Tagger in EmoTag, such as the reduced number of emotions and the idea of the emotion associated to characters. We can include an extra database in which we store the different characters that take part in a story and the emotion related to them.

References

[1] K. Alter, E. Rank, S. Kotz, U. Toepel, M. Besson, A. Schirmer, and A. Friederici. Accentuation and emotions - two different systems? In *Proceedings of the ISCA Workshop on Speech and Emotion*, pages 138–142, Northern Ireland, 2000.

[2] R. Cowie and R. Cornelius. Describing the emotional states that are expressed in speech. In *Speech Communication Special Issue on Speech and Emotion*, 2003.

[3] R. Cowie, E. Douglas-Cowie, and A. Romano. Changing emotional tone in dialogue and its prosodic correlates. In *Proc ESCA International Workshop on Dialogue and prosody*, Veldhoven, The Netherlands, 1999.

[4] P. Gervás, B. Díaz-Agudo, F. Peinado, and R. Hervás. Story plot generation based on CBR. In A. Macintosh, R. Ellis, and T. Allen, editors, *12th Conference on Applications and Innovations in Intelligent Systems*, Cambridge, UK, 2004. Springer, WICS series.

[5] H.Liu, H. Lieberman, and T. Selker. A model of textual affect sensing using real-world knowledge. In *Proceedings of IUI*, Miami, Florida, 2003.

[6] C. Izard. *The face of emotion*. Appleton-Century-Crofts, New York, 1971.

[7] G. Miller. Wordnet: a lexical database for english. *Communications of the ACM*, 38:39–41, 1995.

[8] F. Peinado, P. Gervas, and B. Daz-Agudo. A description logic ontology for fairy tale generation. In F. P. P. T.Veale, A.Cardoso, editor, *Procs. of the Workshop on Language Resources for Linguistic Creativity*, pages 56–61, Lisboa, Portugal, 29th May, 2004. LREA.

[9] Porter. An algorithm for suffix stripping, program. 14:130–137, 1980.

[10] J. Russell. A circumflex model of affect. *Journal of Personality and Social Psychology*, 39:1161–1178, 1980.

[11] K. Scherer. *On the nature and function of emotion: A component process approach*. Scherer and K.R. and Ekman P and editors, Erlbaum, Hillsdale, NJ, 1984.

Towards a Framework for Change Detection in Data Sets

Mirko Böttcher, Detlef Nauck, Dymitr Ruta, Martin Spott

Intelligent Systems Research Centre, BT Research and Venturing

Ipswich, United Kingdom

Abstract

Since the world with its markets, innovations and customers is changing faster than ever before, the key to survival for businesses is the ability to detect, assess and respond to changing conditions rapidly and intelligently. Discovering changes and reacting to or acting upon them before others do has therefore become a strategical issue for many companies. However, existing data analysis techniques are insuffient for this task since they typically assume that the domain under consideration is stable over time. This paper presents a framework that detects changes within a data set at virtually any level of granularity. The underlying idea is to derive a rule-based description of the data set at different points in time and to subsequently analyse how these rules change. Nevertheless, further techniques are required to assist the data analyst in interpreting and assessing their changes. Therefore the framework also contains methods to discard rules that are non-drivers for change and to assess the interestingness of detected changes.

1 Introduction

Data mining methods assume implicitly that the domain under consideration is stable over time and thus provide a rather static view on the patterns and knowledge hidden in gathered data. This is undesirable in timestamped domains, since the data then captures and reflects external influences like management decisions, economic and market trends, and changes in customer behaviour. Data mining methods should account for this dynamic behaviour and hence consider the data as a sequence along the time axis. Such domains are very common in practice, since data is almost always collected over long periods.

From this perspective the question *Which patterns exist?* as it is answered by state-of-the-art data mining technology is replaced by *How do patterns change?* In customer churn management, for example, the analysis of pattern change would enable a business to answer questions like: which factors are gaining more influence on customer churn and may be significant *in the future?* Generally, systematic pattern change is a pattern itself and obviously of high interest in the decision making process: its predictive nature allows for proactive business decisions on a middle and long term scale. In fact, the detection of interesting and previously unknown changes in data—for which this paper proposes a general framework—not only allows the user to monitor the impact of past business decisions but also to prepare today's business for tomorrow's needs.

1.1 Association Rule Discovery

A broadly used approach to perform a nearly exhaustive search for patterns within a data set is *association rule discovery* [1]. Its goal is to detect all those attribute values which frequently occur together and to form rules which predict their co-occurrence. The advantage of association rule discovery is the completeness of its results: it finds the exhaustive set of all patterns which exceed specified thresholds on certain significance metrics. For this reason it provides a rather detailed description of a data set's structure. On the other hand, however, the set of discovered rules is typically vast.

Formally, association rule mining is applied to a set $\mathcal{D}$ of *transactions* $T \in \mathcal{D}$. Every transaction T is a subset of a set of items $\mathcal{L}$. A subset $\mathcal{X} \subseteq \mathcal{L}$ is called *itemset*. It is said that a transaction T *supports* an itemset $\mathcal{X}$ if $\mathcal{X} \subseteq T$.

An association rule r is an expression $\mathcal{X} \rightarrow \mathcal{Y}$ where $\mathcal{X}$ and $\mathcal{Y}$ are itemsets, $|\mathcal{Y}| > 0$ and $X \cap Y = \varnothing$. Its meaning is quite intuitive: Given a database $\mathcal{D}$ of transactions the rule above expresses that whenever $\mathcal{X} \subseteq T$ holds, $\mathcal{Y} \subseteq T$ is likely to hold too. We just focus on association rules whose consequent is a 1-itemset, since such rules are generally sufficient for most business applications. A rule is then written as $\mathcal{X} \rightarrow y$, with $\mathcal{X} \subset \mathcal{L}$ and $y \in \mathcal{L}$. If for two rules $r : \mathcal{X} \rightarrow y$ and $r' : \mathcal{X}' \rightarrow y$, $\mathcal{X} \subset \mathcal{X}'$ holds, then it is said that r is a *generalization* of r'. This is denoted by $r' \prec r$.

As usual, the reliability of a rule $r : \mathcal{X} \rightarrow y$ is measured by its *confidence* conf(r), which estimates $P(y \in T \mid \mathcal{X} \subset T)$, or short $P(y \mid \mathcal{X})$. The statistical significance of r is measured by its *support* supp(r) which estimates $P(\mathcal{X} \cup \{y\} \subseteq T)$, or short $P(\mathcal{X}y)$. We also use the support of an itemset $\mathcal{X}$ denoted by supp$(\mathcal{X})$.

1.2 Histories of Association Rule Measures

The underlying idea of our framework is to detect interesting changes in a data set by analysing the support and confidence of association rules along the time axis. The starting point of such a *rule change mining* approach is as follows: a timestamped data set is partitioned into intervals along the time axis. Association rule discovery is then applied to each of these subsets. This yields sequences—or *histories*—of support and confidence for each rule, which can be analysed further. Of particular interest are regularities in the histories which we call *change patterns*. They allow us to make statements about the future development of a rule and thus provide a basis for proactive decision making.

Let $\mathcal{D}$ be a time-stamped data set and $[t_0, t_n]$ the minimum time span that covers all its tuples. The interval $[t_0, t_n]$ is divided into $n > 1$ non-overlapping periods $T_i := [t_{i-1}, t_i]$, such that the corresponding subsets $\mathcal{D}(T_i) \subset \mathcal{D}$ each have a size $|\mathcal{D}(T_i)| \gg 1$. Let $\hat{T} := \{T_1, \dots, T_n\}$ be the set of all periods, then for each $T_i \in \hat{T}$ association rule mining is applied to the transaction set $\mathcal{D}(T_i)$ to derive rule sets $\mathcal{R}(\mathcal{D}(T_i))$.

Because the measures, like confidence and support, of every rule $r : \mathcal{X} \to y$ are now related to a specific transaction set $\mathcal{D}(T_i)$ and thus to a certain time period T_i we need to extend their notation. This is done straightforward and yields $\mathrm{conf}(r, T_i) \approx P(y|\ \mathcal{X}, T_i)$ and $\mathrm{supp}(r, T_i) \approx P(\mathcal{X}y|\ T_i)$.

Each rule $r \in \hat{\mathcal{R}}(\mathcal{D}) := \bigcap_{i=1}^{n} \mathcal{R}(\mathcal{D}(T_i))$ is therefore described by n values for each measure. Imposed by the order of time the values form sequences called *confidence history* $H_{conf}(r) := (\mathrm{conf}(r, T_1), \dots \mathrm{conf}(r, T_n))$ and *support history* $H_{supp}(r) := (\mathrm{supp}(r, T_1), \dots \mathrm{supp}(r, T_n))$ of the rule r. These histories are the input to most rule change mining approaches, which then detect interesting change patterns.

1.3 Related Work

In the area of rule change mining the discovery of interesting changes in histories for association rules has been studied by several authors. In [2] a query language for history shapes is introduced. In [3] and [4] efficient algorithms which detect emerging itemsets are proposed. A fuzzy approach to reveal the regularities in how measures for rules change and to predict future changes was presented by [5]. In [6] an algorithm that ranks itemsets based on a change measure derived from the minimum description length principle is presented. [7] proposes a statistical approach to distinguish trend, semi-stable and stable rules with respect to their histories of confidence and support. In [8] a method to detect so-called fundamental rule changes is presented. Most of these methods have limitations that prevent them from being applied in the context of this paper. They either require user interaction, are restricted to only two consecutive time periods or use the wrong kind of tests when looking for trends.

The field of anomaly detection also is related to our paper. It refers to the automatic identification of abnormal phenomena embedded in a large amount of temporal data [9]. Anomality detection approaches assume that a description of what is normal is available, e.g. as training data. Our system was designed for corporate data which constantly changes due to a manifold of external influences. For this reaseon, a description of normality is nearly impossible to obtain. Anomality detection methods cannot be used.

2 Framework for Change Detection

As already mentioned above our approach builds upon the idea of deriving association rules at different points in time, which are then analysed for changes. To derive a history, data sets collected during many consecutive periods have to be analysed for association rules. After each analysis session the discovered rules have to be compared to those discovered in previous periods and their histories have to be extended. On the other hand, history values may be discarded

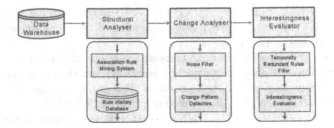

Figure 1: Detailed design of each layer.

if their age exceeds an application dependent threshold. Therefore, rules and histories have to be stored on a long term basis. Taking all of the aforesaid into account the first task of our framework is:

1. Association rules have to be *discovered* and their histories efficiently stored, managed and maintained.

If histories with a sufficient length are available, the next task is straightforward and constitutes the core component of rule change mining:

2. Histories that exhibit specific change patterns have to be reliably *detected*.

Association rule discovery is generally connected with two problems. In the first place, a vast number of rules will be detected, which is also referred to as the *rule quantity problem*. Secondly, rules may be obvious, already known or not relevant, which is also referred to as the *rule quality problem*.

Since a history is derived for each rule, the rule quantity problem also affects rule change mining: it has to deal with a vast number of histories and thus it is likely that many change patterns will be detected. Moreover, as we will briefly discuss in Section 3, methods that were developed to deal with this problem for association rules cannot be used in rule change mining. Furthermore, there is also a quality problem: not all of the detected change patterns are equally interesting to a user and the most interesting are hidden among many irrelevant ones. Overall, the third task is:

3. Histories with a change pattern have to be analysed for redundancies and *evaluated* according to their interestingness.

Because the aforementioned tasks build upon each other, they can be seen as layers of a processing framework. According to their task the layers are termed *Structural Analyser*, *Change Analyser* and *Interestingness Evaluator*, respectively. Figure 1 illustrates them and summarises the workflow.

3 Structural Analyser

Given a timestamped data set collected during a certain period, the task of the Structural Analyser is to discover and store the association rules hidden in it. Therefore, the first component of this layer is an association rule mining system, its second component is a database that stores and manages rules and their histories. Both components, but also the choice of the time periods, will be explained in the following.

In order to obtain the data set, the period length has to be chosen. Two aspects have to be considered. Long periods lead to many transactions in the individual data sets for the different periods and thus can enhance the reliability of the metrics used. Short periods allow to measure a rule's statistics more frequently, which may lead to a more reliable detection of change patterns. The choice of periods length should therefore depend on the application.

After the data set is available, association rule mining is applied to it. A typical system for association rule mining may not only consist of the rule miner itself, but also of methods for pruning, constrained mining and interestingness assessment. Such methods have been developed to cope with the rule quantity and rule quality problem, respectively, in each period.

However, the rule quality obviously does not affect rule change mining: whether or not a rule is interesting in a certain period does not directly influence the interestingness of its history. In fact, we assume that the interestingness of a change pattern primarily influences the interestingness of the underlying rule. Therefore interestingness measures for association rules should not be part of the rule mining system used within the scope of rule change mining.

On the other hand, the rule quantity problem affects rule change mining. A huge number of histories has to be processed and consequently far too many change patterns will be reported. In order to cope with this problem, pruning methods are used to constrain the set of generated rules. From the perspective of rule change mining such pruning methods treat rule sets independently from another. However, in rule change mining we have many, temporally ordered rule sets. Thus the rule property utilized for pruning—in general a measure based on rule statistics—may vary for some rules over time, but still match the pruning criterion in each rule set. Although these variations may render rules interesting, they are discarded by approaches for association rule pruning. Consequently, conventional pruning approaches should not directly be used in conjunction with rule change mining.

4 Change Analyser

The task of the *Change Analyser* is to discover change patterns in rule histories. In this paper, however, we only discuss how histories are detected that are stable or exhibit a trend. The Change Analyser fulfills its task by a two step approach. In the first step a filter is applied to the histories to reduce the noise contained in them. In a second step statistical tests for trend and stability are conducted.

Rule histories inherently may contain random *noise*. Random noise may influence subsequent analysis steps in such a way that wrong and misleading results are produced. To reduce this effect we use *double exponential smoothing* [10] in order to reveal more clearly any trend or stability. It is a simple and fast, yet effective method, which can easily be automated. Nevertheless, it has to be considered that after smoothing association rule measures may be inconsistent with each other. For example, the confidence of a rule can in general not be obtained anymore by dividing the rule's support by the support of its antecedent itemset.

A trend is present if a sequence exhibits steady upward growth or a downward decline over its whole length. This definition is rather loose, but in fact there exists no fully satisfactory definition for trend [10]. From a data mining perspective a trend describes the pattern that each value is likely to be larger or smaller than all its predecessors within a sequence, depending on whether the trend is upward or downward. Hence it is a qualitative statement about the current and likely future development of a sequence. However, taking aspects of interpretability and usefulness into account, such a statement is sufficient in the case of rule change mining. When faced with a vast number of rules and their histories, a user often has a basic expectation whether they should exhibit a trend and of what kind. By comparing his expectations with reality he will mostly be able to roughly assess the implications for its business. On the other hand, a user will rarely know in advance how trends should look like quantitatively, e.g., their shape or target values. Thus he may be unable to exploit the advantages of more sophisticated trend descriptions, like regression models.

To choose a method for trend detection, it has to be taken into account that the number of sequences to examine is huge. Whenever a trend is reported the user is basically forced to rely on the correctness of this statement, because it is infeasible for him to verify each trend manually. In addition to the requirement of reliable detection, the method should incorporate no assumptions about any underlying model, because it is very unlikely that it will hold for all or at least most sequences. Therefore non-parametric statistical tests are the appropriate choice for trend detection.

Within our framework we provide two statistical tests for trend, the *Mann-Kendall test* [11] and the *Cox-Stuart test* [12]. The Cox-Stuart test exploits fewer features of the sequence, leading to a computational effort that increases linearly with the sequence length. Although this may render the Cox-Stuart test susceptible to noise, because the influence of artefacts on the test result is stronger, it is considerably faster for long sequences. In contrast to this, the Mann-Kendall test is much more robust, but its computational effort increases quadratically with the sequence length. Therefore it has to be determined which of the two issues—speed or robustness—is more important depending on the actual application scenario.

Roughly speaking, a history is considered stable if its mean level and variance are constant over time and the variance is reasonably small. Similar to trends, a clear definition of stability is difficult. For example, a sequence may exhibit a cyclical variation, but may nevertheless be stable on a long term scale. Depending on the problem domain, either the one or the other may have to be emphasised. From a data mining perspective stability describes the pattern that each value is likely to be close to a constant value, estimated by the mean of its predecessors. Thus it is, like a trend, a qualitative statement about the future development of a sequence. However, in contrast to a trend, it can easily be modeled in an interpretable and useful way, e.g., by the sequence's sample mean and variance. Generally, stable rules are more reliable and can be trusted—an eminently useful and desirable property for long term business planning.

To test for stability we use a method based on the well-known χ^2 test. However, since the χ^2 test does not take the inherent order of a history's values into account, our method may infrequently also classify histories as stable, which actually exhibit a trend. Therefore, we chose to perform the stability test as the last one in our sequence of tests for change patterns.

5 Interestingness Evaluator

Since usually a vast number of change patterns will be detected, it is essential to provide methods which reduce their number and identify potentially interesting ones. This is the task of the *Interestingness Evaluator*. To reduce the number of change patterns the Interestingness Evaluator contains a novel redundancy detection approach, based on so-called derivative histories. Although this approach proves to be very effective, the number of rules may still be too large for manual examination. Therefore a component for interestingness evaluation is provided, which contains a set of interestingness measures.

5.1 Non-derivative Rules Filter

Generally, most changes captured in a history—and consequently also change patterns—are simply the snowball effect of the changes of other rules. Suppose we are looking at churn prevention and our framework would discover that the support of the rule

$$r_1 : \text{AGE} > 50 \Rightarrow \text{COMPLAIN=YES}$$

shows an upward trend. That is, the fraction of customers over 50 who complain increased. However, if the fraction of males among all over 50 year old complaining customers is stable over time, the history of

$$r_2 : \text{AGE} > 50, \text{GENDER=MALE} \Rightarrow \text{COMPLAIN=YES}$$

shows qualitatively the same trend. In fact, the history of rule r_2 can be *derived* from the one of r_1 by multiplying it with a gender related constant factor. For this reason, the rule r_2 is *temporally redundant* with respect to its history of support.

It is reasonable to assume that a user will generally be interested in rules with non-derivative and thus non-redundant histories, because they are likely key drivers for changes. Moreover, derivative rules may lead to wrong business decisions. In the above example a decision based on the change in rule r_2 would account for the gender as one significant factor for the observed trend. In fact, the gender is completely irrelevant. Therefore, the aim is to find rules that are non-redundant in the sense that their history is not a derivative of related rules' histories. In a way, the approach is searching and discarding rules that are not the root cause of a change pattern which, in turn, can be seen as a form of pruning. In order to find derivative rules we have to answer the following questions. First, what is meant by *related* rules, and second, what makes a history a *derivative* of other histories. Regarding the first question, a natural relation between association rules is *generalization*. We therefore define that a rule r' is *related to a rule* r iff r' is more general than r, i.e. $r \prec r'$.

The following definition for derivative measure histories includes those of itemsets as a generalization from rules. Thereby, the superset relation is used to define *related itemsets*: an itemset $\mathcal{Y}$ is related to an itemset $\mathcal{X}$ iff $\mathcal{X} \prec \mathcal{Y} := \mathcal{X} \supset \mathcal{Y}$. As before, $\mathcal{X}\mathcal{Y}$ is written for $\mathcal{X} \cup \mathcal{Y}$.

Definition 1 *Let* $s, s_1, s_2 \ldots s_p$ *be rules or itemsets with* $s \prec s_i$ *for all i and* $p > 0$. *In case of rules, let the antecedent itemsets of the s_i be pairwise disjoint, in case of itemsets let the s_i be pairwise disjoint. Let m be a measure like support or confidence,* $m(T) := m(s, T)$ *and* $m_i(T) := m(s_i, T)$ *its functions over time and* $\mathcal{M} := \{g : \mathbb{R} \longrightarrow \mathbb{R}\}$ *be the set of real-valued functions over time. The history $H_m(s)$ regarding the measure m is called* derivative *iff a function* $f : \mathcal{M}^p \longrightarrow \mathcal{M}$ *exists such that for all* $T \in \hat{T}$

$$m(T) = f(m_1, m_2, \ldots, m_p)(T) \tag{1}$$

For simplicity, we call a rule or itemset *derivative with respect to a measure* m iff its history of m is derivative. The temporal redundancy of a rule therefore depends on the measure under consideration, e.g. a rule can be redundant (derivative) with respect to its support history, but not redundant (not derivative) with respect to its confidence history. This in turn is consistent with existing rule change mining approaches, because they typically process histories of different measures independently from another.

The main idea behind the above definition is that the history of a rule (itemset) is derivative, if it can be constructed as a mapping of the histories of more general rules (itemsets). To compute the value $m(s, T)$ the values $m(s_i, T)$ are thereby considered. The definition above does not allow for a pointwise definition of f on just the $T \in \hat{T}$, but instead states a general relationship between the measures of the rules independent from the point in time. It can therefore be used to predict the value of, for example, supp(s) given future values of the supp(s_i). A simple example we will see below is $m = f(m_1) = c\, m_1$, i.e. the history of a rule can be obtained by multiplying the history of a more general rule with a constant c.

In the following we introduce three criteria for detecting derivative histories which can be used in combination or independently from another. The first two criteria deal with itemsets and can therefore be directly applied to the support of rules, as well. The last criterion is related to histories of rule confidences. The functions f are quite simple and we make sure that they are intuitive.

The first criterion checks if the support of an itemset can be explained with the support of exactly one less specific itemset.

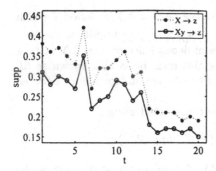 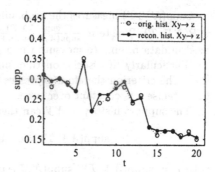

Figure 2: Histories of the rule $\mathcal{X} \rightarrow z$ and its derivative rule $\mathcal{X}y \rightarrow z$

Figure 3: Reconstructed history of $\mathcal{X}y \rightarrow z$ using the history of $\mathcal{X} \rightarrow z$

Criterion 1 *The term* $\operatorname{supp}(\mathcal{X}\mathcal{Y}, T)/\operatorname{supp}(\mathcal{Y}, T)$ *is constant over* $T \in \hat{T}$ *given disjoint itemsets* $\mathcal{X}$ *and* $\mathcal{Y}$.

The meaning of the criterion becomes clear when being rewritten as $c = \operatorname{supp}(\mathcal{X}\mathcal{Y}, T)/\operatorname{supp}(\mathcal{Y}, T) = P(\mathcal{X}\mathcal{Y}|T)/P(\mathcal{Y}|T) = P(\mathcal{X}|\mathcal{Y}T)$ with a constant c. The probability of $\mathcal{X}$ is required to be constant over time given $\mathcal{Y}$, so the fraction of transactions containing $\mathcal{X}$ additionally to $\mathcal{Y}$ constantly grows in the same proportion as $\mathcal{Y}$. This definition is also closely related to confidence, and states that the confidence of the rule $\mathcal{Y} \rightarrow \mathcal{X}$ should not change. For this reason the influence of $\mathcal{X}$ in the itemset $\mathcal{X}\mathcal{Y}$ on the support history is not important. Due to

$$\operatorname{supp}(\mathcal{X}\mathcal{Y}, T) = c \cdot \operatorname{supp}(\mathcal{Y}, T) \tag{2}$$

with $c = \operatorname{supp}(\mathcal{X}\mathcal{Y}, T)/\operatorname{supp}(\mathcal{Y}, T)$ for any $T \in \hat{T}$, $\mathcal{X}\mathcal{Y}$ is obviously a derivative of $\mathcal{Y}$ with respect to support history as defined in Definition 1.

Figures 2 and 3 show an example of a derivative support history of a rule. Figure 2 shows the support histories of the less specific rule at the top and the more specific rule underneath over 20 time periods. The shape of the two curves is obviously very similar and it turns out that the history of the more specific rule can be approximately reconstructed using the less specific one based on (2). As shown in Figure 3, the reconstruction is not exact due to noise. A suitable statistical test was proposed in [13].

Opposed to the criterion above, the following is based on the idea of explaining the support of an itemset with the support values of two subsets.

Criterion 2 *The term* $\frac{\operatorname{supp}(\mathcal{X}\mathcal{Y}, T)}{\operatorname{supp}(\mathcal{X}, T)\operatorname{supp}(\mathcal{Y}, T)}$ *is constant over* $T \in \hat{T}$ *given disjoint itemsets* $\mathcal{X}$ *and* $\mathcal{Y}$.

supp($\mathcal{XY}, T$) measures the probability of the itemset $\mathcal{XY}$ in period T which is $P(\mathcal{XY} | T)$. The term $\frac{\text{supp}(\mathcal{XY},T)}{\text{supp}(\mathcal{X},T),\text{supp}(\mathcal{Y},T)} = \frac{P(\mathcal{XY}|T)}{P(\mathcal{X}|T)P(\mathcal{Y}|T)}$ is quite extensively used in data mining to measure the degree of dependence of $\mathcal{X}$ and $\mathcal{Y}$ at time T. Particularly in association rule mining this measure is also known as *lift* [14]. The criterion therefore expresses that the degree of dependence between both itemsets is constant over time.

The support history of $\mathcal{XY}$ can then be constructed using

$$\text{supp}(\mathcal{XY}, T) = c \cdot \text{supp}(\mathcal{X}, T) \, \text{supp}(\mathcal{Y}, T) \tag{3}$$

with $c = \text{supp}(\mathcal{XY}, T)/(\text{supp}(\mathcal{X}, T) \, \text{supp}(\mathcal{Y}, T))$ for any $T \in \hat{T}$, that is the individual support values of the less specific itemsets are used corrected with the constant degree of dependence on another. According to Definition 1 the support history of $\mathcal{XY}$ is therefore derivative.

Overall, an itemset is considered derivative with respect to support if more general itemsets can be found, such that at least one of the Criteria 1 or 2 holds.

Finally, the last criterion deals with derivative confidence histories of rules.

Criterion 3 *The term $\frac{\text{conf}(r,T)}{\text{conf}(r',T)}$ is constant over $T \in \hat{T}$ given two rules r and r' with $r \prec r'$.*

Assuming the rules $r : \mathcal{XY} \rightarrow z$ and $r' : \mathcal{Y} \rightarrow z$ with disjoint itemsets $\mathcal{X}$ and $\mathcal{Y}$, the criterion translates to $\frac{P(z|\mathcal{XY}T)}{P(z|\mathcal{Y}T)}$ being constant over time. This basically means that the contribution of $\mathcal{X}$ in addition to $\mathcal{Y}$ to predict z relative to the predictive power of $\mathcal{Y}$ remains stable over time and can therefore be neglected. The confidence history of r is derivative because of the following. Be $c = \text{conf}(r, T)/\text{conf}(r', T)$ for any $T \in \hat{T}$, then for all $T \in \hat{T}$

$$\text{conf}(r, T) = c \cdot \text{conf}(r', T) \tag{4}$$

5.2 Interestingness Measures

To assess the interestingness of detected trends and stabilities it has to be considered that each history is linked to a rule, which, prior to rule change mining, has a certain relevance to a user. However, the detection of a specific change pattern may significantly influence this prior relevance. In this sense a rule can have different degrees of interestingness, each related to another history. However, there is no broadly accepted and reliable way of measuring a rule's interestingness up to now [15]. Therefore we consider any statement about the interestingness of a history also as a statement about the interestingness of its related rule.

To assess stable histories two things should be considered. Firstly, association rule discovery typically assumes that the domain under consideration is stable over time. Secondly, measures like support and confidence are interestingness measures for rules themselves. Taking all this into account, a stable

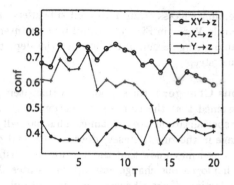

Figure 4: Examples of interesting histories which exhibit a trend.

history is in some way consistent with the abovementioned assumption of association rule mining. It is summarised by the mean of its values, which in turn can then be treated as an objective interestingness measure. Here the variance of the history can be neglected, since it is constrained by the stability detection method.

To develop objective interestingness measures for trends is more complex due to their richness of features. For identifying salient features of a given trend, it is essential to provide reference points for comparison. As such we chose the assumptions a user naively makes in the absence of any knowledge about the changes in rule histories. From a psychological perspective they can be seen as the anchors relative to which histories with a trend are assessed: a trend becomes more interesting with increasing inconsistency between its features and the user's naive assumptions. We identified three such assumptions and defined heuristic measures for the discrepancy between a history and an assumption:

- **Stability:** Unless other information is provided, a user assumes that histories are stable over time. This assumption does not mean that he expects no trends at all, but expresses his naive expectations in the absence of precise knowledge about a trend. It should be noted that this is consistent with conventional association rule mining, which implicitly assumes that the associations hidden in the data are stable over time. The confidence histories of the rule $\mathcal{XY} \Rightarrow z$ in Figure 4 would violate the stability assumption because its trend is very clear.

- **Non-rapid Change:** Since a user shapes his business, he will be aware that the domain under consideration changes over time. However, he will assume that any change is continuous in its direction and moderate in its value. For example, if a business starts a new campaign, it will probably assume that the desired effect evolves moderately, because, for instance, not all people will see a commercial immediately. On the other hand, a rapid change in this context attracts more attention, because it may hint at an overwhelming success or an undesired side effect. For example, the history of the rule $\mathcal{Y} \Rightarrow z$ in Figure 4 would be very interesting according to the non-rapid change assumption because the depicted trend is very pronounced and steep.

- **Homogeneous Change:** If the support of a rule (itemset) changes over time, it is assumed that the rate and direction of changes in the support of all its specialisations are the same. This basically means that the observed change in the rule (itemset) does not depend on further items. For example, a user may know that the fraction of satisfied customers increases. The homogeneous change assumptions states that the observed change in satisfaction affects all customers and not only selected subpopulations, e.g. females over forty. If, on the other hand, the confidence of a rule changes over time, it is assumed that the confidence of all more specialised rules changes at the same rate. For example, the history of the rule $\mathcal{XY} \Rightarrow z$ in Figure 4 would be very interesting because its shape is completetly different from those of its more general rules.

6 Evaluation

To evaluate our framework we chose a representative real-life dataset from the CRM (Customer Relationship Management) domain. The dataset contains answers of customers to a survey collected over a period of 40 weeks. Each tuple is described by 33 nominal attributes with a domain size between 2 and 39. We transformed the dataset into a transaction set by recoding every (attribute, attribute value) combination as an item. Then we split the transaction set into 20 subsets, each corresponding to a period of two weeks. The subsets contain between 1480 and 2936 transactions. To each subset we applied the well-known *apriori* algorithm [1] with the same parameter settings. From the obtained 20 rule sets we created a compound rule set by intersecting them. Its size is 77401 for the parameters $\text{supp}_{\min} = 0.05$ and $\text{conf}_{\min} = 0.2$, respectively. Subsequently we applied the proposed framework. Thereby two objectives are linked with our evaluation. First, the number of trends and stabilities contained in histories has to be determined. Second, the number of derivative rule histories has to be determined.

The results for trend are shown in Table 1 whereby we only show the results for the Mann-Kendall test. Furthermore, the results for stability detection are included, since they depend on the outcome of a prior test for trend. By comparing the corresponding columns for unsmoothed and smoothed histories it can be seen that the number of change patterns detected is a bit but not significantly larger for smoothed histories. Roughly 50% of support histories exhibit a trend, whereas the number of confidence histories with a trend is considerably smaller. On the other hand, around 30% of confidence histories are stable, compared to under 3% for support. The significant difference can be explained with the density of the data. Since some items are highly correlated,

	no smoothing				smoothing			
	trend(%)			stable(%)	trend(%)			stable(%)
	down	up	all		down	up	all	
conf	21.2	18.0	39.3	28.1	25.12	20.5	45.6	32.6
supp	37.5	17.1	54.7	2.6	40.07	18.1	58.2	5.1

Table 1: Fraction of unsmoothed and smoothed histories with trend or stability.

	Support		Confidence	
Pattern	#histories	deriv.(%)	#histories	deriv.(%)
trend	42307	66.3	30387	40.7
stable	2019	39.6	21753	26.7

Table 2: Fraction of derivative histories among all histories which have a trend or are stable.

it is very likely that many rules have a stable history of high confidence values. The support history of such rules, nonetheless, may exhibit a trend.

Only histories which exhibit change patterns were tested if they are a derivative of another history. The first row of Table 2 shows the obtained results for trends separately for support and confidence histories. As it can be seen between 40.7% (for confidence) and 66.3% (for support) of the histories are derivative. The second row shows that these numbers are considerably smaller for stable histories; ranging from 26.7% (for confidence) to 39.6% (for support).

7 Conclusions

The application of advanced data mining techniques in businesses has been slow due to the complex nature of available software. The approach presented in this paper complements and extends our work in automating data analysis and making it available to business users [16].

It is crucial for businesses to detect relevant changes in their process and customer data early and automatically so they can react in time. In this paper we presented a framework that pro-actively and automatically discovers interesting trends and stabilities in the support and confidence histories of association rules. The capabilities of this framework go far beyond of what is offered by state-of-the-art data analysis software today.

We have implemented the framework and tested it in a business context where we successfully applied it to internal data. In our ongoing research we are working on extending the framework to other data mining techniques.

References

[1] Agrawal R., Imielinski T., Swami A. Mining association rules between sets of items in large databases. In *Proc. of the ACM SIGMOD Intl. Conf. on Management of Data*, pages 207–216, Washington D.C., May 1993.

[2] Agrawal R., Psaila G. Active data mining. In *KDD 1995*, pages 3 8, 1995.

[3] Dong, G.,Li, S. Efficient mining of emerging patterns: discovering trends and differences. In *Proc. of the 5th ACM SIGKDD Intl. Conf. on Knowledge Discovery and Data Mining*, pages 43–52, 1999.

[4] Zhang, X., Dong, G., Kotagiri, R. Exploring constraints to efficiently mine emerging patterns from large high-dimensional datasets. In *Proc. of the 6th ACM SIGKDD Intl. Conf. on Knowledge Discovery and Data Mining*, pages 310–314, 2000.

[5] Au, W.-H., Chan K.C.C. Mining changes in association rules: a fuzzy approach. *Fuzzy Sets and Systems*, 149(1):87–104, 2005.

[6] Chakrabarti, S., Sarawagi, S., Dom, B. Mining surprising patterns using temporal description length. In *Proc. of VLDB 1998*, pages 606–617. Morgan Kaufmann Publishers, 1998.

[7] Liu, B., Ma, Y., Lee, R. Analyzing the interestingness of association rules from the temporal dimension. In *Proc. of IEEE ICDM 2001*, pages 377 384, 2001.

[8] Liu, B., Hsu, W., Ma, Y. Discovering the set of fundamental rule changes. In *Proc. of the 7th ACM SIGKDD Intl. Conf. on Knowledge Discovery and Data Mining*, pages 335–340, 2001.

[9] Markou, M., Singh, S. Novelty detection: A review part 1: Statistical approaches. *Signal Processing*, 83(12):2481–2497, 2003.

[10] Chatfield, C. *Time-Series Forecasting*. Chapman and Hall/CRC, 2001.

[11] Mann, H.B. Nonparametric tests against trend. *Econometrica*, 13:245 259, 1945.

[12] Cox, D.R., Stuart, A. Some quick sign tests for trend in location and dispersion. *Biometrika*, 42:80–95, 1955.

[13] Böttcher, M., Spott, M., Nauck, D. Detecting temporally redundant association rules. In *Proc. of 4th ICMLA*, pages 397–403, Los Angeles, USA, 2005. IEEE Computer Society.

[14] Webb, J.I. Efficient search for association rules. In *Proc. of the 6th ACM SIGKDD Intl. Conf. on Knowledge Discovery and Data Mining*, pages 99 107, 2000.

[15] Tan, P.N., Kumar, V., Srivastava, J. Selecting the right objective measure for association analysis. *Information Systems*, 29(4):293–313, 2004.

[16] Spott, M., Nauck, D. On choosing an appropriate data analysis algorithm. In *Proc. of FUZZ-IEEE 2005*, pages 597–602, 2005. IEEE Computer Society.

Incremental Inductive Learning in a Constructivist Agent

Filipo Studzinski Perotto and Luís Otávio Álvares
Universidade Federal do Rio Grande do Sul
Porto Alegre, Brasil
http://www.inf.ufrgs.br
{fsperotto, alvares}@inf.ufrgs.br

Abstract

The constructivist paradigm in Artificial Intelligence has been definitively inaugurated in the earlier 1990's by Drescher's pioneer work [10]. He faces the challenge of design an alternative model for machine learning, founded in the human cognitive developmental process described by Piaget [x]. His effort has inspired many other researchers.

In this paper we present an agent learning architecture situated on the constructivist approach. We present details about the architecture, pointing the autonomy of the agent, and defining what is the problem that it needs to solve. We focus mainly on the learning mechanism, designed to incrementally discover deterministic environmental regularities, even in non-deterministic worlds. Finally, we report some experimental results and discuss how this agent architecture can lead to the construction of more abstract concepts.

1. Introduction

On the last decade, Artificial Intelligence (AI) has seen the emergence of new approaches and methods, and also the search for new theoretical conceptions The Constructivist AI paradigm is a product of this renovation process, comprising all works that refer to the psychological theory established by Jean Piaget [22], [23] and [24]. According to this conception, the human being is born with a few cognitive structures, but this initial knowledge, combined with some special learning functions, enables the subject to build new cognitive structures through the active interaction with the environment. Intelligence is the set of mechanisms that allows the intellectual development, providing adaptation capabilities to the subject. The elementary cognitive structure is called "schema", and it is the mental construct from which behavior emerges. A schema is all that, in an action, can be differentiated, generalized and applied to other situations [17]. It represents an environmental regularity observed by the subject.

There is a continuous and interactive regulation between the subject and the environment, constituted by internal processes of organization and re-organization of the set of schemas. Sometimes the subject's expectation fails, compelling him to a schema modification, but the change must preserve the general structure and the previous correct knowledge. Thus, at the same time that the schemas integrate novelties, they also maintain what they already know. Furthermore, the intelligence has an active role in the comprehensive process. The subject needs to be creative, constructing new concepts to organize the experience. To deal with the enormous complexity of the real world, the intelligence needs to surpass the limit imposed by the direct sensorial perception, creating more abstract levels of representation. Some theoretical discussions on the meaning of the incorporation of piagetian principles by AI are presented in [4] and [12].

In this paper we present an agent learning architecture situated on the constructivist approach. Other previous related works that propose similar solutions. However, we develop an innovative learning mechanism to discover environment regularities, based on deterministic induction, performed by three combined methods: *differentiation*, *adjust* and *integration*.

The paper is organized as follows. Section 2 presents an overview of related works, introducing our model and pointing its innovative differences. Section 3 presents a brief discussion about agent autonomy provided by embodiment and intrinsic motivation. Section 4 describes the schema, which is the form of knowledge representation implemented in our agent, and defines what is the problem that the agent needs to solve. Section 5 explains the learning mechanism, showing details about the proposed method. Section 6 presents experimental results. Section 7 extends the basic learning mechanism to treat high-level regularities. Finally, section 8 concludes the paper, speculating that the induction of hidden properties is a step toward more abstract intelligence.

2.   Related Works

The pioneer work on Constructivist AI has been presented by Gary Drescher [10]. He proposed the first constructivist agent architecture, called "Schema Mechanism", and defined a computational version for the piagetian schema. The learning occurs by exhaustive statistical analysis of the correlation between all the context elements observed before each action, combined with all resulting transformations. If the presence or absence of some element seems to influence some event probability, then the mechanism creates a schema to represent that. The Schema Mechanism has, moreover, capability to discover hidden properties by creating "synthetic items", that characterize a kind of abstraction. These new elements enlarge the initial representational vocabulary, allowing the learning of some high-level aspects of the dynamics of the environment that are not apprehensible in terms of direct perceptions. The main restriction of his model is the computational cost of the kind of operations used in the algorithm. The need of space and time resources increase exponentially with the problem size. So, for a little bit more complex environments, the solution is not viable. Nevertheless, Drescher's model inspired many other constructivist AI researchers.

Wazlawick [29] replaced the correlation calculus by an evolutionary mechanism, where there is a population of schemas, and these schemas compete to represent the knowledge. His system is based on the combination of genetic algorithms with auto-organization maps. Birk and Paul [3] modified the original Drescher's schema mechanism by the introduction of genetic programming to create new schemas. Chaput [31] presented the Constructivist Learning Architecture (CLA), which also modifies Drescher's agent. CLA is built by interconnecting a hierarchy of self-organization maps, and this kind of representation improves the CLA performance when compared with Drescher's mechanism because CLA clusters its knowledge into finite layers, forming different levels of representation. Holmes and Isbell [11] extended Drescher's original architecture to learn more accurate predictions by using improved criteria for discovery and refinement of schemas as well as for creation and maintenance of hidden states using predictions. Other related works are presented in [19], [2], [9], [18] and [6].

We divide the previous works in two approaches: (a) the statistical approach proposes learning methods based on the direct analysis of distribution of frequencies; (b) the evolutive approach combines genetic algorithms with clustering. Our model differs from the previous works because it is mainly guided by a kind of direct induction. Our approach is designed to discover deterministic regularities occurring even in partially-deterministic environments, and it has the advantage of reducing computational costs preserving efficiency. We would to argue that our mechanism could be more easily extended to find high-level regularities. A previous related work has been presented in [21].

3.   Agent Architecture

The agent architecture proposed is designed for the situatedness problem [28]. The term situated refers to an agent that is an entity embedded in and part of a dynamic and complex environment, which is only partially observable through its sensorial perception, and only partially liable to be transformed by its actions. Due the fact that sensors will be limited in some manner, it is entirely possible that a situated agent can find itself unable to distinguish between differing states of the world. A situation could be perceived in different forms, and different situations could seem the same. This confounding of states, also referred to as "perceptual aliasing", has serious effects on the ability of most of learning algorithms to construct consistent knowledge and stable policies [7].

In the intention of creating a self-motivated agent, we subscribe to the idea of using emotions to perform the role of internal drives. This issue refers to the distinction between extrinsic and intrinsic motivation. Extrinsic motivation means being moved to do something because of some specific rewarding outcome, while intrinsic motivation refers to being moved to do something because it is inherently enjoyable. Intrinsic motivation leads an organism to act over the environment, trying to satisfy internal needs. These signals play the role of a critic, saying what is good and what is bad to the organism. They are determined by processes within the agent, which monitor not only the external state but also the internal state [26].

Our agent is also embodied. The agent has a "body", which does the interface between the world and the mind. The body constitutes an internal environment, and, moreover, it supports the agent's set of sensors and effectors. The internal environment is composed of its own properties, and metabolic processes that control the variation of these properties. Sensors perceive the world (external sensors) and the body (internal sensors), and effectors act over the world (external effectors) and over the body (internal effectors).

The combination of embodiment and intrinsic motivation provides a real kind of autonomy to an agent because all intentionality is an emergent result of its own mechanisms [27], [1]. This idea is according to studies of cognitive research [8], [14] where it is claimed the mutual dependence between body and mind, and between knowledge and affectivity in the intelligent behavior.

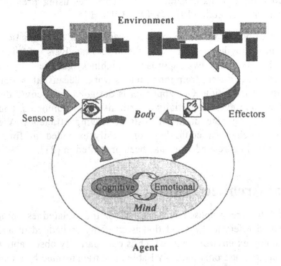

Figure 1. Proposed agent architecture. a) agent-environment interaction; b) body-mind interaction; c) cognitive-emotional interaction

The "mind" of our agent is divided into two parts: an emotional system and a cognitive system. These systems interact with each other. The emotional system senses the body and sends an evaluative signal to the cognitive system. It is the responsible for guiding the agent's actions, conferring an affective meaning to the knowledge and enabling the agent to have its own objectives. The cognitive system stores the actual knowledge, and it performs both the decision making process (choosing the action to execute) and the learning process (improving the knowledge). Figure 1 shows the agent's structure, with a body mediating interface between the mind and the environment, and with the emotional system interacting with the cognitive system.

4.   Knowledge Representation

Our constructivist agent is designed to incrementally learn the patterns in the world dynamics. We make the philosophical assumption that, in natural problems, there are a lot of deterministic regularities. We think that the real world is a great and complex environment, and, despite of the existence of many chaotic or non-deterministic events, it is reasonable to suppose that some other events can be better represented by deterministic beliefs. In this way, the agent must construct knowledge to represent all the deterministic environmental regularities perceived through interaction, even if it is situated in "partially-deterministic" worlds (that mix both deterministic and non-deterministic events).

The elementary piece of knowledge is called "schema", which is composed of three vectors: "context", "action" and "expectation". Both context and expectation vectors have the same length, and each of their elements are linked with one sensor. The action vector has their elements linked with the effectors. In a given schema, the context vector represents the set of equivalent situations where the schema is applicable. The action vector represents a set of similar actions that the agent can carry out in the environment. The expectation vector represents the expected result after executing the given action in the given context.

Each element vector can assume any value in a discrete interval defined by the respective sensor or effector. In addition, the element vector can undertake an undefined value. For example, an element linked with a binary sensor must have one of three values: true, false or undefined (represented, respectively, by '1', '0' and '#'). This form is quite similar to that proposed by Holland [30].

The undefined value generalizes the schema because it allows ignoring some properties to represent a set of world states as the same class. For example, a schema which has the context vector = (100#) is able to assimilate the situations (1000) e (1001). There is "compatibility" between a schema and a certain situation when the schema's context vector has all defined elements equal to those of the agent's perception. Note that compatibility does not compare the undefined elements. So there is no need of considering each possible perception combination, reducing the problem complexity.

The use of undefined values, and the consequent capability to create generalized representations to similar situations, enables the construction of a "schematic tree". Each node in that tree is a schema, and relations of generalization and specialization guide its topology. The root node represents the most generalized situation, which has the context and action vectors completely undefined. Adding one level in the tree is to specialize one generalized element, creating a branch where the undefined value is replaced by different already experimented defined values. This specialization occurs either in the context vector or in the action vector. The structure of the schemas and their organization as a tree are presented in Figure 2.

134

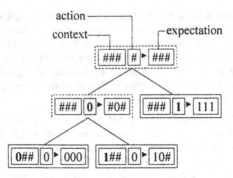

Figure 2. Schemas Tree. Each node is a schema composed of three vectors: context, action and expectation. The leaf nodes are decider schemas.

The schematic tree structure resembles other classic models of AI, such as decision trees [25] and discrimination trees [32], where each branch imposes an additional restriction to the concept description, forming paths between the general root node and the specialized leaf nodes, which represent the classes. However, there are significant differences between the three models, once each one was conceived to represent different things. Decision trees usually put actions as labels in the leaf nodes. The tree is so used to classify what action to do in each kind of situation. In a schematic tree, context and action are put together, and the classes are formed by situations that have the same expectation. The class is an expectation, and expectations are also related by generalization and specialization degrees. This introduces a kind of relation that is not considered in decision trees. Moreover, the construction process is very different because the most part of decision trees induction algorithms are not incremental, requiring the complete set of examples. Furthermore, the schema expectation can change (and consequently the class of the situation represented by the schema), and the mechanism needs to be able to reorganize the tree when this change occurs. When inducing a decision trees it is not necessary to consider this issue, because the labels are supposed to be fixed. Discrimination trees are used to create clusters, a kind of class based only on the instances similarity.

The decision-making process works as follows: at each instant, the context the agent perceives through its sensors is "applied" in the tree, exciting all the decider schemas that have a compatible context vector. This process defines a set of excited schemas, each one suggesting a different action to do in the given situation. The cognitive systems will choose one to activate, and then the schema's action will be performed through the agent's effectors. Appended on each decider schema, there is a memory representing the specific really experimented situations, which happened in the past. The relation between the decider and this memory is similar to that analyzed by Mitchell [16] in version spaces. Deciders represent "maximally general consistent generalization", and the memory of associated situations represent "maximally specific consistent generalizations".

Any incremental learning agent needs to solve the exploration-exploitation dilemma. Sometimes it is better to experiment a new action, exploring alternatives to the situation, but sometimes it is better to use the actual knowledge to feel good. In our agent there is a curiosity parameter that defines the agent tendency to explore or exploit. When exploring, the choice of what excited schema must be activated is based on the schema stability. Schemas with low stability are preferred, supposing they need to be tested more times until it becomes stable. A schema is stable when its expectations have been fully corresponded after the last activations. Therefore, a schema stability value also indicates its reliability. When exploiting, the choice is based on the emotional value attributed to the schema expectation. So, schemas supposed to lead to pleasant situations are preferred.

5. Learning Methods

The learning process happens through the refinement of the set of schemas. The agent becomes more adapted to its environment as a consequence of that. After any situation, the agent's cognitive system checks if the result (context perceived at the instant following the action) is according to the expectation of the activated schema. If it fails in its prediction, the error between the result and the expectation serves as parameter to correct the tree or to adjust the schema. If we consider context, action and expectation as a triple search space, then the learning problem is to induce a set of schemas in this search space that represents the environment regularities.

Our learning method combines top-down and bottom-up strategies. The context and action vectors are put together and this concatenated vector identifies the node in the schematic tree. The tree grows up using the top-down strategy. The agent has just one initial schema. This root schema has the context vector completely general (without any differentiation) and expectation vector totally specific (without any generalization), created at the first situation experienced, according the result directly observed after the action. The context vector will be gradually specialized and differentiated. In more complex environments, the number of features the agent senses is huge, and, in general, only a few of them are relevant to identify the situation. The top-down strategy is better in this kind of environment, because it is a shorter way to begin with an empty vector and searching for these few relevant features, than to begin with a full vector and having to eliminate a lot of not useful elements. Moreover, top-down strategy facilitates the incremental characteristic of the algorithm. The expectation vector is equivalent to labels on the leaf nodes of the tree (decider schemas).

The evolution of expectations uses the bottom-up strategy. Initially all different expectations are considered as different classes, and they are gradually generalized and integrated with others. The agent has two alternatives when the expectation fails. In a way to make the knowledge compatible with the experience, the first alternative is to try to divide the scope of the schema, creating new schemas with more specialized contexts. Sometimes it is not possible, and then the second alternative to solve the inconsistence is to reduce the schema expectation.

Three basic methods compose the learning function: *differentiation, adjust* and *integration*. Differentiation is a necessary mechanism because a schema responsible for a too general context can have imprecise expectations. If a general schema does not work well, the mechanism divides it into new schemas, differentiating them by some element. The algorithm needs to choose some differentiator element from either the context vector or the action vector. Actually, the differentiation method takes an unstable decider schema and changes it into a two level sub-tree. The 'parent' schema in this sub-tree preserves the context of the original schema. Its branches sustain the 'children', which are the new decider schemas. These new deciders have their context vectors more specialized than their parent. They attribute different defined values to the differentiator element, which is undefined in the original schema. This procedure divides the domain of the parent schema among the children. Each level of the tree represents the introduction of some constraint into the parent context vector. In this way, the previous correct knowledge remains preserved, distributed among the new deciders, and the discordant situation is isolated and treated only in its specific context. Figure 3 illustrates the differentiation process.

```
DIFFERENTIATION Method

  Let S be the agent activated decider schema;
  Let N be a new schema;
  Let E be a differentiator element;

  if Failed(S) then
    Remove decider status from S;
    For each defined value i to E do
    Create a new schema N[i];
    Make N a son of S;
    Give to N the decider status;
    Correct N expectation vector;
```

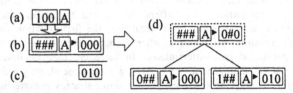

Figure 3. Differentiation method; (a) experimented situation and action; (b) activated schema; (c) real observed result; (d) sub-tree generated by differentiation.

When some schema fails and it is not possible to differentiate it, then the cognitive system executes the adjust method. This method reduces the expectations of an unstable decider schema in order to make it more reliable. The algorithm simply compares the activated schema's expectation and the real result perceived by the agent after the application of the schema and changes the elements that are not compatible to each other for the undefined value '#'. As the mechanism always creates schemas with expectations totally determined and equal to the result of its first application, the walk performed by the schema is a reduction of expectations, up to the point it reaches a state where only those elements that really represent the regular results of the action carried out in that context remain. Figure 4 illustrates that.

```
ADJUST Method

  Let P be the agent perception vector;
  Let S be the agent activated decider schema;
  Let E be the expectation vector of S;

  For each element i of E do
    if E[i] <> P[i] then
      E[i] := #;
```

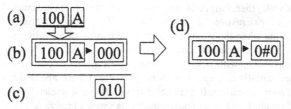

Figure 4. Adjust method; (a) experimented situation and action; (b) activated schema; (c) real observed result; (d) schema expectation reduction after adjust.

Finally, successive adjustments in the expectations can reveal some unnecessary differentiations. When the cognitive system finds two schemas with similar expectations to approach different contexts, the integration method comes into action, merging these schemas into only one, and eliminating the differentiation. The method operates as shown in figure 5.

```
INTEGRATION Method

  Let S1 and S2 be deciders and brothers;
  Let E1 and E2 be their expectation vectors;
  Let P be the parent of S1 and S2;

  if E1 = E2 then
    Delete S1 and S2;
    Give to P the decider status;
```

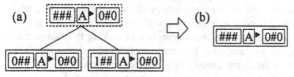

Figure 5. Integration method; (a) sub-tree after some adjust; (b) an integrated schema substitutes the sub-tree.

6. Experimental Results

The agent is inserted in a bidimensional environment where it should learn how to move itself, avoiding collisions and exhaustion, and looking for pleasure. The environment cells are either empty spaces or obstacles. At each time step, the agent can do one of two possible actions: give a step forward, or turn itself (randomly to left or to right). The agent walks freely through empty spaces, but it collides when tries to go against an obstacle. Figure 6 shows the simulation environment, where dark cells are obstacles, clear cells are empty spaces. and the circular cell is the agent, seeing one cell ahead.

The agent has just one external perception: the vision of what is in front of it. The agent's body has four properties: pain, fatigue, exhaustion and pleasure. All of these properties have corresponding internal perceptions. Pain occurs when the agent collides with an obstacle, and it lasts just one instant. The body metabolism eliminates the sensation of pain in the next time step. When the agent repeats many times the action of walk, then fatigue is activated, and if the agent continues walking, the sensation of exhaustion is finally activated. These sensations disappear after a few instants when the walk action ceases. Pleasure occurs always when the agent walks. The emotional system defines that both pain and exhaustion cause bad sensations, with negative values, while pleasure causes a positive emotional value. Initially the agent does not know anything about the environment or about its own sensations. It does not distinguish the obstacles from the free ways, and also does not know what consequences its actions imply.

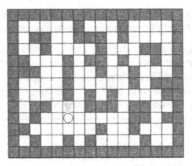

Figure 6. Simulation environment.

Exhaustive repetitions of the experience have shown that the agent ever converges to the expected behavior, constructing correct knowledge to represent the environment regularities, as well as the regularities of its body sensations, and also the regular influence of its actions over both. At the end of a short interaction period, the agent builds a set of schemas that prevents it of making the moves that lead to pain in each visual context, and prevents it of being exhausted when fatigue appears. Otherwise, the agent prefers to walk, because it is pleasant. We may consider our results were successful, once the agent has learned about the consequences of its actions in different situations, avoiding emotionally negative situations, and pursuing those emotionally positive. Figure 7 presents the experimental results. The first graphic (on the top) represents the cognitive transformation during the time. 7000 time steps are represented in the time axis, and the mind stabilizes thereabout 2000 time steps. The last three graphics (on the bottom) shows respectively collisions, exhaustion and pleasure. Some of these bad events occur even after mind stabilization. It is caused by the exploratory behavior, illustrated by the second graphic, which shows decisions made by curiosity.

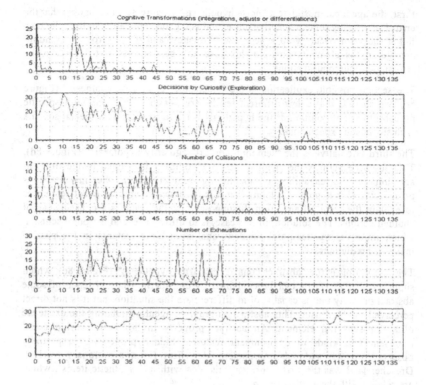

Figure 7. Simulation results.

7. Abstraction Capabilities

The learning methods presented can be extended to be able to detect high-level regularities. Actually they can induce only stationary, deterministic, instantaneous and sensorimotor regularities. Therefore, we introduce on our agent the following capabilities: temporal analysis, abstract concept creation, and probabilistic features. Furthermore, the cognitive mechanism can be improved to chain the schemas, forming action sequences, and permitting the agent to create plans instead just reacting.

In the presented method, when some schema fails the first alternative is to differentiate it. If it is not possible, the mechanism repairs the schema by reducing its expectation. This alternative supposes that there is no regularity and the analyzed result is unpredictable. It is a possible explication to the fail, called "unpredictability hypothesis" (Figure 8a), but it is not necessarily true. In fact, there is no deterministic, instantaneous, sensorimotor regularity, but the agent must considering some alternative hypotheses, which represent other kind of regularities, and which can explain the fail.

First, the agent can postulate a "noise hypothesis" (Figure 8b). It supposes that the error is caused by some perceptive noise, and is a good explication to the schema's fail if the error occurs with a very low frequency, and if the error is a random change in the element value. In this case, the best answer is to preserve the schema without modifications.

The second possible explication is the "stochastic regularity hypothesis" (Figure 8c), which says that a few different results are possible, each one with specific probabilities. The solution, if the hypothesis is right, is to create a special schema with stochastic expectations.

The third alternative is the "temporal context regularity hypothesis" (Figure 8d). This resource permits the agent to perceive contexts distributed in the time, in addition to the capability of identifying regularities in the instantaneous perception. This hypothesis claims that it is necessary to observe event sequences to explain the result of an action. It supposes that the result is a consequence of chained actions. The solution, in this case, is to utilize a special temporal schema, which improves the temporal window, analyzing more instants in the past to make its predictions.

The last option is the "abstract context regularity hypothesis" (Figure 8e), which supposes that the error can be explained by considering the existence of some abstract property that is capable of to differentiate the situation, but it is not direct perceived by the sensor. This abstraction requires agent postulating the existence of a non-sensorial element. An abstract property in the agent's mind could represent two kinds of environment features: hidden properties (in partially observed worlds) and sub-environment identifiers (in non-stationary worlds). Drescher [10] was the first to present this idea with the 'synthetic items', which are related with the agent's action.

With these new capabilities, the agent becomes able to overpass the sensorial perception constructing abstract concepts. By forming these new knowledge elements, the agent acquires new forms to structure the comprehension of its own reality in more complex levels.

After postulating these hypotheses, the agent needs to discover what of them is the correct one. It is not possible to do this a priori. The solution is to use a selectionist idea. During some time, the agent preserves all the hypotheses, and evaluates them. At the end, the best solution survives.

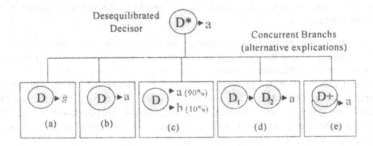

Figure 8. Set of alternative hypotheses to explain the failure.

8. Conclusions

We have shown an agent architecture based on constructivist AI principles. Our model provides adaptive capability because the agent constructs its knowledge incrementally, by interaction with its environment. This autonomy of cognitive construction is associated to motivational autonomy, given by an embodied and intrinsically motivated architecture. We have presented a learning method composed by three functions: differentiation, adjust and integration. These functions operate over a schemas tree, which is transformed during the agent life in a way to describe the observed regularities of the world. Some experimental results have been exposed, corroborating the mechanism ability to discover regularities and use this knowledge to adapt the agent behavior. Finally, we have discussed what kind of regularity is apprehensible by the basic method, and an extension of it is proposed to treat high-level regularities, like stochastic, temporal and abstract events.

References

1. Barandiaran, X. 2004. Behavioral Adaptive Autonomy: a milestone on the ALife route to AI? Proceedings of the 9th International Conference on Artificial Life. MIT Press, Boston, Massachussets, pp. 514-521.
2. Belpaeme, T., Steels, L., & van Looveren, J. 1998. The construction and acquisition of visual categories. In Birk, A. and Demiris, J., editors, Learning Robots, Proceedings of the EWLR-6, Lecture Notes on Artificial Intelligence 1545. Springer.
3. Birk, Andreas & Paul, Wolfgang. 2000. Schemas and Genetic Programming. Ritter, Cruse, Dean (Eds.), Prerational Intelligence: Adaptive Behavior and Intelligent Systems without Symbols and Logic, Volume II, Studies in Cognitive Systems 36, Kluwer.
4. Boden, M. 1979. Piaget. Glasgow: Fontana Paperbacks.
5. Booker, L. B. Goldberg, D. E. & Holland, J. H. 1989. Classifier Systems and Genetic Algorithms. Artificial Intelligence, vol. 40, p. 235-282.
6. Buisson J.-C. 2004. A rhythm recognition computer program to advocate interactivist perception. Cognitive Science, 28:1, p.75-87.
7. Crook, P. & Hayes, G. 2003. Learning in a State of Confusion: Perceptual Aliasing in Grid World Navigation. In Proceedings of Towards Intelligent Mobile Robots, UWE, Bristol.
8. Damasio, A. 1994. Descartes' Error: Emotion, Reason and the Human Brain. New York: Avon Books.
9. DeJong, E. D. 1999. Autonomous Concept Formation. In: Proceedings of the Sixteenth International Joint Conference on Artificial Intelligence IJCAI.
10. Drescher, Gary. 1991. Mide-Up Minds: A Construtivist Approach to Artificial Intelligence. MIT Press.
11. Holmes & Isbell. 2005. Schema Learning: Experience-based Construction of Predictive Action Models. In Advances in Neural Information Processing Systems, volume 17.
12. Inhelder B. & Cellerier G. 1992. Le cheminement des découvertes de l'enfant. Neuchâtel: Delachaux et Niestlé.

13. Kohonen, Teuvo. Self-Organization and Associative Memory. Berlin: Springer-Verlag, 1989.
14. LeDoux, J.E. 1996. The Emotional Brain. New York: Simon and Schuster.
15. Langley, P. Zytkow, J. 1989. Data-Driven Approaches to Empirical Discovery. Artif. Intell. 40(1-3): 283-312.
16. Mitchell, T. 1982. Generalization as search. Artificial Intelligence, 18, p.203-226.
17. Montangero, J., & Maurice-Naville, D. 1997. Piaget or the advance of knowledge. New York: Lawrence. Erlbaum Associates.
18. Morrison, C. Oates, T. & King, G. 2001. Grounding the Unobservable in the Observable: The Role and Representation of Hidden State in Concept Formation and Refinement. In Working Notes of AAAI Spring Symposium Workshop: Learning Grounded Representations.
19. Müller, J.-P. & Rodriguez, M. 1996. A constructivist approach to autonomous systems, Growing Mind Symposium (Piaget Centenary), Geneva.
20. Muñoz, Mauro H. S. 1999. Proposta de Modelo Sensório Cognitivo inspirado na Teoria de Jean Piaget. Porto Alegre: PGCC/UFRGS. (Thesis)
21. Perotto, F. Alvares, L. O. 2006. Learning Environment Regularities with a Constructivist Agent. Fifth International Joint Conference on Autonomous Agents and Multi Agent Systems (AAMAS 2006). Hakodate, Japan.
22. Piaget, Jean. 1951. Symbol Formation - Play, Dreams and Imitation in Childhood. London: Heinemann.
23. Piaget, Jean. 1953. The Origins of Intelligence in the Child. London: Routledge & Kegan Paul.
24. Piaget, Jean. 1957. Construction of Reality in the Child. London: Routledge & Kegan Paul.
25. Quinlan, J. 1986. Induction of Decision Trees. Machine Learning, vol. 1, p.81-106.
26. Singh, S., Barto, A.G. & Chentanez, N. 2004. Intrinsically Motivated Reinforcement Learning. 18th Annual Conference on Neural Information Processing Systems (NIPS), Vancouver, B.C., Canada.
27. Sloman, Aaron. 1999. Review of Affective Computing. AI Magazine 20 (1): 127-133.
28. Suchman, L. A. 1987. Plans and Situated Actions. Cambridge: Cambridge University Press.
29. Wazlawick, R. Costa, A. C. R. 1995. Non-Supervised Sensory-Motor Agents Learning. In: Artificial Neural Nets and Genetic Algorithms. New York: Springer-Verlag: 49-52.
30. Holland, J. Holyoak, K. Nisbett, R & Thagard, P. 1986. Induction: Processes of Inference, Learning, and Discovery. MIT Press, Cambridge.
31. Chaput, H. 2004. The Constructivist Learning Architecture. PhD Thesis. University of Texas.
32. Gennari, J. H. Langley, P. & Fisher, D. H. 1989. Models of incremental concept formation. Artificial Intelligence, 40, 11-61.

SESSION 2b:

ARGUMENTATION, DIALOGUE GAMES AND OPTIMISATION

Argument Based Contract Enforcement

Nir Oren, Alun Preece, Timothy J. Norman

Department of Computing Science, University of Abedeen

Aberdeen, Scotland

Abstract

Agents may choose to ignore contract violations if the costs of enforcing the contract exceed the compensation they would receive. In this paper we describe an argumentation based framework for agents to both decide whether to enforce a contract, and to undertake contract enforcement actions. The framework centres around agents presenting beliefs to justify their position, and backing up these beliefs with facts as necessary. Presenting facts costs an agent utility, and our framework operates by using a reasoning mechanism which is based on the agent comparing the utility it would gain for proving a set of literals with the costs incurred during this process.

1 Introduction

Open environments may contain self–interested agents with different levels of trustworthiness. While self–interested, these agents may both cooperate and compete so as to increase their own utility. Many mechanisms have been proposed to ensure correct agent behaviour in such environments, and most make use of some form of implicit or explicit contract between the agents [1, 6]. The purpose of such a contract is to lay out what is expected from each contracting party. Given norm-autonomous agents, i.e. agents which are able to decide whether to fulfil their normative requirements, contracts also allow for the imposition of penalties and compensation to the wronged party if any deviations from the agreed upon behaviour occurs. Sanctioning of agents often takes place through the use of a trust or reputation framework [12], or some monetary mechanism.

In the real world, minor contract violations are often ignored, either due to the loss in trust that would arise between the contracting parties, or due to the small compensation the wronged party would receive when compared to the overhead of enforcing the contract. Even major violations might not result in the wronged party being (fully) compensated, or the guilty party being penalised as the cost of proving the violation might exceed the compensation which would have been obtained by the victim, resulting in them not attempting to enforce the contract. While the former behaviour might be useful to replicate within multi-agent systems (due to increased efficiency), at first glance the latter behaviour seems undesirable. Such behaviour is however rational (and thus desirable in many settings), as it maximises an agent's gain. It could be argued that loss making contract enforcement actions, which might increase the society's welfare as a whole, are the responsibility of some "pro-bono" third party agents, rather than contract participants.

Contract enforcement costs are not constant in many scenarios. Referring again to a typical real world example, if a contract case goes to court, extra costs are incurred due not only to lawyer's fees, but also due to the cost of gathering evidence. As the case progresses, additional evidence might be needed, leading to further escalating costs. Some legal systems avoid this by having the loser of a case pay its opponent's fees.

The increasing complexity of artificial agent environments means that many of these scenarios have analogies within the agent domain. Agents interacting with each other on the web, virtual marketplace or a Grid do not trust each other and sign contracts before providing and consuming services. If one agent believes another did not fulfil its obligations, it may need to verify its belief by gathering large amounts of evidence. This evidence gathering might cost it not only computational, but also monetary resources as it might have to purchase information from other agents. In a similar manner, it might cost the accused agent resources to defend itself. Allowing for such behaviour can increase both the efficiency and robustness of agent environments.

In this paper we examine multiple issues related to this type of contract enforcement. We provide an argumentation/dialogue game based framework which allows agents to both decide and undertake contract enforcement actions. We also look at how aspects of this framework can tie into contracting languages. Our work forms part of the CONOISE-G project [13]. CONOISE-G centres around the creation and implementation of technologies designed to improve the performance and robustness of virtual organisations. Agents operating within the environment have their behaviour regulated by contracts, and contract monitoring and enforcement thus form a major part of the project focus.

An agent monitors a contract, and, if it believes that it can gain utility by starting a contract enforcement action (e.g. due to clauses where it would gain utility coming into force, or clauses wherein another agent should pay it a penalty), it will start such an action. At each stage of the dialogue, it calculates the amount of utility it would (lose) gain by (not) enforcing the contract. While a net utility gain exists, the agent maintains its enforcement action, bringing forward evidence as required. The action of probing the environment for evidence decreases the agent's utility. The accused agent(s) follow a similar process, computing how much utility they would lose by not defending themselves, and paying for evidence they use in their defence. This process ends when the accusing or defending agents capitulate, or no further evidence can be presented, after which a decision regarding the status of the contract can be reached. While the method we propose in this paper is simple, we believe it can both be useful in a large number of scenarios, as well as provide the basis for more complicated techniques.

This work is based on [11]. A major difference between the work presented there and this work is that the formalism described in this paper allows agents to reason about multiple goals simultaneously. This leads to agents which can reason about more than one contract clause at a time. The ability to reason about multiple (possibly conflicting) clauses is critical in all but the simplest of contracts.

In the next section we formalise our framework, after which an small example is presented. Section 4 looks at the features of our framework, and places it within the context of related work. Finally, possible extensions to this work are discussed.

2   The Formalism

In this section, we describe our approach. We are primarily interested in only one section of the contract enforcement stage, namely the point at which an agent attempts to prove that another agent has (or has not) broken a contract. Informally, the agent begins by determining how much utility it would gain by proving that it has been wronged, as well as what the net utility gain would be for not being able to prove its claims. A dialogue then begins between the involved agents. In the course of this dialogue, evidence is presented from outside sources. Presenting this evidence costs utility, imposing an ordering on the best way to present the evidence, as well as possibly causing an agent to give up on its claims. Once the agents have made all the utterances they desire, an adjudication process can take place, determining whether an agent has been able to prove its case. The work presented here is an extension of the work described in [8, 9].

We begin by describing the logical layer in which interaction takes place, and the way arguments interact with each other. We decided against using an abstract argumentation framework (such as the one described by Dung [3]) or a legal based argumentation framework (such as Prakken and Sartor's [16]) as our arguments are grounded and do not make use of any default constructs. Making use of our own logical formalism also helps simplify the framework.

After describing the logical level, we specify the dialogue game agents can use to perform contract monitoring actions, examining strategies agents can use to play the game, as well as looking at how to determine the winners and losers of an instance of the game. It should be noted that we discuss very few of our design decisions in this section, instead simply presenting the framework. An in depth examination of the framework is left for Section 4. The section concludes by describing how to transform a contract into a form usable by the framework.

2.1   The Argumentation Framework

Argumentation takes place over the language Σ, which contains propositional literals and their negation.

Definition 1 *Argument.* *An argument is a pair (P, c), where $P \subseteq \Sigma \cup \{\top\}$*

and $c \in \Sigma$ such that if $x \in P$ then $\neg x \notin P$. We define $Args(\Sigma)$ to be the set of all possible arguments derivable from our language.

P represents the premises of an argument (also referred to as an argument's support), while c stands for an argument's conclusion. Informally, we can read an argument as stating "if the conjunction of its premises holds, the conclusion holds". An argument of the form $(\top, a)$ represents a conclusion requiring no premises (for reasons detailed below, such an argument is not necessarily a fact).

Arguments interact by supporting and attacking each other. Informally, when an argument attacks another, it renders the latter's conclusions invalid.

An argument cannot be introduced into a conversation unless it is grounded. In other words, the argument $(\{a, b\}, c)$ cannot be used unless a and b are either known or can be derived from arguments derivable from known literals. Care must be taken when formally defining the concept of a grounded argument, and before doing so, we must (informally) describe the proof theory used to determine which literals and arguments are justified at any time.

To determine what arguments and literals hold at any one time, let us assume that all arguments refer to beliefs. In this case, we begin by examining grounded beliefs and determining what can be derived from them by following chains of argument. Whenever a conflict occurs (i.e. we are able to derive literals of the form x and $\neg x$), we remove these literals from our derived set. Care must then be taken to eliminate any arguments derived from conflicting literals. To do this, we keep track of the conflicting literals in a separate set, and whenever a new conflict arises, we begin the derivation process afresh, never adding any arguments to the derived set if their conclusions are in the conflict set.

Differentiating between beliefs and facts makes this process slightly more complicated. A literal now has a chance of being removed from the conflict set if it is in the set of known facts.

More formally, an instance of the framework creates two sets $J \subseteq Args(\Sigma)$ and $C \subseteq \Sigma$, while making use of a set of facts $F \subset \Sigma$ such that if $l \in F$ then $\neg l \notin F$ and if $\neg l \in F$ then $l \notin F$ (i.e. F is a consistent set of literals). J and C represent justified arguments and conflicts respectively.

Definition 2 Derivation. *An argument $A = (P_a, c_a)$ is derivable from a set S given a conflict set C (written $S, C \vdash A$) iff $c_a \notin C$ and $(\forall p \in P_a (\exists s \in S$ such that $s = (P_s, p)$ and $p \notin C)$ or $P_a = \{\top\})$.*

Clearly, we need to know what elements are in C. Given the consistent set of facts F and a knowledge base of arguments $\kappa \subseteq Args(\Sigma)$[1], this can be done with the following reasoning procedure:

$$J_0 = \{A | A \in \kappa \text{ such that } \{\}, \{\} \vdash A\}$$
$$C_0 = \{\}$$

---

[1] We assume that κ contains all our facts, i.e. $\forall f \in F, f \in \kappa$

Then, for $i > 0, j = 1 \ldots i$, we have:

$$C_i^* = C_{i-1} \cup \{c_A, \neg c_A | \exists A = (P_A, c_A), B = (P_B, \neg c_A) \in J_{i-1}\}$$
$$C_i = C_i^* \backslash (C_i^* \cap F)$$
$$X_{i0} = \{A | A \in \kappa \text{ and } \{\}, C_i \vdash A\}$$
$$X_{ij} = \{A | A \in \kappa \text{ and } X_{i(j-1)}, C_i \vdash A\}$$
$$J_i = X_{ii}$$

The set X allows us to recompute all derivable arguments from scratch after every increment of i^2. Since i represents the length of a chain of arguments, when $i = j$ our set will be consistent to the depth of our reasoning, and we may assign all of these arguments to J. Eventually, $J_i = J_{i-1}$ (and $C_i = C_{i-1}$) which means there are no further arguments to find. We can thus define the conclusions reached by a knowledge base κ as $K = \{c | A = (P, c) \in J_i\}$, for the smallest i such that $J_i = J_{i+1}$. We will use the shorthand $K(\kappa, F)$ and $C(\kappa, F)$ to represent those literals which are respectively derivable from, or in conflict with a knowledge base κ and fact set F. C_i^* represents the conflict set before facts are taken into account.

2.2 The Dialogue Game

Agents make use of the argumentation framework described above in an attempt to convince others of their point of view. An agent has an associated private knowledge base (KB) containing its beliefs, as well as a table listing the costs involved in probing the system for the value of literals (M). An instance of the argumentation dialogue is centred around agents trying to prove or disprove a set of goals G. Utility gains and losses are associated with succeeding or failing to prove these goals. The environment also contains a public knowledge base recording the utterances made by the agents. This knowledge base performs a role similar to a global commitment store, and is thus referred to as CS below.

Definition 3 Environment. *An environment is a tuple* $(Agents, CS, F, S)$ *where Agents is the set of agents participating in the dialogue,* $CS \subseteq Args(\Sigma)$ *is a public knowledge base and* $F \subset \Sigma$ *is a consistent set of literals known to be facts.* $S \subseteq \Sigma$ *contains literals representing the environment state.*

Definition 4 Agent. *An agent* $\alpha \in Agents$ *is composed of a tuple* $(Name, KB, M, G, T)$ *where* $KB \subseteq Args(\Sigma)$, M *is a function allowing us to compute the cost of probing the value of a literal.* G *is a goal function (described in Definition 6) allowing the agent to calculate its utility at various stages in the argument.* $T \in \mathbf{R}$ *keeps track of the total costs incurred by an agent during the course of the argument.*

---

[2]This allows us to get rid of long invalid chains of arguments, as well as detect and eliminate arbitrary loops.

The monitoring cost function M expresses the cost incurred by an agent when it must probe the environment for the value of a literal. It maps a set of literals to a real number:

Definition 5 Monitoring costs. *The monitoring cost function M is a domain dependent function $M : 2^{\Sigma} \to \mathbf{R}$*

Representing monitoring costs in this way allows us to discount multiple probing actions, for example, it might be cheaper for an agent to simultaneously determine the cost of two literals than to probe them individually in turn.

We assign a utility to a goal state based on the literals that can be derived within that state, and the literals in conflict within that state. More formally,

Definition 6 Goal function. *The utility function G is a domain dependent function $G : KS \to \mathbf{R}$ where $KS = \{(K, C) | K \in 2^{\Sigma}, C \in 2^{\Sigma}$ such that if $c \in C$ then $\neg c \in C$, and if $\{c, \neg c\} \in C$ then $\{c, \neg c\} \cap K = \{\}\}$*

Agents take turns to put forward a line of argument and ascertain the value of a literal by probing the environment. For example $\{((\top, a), (a, b)), b)\}$ is a possible utterance an agent could make, containing the line of argument $\{(\top, a), (a, b)\}$ and probing the environment for whether b is indeed in the environment state. Alternatively, an agent may pass by making an empty utterance $\{,\}$. The dialogue ends when CS has remained unchanged for as many turns as there are players, i.e. after all players have had a chance to make an utterance, but didn't. Once this has happened, it is possible to compute the literals derivable from CS and F, determine the status of an agent's goal expression, and thus compute who won the dialogue.

Definition 7 Utterances. *The utterance function*

$$utterance : Environment \times Name \to 2^{Args(\Sigma)} \times \Sigma$$

accepts an environment and an agent name, returns the utterance made by the agent. The first part of this utterance lists the arguments advanced by the agents, while the second lists the probed environment states.

Given an agent with a monitoring cost function M, we may compute the cost to the agent of making the utterance (Ar, Pr), where Ar is the line of argument advanced by the agent and Pr is the set of literals the agents would like to probe, as $M(Pr)$.

Definition 8 Turns. *The function*

$$turn : Environment \times Name \to Environment$$

takes an environment and an agent label, and returns a new environment containing the effects of the agent's utterance.

Given an environment $Env = (Agents, CS, F, S)$ and an agent
$\alpha = (Name, KB, M, G, T) \in Agents$, *we define the turn function as follows*

$turn(Env, Name) = (NewAgents, CS \cup Ar, F \cup (Pr \cap S), S)$ *where Ar, Pr*

are computed from the function $utterance(Env, Name) = (Ar, Pr)$, and

$NewAgents = Agents \backslash \alpha \cup (Name, KB, M, G, T + M(Pr))$

We may assume that the agents are named $Agent_0, Agent_1, \ldots, Agent_{n-1}$ where n is the number of agents participating in the dialogue. It should be noted that the inner workings of the *utterance* function are dependent on agent strategy, and we will describe one possible game playing strategy below. Before doing so however, we must define the dialogue itself. Each turn of the dialogue game results in a new environment, which is used during later turns.

Definition 9 Dialogue game. *The dialogue game can be defined in terms of the turn function as follows:*

$turn_0 = turn((Agents, CS_0, F_0, S), Agent_0)$

$turn_{i+1} = turn(turn_i, Agent_{i \bmod n})$

The game ends when $turn_i \ldots turn_{i-n+1} = turn_{i-n}$.

CS_0 and F_0 contain the initial arguments and facts, and are usually empty. Note that the agent may make a null utterance $\{,\}$ during its move to (eventually) bring the game to an end.

For any state, we can compute an agent's utility by combining the amount of utility it gains for the state together with T, the amount of utility it has expended to achieve that state.

Definition 10 Agent utility. *Given an environment $= (Agents, CS, F, S)$, and abbreviating an agent definition $(Name, KB, M, G, T)$ as α, an agent's net utility is defined as*

$$U(CS, F, T) = G(K(CS, F), C(CS, F)) - T$$

2.3 The Heuristic

We are now in a position to define one possible technique for taking part in the dialogue game. We assume that our agent is rational and will thus attempt to maximise its utility. By using the reasoning procedure described in Section 2.1 over the environment's knowledge base CS, its knowledge base KB and the set of known facts F, an agent can both determine what literals are currently in force and in conflict, as well as determine the effects of its arguments. To compute what utterance to make, an agent determines what the utility of the resultant state would be, and advances the argument that maximises this utility. One difficulty encountered here is that the agent does not know what facts probing the environment will yield. To overcome this, we assume optimistic agents, that is, an agent believes that all environment probes will yield results most favourable to it.

Given a set of possible utterances with equal utility, we use a secondary heuristic (as described in [9]) to choose between them: the agent will make the utterance which reveals as little new information to the opponent as possible. More formally,

Definition 11 Making utterances. *For an environment* $(Agent, CS, F, S)$ *and an agent*
$\alpha = (Name, KB, M, G, T)$, *let the set of possible utterances be* $PA = 2^{KB}$. *Then for each* $pa \in PA$, *we define the set of possible facts that the agent can probe as*[3]

$$PP_{pa} = \{f, \neg f | f \text{ or } \neg f \in (K(CS \cup pa) \cup C(CS \cup pa)) \backslash F\} \text{ and } \{f, \neg f\} \cap S \neq \{\}$$

Then the set of possible facts can be computed as $PF_{pa} = 2^{PP_{pa}}$ *such that if* $f \in PF_{pa}, \neg f \notin PF_{pa}$ *and vice-versa. We can compute the utility for an utterance* (pa, Pr) *where* $Pr \in PP_{pa}$ *as* $max_{pf \in PF_{pa}}(U(CS \cup pa, F \cup pf, T + M(Pr)))$, *and advance the argument that maximises utility over all* $pa \in PA$.

If multiple such possible utterances exist, we will choose one such that $K(pa \cup CS) - K(CS) + C(pa \cup CS) - C(CS)$ *is minimised.*

Assuming that every probing action has an associated utility cost, such an agent would begin by attempting to argue from its beliefs, probing the environment only as a last resort. This behaviour is reminiscent of the idea put forward by Gordon's pleadings game [4], where agents argue until certain irreconcilable differences arise, after which they approach an arbitrator to settle the matter. However, when multiple issues are under debate (as in the example provided later), probing may be interleaved with arguing from beliefs.

2.4 Contracts

To utilise such a framework in the context of contracting requires a number of additional features:

1. S, the set of facts which can be probed must be defined.

2. T the agent's cost for performing the probing must also be determined.

3. G the set of agent goals must be computed.

4. Utilities must be set appropriately.

5. The agent's knowledge bases KB must be created to reflect the content of the contract, as well as any initial beliefs held by the agents regarding the environment state.

---

[3]The second part of the condition allows us a way of limiting the probing to only those facts which are in fact accessible, without having to know their value

6. F_0, the set of known facts must be generated.

While all of these are contract specific, some guidelines can be provided due to the features of the framework. The set of facts which can be probed is totally environment dependent, as is the cost for probing. All probe-able literals should be placed (with their "true" value) within the environment's S. Contract clauses, together with an agent's beliefs about the state of the world are used to determine an agent's KB. F_0 (and thus CS_0) will not be empty if certain facts about the environment state are already known.

Assume that an agent gains r utility for proving a certain literal. This means that the other agent will lose r utility for this literal being shown. It could be argued that ensuring that the other agent is unable to prove this literal would thus gain the agent r utility. Legal systems usually require that a plaintiff prove its case either beyond reasonable doubt, or on the balance of probabilities. Due to the binary nature of our system, this means that an agent must show that a literal is justified to gain its reward. This means that if a contract associates a reward r with a literal l, the agent wanting to gain the reward will have l within the K component of G, while the other agent will have l in C, and will also assign a utility r to states where l does not appear in K.

At this stage, contract enforcement is possible using the framework. We will now provide a short example to illustrate the framework in operation.

3   Example

We now examine the functionings of our framework using a simplified example inspired by the CONOISE domain [13]. Assume that a supplier has agreed to provide movie services to a consumer, subject to restrictions on the framerate. A simplified version of the contract may look as follows:

$$fr25 \rightarrow payPerson$$
$$\neg fr25 \rightarrow giveWarning1$$
$$wrongMovie \rightarrow giveWarning2$$
$$giveWarning1 \land giveWarning2 \rightarrow penalty$$

We assume that monitors exist for $fr25, giveWarning1$ and $giveWarning2$ at a cost of 7,10 and 27 respectively (in fact, they cost half this, as both the literal and its negation must be probed). Finally, let the penalty for contract violation be 30 units of currency, while $payPerson$ would cost the consumer 10 units of currency.

Now let us assume that the consumer believes that it has been given the incorrect movie, and when the movie finally arrived, its framerate was below 25 frames per second (i.e. the literal $\neg fr25$ evaluates to true). The provider on the other hand, believes that it has fulfilled all of its obligations, and should be paid. After converting the contract and agent beliefs to a format usable by the framework, the provider's goal set thus includes the following:

$((payPerson),(),(),10),((payPerson),(penalty),(),10),$
$((payPerson),(),(penalty),-20),((),(payPerson,penalty),(),0),$
$((),(payPerson),(penalty),-30),((),(),(penalty),-30)$

If the supplier initiates a contract enforcement action, the dialogue will proceed as follows (brackets are omitted in places for the sake of readability):

$(S1)$ $(\{(\top,fr25),(fr25,payPerson)\},\{\})$
$(C2)$ $(\{(\top,\neg fr25),\},\{\})$
$(S3)$ $(\{\},\{\neg fr25,fr25\})$
$(C4)$ $(\{wrongMovie,giveWarning2\},$
$\{(giveWarning1,giveWarning2),penalty\},\{\})$
$(S4)$ $(\{\top,\neg wrongMovie\},\{\})$
$(C5)$ $(\{\},\{\neg giveWarning2,giveWarning2\})$
$(S6)$ $(,)$
$(C7)$ $(,)$

The supplier begins by claiming it should be paid. While the consumer believes that the supplier should pay it a penalty, probing the monitors to show this would be more expensive than the compensation it could gain, and it thus only refutes the supplier's claim. At this stage, the supplier probes the state of the frame rate literal, hoping to win the argument. Instead, it opens the way for the consumer to pursue penalties. The supplier attempts to defend itself by claiming that it provided the correct movie, but the consumer probes the environment (indirectly) to show this was not the case.

4 Discussion

While we have focused on using our framework for contract enforcement, it can also be used in other settings. For example, given a non-adversarial setting where probing sensors still has some associated cost (for example, of network resources or time), an agent can reason with the framework (by generating an argument leading to its goals) to minimise these sensing costs.

The contract enforcement stage is only part of the greater contracting life-cycle. With some adaptation, our framework can also be used in the contract monitoring stage: by constantly modifying its beliefs based on inputs from the environment, an agent could continuously attempt to prove that a contract has failed; once this occurs contract enforcement would begin.

Contract enforcement and monitoring has been examined by a number of other researchers. Given a fully observable environment in which state determination is not associated with a utility cost, the problem reduces to data mining. Research such as [19] operates in such an environment, but focus more on the problem of predicting imminent contract failure. Daskalopulu et al. [2] have suggested a subjective logic [5] based approach for contract enforcement in partially observable environments. Here, a contract is represented as a finite state machine, with an agent's actions leading to state transitions. A central monitor assigns different agents different levels of trust, and combines reports from them to determine the most likely state of the system. While some weaknesses exist with this approach, most techniques for contract enforcement are similar in nature, making use of some uncertainty framework to determine what the most likely system state is, then translating this state into a contract state, finally determining whether a violation occurred. An argumentation based approach potentially has both computational as well as representational advantages over existing methods. In earlier work [10], we described a contracting language for service level agreements based on semantic web standards (called SWCL). One interesting feature of that work is the appearance of an explicit monitoring clause describing where to gather information regarding specific environment states. Most other contracting languages lack such a feature, and the (trivial) addition of a monitoring cost would allow SWCL to be used as part of our framework. A related feature of our framework which, in a contracting context would require a language with appropriate capabilities, is the ability to assign different monitoring costs for determining whether a literal or its negation holds. In an open world environment, such a feature is highly desirable.

Argumentation researchers have long known that a dialogue should remain relevant to the topic under discussion [7]. This trait allows dialogue based systems to rapidly reach a solution. The approach presented here enforces this requirement due to the nature of the heuristic; any extraneous utterances will lead to a reduction in an agent's final utility. One disadvantage of our approach is that, as presented, the computational complexity of deciding what utterance to make is exponential in nature. Simple optimisations can be implemented to reduce the average case complexity, but in the worst case, all possible arguments must still be considered. Mitigating this is the fact that the number of clauses involved in a contract enforcement action is normally relatively small, making its use practical in the contracting domain.

Many different argumentation frameworks have been proposed in the literature ([17] provides an excellent overview of the field). We decided to design our own framework rather than use an existing approach for a number of reasons. First, many frameworks are abstract in nature, requiring the embedding of a logic, and then making use of some form of attacking relation to compute which arguments are, or are not in force. Less abstract frameworks focus on the non–monotonic nature of argument, often requiring a default logic be used. The manner in which agents reason using our heuristic, as well as the grounded nature of the subject of arguments in our domain makes the argumentation framework presented here more suitable than others for this type of work. However, we intend to show the relationship between our framework and sceptical semantics in existing argumentation frameworks in future work.

Legal argumentation systems often grapple with the concept of burden of proof (e.g. [14, 15, 18]). We attempt to circumnavigate the problem of assigning responsibility for proving the state of a literal to a specific agent by having agents probe for the value themselves as needed. This approach will not work in more complicated scenarios with conflicting sensors, and extending the framework to operate in such environments should prove interesting. One real world feature which we also ignore, and should be taken into account, is the concept of "loser pays". In many real world court systems, the loser of a case must pay the winner's costs, and integrating such concepts into the reasoning mechanism will require further extensions to our approach.

One quirk of our framework is that we do not do belief revision when agents are presented with facts. While adapting the method in which $NewAgents$ are created in Definition 8 is possible by setting the new agent's KB to be $KB \cup (\top, f)\forall f \in F$, and even remove any "obviously conflicting" beliefs, we are still unable to remove beliefs that arise from the application of chains of arguments. We would thus claim that an agent's beliefs are actually a combination of its private knowledge base KB, the public knowledge base CS and the set of presented facts F, rather than being solely a product of KB. Overriding beliefs with facts means our framework assigns a higher priority to fact based argument than belief based argument. This is reminiscent of many existing priority based argumentation frameworks such as [16]. We plan to investigate more complicated forms of belief revision in upcoming work. Other enhancements, such as the ability to withdraw utterances from CS would also be useful.

By computing the utility gained for making an utterance, our agents plan one step ahead. It would be useful to plan further, but this requires some form of opponent modelling. This could range from reasoning about the opponent's goals (which we already do implicitly due to the way in which utility is assigned to states), to in depth knowledge about the opponent's KB.

Finally, the procedure used to transform a contract into an environment and agents for argumentation is very simple. Enhancing this procedure to make use of the full power of the argumentation framework requires further examination. This enhancement will allow for both the representation of, and dialogue regarding, more complex contracts, further increasing the utility of the framework. Another area of future work involves n–party contracts. While our framework provides support for dialogue between more than two agents, we have not examined what such contracts would look like, and this might be an interesting research direction to pursue.

5   Conclusions

Explicit or implicit contracts are the dominant method for specifying desired agent behaviour within complex multi-agent systems. Contract enforcement is necessary when agents are able to renege on their obligations.

In this paper we have presented an argumentation based framework for contract enforcement within partially observable environments for which querying sensors has an associated cost. Our agents are able to reason about multiple goals, which is a desirable quality in all but the simplest contracts. This work can prove useful in a variety of settings, including untrusted (and trusted) distributed computing environments such as the Grid. While many interesting research questions remain, we believe that our framework provides a good starting point to model, and reason about such environments.

References

[1] R. K. Dash, N. R. Jennings, and D. C. Parkes. Computational–mechanism design: A call to arms. *IEEE Intelligent Systems*, 18(6):40–47, 2003.

[2] A. Daskalopulu, T. Dimitrakos, and T. Maibaum. Evidence-based electronic contract performance monitoring. *Group Decision and Negotiation*, 11(6):469–485, 2002.

[3] P. M. Dung. On the acceptability of arguments and its fundamental role in nonmonotonic reasoning, logic programming and n-person games. *Artificial Intelligence*, 77(2):321–357, 1995.

[4] T. F. Gordon. The pleadings game: formalizing procedural justice. In *Proceedings of the fourth international conference on Artificial intelligence and law*, pages 10–19. ACM Press, 1993.

[5] A. Josang. Subjective evidential reasoning. In *Proceedings of the 9th International Conference on Information Processing and Management of Uncertainty in Knowledge-Based Systems*, pages 1671–1678, July 2002.

[6] M. J. Kollingbaum and T. J. Norman. Supervised interaction – creating a web of trust for contracting agents in electronic environments. In *Proceedings of the First International Joint Conference on Autonomous Agents and Multi-Agent Systems*, pages 272–279, 2002.

[7] D. Moore. *Dialogue game theory for intelligent tutoring systems*. PhD thesis, Leeds Metropolitan University, 1993.

[8] N. Oren, T. J. Norman, and A. Preece. Arguing with confidential information. In *Proceedings of the 18th European Conference on Artificial Intelligence*, Riva del Garda, Italy, August 2006. (To appear).

[9] N. Oren, T. J. Norman, and A. Preece. Loose lips sink ships: a heuristic for argumentation. In *Proceedings of the Third International Workshop on Argumentation in Multi-Agent Systems (ArgMAS 2006)*, pages 121–134, Hakodate, Japan, May 2006.

[10] N. Oren, A. Preece, and T. J. Norman. Service level agreements for semantic web agents. In *Proceedings of the AAAI Fall Symposium on Agents and the Semantic Web*, pages 47–54, 2005.

[11] N. Oren, A. Preece, and T. J. Norman. A simple argumentation based contract enforcement mechanism. In *Proceedings of the Tenth International Workshop on Cooperative Information Agents*, 2006. (to appear).

[12] J. Patel, W. Teacy, N. Jennings, and M. Luck. A probabilistic trust model for handling inaccurate reputation sources. In *Proceedings of Third International Conference on Trust Management*, pages 193–209, 2005.

[13] J. Patel, W. T. L. Teacy, N. R. Jennings, M. Luck, S. Chalmers, N. Oren, T. J. Norman, A. Preece, P. M. D. Gray, Shercliff, P. J. G., Stockreisser, J. Shao, W. A. Gray, N. J. Fiddian, and S. Thompson. Agent-based virtual organisations for the grid. *International Journal of Multi-Agent and Grid Systems*, 1(4):237–249, 2005.

[14] H. Prakken. Modelling defeasibility in law: Logic or procedure? *Fundamenta Informaticae*, 48(2-3):253–271, 2001.

[15] H. Prakken, C. A. Reed, and D. N. Walton. Argumentation schemes and burden of proof. In *Workshop Notes of the Fourth Workshop on Computational Models of Natural Argument*, 2004.

[16] H. Prakken and G. Sartor. A dialectical model of assessing conflicting arguments in legal reasoning. *Artificial Intelligence and Law*, 4:331–368, 1996.

[17] H. Prakken and G. Vreeswijk. Logics for defeasible argumentation. In D. Gabbay and F. Guenthner, editors, *Handbook of philosophical logic, 2nd Edition*, volume 4, pages 218–319. Kluwer Academic Publishers, 2002.

[18] D. N. Walton. Burden of proof. *Argumentation*, 2:233–254, 1988.

[19] L. Xu and M. A. Jeusfeld. *Pro-active monitoring of electronic contracts*, volume 2681 of *Lecture notes in Computer Science*, pages 584–600. Springer-Verlag GmbH, 2003.

Negotiating Intelligently

John Debenham & Simeon Simoff

Faculty of IT, University of Technology, Sydney, Australia.
{debenham,simeon}@it.uts.edu.au
WWW home page: http://e-markets.org.au/

Abstract. The predominant approaches to automating competitive interaction appeal to the central notion of a utility function that represents an agent's preferences. Agent's are then endowed with machinery that enables them to perform actions that are intended to optimise their expected utility. Despite the extent of this work, the deployment of automatic negotiating agents in real world scenarios is rare. We propose that utility functions, or preference orderings, are often not known with certainty; further, the uncertainty that underpins them is typically in a state of flux. We propose that the key to building intelligent negotiating agents is to take an agent's historic observations as primitive, to model that agent's changing uncertainty in that information, and to use that model as the foundation for the agent's reasoning. We describe an agent architecture, with an attendant theory, that is based on that model. In this approach, the utility of contracts, and the trust and reliability of a trading partner are intermediate concepts that an agent may estimate from its information model. This enables us to describe intelligent agents that are not necessarily utility optimisers, that value information as a commodity, and that build relationships with other agents through the trusted exchange of information as well as contracts.

1 Introduction

The potential value of the e-business market — including e-procurement — is enormous. Given that motivation and the current state of technical development it is surprising that a comparatively small amount of automated negotiation is presently deployed.[1] Technologies that support automated negotiation include multiagent systems and virtual institutions, game theory and decision theory.

Multiagent systems technology [1] — autonomous, intelligent and flexible software agents — provides the basis for constructing automated negotiation agents. Of particular significance are deliberative architectures that incorporate proactive planning systems [2]. *Virtual Institutions* are software systems composed of autonomous agents, that interact according to predefined conventions on language and protocol, and that guarantee that certain norms of behaviour are enforced. Norms may be specified that regulate the interactions, and so protect the integrity of the commitments exchanged. A Virtual Institution is in

---

[1] Auction bots such as those on eBay, and automated auction houses do a useful job, but do not automate negotiation in the sense described here.

a sense a natural extension of the social concept of institutions as regulatory systems that shape human interactions [3].

Game theory tells an agent what to do, and what outcome to expect, in many well-known negotiation situations [4], but these strategies and expectations are derived from assumptions about the agent's preferences and about the preferences of the opponent. One-to-one negotiation is generally known as *bargaining* [5] — it is the natural negotiation form when the negotiation object comprises a number of issues. For example, in bargaining over the supply of steel issues could include: the quantity of the steel, the quality of the steel, the delivery schedule, the settlement schedule and, of course, the price. Beyond bargaining there is a wealth of material on the theory of *auctions* [6] for one-to-many negotiation, and *exchanges* for many-to-many negotiation. Fundamental to this analysis is the central role of the utility function, and the notion of rational behaviour by which an agent aims to optimise its utility, when it is able to do so, and to optimise its *expected* utility otherwise.

We propose that utility functions, or preference orderings, are often not known with certainty; further, the uncertainty that underpins them is typically in a state of flux. We propose that the key to building intelligent negotiating agents is to take an agent's historic observations as primitive, to model that agent's changing uncertainty in that information, and to use that model as the foundation for the agent's reasoning. We call such agents *information-based agents*. In Sec. 2 we describe the ideas behind these agents, and formalise these ideas in Sec. 3. Sec. 4 relates commitments made to their eventual execution, this leads to a formalisation of trust. Strategies for information-based agents are discussed in Sec. 5.

2 The foundation of information-based agents

We discuss the issues that an intelligent negotiating agent should be designed to address, and give informal descriptions of how information-based agents address those issues. This section provides the rationale for the formal work that follows.

Percepts, the content of messages, are all that an agent has to inform it about the world and other agents. The validity of percepts will always be uncertain due to the reliability of the sender of the message, and to the period that has elapsed since the message arrived. Further, the belief that an agent has in the validity of a percept will be determined by the agent's level of individual *caution*. The information-based agent's *world model* is deduced from the percepts using *inference rules* that transform percepts into statements in probabilistic logic. These rules are peculiar to the agent. These world models are expressed in first-order logic where the validity of statements is expressed as a probability distribution over some valuation space that is not necessarily true/false and may have no natural ordering. The agent's personal *caution* is a component of these epistemic probabilities.

The integrity of percepts decreases in time. The way in which it decreases will be determined by the type of the percept, as well as by the issues listed in the previous paragraph including 'caution'. An agent may have background knowledge concerning the expected integrity of a percept as $t \to \infty$. Information-based agents represent this background knowledge as a *decay limit distribution*. If the background knowledge is incomplete then one possibility for an agent is to assume that the decay limit distribution has maximum entropy [7] whilst being consistent with the data.

All messages are valueless unless their integrity can be verified to some degree at a later time, perhaps for a cost. To deal with this issue we employ an *institution agent* that always reports promptly and honestly on the execution of all commitments, forecasts, promises and obligations. This provides a conveniently simple solution to the integrity verification issue. The institution agent also takes care of "who owns what". This enables the agents to negotiate and to evaluate the execution of commitments by simple message passing.

An agent's percepts generally constitute a sparse data set whose elements have differing integrity. An agent may wish to induce tentative conclusions from this sparse and uncertain data of changing integrity. Percepts are transformed by inference rules into statements in probabilistic logic as described above. Information-based agents may employ entropy-based logic [8] to induce complete probability distributions from those statements. This logic is consistent with the laws of probability, but the results derived assume that the data is 'all that there is to know' — Watt's Assumption [9].

It may be necessary to establish the *bona fide* of a commitment by including a 'default' obligation that an agent is forced to perform by an authority external to the multiagent system in the event that a commitment is not executed correctly. We do not address this issue here, and assume that defaults can be specified, and that some legal mechanism can be invoked if necessary.

In considering a proposed commitment or promise, an agent evaluates that commitment in some way, perhaps in utilitarian terms. Information-based agents express evaluations as probability distributions over some evaluation space that may not be totally ordered. An *evaluation space* is a complete disjoint set whose elements may be qualitative. An evaluation space may have a lattice ordering that represents an agent's known preferences. An agent may not have sufficient information to determine its preferences. If subjective judgement is required then an agent may be ambivalent. If there is a temporal consideration, such as in selecting a trading partner for a long-term relationship, then an agent may have no clear preference. If a negotiation object involves multiple issues then an agent may know its preference along each dimension, but not across the entire space. If an agent's goals are expressed at a high-level, such as 'the goal of this organisation is to achieve world domination', then such a goal may not translate into preferences that enable an agent to choose between two different types of pencil to purchase, for example. Further, preferences, like everything else, are derived from the agent's information and so may change in time — this may mean that an attempt to be a 'utility optimiser' is flawed by the fact that the utility function is uncertain, and its uncertainty is in a state of flux. To place utility optimisation in perspective — it aims to optimise an inherently uncertain function of permanently changing integrity that takes no account of the value of information exchange.

Information is strategic. It has value as information. With the exception of highly cautious messages such as "make me an offer" in simple bargaining, *everything* that an agent says gives away information. This is a central issue here — the exchange of information is a strategic component of competitive interaction. Information-based agents evaluate information received as the reduction in entropy of the agent's current world model. Information transmitted is evaluated as the agent's expectation of the reduction of entropy in the recipient's world model (by assuming that the recipient's reasoning apparatus mirrors its own).

In deciding how to act, an agent takes account of the value of the inflow and outflow of information; it takes account of its personal preferences, and, if these preferences may be totally ordered then they may be represented as a utility function. It also takes account of functions that evaluate trust and other parameters. From its information an information-based agent extracts: information measures, trust measures, measures of preference, utility or monetary value, all being expressed as probability distributions that represent the changing uncertainty in an agent's belief in the integrity of all of its information. Measures of the value of information, and utilitarian measures of the value of contracts, should not be unified into one overall measure. They are different and orthogonal concepts. Information-based agents exploit this orthogonality.

An agent will form expectations of other agents' behaviours by observing the difference between commitments encapsulated in contracts, promises and statements of intent, and their subsequent execution. These observations may take account of whether those differences, if any, are 'good' or 'bad' for the agent. In Sec. 4 we describe various measures for doing this. Some of these measures involve ideas from information theory.

An agent acts in response to some *need* or needs. A need may be exogenous such as the agent's 'owner' needs a bottle of wine, or a message from another agent offering to trade may trigger a latent need to trade profitably. A need may also be endogenous such as the agent deciding that it owns more wine that it requires. An agent may be attempting to satisfy a number of needs at any time, and may have expectations of its future needs. A need may involve acquiring some physical object, it may also be a need to acquire information or to develop some on-going relationship. Information-based agents have a planning system that is invoked to aim to satisfy needs — the planning system is flexible and explores a number of (possibly inter-related) options at the same time, and devotes resources (if necessary) to the most promising. One component of the world model will necessarily be an estimate of the expectation that some contract will subsequently satisfy a need in an acceptable way — this will be in the form of a probability distribution over some evaluation space that measures 'the expectation of the acceptability of the execution of a contract with respect to the satisfaction of that need'.

In general there will be many 'acceptable' ways of satisfying an agent's needs. An agent has strategies that aim to reach acceptable outcomes that are in some

sense 'good'. In a one-one negotiation, strategies determine the dynamic sequence in which an agent makes acceptable proposals to another agent. and a
mechanism for accepting proposals from that agent. Information-based agents'
strategies exploit the orthogonality between information in proposals and preferences (possibly the utility) of proposals. For example, if our agents wish to
make an offer at some 'preference level' then they may select from the available
equi-preferable offers on the basis of their information revelation (an agent may
wish this to be high, low) or selected from some section of the ontology. Alternatively, an agent may wish to make an offer at some 'information revelation level'
— for example, the equitable information revelation strategy [10]. That strategy
responds to a message with a response that gives the recipient expected information gain similar to that which the message gave to the agent — in single-issue
bargaining if the opponent works with a fixed increment/decrement then the
equitable information revelation strategy will respond likewise.

Strategies also address the issue of choosing which agent to attempt to negotiate with, and how needs may be met in the future. We have described trust
and honour models for information-based agents [11]. This leads on to the development of business relationships that we believe are founded on the trust that
grows both from an expectation of 'good' contracts and contract executions, and
from an expectation of valuable and reliable information exchange.

Not withstanding the sequence of the discussion above, the strategies will
determine the agent's world model. The agent's dynamic world model provides
the 'data' for the strategies. The communication language determines the sorts of
percept that an agent may receive, and the strategies determine the probability
distributions in the world model. So the communication language and a strategy
will together determine the requirements for the inference rules.

3 The architecture of information-based agents

The architecture of our information-based agent is shown in Fig. 1. The agent
begins to function in response to a percept (received message) that expresses a
need $N \in \mathcal{N}$. A *need* can be either exogenous (typically, the agent receives a
message from another agent $\{\Omega_1, \ldots, \Omega_o\}$), or endogenous. The agent has a set
of pre-specified *goals* (or *desires*), $G \in \mathcal{G}$, from which one or more is selected to
satisfy its perceived needs. Each of these goals is associated with one or more
plans, $s \in S$. This is consistent with the BDI model [1], and we do not detail
these aspects here. The agent in Fig. 1 also interacts with information sources
$\{\theta_1, \ldots, \theta_t\}$ that in our experiments[2] include unstructured data mining and text
mining 'bots' that retrieve information from the agent market-place and from
general news sources.

Finally the agent in Fig. 1 interacts with an 'Institution Agent', ξ, that
reports honestly and promptly on the fulfilment of contracts. The Institution
Agent is a conceptual device to prevent the requirement for agents to have 'eyes'

---

[2] http://e-markets.org.au

164

Fig. 1. Agent architecture.

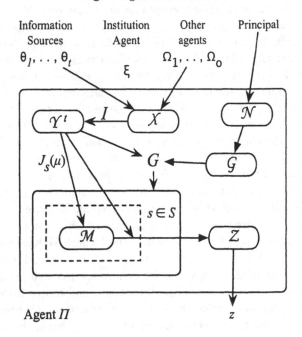

and effectors. For example, if agent Π wishes to give an object Y to agent Ω_k then this is achieved by Π sending a message to ξ requesting the transfer the ownership of Y from Π to Ω_k, once this this is done, ξ sends a message to Ω_k advising him that he now owns Y. Given such an Institution Agent, agents can negotiate and evaluate trade by simply sending and receiving messages.

Π has two languages: $\mathcal{C}$ and $\mathcal{L}$. $\mathcal{L}$ is a first-order language for internal representation — precisely it is a first-order language with sentence probabilities optionally attached to each sentence representing Π's epistemic belief in the validity of that sentence. $\mathcal{C}$ is an illocutionary-based language for communication [12]. Messages expressed in $\mathcal{C}$ from $\{\theta_i\}$ and $\{\Omega_i\}$ are received, time-stamped, source-stamped and placed in an *in-box* $\mathcal{X}$. The illocutionary particles in $\mathcal{C}$ are:

– Offer(Π, Ω_k, δ). Agent Π offers agent Ω_k a contract $\delta = (\pi, \varphi)$ with action commitments $\pi \in \mathcal{L}$ for Π and $\varphi \in \mathcal{L}$ for Ω_k.

– Accept(Π, Ω_k, δ). Agent Π accepts agent Ω_k's previously offered contract δ.

– Reject($\Pi, \Omega_k, \delta[, info]$). Agent Π rejects agent Ω_k's previously offered contract δ. Optionally, information *info* $\in \mathcal{L}$ explaining the reason for the rejection can be given.

– Withdraw($\Pi, \Omega_k[, info]$). Agent Π breaks down negotiation with Ω_k. Extra *info* $\in \mathcal{L}$ justifying the withdrawal may be given.

– Inform($\Pi, \Omega_k, info$). Agent Π informs Ω_k about *info* $\in \mathcal{L}$ and commits to the truth of *info*.

– Reward($\Pi, \Omega_k, \delta, \circ[, info]$). Intended to make the opponent accept a proposal with the promise of a future compensation. Agent Π offers agent Ω_k a contract δ. In case Ω_k accepts the proposal, Π commits to make $\phi \in \mathcal{L}$ true. The intended meaning is that Π believes that worlds in which ϕ is true are somehow desired by Ω_k. Optionally, additional information in support of the contract can be given.

– Threat($\Pi, \Omega_k, \delta, \phi, [info]$) Intended to make the opponent accept a proposal with the menace of some sort of retaliation. Agent Π offers agent Ω_k a contract δ. In case Ω_k does not accept the proposal, Π commits to make $\phi \in \mathcal{L}$ true. The intended meaning is that Π believes that worlds in which ϕ is true are somehow *not* desired by Ω_k. Optionally, additional information in support of the contract can be given.

– Appeal($\Pi, \Omega_k, \delta, info$) Intended to make the opponent accept a proposal as a consequence of the belief update that the accompanying information might bring about. Agent Π offers agent Ω_k a contract δ, and passes information in support of the contract.

The accompanying information, *info*, can be of two basic types: (i) referring to the process (plan) used by an agent to solve a problem, or (ii) data (beliefs) of the agent including preferences. When building relationships, agents will therefore try to influence the opponent by changing their processes (plans) or by providing new data.

3.1 World model

Everything that Π has at its disposal is derived from the messages in the inbox $\mathcal{X}$. As messages age, the degree of belief that Π associates with them will decrease. We call this *information integrity decay*. A factor in the integrity of a message will be the reliability of the source. This subjective decay is a feature of the agent, and agents will differ in their subjective estimates.

Each plan is driven by its expectations of the state of the world, and by the states of the other agents. These states will generally be quite numerous, and so we assume that at any time the agent's active plans will form expectations of certain *features* only, where each feature will be in one of a finite number of states[3]. Suppose that there are m such features, introduce m random variables, $\{X_i\}_{i=1}^m$. Each value, $x_{i,j}$, of the i'th random variable, X_i, denotes that the i'th feature is in the j'th perceivable state, or *possible world*, of that feature.

The messages in $\mathcal{X}$ are then translated using an *import function* I into sentences expressed in $\mathcal{L}$ that have integrity decay functions (usually of time) attached to each sentence, they are stored in a *repository* $\mathcal{Y}^t$. And that is all that happens until Π triggers a goal.

In general Π will be uncertain of the current state of each feature. Π's *world model*, $M \in \mathcal{M}$, consists of probability distributions over each of these random variables. If these m features are independent then the overall uncertainty, or

---

[3] We thus exclude the possibility of continuous variables.

entropy, of Π's world model is:

$$\mathbb{H}^t(M) = -\sum_{i=1}^{m} \mathbb{E}(\ln \mathbb{P}^t(X_i)) = -\sum_{i=1}^{m}\sum_{j=1}^{n_i} \mathbb{P}^t(X_i = x_{i,j}) \ln \mathbb{P}^t(X_i = x_{i,j})$$

The general idea is that if Π receives new information then the overall uncertainty of the world model is expected to decrease, but if Π receives no new information then it is expected to increase.

3.2 Reasoning

Consider first what happens if Π receives no new information. Each distribution, $\mathbb{P}^t(X_i)$, is associated with a *decay limit distribution*, $\mathbb{D}(X_i)$, that represents the expected limit state of the i'th feature in the absence of any observations of the state of that feature: $\lim_{t\to\infty} \mathbb{P}^t(X_i) = \mathbb{D}(X_i)$. For example, if the i'th feature is whether it is raining in Sydney, and $x_{i,1}$ means "it is raining in Sydney" and $x_{i,2}$ means "it is not raining in Sydney" — then if Π believes that it rains in Sydney 5% of the time: $\mathbb{D}(X_i) = (0.05, 0.95)$. If Π has no background knowledge about $\mathbb{D}(X_i)$ then the decay limit distribution is the maximum entropy, "flat", distribution. In the absence of incoming information, $\mathbb{P}(X_i)$ decays by:

$$\mathbb{P}^{t+1}(X_i) = \Delta_i(\mathbb{D}(X_i), \mathbb{P}^t(X_i))$$

where Δ_i is the *decay function* for the i'th feature satisfying the property that $\lim_{t\to\infty} \mathbb{P}^t(X_i) = \mathbb{D}(X_i)$. For example, Δ_i could be linear:

$$\mathbb{P}^{t+1}(X_i) = (1 - \nu_i)\mathbb{D}(X_i) + \nu_i \times \mathbb{P}^t(X_i) \tag{1}$$

where $\nu_i < 1$ is the decay rate for the i'th feature. Either the decay function or the decay limit distribution could also be a function of time: Δ_i^t and $\mathbb{D}^t(X_i)$.

If Π receives a message expressed in $\mathcal{C}$ then it will be transformed by inference rules into statements expressed in $\mathcal{L}$. We introduce this procedure with an example. Preference information is a statement by an agent that it prefers one class of contracts to another where contracts may be multi-issue. Preference illocutions may refer to particular issues within contracts — e.g. "I prefer red to yellow", or to combinations of issues — e.g. "I prefer a car with a five year warranty to the same car with a two year warranty than costs 15% less". An agent will find it useful to estimate which contract under consideration is favoured most by the opponent. Preference information can assist with this estimation as the following example shows. Suppose Π receives preference information from Ω_k through an Inform$(\Omega_k, \Pi, info)$ illocution: $info =$ "for contracts with property Q_1 or property Q_2, the probability that the contract Ω_k prefers most will have property Q_1 is z" — the ontology in $\mathcal{C}$ is assumed to contain an illocutionary particle that can express this statement. What happens next will depend on Π's plans. Suppose that Π has an active plan $s \in S$ that calls for the probability distribution $\mathbb{P}^t(\text{Favour}(\Omega_k, \Pi, \delta)) \in M$ over all δ, where $\text{Favour}(\Omega_k, \Pi, \delta)$

means that "δ is the contract that Ω_k prefers most from Π". Suppose Π has a prior distribution $q = (q_1, \dots)$ for $\mathbb{P}^t(\text{Favour}(\cdot))$. Then s will require an inference rule: $J_s^{\text{Favour}}(info)$ that is the following linear constraint on the posterior $\mathbb{P}^t(\text{Favour}(\Omega_k, \Pi, \delta))$ distribution:

$$z = \frac{\sum_{\delta:Q_1(\delta)} p_\delta}{\left(\sum_{\delta:Q_1(\delta)} p_\delta\right) + \left(\sum_{\delta:Q_2(\delta)} p_\delta\right) - \left(\sum_{\delta:Q_1 \wedge Q_2(\delta)} p_\delta\right)} \qquad (2)$$

and is determined by the *principle of minimum relative entropy* — a form of Bayesian inference is that is convenient when the data is sparse [13] — as described generally below. The inference rule $J_s^{Favour}(\cdot)$ infers a constraint on a distribution in M from an illocution expressed in $\mathcal{C}$. Inferences of this sort are necessary for Π to operate, but their validity is a personal matter for Π to assume.

Now, more generally, suppose that Π receives a percept μ from agent Ω_k at time t. Suppose that this percept states that something is so with probability z, and suppose that Π attaches an epistemic belief probability $\mathbb{R}^t(\Pi, \Omega_k, \mu)$ to μ. Π's set of active plans will have a set of model building functions, $J_s(\cdot)$, such that $J_s^{X_i}(\mu)$ is a set of linear constraints on the posterior distribution for X_i where the prior distribution is $\mathbb{P}^t(X_i) = q$. Let $p = (p_1, \dots)$ be the distribution with minimum relative entropy with respect to q: $p = \arg\min_p \sum_j p_j \log \frac{p_j}{q_j}$ that satisfies the constraints $J_s^{X_i}(\mu)$. Then let r be the distribution:

$$r = \mathbb{R}^t(\Pi, \Omega_k, \mu) \times p + (1 - \mathbb{R}^t(\Pi, \Omega_k, \mu)) \times q$$

and then for a small time step δt let:

$$\mathbb{P}^{t+\delta t}(X_i) = \begin{cases} r & \text{if } \mathbb{K}(r\|\mathbb{D}(X_i)) > \mathbb{K}(\mathbb{P}^t(X_i)\|\mathbb{D}(X_i)) \\ q & \text{otherwise} \end{cases} \qquad (3)$$

where $\mathbb{K}(x\|y) = \sum_j x_j \ln \frac{x_j}{y_j}$ is the Kullback-Leibler distance between two probability distributions x and y. The idea in Eqn. 3 is that the vector r will only update $\mathbb{P}^t(X_i)$ if it contains more information with respect to the decay limit distribution than the prior q. Then combining Eqn. 3 with Eqn. 1 let:

$$\mathbb{P}^{t+1}(X_i) = (1 - \nu_i)\mathbb{D}(X_i) + \nu_i \times \mathbb{P}^{t+\delta t}(X_i) \qquad (4)$$

and note that this procedure has dealt with integrity decay, and with two probabilities: first, the probability z in the percept μ, and second the epistemic belief probability $\mathbb{R}^t(\Pi, \Omega_k, \mu)$ that Π attached to μ. Given a probability distribution q, the *minimum relative entropy distribution* $p = (p_1, \dots, p_I)$ subject to a set of J linear constraints $g = \{g_j(p) = a_j \cdot p - c_j = 0\}, j = 1, \dots, J$ (that must include the constraint $\sum_i p_i - 1 = 0$) is: $p = \arg\min_p \sum_j p_j \log \frac{p_j}{q_j}$. This may be calculated by introducing Lagrange multipliers λ: $L(p, \lambda) = \sum_j p_j \log \frac{p_j}{q_j} + \lambda \cdot g$. Minimising L, $\{\frac{\partial L}{\partial \lambda_j} = g_j(p) = 0\}, j = 1, \dots, J$ is the set of given constraints g, and a solution to $\frac{\partial L}{\partial p_i} = 0, i = 1, \dots, I$ leads eventually to p.

3.3 Estimating $\mathbb{R}^t(\Pi, \Omega_k, \mu)$

Π attaches an epistemic belief probability $\mathbb{R}^t(\Pi, \Omega_k, \mu)$ to each message μ. A historic estimate of $\mathbb{R}^t(\Pi, \Omega_k, \mu)$ may be obtained by measuring the 'difference' between commitment and execution. Π's plans will have constructed a set of distributions. We measure this 'difference' as the error in the effect that μ has on each of Π's distributions. Suppose that μ is received from agent Ω_k at time u and is verified at some later time t. For example, μ could be a chunk of information: "the interest rate will rise by 0.5% next week", and suppose that the interest rate actually rises by 0.25% — represent what the message should have been μ'. What does all this tell agent Π about agent Ω_k's reliability? Consider one of Π's distributions for X that is $\boldsymbol{q}^u$ at time u. Let $\boldsymbol{p}^u_\mu$ be the posterior minimum relative entropy distribution subject to the constraint $J^X_s(\mu)$, and let $\boldsymbol{p}^u_{\mu'}$ be that distribution subject to $J^X_s(\mu')$. We now estimate what $\mathbb{R}^u(\Pi, \Omega_k, \mu)$ should have been in the light of knowing *now*, at time t, that μ should have been μ'.

The idea of Eqn. 3, is that the current value of $\mathbb{R}^t(\Pi, \Omega_k, \mu)$ should be such that, *on average*, $\boldsymbol{p}^u_\mu$ will be "close to" $\boldsymbol{p}^u_{\mu'}$ when we eventually discover μ' — no matter whether or not μ was used to update the distribution for X, as determined by the acceptability test in Eqn. 3 at time u. The *observed reliability* for μ and distribution X, $\mathbb{R}^t_X(\Pi, \Omega_k, \mu)|\mu'$, on the basis of the verification of μ with μ', is the value of r that minimises the Kullback-Leibler distance:

$$\mathbb{R}^t_X(\Pi, \Omega_k, \mu)|\mu' = \arg \min_r \mathbb{K}(r \cdot \boldsymbol{p}^u_\mu + (1 - r) \cdot \boldsymbol{q}^u \| \boldsymbol{p}^u_{\mu'})$$

If $\mathbf{X}(\mu)$ is the set of distributions that μ affects, then the overall *observed reliability* on the basis of the verification of μ with μ' is:

$$\mathbb{R}^t(\Pi, \Omega_k, \mu)|\mu' = 1 - (\max_{X \in \mathbf{X}(\mu)} |1 - \mathbb{R}^t_X(\Pi, \Omega_k, \mu)|\mu'|)$$

Then for each ontological context o_j, at time t when μ has been verified with μ':

$$\mathbb{R}^{t+1}(\Pi, \Omega_k, o_j) = (1 - \nu) \times \mathbb{R}^t(\Pi, \Omega_k, o_j) + \nu \times \mathbb{R}^t(\Pi, \Omega_k, \mu)|\mu' \times \mathrm{Sim}(o_j, O(\mu))$$

where Sim measures the semantic distance between two sections of the ontology, and ν is the learning rate. Over time, Π notes the ontological context of the various μ received from Ω_k, and over the various ontological contexts calculates the relative frequency, $\mathbb{P}^t(o_j)$, of these contexts, $o_j = O(\mu)$. This leads to an overall expectation of the *reliability* that agent Π has for agent Ω_k:

$$\mathbb{R}^t(\Pi, \Omega_k) = \sum_j \mathbb{P}^t(o_j) \times \mathbb{R}^t(\Pi, \Omega_k, o_j)$$

4 Commitment and Execution

The interaction between agents Π and Ω_k will eventually lead to some sort of *contract*: $\delta = (\pi, \varphi)$ where π is Π's commitment and φ is Ω_k's commitment.

No matter what these commitments are, Π will be interested in any variation between Ω_k's commitment, φ, and what actually happens, the execution, φ'. The form of this commitment could be a promise to deliver goods, or abide by certain trading terms that extend over a period of time, or that some information that may, or may not, prove to be correct. We denote the relationship between commitment and execution, $\mathbb{P}^t(\text{Execute}(\varphi')|\text{Commit}(\varphi))$ simply as $\mathbb{P}^t(\varphi'|\varphi)$. In general we assume that such commitment and execution takes place in the context of a *relationship* ρ between Π and Ω_k.

Beliefs 'evaporate' as time goes by. If we don't keep an ongoing relationship, we become unsure how *trustworthy* a trading partner is. This decay is what justifies a continuous relationship between agents. The conditional probabilities, $\mathbb{P}^t(\varphi'|\varphi)$, should tend to ignorance as represented by the *decay limit distribution* $d = \{d_i\}$. If we have the set of observations $\Phi = \{\varphi_1, \varphi_2, \ldots, \varphi_n\}$ then complete ignorance of the opponent's expected behaviour means that given the opponent commits to φ, the conditional probability for each observable outcome φ' becomes $d_i = \frac{1}{n}$, but Π may have background beliefs about Ω_k's decay limit distribution. This natural decay of belief is offset by new observations. We define the evolution of the probability distribution as: $\mathbb{P}^{t+1}(\varphi'|\varphi) = ((1 - \nu) \cdot d + \nu \cdot \mathbb{P}^t_+(\varphi'|\varphi))$, where $\nu \in [0,1]$ is the learning rate, and $\mathbb{P}^t_+(\varphi'|\varphi)$ represents the posterior distribution for $(\varphi'|\varphi)$ given an observed contract execution as the following shows.

Suppose that Π has a business relationship ρ with agent Ω_k, that Ω_k commits to φ, and this commitment is sound. The material value of φ to ρ will depend on the future use that Π makes of it, and that is unlikely to be known. So Π estimates the value of φ to the relationship ρ he has with Ω_k using a probability distribution $(p_1, \ldots, p_n)$ over a *relationship evaluation space* $E = (e_1, \ldots, e_n)$ that could range from "that is what I expect from the perfect trading partner" to "it is totally useless" — E may contain hard or fuzzy values. $p_i = w_i(\rho, \varphi)$ is the probability that e_i is the correct evaluation of the enactment φ in the context of relationship ρ, and $w : \mathcal{L} \times \mathcal{L} \to [0,1]^n$ is the *evaluation function*.

Let $(\varphi_1, \ldots, \varphi_m)$ be the set of possible contract executions in some order. Then for a given φ_k, $(\mathbb{P}^t(\varphi_1|\varphi_k), \ldots, \mathbb{P}^t(\varphi_m|\varphi_k))$ is the prior distribution of Π's estimate of what will actually occur if Ω_k committed to φ_k occurring and $w(\rho, \varphi_k) = (w_1(\rho, \varphi_k), \ldots, w_n(\rho, \varphi_k))$ is Π's evaluation over E with respect to the relationship ρ of Ω_k's commitment φ_k. Π's expected evaluation of what will occur given that Ω_k has committed to φ_k occurring is:

$$
w^{\exp}(\rho, \varphi_k) = \left(\sum_{j=1}^m \mathbb{P}^t(\varphi_j|\varphi_k) \cdot w_1(\rho, \varphi_j), \ldots, \sum_{j=1}^m \mathbb{P}^t(\varphi_j|\varphi_k) \cdot w_n(\rho, \varphi_j) \right).
$$

Now suppose that Π observes the event $(\phi'|\phi)$ in another relationship ρ' also with agent Ω_k. Eg: Π may buy wine and cheese from the same supplier. Π may wish to revise the prior estimate $w^{\exp}(\rho, \varphi_k)$ in the light of the observation $(\phi'|\phi)$ to:

$$
(w^{\text{rev}}(\rho, \varphi_k) \mid (\varphi'|\varphi)) = g(w^{\exp}(\rho, \varphi_k), w(\rho', \phi), w(\rho', \phi'), \rho, \rho', \varphi, \phi, \phi'),
$$

for some function g — the idea being, for example, that if the commitment, ϕ, concerning the purchase of cheese, ρ', was not kept then Π's expectation that the commitment, φ, concerning the purchase of wine, ρ, will not be kept should increase. We estimate the posterior $\mathbb{P}^t_+(\varphi'|\varphi)$ by applying the principle of minimum relative entropy: $\left(\mathbb{P}^t_+(\varphi_j|\varphi)\right)^m_{j=1} = \arg\min_p \sum^m_{i=1} p_i \log \frac{p_i}{\mathbb{P}^t(\varphi_i|\varphi)}$ where $p = (p_j)^m_{j=1}$, satisfies the n constraints:

$$\sum^m_{j=1} p_j \cdot w_i(\rho, \varphi_j) = g_i(w^{\exp}(\rho, \varphi_k), w(\rho', \phi), w(\rho', \phi'), \rho, \rho', \varphi, \phi, \phi')$$

for $i = 1, \ldots, n$. This is a set of n linear equations in m unknowns, and so the calculation of the minimum relative entropy distribution may be impossible if $n > m$. In this case, we take only the m equations for which the change from the prior to the posterior value is greatest. That is, we attempt to select the most significant factors.

Consider a distribution of expected fulfilment of commitments that represent Π's "ideal" for a relationship with Ω_k, in the sense that it is the best that Π could reasonably expect Ω_k to do. This distribution will be a function of Ω_k, Π's history with Ω_k, anything else that Π believes about Ω_k, and general environmental information including time — denote all of this by e, then we have $\mathbb{P}^t_I(\varphi'|\varphi, e)$. For example, if Π considers that it is unacceptable for the execution φ' to be less preferred than the commitment φ then $\mathbb{P}^t_I(\varphi'|\varphi, e)$ will only be non-zero for those φ' that Π prefers to φ. The distribution $\mathbb{P}^t_I(\cdot)$ represents what Π expects, or hopes, Ω_k will do. *Trust* is the relative entropy between this ideal distribution, $\mathbb{P}^t_I(\varphi'|\varphi, e)$, and the distribution of the observation of fulfilled commitments, $\mathbb{P}^t(\varphi'|\varphi)$. That is:

$$\text{Trust}(\Pi, \Omega_k, \varphi) = 1 - \sum_{\varphi'} \mathbb{P}^t_I(\varphi'|\varphi, e) \log \frac{\mathbb{P}^t_I(\varphi'|\varphi, e)}{\mathbb{P}^t(\varphi'|\varphi)} \tag{5}$$

where the "1" is an arbitrarily chosen constant being the maximum value that trust may have. This equation defines trust for one, single commitment φ — for example, my trust in my butcher if he commits to provide me with a 10% discount for the rest of the year. It makes sense to aggregate these values over a class of commitments, say over those φ that are subtypes of a particular relationship ρ, that is $\varphi \leq \rho$. In this way we measure the trust that I have in my butcher in relation to the commitments he makes for red meat generally:

$$\text{Trust}(\Pi, \Omega_k, \rho) = 1 - \frac{\sum_{\varphi:\varphi\leq\rho} \mathbb{P}^t(\varphi) \left[\sum_{\varphi'} \mathbb{P}^t_I(\varphi'|\varphi, e) \log \frac{\mathbb{P}^t_I(\varphi'|\varphi,e)}{\mathbb{P}^t(\varphi'|\varphi)}\right]}{\sum_{\varphi:\varphi\leq\rho} \mathbb{P}^t(\varphi)}$$

where $\mathbb{P}^t(\varphi)$ is a probability distribution over the space of commitments that the next commitment Ω_k will make to Π is φ. Similarly, for an overall estimate of Π's trust in Ω_k:

$$\text{Trust}(\Pi, \Omega_k) = 1 - \sum_{\varphi} \mathbb{P}^t(\varphi) \left[\sum_{\varphi'} \mathbb{P}^t_I(\varphi'|\varphi, e) \log \frac{\mathbb{P}^t_I(\varphi'|\varphi, e)}{\mathbb{P}^t(\varphi'|\varphi)}\right]$$

5 Strategies

An agent requires *strategies* for deciding who to interact with, and for deciding how to manage interaction using the language $\mathcal{C}$. In $\mathcal{C}$ as defined in Sec. 3, contracts may be for a single trade, or may encapsulate an on-going trading relationship. Interaction is normally bound by an *interaction protocol* that moderates the interaction sequence, and so may limit the range of model building functions, $J_s(\cdot)$. Consider the protocol in which statements in $\mathcal{C}$ are exchanged between pairs of agents, and Offer($\cdot$) statements are binding until countered, or until one of the pair issues a Quit($\cdot$). That is, an agent would only enter into a negotiation — ie: offer exchange — if it were prepared to commit. To manage this protocol, agent Π requires the following probability estimates in M where Π is bargaining with opponent Ω_k, in satisfaction of some need $N \in \mathcal{N}$:

1 $\mathbb{P}^t(val(\Pi, \Omega_k, N, \delta) = v_i)$ — for any deal, δ, the probability distribution over some valuation space $\{v_i\}$ that measures how "good" the deal δ is to Π.
2 $\mathbb{P}^t(acc(\Pi, \Omega_k, \delta))$ — for any deal, δ, the probability that Ω_k would accept δ.
3 $\mathbb{P}^t(conv(\Pi, \Omega_k, \Delta))$ — for any sequence of offer-exchanges, Δ, the probability that that sequence will converge to an acceptable deal.
4 $\mathbb{P}^t(trade(\Pi, \Omega_k, o_j) = u_i)$ — for an ontological context o_j, the probability distribution over some valuation space $\{u_i\}$ that measures how "good" Ω_k is as a trading partner to Π for deals in ontological context o_j.

The estimation of these distributions has been described previously [10]. Π's strategy determines how it uses these distributions. An approach to issue-tradeoffs is described in [14]. That strategy attempts to make an acceptable offer by "walking round" the iso-curve of Π's previous offer (that has, say, an acceptability of α) towards Ω_k's subsequent counter offer. In terms of the machinery described here: $\arg\max_\delta \{ \mathbb{P}^t(acc(\Pi, \Omega_k, \delta)) \mid \mathbb{E}^t(val(\Pi, \Omega_k, N, \delta)) \approx \alpha \}$. By including the "information dimension" Π can implement strategies that go beyond utilitarian thinking. Π evaluates every illocution for its utilitarian value, and for its value as information. For example, the *equitable information revelation* strategy [10] responds to a message μ with a message that gives the recipient expected information gain similar to that which μ gave to Π; these responses are also "reasonable" from a utilitarian point of view. An information-based agent evaluates all exchanges in terms of both their estimated utilitarian value, and their information value.

Estimations of trust — Sec. 4 — may be used to select a trading partner. One interesting question is to determine a set of partners to maintain for deals from a particular section of the ontology — this is a question of risk management. Having identified such a set, the agent then has to decide which one of these partners to use for the next negotiation. A nice strategy is to choose the partner with a probability equal to the probability that they are the best choice — as determined by trust, or some other means.

An information-based agent additionally requires strategies to manage the exchange of information, and to be strategic in their information acquisition. This includes strategies for dealing with the information sources $\{\theta_1, \ldots, \theta_t\}$, which becomes interesting if those sources are not always available, charge a fee, or take some time to deliver. This also includes strategies for the acquisition of information by both covert and overt strategic interaction with other agents $\{\Omega_1, \ldots, \Omega_o\}$. These information strategies are the subject of current research.

6 Conclusion

We do not claim that this is the end of the matter in deploying automated negotiators, and the approach described here has yet to be trialed extensively. But we do maintain the strategic apparatus of intelligent negotiating agents should include the intelligent use of information. We have proposed a theoretical basis for managing information in the context of competitive interaction, and have shown how that theory may be computed by an intelligent agent. Information theory provides the theoretical underpinning that enables such an informed agent to value, manage and exchange her information intelligently.

References

1. Wooldridge, M.: Multiagent Systems. Wiley (2002)
2. Ghallab, M., Nau, D., Traverso, P.: Automated Planning : Theory and Practice. Morgan Kaufmann (2004)
3. Arcos, J.L., Esteva, M., Noriega, P., Rodríguez, J.A., Sierra, C.: Environment engineering for multiagent systems. Journal on Engineering Applications of Artificial Intelligence 18 (2005)
4. Rosenschein, J., Zlotkin, G.: Rules of Encounter. MIT Press (1998)
5. Muthoo, A.: Bargaining Theory with Applications. Cambridge UP (1999)
6. Klemperer, P.: The Economic Theory of Auctions : Vols I and II. Edward Elgar (2000)
7. Paris, J.: Common sense and maximum entropy. Synthese 117 (1999) 75 – 93
8. Jaynes, E.: Probability Theory — The Logic of Science. Cambridge University Press (2003)
9. Jaeger, M.: Representation independence of nonmonotonic inference relations. In: Proceedings of KR'96, Morgan Kaufmann (1996) 461–472
10. Debenham, J., Simoff, S.: An agent establishes trust with equitable information revelation. In Subrahmanian, V., Regli, W., eds.: Proceedings of the 2005 IEEE 2nd Symposium on Multi-Agent Security and Survivability, Drexel University, Philadelphia, USA, IEEE (2005) 66 – 74
11. Sierra, C., Debenham, J.: Trust and honour in information-based agency. In: Proceedings Fifth International Conference on Autonomous Agents and Multi Agent Systems AAMAS-2006, Hakodate, Japan, ACM Press, New York (2006)
12. Sierra, C., Jennings, N., Noriega, P., Parsons, S.: A framework for argumentation-based negotiation. In: Intelligent Agents IV: Agent Theories, Architectures, and Languages (ATAL-97), Springer-Verlag: Heidelberg, Germany (1998) 177–192
13. Cheeseman, P., Stutz, J.: On The Relationship between Bayesian and Maximum Entropy Inference. In: Bayesian Inference and Maximum Entropy Methods in Science and Engineering. American Institute of Physics, Melville, NY, USA (2004) 445 – 461
14. Faratin, P., Sierra, C., Jennings, N.: Using similarity criteria to make issue tradeoffs in automated negotiation. Journal of Artificial Intelligence 142 (2003) 205–237

Avoiding Long and Fruitless Dialogues in Critiquing

David McSherry[1] and David W. Aha[2]

[1]School of Computing and Information Engineering
University of Ulster, Coleraine BT52 1SA, Northern Ireland
dmg.mcsherry@ulster.ac.uk

[2]Navy Center for Applied Research in Artificial Intelligence
Naval Research Laboratory, Code 5515, Washington DC 20375, USA
david.aha@nrl.navy.mil

Abstract

An important issue in critiquing approaches to product recommendation is how to avoid long and fruitless critiquing dialogues when none of the available products are acceptable to the user. We present a new approach called *progressive* critiquing in which the non-existence of a product that satisfies all the user's critiques triggers an explanation alerting the user to the possibility that none of the available products may be acceptable. A recovery mechanism based on implicit relaxation of constraints ensures that progress can again be made if the user is willing to compromise. Our empirical results show that progressive critiquing is most effective when users give priority to critiques on attributes whose values they are least inclined to accept.

1 Introduction

Critiquing is an approach to eliciting user requirements in recommender systems which has attracted significant research interest in case-based reasoning (CBR) and other disciplines (e.g., [1-11]). The idea is that it is often easier to critique (or *tweak*) an example product than to construct queries. Simply by pointing to a car on display in a showroom and saying *Like this but cheaper*, a customer reveals important clues about her automobile preferences (e.g., make, class, color) as well as the maximum price she is prepared to pay. A natural response for the salesperson is to show the customer a car that is less expensive but otherwise similar to the one that attracted her attention.

In a recommender system based on critiquing, the user may be invited to critique an already familiar product or one retrieved in response to an initial query. An early example is *Entrée*, a restaurant recommender that supports both *directional* critiques (e.g., *cheaper*, *livelier*, *quieter*) and *replacement* critiques such as one that allows the user to select a different *cuisine* [3]. The product retrieved in response to a critique is usually one that satisfies the critique and is most similar to the critiqued product. If not prepared to accept the product now recommended, the user can continue critiquing the system's recommendations as long as she wishes.

As we show in Section 2, one problem in critiquing is that progress towards an acceptable product — if such a product exists — can be surprisingly slow even when the number of available products is very small. Techniques for increasing the efficiency of critiquing include taking account of the user's previous critiques when responding to her current critique [9] and multi-attribute critiques that enable the user to move more quickly through the product space [7].

A problem which appears to have received less attention is how to avoid long and fruitless dialogues when none of the available products are acceptable to the user. In a holiday recommender, for example, a user seeking a skiing holiday for two in December costing less than £600 may be unable to compromise on holiday type, number of persons, or price. If there is no skiing holiday for two costing less than £600 then none of the available holidays are acceptable. In this situation, it is reasonable to expect that the *non-existence* of an acceptable product should be recognizable by the user from feedback provided by the system in response to her critiques.

Of course, any critiquing system must inform the user if there is no product that satisfies the user's *current* critique. In most critiquing systems, however, no other mechanism is provided to help users recognize the non-existence of an acceptable product. The knowledge-intensive approach used in Hammond *et al.*'s [4] *Car Navigator* to explain known trade-offs in the automobile domain, such as that between horsepower and fuel economy, is one exception. Though clearly of benefit to users whose expectations may be unrealistic, such explanations cannot account for recommendation failures caused by lack of coverage of the product space.

To address this issue, we present a new approach called *progressive* critiquing in which the non-existence of a product that satisfies all the user's critiques is recognized as a *progression failure*. An explanation of the failure is provided to alert the user to the possibility that none of the available products may be acceptable. This is followed by a *recovery* process based on implicit relaxation of constraints to ensure that progress can again be made if the user is willing to compromise.

In Section 2, we use examples based on property recommendation to illustrate the difficulty of recognizing the non-existence of an acceptable product in critiquing dialogues. We also discuss potential problems related to user critiquing behavior before concluding with a brief discussion of related work. In Section 3, we present a detailed account of progressive critiquing and demonstrate the approach in a recommender system called *Tweak*. In Section 4, we evaluate the performance of progressive critiquing when none of the available products may be acceptable, and investigate the extent to which the effectiveness of critiquing dialogues may be affected by the user's critiquing choices. Our conclusions are presented in Section 5.

2 Problems in Critiquing

In CBR recommender systems — which have often been the focus of critiquing research — descriptions of available products are stored in a product case base. Figure 1 shows an example case base in the property domain which we use to demonstrate that recognizing the non-existence of an acceptable product can be surprisingly difficult even when the number of available products is very small. Another limitation of standard critiquing dialogues highlighted by our discussion is that progress towards an acceptable product, if one exists, can be much slower than might be expected.

	Loc	Beds	Type	RRs
Case 1	A	3	sem	2
Case 2	B	3	det	2
Case 3	B	4	sem	2
Case 4	B	3	sem	3
Case 5a	B	3	sem	2

Figure 1. Example case base in the property domain

Attributes in the example case base are location (A or B), bedrooms (3 or 4), type (semi-detached or detached), and reception rooms (2 or 3). The attributes are equally weighted and the similarity between two cases is the number of matching features. In the example critiquing dialogue that we now present, the user is looking for a 4 bedroom detached property in location A with 3 reception rooms (A 4 det 3). Her initial query is loc = A and the case initially recommended by the system is Case 1 (A 3 sem 2). The available critiques are *more* and *less* critiques for beds and reception rooms (RRs) and replacement critiques for loc and type.

We assume a basic critiquing algorithm in which:

- Each critique is applied only to a single attribute
- The case retrieved in response to a critique, if any, is one that satisfies the critique and is most similar to the critiqued case
- No account is taken of any previous critiques or initial query
- Previously recommended cases are eliminated from further consideration

For such a critiquing algorithm, Figure 2 shows the cases recommended in response to a sequence of critiques with Case 1 as the initially recommended case. The user's critiquing choices are entirely reasonable, but after three critiques, she has made no progress towards her goal. The case recommended in response to her final critique — like all the other cases she has seen — satisfies only one of her requirements.

Figure 2. Cases recommended in a critiquing dialogue with Case 1
as the initially recommended case.

The user also has no way of telling if there is a case that satisfies her requirements (A 4 det 3). In fact, there is no such case in the example case base. But the system's responses to the user's critiques (Figure 2) would be the same with Case 5a replaced by a case that exactly matches the user's requirements:

| Case 5b | A | 4 | det | 3 |

For example, Case 2 would still be recommended in response to the first critique as it is more similar to Case 1 (the critiqued case) than Case 5b.

In progressive critiquing, the approach we present in Section 3, the non-existence of a case that satisfies all the user's critiques — and any constraints in her initial query — is recognized as a progression failure, and triggers an explanation alerting the user to the possibility that none of the available cases may be acceptable. By insisting that, if possible, the case recommended in response to a critique must also satisfy any previous critiques and query constraints, progressive critiquing also enables quicker progress towards an acceptable case if one exists. With Case 5a replaced by Case 5b in the example case base, only a single critique is needed in progressive critiquing to reach a case that exactly matches the user's requirements.

Progressive critiquing also includes a mechanism for recovering from progression failures based on implicit relaxation of constraints. Of course, recovery is possible only if the user is willing to compromise. We will refer to a case that satisfies all the user's hard constraints as a *feasible* case. Whether such a case, if one exists, is acceptable to the user may depend on the extent to which it satisfies her *soft* constraints. However, the non-existence of a feasible case implies the non-existence of an acceptable case.

2.1 User Critiquing Behavior

Surprisingly little appears to be known about the effects of the user's critiquing choices on the efficiency of critiquing dialogues. However, possible pitfalls that seem likely to reduce the effectiveness of a critiquing algorithm include:

- Early critiques on attributes that fail to satisfy soft constraints may result in progression failures that impede progress towards a feasible case if one exists

- By over-critiquing an attribute (e.g., price) whose current value is acceptable, the user may find herself in an area of the product space where none of her other requirements are satisfied

- If some of the user's critiques are inconsistent with her requirements, there may be a case that satisfies all her requirements but not all her critiques

Some of these pitfalls could perhaps be avoided by providing users with guidelines for more effective critiquing, such as focusing initially on attributes whose values they are least inclined to accept. This is one of the issues we investigate in our evaluation of progressive critiquing in Section 4.

2.2 Related Work

Maintaining a history of the user's previous critiques is a feature that progressive critiquing shares with incremental critiquing [9]. Retrieval in the latter approach is based on a single *compatibility* measure that takes account of each case's similarity to the critiqued case and the number of previous critiques, in addition to the current critique, that it satisfies. However, because a highly similar case may dominate other cases that satisfy more critiques, the case recommended in response to a critique may not satisfy all the user's critiques even if such a case exists. Salamó *et al.* [10] propose an approach to addressing this issue in which similarity to the critiqued case is used as a secondary retrieval criterion. Also in contrast to progressive critiquing, there is no recognition or explanation of progression failures in incremental critiquing.

As in incremental critiquing [9], previously recommended cases are currently eliminated in progressive critiquing, though it may be argued that critiquing a recommended product does not amount to *rejection* of the product by the user. In future work we plan to investigate the potential benefits and drawbacks of allowing previous recommendations to be repeated in progressive critiquing.

Bridge and Ferguson [1] examine problems associated with the lack of a clear semantics for directional critiques, such as how to adjust the user's preferred price in response to a *Like this but cheaper* critique. As we show in Section 3.1, progressive critiquing avoids the problem of adjusting preferences in response to directional critiques for certain types of attributes by adapting only the user's *constraints* in response to such critiques.

Separate modeling of user preferences and constraints, as described in Section 3, is a feature that progressive critiquing shares with compromise driven retrieval (CDR) [8, 12], and one that plays an important role in enabling constraints to be relaxed without affecting the system's understanding of the user's preferences.

3 Progressive Critiquing

Following a detailed account of progressive critiquing and features that characterize the approach (e.g., separate modeling of user preferences and constraints, explanation of progression failures, and implicit relaxation of constraints), we use a well-known case base to demonstrate the approach in a recommender system called *Tweak*.

3.1 Attributes and Critiques

In most recommender systems, attributes of various types are used to describe the available products. For example, a *nominal* attribute is one whose values do not have a natural ordering that determines their similarity (e.g., the type or make of a personal computer). A *more-is-better* (MIB) attribute is one that most users would prefer to maximize, such as memory or processor speed. A *less-is-better* (LIB) attribute is one that most users would prefer to minimize (e.g., price). A *nearer-is-better* (NIB) attribute (e.g., screen size) is one for which most users have in mind an ideal value and prefer values that are closer to their ideal value.

Critiques currently supported in *Tweak* are *more* and *less* critiques on NIB attributes, *more* critiques on MIB attributes, *less* critiques on LIB attributes, and *replacement* critiques on nominal attributes. A replacement critique [1] is one in which the user specifies a preferred value (e.g., *type* = laptop) for one of the attributes in the critiqued case. The available critiques are dynamically generated in each recommendation cycle to ensure that the user is offered only critiques that are satisfied by at least one of the remaining cases. For example, if a recommended PC has more memory than any remaining case, then it is pointless to offer the user a *more memory* critique.

McSherry [12-13] proposes a CBR approach to assessment of similarity with respect to LIB and MIB attributes in which there is no need for preferred values to be elicited from the user. Instead, the preferred value of a LIB attribute (e.g., price) is assumed to be the *lowest* value in the case base, and the preferred value of a MIB attribute (e.g., speed) is assumed to be the *highest* value in the case base. This is the approach we use in progressive critiquing. One advantage is that assumed preferences for MIB and LIB attributes can be used to guide the retrieval of an initially recommended case if the user declines to enter an initial query. Another advantage is that no updating of the user's preferences is needed in response to *more* critiques on MIB or *less* critiques on LIB attributes. In progressive critiquing, only the user's *constraints* are updated in response to such critiques.

3.2 User Preferences and Constraints

In progressive critiquing, the system's understanding of the user's preferences and constraints is based on her initial query, if any, and critiques of previously recommended cases. An initial query in *Tweak* may include upper limits for LIB attributes (e.g., *price* ≤ 700), lower limits for MIB attributes (e.g., *memory* ≥ 128), and ideal values for NIB or nominal attributes (e.g., *screen* = 17, *make* = Dell). An ideal value for a NIB or nominal attribute is treated as both a preference and a constraint.

Figure 3 shows the currently recommended case in a progressive critiquing session based on the personal computer (PC) case base [14] in which the initial query is *make* = Dell, *price* ≤ 1000 and the user's critiques of previously recommended cases are *type* = laptop and *more screen*. Also shown are the current models of the user's preferences and constraints on which *Tweak*'s recommendation is based. As indicated by the entries (Y or N) to the right of the current constraints, the recommended case satisfies all the current constraints except *type* = laptop.

Recommended Case	Current Constraints		Preferences	
make = Dell	make = Dell	Y	make = Dell	E
price = 719	price ≤ 1000	Y	price = 658	A
type = desktop	type = laptop	N	type = laptop	E
screen = 15	screen > 12	Y	screen = 13.3	P
speed = 1.6			speed = 2.2	A
memory = 512			memory = 2000	A
hard disk = 20			hard disk = 120	A
chip = Intel Pentium				

Figure 3. Currently recommended case in a progressive critiquing session and models of the user's constraints and preferences on which the system's recommendation is based

In progressive critiquing, the assessment of a retrieved case's similarity takes account of *explicit* preferences (E), if any, in the initial query and replacement critiques, *assumed* preferences for MIB and LIB attributes (A), and preferences *predicted* from critiques on NIB attributes (P). Retrieval also takes account of preferences that are *implicit* in the user's request to see another case that is like a recommended case but satisfies her critique. For example, *Tweak*'s response to a *more speed* critique on the recommended case in Figure 3 would take account of the implicit preference *chip* = Intel Pentium. However, only assumed, explicit, and predicted preferences are represented in *Tweak*'s model of the user's preferences, and these are given priority over implicit preferences whenever there is a conflict.

Tweak's understanding of the user's preferences and constraints is continually revised in light of the user's critiques. For example, a replacement critique *a* = *v* on a nominal attribute *a* results in *a* = *v* replacing any existing constraint on the value of *a* and *a* = *v* replacing any existing preference with respect to *a*.

In contrast to replacement critiques (e.g., *type* = laptop), directional critiques provide only imprecise information about the user's preferences and constraints. For example, a *more screen* critique does not determine precisely the preferred screen size, or the minimum screen size that the user may be prepared to accept. In the case of a NIB attribute (e.g., *screen*), we use the knowledge stored in cases to adapt the system's understanding of the user's preferences in response to *more* and *less* critiques. In response to a *more* critique on a NIB attribute, the preferred value — if not already consistent with the critique — is predicted to be the *successor* of the value in the critiqued case; that is, the next highest value in the case base. Likewise in response to a *less* critique on a NIB attribute, the preferred value is predicted to be the *predecessor* of the value in the critiqued case.

As the preferred value of a MIB attribute is assumed to be the highest value in the case base, no updating of the user's preferences is required in response to a *more* critique on a MIB attribute. Similarly, no updating of the user's preferences is required in response to a *less* critique on a LIB attribute.

In response to a *more* critique on a MIB or NIB attribute a, the constraint $a > v_1$ replaces any existing constraint of the form $a > v_2$, where v_1 is the value of a in the critiqued case. A similar process is used to update the user's constraints in response to a *less* critique on a LIB or NIB attribute.

3.3 Explanation of Progression Failures

As mentioned in Section 2.2, previously recommended cases are currently eliminated in progressive critiquing. The case retrieved in response to a critique is the most similar of the remaining cases, if any, that satisfies all the current constraints, including the current critique. If no such case exists, the case retrieved is the most similar case that satisfies the current critique. If there is a tie between equally similar cases, the retrieved case is randomly selected from these cases.

If no remaining case satisfies all the current constraints, this is recognized as a progression failure and triggers an explanation of why the system is recommending a case that fails to satisfy all the user's constraints. In Figure 3, for example, the case recommended in response to the user's *more screen* critique satisfies all the current constraints except *type* = laptop. A progression failure has therefore occurred, and this triggers the explanation:

> *There is no remaining case with make = Dell, price ≤ 1000, type = laptop, and screen > 12, but you may wish to consider Case 35, which satisfies all of these constraints except type = laptop.*

As shown by our empirical results in Section 4, such explanations often enable the non-existence of an acceptable case to be recognized at an early stage of the recommendation dialogue. In the above example, it should be clear to the user that unless she is willing to compromise on make, price, type, or screen size, then there is no point in continuing the recommendation dialogue.

Dynamic generation of the available critiques in each recommendation cycle, as described in Section 3.1, provides another way for users to recognize the non-existence of an acceptable case. For example, if the price of a recommended case is more than the user is prepared to pay, and a *less price* critique is not available, it should be clear to the user that none of the remaining cases meet her requirements.

Only some of the user's previous critiques are maintained as constraints in progressive critiquing. For LIB, MIB, and nominal attributes, only the constraint from the most recent critique on the attribute is maintained. For a NIB attribute, at most two constraints (e.g., *screen* > 12 and *screen* < 15) from the most recent *more* and *less* critiques on the attribute are maintained. Limiting the number of current constraints has the advantage of simplifying explanations of local critiquing failures, thus making it easier to recognize the non-existence of an acceptable case.

3.4 Implicit Relaxation of Constraints

A mechanism for *recovering* from progression failures is needed to ensure that progress can again be made following explanation of the failure and recommendation of a case that satisfies the current critique. In the absence of such a recovery mechanism, critiquing an attribute not mentioned in a previous critique or in the initial query can only result in another progression failure.

Our solution to this problem, which we refer to as *implicit relaxation*, is based on the idea that by critiquing a case, the user implicitly accepts any compromises it involves. Thus when the user critiques a recommended case, any current constraints that are not satisfied by the recommended case are relaxed (i.e., removed from the list of current constraints). For example, by critiquing the recommended case in Figure 3 on *speed* or *hard disk* the user is deemed to have accepted the compromise on *type*. However, the system's understanding of the user's *preference* (i.e., *type* = laptop) is unaffected by relaxation of the corresponding constraint.

Of course, the user may not be prepared to compromise on *type*. If so, she can ensure that the constraint *type* = laptop remains in force by critiquing the recommended case on *type*.

3.5 Progressive Critiquing in Tweak

The example case base that we use to demonstrate the recommendation process in *Tweak* is McCarthy *et al.*'s [7] digital camera case base, which contains the descriptions of 210 cameras. Attributes in the case base and weights assigned to them in *Tweak* are make (1), price (8), format (1), resolution (1), optical zoom (1), digital zoom (1), weight in grams (1), storage type (1), and memory (1). Resolution, optical zoom, digital zoom, and memory are treated as MIB attributes in *Tweak*, and price and weight as LIB attributes. Make, format, and storage type are treated as nominal attributes. Though also available in the case base as part of a camera's description, the model identifier plays no part in the recommendation process.

The example dialogue in Figure 4 shows how explanatory feedback provided by *Tweak* may enable the user to recognize early in a recommendation dialogue that none of the available cases are acceptable. In the example dialogue, the user is looking for a compact *Pentax* camera with a resolution of at least 5 mega-pixels and is prepared to pay up to 400 euro. She would also prefer a lightweight camera with an optical zoom of at least 4, but is prepared to compromise on these features. Retrieval of Case 188 as the initially recommended case is based on the user's initial query (*make* = Pentax) and assumed preferences with respect to price, resolution, optical zoom, digital zoom, weight, and memory.

Tweak:	Please enter your query:
User:	make = Pentax
Tweak:	The following case is recommended:
	Case 188: Pentax, Optio 450, 359, compact, 3.9, 4.9, 4, 250, SC, 16
User:	**more** resolution
Tweak:	The following case is recommended:
	Case 186: Pentax, Optio 550, 447, compact, 5, 4.9, 4, 250, SC, 16
User:	**less** price
Tweak:	The following case is recommended:
	Case 182: Pentax, Optio S4, 352, ultra compact, 4, 3, 4, 115, IMSC, 11
User:	**more** resolution
Tweak:	There is no case with:

make = Pentax
price < 447
resolution > 4

but you might like to consider Case 149:

Case 149: Konica Minolta, KD-500 Zoom, 329, ultra compact, 5, 3, 4, 235, IMSC, 2

Figure 4. Example dialogue in *Tweak* showing how explanatory feedback may enable the user to recognize that none of the available cases are acceptable

On learning that there is no Pentax camera costing less than 447 euro with a resolution of more than 4 mega-pixels, it should be clear to the user that none of the available cameras meet her requirements and that there is no point in continuing the dialogue. In this example, the non-existence of an acceptable case is recognizable after only three critiques, with no need for the user to critique on format, optical zoom or weight.

4 Empirical Results

Progressive critiquing uniquely combines the use of explanatory feedback to help users recognize the non-existence of an acceptable product with a mechanism for recovering from progression failures based on implicit relaxation of constraints. In the absence of any comparable approach, our evaluation of progressive critiquing focuses on its performance in conditions which, by design, are least favorable to the critiquing process:

- None of the available cases may be acceptable to the user
- An initial query is not provided by the user
- The initially recommended case is the one that is *least* similar to the left-out case from which the simulated user's requirements are generated

- The target case, if any, is unknown to the simulated user

Performance measures of interest include the average length of critiquing dialogues required to reach a feasible case — if one exists — and to recognize the non-existence of a feasible case if no such case exists. Aiming to identify conditions in which progressive critiquing provides most benefits, we also examine the effects of the user's critiquing choices on the effectiveness of critiquing. For example, our expectation is that critiquing performance is likely to be adversely affected if priority is not given to attributes that fail to satisfy hard constraints. We also expect critiquing performance to degrade if the user *over-critiques* attributes that already satisfy her constraints.

Our experiments are based on the personal computer (PC) case base [14], which includes attributes of all the types discussed in Section 3. The attributes and weights assigned to them in our experiments are: make (1), chip (1), speed (1), screen size (1), type (1), memory (1), drive (1), and price (7). Speed, memory, and drive are treated as MIB attributes, price as a LIB attribute, and screen size as a NIB attribute. Make, type, and chip are treated as nominal attributes.

We use a leave-one-out cross validation approach in which each of the 120 cases in the PC case base is temporarily removed and used to represent the requirements of a simulated user interacting with *Tweak*. The value of a LIB attribute in a left-out case is treated as an upper limit (e.g., *price* ≤ 700), the value of a MIB attribute as a lower limit (e.g., *speed* ≥ 1.3), and the value of a nominal or NIB attribute (e.g., *make* = Dell, *screen* = 14) as both a constraint and a preferred value. We randomly select 4 of the 8 constraints generated from a left-out case as the simulated user's *hard* constraints. This step is repeated five times for each left-out case, giving a total of 600 simulated dialogues.

Before an initially recommended case is presented to the simulated user by *Tweak*, we use the hard constraints generated from the left-out case to determine if one or more cases may be acceptable to the simulated user. If so, we select one of them as a *target* case. In the unlikely event that a target case cannot be uniquely identified, there may be more than one target case.

If there is an *exactly matching* case (i.e., one that satisfies all the simulated user's constraints), then the target case is the exactly matching case that is most similar to the left-out case. If there is a *feasible* case (i.e., one that matches all the user's hard constraints) but no exactly matching case, then the target case is the feasible case that is most similar to the left-out case. If no feasible case exists, then there is *no* target case.

The case that is least similar to the left-out case is now presented to the simulated user as the initially recommended case. The critiquing dialogue that follows continues until a target case is recommended or the non-existence of a feasible case is recognized by the simulated user.

As we have shown in Section 3, the non-existence of a feasible case among the remaining cases is recognizable from *Tweak*'s explanation of a progression failure if the unsatisfied set of constraints is a *subset* of the user's hard constraints, or *weaker* than the user's hard constraints. It is also recognizable if the critiques from which the user is invited to select do not include a *less* critique on a LIB attribute that fails to satisfy a hard constraint, a *more* critique on a MIB attribute that fails to satisfy a hard constraint, or a more/less critique on a NIB attribute whose value is less/more than the only value the user is prepared to accept.

We repeat the above experiment with simulated users in each of the following categories:

Class 1. Choose only critiques on attributes that fail to satisfy their constraints, and give priority to attributes that fail to satisfy their hard constraints

Class 2. Choose only critiques on attributes that fail to satisfy their constraints

Class 3. Choose only critiques on attributes that fail to satisfy their constraints or LIB/MIB attributes that already satisfy their constraints

Thus Class 3 differs from Class 2 only in that Class 3 users may *over-critique* LIB or MIB attributes that already satisfy their constraints.

For simulated users in Classes 1-3, Figure 5 shows the average lengths of critiquing dialogues required to reach a feasible case, reach a target case, and recognize the non-existence of a feasible case. The target case was unique in almost 99% of dialogues in which there was a feasible case, and the number of target cases was never more than 2. There was no feasible case — and therefore no target case — in 22% of all dialogues.

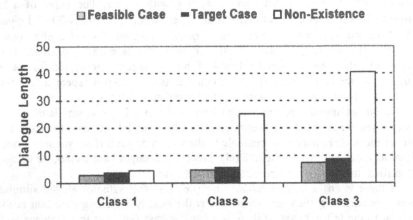

Figure 5. Average lengths of progressive critiquing dialogues on the PC case base for simulated users in Classes 1-3

A striking feature of the results is that average dialogue lengths in Class 1 are very small. Only 3 critiques were required on average to reach a feasible case, 3.8 to reach a target case, and 4.6 to recognize the non-existence of a feasible case.

In Class 2, not giving priority to attributes that fail to satisfy hard constraints resulted in minor increases (less than 2) in the average numbers of critiques required to reach a feasible case and to reach a target case. However, it had a major impact on the average number of critiques required to recognize the non-existence of a feasible case (25.2 compared to 4.6 for Class 1). It can be seen from the results for Classes 2 and 3 that over-critiquing also had a major impact on this aspect of critiquing performance, with the average number of critiques required to recognize the non-existence of a feasible case increasing from 25.2 to 40.5. Once again, increases in the average numbers of critiques required to reach a feasible case and to reach a target case were relatively minor.

These findings support our hypothesis that the effectiveness of critiquing is adversely affected by not giving priority to critiques on attributes that fail to satisfy hard constraints and over critiquing attributes whose values are acceptable. The critiquing choices of Class 2 and Class 3 users had most impact on their ability to recognize the non-existence of an acceptable case even with the benefit of the explanatory feedback provided in progressive critiquing. This is therefore an aspect of critiquing performance that might be improved by providing users with guidelines for more effective critiquing.

That progressive critiquing is most effective when priority is given to critiques on attributes that fail to satisfy hard constraints is clear from the average dialogue lengths for Class 1 users in Figure 5. As shown in Figure 6, the number of critiques required to recognize the non-existence of a feasible case ranged from 2 to 10. It was more than 6 in less than 10% of dialogues.

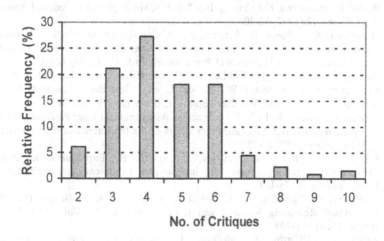

Figure 6. Numbers of critiques required for Class 1 users to recognize the non-existence of a feasible case in the PC case base

In Class 1 dialogues in which a feasible case did exist, the number of critiques required to reach a feasible case ranged from 1 to 10, and was more than 5 in less than 10% of such dialogues.

5 Conclusions

Progressive critiquing is a new approach to critiquing in which explanations of *progression failures* alert users to the possibility that none of the available products may be acceptable. An important benefit is that the non-existence of an acceptable product can often be recognized at an early stage of a critiquing dialogue. As also shown by our empirical results, progressive critiquing is very quick to locate a product that satisfies all the user's hard constraints if one exists, particularly when the user gives priority to critiques on attributes that fail to satisfy her hard constraints. However, an important issue highlighted by our results is that the ability to recognize the non-existence of an acceptable product — and other aspects of critiquing performance — may depend as much on the user's critiquing choices as on the system's responses to her critiques. It therefore seems likely that some users may benefit from guidelines for more effective critiquing.

References

1. Bridge, D., Ferguson, A.: An Expressive Query Language for Product Recommender Systems. Artificial Intelligence Review **18** (2002) 269-307
2. Burke, R.: Interactive Critiquing for Catalog Navigation in E-Commerce. Artificial Intelligence Review, **18** (2002) 245-267
3. Burke, R., Hammond, K.J., Young, B.: The FindMe Approach to Assisted Browsing. IEEE Expert **12** (1997) 32-40
4. Hammond, K.J., Burke, R., Schmitt, K.: A Case-Based Approach to Knowledge Navigation. In: Leake, D.B. (ed.) Case-Based Reasoning: Experiences, Lessons & Future Directions. AAAI Press/MIT Press, Menlo Park, CA (1996) 125-136
5. Hurley, G., Wilson, D.C.: DubLet: An Online CBR System for Rental Property Recommendation. In: Aha, D.W., Watson, I. (eds.) Case-Based Reasoning Research and Development. LNAI, Vol. 2080. Springer, Berlin (2001) 660-674
6. Linden, G., Hanks, S., Lesh, N.: Interactive Assessment of User Preference Models: The Automated Travel Assistant. Proceedings of the 6th International Conference on User Modeling (1997) 67-78
7. McCarthy, K., Reilly, J., McGinty, L., Smyth, B.: Experiments in Dynamic Critiquing. Proceedings of the 10th International Conference on Intelligent User Interfaces (2005) 175-182
8. McSherry, D.: Similarity and Compromise. In: Ashley, K.D., Bridge, D.G. (eds.) Case-Based Reasoning Research and Development. LNAI, Vol. 2689. Springer, Berlin (2003) 291-305
9. Reilly, J., McCarthy, K., McGinty, L., Smyth, B.: Incremental Critiquing. Knowledge-Based Systems **18** (2005) 143-151
10. Salamó, M., Reilly, J., McGinty, L., Smyth, B.: Improving Incremental Critiquing. Proceedings of the 16th Irish Conference on Artificial Intelligence and Cognitive Science (2005) 379-388
11. Shimazu, H.: ExpertClerk: A Conversational Case-Based Reasoning Tool for Developing Salesclerk Agents in E-Commerce Webshops. Artificial Intelligence Review **18** (2002) 223-244
12. McSherry, D.: On the Role of Default Preferences in Compromise-Driven Retrieval. Proceedings of the 10th UK Workshop on Case-Based Reasoning (2005) 11-19
13. McSherry, D.: Incremental Nearest Neighbour with Default Preferences. Proceedings of the 16th Irish Conference on Artificial Intelligence and Cognitive Science (2005) 9-18
14. McGinty, L., Smyth, B.: Comparison-Based Recommendation. In: Craw, S., Preece, A. (eds.) Advances in Case-Based Reasoning. LNAI, Vol. 2416. Springer, Berlin (2002) 575-589

LSA-based Landscape Analysis for Multicast Routing

Mohammed S. Zahrani
University of Hertfordshire
School of Computer Science
Hatfield, AL10 9AB, UK

Martin J. Loomes
Middlesex University
School of Computing Science
London NW4 4BT, UK

James A. Malcolm
University of Hertfordshire
School of Computer Science
Hatfield, AL10 9AB, UK

Andreas A. Albrecht
School of Computer Science
University of Hertfordshire
Hatfield, Herts AL10 9AB, UK

Abstract

Over the past few years, several local search algorithms have been proposed for various problems related to multicast routing in the off-line mode. We describe a population-based search algorithm for cost minimization of multicast routing. The algorithm utilizes the partially mixed crossover operation (PMX) under the elitist model: for each element of the current population, the local search is based upon the results of a landscape analysis that is executed only once in a pre-processing step; the best solution found so far is always part of the population. The aim of the landscape analysis is to estimate the depth of the deepest local minima in the landscape generated by the routing tasks and the objective function. The local search then performs alternating sequences of descending and ascending steps for each individual of the population, where the length of a sequence with uniform direction is controlled by the estimated value of the maximum depth of local minima. We present results from computational experiments on two different routing tasks, and we provide experimental evidence that our genetic local search procedure performs better than algorithms using either Simulated Annealing or PMX only.

1 Introduction

Multicast routing has become an important topic in combinatorial optimisation. A recent overview on multicast routing and associated optimisation algorithms has been presented by Oliveira and Pardalos [18]. The focus of this overview, as in most papers on multicast routing, is on on-line algorithms. An early summary of problems and technical solutions related to multicast communication was given by Diot et al. [5]. Great effort has been undertaken to incorporate quality of service (QoS) into ATM and IP networks [4, 21, 24]. Many multicast applications, such as video conferencing, distance-learning, and multimedia broadcasting are QoS-sensitive in nature and thus they will benefit from the QoS support of the underlying networks.

Designing multicast routing algorithms is a complex and challenging task. Among the various issues involved are the design of optimal routes taking into consideration different cost functions, the minimisation of network load and the avoidance of loops and traffic congestion, and the provision of basic support for reliable transmission. The problem of minimizing the tree costs of single requests under the constraint that all path capacities are within a user-specified capacity bound, i.e. the requests are executed simultaneously, is referred to as the capacity constrained multicast routing problem (CCMRP) [5, 18].

The CCMRP can be formalised as a constrained Steiner tree problem, which is known to be NP-complete [14]. We note that in applications like video conferencing, multimedia broadcasting, and distance-learning the routing procedure is updated only from time to time, e.g. when new customers register to use one of the services. In such cases, off-line routing algorithms are an appropriate way to solve the routing problem. Since we are dealing with an NP-complete problem, local search methods are a natural choice to approach the problem. For an overview on search methods, in particular, genetic algorithms applied to various problem settings in multicast routing, we refer the reader to [13]; cf. p.20–21 therein.

The genetic algorithms proposed in [7, 25] assume that several messages have to be transferred from several sources to multiple destinations each, which has to be executed simultaneously without any order or priority for certain messages. The genetic algorithm uses a population of chromosomes, where each chromosome is a permutation of the numbers that are assigned to the requests. The search-based methods from [7, 25] are, in part, incorporated into our approach and are discussed in more detail in Section 4.1.

We propose a genetic local search algorithm to solve multicast routing problems. The general structure of the algorithm follows the approach presented by Merz and Freisleben [17]: a classical local search is executed for each individual of a population and combined with a crossover operation, where a key element constitutes a thorough analysis of the underlying landscape. In our heuristic, the local search executes descending steps in the landscape until a potential local minimum is reached; then it performs ascending steps only, where the maximum number of steps is guided by a parameter that is derived from the landscape analysis; then it switches again to descending steps and repeats the procedure. At intermediate steps, the partially mixed crossover operation is applied.

The landscape analysis is performed in a pre-processing step and utilizes logarithmic simulated annealing (LSA). The annealing procedure allows us to estimate the depth of the deepest local minima. As widely accepted, simulated annealing is an appropriate tool to tackle NP-hard problems from Combinatorial Optimisation [1]. Recently, simulated annealing algorithms, in particular variants based on inhomogeneous Markov chains (a special case is logarithmic simulated annealing), have been used to investigate problems from Computational Biology in the context of landscape analysis; cf. [23] and the literature therein. Another motivation for choosing simulated annealing is based upon recent advances in genetic algorithms research [22]: in order to ensure the convergence of genetic algorithms to optimum solutions, simulated annealing-based selection has to be employed in one or another way (see Section 10 in [22] for a summary of results).

We performed computational experiments on two instances of the OR library [2] (steinb10 and steinb18). The results provide evidence that our genetic local search heuristic performs better than "pure" logarithmic simulated annealing, and for most of the instances, LSA produces better results than the use of PMX crossover only.

2   Basic Definitions

Communication networks consist of nodes connected through links. The nodes are the originators and receivers of information, while the links serve as the transport between nodes. Nodes can be either endpoint nodes or intermediary nodes. Both nodes and links have a certain capacity of information flow they can handle. The typical approach to solve the point-to-multipoint routing problem is through the separation of the problem into several point-to-point routing problems, according to the number of destination points. This simple method is very inefficient. The same information might flow on the same link many times. It creates unnecessary traffic on the link, which could be avoided. Therefore, we consider the simultaneous execution of requests, where messages from a single source are combined to form a single request.

Given a graph $G = (V, E)$ that represents a communication network with node set V and edges E, we define two non-negative weight functions $Co :$ $E \to \Re$ and $Ca : E \to \Re$, where Co is the cost function and Ca is the capacity function on E, respectively.

Each of the point-to-multipoint requests has a source node $s \in V$ and a set of destination nodes $D \subseteq V$. We define a multicast request R by setting

$$
\begin{aligned}
R &= [v_s \Rightarrow (v_1, v_2, ..., v_n); C], \quad \text{where} \\
v_s &= \text{the source node of } R; \\
D &= \{v_1, ..., v_n\} = \text{the destination nodes}; \\
C &= \text{the capacity required by each } v_s \Rightarrow v_i.
\end{aligned}
\tag{1}
$$

The multicast problem P is then defined by

$$
\mathsf{P} = [G; Co; Ca; R_1, ..., R_n].
\tag{2}
$$

Usually, multicast routing algorithms are based on the following assumptions [5, 7, 18, 25]: each R from P is routed separately by a minimum Steiner tree with root v_s and leaves $D(R)$. The cost of the Steiner tree is the sum $\sum_e Co(e)$ of the costs of the edges in the tree, while the capacity $Ca(e)$ on each edge on a path from v_s to each $v_i \in D$ obeys $Ca(e) \geq C(R)$, see (1).

However, to minimize $\sum_e Co(e)$ for given G, v_s, D, Co, and Ca is NP-complete [14]. Numerous heuristics have been devised to find good approximations of minimum solutions efficiently [10, 16, 19]. Since in our approach single requests may have to be rerouted many times in order to satisfy capacity constraints, we employ the simple but efficient KMB algorithm [16]. It has been estimated that the cost of a tree generated by the KMB algorithm averages 5% more than the cost of a Steiner minimal tree [6]. Of course, the KMB algorithm we are using can be substituted by any efficient Steiner tree algorithm.

3 LSA Pre-processing

Simulated annealing was introduced as an optimisation tool independently in [15] and [3]; see also [1]. The underlying algorithm acts within a configuration space in accordance with a specific neighbourhood structure, where the transition steps are controlled by the objective function.

3.1 Simulated annealing in the multicast routing context

The configuration space consists of all feasible solutions for a given multicast problem $P = [G; Co; Ca; R_1, ..., R_n]$, i.e. the capacity conditions according to (1) are not violated. We denote the configuration space by

$$M = \{S | S = [R_{i_1}, ..., R_{i_n}]; R_{i_1}, ..., R_{i_n} \text{ are SMT-routed}\}. \tag{3}$$

Here, SMT-routed means that each R_{i_j} from the ordered sequence S is routed by the KMB algorithm [16] that approximates a Steiner minimal tree (SMT) in accordance with the capacity constraints and the given cost function.

By N_S we denote the neighbourhood of S, and $Z(S)$ denotes the underlying objective function; both are specified in Section 3.2. The neighbours N_S are all required to be feasible, and S itself is an element of N_S.

The probability of performing a transition from S to $S' \in N_S$ is defined by

$$\mathbf{Pr}\{S \to S'\} = \begin{cases} G[S, S'] \cdot A[S, S'], & \text{if } S' \neq S; \\ 1 - \sum_{H \neq S} G[S, H] \cdot A[S, H], & \text{otherwise,} \end{cases} \tag{4}$$

where G denotes the probability of generating a specific neighbour from N_S, and A is the probability of accepting the neighbour once it has been generated according to G. The generation probability is uniform and defined by

$$G[S, S'] := \begin{cases} \frac{1}{|N_S|}, & \text{if } S' \in N_S; \\ 0, & \text{otherwise.} \end{cases} \tag{5}$$

The "uniform" definition assumes that all potential neighbours are tested if they are feasible or not in order to determine N_S and $| N_S |$, which would require a large number of SMT calculations. In the actual implementation (see Section 3.5), a potential neighbour is chosen randomly and its feasibility is tested. If conflicts arise in simultaneous routing, a new potential neighbour is chosen; see Section 3.2.

The acceptance probabilities $A[S, S']$, $S' \in N_S$, are derived from the underlying analogy to thermodynamic systems:

$$A[S, S'] := \begin{cases} 1, & \text{if } Z(S') - Z(S) \leq 0, \\ e^{-(Z(S')-Z(S))/c}, & \text{otherwise,} \end{cases} \tag{6}$$

where c is a control parameter having the interpretation of a *temperature* in annealing procedures. The actual decision, whether or not S' should be accepted in case of $Z(S') > Z(S)$, is performed in the following way: S' is accepted, if

$$e^{-(Z(S') - Z(S))/c} \geq \rho, \tag{7}$$

where $\rho \in [0, 1]$ is produced by a random number generator. The value ρ is generated in each trial in case of $Z(S') > Z(S)$.

Let $\mathbf{a}_S(k)$ denote the probability of being in configuration $S \in \mathrm{M}$ after k steps according to (4),...,(7). The probability $\mathbf{a}_S(k)$ is given by

$$\mathbf{a}_S(k) := \sum_H \mathbf{a}_H(k-1) \cdot \mathbf{Pr}\{H \rightarrow S\}, \tag{8}$$

where $\mathbf{Pr}\{H \rightarrow S\}$ is from (4). The recursive application of (8) defines a Markov chain of probabilities $\mathbf{a}_S(k)$, where $S \in \mathrm{M}$ and $k = 1, 2, \ldots$. If the parameter $c = c(k)$ in (6) is a constant c, the chain is said to be a *homogeneous* Markov chain; otherwise, if $c(k)$ is lowered at each step, the sequence of probability vectors $\vec{\mathbf{a}}(k)$ is an *inhomogeneous* Markov chain.

We consider a special type of inhomogeneous Markov chains only. The motivation for this choice is based upon the convergence properties of the two types of Markov chains: Convergence propositions about homogeneous Markov chains rely on an infinite number of transitions at fixed "temperatures" c. The probability distribution approached in the limit is the Boltzmann distribution $e^{-Z(S)/c}/V$, where V is a normalisation value. If $c \rightarrow 0$, the Boltzmann distribution tends to the distribution over optimum configurations. In practice, however, it is infeasible to perform an infinite number of transitions at fixed temperatures. The convergence analysis of inhomogeneous Markov chains avoids the intermediate step, and in our approach the "temperature" $c(k)$ changes in accordance with

$$c(k) = \frac{\Gamma}{\ln(k + 2)}, \quad k = 0, 1, \ldots. \tag{9}$$

The choice of $c(k)$ is motivated by Hajek's theorem [9] on logarithmic cooling schedules. We denote by $F_{\min}$ the set of optimum solutions. Basically, Hajek's theorem states

Theorem 1 *Under some natural assumptions about the configuration space* F *and the neighbourhood* N_f, *the asymptotic convergence* $\sum_{f \in F_{\min}} \mathbf{a}_f(k) \xrightarrow[k \rightarrow \infty]{} 1$ *of logarithmic simulated annealing is guaranteed if and only if* Γ *from (9) is lower bounded by the maximum value of the minimum escape height from local minima.*

Unfortunately, due to the complex nature of our configuration space M, we cannot decide the question whether or not Theorem 1 applies to M. However, logarithmic simulated annealing has proved to be an efficient method in similar settings.

3.2 Neighbourhood and objective function

There are numerous ways to define the neighbourhood relation; in the present study, we focus on one example only. Given $S \in M$ by $S = [R_{i_1}, ..., R_{i_n}]$, the neighbourhood N_S includes S itself and is defined by the following procedure:

> Two integers a and b, $1 \leq a < b \leq n$, are randomly chosen, and the order of all requests from number i_a to number i_b is reversed; a new potential configuration S' is generated.

> The potential configuration S' is validated for feasibility, i.e. we try to simultaneously schedule all the requests from R_{i_b} upwards. If a conflict occurs, a new pair (a, b) is generated.

> If S' indeed belongs to M, the objective function $Z(S)$ is calculated.

The objective function is chosen as in [7, 25] and represents a combined measure of transmission costs and capacity constraints: let $T(R)$ denote the set of edges of the tree associated with the request R from configuration $S \in M$. We first define

$$W(R) := C \cdot \sum_{e \in T(R)} Co(e), \tag{10}$$

where Co is from (2) and C the capacity request of R; see (1). The value of the objective function $Z(S)$, $S \in M$, is then simply given by

$$Z(S) := \sum_{R \text{ from } S} W(R). \tag{11}$$

3.3 Initial feasible solutions

We randomly select an order $(i_1, i_2, ..., i_n)$ of $i_j \in [1, ..., n]$. If the request R_{i_j} has been scheduled successfully by the KMB algorithm [16], $j \geq 1$, then the capacity function Ca is updated by

$$\forall e \, (e \in E \rightarrow Ca(e) := Ca(e) - C), \tag{12}$$

where $C = C(R_{i_j})$ is the capacity request of R_{i_j}. We then try to schedule request $R_{i_{j+1}}$ by the KMB algorithm. Before KMB is applied, all edges $E \in G$ with updated values $Ca(e) < C(R_{i_{j+1}})$ are removed from G, i.e. the underlying network is modified in accordance with $[R_{i_1}, ..., R_{i_j}]$. If capacity constraints are violated, i.e. $R_{i_{j+1}}$ cannot be scheduled by KMB, a new random order $(i'_1, i'_2, ..., i'_n)$ is generated, and we start again with R_{i_1}. After 100 unsuccessful attempts, the search for a feasible solution of $P = [G; Co; Ca; R_1, ..., R_n]$ is terminated.

3.4 Landscape analysis

Merz and Freisleben [17] present different methods of landscape analysis as part of genetic local search methods. We introduce a new method that basically estimates Γ in (9), i.e. provides an upper bound for the maximum escape height from local minima.

To estimate Γ, we first have to decide about the number of transitions T after starting with a solution S_0 generated by the procedure described in Section 3.3. We decided to choose T in the region of $T \approx 10^4, ..., 2 \cdot 10^4$, which has been confirmed by our computational experiments.

For a pre-defined number of transitions T, we employ the following procedure in order to find an estimation of Γ: first, the procedure tries to estimate the intermediate increase G_{est} of the objective function between two successive improvements of the best value $Z(S)$ found so far. Then, we establish a conjecture about Γ_{est} that is based on G_{est}, and subsequent computational experiments are executed for different settings of Γ in (9); see Section 3.5. To find at first a value for G_{est}, we proceed as follows:

Two initial solutions S_0^1 and S_0^2 are generated by the procedure from Section 3.3, and $G_{est} := |Z(S_0^1) - Z(S_0^2)|$ is the initial estimation, where we assume $Z(S_0^1) \neq Z(S_0^2)$.

We set $S_{best} := S_0^i$, where $Z(S_0^i)$ is the smaller value out of $\{Z(S_0^1), Z(S_0^2)\}$, $i \in \{1, 2\}$. The procedure from Section 3.1 is started with S_{best} and G_{est} in (9); an auxiliary parameter $\Delta_0 := 0$ is initialized.

At each step $k \leq T$, if $Z(S_k) > Z(S_{k-1})$ and $Z(S_{best}) + \Delta_s < Z(S_k)$, we update Δ_s by $\Delta_s := Z(S_k) - Z(S_{best})$, $0 \leq s \leq k$.

At each step $k \leq T$, if $Z(S_k) < Z(S_{k-1})$, $Z(S_k)$ is compared to $Z(S_{best})$: if $Z(S_k) < Z(S_{best})$, then we set $S_{best} := S_k$, we update $G_{est} := \max\{\Delta_s, G_{est}\}$, and we initialize again $\Delta_{s+1} := 0$.

After step $k = T$, we set $G_{est} := \max\{\Delta_{s(T)}, G_{est}\}$, where $\Delta_{s(T)}$ is the latest update of Δ.

Thus, every time the value $Z(S_{best})$ is updated, i.e. when a potential local minimum has been reached, a new estimation of G_{est} is started. If the initial value $G_{est} := |Z(S_0^1) - Z(S_0^2)|$ appears to be too small, the initial estimation can be chosen in the region of $c \cdot |Z(S_0^1) - Z(S_0^2)|$, where $c \approx 3, ..., 5$.

We recall that Γ itself is related to the maximum value of the minimum escape height from local minima; cf. Theorem 1. It is unlikely that G_{est} is close to the minimum escape height, and therefore further experiments are required to establish a relationship between Γ and G_{est}. On the other hand, G_{est} provides some information about the structure of the underlying landscape. Thus, G_{est} together with different settings for Γ in (9) are used to find an estimation Γ_{est}.

3.5 Computational experiments for LSA pre-processing

The algorithm described in Section 3.1 until Section 3.4 has been implemented in Java. Particular attention has been paid to the implementation of the KMB algorithm, which uses Dijkstra's shortest path algorithm and Kruskal's minimal spanning tree algorithm. The experiments were executed on a 2 GHz Pentium4 Processor with 512 MB RAM.

Table 1: Set of single requests for steinb10.

R-No.	v_s	Destination Node(s)	Capacity
1	36	7, 23, 25, 40	3
2	17	15, 30, 31, 40, 41, 46	2
3	48	36, 58	8
4	41	13, 22, 27, 35, 50	2
5	2	6, 14, 18, 23, 27, 33, 47, 49	4
6	13	28	7
7	50	5, 12, 28, 31, 44, 45	2
8	24	20, 29, 30	3
9	52	9, 13, 22, 55	2
10	53	13, 14, 28, 41, 52, 55	1
11	10	5, 20, 31, 40	3
12	66	18, 20, 22, 23	2
13	14	6, 16, 36	4
14	61	15, 20, 33, 38	6
15	55	4, 21, 41	5
16	14	9, 16, 31, 43, 44	3
17	67	23, 29	6
18	9	4, 6, 7, 30, 31, 35	2
19	69	10, 40, 54	2
20	75	33, 57	7

The underlying graphs are the instances no. steinb10 and steinb18 from the OR library [2]. The graphs have $75 - 100$ nodes and $150 - 200$ edges. Each edge was randomly assigned a cost value $Co(e) \in \{1, 2, ..., 10\}$; the capacity of edges was set by $Ca(e) = 12$.

Table 2: Z_{best} for different Γ (steinb10).

P_i	G_0	$T = 2 \cdot 10^4$			
No.	values	$G_0/8$	$G_0/16$	$G_0/20$	$G_0/32$
15	156	2086	2080	2080	2080
16	156	2251	2238	2238	2238
17	156	2320	2314	2314	2314
18	178	2468	2448	2442	2442
19	190	2524	2520	2516	2516
20	194	2636	2636	2632	2632

For each of the steinb-instances, 20 requests were generated randomly. For steinb10, the set of requests $\{R_1, ..., R_{20}\}$ is given in Table 1. From the 20 requests, we derived 6 multicast routing problems P_i, with P_{15} defined by $\{R_1, R_2, ..., R_{15}\}$ and P_{20} defined by $\{R_1, R_2, ..., R_{20}\}$. For each of the two values $T = 10^4, 2 \cdot 10^4$, the experiments were executed for 4 different values of Γ in (9), where $\Gamma := G_0/c$ for $c = 8, 16, 20, 32$, and $G_0 := |Z(S_0^1) - Z(S_0^2)|$.

In Table 2, we present a complete picture of runs for steinb10 and P_i, $i = 15, ..., 20$, with $T = 2 \cdot 10^4$ and $\Gamma := G_0/c$ for $c = 8, 16, 20, 32$. We note that for $G_0/20$ we obtain already the best values for $Z(S_{best})$.

Finally, we estimated Γ by the procedure described in Section 3.4, i.e. $\Gamma := G_{est} := \max\{\Delta_{s(T)}, G_{est}\}$, and the implementation was executed for both values of T and each P_i, $i = 15, ..., 20$; cf. Table 3. If we now compare the outcomes for $G_0/20$ in Table 2, where we obtain the best results for $Z(S_{best})$, and for G_{est} in Table 3, and if we take into account the relation between G_{est} and $G_0/20$, we conclude that

$$\Gamma_{est} \approx \frac{G_{est}}{10} \qquad (13)$$

is an appropriate choice for Γ in (9).

Table 3: Z_{best} for G_{est} and $\Gamma_{est} \approx G_{est}/10$ (steinb10).

| P_i | G_{est} | Z_{best} values for G_{est} | | Z_{best} values for Γ_{est} | |
No.	values	$T = 10^4$	$T = 2 \cdot 10^4$	$T = 10^4$	$T = 2 \cdot 10^4$
15	71	2163	2135	2113	2084
16	143	2314	2279	2249	2242
17	146	2391	2355	2331	2319
18	157	2531	2486	2462	2451
19	169	2573	2567	2540	2521
20	171	2721	2693	2648	2636

In Table 4 and Table 5 we present the corresponding results for steinb18. The results demonstrate that the estimation according to (13) is relatively independent of the underlying network structure.

Table 4: Z_{best} for different Γ (steinb18).

| P_i | G_0 | $T = 2 \cdot 10^4$ | | | |
No.	values	$G_0/8$	$G_0/16$	$G_0/20$	$G_0/32$
15	224	2179	2173	2170	2170
16	312	2370	2354	2327	2327
17	374	2578	2556	2528	2528
18	309	2671	2653	2637	2637
19	504	2791	2776	2732	2732
20	576	2993	2977	2958	2958

Table 5: Z_{best} for G_{est} and $\Gamma_{est} \approx G_{est}/10$ (steinb18).

| P_i | G_{est} | Z_{best} values for G_{est} | | Z_{best} values for Γ_{est} | |
No.	values	$T = 10^4$	$T = 2 \cdot 10^4$	$T = 10^4$	$T = 2 \cdot 10^4$
15	203	2279	2263	2245	2234
16	206	2423	2414	2407	2389
17	235	2638	2607	2586	2562
18	302	2724	2695	2686	2670
19	329	2817	2802	2791	2755
20	418	3112	3076	3048	3009

Thus, for a given multicast routing problem P with fixed edge capacities, as defined in (2), one can proceed as follows: firstly, the simulated annealing-based algorithm is executed for $\Gamma = G_0$ as described in Section 4, where G_{ext} is estimated according to the procedure from Section 3.4. Secondly, the calculations are repeated for $\Gamma = G_{ext}/10$, i.e. the total number of runs is reduced to two.

4   Genetic Local Search for Multicast Routing

Genetic algorithms (GA) are based on nature's selection process and the concept of survival of the fittest [8, 12]. GAs utilize random mutation, crossover and selection procedures to create better solutions from a random starting population. The population contains several initial solutions. Each solution is evaluated and its fitness is calculated. Then a new generation is created from the current population by crossover and mutation, where usually the size of the population is kept unchanged by applying the fitness function. Based on a convergence result by G. Rudolph [20], the best solution found so far is always maintained in the population, i.e. we follow the so-called elitist approach.

4.1   The partially mixed crossover (PMX) operation

Since we rely on similar notations and basically the same configuration space as in [25, 7], we explain in more detail their GA-based method. The key element of the method is the partially mixed crossover (PMX) operation. The algorithm starts with a randomly chosen population. To pairs of ividuals the partially mixed crossover is applied: Two strings are aligned and two crossing sites are picked uniformly at random along the strings. Let positions P_1 and P_2 define a matching section where the requests are exchanged position by position. This operation may generate duplicate occurrences of requests. Therefore, to the rest of the positions (outside the matching section), the following procedure is applied: if R has a duplicate R' in the same string, then the duplicate R' outside the matching region is substituted by the request R'' from the other offspring that was swapped with R.

Finally, the new population of the same fixed size is then generated by roulette wheel selection, where a sector of a "roulette wheel" is assigned to each offspring whose size is proportional to the fitness measure.

Zhu et al. [25] employ this operation in the following procedure: starting from a random initial population, where each individual has only $k < n$ requests from the same k-subset of n requests, the algorithm executes a fixed number of PMX operations. Then k is increased by one in order to check whether $(k+1)$ requests can be scheduled conflict-free, and the same fixed number of PMX operations is applied, until either $k = n$ or repeated attempts to schedule simultaneously $k + x < n$ requests are unsuccessful. The heuristic was evaluated for a population size is 100 and 100 crossover/selection steps for each $k \leq n = 20$. The $n = 20$ requests were defined in a network with 61 nodes and 133 edges. Each request R has at least eight destination nodes, and the capacity C was between five and nine; see [25]. Feasible solutions were found for $k \leq 18$.

4.2   Genetic local search

Recently, genetic local search has been investigated in the context of a variety of combinatorial optimisation problems; cf. [7, 17] and the literature therein. The basic idea is relatively simple: a (quasi-)deterministic local search with continuous improvements of the objective function is executed for all individuals of a population; if the individual runs are stuck in local minima, a crossover operation is applied in order to leave local minima. Here, quasi-deterministic means that the "downward" steps may have a random component, i.e. the neighbours with improved values of the objective function might be chosen randomly.

Figure 1: The genetic local search description.

Read all the network information; choose Γ.
Determine an initial feasible solution; see Section 3.3.
repeat

    Run M computations for a predefined number of steps K;
    Generate a neighbour S' from the current S; see Section 3.2;
    Find Steiner trees using KMB Algorithm for requests of S';
    if S' is feasible **then**
    determine $Z(S')$; see (10) and (11); **else** select new S'
    end if

        First mode: do only downward steps:
        if $Z(S') \leq Z(S)$ **then**
            S' is accepted and move to S';
            if local minimum is reached **then**
            goto second mode;
            else goto first mode **end if**
        else
            ignore S' and select a new neighbour;
            if no S' with $Z(S') < Z(S)$ has been found
            after L trials **then**
            treat S as a local minimum;
            goto second mode **end if**
        Second mode: do only upward steps:
        if $Z(Local\,minimum) + \Gamma$ is reached **then**
        switch to first mode **else goto** new round of second
        mode **end if**

until K steps done for all M computations.
for each pair of intermediate solutions
apply partially mixed crossover (PMX); **end for**
Restart again K steps with the M best solutions from PMX crossover, including elitist solution.
Repeat N times (thus, for a single strain of computations $K * N$ steps).
After N times K steps, take the best solution out of the M results.

In our heuristic, we employ such a "modest random" procedure. The parameters of our genetic local search procedure are:

1. A multicast routing problem P as defined in Eqn. (2), i.e. with n requests as defined in Eqn. (1);

2. Γ_{est} as defined in Section 3.4 and estimated in Eqn. (13);

3. The population size M;

4. The number K of maximum steps between two successive executions of the PMX operations;

5. The number N of maximum executions of the PMX operation applied to a single element of the population.

Due to the extremely large number of potential neighbours, we do need two more auxiliary parameters: if after $L = 50$ unsuccessful trials no neighbour with a better value of the objective function could be found, the current solution with objective value $Z(S)$ is declared to be a potential local minimum, and the procedure switches from downward steps to a sequence of upward steps. The upward steps are executed until either an S' with $Z(S') \geq Z(S) + \Gamma_{est}$ has been reached, or after $L = 50$ unsuccessful trials no neighbour with a larger value of the objective function could be found. In either of the two cases, the procedure switches back to downward steps. Thus, for each individual a random walk through the landscape is executed, and after K steps, the walk is interrupted by an PMX operation in order to generate a new population of the same size in the elitist model. The heuristic is described in Algorithm 1.

4.3 Computational experiments

The implementation decribed in Section 3.5 has been extended by the PMX crossover algorithm and modified with respect to to the quasi-deterministic local search presented in Algorithm 1. The multicast routing problems are the same as in Section 3.5, i.e. we analyze 6 routing tasks defined for two networks that are based on the instances no. steinb10 and steinb18 from the OR library [2]; cf. Table 1 for steinb10.

The parameters M, K, and N were chosen in such a way ($L = 50$ is fixed) that $M \cdot K \cdot N$ is in the region of T from our experiments with logarithmic simulated annealing; cf. Table 3 till Table 5 in Section 3.5. Thus, the particular parameter settings were $M = 7, 10$, $K = 70, 80$, and $N = 20, 25$.

Table 6: Z_{best} (GLS: elitist PMX, steinb10).

No. of P_i	$N = 20$, $K = 70$, $L = 50$, $M = 7$ GLS	$N = 25$, $K = 80$, $L = 50$, $M = 10$ GLS	PMX only
15	2082	2080	2086
16	2242	**2236**	2249
17	2316	2314	2340
18	2446	2442	2454
19	2520	2516	2528
20	2636	**2626**	2640

In Table 6 and Table 7, the numbers in bold face indicate improvements in comparison to the results obtained by logarithmic simulated annealing, as shown in Table 2 and Table 4. The genetic local search with LSA pre-processing performs better on larger multicast routing instances compared to applications of either LSA or PMX only, especially for a total number of operations $M \cdot K \cdot N$ that is equivalent to $T = 2 \cdot 10^4$. For most of the instances, LSA produces better results than the use of PMX crossover only. We note that omitting elitist solutions produces worse results compared to LSA-based search.

Table 7: Z_{best} (GLS: elitist PMX, steinb18).

Size of P_i	$N=20$, $K=70$, $L=50$, $M=7$	$N=25$, $K=80$, $L=50$, $M=10$	
	GLS	GLS	PMX only
15	2216	2204	2218
16	2379	2375	2385
17	2523	**2500**	2539
18	2646	**2634**	2653
19	2736	**2723**	2749
20	2967	**2947**	2993

5 Conclusion

We introduced a genetic local search heuristic that utilizes logarithmic simulated annealing in a pre-processing step for an analysis of the landscape generated by a multicast routing problem and the associated objective function. The genetic local search employs the partially mixed crossover (PMX) operation in-between sequences of downward and upward search steps, where the elitist model is applied. The PMX operation seems to be particularly suited to problems like multicast routing, since the outcome of the operation is always defined for two given parent routing orders. The computational experiments were executed on two synthetic networks that are based on the instances steinb10 and steinb18 from the OR library. The results show that the random walk that is guided by a parameter obtained from the landscape analysis together with the PMX operation provide better results on most routing instances compared to "pure" simulated annealing-based search as well as to applications of PMX crossover only. We note that to achieve these results the elitist approach was essential. Future research will concentrate on implementations in distributed systems, where the size of the population can be chosen much larger than in the present study.

References

[1] E. Aarts. *Local Search in Combinatorial Optimization*. Wiley & Sons, New York, 1998.

[2] J. Beasley. OR library: http://people.brunel.ac.uk/~mastjjb/jeb/info.html.

[3] V. Cerny. A thermodynamical approach to the travelling salesman problem: An efficient simulation algorithm. *Journal of Optimization Theory and Applications*, 45:41–51, 1985.

[4] D. Chakraborty, G. Chakraborty, and N. Shiratori. A dynamic multicast routing satisfying multiple QoS constraints. *International Journal of Network Management*, 13:321–335, 2003.

[5] C. Diot, W. Dabbous, and J. Crowcroft. Multipoint communication: A survey of protocols, functions, and mechanisms. *IEEE Journal on Selected Areas in Communication*, 15:277–290, 1997.

[6] M. Doar and I. Leslie. How bad is naïve multicast routing? In *Proc. of IEEE INFOCOM'93*, pp. 82–89, 1993.

[7] P. Galiasso and R. Wainwright. A hybrid genetic algorithm for the point to multipoint routing problem with single split paths. In *Proc. of ACM Symposium on Applied Computing (2001)*, pages 327–332, 2001.

[8] D. Goldberg. *Genetic Algorithms in Search.* Addison-Wesley Publishing Co., Reading, MA, 1989.

[9] B. Hajek. Cooling schedules for optimal annealing. *Mathematics of Operations Research*, 13:311–329, 1988.

[10] S. Hakimi. Steiner's problem in graphs and its implications. *Networks*, 1:113 133, 1971.

[11] T. Harrison and C. Williamson. A performance study of multicast routing algorithms for ATM networks. In *Proc. of 21st Annual IEEE Conference on Local Computer Networks*, p. 191, 1996.

[12] J. Holland. Genetic algorithms. *Scientific American*, 267(1):66 72, 1992.

[13] P. Kampstra. Evolutionary computing in telecommu- nications. In *BMI paper (Vrije U. Amsterdam)*, 2005.

[14] R. Karp. Reducibility among combinatorial problems. In *Complexity of Computer Computations*, pp. 85–103. Plenum Press, 1972.

[15] S. Kirkpatrick, C. G. Jr., and M. Vecchi. Optimization by simulated annealing. *Science*, 220:671–680, 1983.

[16] L. Kou, G. Markowsky, L. Berman. A fast algorithm for Steiner trees. *Acta Informatica*, 15:141–145, 1981.

[17] P. Merz and B. Freisleben. Fitness landscapes, meme- tic algorithms, and greedy operators for graph bipar- titioning. *Evolutionary Computation*, 8(1):61 81, 2000.

[18] C. Oliveira and P. Pardalos. A survey of combinatorial optimization problems in multicast routing. *Comput. & Operations Research*, 32:1953 1981, 2005.

[19] H. Prömel, A. Steger. A new approximation algorithm for the Steiner tree problem with performance ratio 5/3. *Journal of Algorithms*, 36:89 101, 2000.

[20] G. Rudolph. Convergence analysis of canonical genetic algorithms. *IEEE Transactions on Neural Networks*, 5:96 101, 1994.

[21] H. Salama, D. Reeves, and Y. Viniotis. Evaluation of multicast routing algorithms for real-time communi- cation on high-speed networks. *IEEE Journal on Selected Areas in Communications*, 13:332–345, 1997.

[22] L. Schmitt. Theory of genetic algorithms. *Theoretical Computer Science*, 259:1 61, 2001.

[23] M. Wolfinger, W. Svrcek-Seiler, C. Flamm, I. Hofacker, and P. Stadler. Exact folding dynamics of RNA secondary structures. *Journal of Physics A: Mathematics and General*, 37:4731–4741, 2004.

[24] C. Yeo, B. Lee, and M. Er. A framework for multicast video streaming over IP networks. *Journal of Network and Computer Applications*, 26:273 289, 2003.

[25] L. Zhu, R. Wainwright, and D. Schoenefeld. A genetic algorithm for the point to multipoint routing problem with varying number of requests. In *Proc. of IEEE International Conference on Evolutionary Computation*, pp. 171–176, 1998.

SESSION 3:

KNOWLEDGE REPRESENTATION
AND MANAGEMENT

Dependent Record Types for Dynamic Context Representation

Richard Dapoigny

LISTIC/ESIA, University of Savoie

P.O. Box 806 74016 Annecy (France)

Patrick Barlatier

LISTIC/ESIA, University of Savoie

P.O. Box 806 74016 Annecy (France)

Abstract

The context paradigm emerges from different areas of Artificial Intelligence (AI). However, while significative formalizations have been proposed, contexts are either mapped on independent micro-theories or considered as different concurrent viewpoints with mappings between contexts to export/import knowledge. These logical formalisms focus on the semantic level and do not take into account dynamic low-level information such as those available from sensors via physical variables. This information is a key element of contexts in pervasive computing environments. In this paper, we introduce a formal framework where the knowledge representation of context bridges the gap between semantic high-level and low-level knowledge. The logical reasoning based on intuitionistic type theory and the Curry-Howard isomorphism is able to incorporate expert knowledge as well as technical resources such as computing variable properties.

1 Introduction

There is a wide consensus in the AI literature agreing on the fact that most cognitive processes are contextual in the sense that they depend on their environment. After a summary on common concepts required for the design of well-formed context theories and a brief recall of major logic-based approaches for reasoning about context, a new proposal centered on Intuitionistic Type Theory is introduced.

There is no consensus on how the context must appear in logical formalisms. A well-designed context model must incorporate a number of basic constraints common to a wide spectrum of domains as highlighted in [24]. For a complete understanding of context, concepts such as location, identity and time must be addressed. Another important constraint concerns the distributed computation where an uniform context model must facilitate context sharing for an interoperability of applications. Obviously, this constraint reveals the ontological nature of the context model. The need for a standardization in context modelling has been pointed out by some authors[19] which have proposed several ontological implementations. In order to avoid failures in Knowledge-based systems, there must exist an explicit representation of context [23][8]. This representation must include objects of the domain together with relevant information for a given task to be achieved successfully. Alternatively, the context modelling ranges from a cognitive view where context models interactions and situations in a given world, to an engineering view where context reasons about a restricted space in order to solve a particular problem. Therefore, contexts must take in account different abstraction levels. It appears also that contexts must reconcile a dynamic part (during a real process) with a static part including the past (history) and background knowledge (ontological part). In order to use knowledge across contexts, a decontextualization is needed, in which a piece of knowledge is abstracted from context at a higher level covering the previous one [17]. Another central issue concerns the relation between contexts and their organization. For example, contexts may be encapsulated (a context may be part of another one), relations between contexts need to be specified and the local nature of rules must be explicit. Finally, context is the concept which gives meaning to data in a process transforming data into information. As a result, it appears that context modelling and reasoning requires the specification of a logical framework which incorporates multi-level representations (different abstraction levels), static and dynamic aspects and ontological abilities.

In logic-based systems, contextual information is introduced, updated and deleted in terms of facts or inferred from a set of rules. In the early ninety, the most significant general foundations for reasoning about contexts have explored logics rooted in the Situation Calculus. In [17], contexts are first class objects where the formula $ist(c, p)$ asserts that the formula p is true in the context c. Lifting rules are able to relate the truth in one context to the truth in another one. In addition, operations such as entering and leaving contexts were introduced. This work was the starting point for a formalization in propositional logic [5] extended to first-order languages [6]. Alternatively, a quite different approach has been explored in [13][12] where the formalization relies on two assumptions, namely the locality principle where reasoning happens inside a context and the principle of compatibility where relationships can occur between reasoning processes in different contexts. The approach known as Multicontext Systems considers a context as a subset of the complete state of an individual. More precisely, contexts are seen as partial theories which can interact with each other through bridge rules allowing to infer a conclusion in one context from a premise in another one. More recently, an approach of contexts exploring type-theoretic ideas has been proposed in [26][27]. Three primitive syntactic constructions are derived from type theory, namely identity, functional application and lambda abstraction. Built on a previous work on intensional logic [18], propositions are defined as sets of possible worlds and a context is identified with a set of propositions.

While the above approaches cover a wide spectrum of AI modelling, they show some difficulty to manage the intensional aspect where most of them present modality as a solution. Let us consider the domain of Engineering/Physical processes which cover a wide spectrum of real applications of AI including pervasive computing [24]. Starting from the observation that physical variables are a central element of process activity and building on recent works in Natural language Processing (NLP) [2][22][28], a context model based on intuitionistic type theory is proposed. Each physical variable is described by a record where the fields detail the physical context of that variable. As a result, it provides a simultaneous access to information about the physical process (semantic part) and to meta-information about the variable itself (syntactic part). These parts are defined in the framework of type theory through dependent records. The ability of dependent record types to provide a simple structure that can be reused to specify different kinds of structured semantic objects is very attractive. Unlike previous approaches in which contexts are defined within situations, we adopt a rather different perspective stating that pairs of contexts are the central element of the theory within an event-like formalism. This model bridges the gap between software engineering and classical real-world models by introducing syntactical and semantical parts attached to each variable. Record types and tokens are introduced to separate the specification of potential contexts (types) with its implementation. A further attraction is that this subdivision is also able to support ontological engineering for the specification (during the design step). The second section presents an account of contexts in Intuitionistic Type Theory with dependent record types, and introduces the physical contexts with their properties. In the third section, a formal topologies of contexts with specific connectors is detailed. The fourth section presents implementation features. Finally, in the last section, we discuss major benefits of the model and some future work in progress.

2 Contexts and dependent Record types

2.1 Dependent Record Types

The analysis of contextual reasoning requires sound and expressive formalisms. Widely used in Natural Language processing [2][22][28] and in Programming Languages [3][20] [10], Intuitionistic Type Theory [16] seems appropriate to support the linguistic nature of physical variables together with their functional framework. Moreover, it provides an intensional type theory for representing most of the features characterizing contexts in an AI perspective. The theory of types has been extended with dependent record types [1][15] which formalize a proof of a basic property of groups. A record corresponds to a number of kinds of entities. In order to be as general as possible, we must consider dependent record types.

Definition 1 *A dependent record type is a sequence of fields in which labels l_i correspond to certain types T_i, that is, each successive field can depend on the values of the preceding fields:*

$$< l_1 : T_1, l_2 : T_2(l_1) \ldots, l_n : T_n(l_1 \ldots l_{n-1}) > \qquad (1)$$

where the type T_i may depend on the preceding labels $l_1, ..., l_{i-1}$.

Notice first that a term like $l_2 : T_2(l_1)$, is in fact the abbreviation for

$$l_2 : \lambda r : [l_1 : T_1](T_2(r.l_1))$$

where r stands for a record r of type T_2. To avoid complex representation, we have adopted the simplified notation in (1). Notice also that this formalism which can be seen as a logic of dependence, captures most of the concepts involved in context theories. While T_1 is a set, each other field is a family of sets. A similar definition holds for record tokens where a sequence of values is such that a value v_i can depend on the values of the preceding fields $l_1, ..., l_{i-1}$:

$$< l_1 = v_1, ..., l_n = v_n > \tag{2}$$

The empty sequence $<>$ is a record type and the type T_i is a family of types over the record type $l_1 : T_1, ..., l_{i-1} : T_{i-1}$. Assuming that Γ is a valid context[1], we can express the record type formation rules provided that l is not already declared in R :

$$\frac{}{\Gamma \vdash <>: record - type} \qquad \frac{R : record - type}{\Gamma \vdash R \sqsubseteq <>}$$

$$\frac{\Gamma \vdash R : record - type \quad \Gamma \vdash T : record - type \rightarrow type}{\Gamma \vdash < R, l : T >: record - type}$$

$$\tag{3}$$

The record type generalizes the concept of Σ-type.

2.2 Physical contexts as records

In what follows, we assume that the general rules of construction for *Set* and *Prop* types are valid and that primitive syntactic constructions (i.e., equality, functional application and lambda abstraction) hold (for more details see [16]). In engineering systems modelling, the context information is related to each physical variable describing a part of the physical process. The basic idea is to think of a physical variable as describing a given entity of the real world together with a computational entity having type properties. Contexts can be considered at different abstraction levels [4][25] ranging between a data level to a semantic level. The proposed definition unifies two notions of contexts, the programming language perspective in which a context is known as an environment, and the knowledge representation formalisms (e.g., ontologies, situation-based theories) in which context is additional knowledge. As a result, a formal definition of a physical context type c includes a semantic part denoted *sem* (what the variable is supposed to represent) and a syntactic part denoted *syn* (how the variable is represented):

$$c = (sem(c), syn(c))$$

---

[1]A valid context in type theory is a sequence $x_1 : T_1, ... x_n : T_n$ such that there is a judgment having it as left side of a sequent.

A physical variable must include at least a physical property and its related physical entities (at least one). In order to support a contextual definition in the classical meaning, that is to express situational properties, propositions are added to the previous structure. We can use the previous notion of typehood to offer the most rudimentary notion of physical context, namely that it is a record which carries information about semantic and syntactic parts of any physical variable. We introduce the Physical Context type (PC-type, for short) as a sub-family of record type:

$$c : PC - type \ \ with \ \ PC - type \sqsubseteq record - type$$

Notice that types describe potential properties of the real world while tokens are dedicated to the run-time process. From some basic ground types, i.e., Ind (Individual), $Phys\_Quality$ (physical quality), ... complex PC-types can be composed with more than one variable. Propositions are treated as individuals that can be arguments of predicates. Let us consider the pressure measurement via a pressure sensor (e.g., a Pitot tube) in a small volume $SFA1$ of a water channel. Ground types generate the respective PC-types and tokens:

$$
\begin{array}{llll}
& x : & Ind & \qquad x = & P_s \\
& \psi_1 : & Ind & \qquad \psi_1 = & SFA_1 \\
& q : & StatPressure(\psi_1) & \qquad q = & p_0 \\
& s_1 : & liquid(\psi_1) & \qquad s_1 = & p_1 \\
PC\text{-type}: & t : & Numeric(x) & PC\text{-token}: \quad t = & p_2 \\
& u : & Unit & \qquad u = & Pa \\
& r : & Domain & \qquad r = & infinite \\
& m : & Input(x) & \qquad m = & p_3 \\
& n : & Address & \qquad n = & node_1
\end{array}
$$

where q, p_1, p_2 and p_3 are the respective proofs of $StatPressure(SFA_1)$, $liquid(SFA_1)$, $Numeric(P_s)$ and $Input(P_s)$. Since the Curry-Howard isomorphism identifies proofs with programs, it can be used to prove a specification, that is to say, to select which definitions are needed for the specification to work properly.

2.3 Context extension

The extension of a physical context type needs to define first the basic rules of construction. The first rule asserts that a concatenation of PC types is again a PC type. The second rule states that any PC-type is a sub-type of the empty sequence (since a PC type with no labels doesn't impose any constraints on its objects). The two remaining rules specify that any concatenation of PC types is a subtype of each one of its component PC type since the former contains more specific information.

$$\frac{\Gamma \vdash c_1 : PC - type \quad \Gamma \vdash c_2 : PC - type}{\Gamma \vdash c_1 \oplus c_2 : PC - type}$$

$$\frac{\Gamma \vdash c : PC - type}{\Gamma \vdash c \sqsubseteq <>}$$

$$\frac{\Gamma \vdash c_1 \oplus c_2 : PC - type}{\Gamma \vdash c_1 \oplus c_2 \sqsubseteq c_1} \qquad \frac{\Gamma \vdash c_1 \oplus c_2 : PC - type}{\Gamma \vdash c_1 \oplus c_2 \sqsubseteq c_2}$$

The extension of a physical context type c to a context type c' corresponds to the process of getting more information. These rules are extensible to any number of context types.

2.4   Non-monotonic characteristics

Roughly speaking, monotonicity indicates that learning a new information cannot reduce the set of known information. During context extension, if the assumptions that hold in the added PC contradict judgments of the initial PC, non-monotonicity occurs. As a consequence, a lifted judgment formally derives the absurd type ($\perp$). We face a belief revision process since beliefs have to be changed to accommodate the new belief otherwise inconsistency can occur. An efficient way to cope with non-monotonic situations as suggested in [2], consists either in declaring the extended PC as impossible, in other words to discard the extension, or alternatively, to revise the belief leading to a contradiction in the initial context. Anyway, one PC has to be declared as impossible context.

3   Causal relation in Contexts

3.1   Causal Dependencies

Following the ideas expressed in NLP where the dynamic meaning of a sentence is represented by pairing two context types [9][11], a dynamic model must include relations between PCs. Causal relations between physical contexts are to be regarded as record types involving the relevant field(s) of connected PCs. For engineering systems for example, we consider the field denoting the proof of the physical quality of an individual which is the basis for semantic dependency.

Definition 2 *Assuming an input PC type resulting from multiple extensions* $c_i, \ldots, c_j$, *an output PC type* c_k *can be connected to the input PC type if there exists a dependence relation between a field* q_k *in* c_k *with the correspondent fields* $q_i, \ldots, q_j$ *of the physical contexts* $c_i, \ldots, c_j$ *that is, it depends on the proofs of the preceding fields:*

$$\Gamma, \Delta_i, c_i : (C\Delta_i) \vdash (q\, c_i) : Prop$$

$$\vdots$$

$$\frac{\Gamma, \Delta_j, c_j : (C\Delta_j) \vdash (q\, c_j) : Prop}{\Gamma, \Delta_k, c_k : (C\Delta_k) \vdash (q\, c_k) : Prop(q\, c_i, \ldots q\, c_j)}$$

$$\Delta_k = \bigcup_{l=i}^{l=j} \Delta_l \tag{4}$$

where C denotes the family of PC-types, q, the physical quality label and Δ_i, the context extension of Γ for the physical context c_i.

Considering the measurement of static pressure and dynamic pressure in a water channel, the Bernoulli equation states that one can approximate[2] the velocity of the liquid volume surrounding the pressure sensors by:

$$V = \sqrt{\frac{2(P_d - P_s)}{\rho}} \tag{5}$$

where P_d, P_s and ρ denote respectively the dynamic pressure, the static pressure and the fluid density (constant). The resulting PC types, respectively c_1, c_2 and c_3 can be:

x_1 :	Ind	x_2 :	Ind	x_3 :	Ind
ψ_1 :	Ind	ψ_2 :	Ind	ψ_3 :	Ind
q :	$DynPressure(\psi_1)$	q :	$StatPressure(\psi_2)$	q :	$Velocity(\psi_3)$
s :	$liquid(\psi_1)$	s :	$liquid(\psi_2)$	s :	$liquid(\psi_3)$
t :	$Numeric(x_1)$	t :	$Numeric(x_2)$	t :	$Numeric(x_3)$
u :	$Unit$	u :	$Unit$	u :	$Unit$
r :	$Domain$	r :	$Domain$	r :	$Domain$
m :	$Input(x_1)$	m :	$Input(x_2)$	m :	$Input(x_3)$
n :	$Address$	n :	$Address$	n :	$Address$

From 4, the dependence can be expressed as:

$$Velocity(\psi_3) : Prop(StatPressure(\psi_2), DynPressure(\psi_1)) \tag{6}$$

where ψ_2, ψ_1 and ψ_3 are of types volume of liquid in the static flow area, the dynamic flow area and the flow area surrounding the sensors. It amounts to say that q in c_3 is a proof of $Velocity(\psi_3)$ if it is also a proof that q in c_1 is a proof of $StatPressure(\psi_2)$ and that q in c_2 is a proof of $DynPressure(\psi_1)$.

Non-monotonicity can results in the output context, and in that case it is the input context which has to be discarded, since the output is the referent for the updated situation. More than a single relation can exists between input PCs and the output one. The designer's task is restricted to describe conventionally acceptable patterns of interaction (protocols), in terms of possible connections between PC types. The basic units of connection are relations between PCs that specify how one PC configuration can be modified into another. These relations could be physical equations between PCs, control laws in engineering processes or business laws between PCs (in that case, PCs can be performance indicators). In order to formalize these relations and to extend the previous definition, a new record type, the connector-type C, is introduced as the basic tool we use in decomposing protocols. The connector-type includes input PC types, output PC type and one or more relations between input and output

---

[2]provided that the flow is steady, density is constant and friction losses are negligible

fields together with additional constraints about the possible connection. The connector-type (*Connect*) type is defined as a sub-family of record type :

$$t : Connect - type, \quad with \quad connect - type \sqsubseteq record - type$$

$$t \quad = \quad < in : PC - type, out : PC - type \ldots, l_i : T_i(in.l_1 \ldots out.l_k), \ldots >$$
$$= \quad < in : PC - type, out : PC - type, conds : Prop - type > \qquad (7)$$

where $in.l_1$ is a field of the input PC, $out.l_k$, a field of the output PC, *Prop−type* a record where each field is of type *Prop* and *conds*, a record type including propositions expressing the constraints which can depend on the fields of both input and output context. For the previous example, a typical connector type could be as follows:

$$
\begin{array}{lcl}
c_1 \oplus c_2 & : & PC - type \\
c_3 & : & PC - type \\
velocity(c_3.q) & : & Prop(c_2.q, c_1.q) \\
\ldots
\end{array}
$$

3.2 Causality and connection rules

The causality between Physical Contexts can be formally addressed with basic rules. The first rule is the introduction rule for causality between PCs through the connect type. The second rule defines an initial PC-type, O_c vacuously satisfied and states that any PC type can be connected to the initial PC type without any condition. The third rule expresses the fact that if a concatenation of PCs causally precedes a given PC, then each of them precedes this PC. The fourth rule formulates the reciprocal. Finally, the last one asserts that the transitivity holds for connected pairs of PCs.

$$\frac{\Gamma \vdash c_1 : record - type \quad c_2 : record - type}{\Gamma \vdash c_1 \preceq c_2 : Prop}$$
$$t : connect - type[in := c1, out := c2]$$

$$\overline{0_c : PC - type} \qquad \frac{t : connect - type[in := 0_c, out := c]}{t : connect - type[conds := \top]}$$

$$\frac{\Gamma \vdash c_1 : record - type \quad c_2 : record - type \quad c_3 : record - type}{\Gamma \vdash c_1 \preceq c_3 : Prop \ \& \ c_2 \preceq c_3 : Prop}$$
$$t : connect - type[in := c1 \oplus c2, out := c3]$$

$$\frac{\Gamma \vdash c_1 : record - type \quad c_2 : record - type \quad c_3 : record - type}{\Gamma \vdash c_1 \oplus c_2 \preceq c_3 : Prop}$$
$$c_1 \preceq c_3 : Prop \quad c_2 \preceq c_3 : Prop$$

$$\frac{\Gamma \vdash c_1 : record - type \quad c_2 : record - type \quad c_3 : record - type}{\Gamma \vdash c_1 \preceq c_3 : Prop}$$
$$c_1 \preceq c_2 : Prop \ \& \ c_2 \preceq c_3 : Prop$$

3.3 Discussion

As presented in the previous sections, contexts as dependent record types are subject to different relation types. First, a subsumption relation "sub-context-of" holds locally[3] between contexts (see subsection 2.3). This relation allows to extend contexts provided that the issue of non-monotonicity is solved. Second, the causality is expressed by a "precede" relation ($\preceq$) which connects context types (see subsections 3.1-3.2). This relation must be a partial order to cope with distributivity. Since there is an implicit time order which holds between contexts, each of them can include contradictory propositions.

The present logic models the potential constraints in which physical processes occur. The Intuitionistic Logic and its implementation through Dependent Record Types (DRT) presents some benefits. It provides a simple logical architecture which has been thoroughly investigated by logicians. Since DRT have been investigated in NLP, its extension to physical processes facilitates linguistic applications of the context logic. The highly structured ontology of types is potentially useful in formalization. Checking the existence of entities with their properties (i.e. propositions) at run-time with a theorem prover written in OCaml (see next section) makes this approach suitable for context-aware applications.

4 Software Implementation

4.1 Main Components

Based on Intuitionistic Type Theory, we have developed an intelligent Graphical User Interface (GUI), known as the *SoftWeaver* Research Project, to collect from the users'interface some context-based information through PC types. Figure 2 outlines the main components and information flows in a three layers GUI architecture. The topmost layer allows a user to describe intelligent nodes with relevant information about the physical environment and to store them in Knowledge Base. The middle layer is dedicated to the checking of the user functional models via a theorem prover. The bottom layer consists of a compiler which produces executable code.

4.2 The top layer

A shared Knowledge Base is accessed by the top layer to register Physical Context types. This Base contains the Domain Ontology of a given node through PC types. This work has been motivated by the search of an ontological model featured by an efficient implementation and able to describe the calculus of individuals which is required to support part-of relations between the structural components. There are currently many generic ontology languages able

---

[3] here, we mean a spatial locality.

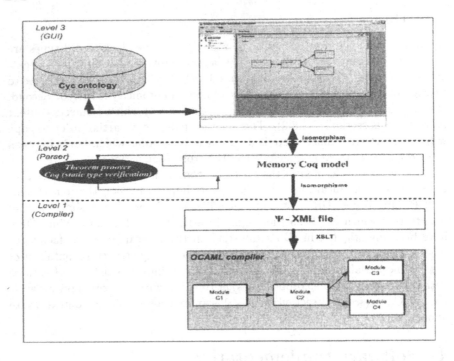

Figure 1: Overview of the Software Architecture

to support domain ontologies, such as *OWL* [29], *KIF* or *Cyc*. *OWL* which is the most common language, offers a lot of concepts suitable in an ontological perspective and covers most of the features for the modelling of Web Services. However, it is unable to cope with part-of relations and implementations of serializations within relational databases through tools such as *Xerces* appear to be inefficient. Alternatively, the *Cyc* language through the *OpenCyc* tool, provides an efficient tool for information sharing across networks and supports the modelling of part-of relations. As a consequence, the *OpenCyc* software tool (with the *CYC* language) has been selected as a knowledge base on which *SoftWeaver* relies. Physical context types are described and manipulated as micro-theories and intelligent nodes, as individuals. These two concepts can be considered as individuals and therefore, can be divided into parts. The user has the availability through the GUI, to describe the required topological relations between PC types in order to achieve a given goal. The PC types are basically the object type on which an action can be defined. The node(s) and the physical entities that the PC type can access correspond to the physical environment[4]. Other relevant components of a PC type are its generic address (e.g., a network address) and one or more physical entities resulting locally in

---

[4] the part-whole relationship define the structural model

a context token.

4.3 The middle layer

The middle layer deals with the memory model implemented with the *COQ* language (Theorem prover written in *CAML*). The language contains both dependent types theory and dependent record types. Therefore, it acts like a static type compiler where the model is automatically checked. It could have been possible to produce roughly, through the *COQ* assistant, *CAML* code but this code doesn't longer include the propositional types. Since propositional types are required to dynamically check types at run-time, the *COQ* assistant cannot be assigned this task.

4.4 The bottom layer

The central goal of the bottom layer is to produce a model from the middle layer in an XML output form. The XML format is useful for data exchange, as input for another software tool or to be converted through *XSLT* in an *OCAML* file. The PC types are implemented as parametric modules in the *OCAML* language. The *Prop* type is defined in a main module called *SOFTWEAVER*, as the signature of all other modules. More precisely, PC types are stored in an XML description file($\Phi - XML$) and with *OCAML* parametric modules (notice that the conversion between the $\Phi - XML$ model and the *OCAML* modelling is achieved by a compiler written in *XLST*). The implementation of an OCAML compiler has a dual advantage. First, it is used by a meta-language, and second, it is able to output optimal source code. The dynamic typing model allows to deliver at run-time a meta model for the node and PC types. This meta model enable self observation and self modification for the system (reflection) which results in run-time flexibility (context awareness) and reification capability. For this purpose, PC types make use of their knowledge about the external world (resulting from the structural model of individuals). These individuals require logical properties to determine their state and notify their availability to the PC type. If a PC type is not available, the software may look for a local substituting solution or question other nodes.

5 Conclusion

Among the works which report on Type Theory to describe contexts, [27] didn't follow the intuitionistic paradigm, but rather, builds on Montague's work [18] about Intensional Logic by introducing a Contextual Intensional Logic. Contexts are treated as modal operators where an additional primitive type is added, the type i of indices. However, its logic is not sufficient to cover all aspects of contextual reasoning such as partiality, dynamic operators and non-monotonic features. Alternatively, in [2], the author suggests to define contexts with Intuitionistic Type Theory, and details significant advantages of the model upon the classical context theories. Notice that this model doesn't take advantage of the powerful dependent types. We have shown in this paper, how dependent records types can be used to specify physical contexts in real world applications. These contexts relate static meaning (through types) with dynamic meaning (through tokens). While a number of methods modelling physical processes already exist, the present approach promotes reuse to its ontological nature (through types and tokens), separates the functional aspect (intended context type connections) with its behavior (run-time token connections) and allows for dynamic reasoning on context types. Moreover, the Intuitionistic Type Theory provides an improved formulation of possible planning sequences for use in planning. Most characteristics of context reasoning models are addressed with PC-types. The dynamic change of context is reflected by the dynamic pairing of PC types conditioned by constraints. Non-monotonicity has been formulated in a specific way. The type-based approach has an immediate computational impact since type-theory is implemented in many proof systems. Finally, the partial validation is addressed through the basic nature of records types and their sub-typing properties.

This work about contexts is a first step toward a goal modelling in which context formalization yields computable and well-founded programs. Further works include first a goal modelling in which goals are both modelled by record types and related to the context model within an ontological framework, second, a rapid prototyping graphical user interface to overcome the difficulties of type programming and third, an implementation of a distributed agent-based version.

References

[1] Betarte G.,: Type checking dependent (record) types and subtyping. Journal of Functional and Logic Programming (2000) **10** (2) 137–166

[2] Boldini, P.: Formalizing Context in Intuitionistic Type theory. Fundamenta Informaticae (2000) **42** 1–23

[3] Bove A., Capretta, V.: Nested General Recursion and Partiality in Type Theory TPHOL (2001) R.J. Boulton and P.B. Jackson eds. LNCS 2152 121135 Springer

[4] Brézillon P., Abu-Hakima S.: Using Knowledge in its Context: Report on the IJCAI'93 Workshop. AI Magazine (1995) **16**(1) 87–91

[5] Buvac S., Buvac V., Mason I.A.: Metamathematics of Contexts. Fundamentae Informaticae **23**(3) (1995) 412–419

[6] Buvac S.: Quantificational logic of context. Procs. of the 13th National Conference on Artificial Intelligence (1996)

[7] Cederquist J.: A Pointfree Approach to Constructive Analysis in Type Theory. PhD thesis Chalmers Univ. Sweden (1997)

[8] Bouquet P., Serafini L., Brézillon P., Benerecetti M., Castellani F.: Modeling and Using Context, Second International and Interdisciplinary Conference, CONTEXT'99 Trento Italy (1999) Springer LNCS 1688

[9] Cooper R.: Mixing Situation Theory and Type Theory to Formalize Information States in Dialogue Exchanges. in Procs of TWLT 13/Twendial '98: Formal Semantics and Pragmatics of Dialogue (1998)

[10] Coquand C., Coquand T.: Structured type theory. Workshop on Logical Frameworks and Meta-languages (1999)

[11] Ginzburg J.: Abstraction and Ontology: Questions as Propositional Abstracts in Type Theory with Records. Journal of Log. Comput. **15**(2) (2005) 113-130

[12] Giunchiglia F.: Contextual Reasoning. Istituto per la Ricerca Scientifica e Technologica (1992) 9211-20

[13] Ghidini C., Giunchiglia F.: Local Models Semantics, or Contextual Reasoning = Locality + Compatibility. Artificial Intelligence (2001) **127**(2) 221–259

[14] Guha R.V.: Contexts: a Formalization and some Applications. Stanford Computer Science Departement **STAN-CS-91-1399** (1991)

[15] Kopylov A.: Dependent Intersection: A New Way of Defining Records in Type Theory. in Procs. of the 18th Annual IEEE Symposium on Logic in Computer Science (2003) 86–95

[16] Martin-Lof, P.: Constructive Mathematics and Computer Programming. Logic, Methodology and Philosophy of Sciences (1982) **6** 153–175

[17] McCarthy J.: Notes on Formalizing Context. Procs. of the 13th Int. Joint Conf. on Artificial Intelligence (1993) 555–560

[18] Montague R.: Pragmatics and intensional logic, Synthèse **22** (1970) 68–94

[19] Ozturk P., Aamodt A.: A context model for knowledge-intensive case-based reasoning International Journal of Human Computer Studies (1998) **48** 331–355

[20] Paulson L.C.: The Foundation of a Generic Theorem Prover. Journal of Automated Reasoning (1989) **5** 363–397

[21] Ranta, A.: Constructing Possible Worlds. Theoria **57**(1/2) (1991) 77–99

[22] Ranta, A.: Grammatical Framework: A Type-Theoretical Grammar Formalism. Journal of Functional Programming (2004) **14**(2) 145–189

[23] Drabble B., et al.: Reports on the AAAI 1999 Workshop Program. AI Magazine **21**(1) (2000) 95-100

[24] Strang T., Linnhoff-Popien C.: A Context Modeling Survey. Sixth International Conference on Ubiquitous Computing (UbiComp2004) (2004) 34–41

[25] Terziyan V.Y., Puuronen S.: Formal Aspects of Context. P. Bonzon, M. Cavalcanti and R. Nossum eds. Kluwer Academic (2000)

[26] Thomason R.H.: Representing and Reasoning with Context. Procs. of the International Conference on Artificial Intelligence and Symbolic Computation (1998) 1476 LNCS 29–41 Springer

[27] Thomason R.H.: Type theoretic foundations for context, part 1: Contexts as complex typetheoretic objects. Modeling and Using Contexts Paolo Bouquet et al. eds., (1999) 352-374 Springer

[28] Villadsen, J.: Multi-dimensional Type Theory: Rules, Categories, and Combinators for Syntax and Semantics. Int. Workshop on Constraint Solving and Language Processing (2004) H. Christiansen et al. eds. 160–165

[29] OWL Web Ontology Language - Semantics and Abstract Syntax. Recommendation 10 (2004) http://www.w3.org/TR/owl-semantics/

Adjusting game difficulty level through Formal Concept Analysis *

Marco A. Gómez-Martín, Pedro P. Gómez-Martín
Pedro A. González-Calero and Belén Díaz-Agudo,
Dep. Sistemas Informáticos y Programación
Universidad Complutense de Madrid
Madrid, Spain
email: {marcoa,pedrop,pedro,belend}@sip.ucm.es

Abstract

In order to reach as many players as possible, videogames usually allow the user to choose the difficulty level. To do it, game designers have to decide the values that some game parameters will have depending on that decision. In simple videogames this is almost trivial: minesweeper is harder with longer board sizes and number of mines. In more complex games, game designers may take advantage of data mining to establish which of all the possible parameters will affect positively to the player experience. This paper describes the use of Formal Concept Analysis to help to balance the game using the logs obtained in the tests made prior the release of the game.

1 Introduction

Nowadays, the number of available videogames is impressive. If game developers want to increase the number of sold copies, they must make them suitable for a big amount of players, with different game skills, interests, and time available.

In fact, loads of people miss some kind of help when playing games. All players have inevitably got stuck some time, and have finally given the game(s) up. The evidence is the great amount of game magazines and Internet sites that offer the visitors guides, cheats, hints and walkthroughs of games.

There are players that argue that these difficulties are the essence of games, but most of them belongs to the so-called "hard-core" gamers groups, people who play many hours per week and have a great intuition about games.

The effort required to finish a game affects the player amusement, so designers must balance the games trying to make them not too easy nor too hard.

*Supported by the Spanish Committee of Education & Science (TIN2005-09382-C02-01)

But, on the other hand, the time needed to overcome a level or defeat an enemy greatly differs depending on the player ability. Due to both facts, it is common practise to add different difficulty levels to games.

Obviously, this is an advantage for users. But, being quite difficult to balance a game, this multiplies the design work. Clearly, in simple games, the decision to adjust the difficulty level is light. For example, in the well-known game of Pac-Man, an evident way to simplify each session consists on decreasing the number of ghosts and their speed, or increasing the number of ghostbuster pills.

But when the game complexity increases, the number of *adaptable design parameters* is higher. This supposes an exponential explosion that makes common sense useless.

In this paper we propose a way to help in the difficulty balance of a game using Formal Concept Analysis (FCA), a mathematical method for data analysis, knowledge representation and information management. Specifically, we apply FCA in the inspection of betatesters plays logs. We claim that the conclusions we extract with FCA can be useful in several areas of game tuning.

The outline of the paper is as follows. Section 2 introduces the game designer work, and formalises it in order to serve as a basis for the rest of the paper. Section 3 describes FCA, and section 4 the way we use it for helping the game design. These exposed ideas are apply in Section 5 in a concrete example involving the well known Tetris game. Section 6 analyses where our method is applicable. Finally, Section 7 presents some conclusions and ends the paper.

2   The Game Designer Work Formalised

The effort to defeat opponents or to overcome levels has important effects on the entertainment perceived by players. Novice or casual players usually prefer challenging but beatable enemies, while strong players enjoy difficult ones.

Game designers have traditionally added games with several difficulty levels. At the beginning of the game session, users choose the category where they feel they belong to, and game opponents adjust their difficulty accordingly.

However, the parameters the game changes depending on that level are stated by game designers using their intuition. This is an easy task only in very simple games. For example, it seems clear that in the well-known minesweeper game altering board size or the number of mines affects the complexity of the game. So, there is a dependency between the size of a board and its difficulty.

In non trivial games, this link between game parameters and game complexity may not be so clear. Game designers have to find out, usually guided by their intuition, which parameters determine the difficulty.

As a first step forward an atomatic tool for helping in this game balance, in this section we will formalise the task of configuring the different difficulty levels using a mathematical notation.

The first decision to be taken is the number of difficulty levels the game will have. In our formalization, we will consider L as the set of de different levels, for example:

$$L = \{easy, normal, hard\}$$

As it has been told previously, the designer is able to change different game parameters to establish the difficulty level. For example, in a first person shooter (FPS), the designer may alter the number of enemies in one map, or the accuracy of the player gun. From now, we will name P the set of the design parameters that can be changed.

Every member of P (p_i) has a specific domain, $D(p_i)$. For example, the domain of the number of enemies in a map takes its values from positive natural numbers:

$$D(\text{number of enemies}) = \mathbb{N}^+$$

The designer task is to establish, for each element $l_i \in L$, a value for all the parameters $p_i \in P$. That can be seen as defining the functions:

$$t_i : L \to D(p_i)$$

or, grouping all them together:

$$t : L \to D(p_1) \times \ldots \times D(p_n)$$

that is a function that receives the difficulty level and provides a tuple with the value of all the game parameter for it. As a mnemonic, the function name t comes from designer task.

As said before, this association between difficulty level and values in the design parameters has been traditionally done in a *ad hoc* way, using the intuition and common sense.

For simple games, this is enough, but it is quite scarce when the complexity increases. In that case, it is common practise to use *focus groups* in the initial stages of the development. A *focus group* consists in a set of people with different videogame backgrounds who is faced to a preliminary version of the project. Game designers look over the shoulder of the testers, taking notes that can help them to understand *how people play their game*. The version of the game itself is in charge of saving a big amount of log information to later off-line processing.

We will denote this group of *testers* as T. They initially estimate their own skill in the game based in their experience with similar games and preferences. Assuming that the different available categories are what we previously called L, we will designate:

$$s : T \to L$$

as the function that links each tester with her *skill level*.

The logs created by the program used by the focus group annotate different measures about the way each tester evolves in the game. In our running FPS example, some of them could be the number of killed enemies, time to overcome a level, final health state or the shot average to hit somebody. We will denote the set of measures as M. Each value in M belongs to a specific domain $D(m_i)$.

The formalisation of these logs consists on a group of functions f_i relating each tester with a measure m_i:

$$f_i : T \to D(m_i)$$

or, grouping all of them in a generalized funcion returning a tuple:

$$f : T \to D(m_1) \times \ldots \times D(m_n)$$

All this information is collected and analysed by designers. They must use their knowledge about statistics to filter the logs (f) and extract the interesting information. Their conclusions would be, for example, that novice FPS players need a big amount of shots to kill an enemy, or very experienced gamers can overcome a level without kill anybody. These conclusions are objective to some extent, except due to the fact that the testers have arranged themselves in the different skill groups.

In this points, it's worth remembering that the final task of the designers is to specify the t function, relating difficulty level (L) and adjustable game parameters (P). Therefore, using the previously acquired conclusions, designers can decide, for example, that initial levels should have a big amount of ammo, but it should be scarce in the harder ones in order to force gamers to play as the experts do.

Again, this t is determined using common-sense. A hypothesis is hidden in all this process. Measured values in the focus group (M) are supposed to be, in some way, dependent with the different changeable design parameters P. In other words, for a specific gamer g_i, the value of $f(g_i)$ would be different if any parameter in P is changed in the game used to test it. In that sense, examples of *useless* measures in a FPS would be the number of unnecessary jumps, or the times the player pauses the game.

The information collected by the logs is potentially huge. In order to help game designers to use them, some kind of data analysis may be used. Our method consists on using Formal Concept Analysis (FCA) to process them and giving hints to be applied while balancing the game. To make this paper self-contained, next section describes FCA, that we will use in Section 4.

3 Formal Concept Analysis

Formal Concept Analysis (FCA) is a mathematical method for data analysis, knowledge representation and information management. It was invented by Rudolf Wille [11] and during the last two decades it has been applied in numerous applications in different domains, like psychology, medicine, linguistics and computer sciences among others. In general, FCA may be useful in knowledge discovery in databases [9]. In previous papers [3, 8, 2] we have used FCA as a particular and very adequate technique to organize and discover knowledge embedded in Case Based Reasoning (CBR) applications.

FCA can be applied to any collection of items described by properties and provides a way to identify groupings of objects with shared properties. FCA applied on a data set provides an internal sight of the conceptual structure and allows finding patterns, regularities and exceptions among the cases. In FCA, data is structured into formal abstractions called *concepts*. These formal concepts have the property that they form a concept lattice, ordered by a subconcept-superconcept relation.

As we explain in next subsection, besides conceptual abstractions, FCA also allows to elicit the attribute co-appearance knowledge between the properties describing the objects. First, we describe the basis of the FCA technique. See [4] for a concise textbook treatment. Second, we illustrate FCA with a simple example of experience indexing in the Tetris case study that is used in Section 5.

3.1 Context, concept lattices and rules

In FCA, a *formal context* is defined as a triple $\langle G, M, I \rangle$ where there are two sets G (of objects) and M (of attributes), and a binary (incidence) relation $I \subseteq G \times M$, expressing which attributes describe each object (or which objects are described using an attribute), i.e., $(g, m) \in I$ if the object g carries the attribute m, or m is a descriptor of the object g. When the sets are finite, the context can be specified by means of a cross-table. When we have to deal with numbers we use standard techniques for discretizing numeric attributes [12] as we do in Section 5.

With a general perspective, a concept represents a group of objects and is described by using *attributes* (its intent) and *objects* (its extent). The extent covers all objects belonging to the concept while the intent comprises all attributes (properties) shared by all those objects. With $A \subseteq G$ and $B \subseteq M$ the following operator (*prime*) is defined as:

$$A' = \{m \in M \mid (\forall g \in A)(g, m) \in I\}$$

$$B' = \{g \in G \mid (\forall m \in B)(g, m) \in I\}$$

A pair (A,B) where $A \subseteq G$ and $B \subseteq M$, is said to be a *formal concept* of the context $\langle G, M, I \rangle$ if $A' = B$ and $B' = A$. A and B are called the *extent* and the *intent* of the concept, respectively.

It can also be observed that, for a concept (A, B), $A'' = A$ and $B'' = B$, which means that all objects of the extent of a formal concept, have all the attributes of the intent of the concept, and that there is no other object in the set G having all the attributes of (the intent of) the concept.

The set of all the formal concepts of a context $\langle G, M, I \rangle$ is denoted by $\beta(G, M, I)$. The most important structure on $\beta(G, M, I)$ is given by the subconcept - superconcept order relation denoted by $\leq$ and defined as follows:

	b	i	e	w	$\overline{w}$	$<_{50\%}$	$\geq_{50\%}$
player 1			■	■		■	
player 2		■		■			■
player 3	■				■		■
player 4			■	■		■	
player 5			■	■			■

b ≡ beginner   i ≡ intermediate   e ≡ expert

w ≡ wins $\overline{w}$ ≡ looses

Table 1: Formal context of a simple Tetris example

$$(A1, B1) \leq (A2, B2)$$

if $A1 \subseteq A2$ (which is equivalent to $B2 \subseteq B1$ see [4]).

The Basic Theorem for Concept Lattices concepts of a given context can be ordered using the subconcept–superconcept relation and can be represented as a lattice, like the one shown in Figure 1.

3.1.1 Dependency Rules

Though the formal concepts and lattice structure could be useful on their own [3], we use the capacity of mining association rules from it. An association rule is an expression $A \rightarrow B$ where both A and B are sets of attributes. They means that objects having all the attributes in A will probably have those attributes in B.

Association rules are characterized by two parameters: confidence and support. Confidence express the *probability* of that rule to hold, or in other words, the percentage of objects that, having all the attributes in A also have those in B. On the other hand, support indicates the number of objects where the rule is applicable, formally speaking, the number of objects with attributes in A and B divided by the total number of objects.

Rule extraction algorithms based on FCA are able to efficiently extract all the association rules that have a confidence above a threshold. There are several algorithms, though we have used Duquenne–Guigues [5] to extract exact association rules (100% of confidence) and Luxenburguer [6] for non-exact ones.

3.2 A simple example FCA application

Just to illustrate with a concrete example all these concepts, we provide a simple example. Let's suppose we want to analyse how five people (one beginner, one intermediate and three expert players) plays a reduced version of Tetris. We materialize the information about the games in an incidence table (formal context) shown in Table 1.

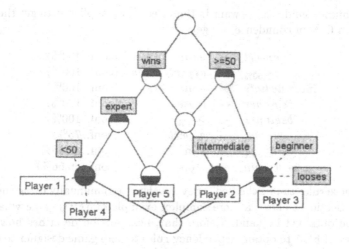

Figure 1: Lattice from formal context in Table 1

Let's assume that our version of Tetris ends when the user completes 100 lines or the blocks reach the top of the screen. The formal context store a formal object (row) for each game session. There are three formal attributes (columns) which encode the player level ('b' means *beginner*, 'i' stands for *intermediate* and 'e' is used for *expert* players). Two attributes express whether the user wins the game (w) or looses it ($\overline{w}$). Finally, two attributes indicates whether the percentage of occupied squares on the screen at the end of the game was above a 50% or not.

With this in mind, we produce the cross table from the game evaluation experience: a cell contains X if and only if the user evaluation experience has resulted in this feature. For example, columns b, i and e indicate that players 1,4 and 5 are experts players, whereas player 3 is a beginner and player 2 belongs to the intermediate level.

Figure 1 shows the lattice extracted from the formal context. It can be used to mining the exact association rules (those with a confidence of 100%). In particular, we can read the dependence rules in the lattice as follows:

- Each line between nodes labeled with attributes means a dependence rule between the attributes from the lower node to the upper one.

- When there are several attributes in the same label it means that there is a co-appearance of all these attributes for all the cases in the sample.

Therefore, from the lattice in Figure 1, we can read (among others) rules like:

$$expert \;\rightarrow\; wins$$
$$beginner \;\leftrightarrow\; looses$$

FCA allows us to obtain also non-exact rules (those with confidence below 100%), using the Luxenburger algorithm [6]. This method is parametrizied by the minimum confidence we want in the rules. If we applied it to get those with more than 60% of confidence, we get:

$$
\begin{array}{rcl}
expert & \rightarrow & wins \qquad\qquad\; \text{(conf. 100\%)}\\
<_{50\%} & \rightarrow & expert,\; wins \quad \text{(conf. 100\%)}\\
intermediate & \rightarrow & wins,\; \geq_{50} \quad\;\; \text{(conf. 100\%)}\\
beginner & \leftrightarrow & looses \qquad\quad\; \text{(conf. 100\%)}\\
beginner & \rightarrow & \geq_{50\%} \qquad\qquad \text{(conf. 100\%)}\\
win & \rightarrow & expert \qquad\quad\; \text{(conf. 75\%)}\\
\geq_{50\%} & \rightarrow & win \qquad\qquad\; \text{(conf. 66.66\%)}\\
expert,\; win & \rightarrow & <_{50\%} \qquad\qquad \text{(conf. 66.66\%)}
\end{array}
$$

All these rules can be checked (or even calculated) manually using the formal context. Section 5 shows a more complex example of Tetris game where rules cannot be obtained by hand. Before that, next section describes how we use the ability of FCA to obtain dependency rules to help game designer to do their task.

4 Helping game designers with FCA

A naive and usual way to make use of the focus group test is just to ask the players about specific aspects of the game, such as if they find it difficult, or what kind of behaviour they would change.

When a log is available, however, designers can analyse all this information and use it to make their decisions. In particular, they usually calculate averages of some parameters and manually explore them to get some conclusions.

We propose the use of FCA for extracting these conclusions in the form of dependency rules. The analysis of these rules may help the designer to determine the function t described in Section 3, that relates the difficulty level of the game with the value of their parameters.

The goal of our method is to find dependency rules with the form:

$$l_i \rightarrow b_1 \ldots b_n \qquad \text{(confidence c\%)}$$

where l_i expresses one of the different available difficulty levels, and $b_1 \ldots b_n$ are attributes that encoded some concrete values of parameters in the log (elements of P).

Using FCA to obtain these rules implies the creation of a formal context that represents log information. In that sense, we consider every game play as a formal object, an every attribute encoded a particular piece of information contained in the log. As these values usually have a continuous domain, a previous step of discretization should be done. To do it, the designer may choose fixed intervals using the lower and greater values of the samples, or to use some information gain method.

As additional attributes, we encoded the skill level declared by the tester that play the game. Dependency rule extraction will give us rules involving both, concrete values of the measured parameters and the level of skills.

Instead of detailing the method in an abstract way, next section exemplify it using the well-known Tetris game.

5   Case of study: Tetris

In order to demonstrate how our method works, we have used it to analyse information recovered from an adapted implementation of the Tetris Game.

Tetris gameplay is well known; as explain [10], seven randomly chosen tetraminoes fall down the playing field. The object of the game is to manipulate these tetrominoes with the aim of creating a horizontal line of blocks without gaps. When such a line is created, it disappears, and the blocks above (if any) fall. As the game progresses, the tetrominoes fall faster, and the game ends when the stack of Tetrominoes reaches the top of the playing field and no new Tetrominoes are able to enter.

Though Tetris has been extensively studied and its ability to keep player attention is no questionable, having simple rules allow us to exemplify our technique.

Our experiment starts with a Tetris clone called U61 [7] developed by Christian Mauduit under the GNU General Public License. We chose this particular implementation because the complete code is available, so we could adapt it to generate game logs.

These logs contain the attributes of each game session, that constitutes, according to Section 2 terminology, the set M:

- The name of the player.

- The score she got.

- The total number of tetraminoes.

- The average time spent in placing each shape.

- The average of the number of rotations per shape.

- The average of the number of changes in the direction of a tetraminoe. When a shape is falling down, the player may choose to move it towards one direction, and change her mind afterwards starting to move it to the other one. This measure express the number of times she do this per shape.

- Number of hits to the walls or other shapes when moving the tetraminoe left or right.

- Number of hits to the walls or other shapes when rotating the tetraminoe.

- Average number of holes leaving per shape.

	Number of players	Number of plays	Score average
Beginner	7	17	1333
Intermediate	3	7	4327
Expert	4	6	10105

Table 2: Focus group

	b	i	e	$<_3$	$<_4$	$<_5$	$<_6$	$<_7$	$<_8$	$<_9$	$\geq_9$
player 1		■	■	■	■	■	■	■	■	■	
player 2	■					■	■	■	■	■	
player 3		■						■	■	■	
player 4	■										■
$\vdots$	$\vdots$	$\vdots$	$\vdots$	$\vdots$	$\vdots$	$\vdots$	$\vdots$	$\vdots$	$\vdots$	$\vdots$	$\vdots$

b ≡ beginner   i ≡ intermediate   e ≡ expert

Table 3: Formal context containing the average time per shape.

We worked with a *focus group* of 14 people, each of whom declared her level playing Tetris (function s in Section 2) between *beginner*, *intermediate* and *expert* (values of L). Players were told to play one or more games; the number of players and games per level is showed in Table 2. It has also a column with the score average per group; that confirms that the *subjective* decision of players grouping in their levels is correct, because beginner group gets less score than intermediate and expert group.

Using FCA, we process the logs to extract dependency rules that relates those players belonging to one level and the value of certain parameters retrieved from the log.

To illustrate the process, we will describe how we have analyzed three of those parameters: time per shape, number of hits when moving a tetraminoe to the left, and changes in the direction of the shape.

For all of them, we create a *formal context* that contains an object per player and two groups of attributes. The first one expresses the skill of the player (beginner, intermediate or expert). The second one codifies the value of each previous parameter.

As the values got from the log are real numbers, we scaled them. Table 3 partially shows the formal context created to analyze the time parameter.

Once we have built the formal context scaling the real values, we apply FCA and the dependency rules extractor. Most of the rules extracted by the algorithm are related to the scaling mechanism. For example, we got exact rules like:

$$<_7 \; \rightarrow \; <_8, <_9 \qquad \text{(conf. 100\%)}$$

Our method retrieves more interesting rules; the game designer may conclude that the level of a player is strongly related to the average time she takes to place each shape, according to the rules from the formal context[1]:

$$
\begin{aligned}
beginner &\rightarrow\ <_8 &&(\text{conf. }85.71\%) \\
intermediate &\rightarrow\ <_8 &&(\text{conf. }100\%) \\
expert &\rightarrow\ <_5 &&(\text{conf. }100\%) \\
expert &\leftrightarrow\ <_4 &&(\text{conf. }75\%) \\
<_3 &\rightarrow\ expert &&(\text{conf. }100\%) \\
\geq_9 &\rightarrow\ beginner &&(\text{conf. }100\%)
\end{aligned}
$$

With these rules, game designer is confident when stating that the game parameter that fixed the speed of the falling down shape (a game parameter in P) has a strong effect in the player experience. This is deduced because the designer can inferred from the previous rules that expert gamers spent much less time per shape than beginners. Increasing the tetraminoes speed in advanced level makes the game to force *implicitly* the player to place the shapes faster, as *only* experts do.

If we analyze the measure of the average number of hits produced by lateral movements to the left, the designer can conclude that these values are also strongly related to the skill of the player, but in a unusual way: expert players hit the wall more often than intermediate and beginner players[2]. The designer may then think about let the shape fall down one position when it hits the wall, because that will make things more difficult to experts while hardly affecting beginners and intermediate players.

Finally, in Section 2 we mentioned the importance of log measures (in M) dependent on the adaptable design parameters (P). In order to test if FCA would detect useless measures, we added some of them that common sense says that are not too relevant. For example, when analysing the dependency rules of the number of direction changes made by the player the algorithm does not report any significant rule above the 60% of confidence that relates the player level with the value of the parameter.

6 Discussion

Formal Concept Analysis allows us to get dependency rules between the skill level of the testers and the parameters measured in the special version of the game that generates the log files.

The more significant aspect here is that these rules are *automatically* extracted. Game designers must decide what meassures should be taken using the focus group (M), and how to *discretise* the results (converting the continuous domains of some of them to intervals). Once this is done, *no more work is needed* to get the rules, specially no statistics knowledge is required.

---

[1] These are the entire list of rules form the context of Table 3 that involve the level of the player

[2] We think that is related to the intensive use that expert players made of keyboard repetition.

However, there are some points that are important to keep in mind when using this method because we envision that they could be, to some extent, problematic:

- Game designer still has to decide the number of levels (set L in Section 2) she wants to include in the game.

- The function that relates players on the focus group with their skill level (called s in Section 2) may be very subjective or not available at all. In our experiment about Tetris in the previous section, we confront the level state by the players with the score they got (see Table 3), just to assure that the function set the players' level correctly. In some games, players must not know their skill (for example in videogames with highly original concepts) or a method may not be available to confirm that the association was done correctly.

- *Focus group* tests are usually made with a reduced group of people. Though in our case, fourteen people has been enough to get significant results, in more complex games that number can limit the conclusions of the method. By contrast, there is a specific videogame genre where crowed focus groups can be used: Massively Multiplayer Online Role-Playing Games (MMORPG). In order to test the correction of the game rules and servers load capacity, massive tests are performed during different development stages, involving people all around the world. It would be very interesting to have access to their logs in order to see how FCA reacts.

- In some games the difficulty has nothing to do with the values of certain parameters but with the game rules themselves. For example, strategy games has established rules, and game evolves according to user actions and rules. Game designer has to worried also whether rules make the game too hard to play. Our method is not able to obtain any conclusion about that. Related to that, [1] makes a clever comparison: the well-known game of Pong (dated from 1972) had simple instructions: "Insert coin", "Press start", "Avoid missing ball for high score" while the "Falcon 4.0" manual, a flight simulator created in 1998, contained about 600 pages. Obviously, one important aspect of the flight simulator difficulty are the rules themselves, not just the different design parameters as plane maneuverability.

- There are some games where the assumption of the existence of relationships between changeable design parameters (P) and measurable values (M) in the focus group is not valid. For example, when implementing games of perfect information like chess, a natural way to change the difficulty level is by increasing the deep in the search tree of the minimax (or alpha-beta) algorithm. Another possibility is to change the static *position evaluation function* (which is a heuristic), altering the weight of its addends. Being "design parameters", all of them would belong to our set

P. But, it's unclear if some meaningful measure exists in M to log with the focus group.

7 Conclusions

This papers has described the increasing effort that game designers are obliged to make in order to balance their games. This work is even higher when the game provides different difficulty levels to adapt to a wider market.

In complex games, the number of design parameters that can be changed in order to adjust its behaviour can be quite numerous. Fine tuning their values overcomes the only natural resource available for designers: common sense. To solve the problem, focus groups are usually used, so testers with different gaming background provide information about the game itself. The result is a huge amount of data, that usually must be manually analysed in order to get useful information.

In this paper we have proposed to ease this task using Formal Concept Analysis, a mathematical method for data analysis and information management. In order to test our ideas, we have exemplified them with a modest but useful example: the Tetris Game. It has demonstrated that FCA can automatically extract the expected *dependency rules* between player skills and the way in which they play. Also, it has dropped away some useless collected data, and, even more interesting, discovered a non-foreseen characteristic in the way expert users play.

8 Acknowledgements

We would like to express our gratitude to all those people that acceded to play Tetris, knowing that they were being logged. We also are in debt to Christian Mauduit, who implemented his Tetris version, U61, and makes it available through the GPL license.

References

[1] M. Bopp. *The Future of Learning: Affective and Emotional Aspects of Human-Computer Interaction*, volume 1, chapter Didactic Analysis of Digital Games and Game-Based Learning, pages 8–37. IOS Press, 2006.

[2] B. Díaz-Agudo, M. A. Gómez-Martín, P. P. Gómez-Martín, and P. A. González-Calero. Formal concept analysis for knowledge refinement in case based reasoning. In M. Bramer, F. Coenen, and T. Allen, editors, *XXV International Conference on Innovative Techniques and Applications of Artificial Intelligence (AI 2005)*, pages 233–245. Springer, 2005.

[3] B. Díaz-Agudo and P. A. González-Calero. Formal Concept Analysis as a Support Technique for CBR. In *Knowledge-Based Systems, 14 (3-4)*, pages 163–172. Elsevier, June 2001.

[4] B. Ganter and R. Wille. Formal concept analysis.

[5] J.-L. Guigues and V. Duquenne. Familles minimales d'implications informatives resultant d'un tableau de données binaires. *Math. Sci. Humanies 95, 1986, 5-18.*

[6] M. Luxenburguer. Implications partielles dans un contexte. *Mathématiques, Informatique et Sciences Humaines*, 113(29):35–55, 1991.

[7] C. Mauduit. U61. Available at http://www.ufoot.org/u61 (last access, June 2006).

[8] J. A. Recio-García, M. A. Gómez-Martín, B. Díaz-Agudo, and P. A. González-Calero. Improving annotation in the semantic web and case authoring in textual cbr. In *8th European Conference on Case-Based Reasoning (ECCBR'06)*. Springer Verlag, 2006.

[9] G. Stumme. Efficient data mining based on formal concept analysis. In A. Hameurlain, R. Cicchetti, and R. Traunmüller, editors, *Database and Expert Systems Applications, 13th International Conference*, volume 2453 of *Lecture Notes in Computer Science*. Springer, September 2002.

[10] Wikipedia, the free encyclopedia. Tetris entry. Available at http://en.wikipedia.org/wiki/Tetris.

[11] R. Wille. *Restructuring Lattice Theory: an approach based on hierarchies of concepts*. Ordered Sets, 1982.

[12] I. Witten and E. Frank. *Data Mining, practical machine learning tools and techniques wiht Java Implementations*. 2000.

Ontology Constraint Satisfaction Problems using Conceptual Graphs

Madalina Croitoru

Department of Computing Science, University of Aberdeen

Aberdeen, UK

Ernesto Compatangelo

Department of Computing Science, University of Aberdeen

Aberdeen, UK

Abstract

In this paper we present a visual formalism for representing constraints over knowledge intensive domains. Our approach is based on Conceptual Graphs and consequently benefits from their visual and semantic properties. By expressing constraint satisfaction problems using conceptual graphs we can use effective hybrid strategies to solve them. Central to this approach is the possibility of using projection (i.e. subsumption) to reason with constraints in conjunction with other CSP strategies. We present our framework formally, illustrating it with an example, and then discuss its limitations, as well as possible future work.

1 Motivations and rationale

This paper's contribution is a visual representation for constraints in a knowledge rich domain (e.g. ontologies etc.). Our claim is that, for applications dealing with such domains (e.g. Semantic Web applications etc.), constraint satisfaction problems should be addressed in a domain oriented manner. This means exploiting the ontological information encoded in the knowledge representation formalism.

We formally introduce a visual mechanism able to build upon the knowledge repositories described by chosen representation languages. If we consider ontology applications then these languages can either be RDF [20] based, OWL [23] based, DLs [1] based etc.

Our visual framework for representing constraint satisfaction problems uses a Conceptual Graph (CG) model. Conceptual Graphs [18, 17] are a powerful knowledge representation formalism with attached first order logic semantics. They allow for both visual depiction of knowledge and the ability of reasoning over the described information.

Since our work is specifically looking at visually representing constraints over knowledge rich domains the choice of Conceptual Graphs is motivated as follows:

- Due to their visual capabilities CGs allow for easy knowledge acquisition.

- CGs reuse, by the means of wrappers, existing ontological knowledge expressed in different languages.

- The attached semantics of Conceptual Graphs make them a powerful reasoning knowledge representation formalism.

Consequently the advantage of employing Conceptual Graphs is two-fold:

1. The user is able to clearly see the constraints (s)he is working with.

2. Conceptual Graphs reasoning mechanisms can be viewed as an intermediate layer in the solving process.

Constraint satisfaction problems (CSPs) cover a wide range of computational problems from many different application areas. Generally speaking a CSP consists of a a collection of variables which have to be assigned values from certain domains, subject to specified restrictions (constraints). Our work is looking at visually representing the constraints over knowledge rich domains such as ontologies. Our framework allows the representation of "conceptual" constraints: star graphs extracted from the domain's background knowledge. This initial phase of modelling is useful from both a knowledge acquisition view point and from a CSP solving point of view.

From a knowledge acquisition view point we can make use of the background (domain knowledge) due to the nature of the Conceptual Graph formalism which plugs in on top of a "knowledge repository" - the support. Another advantage is that by considering the constraints using our formalism we address another important problem when defining constraints over such domains: the identification of variables / domains. We solve this by representing constraints differently using mappings rather then traditional CSP formulations.

From a CSP solving view point CG reasoning mechanisms can avoid whole backtracking steps when type checking. We show how to make use of (partial) existing solutions and reuse available information given by the CSP instance solutions. More complicated constraints are represented by "functional" relations defined on existing concepts. These constraints are to be addressed using traditional CSP methods, accordingly adapted for our CG model.

This paper is structured as follows: Section 2 presents existing work both in the field of CSPs for knowledge rich domains and Conceptual Graphs. In section 3 we provide a real world example to illustrate our modelling approach which is then formalised in Section 4. Section 5 concludes the paper and lays down future work directions.

2 Existing work

This work ties together two research strands: constraint satisfaction problems for rich domain models and Conceptual Graphs. In this section, we will discuss existing and related research in both of these fields.

2.1 Constraint representation in rich knowledge domains

Constraint programming (CP) is a modelling framework for solving a specific class of combinatorial problems. These problems arise in many practical applications (planning, scheduling, time tabling, etc) which are using computer assisted decision-making techniques [16].

Solving a problem within the constraint-based programming (CP) framework consists of providing a user-defined model of the problem at hand. This is done by declaring the problem's constitutive variables along with the constraints that relate them. Once the problem is modelled, a specialized solver is responsible for the resolution process.

These problems are known as constraint-satisfaction problems (CSP). Their input consists of a set of variables, a set of possible values for the variables, and a set of constraints between the variables. The challenge is to determine whether there is an assignment of values to the variables that satisfies the given constraints. Constraint satisfaction is an important area of artificial intelligence (AI) because many AI problems can be modelled as constraint-satisfaction problems [19].

In its full generality, a constraint satisfaction is an NP-complete problem. For this reason, researchers have focused both on heuristics for constraint satisfaction problems and on tractable cases obtained by imposing restrictions on constraints [8, 13].

Recent projects [4, 9] address the problem of constraints visualization for ontological knowledge, mainly with a focus on knowledge acquisition [15] and user validation. Most of these systems use OWL for knowledge representation and SWRL [21] for expressing rules / constraints on the data. This approach suffers from a series of drawbacks due to the expressiveness and visual capabilities of SWRL. Visualization is extremely important when attempting constraint user validation. However, SWRL as a representation language (built on OWL constructs) was not intended to be visually displayed as such. Figure 1 depicts the graph for a simple scheduling CSP[1]. This calls for a further visualization layer that depicts the rules / constraints in the ontology. The main drawback however is the expressivity capabilities of SWRL. Being developed as a way of writing rules, it can be only used to represent constraints so long as these constraints are conjunctive and evaluate, as a whole, to true or false. Extensions have been proposed in the literature but they are hard to manipulate visually [10].

---

[1]Generated from OWL found at http://www.csd.abdn.ac.uk/~schalmer/akt/

234

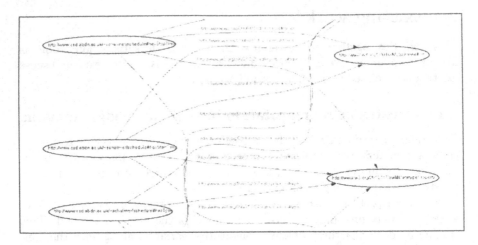

Figure 1: Visual rendering of a scheduling CSP

2.2 Conceptual Graphs

An example of a Conceptual Graph is given in Figure 2. This graph represents the fact that a postgraduate student teaches a course which has a topic. The main represented concepts (postgraduate student, teaches, course etc.) are defined in hierarchies that describe the domain of interest. Conceptual Graphs (CGs), as a knowledge representation formalism, make the distinction between the domain knowledge – the support (viewed as concepts and relations hierarchies, together with a set of instance names) – and the facts defined over the support's encoded knowledge. These facts are depicted as a bipartite graph. This distinction led to the idea of employing Conceptual Graphs for CSP (constraint satisfaction problems) modelling. We believe that such distinction can prove beneficial in manipulating constraints in knowledge rich applications.

It is well-known that the problem of deciding if a given CSP has a solution and the problem of projection checking between two given conceptual graphs are polynomial equivalent [6]. However, our aim is to provide a CG modelling framework for CSPs.

Conceptual Graphs have been previously used to represent constraints [2, 3]. Constraints were represented as bicolored conceptual graphs. By only employing conceptual graphs reasoning mechanisms (i.e. projection) this approach does not allow for hybrid CSP solving techniques. Our method allows for better representation of composite constraints [14], hierarchical constraints (eventually employing Layered Conceptual Graphs [7]) or dynamic constraints [11]. Novel syntactic CG constructs are required for CG manipulation within this CSP scope. From a reasoning view point we benefit from both the projection mechanism of CGs and from previously discovered solutions which are integrated in the solving process. These results are also given in Section 4(see Proposition 5 and 6).

3 Working example

We will motivate our theoretical approach with a real-world CSP example. Let us consider a simple example of Conceptual Graph, which states that a postgraduate student teaches a course dealing with a given a topic. This is shown in Figure 2. The represented domain concepts (*e.g.*, PStudent, Course, Topic) and the relationships between them (*e.g.*, teaches, has) are arranged in separate hierarchies — namely, a *type* hierarchy and a *relation* hierarchy — that describe the domain of interest.

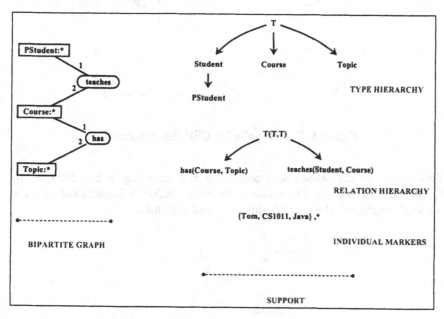

Figure 2: An example of simple Conceptual Graph

The problem we are trying to model is the following: a set of postgraduate students need to be assigned for teaching a set of courses. The students have a given workload (full-time, part-time) and a certain background (programming, maths, artificial intelligence etc.). The courses, at their turn have a duration (half-term, full-term etc.), a topic (maths, AI, etc.) and a degree of difficulty (marking, office hours, big classes etc.). For simplicity reasons, the students background corresponds to the courses topics; and student's preferences are not considered. This information is modelled using conceptual graphs as shown in Figure 3. For every restriction a star graph is built depicting the corresponding information.

These graphs are bound together and integrated in the conceptual graph that will depict all the constraints over the data and their relationships. This graph is shown in Figure 4. Please note the special node "function" which can be subsequently introduced for representation of certain functional relations.

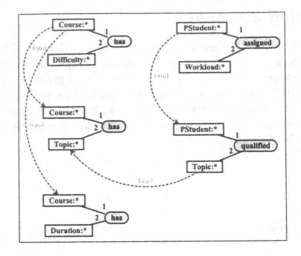

Figure 3: Star Graphs for CSP Representation

These relations are defined as a procedure and are going to be addressed by traditional CSP solvers. The relation "function" defines a formula between the student's workload, the course's duration and difficulty.

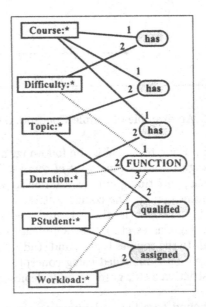

Figure 4: Conceptual Graph for CSP Representation

4 Formalising CSPs with Conceptual Graphs

4.1 Preliminary notions on CGs

An ordered bipartite graph is a triple which consists of a set of concept nodes, a set of relation nodes and a mapping between the relation nodes and nonempty finite sequences over concept nodes. An ordered bipartite graph with just one relation node is called a star graph. We consider a special kind of subgraphs for our modelling purposes, namely spanned subgraphs. A spanned subgraph induced by a set of relation nodes consists of the set of relation nodes, the edges incident with these and the corresponding concept nodes.

Definition 4.1 (Ordered Bipartite Graph) *A triple $G = (V_C, V_R, N_G)$ is called an* ordered bipartite graph *if*
- V_C and V_R are finite disjoint sets, ($V_G := V_C \cup V_R$ is the vertices set *of G), and*
- $N_G : V_R \to V_C^+$ is a mapping, where V_C^+ denotes the set of all finite nonempty sequences over V_C.

For $r \in V_R$ with $N_G(r) = c_1 \ldots c_k$, $d_G(r) := k$ is the degree *of r in G and $N_G^i(r) := c_i$ is the i-neighbour of r in G. The set of (distinct) neighbours of r is denoted $\overline{N}_G(r)$.*
The multiset E_G of edges of G is $E_G = (\{c,r\}|c \in V_C, r \in V_R$ and $\exists i$ such that $N_G^i(r) = c)$.
We further assume that for each $c \in V_C$ there is $r \in V_R$ and $i \in \mathbb{N}$ such that $c = N_G^i(r)$ (G has no isolated vertices).

If $G = (V_C, V_R, N_G)$ is an ordered bipartite graph with $|V_R| = 1$, then G is called a star graph.

If $G = (V_C, V_R, N_G)$ is an ordered bipartite graph and $A \subseteq V_R$, the subgraph spanned by A in G is the graph $G[A] := (V_C^1, A, N_G^1)$, where N_G^1 is the restriction of N_G to A and $V_C^1 = \{c \in V_C | \exists r \in A$ and $\exists i \in \mathbb{N}$ such that $c = N_G^i(r)\}$.
If $A = \{r\}$, then we simply write $G[r]$, which is referred to as the star subgraph spanned by r in G. *Clearly, the graph G can be expressed as the union of its star subgraphs: $G = \cup_{r \in V_R} G[r]$.*

The next two definitions introduce the concepts of support and conceptual graphs. A support is a structure that provides the background knowledge about the information to be represented in the conceptual graph. It consists of a concept type hierarchy , a relation type hierarchy (properties in OWL) , a set of individual markers that refer to specific concepts (instance names) and a generic marker, denoted by *, which refers to an unspecified concept.

Definition 4.2 (Support) *A support is a 4-tuple $S = (T_C, T_R, \mathcal{I}, *)$ where:*

- T_C is a finite partially ordered set (poset), $(T_C, \leq)$, of concept types, defining a type hierarchy (specialization hierarchy: $\forall x, y \in T_C \; x \leq y$ means that x is a subtype of y) and which has a greatest element $\top_C$, the universal type.

- T_R is a finite set of relation types partitioned into k posets $(T_R^i, \leq)_{i=1,k}$ of relation types of arity i $(1 \leq i \leq k)$, where k is the maximum arity of a relation type in T_R. Each $(T_R^i, \leq)_{i=1,k}$ has a greatest element, the universal type $\top_{T_R^i}$.

- $\mathcal{I}$ is a set of countable set of individual markers, used to refer specific concepts.

- $*$ is the generic marker used to refer to an unspecified concept (having, however, a specified type).

- The sets T_C, T_R, $\mathcal{I}$ and $\{*\}$ are mutually disjoint and $\mathcal{I} \cup \{*\}$ is partially ordered by $x \leq y$ iff $x = y$ or $y = *$.

We describe the posets $(T_C, \leq)$ and $(T_R^i, \leq)_{i=1,k}$ by specifying their Hasse's diagrams, yet more practical representations based on ontology technology [12] or formal concept analysis [22] are possible.

A conceptual graph is a structure that depicts factual information about the background knowledge described by its support. This information is presented in a visual manner as an ordered bipartite graph, whose nodes have been labelled with elements from the support. The label $\lambda(v)$ is inserted in the shape representing the vertex v.

Definition 4.3 (Conceptual graph) *A (simple) conceptual graph (CG) is a triple $SG = [S, G, \lambda]$, where:*

- *$S = (T_C, T_R, \mathcal{I}, *)$ is a support;*

- *$G = (V_C, V_R, N_G)$ is an ordered bipartite graph;*

- *λ is a labelling of the vertices of G with elements from the support S: $\forall r \in V_R, \; \lambda(r) \in T_R^{d_G(r)}; \; \forall c \in V_C, \; \lambda(c) \in T_C \times (\mathcal{I} \cup \{*\})$.*

Conceptual graphs reasoning, which is logically sound [18] and complete [5], is based on a conceptual graph operation called projection. This is a labelled graph homomorphism which defines a generalization-specialization relation over conceptual graphs. A structure G is more general than a structure H (denoted as $G \geq H$) if there is a projection from G to H. The $\geq$ symbol is interpreted as "greater than" in the sense that a human is more generic (i.e. broader) than a student.

Projection checking translates to a graph homomorphism between the two graphs (defined on the same support) which makes use of the sub/super class information given by the support. Figure 5 depicts a very simple projection between two graphs. One graph states that a student is teaching a course on a certain topic, the other represents the fact that a postgraduate student is teaching a course. The common support is not shown for simplicity reasons, being the same with the support depicted in Figure 2.

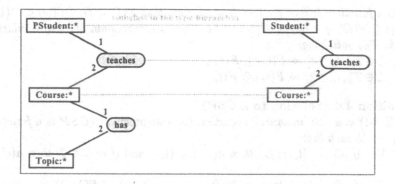

Figure 5: Conceptual Graph Projection

Definition 4.4 (Projection, Subsumption relation)
If $SG = [S, G, \lambda_G]$, and $SH = [S, H, \lambda_H]$ are two CG's defined on the same support S, then a projection from SG to SH is a mapping

$$\pi : V_C(G) \cup V_R(G) \rightarrow V_C(H) \cup V_R(H)$$

such that

- $\pi(V_C(G)) \subseteq V_C(H)$ and $\pi(V_R(G)) \subseteq V_R(H)$;

- $\forall c \in V_C(G), \forall r \in V_R(G)$ if $c = N_G^i(r)$ then $\pi(c) = N_H^i(\pi(r))$;

- $\forall v \in V_C(G) \cup V_R(G)$ $\lambda_G(v) \geq \lambda_H(\pi(v))$.

If there is a projection from SG to SH then SG subsumes SH, denoted $SG \geq SH$. This subsumption relation is a preorder on the set of all CG's defined on the same support.

4.2 CGs for Constraint Satisfaction Problems

The following 3 definitions present the formalization of a constraint satisfaction problem(CSP) and its (partial) solution using conceptual graphs (CGs). A CSP is defined as a pair consisting of a conceptual graph and a model for the support the conceptual graph is defined on. The model maps the support elements to appropriate structures defined on a finite domain. A solution to a CSP is defined as a function that associates the CG's concept nodes to the domain in such way that the model's mappings are preserved.

Definition 4.5 (CSP instance) *A Constraint Satisfaction Problem (CSP) instance is a pair $CSP = (SG, \mathcal{M})$, where $SG = [S, G, \lambda]$ is a conceptual graph and $\mathcal{M}$ is a model for the support $S = (T_C, T_R, \mathcal{I}, *)$, that is, a pair $\mathcal{M} = (D, F)$ where*
- D is a finite set of objects called the domain or universe of $\mathcal{M}$,

- F is a function defined on $T_C \cup T_R \cup \mathcal{I}$ such that $F(\mathcal{I}) \subseteq D$, $F(T_C) \subseteq \mathcal{P}(D)$, $F(T_R^i) \subseteq \mathcal{P}(D^i)$ for each $i \in \{1, \ldots, k\}$ (k is the maximum arity of a relation type in T_R) satisfying:

- $\forall t_c, t_c' \in T_C, t_c \leq t_c' \Rightarrow F(t_c) \subseteq F(t_c')$,
- $\forall t_r, t_r' \in T_R^i, t_r \leq t_r' \Rightarrow F(t_r) \subseteq F(t_r')$.

Definition 4.6 (Solution to a CSP)
If $(SG, \mathcal{M})$ is a CSP instance, a solution (or assignment) to CSP is a function $a : V_C \to D$ such that
-$\forall c \in V_C$, if $\lambda(c) = (t_c, ref_c)$ then $a(c) \in F(t_c)$, and if $ref_c \in \mathcal{I}$ then $a(c) = F(ref_c)$;
-$\forall r \in V_R$, if $deg_G(r) = i$ then $(a(N_G^1(r)), \ldots, a(N_G^i(r))) \in F(\lambda(r))$.
The set of all solutions to CSP is denoted $\mathcal{A}(SG, \mathcal{M})$. If $\mathcal{A}(SG, \mathcal{M}) \neq \emptyset$ then SG holds in $\mathcal{M}$ and is denoted $\mathcal{M} \models SG$.

Finding a solution to a given CSP instance $CSP = (SG, \mathcal{M})$ means specifying the objects corresponding to the concept vertices $V_C(*)$ of the conceptual graph SG. These concepts need to be consistent with the relations on D obtained by the $\mathcal{M}$ interpretation.

Note that objects corresponding to vertices in $V_C \setminus V_C(*)$ are established by the model $\mathcal{M}$ and therefore the following proposition holds trivially.

Proposition 1 Let $CSP = (SG, \mathcal{M})$ be a CSP instance such that $V_C(*) = \emptyset$. If $\mathcal{M} \models SG$, then the CSP instance has an unique solution, $\mathcal{A}(SG, \mathcal{M}) = \{a\}$, where $a(c) = F(ref_c)$, for each concept vertex c with $\lambda(c) = (t_c, ref_c)$.

A partial solution to a CSP with a scope A (where A is a subset of generic concept nodes) is defined as a function that associates A's concept nodes to the domain in such way that the model's mappings are preserved. Any partial solution must assign the value prescribed by the model to concept nodes labelled by individual markers, and also must be consistent with respect to all relation vertices having the set of (concept) neighbors contained in A or labelled by individual markers.

Definition 4.7 (Partial solution to a CSP)
Let $CSP = (SG, \mathcal{M})$ be a CSP instance, and $A \subseteq V_C(*)$. A partial solution with scope A (or partial A-assignment) to CSP is a function $a' : A \cup (V_C \setminus V_C(*)) \to D$ such that
-$\forall c \in V_C \setminus V_C(*)$ $a'(c) = F(ref_c)$;
-$\forall c \in A$, if $\lambda(c) = (t_c, *)$ then $a'(c) \in F(t_c)$;
-$\forall r \in V_R$, if $deg_G(r) = i$ and $\overline{N}(r) \subseteq A \cup (V_C \setminus V_C(*))$ then
$(a'(N_G^1(r)), \ldots, a'(N_G^i(r))) \in F(\lambda(r))$.

The next definition introduces the notion of comparing two models for a given support. This can be used to pave the way for CSP reasoning using the projection operation for CGs.

Definition 4.8 (Comparing Models)

Let $S = (T_C, T_R, \mathcal{I}, *)$ be a support and $\mathcal{M}_1 = (D, F_1)$ and $\mathcal{M}_2 = (D, F_2)$ two models for S. We say that $\mathcal{M}_1$ is a submodel of $\mathcal{M}_2$, denoted $\mathcal{M}_1 \le \mathcal{M}_2$, if for each $i \in \mathcal{I}$ we have $F_1(i) = F_2(i)$ and for each $x \in T_C \cup T_R$ we have $F_1(x) \subseteq F_2(x)$.

It is easy to see from the previous definitions that the following proposition holds.

Proposition 2 Let $CSP_i = (SG, \mathcal{M}_i)$, $i = 1, 2$ two CSP instances, where $\mathcal{M}_1 \le \mathcal{M}_2$. Then $\mathcal{A}(SG, \mathcal{M}_1) \subseteq \mathcal{A}(SG, \mathcal{M}_2)$. In particular, $\mathcal{M}_1 \models SG \Rightarrow \mathcal{M}_2 \models SG$.

Proof. Let $a \in \mathcal{A}(SG, \mathcal{M}_1)$. Since $\mathcal{M}_1 \le \mathcal{M}_2$, we have $a(c) = F_1(ref_c) = F_2(ref_c)$ for each $c \in V_C \setminus V_C(*)$. If $c \in V_C(*)$, that is $\lambda(c) = (t_c, *)$, then $a(c) = F_1(t_c) \subseteq F_2(t_c)$. Also for each $r \in V_R$, with $d_G(r) = k$, we have $(a(N_G^1(r)), \ldots, a(N_G^i(r))) \in F_1(\lambda(r)) \subseteq F_2(\lambda(r))$. We have therefore verified that $a \in \mathcal{A}(SG, \mathcal{M}_2)$.

A common way to use the above proposition is the backtracking solution search for a CSP instance. The task of extending a current partial assignment a' can be interpreted as solving a new CSP instance with a new model for the support. This is obtained from the current model, by considering a submodel which respects the work done for the finding of a'. More precisely, we have the following:

Proposition 3 Let $CSP = (SG, \mathcal{M})$ be a CSP instance, $A \subset V_C(*)$, and a' a partial A-assignment to CSP. Let $\mathcal{M}'$ the submodel of $\mathcal{M}$ obtained by considering $F'(ref_c) = \{a'(c)\}$ for each $c \in A$, and $F'(x) = F(x)$ for the remaining elements $x \in T_C \cup T_R$. Then,

$$\mathcal{A}(SG, \mathcal{M}') = \{a | a \in \mathcal{A}(SG, \mathcal{M}), a|_A = a'\}.$$

Proof. By the construction of $\mathcal{M}'$, the restriction of each solution $a \in \mathcal{A}(SG, \mathcal{M})$ on the set A, denoted $a|_A$, is a solution in $\mathcal{A}(SG, \mathcal{M}')$, therefore we have $\{a | a \in \mathcal{A}(SG, \mathcal{M}), a|_A = a'\} \subseteq \mathcal{A}(SG, \mathcal{M}')$. The converse inclusion is a consequence of the above proposition, because $\mathcal{M}' \le \mathcal{M}$.

Another useful tool for a decomposition approach to the task of obtaining the solutions of a CSP instance can be described as follows.

Let $CSP = (SG, \mathcal{M})$ be a CSP instance, and (R_1, R_2) be a partition of the set V_R of relation vertices of the conceptual graph G. If we denote G_i ($i = 1, 2$) the subgraph spanned by R_i in G and by SG_i the corresponding simple conceptual graph (λ_i is the restriction of the labeling function λ on the vertices of G_i), then we obtain two CSP instances $CSP_i = (SG_i, \mathcal{M})$ ($i = 1, 2$). These can be solved independently giving partial solutions of the initial problem. The set of solution of the initial CSP instance can be constructed by joining the "compatible" partial solutions. More precisely, we have the following:

Proposition 4 *Let* $CSP = (SG, \mathcal{M})$ *be a CSP instance,* (R_1, R_2) *a partition of the set* V_R *of relation vertices of the conceptual graph* G, *and* $CSP_i = (SG_i, \mathcal{M})$ $(i = 1, 2)$ *the corresponding induced subinstances . Then,*
$$\mathcal{A}(SG, \mathcal{M}) = \{a : V_C \to D | \exists a_i \in \mathcal{A}(SG_i, \mathcal{M}) \ s.t.$$
$$a|_{N_G(R_i)} = a_i \ (i = 1, 2) \ and$$
$$a_1|_{N_G(R_1) \cap N_G(R_2)} = a_2|_{N_G(R_1) \cap N_G(R_2)}\}.$$

Conceptual Graphs reasoning mechanisms (projection) can be highlighted by the following proposition.

Proposition 5 *Let* $CSP_i = (SG_i, \mathcal{M})$, $i = 1, 2$ *two CSP instances with* $SG_2 \geq SG_1$. *If* π *is a projection from* SG_2 *to* SG_1, *then for each* $a \in \mathcal{A}(SG_1, \mathcal{M})$ *we have* $a \circ \pi \in \mathcal{A}(SG_2, \mathcal{M})$. *In particular,* $\mathcal{M} \models SG_1 \Rightarrow \mathcal{M} \models SG_2$.

Proof. Since π is a projection from SG_2 to SG_1, then $F(c) \geq F(\pi(c))$, and therefore $a \circ \pi(c) = a(\pi(c)) \in F(\pi(c)) \subseteq F(c)$. The concept nodes of SG_1 labelled by individual markers are projected in concept nodes labelled by the same individual markers. Since π decreases the labels of relation nodes too, it is easy to see that $(a \circ \pi(N_{G_2}(r)), \ldots, a'(N_{G_2} i(r))) \in F(\lambda(\pi(r)))$ for each $\forall r \in V_R^2$ with $deg_{G_2}(r) = i$. Therefore $a \circ \pi$ is a solution in $\mathcal{A}(SG_2, \mathcal{M})$.

The above proposition states that, if there is a projection between two conceptual graphs which are describing two CSP instances, then, for each solution of the second instance we can find a solution for the former by using the graph homomorphism given by the projection. A special case is to use of a previously discovered solution, which is present in the knowledge base. Then, the following corollary holds:

Corollary 4.1 *Let* $CSP = (SG, \mathcal{M})$ *be a CSP instance. If* $CSP_1 = (SH, \mathcal{M})$ *is a CSP instance such that* $V_C^H(*) = \emptyset$ *and* $SG \geq SH$, *then for each projection* π *from* SG *to* SH, *the function* a *defined by* $a(c) = F(i)$, *for each concept vertex* $c \in V_C^G$ *with* $\lambda(c) = (t_c, i)$, *is a solution to* CSP.

This corollary states that if CSP_1 has already been solved (there are no more variables, that is, generic nodes labeled by $*$) and if there is a projection between the two conceptual graphs associated to CSP and CSP_1, then we can always build a solution to CSP. This is an important result, giving a new way of solving a CSP instance. Finding all the solutions to a CSP instance reduces to finding all the conceptual graphs SH without generic nodes, with the property that the graph associated to the CSP instance projects to SH. The following proposition holds:

Proposition 6 *Let* $CSP = (SG, \mathcal{M})$ *be a CSP instance. If*
$\mathcal{SG} = \{SH | SG \geq SH, V_C^H(*) = \emptyset, \ and \ \mathcal{A}(SH, \mathcal{M}) \neq \emptyset\}$ *and for each* $SH \in \mathcal{SG}$,
$\{a_{SH}\} := \mathcal{A}(SH, \mathcal{M})$ *and* $\Pi(SG, SH) := \{\pi | \pi \ is \ a \ projection \ from \ SG \ to \ SH\}$,
then
$$\mathcal{A}(SG, \mathcal{M}) = \cup_{SH \in \mathcal{SG}} \cup_{\pi \in \Pi(SG, SH)} \{a_{SH} \circ \pi\}.$$

5 Discussion

This paper has presented a visual way of representing CSP instances using a CG derived model. We have expressed, by the means of graphs the variables, their corresponding domains and the constraints. This representation gives, as such, a static view over the CSP instance to be addressed. From this point of view, the advantage of our framework is that arbitrary constraint satisfaction methods can be employed. This also includes local search methods.

On the other side, the static representation complicates the constraints in case of alternative scenarios (tasks like scheduling, planning, configuration etc.). In this case we need to extend the CG model, introduce new syntactic operations etc. One way of solving this problem is to design a dynamic representation which allows real-world scenarios depiction. We are developing Conceptual Graph Assemblies (CGAs), a structure which contains a Conceptual Graph (CG) along with a combinatorial structure on its relation nodes. This structure is used to capture alternative knowledge views on data, as opposed to static, "snapshot" like, facts.

We believe that bringing together the CSP realm and visual knowledge representations has research potential both from a theoretical and an application point of view. In this context, our goal is neither to provide competitive results, nor to propose specific problem driven combinations which compete with state of art solvers, but to illustrate the use of this framework in designing hybrid strategies to addressing CSPs.

References

[1] F. Baader et al., editors. *The Description Logic Handbook*. Cambridge Univ. Press, 2003.

[2] J.-F. Baget and M.-L. Mugnier. Extensions of Simple Conceptual Graphs: the Complexity of Rules and Constraints. *Jour. of Artif. Intell. Res.*, 16:425–465, 2002.

[3] J.-F. Baget et al. A Pure Graph-Based Solution to the SCG-1 Initiative. In *Proc. of the 7th Int'l Conf. on Conceptual Structures (ICCS'99)*, pages 355–376, 1999.

[4] S. Bechhofer et al. OilEd: a Reason-able Ontology Editor for the Semantic Web. In *Proc. of the Joint German/Austrian Conf. on Artif. Intell. (KI'2001)*, number 2174 in Lect. Notes in Comp. Sci., pages 396–408. Springer, 2001.

[5] M. Chein and M.-L. Mugnier. Conceptual graphs: Fundamental notions. *Revue d'Intelligence Artificielle*, 6(4):365–406, 1992.

[6] M. Chein and M.-L. Mugnier. Conceptual Graphs are also Graphs. Research report, LIRMM, 1995.

[7] M Croitoru et al. Hierarchical knowledge integration using layered conceptual graphs. In *Proc. of the 13th Int'l Conf. on Conceptual Structures (ICCS'2005)*, number 3596 in Lect. Notes in Artif. Intell., pages 267–280. Springer, 2005.

[8] Rina Dechter. *Constraint Processing*. Morgan Kaufmann, 2003.

[9] D. W. Fowler et al. The Designers' Workbench: Using Ontologies and Constraints for Configuration. In *AI2004: The Twenty-fourth SGAI International Conference on Innovative Techniques and Applications of Artificial Intelligence*, Cambridge, UK, December 2004.

[10] C. McKenzie et al. Extending swrl to express fully-quantified constraints. In G Antoniou and H. Boley, editors, *Rules and Rule Markup Languages for the Semantic Web (RuleML 2004)*, pages 139–154. Springer, 2004.

[11] S. Mittal and B. Falkenhainer. Dynamic constraint satisfaction problems. In *Proceedings of the 8th National Conference on Artificial Intelligence*, pages 25–32. AAAI Press, 1989.

[12] Natalya F. Noy et al. Creating semantic web contents with protege-2000. *IEEE Intell. Syst.*, 2(16):60–71, 2001.

[13] J. K. Pearson and P. G. Jeavons. A survey of tractable constraint satisfaction problems. Technical Report CSD-TR-97-15, Royal Holloway University of London, 1997.

[14] D. Sabin and E. D. Freuder. Configuration as Composite Constraint Satisfaction. In George F. Luger, editor, *Proceedings of the (1st) Artificial Intelligence and Manufacturing ResearchPlanning Workshop*, pages 153–161. AAAI Press, 1996, 1996. ISBN 1-57735-003-0.

[15] Derek Sleeman and Stuart Chalmers. Assisting domain experts to formulate & solve constraint satisfaction problems. In *To appear: 15th International Conference on Knowledge Engineering and Knowledge Management*, Podebrady (near Prague), Czech Republic, October 2006.

[16] B. Smith. Modelling for Constraint Programming. 1st Constraint Programming Summer School, September 2005.

[17] J. Sowa. *Knowledge Representation: Logical, Philosophical, and Computational Foundations*. Brooks Cole Publishing Co., 2000.

[18] J. F. Sowa. *Conceptual Structures: Information Processing in Mind and Machine*. Addison-Wesley, 1984.

[19] E. P. K. Tsang. *Foundations of Constraint Satisfaction*. Academic Press, 1993.

[20] W3C RDF Primer. RDF Primer — W3C Recommendation 10/2/2004, 2004. URL http://www.w3.org/TR/rdf-primer/.

[21] W3C SWRL. SWRL: A Semantic Web Rule Language Combining OWL and RuleML, 2004. URL http://www.w3.org/Submission/SWRL/.

[22] R. Wille. Conceptual Graphs and Formal Concept Analysis. In *Proc. of the 5th Int'l Conf. on Conceptual Structures (ICCS'97)*, pages 290–303, 1997.

[23] World Wide Web Consortium. Web Ontology language (OWL), current Aug. 2005. URL http://www.w3.org/2004/OWL/.

Integrating Uncertain Knowledge in a Domain Ontology for Room Concept Classifications

Joana Hois
Universität Bremen, Germany
joana@informatik.uni-bremen.de
www.informatik.uni-bremen.de/~joana

Kerstin Schill
Universität Bremen, Germany
kschill@informatik.uni-bremen.de
www.informatik.uni-bremen.de/cog_neuroinf

John A. Bateman
Universität Bremen, Germany
bateman@uni-bremen.de
www.uni-bremen.de/~bateman

Abstract

Ontologies provide a representation of precise knowledge about concepts, their attributes and relations. The Dempster-Shafer theory provides a representation of epistemic plausibilities. In AI both representations are typically developed separately on purpose, which is appropriate unless their combination is required. Real world applications, however, sometimes require a combination of both.

In this paper we will present such a combination of a domain ontology and uncertain knowledge. Our approach arises from the need of a room classification system for representing room concepts (in the sense of classifying names that are cognitively assigned to rooms, such as "kitchen", "laboratory", "office") that can be derived from objects occurring in the rooms. These room concepts can only be determined with a certain degree of belief, not so much depending on the system's quality as depending on ambiguities in the cognitive assignment of room concepts. Hence, uncertainty about concepts that exist in reality also needs to be represented in the application.

1. Introduction

Our aim is to develop a system that identifies the *room concept* of a room on the basis of visual information in order to accomplish further tasks based on this classification. Room concepts (cf. [12]) are distinguished by means of the functional role that is associated with actions that can be performed in such rooms.

In turn, the functions and actions depend on several physical objects that have to be in the room. The objects occurring in a room therefore imply the room's room concept. For example, a kitchen is a place where you can make coffee, wash dishes, or cook. These activities depend on certain objects, namely interior furniture, equipment, or ingredients. In our example, the activity "make coffee" depends on a coffee machine, a mug, sugar, milk, water, or similar objects. Hence, the perception of the concepts of a room depend on its contained objects as they indicate possible functional aspects [14] and consequently the functional role, i.e. the room concept itself.

This analysis provides significant opportunities for cognitive, spatially aware systems. For instance, intelligent buildings using this system are able to answer user requests, such as "Where can I find an unoccupied kitchen?" or "Tell me all possible seminar rooms that have at least a video projector and a white board." Or autonomous robots can respond to tasks that refer to special activities they can perform considering the respective room concepts and occurring objects. Both examples also show a strong connection to human-computer interaction, possibly realised with natural language dialogues, which can directly access the concepts described above. Autonomous robots, however, can also use the room concept classification for an independent exploration of their environments in dynamic contexts, especially in which they have to react to changes.

For representing necessary concepts of rooms and objects in our application we decided to develop a domain ontology for rooms of a university building. The decision to use an ontology is based upon its advantage for formal representation of objects and their relations and its direct support of re-usability and knowledge sharing [7]. For the latter, our domain ontology is guided by an upper ontology for linguistic and cognitive engineering [13], which also offers a solid basis for further development. That linguistic terms also have a strong impact on the types of room concepts and objects confirms our decision for using a domain ontology as it can provide a mapping to a linguistic ontology and can be used within a dialogue system [8].

However, we must also represent degrees of uncertainty for each room concept because of the possibility of one room providing multiple functions and uncertain evidence. Thus, the analysis of a room indicates room concepts with a certain degree of belief. This is due to the fact that a room scene tends to be compatible with more than just one room concept. For example, when the system recognises a room full of chairs and tables it may be confronted with a study room, a lecture hall, or a seminar room. In fact, this does not eliminate the possibility of one room having more than one room concept at the same time. A room can provide functionality for a lecture hall as well as a seminar room, for instance, by having enough chairs, tables, and blackboard or projection facilities. But a room with a fridge, a microwave, a sink, tables, and cabinets might not serve as a kitchen and a chemical laboratory simultaneously (because of safety issues). Accordingly, different room concepts can be mutually exclusive, which is why we are often not able to make distinct definitions of a unique room concept and we specify the evidence for a certain room concept instead. In our work this evidence is represented by the Belief function of the Dempster-Shafer theory [18]. A room concept is then classified with respect to statistic data about prototypic room samples, their contained objects and their room concepts.

In the following, we will give detailed description of the ontological representation within our system as well as the representation of uncertain knowledge, and we will demonstrate a combination of a domain ontology and uncertain knowledge considering our application as example.

2. Ontology

Ontologies are nowadays widely used in different applications ranging from the attempt to represent complete general knowledge and common sense, such as OpenCyc[1], to the use in particular domains to represent specific concepts, such as Medical Information[2]. [9] specify several principles by which ontologies can be modelled and classified and they give a detailed overview of technical issues and applications using ontologies hitherto. This spread of ontological applications also results from the development of the Semantic Web [5], which is intended to provide a navigable structure aligned by its semantic concepts.

As we have to represent rooms, their interior objects, and the room concepts they support, we require a taxonomical and partonomical structure: The room concepts can be grouped hierarchically in a taxonomy, whereas interior objects are parts of the respective rooms. This representation is also affected by linguistic expressions of the represented concepts caused by the intended dialogue between a user and the system, as we have mentioned with the intelligent building example above. Therefore, the structure has to take into account also the semantics of those expressions corresponding with the room scenes. Further considerations are reasoning strategies that are inherently supported by the structure. As all of these requirements are covered by ontological structures (see [9]) and because of the reasons we gave in the introduction, we decided to develop a domain ontology for representing scenes, objects, and room concepts. We finally have to consider the particular modelling of a domain ontology for our application.

Besides the different ontology principles, the role of an ontology can be outlined as "(i) to set out a consistent and well-specified general modelling scheme which is free of contradiction and from which follows a set of generic properties that necessarily hold over the entities covered and, (ii) to support problem solving and inference within the domain of concern"[3]. Yet a realisation of the first claim is not thus simple. Although there are several guidelines for the design of ontologies (for instance [20]), there are still problems about consistency and coherence throughout various ontologies. Complications usually arise in case of ontology mappings and it becomes difficult to mediate between different ontologies because they are not easily interchangeable. Hence, the sharing of ontological knowledge becomes complex and ontologies are rather remade than re-used. Recently, different approaches try to provide not just guidance but a systematic frame for

---

[1] http://www.opencyc.org/
[2] http://www.ifomis.uni-saarland.de

designing ontologies. As we do not want to encounter the problems of indiscriminately designed ontologies, our developed ontology for rooms and their objects will be integrated into an ontology framework that already provides a more abstract scope for linguistic and cognitive engineering, namely DOLCE [13].

2.1 Domain Ontology Modelling

DOLCE was originally developed as a part of the WonderWeb project[3] with a strong influence from natural language and human common sense. The basic categories of DOLCE are *Perdurants*, *Endurants*, *Qualities*, and *Abstracts*. Perdurants describe entities that unfold in time (e.g., an event of some kind), whereas Endurants describe entities that are wholly present at each point in time (e.g., a cup, a glass, a desk, etc.). Qualities inhere in entities, which means that every entity can have certain qualities, even Qualities themselves. The value of these qualities are expressed by entities of the Abstract concept, called *quale*.

The rooms we will analyse will be classified as an instance of *Non-Agentive Physical Object* (a subclass of Endurant) as it defines physical objects that have direct spatial qualities, a life (exist over time), and we do not ascribe intentions, beliefs, or desires to them (in contrast to *Agentive Objects*). The objects that occur in a room will be an instance of Non-Agentive Physical Object as well because we are currently omitting humans or robots in rooms as their attendance is mostly not indicative enough.

Starting from this we created a hierarchy of specific non-agentive physical objects, to wit physical rooms and their contained objects. Physical rooms in this case define the bare rooms that are characterised by their walls, floors, ceilings, and dimensions and that can contain further physical objects (such as chairs, desks, shelfs, etc.)[4]. These physical rooms are not distinguished by their functional role yet. Instead the hierarchy of possible room concepts are classified as an instance of Abstract. This distinction between physical rooms (that contain objects) and the abstract room concepts (that can be represented by a physical room) is quite crucial. It is a precise modelling of the relations between rooms and their room concepts and results in physical rooms having a quality that specifies the room concept it may support owing to its contained objects (or in fact the functions that the objects are indicating). This physical room quality also resembles the concept of a so-called *niche* [2, 19]. In our application, we use a Quality to represent this concept, as we presuppose all rooms of a university building supporting at least one specific room concept and by allowing an empty room concept. Figure 1 illustrates the described ontological concepts and their relations. To keep the classification

---

[3] http://wonderweb.semanticweb.org/
[4] Although this "contained in" relation is time-dependent, i.e., an object is contained in a room during a specific time duration, and should therefore include a time parameter, we omit this data for simplicity, because our room concept classification is done ad hoc and thus independent of previous results or changes of objects.

system deterministic and executable, our domain ontology is developed in description logic using OWL DL in combination with DOLCE-Lite[5].

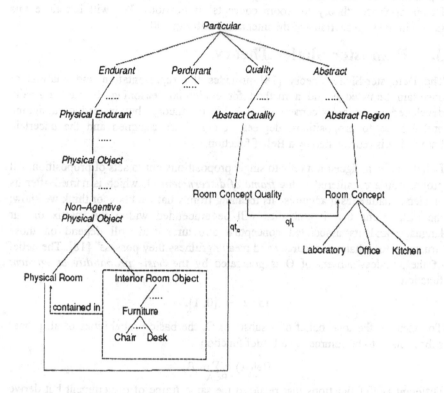

Figure 1 Ontological room concepts of the domain ontology. The concepts in italic are indicating DOLCE's concepts. Lines represent taxonomical relations, arrows represent other relations between concepts

This domain ontology design facilitates the representation of our application concern though the supported room concepts of a physical room cannot be classified uniquely by the system. Imagine a room having a table with chairs surrounded and some pictures on the walls or the like. Without further information it may serve as a dining room, a seminar room, a day room, or all of them as the occurring objects do not give much indication to possible actions that can be performed in this room. Even if the attributes of all room concepts were defined exhaustively, an explicit classification would not be possible. Although the more precise the information about room concepts in the domain ontology, the better the result of the classification, under real world conditions there is little or no reasonable chance of having unambiguous situations. A room can still be used as a kitchen if it looses its oven. And it is still not a chemical laboratory, although necessary equipment for respective activities is present. In lieu of exactly

---

[5] http://www.loa-cnr.it/ontologies/DOLCE-Lite.owl

determining the supported room concepts the application is instead able to indicate them with a certain degree of belief. Hence, these values also need to be represented in our domain ontology. In fact, we integrate belief values of the Dempster-Shafer theory for room concepts' indications. We will introduce this theory in the next section and the integration subsequently.

3. Dempster-Shafer Theory

The Dempster-Shafer theory [18] provides the representation and analysis of uncertain knowledge and a method for evidential reasoning. It was originally developed as an enhancement of probabilistic theory, but instead of assigning probabilities to propositions, degrees of belief are assigned and the uncertain knowledge is represented by a Belief function.

Belief can be assigned not only to single propositions but to sets of proposition. All proposition are gathered in the *frame of discernment* Θ, which is named after its epistemic nature, as it acquires "its meaning from what we know or think we know; the distinctions that it embodies will be embedded within the matrix of our language and its associated conceptual structures and will depend on those structures for whatever accuracy and meaningfulness they possess" [18]. The belief of the smallest subsets of Θ is generated by the *basic probability assignment* function

$$m : 2^{\Theta} \to [0, 1].$$

To calculate the total belief of a subset of Θ, the basic probabilities of all proper subsets have to be summed in a Belief function

$$Bel(A) = \sum_{B \subset A} m(B)$$

Different Belief functions that relate to the same frame of discernment but derive from distinct bodies of evidence can be combined by using *Dempster's Rule of Combination*, which is a belief function based on the combined evidences for computing their orthogonal sum. For the combination of different belief this function $((\cdots (Bel_1 \otimes Bel_2) \cdots) \otimes Bel_{n-1}) \cdots Bel_n$ combines the belief Bel_1, ..., Bel_n pairwise. For instance, if we have the result of two analyses from distinct points of view of the room, both indicating that the room supports the room concept "office"; viewpoint A with an evidence of 0.7, viewpoint B with an evidence of 0.9. Then we can combine both as shown in Table 1. Hence, the total evidence for the room concept "office" is 0.97 (the sum of each supporting evidence). For a more detailed presentation of Dempster's Rule, we refer the reader to [18], chapter 3, §1.

A major advantage of the Dempster-Shafer theory is its explicit representation of ignorance [4] as it makes a clear distinction between the lack of knowledge and the assignment of degrees of belief to the negation of a proposition. Hence, there is no need for the belief of a proposition and the belief of its negation to sum up to 1 because remaining propositions will not be affected without explicit assignments. In our application the belief that a physical room may be used as an office for a certain degree does not determine the belief of other possible room concepts, for instance, a study room (especially as the physical room may be used as both room concepts). The use of subjective belief of specialists is also a great benefit if no a priori probabilities are available [16]. This provides the possibility of assigning degrees of belief to physical room concepts depending on occurring objects without the investigation of a vast number of empirically measured physical room data (see for further details the implementation in section 5).

Table 1 Example of using Dempster's Rule of Evidence for combining different evidences for the room concept "office" from viewpoint A and B

	A: "Office" (0.7)	A: Θ (0.3)
B: "Office" (0.9)	0.63	0.27
B: Θ (0.1)	0.07	0.03

When applying Dempster's Rule of Combination new belief can be combined with the old one, which results in a *belief update*. This benefits our system's implementation depending on our application, which analyses one object after another and can therefore calculate current belief distributions iteratively.

It has been observed that "very little has been done to perform reasoning or inferencing with information represented in terms of belief functions" [4]. Hence, using a domain ontology, which already provides a reasoning strategy in its structure to integrate this information seems to be a promising suggestion.

Although a disadvantage of the Dempster-Shafer theory is its computational complexity, simplification algorithms have been developed [1, 10] that restrict the frame of discernment to a hierarchical structure, which already conforms to an ontological structure.

Besides the incidental relation between the frame of discernment's epistemic slope and our cognitively assigned room concepts that rely on linguistic expressions, the reasons mentioned above confirm the adequacy of using Dempster-Shafer's Belief functions for the representation of uncertain knowledge for the room concepts in order to integrate them into an ontology. This integration will be discussed in the next section.

4. Combination of Domain Ontology and Dempster-Shafer Theory

As we have now illustrated the need for both the representation of a domain ontology as well as Dempster-Shafer belief values, we will introduce our approach to integrate belief values of the Dempster-Shafer theory into our developed domain ontology.

The clear separation between physical rooms and abstract room concepts turns out to be not only a precise modelling of the relations between rooms and their room concepts but also a sophisticated foundation for the combination of an ontology and the Dempster-Shafer theory. This allows us to assign belief values to the quale values of the quality that a physical room supports a room concept. This is illustrated in Figure 2: Room Concept Quality can have more than just one quale,

252

which are in turn provided with an additional degree of evidence of the Dempster-Shafer theory, namely a belief value between 0 and 1.

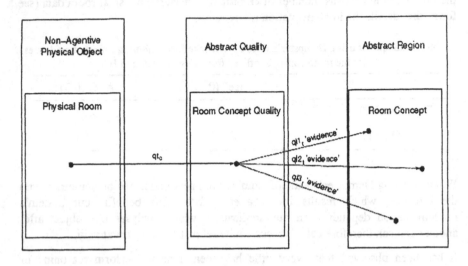

Figure 2 Integrating evidence values into domain ontology

When a physical room with its contained objects is instantiated, the room can have several qualities that relate it to particular room concepts with a specific degree of evidence. In case of new information about the room concepts the evidences can be updated by using Dempster's Rule of Combination[6].

This domain ontology design is characterised by following criteria: First, rooms are represented independently from the room concepts, they support and they are uniquely distinguished by their physical dimensions and properties. For instance, if the furniture of a room is removed from the room it will still retain its identity, only its room concept qualities may change. Similarly, rooms contain objects that are positioned in them and their unique character is not depending on them. Second, the constellation of the contained objects suggests possible functions that can be performed in the rooms and depending on these functional aspects, possible cognitively assigned room concepts can be derived. Third, the quality that a room may support a certain room concept is specified by a belief value with regard to functions that the contained objects indicate or not.

Based on this formal representation, we have developed a visual room concept classification system, which is introduced in the next section.

---

[6] Note: For simplicity the system currently classifies only single concepts. Therefore, we can equate the belief for single propositions (basic probability assignment) with sets of propositions (Belief function).

5. Room Concept Classification System

In our application, the room concept classification is incorporated into a cognitive vision system [17] that analyses and classifies an individual object that is displayed in a 2D-image. This hybrid system performs saccadic eye movements on the image and classifies the represented object after performing a supervised learning phase. We have extended this system for analysing possible room concepts of a given input image by reasoning over the extracted and classified individual objects in the image. As we do not want to consider concrete segmentation algorithms yet, we have created example scenes on the basis of real pictures, in which each single object has its own grey value. We also do not allow overlapping or partially hidden objects yet.

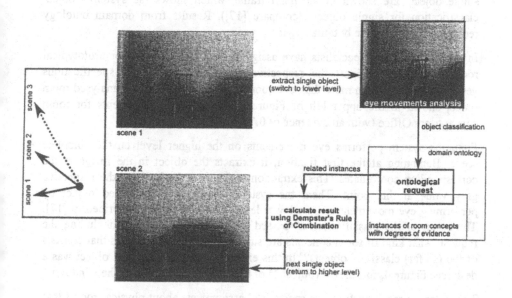

Figure 3 Two-level process of eye movements analysis including the use of ontological and uncertain knowledge

The analysis of a complex scene composed of several objects is divided into two processes: On a higher level the system performs eye movements on the whole scene stopping at each fixation point. On a lower level it extracts the object, which is located at each fixation point, from the complete scene and classifies it by performing eye movements solely on this object depending on a prior learning phase (see [17]). After classifying the single object the system returns to the higher level and resumes eye movement on the complete scene as illustrated in Figure 3. This split between the higher and lower level of eye movements is based on the assumption resulting from experimental results [11, 21] that humans tend to recognize single objects and make conclusions about the scene on a more abstract level than pure visual recognition.

For an illustrative test phase, we used a domain of university building rooms. Available room concepts are Kitchen, Classroom, Lecture Hall, Laboratory, and Office. As the system is instructed to identify them from a given input scene with a certain degree of evidence and all room concepts are pairwise distinct in our modelling, the system uses Demster's Rule of Combination of singleton hypotheses as described in [10]. According to the visual analysis of one object after the other, we compute the respective degrees of belief of each room concept iteratively after every single object classification. This is primarily done for performance, to get a first result of a potential room concept as soon as possible.

The example of a scene analysis that demonstrates the systems behaviour is shown in Figure 4. The physical room scene[7] is displayed in the upper left of the window, in which arrows indicate performed eye movements on the higher level. Analysed single objects are shown in the main frame, which shows the system's object classification for single objects (compare [17]). Results from domain ontology requests are given at the bottom.

In our example, two specialists have assigned their belief values for prototypical room scenes that support the respective room concepts. Their specifications generally tend to assign more than one room concept. In case of the analysed room scene, shown in the upper left of Figure 4, the average assignments for room concepts are Office (with an evidence of 0.75) and Laboratory (0.05).

First, the system performs eye movements on the higher level on the complete scene. Beginning at the first fixation, it extracts the object in the image at the corresponding coordinates. This extraction is done on the basis of the respective grey value at this point. Then, the system classifies the extracted object by performing eye movements on the lower level, which is already described in [17]. The result of the classification is passed to the domain ontology including the request: what kind of room concepts are supported by physical rooms that consists of the (so far) classified objects?[8] In this example, the first classified object was a desk (see Figure 4, fourth row (object 1) of the table at the bottom of the window).

The instances resulting from the specialists' assignments about physical rooms that agree with the analysed contained object are returned and combined by using Dempster's Rule of Combination as described in section 3. In this case we get the following results for possible room concepts of the current scene given the respective belief values in parentheses: Laboratory (0.999), Lecture Hall (0.999), Office (0.999), Classroom (0.999), Kitchen (0.998). The system continues performing its higher level eye movement and extracts and analyses the object in the image at the next fixation point. In the example shown in Figure 4 the analysis shows a sound result of the room supporting the concepts Office (0.99) and Laboratory (0.297) after four steps with respect to the experimental rating of the specialists.

---

[7] For computational simplicity, the images have been abstracted from original pictures taken in university buildings.

[8] Using OWL DL (http://www.w3.org/TR/owl-features) as ontology modelling language and Pellet (http://www.mindswap.org/2003/pellet) as reasoner.

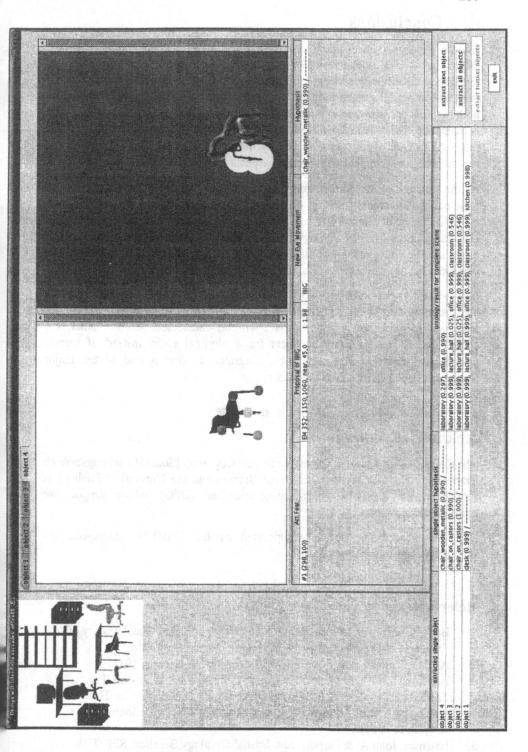

Figure 4 Room concept analysis after four classified objects

6. Conclusions

In this paper we have introduced a first prototype for integrating uncertain knowledge into a domain ontology. However, little work has been done on integrating uncertain knowledge into ontologies as yet. Although two approaches tried to combine Bayesian probabilities [6] or Fuzzy Logic [15] with ontologies, both approaches are more interested in the technical issues concerning this combination than their applicability. In this paper we have emphasised the motivation of our decision influenced by the need of a real world application to represent both ontological and uncertain aspects jointly.

As the structure of our domain ontology evolves from an upper ontology we hope to avoid the commonly arising difficulties for coherence, re-use, mapping and extensibility. Still it is up to future work to determine whether the belief values introduced in our domain ontology are also applicable to similar niche concepts. It might also be necessary for consistency to define a specific quality that specifies whether a quality may have several quales with additional evidences.

Also some computational issues will be investigated further: On the one hand, an automatisation for quality concepts that include an evidence quality value, for instance, by modelling a "meta-class", will be considered. On the other, the calculation of sets of room concepts for a physical room instead of merely calculating single hypotheses will be integrated as this is one of the major advantages of the Dempster-Shafer theory.

Acknowledgements

The Collaborative Research Center for Spatial Cognition (Sonderforschungsbereich Transregio SFB/TR8) of the Universität Bremen and the Universität Freiburg is funded by the Deutsche Forschungsgemeinschaft (DFG), whose support we gratefully acknowledge.

This work has been especially supported by the SFB/TR8 subprojects I1-[OntoSpace] and A5-[ActionSpace].

References

1. Barnett, Jeffrey A. Computational Methods for a Mathematical Theory of Evidence. In Proceedings of the 7th International Joint Conference on Artificial Intelligence, pages 868–875, Vancouver, Canada, 1981.
2. Bateman, John A. Linguistic interaction as ontological mediation. In Zaefferer, Dietmar & Schalley, Andrea (editors), Ontolinguistics. How ontological status shapes the linguistic coding of concepts. Mouton de Gruyter, to appear.
3. Bateman, John A. & Farrar, Scott. Spatial Ontology Baseline. SFB/TR8 internal report I1-[OntoSpace] D2, Collaborative Research Center for Spatial

Cognition, University of Bremen, University of Freiburg, Germany, June 2005.

4. Bhatnagar, Raj K. & Kanal, Laveen N. Handling Uncertain Information: A Review of Numeric and Non-Numeric Methods. In Kanal, Laveen N. & Lemmer, John F. (editors), Uncertainty in Artificial Intelligence, pages 3–26. North-Holland, Amsterdam, 1986.

5. Berners-Lee, Tim & Hendler, James & Lassila, Ora. The Semantic Web. Scientific American, 284(5), May 2001.

6. Ding, Zhongli & Peng, Yun & Pan, Rong. A Bayesian Approach to Uncertainty Modeling in OWL Ontology. In Proceedings of the International Conference on Advances in Intelligent Systems - Theory and Applications, page 9, Luxemburg, November 2004. IEEE.

7. Farrar, Scott & Bateman, John A. General Ontology Baseline. SFB/TR8 internal report I1-[OntoSpace] D1, Collaborative Research Center for Spatial Cognition, University of Bremen, University of Freiburg, Germany, November 2004.

8. Farrar, Scott & Tenbrink, Thora & Bateman, John A. & Ross, Robert J. On the Role of Conceptual and Linguistic Ontologies in Spoken Dialogue Systems. In Symposium on Dialogue Modelling and Generation, Amsterdam, Netherlands, July 2005.

9. Gómez-Pérez, Asunción & Fernández-López, Mariano & Corcho, Oscar. Ontological Engineering with examples from the areas of Knowledge Management, e-Commerce and the Semantic Web. Springer-Verlag, London, 2004.

10. Gordon, Jean & Shortliffe, Edward H. A method for managing evidential reasoning in a hierarchical hypothesis space. Artificial Intelligence, 26:323–357, 1985.

11. Herrmann, Theo. Blickpunkte und Blickpunktsequenzen. Sprache und Kognition, 15:159–177, 1996.

12. Knauff, Markus. Räumliches Wissen und Gedächtnis. Deutscher Universitätsverlag, Wiesbaden, 1997.

13. Masolo, Claudio & Borgo, Stefano & Gangemi, Aldo & Guarino, Nicola & Oltramari, Alessandro. Ontologies library (final). WonderWeb Deliverable D18, ISTC-CNR, Padova, Italy, December 2003.

14. Mulligan, Kevin. Perception, Predicates and Particulars. In Fisette, Denis (editor), Consciousness and Intentionality: Models and Modalities of Attribution, pages 163–194. Kluwer, Dordrecht, 1999.

15. Pan, Jeff Z. & Stamou, Giorgos & Tzouvaras, Vassilis & Horrocks, Ian. A Fuzzy Extension of SWRL. In Proceedings of the International Conference on Artificial Neural Networks (ICANN 2005), Special section on "Intelligent multimedia and semantics", 2005. to appear.

16. Schill, Kerstin. Distributed Reasoning with Uncertain Data. In Ayyub, Bilal M. & Gupta, Madan M. (editors), Uncertainty Analysis in Engineering and the Sciences: Fuzzy Logic, Statistics, and Neural Network Approach, pages 339–351. Kluwer Academic Publisher, Boston, 1997.

17. Schill, Kerstin & Umkehrer, Elisabeth & Beinlich, Stephan & Krieger, Gerhard & Zetzsche, Christoph. Scene Analysis with Saccadic Eye

Movements: Topdown and Bottom-up Modeling. Journal of Electronic Imaging, 10(1):152–160, 2001.

18. Shafer, Glenn. A Mathematical Theory of Evidence. Princeton University Press, Princeton, 1976.

19. Smith, Barry & Varzi, Achille. The niche. Noûs, 33(2):198–222, 1999.

20. Uschold, Mike and Grüninger, Michael. Ontologies: Principles, methods and applications. Knowledge Engineering Review, 11:93–155, February 1996.

21. Yarbus, Alfred L. Eye Movements and Vision. Plenum Press, New York, 1967. Translation: B. Haigh.

SESSION 4:

SEMANTIC WEB

Using AI and Semantic Web Technologies to attack Process Complexity in Open Systems

Simon Thompson, Nick Giles, Yang Li,
Hamid Gharib, Thuc Duong Nguyen.
BT Research and Venturing,
Adastral Park, Ipswich.
Contact: simon.2.thompson@bt.com

Abstract

Recently many vendors and groups have advocated using BPEL and
WS-BPEL as a workflow language to encapsulate business logic.
While encapsulating workflow and process logic in one place is a
sensible architectural decision the implementation of complex
workflows suffers from the same problems that made managing and
maintaining hierarchical procedural programs difficult. BPEL lacks
constructs for logical modularity such as the requirements construct
from the STL [12] or the ability to adapt constructs like pure abstract
classes for the same purpose. We describe a system that uses
semantic web and agent concepts to implement an abstraction layer
for BPEL based on the notion of Goals and service typing. AI
planning was used to enable process engineers to create and validate
systems that used services and goals as first class concepts and
compiled processes at run time for execution.

1. Introduction

When process flows move beyond describing the interactions required to buy a
book they can become very complex. For example, the job allocation workflow
implemented in BT on the CSS system in COBOL requires two sheets of A0 paper
to be plotted with readable fonts. While it is possible to write a job allocation
process as receive task -> choose resource -> allocate task real world issues such as
record maintenance, audit, co-ordination, authentication, health and safety,
reporting, billing, resource management, logistics and cash flow must be included
to make the process operational. The move of business processes into an open
environment of dynamic virtual enterprises has added another problem and another
source of complexity.

Software development attacked the problem of complexity of process flow by
developing abstractions that allowed a degree of agility and reuse to be achieved by
modularity and encapsulation of data and function. Classes as an abstraction in
object orientated programming provide both abstract data types and polymorphism
for use cases such as the abstract factory pattern or template based development.

We have used the concepts of service mark-up and goal orientation that have been
proposed by the Semantic Web and Autonomous Agent communities to implement

an approach to dealing with process complexity (see section 2) This paper describes our approach in detail with an example (section 3) and reports on analytic tools (section 4) and development method (section 5) which are required to support the use of this technology in the context of developing process orientated systems. In particular our tools are designed to help engineers develop and test dynamic, open systems of services, possibly provided by Autonomous Agents.

2. Previous work

BPEL is Turing Complete and is therefore an acceptable machine readable process specification. It is highly portable and widely implemented so it's an appropriate target language for our system.

The non-functional properties of the three types of future computing systems (Grid, Web Services & Ubiquitous Computing) that are currently fashionable are:

- Scale: in all three visions very large numbers of components work together over extended lifecycles.

- Openness: components come and go dynamically programmers have only expectations of runtime availability of functionality.

- Low cost: the hype and excitement surrounding all three visions is driven by an expectation that costs for using these infrastructures will be very low.

These non-functional properties drive the following requirements for the software development systems that are to be used to implement functionality on them.

- They must at least help humans find and select relevant services.

- They must be able to utilize the services that are available to achieve the human's goals.

- They must provide a high degree of automation.

Goal directed agents offer a technological response to these requirements. The canonical style of goal directed agent is the BDI agent, but it is important to stress that the canonical implementation of the BDI architecture, PRS, and PRS style agents implemented with Agentspeak, and its derivatives are only one way to meet the requirements above. PRS based agents are implemented using a planner that selects scripts (plans) from a database based on the current state of the world and the current goals of the Agent. The plan database is created by the Agent developer at compile time. The Agent is therefore unable to take advantage of action effects/services that are unknown to the programmer at compile time and enter its world at run time, because by definition none of the scripts in its plan database feature these effects.

In the past many Agent systems like Decafe [7] and Zeus [5] have featured constructive planners which provide varying degrees of flexibility of behaviour in the face of dynamic sets of service actions. The problem that we have encountered in developing agents with constructive planners that the development of systems that utilize this behaviour is difficult (in the sense that PhDs find it hard), unpredictable (in the sense that committing to deadlines is difficult) and unreliable (in the sense that the system doesn't behave in the desired fashion). Gaia and other similar methodologies do not address agent application deployment although tools like JADE [1] and Retsina [13] do provide mechanisms to distribute and launch agents. The work that we present here integrates a methodology for agent analysis and development with a development, testing and deployment cycle.

2.1 Analytics

Process style mark-up has been used in HTN planners such as SHOP-2 [11], and in a variety of other settings, but we are unaware of any tools that provide analysis to engineers during the creation of system with ad-hoc coalition structures derived by an agent's PSM at run time. The GIPO tool is closest [10] but this is focused on planning primitives and the HTN abstraction only. The numerous algorithms that have been proposed to enable the problem solving agents operation (coalition formation for example [3], planning for example [4], coalition structure discovery for example [6]) indicate that this is a significant area of investigation, so it is surprising that so little attention has been given to designing and implementing tool support for this task.

2.2 Agent Development or Service Composition?

Extending the discussion above we can frame the issue of dealing with the process complexity abstraction issue as that of developing technology for provisioning and utilizing (engineering with) knowledge for a situated agent in a dynamic environment. There is an extensive literature on Semantic Web service composition [9] which describes related technology.

We draw two distinctions:

1. We expect the agent utilizing the planning knowledge that it is gleaning from its domain to act *run time, and to base its compositions on the state of its beliefs about the environment* whereas service composition tools, typically, are used to generate new meta-services at compile time, which are then registered in directories as new capabilities for direct use.
2. We expect the agent to act *autonomously* in the second sense defined by Luck et-al [8]. Goal of the agent are the result of an interaction of the required outcome of a request and the context that the request is made in terms of the availability of the services and the conditions in the environment.

For example, given a scenario for a portal to provide a service for the selection of telecom services based on the features that the customer desires. New products are added, inventory changes, and the customer's circumstances change. The agent managing the portal uses its planner to provide best effort services based on the companies ability to procure and fulfil orders for the equipment and to install it in the required time windows.

3. Approach

The objective of our technology is to handle the complexity of workflow applications in complex contexts. In the telecoms domain drivers of complexity are;

1. different treatments for different user groups,
2. different treatments at different geographical locations, for example based on distance to exchanges;
3. exception handling;
4. varying regimes based on overall order value;
5. bundles of products with variation of treatment depending on the bundle content, for example if one component requires manual installation it can be cheaper to install all manually on the first attempt rather than risk a rework order.

Other domains may have different drivers; for example consumer devices are currently being applied into multiple contexts (home, car, public) where they are required to behave differently; in many domains processes are contingent on the authorities of the human actors that are participating in them.

The enumeration of the portfolio of planning scripts to support planning agents in these different contexts, with different goals is a significant engineering task; the generation of the plans from declarative knowledge structures seems, by inspection, to offer a way to short-circuit this requirement by providing for the development and audit of critical paths in the process and supporting the expectation of the developer and user that the process execution system will be able to deduce the correct actions in other cases, exceptions and contexts.

3.1 Example Application

A broadband consumer wants to move their office from one location to another.

As an example "Simon" wants to cease voice services and use the video calling application and his mobile instead. Alternatively "Nick" requires the voice service because he needs to have a reliable and recorded point of contact which he implements using an answering machine. The permutation of the processes required to effect the required combination of activities to achieve the users goal can be captured in a script or workflow by an engineer. However, in this case the workflow rapidly becomes unmanageable. Given a set of 9 possible targets can be selected.

The combinations of these targets for 1,2,3,4,5,6,7,8 & 9 simultaneous selections are:

$9 + 36 + 84 + 126 + 126 + 84 + 36 + 9 + 1 = 511$

Which gives a total of 511 processes

However:

Targets can that imply other targets (the goals that they are linked to contain the other goals), for example

'Home Security' implies 'Get PSTN', 'Get Broadband', 'Get Home Security WebCam', 'Get Home Security Motion Sensor'

'Move your ADSL' implies 'Move your PSTN'

'Get Broadband' implies 'Get PSTN'

'Get internet radio over a wireless connection' implies 'Get Broadband'

'Get internet radio through a wired connection' implies 'Get Broadband'

Taking account of the implication's due to dependencies the number of paths in the workflow or separate selected workflow scripts is $9 + 28 + 56 + 70 + 56 + 28 + 8 + 1 + 1 = 257$.

3.2   Statement of Task.

3.2.1   Functional Task

A our system can be described as a set of tupels of the form :

$$<gu, ga, components, state>$$

Where

   ga = goals known to be achievable

   gu =goals known to be unachievable

   $components$ = services available

   $state$ = initial state

Goals are the set of states which are to be achievable by the system in response to a human request. Achievable goals are those for which the developer has obtained an executability proof, unachievable goals are those where no proof has been created (which *could* mean that no agent can perform them given these components and state).

state is the set of propositional assertions $<a1, a2,...,an>$ that are true when the proofs of achievability are to be obtained. ax is a proposition of the form :

$$tag(atom1,atom2,...,atomn).$$

Where the tag is a signifier and atoms are either variables, literals or values.

components are a set $<s1, s2,...,sn>$ where sx is an action statement of the familiar form $<precondition, add effect, delete effect, input, output>$ where the semantic of planning layer (pre/add|del) and data layer (in/out) state the transactional semantic of the action sx.

$$<precondition, add, del, input, output>$$

are sets of propositional assertions of the same form as in state.

A proof is a sequence of sets of services :

$$<\{sa1,sa2,...,san\}, \{b1,sb2,...,sbn\},...,\{sx1,sx2,...sxn\}>$$

Such that all preconditions of {sa1,sa2,...,san} are members of state and each sequential member of the proof has a valid unification of all preconditions in its set in the post conditions of the previous member of the set.

4. Tools developed

We developed our system, which we called Kreno, with tools that are used to support the annotation and manipulation of service resources and the definition of goals and their utilization in deployed applications.

- A mechanism for snap-shotting and importing service environment states from (in our implementation) a UDDI server. This allows the developer to work within a specific environment state or set of environment states.

- A service annotation system that allows the mark-up of services with applicability and effect information (preconditions and post-conditions/add effects/delete effects) to facilitate rapid deployment and round tripping of services from deployment to development and back again to facilitate maintenance. The service annotation tool allows services to be configured with plug-ins that implement functionality.

- A wizard for exporting service definitions into a service framework and deploying services into an operational framework.

These tools are editors, straightforward compilers and file/query handlers. They are important in the general picture of the make up of an IDE for agent development, however their detailed description is not the main focus of this paper.

Of more interest are the tools which rely on deductive and analytic algorithms:

- A service composition assistant that provides advice on the applicability and usefulness of services in the current context to assist in the construction of valid proofs.

- A "test" capability which enables the system to produce visualizations of possible plans in response to developer requests. These plans have no first class object status; they are artefacts for the developer's inspection only and are never deployed or saved for later use (they are saved for later reference, inspection and audit).

4.1 Service Composition Assistance Tool

The objective of the service composition tool is to provide developers with advice about why service proofs are not succeeding, or are using unexpected or anomalous means. This is the critical contribution of Kreno, in the past developers have had to perform the necessary unification and checking mentally or on paper.

In order to provide the advice required first a datastructure; the ActionMatchMatrix is generated.

Figure 1. The Service Advice editor implemented on the Eclipse IDE.

For each service make a node <add, del, pre> in a matrix such that;
add=add effects, del=delete effects, pre = preconditions. Add links to the nodes
<node,type> according to the following procedure.
for each node1
for each node2 !=node1
  for each node1.pre
    for each node2.add
    if ∃unifier(node1.pre,node2.add)
      node1.addSupportedBy(node2,add)
      node2.addSupports(node1,pre)
    end if
    end for
  end for
end for
for each node1
for each node2 !=node1
  for each node1.pre
    for each node2.del
    if ∃unifier (node1.pre,node2.del) node1.addContradictedBy (node2,del)
node2.addContradicts(node1,pre)
    end if
    end for
  end for
end for
end for
end for

Figure 2.An Algorithm for Generating the Service Advice
ActionMatchMatrix Data

The ActionMatchMatrix is constructed to contain an node for every service in the current system and a graph of connections to every other node. These links are via the propositions, the propositions link to their matching propositions in other actions, so an action with a postcondition would have a link from that postcondition to all the preconditions of other actions that it supports, from which it can then determine which actions it supports. The links between propositions are of four types: supports, contradicts, supported-by, contradicted by. The links themselves are not bi-directional, but would usually have a complementary counterpart .

Figure 2 shows the algorithm used to construct the ActionMatchMatrix. The procedure is $2(n-1(O))^2$ complex as it consists of two steps each of which requires an evaluation of each of the components in the system against all of the other components of the system. The cost of O is approximately the cost of a unification of the symbols in all the preconditions of one component against the symbols in the add effects and delete effects of the other component for each of the two steps of evaluating support and contradiction.

ActionMatchMatrix is then used to generate the entries for the six panels shown in Figure 1. These panels are unsupported preconditions, sufficient components, supported components, supporting components, blocked components and blocking components for this component s. The data that populates these panels is the result of the query to the ActionMatchMatrix described below:

Unsupported Preconditions : get all the preconditions that do not contain any supportedBy links for s. Formally the set of Unsupported Preconditions, US, displayed on the Service Composition Assistant Tool for component s is :

$US = \{pre_1, pre_2, ..., pre_n\} \mid \forall pre_x \in US \land pre_x \in pre_s \ !\exists \ link \in supportedBy \land link.pre_s = pre_x$

Sufficient Components : get all the components that are linked to by supportedBy links from all of the preconditions of this component.

Formally the set of Sufficient Components, CC, displayed on the Service Composition Assistant Tool is :

$CC = \{s1, s2, ..., sn\} \mid \forall sa \in CC \ \exists linky \in supportedBy \land linky.pre \in pre$

Supported Components: get all the components that are linked to by supports links from any of the add effects of this node.

Formally PC, the set of components that this components add effects support is:

$PC = \{s_1, s_2, ..., s_n\} \mid \forall s_x \in PC \ \exists link \in supports \land link.node = s_x$

Supporting Components: get all the nodes that are linked to by supportedBy link from any of the preconditions of this node.

Formally SC, the set of components that provide some degree of support for this component s by having an add effect that is a precondition of s is:

$SC = \{s_1, s_2, ..., s_n\} \mid \forall s \in SC \ \exists link \in supportedBy \land link.node = s_x$

Blocked Components: Get all the nodes that are linked to by any contradicts links from and of the delete effects of this node.

Formally BC, the set of components that have a precondition which is a delete effect of this component is

$$BC = \{ s_1, s_2, \ldots, s_n \} \mid \forall s \in BC \ \exists link \in contradicts \wedge link.node = s_x$$

Blocking Components: Get all the nodes that are linked by contradictedBy links from any of the preconditions of this node.

Formally IC, the set of components that have a delete effect that is a precondition of this components is :

$$IC = \{ s_1, s_2, \ldots, s_n \} \mid \forall s_x \in IC \ \exists link \in contradicts \wedge link.node = s_x$$

4.2   Proof Visualisation Tool

A proof visualization wizard is used to select sub sets of service and conditions with which to test the reachability of collections of goals. This functionality supports the incremental development of composed services based on the familiar developer procedure of generate (code) and test (with assumptions) to see if it will run. In addition this method allows a process analogous to unit-testing to be applied to the service chains that make up composite functionality in the system.

In Figure 3. the outcome of a "proving" episode is illustrated. An important aspect of Kreno mentioned in section 2.1 is its use for developing logic for context sensitive situated agents. This is facilitated by the editors described in section 4.1 and by the functionality of the proof visualisation wizard which consists of a three step selection process:

select components->select goals ->select conditions

At each step it is possible to design the structure of the goal solving environment that the proof will be constructed for by selecting the groups of assertions represented in the goal collections or in the component selections.

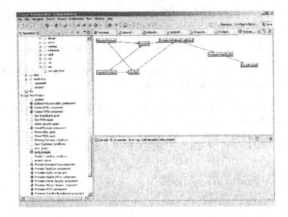

Figure 3.The Proof Visualisation viewer as implemented in the Eclipse IDE using SWT

The proof is developed using a derivative of the Graphplan algorithm [2]. The planning graph is expanded from the conditions at level 0 using a closed world assumption. Solution extraction is done using reverse chaining and only one solution is extracted with a heuristic that prefers the shortest available solution.

This tool is designed to facilitate planning over a business process, and therefore features mark-up for service input/output as well as for pre-conditions and post-conditions. In order for the process to be valid inputs and outputs must be reconciled as well as the logical conditions of the pre-post conditions. This is achieved by generating derived preconditions and add effect which are then asserted into the planning predicates to ensure that only functionally valid compositions are proposed.

We can contrast the two tools (service composition assistant and proof visualisation) as shallow and deep analysis methods for the system. Proof visualisation allows the implications of service chaining to be explored, where as the composition assistant allows developers to consider the local implications of service mark-up.

It is difficult to conduct meaningful performance experiments on this type of system, but it is worth noting some illustrative figures. Over a 10 day period of use the average time for proof visualisation episodes was 569ms. The standard deviation of the time was 349ms with the maximum time taken for a request as 1438ms. Timing was done on a twin Xeno PIII at 2GHz and with 1Gb of memory using the standard Java clock, which has an accuracy (on our implementation) of ~100ms.

There are 257 individual paths through the workflow if the dependencies between the elements of a feasible bundle are taken into account.

In the implementation of the application using the Kreno only 9 individual goals and 32 services were required.

An obvious question is: is this an equivalent system to a hand implemented workflow. We argue that it is not possible to prove equivalence because unless the hand coded system is available with all permutations implemented and is correct. In fact, our experience is that many cases of bundle provision are un-implemented in a workflow and resolved by human intervention.

5. Development Method

The tools reported above have been implemented in order to support a development method for compositional systems. We have identified four distinct phases in the development task; Application Analysis; Application Development; Application Validation & Testing; Application Deployment. We have not addressed change control and maintenance in our tool set at this time.

5.1 Application Analysis

Application analysis in Kreno is performed by examining the features of the required solutions being requested from the system by the user. These are the abstract goals of the system and need to be distilled from the product specifications or requirement lists provided.

No analysis of organizational model or interaction model is required as these are the concerns of the deployment framework and are not considered by the Kreno tools.

5.2 Application Development

The Application Development process in Kreno is listed below.

1. Import test environment from UDDI, including markup; use snapshot macros and Kreno import wizard.
2. Specify goals for system; each goal is specified as a set of propositions in the goal editor page.
3. Create a set of preconditions that are expected to hold for the proofs to be compiled.
4. Select a goal
5. Repeat
6. Identify all the components required to satisfy the propositions in the goal; identify all the preconditions in these services using the Assistant tool or from the service editor precondition pane.
7. If there are no components available with the correct postconditions then a new one will have to be created; use the service editor.
8. Create a conditions set containing all preconditions identified above.
9. Create a proof using the proof visualization tool and wizard.
10. The goal is now the preconditions of the services selected or created in 5/6; if all the preconditions are in the set created in 3 then finish.
11. end repeat
12. Implement component functionality by importing relevant plugins or implementing new plugins in a compatible language – currently Java.

13. Deploy components using the Export Component Wizard into the service directory (UDDI) and application/service container (Apache-Axis)
14. Deploy goals using the Export Goal Wizard to the application framework on Apache-Axis.

5.3 Application Validation & Testing

Application validation and testing was a use case of the Kreno tool that evolved naturally as we used it for application development. Application validation is the process of building a number of test cases that are used to reassure the developer or customer of the validity of the implemented system. The set of cases described in section 4 is implemented in Application Analysis, here we implement cases that are "good tests" of whether the core functionality is correct.

Currently this is done by generating test processes against particular test cases (goal sets, conditions) and storing them in a "testing" directory in the project source tree.

Tool based support for this will be required in the future but is not currently implemented. Kreno does not currently support a "case" data structure that links goals and test conditions. The Proof Visualization wizard should generate this case from the selections made by the user. The case could then be displayed via a separate editor page using the logic for the Proof Visualization wizard, but without the selection process. Other uses of cases could be the compilation of a case set and then validation against a service architecture to produce a test report, as opposed to a graph and visualization.

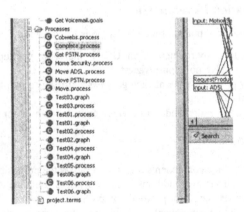

Figure 4. A test case directory developed for validation

5.4 Application Deployment

Components marked up with Kreno are published into a web service server based on Apache Axis. Services are registered by name and invocation interface to a

UDDI directory. Service markup is written to files in specified directories that are served by a web server to requesting clients using HTTP.

A framework is provided to enable developer to implement web-app functionality to enable service requests to be made to a composing agent (using a deployment version of the planner), provisioned with context information from appropriate data sources, and then scheduled using appropriate resource models.

Execution is performed by a process engine over processes written in a BPEL. Exceptions are handled either by on-demand service re-provisioning or by replanning according to the current resourcing model/agent context that pertains.

6.   Conclusion

In this paper we have presented an approach to handling process complexity using AI technologies in an open web services infrastructure. A workbench for editing, administering and round-tripping development episodes and an implementation focused process for modelling declarative business logic was described. The methodology we have developed for application creation was reported along with a motivating example of process complexity in an apparently simple task and a description of how our technology can be applied to it.

In addition to the tools that we have described others will also be needed to tackle process complexity. We have mentioned that role modelling systems are in our opinion orthogonal to Kreno in providing abstractions for organization design, and that technology for protocol modelling and implementation is also well advanced. In addition to these we believe that abstractions for reputation, acquaintance, type, quality of service, environmental evolution, resource management, price and cost maximization (and other market behaviours), and yield will all be needed to realize the full vision of open, reusable, intelligent, service orientated distributed Agent systems.

7.   References

1. Bellifemine,F., Poggi,A. & Rimassa,G. (1999) "JADE - A FIPA-compliant agent framework" In: Proceedings of PAAM'99, London, April 1999, pp.97-108.

2. Blum, A. & Furst,M. (1997) "Fast Planning Through Planning Graph Analysis", Artificial Intelligence, 90:281--300(1997).

3. Blum, A., Sandholm, T., and Zinkevich, M. (2002). "Online Algorithms for Market Clearing". In: *Proceedings of the ACM-SIAM Symposium on Discrete Algorithms (SODA)*, pp. 971-980, San Francisco, CA, January 6-8.

4. Coddington,A.M. & Luck,M. "A Motivation Based Planning and Execution Framework", *International Journal on Artificial Intelligence Tools*, 13(1), 5-25, 2004.

5. Collis, J., Ndumu, D.T. Nwana, H.S., Lee, L. (1998) "The Zeus Agent Building Tool Kit", BT Technology Journal 16(3): 60-68, July 1998. Kulwer.

6. Dang, V.D. & Jennings, N.R. (2004) "Generating coalition structures with finite bound from the optimal guarantees" In : *Proc. 3rd Int. Conf. on Autonomous Agents and Multi-Agent Systems*, New York, USA, 564-571

7. Graham, J., Windley, V., McHugh, D., McGeary, F., Cleaver, D., & Decker, K. "A_Programming and Execution Environment for Distributed Multi Agent Systems." *Workshop on Infrastructure for Scalable Multi-agent Systems at the Fourth International Conference on Autonomous Agents,* Barcelona, Spain, June, 2000

8. Luck, M., D'Inverno, M., Munro, S. "Autonomy, Variable and Generative." In: *Agent Autonomy*, H. Hexmoor, C. Castelfranchi, and R. Falcone (eds.), Kluwer, 9-22, 2003.

9. McIlraith, S.A. & Son, T.C. (2002) "Adapting golog for composition of semantic web services" In: D. Fensel, F. Griunchiglia, D. McGuinness, M.A. Williams (eds) *Proceedings of the 8th International Conference on KR and R (KR-02)*, pp 482-496.

10. McCluskey, T.L., Liu, D. & Simpson, R. "GIPO II: HTN Planning in a Tool-supported Knowledge Engineering Environment" *Proceedings of the International Conference on Automated Planning and Scheduling*, June, 2003

11. Sirin, E., Parsia, B., Wu, D., Hendler, J. and Nau, D. (2004) "HTN planning for web service composition using SHOP2." *Journal of Web Semantics*, 1(4):377-396, 2004.

12. STL 2003 'Introduction to the STL". Available from http://www.sgi.com/tech/stl/stl_introduction.html

13. Sycara, K., Giampapa, J.A., Langley, B. & Paolucci, M. "The RETSINA MAS, a Case Study," Software Engineering for Large-Scale Multi-Agent Systems: Research Issues and Practical Applications, Alessandro Garcia, Carlos Lucena, Franco Zambonelli, Andrea Omici, Jaelson Castro, ed., Springer-Verlag, Berlin Heidelberg, Vol. LNCS 2603, July, 2003, pp. 232--250.

A Semantic Web Blackboard System

Craig McKenzie, Alun Preece, and Peter Gray

University of Aberdeen, Department of Computing Science
Aberdeen AB24 3UE, UK
{cmckenzie,apreece,pgray}@csd.abdn.ac.uk

Abstract. In this paper, we propose a Blackboard Architecture as a means for coordinating hybrid reasoning over the Semantic Web. We describe the components of traditional blackboard systems (Knowledge Sources, Blackboard, Controller) and then explain how we have enhanced these by incorporating some of the principles of the Semantic Web to produce our Semantic Web Blackboard. Much of the framework is already in place to facilitate our research: the communication protocol (HTTP); the data representation medium (RDF); a rich expressive description language (OWL); and a method of writing rules (SWRL). We further enhance this by adding our own constraint based formalism (CIF/SWRL) into the mix. We provide an example walk-though of our test-bed system, the AKTive Workgroup Builder and Blackboard(AWB+B), illustrating the interaction and cooperation of the Knowledge Sources and providing some context as to how the solution is achieved. We conclude with the strengths and weaknesses of the architecture.

1 Introduction & Motivation

Since the Semantic Web (SW) is essentially a symbolic version of the current Web, anyone attempting to use published data is still faced with handling the standard knowledge integration and reuse problems [12, 3]: accommodating errors in the data at either a syntactic or semantic level, incompleteness, inconsistency, intractability, etc. Performing reasoning of various kinds in order to "do the best we can with what we've got" is a hard problem. The primary goal of our research is to investigate the suitability of a Blackboard System as a means of co-ordinating hybrid reasoning over the SW.

The SW is intrinsically hybrid in terms of its knowledge representation formalisms. Our ground data exists as RDF which will normally conform to either an RDF Schema or an OWL ontology[1]. The semantics of these mean that we are able to perform different types of reasoning upon them – ranging from transitive closure right up to full DL (ABox and/or TBox[7]) classification – to better enrich the data by deducing facts that may not have been explicitly stated. Derivation rules, represented using SWRL[2], can also be applied in order to generate additional entailments.

---

[1] http://www.w3.org/2001/sw/
[2] http://www.w3.org/Submission/SWRL/

We believe that reasoning on the SW requires a combination of reasoning methods rather than just a single "super-reasoner". For example, [16] compared a DL reasoner to a first-order theorem prover, and conclused that when dealing with a very expressive OWL DL ontology a combination of both is necessary because there was no known single reasoning algorithm able to adequately cope with the full expressivity possible with the OWL DL language. They also identified slow performance speed as a potential hurdle. Advocacy of a hybrid approach to reasoning predates the SW [1]. However this is not without its problems. How should contradictions be handled? Can conflicting reasoning strategies interfere with one another? Hence, some mechanism is required to help manage such issues. However there is currently nothing in the SW architecture for coordinating this effort, so we believe that the Blackboard architecture is appropriate as it meets our requirements – supporting the use of distributed Knowledge Sources (KSs) responding to a central, shared knowledge base via a control mechanism [13, 2].

Having outlined our reasons for our research, in the following section (Section 2), we introduce the problem domain and our test-bed Blackboard System. In Section 2 we discuss the blackboard architecture and explain the role of each of its constituent parts, then in Section 3 we discuss the changes to this in our Semantic Web approach. In Section 5, we perform a walk-through of the application to illustrate the interplay between the component. Section 6 is a discussion of how we focus the reasoning effort. In Section 7 we describe the issues we encountered and outline our future work before discussing our final conclusions in Section 8.

2 Problem Domain and the AWB+B Application

We needed to decide the problem domain within which to we wished to work. We settled upon the same context as that of the CS AKTive Space [15], namely the Computing Science (CS) community in the UK. The data describes people, their research interests, affiliations, publications and projects at various levels of granularity and completeness.

Our demo application, called the AKTive Workgroup Builder and Blackboard (AWB+B)[3], is a web-based application that utilises disparate RDF based information in constructing a workshop, containing one or more working groups of people, from this pool of known individuals. Each workgroup must adhere to a set of user defined constraints, e.g. "the workgroup must contain between 5 and 11 individuals" or "at least half the members of the workgroup must be students". Since the user is not expected to have knowledge about the lower level operations of the blackboard, we assume that all the necessary RDF information resources (describing the people, constraints, derivation rules, etc) to be included are known to the user and accessible via URIs.

The final aspects of the problem were the representation of constraints. For this, we had already developed an ontology as a means of representing Constraint

---

[3] This is a refinement of the non-blackboard AWB system in [11].

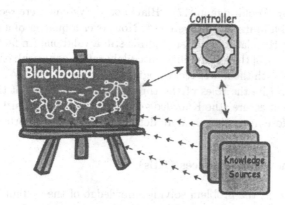

Fig. 1. The core architectural components of a Blackboard System. Each KS can view the contents of the Blackboard but it is the Controller that decides which KS(s) are allowed to contribute.

Satisfaction Problems (CSPs) on the SW[14]. This also builds upon our earlier work, CIF/SWRL [11], in developing a SW representation for fully-quantified, individual constraints. This is based on SWRL and is used for expressing the individual constraints that comprise a CSP.

3 Blackboard Architecture

Back in the late '70s, when Lesser and Erman developed Hearsay-II [10] they conceived the Blackboard Architecture [6,9] as an effective means for collaborative problem solving. The premise was simple: *how would a group of real-life experts work together to solve a complex problem?* Since none of the individuals were capable of solving it on their own, they would all gather around a blackboard, with each person using their knowledge and expertise to contribute by either: decomposing a problem into smaller sub-problems and writing these on the board; or solving an existing problem and writing up the answer. Slowly, the overall problem would be progressed until, finally, it reached a state where it was solved (for a fuller description see [13]). The key aspects of this approach being that the solving process is only possible through collaboration (no individual is capable of solving the problem on their own) and in an incremental manner (progress is made via small steps).

The whole process is overseen by a *Controller* that performs two roles. Firstly, it enforces a protocol for who gets to write on the blackboard and when. Returning to the metaphor, if there is only one piece of chalk, the controller would decide whom gets to use it and when. If there is a whole box of chalk, the controller would ensure that all the writers do not get in one another's way. Secondly, the controller attempts to keep the contents of the blackboard relevant by asking each KS what sort of contribution they can make before deciding to let them make it or not (see Figure 1).

As stated by Wooldridge in [17], "Blackboard Systems were recognisably the earliest form of a Multi-Agent Systems". Now, over a quarter of a century later, we believe that the blackboard paradigm is still a valid one (in fact, recent work has focussed on [4, 5] their suitability for collaborating software), especially when used in concert with the newer technologies that make up the SW. The following subsections describe the roles of the three main components of the traditional Blackboard architecture (the Knowledge Sources, the Blackboard itself and the Controller) before discussing in more detail our SW based approach.

3.1 The Knowledge Sources (KSs)

The KSs represent the problem solving knowledge of the system. Each KS can be regarded as being an independent domain expert with information relevant to the problem at hand. In implementation terms, KSs do not interact with one another, nor even know about any of the others that are present. Also, no assumptions should be made about the capabilities of a KS – conceptually it should be regarded as a black box. Each KS has a precondition, or event trigger, (indicating that it can add something to the blackboard) and an action (what it can add to the blackboard). Due to the tightly coupled nature of the KSs and the Blackboard, all KSs must be "registered" so that they can continually check the blackboard and determine if they can make a contribution. The whole process is driven by the posting of goals which a KS either offers a direct solution to, or breaks down further into sub-goals (indicating that more knowledge is required).

3.2 Knowledge on the Blackboard

The actual blackboard itself can be thought of as a shared data repository representing a communal work area or "solution space" of potential solution components. Since the KSs are required to both view and modify the contents of the blackboard it is also a communication medium. For all this to work efficiently, the data held on the blackboard is structured hierarchically into what were called *abstraction Levels*. If the blackboard contained multiple distinct hierarchies, these were referred to as *panels*.

This organisation served two purposes. Firstly, it aided each KS in checking if it can contribute (i.e. the KS was activated, or triggered, by the propagation of information onto an abstraction level that it was monitoring). Secondly, it helped focus the search for the solution. As the name suggests, each layer is an abstraction using concepts that hide the detail on the layer below it. To clarify, using the domain of speech understanding, suppose the lowest abstraction level could be the phonetic sounds accepted by the system; the level above could be potential combinations of these sounds into letter groups; the next level being single words; the next level could be phrases; with, finally, the topmost level consisting of potential whole sentences. A word-dictionary KS would examine the phonetic letter groups and combine these to form words, which (controller permitting) it would then post onto the level above.

The nature of each abstraction level and the actual entries within each level, can vary from implementation to implementation depending upon the nature of the problem attempted. Instead of the bottom-up approach used in the example, a top-down approach may be required, so the first abstraction level is vague with later ones becoming more refined. Likewise a KS's trigger could span multiple layers with a contribution also affecting one or more layers.

3.3 The Controller

As mentioned already, the decision of what is (or is not) placed on the blackboard is made by the controller. The complexity of this strategy can vary from a simplistic "just action everything" approach to a more complex goal driven algorithm. The key point is that the controller directs the solving process, via goals and sub-goals, that each of the KSs can be triggered by. This also helps to ensure that only relevant information is added. Since the triggering action can be dependent upon information added by a different KS. This results in an opportunistic solving paradigm and also means that a blackboard system is fundamentally backward chaining – it is goal driven. In our case, the initial goal placed on the blackboard is to find a solution to a specified workgroup problem. It should also be noted, that the current implementation of the AWB+B, the blackboard is monotonic, facts are only ever added by the KSs, never retracted.

4 The Semantic Web Approach

Our Semantic Web Blackboard maintains all the principles of a traditional blackboard but improves upon it by incorporating some of the concepts of the SW. The notion of abstraction levels aligns itself well to the hierarchical, structured nature of an ontology. Historically, abstraction levels were developed at design time so their structure was fixed throughout the execution of the system. In the AWB+B, the information represented on the blackboard is stored as a dynamically created RDF graph. RDF statements ("triples") can be added incrementally to the blackboard to gradually build up both ontological information and instance data. For example, we can add the triples

```
<ex:Tim>       <rdf:type>        <ont:Lecturer>
<ont:Lecturer> <rdfs:subClassOf> <ont:Academic>
```

in any order, resulting in the knowledge that some instance Tim is a lecturer (instance-level data) and that a lecturer is a kind of academic (ontological data).

To the best of our knowledge, in the past the blackboard has always been passive with any deductive mechanism performed by the KSs. While not wishing to stray too far from the original concepts of the architecture, we decided to introduce an element of intelligence to the blackboard itself by enabling it to perform reasoning on the ontological structure evolving on it. Four rules are forward chained (here, clauses are RDF triples, and ?x denotes a variable):

i) (?a <rdfs:subClassOf> ?b) & (?b <rdfs:subClassOf> ?c)
$$\Rightarrow \text{(?a <rdfs:subClassOf> ?c)}$$

ii) `(?x <rdfs:subClassOf> ?y)` & `(?a <rdf:type> ?x)` $\Rightarrow$ `(?a <rdf:type> ?y)`

iii) `(?a <rdfs:subPropertyOf> ?b)` & `(?b <rdfs:subPropertyOf> ?c)`
$$\Rightarrow \text{ (?a <rdfs:subPropertyOf> ?c)}$$

iv) `(?a ?p ?b)` & `(?p <rdfs:subPropertyOf> ?q)` $\Rightarrow$ `(?a ?q ?b)`

Here we are only materialising all the transitive sub-class/property relations and all the instance type relations. For example, as per rule (i), if a class C_1 is defined as being a sub-class of C_2 and C_2 is a sub-class of C_3 then the blackboard would assert that C_1 is a sub-class of C_3. The blackboard also has the ability to assert new `<rdf:type>` statements about individuals (rule (ii)). Continuing the previous example, if X is an instance of C_1 and C_1 is a sub-class of C_2 then we can assert that X is also an instance of C_2. Rules (iii) and (iv) are similarly applied for properties.

We elected to only perform this type of reasoning and not a richer type of classification that is possible within OWL (e.g. using property domain and ranges) since this is such a common operation that having it done by the blackboard eliminates the need for frequent call outs to KS that would perform the same function. Unfortunately, enabling the Blackboard to make inferences must be treated with caution. It would be undesirable if the blackboard became a bottleneck while it attempted to fully reason about facts posted upon it while denying all the KSs from contributing (especially if a "denied" KS was attempting to add a fact that would help the reasoning process). This is why we have not increased the blackboard's inference ability any further.

5 A Walk-though of Cooperative Problem Solving

Having now described the components of the blackboard architecture, we now use a couple of the possible KS types in order to present a walk-through of a simplified problem – constructing a single workgroup. This should illustrate the cooperative and incremental nature of a blackboard system. Since the contents of the blackboard in the AWB+B is an RDF graph, we have used a simplified form of RDF to illustrate this throughout.

5.1 Human (User Interface) KS

While not immediately obvious, the user of the system can be regarded as a type of KS representing the "human knowledge" of the system in the form of "human input". In the AWB+B case, this is the user entering the initial system parameters (via a web interface), i.e. the number of workgroups to be built, the size of each workgroup, any associated compositional constraints, derivation rules etc. This information is then transformed into the system's starting goals and posted onto the blackboard.

In the current AWB+B implementation human interaction is limited to that outlined above. However, there is nothing to prevent a more "interactive" human KS. Another variation of a User KS could, for example, continually check the blackboard for inconsistencies and when one is found present the user with pop-up windows asking them to offer a possible resolution, i.e. it gives the user a "view" of inconsistencies found on the blackboard.

Now, for our running example, let us suppose the user wishes to compose a single workgroup, as per the following constraints:

1. Must contain between 3 and 5 members, of type `Person`.
2. Must contain at least 1 `Professor`.
3. Must contain an `expertOn` "Machine Learning".

In addition to this, the user also specifies a SWRL rule, paraphrased as: "if a person is an author of a book and the subject of that book is known, then this implies that the author is an expert on that subject". This is written in SWRL as follows:

```
Person(?p) & authorOf(?p, ?b) & Book(?b) & hasSubject(?b, ?s)
                                        ⇒ expertOn(?p, ?s).
```

All this results in the following skeletal workgroup structure being placed on the blackboard, as well as the class definitions for `Person` and `Professor`, and a property definition for `expertOn` (from the specified constraints):

```
<ex:Wg1>   <rdf:type>   <wg:Workgroup>
<ex:Wg1>   <wg:hasMinMembers>   3
<ex:Wg1>   <wg:hasMaxMembers>   5
<ex:Wg1>   <wg:hasFillerClass>   <ont:Person>
<ex:Wg1>   <wg:hasConstraint>   <ex:OneProfessor>
<ex:Wg1>   <wg:hasConstraint>   <ex:MLExpert>
<ont:Person>   <rdf:type>   <owl:Class>
<ont:Professor>   <rdf:type>   <owl:Class>
<ont:expertOn>   <rdf:type>   <rdf:Property>
```

(Here, `<ex:OneProfessor>` and `<ex:MLExpert>` are references (URIs) to the constraints (2) and (3) above, which are expressed in our CIF/SWRL language.)

5.2 Instance-based KS

This type of KS contains only instance data corresponding to an ontology but not the actual schema itself. This could either be from a simple RDF file, a Web Service or data held in an RDF datastore. We cannot assume that any additional entailments have been generated for the RDF as this KS may or may not have a reasoner attached to it. This KS contributes in the following way:

i) Try to add a solution to a posted (sub-)goal by adding instance data for classes and/or properties defined on the blackboard.

ii) Try to add a solution to classify any property's *direct* subject and/or object which the blackboard does not have a class definition for.

If this KS is a repository of RDF triples (e.g. 3Store [8]) we require a wrapper for it, allowing us to communicate with the datastore via its API. In the case of the

3Store, it has an HTTP interface that accepts SPARQL queries[4]. We transform any blackboard goal into a query, the result of which can be transformed into triples and asserted onto the blackboard.

Since this type of repository can contain a vast amount of information, this raises the issue of the state which that information is in. Since access to the data is via a query mechanism, we are still effectively querying an RDF graph for which we have no means of knowing whether all, some or no additional entailments have been inferred. For example, while an ontology describes a `Professor` as a sub-class of `Academic` and the datastore contains instances of `Professor` for this schema, it might not actually contain the triples saying that `Professor` instances are also `Academics`. Consequently, a SPARQL query for `Academics` would not return the `Professors` as it does not follow sub-class links. The only way around this is to query for all the sub-classes. However this will eventually occur because the Schema based KS (described next) will post the sub-classes as sub-goals which will prompt more refined queries.

Continuing our example, we have three goals on the blackboard (two classes defined, namely `Person` and `Professor`, and a property definition, `expertOn`). If this KS has instances of `Professor`, then it will offer these as solutions (as per (i)). Property definitions work in the same way, but are slightly more complex. Let us assume, our KS has a statement relating to the `expertOn` property, and therefore offers this statement:

`<ex:Tim>  <ont:expertOn>  "Semantic Web"`

However, this gives no information about the subject, `<ex:Tim>`, of that triple (the same would have applied for the object, `"Semantic Web"`, had it not been a literal). This would not be an issue if `<ex:Tim>` was already instantiated on the blackboard, but since it it not, then this KS will subsequently offer (as per (ii)):

`<ex:Tim>  <rdf:type>  <ont:Lecturer>`

Because this KS does not know the underlying schema, it cannot contribute class definition information about the `Lecturer` (e.g. what this might be a sub-class of).

5.3   Schema-based KS

This represents a KS that contains only ontological schema information. Since the blackboard initially contains no ontological structure other than the starting goals, it is the job of this KS to help facilitate the construction of the relevant ontological parts on the blackboard. This type of KS attempts to contribute in the following ways:

i) Attempt to add new sub-goals by looking for ontological sub-classes/sub-properties of those already defined on the blackboard.

ii) Attempt to improve the (limited) reasoning ability of the blackboard by adding `<rdfs:subClassOf>` or `<rdfs:subPropertyOf>` statements connect-

---

[4] http://www.w3.org/TR/rdf-sparql-query/

ing those already defined on the blackboard. These connective statements are only added for *direct* sub-class/sub-property relations.

iii) Attempt to add new sub-goals for any subject/object on the blackboard that does not have a class definition. The sub-goals, in this case, would be the missing class/property definitions.

In (i) and (ii) super-classes/properties are never added to the blackboard as these are deemed irrelevant and would widen the scope of the blackboard contents too much. Likewise, we need to be careful in (iii), as we do not want to simply use a property definition and add the classes specified in its domain and range values as new sub-goals. This is because they could introduce non-relevant goals onto the blackboard, instead, we just use the classes of actual instances that have this property. To clarify, let us suppose that when the ontology was first authored, the `expertOn` property was assigned a domain of `Person` and a range of `<owl:Thing>`. This was because the author believed that only a `Person` is capable of being an expert, but what it is they have expertise in could be anything. Therefore, for simplicity, they just widened the domain to encompass as many classes as possible. If we were to use these domain and range values, we would introduce a sub-goal asking for all instances of `<owl:Thing>` which would result in each KS offering every class instance it knows about. Therefore, in an attempt to narrow the search space as much as possible, only the class definitions of instances with the `expertOn` property are added as sub-goals.

Continuing our running example, based upon the current contents of the blackboard, this KS would see the class definition of `Person` and act upon it by offering to add a sub-goal, as per (i), by defining a sub-class of Person:

```
<ont:Academic>  <rdf:type>  <owl:Class>
```

In blackboard terms, defining the class `Academic` does not automatically specify it as a sub-class of `Person`. This must explicitly be stated on the blackboard. Therefore, this KS would next offer the explicit sub-class link between these two classes (as per (ii)):

```
<ont:Academic>  <rdfs:subClassOf>  <ont:Person>
```

Finally, this KS would see the statement (previously contributed by the Instance KS):

```
<ex:Tim>  <rdf:type>  <ont:Lecturer>
```

The triple already implies that `Lecturer` is a class (although, it could either be a `rdfs:Class` or the more specific `owl:Class`). The KS would then offer the full class definition (as per (iii)), hence re-classifying Tim appropriately and creating a new sub-goal, so from our earlier examples we would now have:

```
<ont:Lecturer>  <rdf:type>  <owl:Class>
<ex:Tim>  <rdf:type>  <ont:Lecturer>
<ex:Tim>  <ont:expertOn>  "Semantic Web"
```

5.4 Rule-based KS

A Rule KS, like all the other KS types, can be viewed as a black box, encapsulating its rules and keeping them private. The ability to derive new information through rules is an extremely important and powerful asset. We achieve this by expressing them using SWRL, although there is no restriction on what rule representation is used (especially since the rules within a KS are private) we elected to use SWRL because it is part of the SW framework.

This KS works by examining the contents of the blackboard to determine if any of the rules that it knows about are required and then attempts to contribute. A rule is required *only* if any of the elements in the consequent (head) are present on the blackboard[5]. The KS attempts to contribute to the blackboard in the following ways:

i) Try to add a "solution" by firing the rule against instances already on the blackboard and asserting the appropriate statement(s).

ii) Try to add new sub-goals to the blackboard by offering class/property definitions that are antecedents of the rule and have not been defined on the blackboard.

Reusing our derivation rule to determine expertise (Section 5.1), and continuing our example, we see that the Blackboard contains a class definition for `Person` but no property definitions (or instances of) the other rule antecedents, i.e. the class `Book` and the properties `authorOf` and `hasSubject`. Therefore, regardless of instance data, the rule is incapable of firing. Hence, this KS would offer the following sub-goals, as per (ii):

```
<ont:Book>  <rdf:type>  <owl:Class>
<ont:authorOf>  <rdf:type>  <rdf:Property>
<ont:hasSubject>  <rdf:type>  <rdf:Property>
```

Once other KSs have contributed instance data for the antecedents, the rule can fire and generate a solution instance for the `expertOn` property (i.e. backward chaining) that has not been explicitly stated in a KS (as per (i)).

5.5   CSP-solving KS

The final component of the AWB+B system is the CSP solving. The constraints for the workgroup(s) are expressed using CIF/SWRL [11] – our Constraint Interchange Format (CIF), which is an RDF based extension of SWRL that allows us to express fully quantified constraints. These constraints are placed on the blackboard by the Human KS when the workgroup is first defined. Since the goal of the AWB+B is to form workgroups that adhere to these specified constraints, a CSP KS was created, having the trigger:

i) Try to add a "solution" by using instance data already on the blackboard to perform CSP solving and assert the appropriate `hasMember` triples to the corresponding instance of the `Workgroup` class.

The triggering mechanism of this KS requires it to continually monitor the blackboard contents and attempt to provide a solution to the CSP. To improve efficiency, we decided that rather than attempting full blown CSP solving each

---

[5] The reason why this is "any head element" is because SWRL allows the consequent to contain a conjunction of atoms.

cycle, the solver should perform a faster check of each of the constraints individually and only if they can all be satisfied, should it attempt the more difficult task of solving them combinatorially. If no solution can be found then this KS will simply not offer a contribution.

In our implementation the CSP solver is unique, in that it is the only KS that can post a solution to the Workgroup goal, initially posted onto the blackboard by the User KS[6]. However, there is no restriction on the number of CSP solver KSs that could be used within the system. In our future work there is also the possibility of greater user interaction (via the User KS) w.r.t to acceptance or rejection of a solution. Here the user could ask the CSP Solver KS to contribute again (provided there are alternate solutions) or accept the current one on the blackboard.

6   Controlling Content

So far we have talked about the contents of the blackboard as merely containing data relating to finding a workgroup solution. In actual fact, the AWB+B blackboard is divided into two panels.

The first panel is the Data Panel which holds the solution-related information. In order to inhibit the actions of the KSs accessing this panel, there are a couple of safeguards in place. The controller will not allow the goal of <owl:Thing> to be placed onto the blackboard and KS access to the blackboard is via a restrictive API that allows the underlying graph to be viewed by the KSs while not allowing it to be modified without the controller's knowledge.

The second panel is the Tasklist Panel, and is used by the controller to coordinate the actions of each KS by storing information about *what* each KS can contribute, based on the current state of the blackboard. Like the Data Panel, this is visible to all the KSs however, unlike the Data Panel, the KSs are allowed to add to this panel directly (but not remove items from it), the purpose of this is to facilitate the controller in directing the solving effort. The KSs add TasklistItems that describe the nature of any contribution they could offer. The controller looks at the items on the Tasklist Panel and determines which KS is allowed to contribute. Once a TasklistItem has been actioned, the controller removes it from the panel. This "request for contribution" and "make your contribution" sequence is applied using a Java interface, which each registered KS must implement and consists of the two method calls: canContribute and makeContribution.

When a KS's canContribute method is called it first determines *what* it can contribute (as per the steps previously outlined in the KS descriptions) and then checks, in the following order, if its "current" proposed contribution is not

---

[6] It is possible that an instance-based KS could contain instances of workgroups and offers to contribute those. In our case, because the user specifies the KSs at the start, we assume that none of the KSs contain workgroup instances. Similarly, a workgroup could be formulated based on a rule set within a rule-based KS and offered as a solution.

on the blackboard already; has not been contributed previously by itself; and is not already on the Tasklist, i.e. already proposed by another KS. Only if none of these cases apply is a `TasklistItem` created by the KS and added to the Tasklist Panel.

In our current implementation the controller is relatively simple. After all the KSs have been registered, the system "cycles" over each one asking it to populate the Tasklist Panel (by calling its `canContribute` method). Next, the controller examines the contents of the Tasklist and decides which items to action (by calling the appropriate `makeContribution` method of a KS). After actioning the appropriate `TasklistItems` on the Tasklist Panel, the controller has the option of retaining tasks that have not been actioned, or removing any remaining items from the Tasklist completely. This is purely a housekeeping measure as it prevents redundant or "out of date" items remaining on the Tasklist Panel. Then the cycle begins again. If nothing new has been added after a complete cycle, it is assumed that none of the KSs can contribute further and the CSP Solver KS is activated and attempts to find a solution.

7   Issues & Future Work

One issue with the blackboard architecture is that the two step `canContribute` and `makeContribution` process is inefficient. The effort involved to determine whether a contribution can be made is comparable to actually making the contribution itself and even then, depending upon the controller strategy, the contribution my never be asked for. This overhead may be reduced somewhat by caching the result of the `canContribute` step so that if the KS is asked to make its contribution a duplication of effort is not required.

Another important issue is that of contradictory information being placed on the blackboard. In the current implementation of the AWB+B, contradictions are just ignored – they remain unresolved with the blackboard containing both discrepant parts. Should one of these be parts be required in the composition of a solution then it is just used. One possibility to improve upon this is to have a KS continually checking the blackboard, prompting the user should an inconsistency be found. This would enable the user to decide which fact they wish to retain and remove the remaining inappropriate data. At first glance this might appear to be a very appropriate course of action, since a human should be able to do a better job of deciding than a machine. Unfortunately, in the case where a large quantity of contradictions occur this becomes far from ideal, especially from a usability viewpoint since this would very quickly become unworkable. The user would be constantly attending to these notifications, making themselves a bottleneck and impacting the overall performance of the system (not to mention becoming increasingly frustrated). Therefore, a more automated approach is desirable and is an area in which we plan to investigate further.

We have also highlighted the importance of ensuring only relevant items are placed on the blackboard. Since the blackboard system is attempting to centralise distributed SW data it does not want all the available data from each of the KSs;

it is only interested in as small a subset of this as is possible in order to solve the CSP problem. Since it is the job of the controller to ensure that this is the case, in our future work we plan to investigate possible controller strategies to improve relevancy, and therefore enhance the system performance.

8 Conclusions

Since reasoning is hard, we deem that reasoning over a dynamically composed sub-set of all the available data is preferable than just combining all that data *en masse* and processing that. To create as small a sub-set as possible it is important that the collected data is as relevant as possible to the problem at hand. We believe that the Blackboard Architecture is a suitable paradigm for controlling this effort since it not only enables a mix of reasoning methods but also allows them to operate cooperatively. This paradigm also supports the addition and removal of KSs from the process, even during runtime. For example, consider the scenario of a KS that starts to perform reasoning that could take hours, or even days to complete. Normally a system would have to wait until this was resolved before continuing. The Blackboard Architecture guards against the inefficiency of KSs (caused by numerous factors, e.g. tractability, network connections, etc) – the overall process of controlling the problem solving remains with the controller. Had we implemented an asynchronous version of the application, then a time-out mechanism can be added, so if a KS takes an inordinate amount of time to respond it is just ignored. The only adverse effect being on quality of the results.

Our SW Blackboard system is domain independent. Since the content of the blackboard is a dynamically generated RDF graph, a by-product of this is that it contains what is essentially a new *sub-ontology* representing the *relevant* parts of the problem domain too. This may be useful for a system geared more toward information gathering.

Acknowledgements. This work is supported under the Advanced Knowledge Technologies (AKT) IRC (EPSRC grant no. GR/N15764/01) comprising Aberdeen, Edinburgh, Sheffield, Southampton and the Open Universities. http://www.aktors.org

References

1. R. Brachman, V. Gilbert, and H. Levesque. An Essential Hybrid Reasoning System: Knowledge and Symbol Level Accounts of KRYPTON. In *The Ninth International Joint Conference on Artificial Intelligence (IJCAI-85)*, pages 532–539, Los Angeles, California, USA, 1985.
2. N. Carver and V. Lesser. The Evolution of Blackboard Control Architectures. CMPSCI Technical Report 92-71, Computer Science Department, Southern Illinois University, 1992.
3. C. Chweh. Generations ahead: Michael Huhns on cooperative information systems. *IEEE Intelligent Systems*, 12(5):82–84, September/October 1997.

4. D. D. Corkill. Collaborating Software: Blackboard and Multi-Agent Systems & the Future. In *Proceedings of the International Lisp Conference*, New York, New York, October 2003.

5. D. D. Corkill. Representation and Contribution-Integration Challenges in Collaborative Situation Assessment. In *Proceedings of the Eighth International Conference on Information Fusion (Fusion 2005)*, Philadelphia, Pennsylvania, July 2005.

6. R. S. Engelmore and A. J. Morgan, editors. *Blackboard Systems*. Addison-Wesley, 1988.

7. G. D. Giacomo and M. Lenzerini. Tbox and Abox Reasoning in Expressive Description Logics. In *KR-96*, pages 316–327, Los Altos, 1996. M. Kaufmann.

8. S. Harris and N. Gibbins. 3store: Efficient Bulk RDF Storage. In *1st International Workshop on Practical and Scalable Semantic Systems (PSSS'03)*, pages 1–20, 2003.

9. V. Jagannathan, R. Dodhiawala, and L. Baum, editors. *Blackboard Architectures and Applications*. Academic Press, 1989.

10. V. R. Lesser and L. Erman. A Retrospective View of the HEARSAY-II Architecture. In *Fifth International Joint Conference on Artificial Intelligence (IJCAI'77)*, pages 790–800, Cambridge, Massachusetts, August 1977.

11. C. McKenzie, A. Preece, and P. Gray. Extending SWRL to Express Fully-Quantified Constraints. In G. Antoniou and H. Boley, editors, *Rules and Rule Markup Languages for the Semantic Web (RuleML 2004)*, LNCS 3323, pages 139–154, Hiroshima, Japan, November 2004. Springer.

12. J. Myplopoulos and M. Papazoglu. Cooperative Information Systems, Guest Editors' Introduction. *IEEE Intelligent Systems*, 12(5):28–31, September/October 1997.

13. H. P. Nii. Blackboard Systems: The Blackboard Model of Problem Solving and the Evolution of Blackboard Architectures. *AI Magazine*, 7(2):38–53, 1986.

14. A. Preece, S. Chalmers, C. McKenzie, J. Pan, and P. Gray. Handling Soft Constraints in the Semantic Web Architecture. In *Reasoning on the Web Workshop (RoW2006), in the World Wide Web Conference (WWW2006)*, Edinburgh, UK, 2006.

15. N. Shadbolt, N. Gibbins, H. Glaser, S. Harris, and m. schraefel. CS AKTive Space, or How We Learned to Stop Worrying and Love the Semantic Web. *IEEE Intelligent Systems*, 19(3):41–47, 2004.

16. D. Tsarkov and I. Horrocks. DL Reasoner vs. First-Order Prover. In *2003 Description Logic Workshop (DL 2003)*, volume 81, pages 152–159. CEUR (http://ceur-ws.org/), 2003.

17. M. Wooldridge. *An Introduction To MultiAgent Systems*. Wiley, 2002.

Planning with the Semantic Web by fusing Ontologies and Planning Domain Definitions

Marco Cioffi and Simon Thompson[1],
BT Research and Venturing,
Martlesham Heath, Ipswich, UK.
marco@marcocioffi.com
Simon.2.Thompson@bt.com

Abstract

In this paper we describe how we integrated ontological knowledge into a planning domain definition system. We claim that this approach has two main benefits: (i) from the user point of view, existing ontologies previously developed inside the company can be reused (ii) from the planning system point of view ontology semantics can be used to infer domain properties that are not explicitly represented by the user. The specific contribution described in this paper is the use of OWL semantics beyond subsumption to infer knowledge in the planning domain definition. We demonstrate how this is done and describe a system that can utilize the technique to solve practical problems.

1. Introduction

Development in the field of the semantic web has exposed developers to a set of new tools and concepts. In particular ontologies, and the semantic web technologies of RDF and OWL [3] have been widely adopted.In parallel research in the field of service-oriented computing and service orientated architectures have become significant topics of commercial interest. For example BT is adopting a Service Orientated Architecture to underpin its future systems estate. A particularly active community is studying the problem of web-services composition [6] (for example), and in this context previous research on artificial intelligence (primarily on planning) has been used successfully.

The idea of using ontologies to express concepts for general use in various applications (data-integration, concept formation, systems development) and then re-using these concepts within service composition seems attractive. Providing a pre-defined corpus of knowledge for composition that has been generated for other purposes could be an enabler to developing service composition based applications like workflow design analysis, automated workflow design and repair, and ad-hoc on demand service provision. Merging the world of planning and ontologies is not

[1] The authors would like to thank their colleagues at BT for their help in the preparation of this paper and the support provided during the implementation of the software that we report here. We would also like to thank the anonymous referees on the AI-2006 program committee.

new, there was a workshop [5] addressing this issue. Even so work in the area is at an early stage and it seems that no standard approach has yet emerged.

Our question is *"why use ontological knowledge in a planning language?"* PDDL has provided a useful standard notation for planning systems and is constantly being reviewed and extended by the planning community. Literature on planning and ontologies seems to have accepted that using OWL (specifically) is just a natural and Good Thing. That may or may not be true, but in order for an approach to gain wide acceptance a range of motivations that address the concerns of the various communities and stakeholders involved in the development of a technology are required.

OWL is well structured to facilitate cross linking and definition sharing, and this will be important in cross organisation composition, so it can be said that there is a strong natural motivation to explore the topic. On the other hand, there is very little support or utilization of semantic web technology in mainstream web products at the time of writing. It might be quite reasonable to simply reject OWL and utilize an alternative approach to support the knowledge representation required for composing web services.

Our approach is to note that OWL provides a set of semantics which might be commonly used by knowledge engineers to describe their domain and which could be used in a compiler to produce a domain definition for a planner.

For example :

```
<owl:Ontology rdf:about="http://kreno.bt.com/" />
<owl:Class rdf:about="http://kreno.bt.com/#Phone"/>
<owl:Class rdf:about="http://kreno.bt.com/#Hub"/>
<owl:Class rdf:about="http://kreno.bt.com/#CordlessPhone">
  <rdfs:subClassOf rdf:resource="http://kreno.bt.com/#Phone" />
</owl:Class>
<owl:ObjectProperty rdf:ID="connected">
  <rdf:type rdf:resource="&owl;SymmetricProperty" />
  <rdfs:domain rdf:resource="http://kreno.bt.com/#CordlessPhone" />
  <rdfs:range rdf:resource=" http://kreno.bt.com/#Hub" />
</owl:ObjectProperty>
```

Example 1 - definition of ontology, note the use of the symmetric property

```
isa(?thing1,http://kreno.bt.com/#phone)
isa(?thing2,http://kreno.bt.com/#hub)
connected (?thing1,?thing2)
```

Example 1 – concepts expressed in the planning language that reference ontology elements

```
connected (?thing2, ?thing1)
```

Example 1 – a concept inferred from the domain engineers description and the ontology concepts.

We have implemented a planning system that demonstrates how it is possible to exploit the semantics of OWL expressions (manipulated using the JENA parser) in a planning domain description. Specifically, transitive and symmetric relations can be expressed using OWL and when the model is compiled into the planners internal language and semantics these can be expanded. The ideas behind this work are outlined in section 4 of the paper. In section 4.2 the mechanism used to relate ontological definitions in OWL and propositional planning domain operators is explained and in section 4.3 and 4.4 respectively the mechanisms that were used to exploit the OWL property hierarchy and the semantic relations as in Example 1 are explained. In section 5 we present the technical details of how we implemented it using standard web technology (Java, Eclipse, Jena and Tomcat) in order to demonstrate the practical nature of these ideas. Finally in section 6 we provide some comments on the work and directions for further development.

We will give a more complete description of the concerns of this paper in section 2 and 3.

2. Planning Systems

Planning is a research field of artificial intelligence that deals with plan construction. During the paper, the word *plan* will be used to specify a set of actions that an agent should do in order to satisfy its goals. Planning is used every time that an agent detects a mismatch between the current state of the world and its goals.

In the project we have chosen to use a STRIPS-style formalism [2] with an efficient algorithm, GRAPHPLAN [1]. Our motivations for the use of this formalism come from its immediacy and simplicity, its widely accepted and used in planning research.

In STRIPS each action that an agent can execute in order to modify the world, is represented as:

(i)   a preconditions list, a list of clauses that must be true in the current world description to for the action to be executed;

(ii)   an add list, a list of clauses that will be added to the world description once the action is executed;

(iii)   a delete list, a list of clauses that will be deleted from the current world description once the action is executed.

For example: we want to formalise the situation in which an agent has to move through different rooms in order to use some network connections.

The formalisation of the world uses the following predicates:

- *In*, this predicate will specify the current location of the agent, e.g. *In(room1)*
- *Connection*, this predicate will be used to identify a connection, e.g. *Connection(phone)*, *Connection(handy)*.
- *ConnectionIn*, this predicate will be used to specify the current location of the connection, e.g. *ConnectionIn(phone, room1)*, *ConnectionIn(handy, room1)*.
- *Used*, this predicate will be used to specify whether a connection was already used or not, e.g. *Used(phone)*

```
MOVE (?from, ?to)
PRE:  In(?from)
ADD:  In(?to)
DEL:  In(?from)


USE (?object)
PRE:  ConnectionIn(?place, ?object), In(?place)
ADD:  Used(?object)
DEL:  ConnectionIn(?object, ?place)
```

Example 2 – Two simple plan actions using STRIPS formalism

```
Init: Room(room1), Room(room2),
      Connection(phone), Connection(handy),
      ConnectionIn(phone, room1), FoodIn(handy, room2),
      In(room1)
Goal: Used(phone), Used(handy)
--> Generated Plan: USE(phone), MOVE(room1, room2), USE(handy)
```

Example 1 – From an initial condition and a goal the planning engine generate a plan

Two actions can be specified (Example). The first action (*MOVE*) is used to move the agent between the rooms; the second action (*USE*) is used to use the specified connection.

In Example 1, the planning engine takes as input a list of action, an initial state, a goals list and generates a plan as a set of actions that if executed will move the agent from the initial state to a final state, which will contain the goal list.

3. Ontologies

Ontologies are used to describe concepts. In general terms the main benefits that they can bring are: (i) specification of the domain, formalizing the concepts of the system is a first step to its understanding; (ii) establish shared knowledge, during the development of complex systems in which multiple actors are involved a key issue is to share and use the same set of concepts.

OWL is a standard developed by the W3C to define ontologies; there are three variant dialects of OWL: OWL-Lite, OWL-DL and OWL-Full, with growing expressiveness and complexity. We identified a subset of the OWL expressions that could be used to represent knowledge in the domain definition system for the planner. In order to understand the next section, a brief remark of these properties will follow:

- owl:Class, this expression defines a class of objects. The word *class* is used to define a subset of things with same properties; e.g. the class *phone* define an object that can be used to telephone another person, has a numeric keypad, a color, an earphone and so on.
- owl:SubClassOf, this expression defines an hierarchical relation between two classes; e.g. a *cordless phone* is a special kind (a sub class) of *phone*, so it has all the properties of the class *phone* and some additional properties, for example that can be carried with the user.
- owl:ObjectProperty, this expression defines a property. A property is used to create a relation between two concrete things. For example, we can define a property called *line* which indicate that two telephone are connected together, or a property *haveNumber* which create a relation between a physical telephone and a telephone number.
- owl:TransitiveProperty, this expression defines a special property considered transitive. If R is a transitive property and a, b, c three individuals which could be applied to the mentioned property, then:

$$R\,(a,\,b) \wedge R\,(b,\,c) \Rightarrow R\,(a,\,c)$$

For example, a property with the name *In* could be used to define where is an object. In that case, the following could be inferred:

$$In(room1,\ floor1)\ \wedge\ In(floor1,\ building1)\ \Rightarrow\ In(room1,\ building1)$$

- owl:SymmetricProperty, this expression defines a special property considered symmetric. If R is a symmetric property and a, b two individuals which could be applied to the mentioned property, then:

$$R\,(a,\,b) \Leftrightarrow R\,(b,\,a)$$

For example, a property with the name *Connect* could be used to connect two telephone (*telephone1* and *telephone2*) in that case the following is valid:

$$Connect\ (telephone1,\ telephone2)\ \Leftrightarrow\ Connect\ (telephone2,\ telephone1)$$

- owl:inverseOf, this expression defines a special relation between two properties. If $R1$ and $R2$ are two relations and $R2$ is declared as the inverse of $R1$ then:

$$R1\ (a,\,b) \Leftrightarrow R2\ (b,\,a)$$

For example if we define the property *Calling* (meant to indicate that an user is calling another user) as the inverse of the property *Receiving* (meant to indicate that an user is receiving a call from another user) than the following is valid:

Calling (Simon, Marco) ⇔ *Receiving (Marco, Simon)*

- `owl:DatatypeProperty`, this expression defines links between OWL entities and data values.
- `Rdfs:subPropertyOf`, this expression defines an hierarchical relation between two properties; e.g. an *ADSL Connection* between two telephones is a special kind of *Connection*. In that case using the OWL semantic we can infer: *ADSLConnection (tel1, tel2)* ⇒ *Connection (tel1, tel2)*
- `owl:equivalentProperty`, this expression defines a special relation between two properties. If *R1* and *R2* are two relations and *R2* is declared as equivalent of *R1* then: *R1 (a, b)* ⇔ *R2 (a, b)*
  This relation could be used to define, for example, properties with the same name, for example if the property *Connection* is equivalent to the property *Connection*, then

Connection (tel1, tel2) ⇔ *Connected (tel1, tel2)*

- `owl:equivalentClass`, this expression defines two classes as equivalent; if *C1* and *C2* are two classes than all the individuals of *C1* must be individual of *C2* and vice-versa.

In Example 2 we have reported a simple example where we show a simple ontology where we define four classes: *Location, Person, Phone* and *CordlessPhone*; and three properties: *Connect, Friend, In*. Note that the *Connect* and the *Friend* properties are symmetric and the *In* property is transitive, so it is valid what asserted earlier when we presented the `owl:SymmetricProperty` and the `owl:TransitiveProperty`.

4. Using Ontologies in a Planning System

Other work has been published that examines the challenge of moving between OWL and PDDL representations. For example in [4] a system is presented that translates between OWL and OCL. However the hierarchy of properties and relations in the ontology definition are not utilized. The WSMO project [7] has developed a comprehensive modelling system for semantic web services in contrast to our approach of using disjoint modelling techniques (STRIPS operators and Ontologies) as Domain Specific Languages [8].

```
<owl:Ontology rdf:about="http://kreno.bt.com/" />
<owl:Class rdf:about="http://kreno.bt.com/#Location"/>
<owl:Class rdf:about="http://kreno.bt.com/#Person"/>
<owl:Class rdf:about="http://kreno.bt.com/#Phone"/>
<owl:Class rdf:about="http://kreno.bt.com/#CordlessPhone">
  <rdfs:subClassOf rdf:resource="http://kreno.bt.com/#Phone" />
</owl:Class>
<owl:ObjectProperty rdf:ID="Connected">
  <rdf:type rdf:resource="&owl;SymmetricProperty" />
  <rdfs:domain rdf:resource="http://kreno.bt.com/#Phone" />
  <rdfs:range rdf:resource=" http://kreno.bt.com/#Phone" />
</owl:ObjectProperty>
<owl:ObjectProperty rdf:ID="Friend">
  <rdf:type rdf:resource="&owl;SymmetricProperty" />
  <rdfs:domain rdf:resource="http://kreno.bt.com/#Person" />
  <rdfs:range rdf:resource=" http://kreno.bt.com/#Person" />
</owl:ObjectProperty>
<owl:ObjectProperty rdf:ID="In">
  <rdf:type rdf:resource="&owl;TransitiveProperty" />
  <rdfs:domain rdf:resource="http://kreno.bt.com/#Location" />
  <rdfs:range rdf:resource=" http://kreno.bt.com/#Location" />
</owl:ObjectProperty>
```

Example 2 – An Example OWL Ontology

This work is an enhancement of the planning domain definition system that allows the expression of relations between atoms in a more structured way. PDDL provides methods of defining semantics around actions – for example expressing that an action can be executed in parallel with another action, we are interested in adding semantics about the relationships between the things that are being processed and then using this knowledge to create more complete domain definitions.

Our general idea is to use a subset of OWL to express the relations between concepts inside the planning domain. The user can reference this information and knowledge during the creation of a new planning problem and it can be compiled into a more complete definition to help the planners engine to cope with partial problem specification situations (for example, when the state of the world is not fully specified).

There are two reasons to do this :

- A *prescriptive purpose*, using the ontologies information a planning specification can be validated as correct or incorrect. This automation improves the quality of the domain description by enabling a more compact and expressive representation, this improves the user experience and can reduce time spent debugging plans.
- A *deductive purpose*, we can use the ontology information to deduce further knowledge representing the world and then solving problems not fully specified by the user.

4.1 General architecture

A plan editor that bridges between OWL and the STRIPS formalism as described above has been developed as a plug-in for Eclipse. The planning engine is a standalone package developed as plain Java object that uses an extended version of the Graphplan algorithm to produce plans for achieving goals from a particular system state. The integration between OWL and the planning system used the following components:

- An *Owl Import* component, allows the user to import an external ontology inside the project.
- A *Planning Editor* component works natively with OWL files. Thus, all the entities created by the user are stored as OWL knowledge inside a special project file..
- A *planning pre-processor* component was created in order to enable the *inference of relations between objects and properties* described earlier. In particular, the user can use OWL semantics during the design of a new planning problem. Once the planning pre-processor has completed/validated the plan then the standard *Planner* is invoked.

We used the Jena parser [9] to import and export the knowledge in OWL. The planning pre-processor that fuses the ontology and planning domain uses the Jena rule engine.

4.2 Re-use of Existing Knowledge

This feature allows the user to import a previously developed ontology into their project or workspace. For this task, the *Owl Import* component is used. Once the user has imported the ontology through the GUI, then, all the defined classes and relations of the ontology are available.

In our planning definition system we have introduced a special predicate which aims to mark the type of each individuals. We have called this *isa* predicate. In the follc ving example, we use an external ontology with the concepts we want to re-use, suppose for simplicity that this ontology has a root of http://kreno.bt.com/.

Once imported through the GUI, the *OWL Import* component marks the location of the new ontology and it becomes possible to write the following (Example 3) using the proposition editor provided.

```
isa (phoneID078531, http://kreno.bt.com/#Phone)
```

Example 3 – A type definition using the *isa* predicate and the *Phone* concept

Example 4 shows how it is possible to assign a type to an individual; in particular, we are defining the type of the entity phoneID078531 as http://kreno.bt.com/#Phone. Giving an interpretation to the previous example, we can assert that the entity phoneID078531 is an individual of the class http://kreno.bt.com/#Phone. In other words, it is a phone!

In detail, *isa* is the name of the predicate we use to define the type relation; phoneID078531 is the name of the identifier for the entity phoneID078531; http://kreno.bt.com/#Phone is the URI of the concept that we want to use. Note that the URI is composed of two part: the first part identify the ontology and in particular is the base of the ontology (http://kreno.bt.com/), the second part (#Phone) identify instead the concept to use inside the ontology.

The point here is that we are tying the propositional representation of the phone entity to the ontological definition of phone; these entities are then used in constructs that are not available in OWL-FULL, specifically goals and actions.

To make an analogy the isa is to the planning domain definition system what the owl:Individual is to OWL.

4.3 Using the Property Hierarchy

This feature allows exploitation of the relations between classes of objects defined in the ontology in planning. The *Planning Pre-Processor* component can check the consistency of the plan and infers a full description in case of partial plan description.

This component takes in input an ontology definition and a planning domain and as output gives a new planning domain completed with the full description of the world or errors in case of an inconsistent plan. The standard planning engine can then processes this output.

For example, supposing we create a planning domain for the domestic customers. In particular, the focus is to represent the concept of *CordlessPhone* as a special type of *Phone* that can be moved. Using the OWL semantics we can define these concepts as following (Example 4):

```
<owl:Ontology rdf:about="http://kreno.bt.com/" />
<owl:Class rdf:about="http://kreno.bt.com/#Phone"/>
<owl:Class rdf:about="http://kreno.bt.com/#MovableObject"/>
<owl:Class rdf:about="http://kreno.bt.com/#CordlessPhone">
  <rdfs:subClassOf rdf:resource="http://kreno.bt.com/#Phone" />
  <rdfs:subClassOf rdf:resource=http://kreno.bt.com/#MovableObject
 />
</owl:Class>
```

Example 4 – An ontology that define the relation between different kind of phone

In particular, note that the relations between the classes *CoordlessPhone*, *Phone* and *MovableObject*. Once imported this ontology, in the planning system we can define some concrete phone that will be used by the user. In Example 5 three phones phoneID078531, phoneID078532, phoneID078533 are defined. Note that the first and the latter phone are of type http://kreno.bt.com/#CordlessPhone.

```
isa (phoneID078531, http://kreno.bt.com/#CordlessPhone)
isa (phoneID078532, http://kreno.bt.com/#Phone)
isa (phoneID078533, http://kreno.bt.com/#CordlessPhone)
```

Example 5 – A type definition using the isa predicate and the CordlessPhone concept

Since we have defined some entity using the type http://kreno.bt.com/#CordlessPhone and since the planning pre-processor can access to the previously defined ontology (Example 4) then some property of the entity defined (Example 5) can be deduced as follows (Example 6):

```
isa (phoneID078531, http://kreno.bt.com/#MovableObject)
isa (phoneID078531, http://kreno.bt.com/#Phone)
isa (phoneID078533, http://kreno.bt.com/#MovableObject)
isa (phoneID078533, http://kreno.bt.com/#Phone)
```

Example 6 – Deduced property using the define ontology and planning definition

The advantages of this are:

1. The pre-planner can infer the missing relation and the planner can find more solutions by using those relations
2. the user could write generic actions, for example an actions for MovableObjects that apply also to other things which are subclasses of moveable objects according to the ontology

4.4   Using semantic relations

In addition to using the hierarchy of classes and objects to infer missing relations we use other semantic declarations in the ontology. In particular we can use *TransitiveProperty, SymmetricProperty and InverseOf.* Example 1 shows how this works in practice. Given references to relations or objects defined in an ontology the task is to check to see if any of the relations have properties that can lead to an expansion and then to create that expansion by applying an appropriate rule :

Relation1 (A, B)
        →
        Relation1 (A, B) && Symmetric(Relation1)
        THEN
            Relation1 (B, A)
Relation1 (A, B) && Relation1 (B, C)
        →
        Relation1 (A, B) && Relation1 (B, C) && Transitive (Relation1)
        THEN
            Relation1 (A, C)
Relation1 (A, B)
        →
        Relation1 (A, B) && InverseOf (Relation2, Relation1)
        THEN
        Relation2 (B, A)

5.   Implementation into a practical system

As we have previously noted the planning system that consumes the knowledge generated from OWL is a derivative of GRAPHPLAN which generates a WSBPEL workflow as its plan. Service markup in a variant of OWL-S is gathered from references retrieved from UDDI and is unified with domain definition knowledge (context) and user goals to create a planning problem which is then resolved by the planner into a web service orchestration that is monitored and run to achieve the user goals.

Our planner is implemented into two programmes, a run time agent rationality engine that runs under TOMCAT and a programmers workbench that runs under ECLIPSE. We call the overall set of tools and programs "Kreno". The overall objective of the Kreno toolset is to provide a way to define a working application in terms of services and goals, so that the application is independent of the particular services that are used to provide it's functionality at run time.

300

5.1 Import/Export Ontology

Graphical tools are used to import the ontology definitions into the system; Figure 1 shows a dialog selecting OWL ontology definition files for use in the current project.

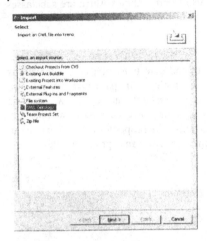
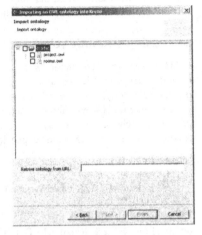

Figure 1. A screenshot of the OWL import component

5.2 Pre-planning tool interface

Once imports have been completed the ontology is parsed using JENA and the model generated is used to provide information for the knowledge editing tools required to provide the propositions for the context, service and goal definitions. Figure 2 shows how imported ontology elements are selected and used to define type information in one of the proposition editors used.

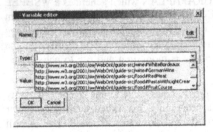

Figure 2 – A screenshot of the variable editor and the proposition editor

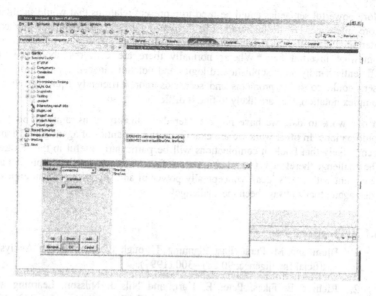

Figure 3. A Goal definition using a transitive relation

The workbench is used to edit the service and goal mark-up that defines the planning domain. Figure 3 shows the typical output of an editing episode, where a proposition :

```
connected(?lineOne, ?lineTwo)
```

is added to a goal. The proposition is marked as symmetric; this leads the editor to derive the consequences

```
connected (?lineOne, ?lineTwo)
connected (?lineTwo, ?lineOne)
```

All relations added to definitions by derivation are recomputed before each planning cycle initiated by the tool, this re-computation procedure is also applied in the Agent based implementation of the planning engine when it is deployed in an application. Plans are produced by the agent as sequences including parallel actions using our planners internal datastructure. This is then rendered into BPEL4WS by syntactic rewriting.

6. Conclusions and Future Work

This paper has reported the use of OWL semantics to support the definition of planning domain definitions in the context of service composition in the semantic web. Jena was used to parse and reason over the OWL definitions. This work represents a useful "widget" in the semantic web developers toolkit, we think that it has practical value for developers on the sematic web, but we don't claim that it is going to revolutionise any aspect of their work!

More powerful semantics could be used to represent relations that would facilitate more inference, but the old trade offs between representational complexity and inferential power, which themselves have influenced the design of OWL are somewhat inverted here. Wheras normally there are concerns about how to efficiently handly more sophisticated logics and notations it seems to us that while users could construct problems and scenarios more efficiently (quickly) with a complex notation, they are likely to find it difficult to do so.

In our work to date we have not considered cardinality; constraints or boolean combinations. In other work we are examining the semantics of agent goals, and it seems likely that boolean combinations will be particularly useful in this context. The challenge therefore is to find abstractions for service and goal concepts that are congruent with user's ideas, conceptually powerful and support useful inferences. Then again, that's always been the challenge!

6.1 References

1. Blum and M. Furst. Fast Planning Through Planning Graph Analysis. Artificial Intelligence, 90:281--300 (1997).

2. Richard E. Fikes, Peter E. Hart, and Nils J. Nilsson, Learning and Executing Generalized Robot Plans. Artificial Intelligence, 3 (1972) 251-288.

3. McGuiness and F. van Harmelen. "OWL Web Ontology Language Overview" W3C Recommendation 10th February 2004. Available from

4. McCluskey, T.L., and Cresswell, S.N. "Importing Ontological Information into Planning Domain Models", In Olivares & Onaindia (eds) *The Role of Ontologies in AI Planning and Scheduling* ICAPS 2005 workshop.

5. J. F. Olivares and E. Onaindia (eds) *The Role of Ontologies in AI Planning and Scheduling* Proceedings, ICAPS05 Workshop, Available from http://icaps05.uni-ulm.de/documents/ws-proceedings/ws2-allpapers.pdf. Downloaded 23/8/06

6. B. Srivastava, J. Blythe, (eds) Proceedings of AAAI 2005 workshop on Exploring Planning and Scheduling for Web Services, Grid and Autnomoic Computing. AAAI Technical Report WS-05-03 56pp

7. J.Domingue, D. Roman, M. Stollberg. (2005). Web Service Modeling Ontology (WSMO) – An Ontology for Semantic Web Services. Position Paper at the W3C Workshop on Frameworks for Semantic Web Services. June 9-10, 2005, Innsbruck, Austria.

8. M. Mernik, J. Heering, A.M. Sloan. "When and how to develop domain-specific languages" ACM Computing Surveys. 37(4), pp 316-344. December 2005.

9. B. McBride. "Jena: Implementing the RDF Model and Syntax Specification" Semantic Web Workshop, WWW 2001.

A Reusable Commitment Management Service using Semantic Web Technology

Alun Preece, Stuart Chalmers, and Craig McKenzie

University of Aberdeen, Computing Science, Aberdeen, UK
{apreece,schalmer,cmckenzie}@csd.abdn.ac.uk
http://www.csd.abdn.ac.uk/research/akt/cif

Abstract. Commitment management is a key issue in service-provisioning in the context of virtual organisations (VOs). A service-provider — which may be a single agent acting within an organisation, or the VO acting as a collective whole — manages particular resources, and commits these resources to meet specific goals. Commitments can be modelled as constraints on resources. Such constraints are often soft: they can be broken if necessary. The goal of the work described in this paper is to create an open, reusable commitment management service (CMS) based on Semantic Web standards. The chief requirement is that the CMS should be reusable in different domains, able to manage commitments over services described in a wide range of domain-specific service ontologies. This paper presents open Semantic Web representations for (1) expressing individual commitments as constraints over service descriptions, (2) capturing a set of commitments as a soft constraint satisfaction problem, and (3) representing and communicating the solution to a soft CSP. A reference implementation of a constraint solver able to operate on (1) and (2) to produce (3) is described, and its reuse is demonstrated in two distinct domains: e-commerce and e-response.

1 Introduction

Commitment management is a key issue in service-provisioning in the context of virtual organisations (VOs). A service-provider — which may be a single agent acting within an organisation, or the VO acting as a collective whole — manages particular resources, and commits these resources to meet specific goals. The issue of commitment management appears throughout the lifecycle of such organisations [14]: when a partner is deliberating whether to bid to join a VO, it must consider its existing commitments, and construct a bid that is compatible with its commitments; when a VO is operating, it must manage its commitments over its collective resources and — when perturbations inevitably occur — the VO must adapt by revising its commitments; finally, when a VO's job is done and it disbands, commitments must be released and cleaned-up. Although the types of services managed in each case are very diverse, commitment management issues arise in VOs in all domains, including e-commerce [13], e-science [6], and e-response[1].

Often, the commitment of resources to goals is governed by service-level agreements. The commitments can be modelled as *constraints* on the resources. Such constraints are often *soft*: they can be broken if necessary [4]. When a service-provider is

---

[1] http://e-response.org/

presented with a new potential commitment, it must perform reasoning to determine if it can take on this commitment, possibly by dropping (breaking) existing commitments (constraints). Hence, the goal of the agent's deliberation procedure becomes to find an optimal solution that satisfies a maximal subset of the constraints [7]. In this context, constraints often have associated *utility values*, indicating the relative importance of satisfying individual constraints or clauses [2, 8]. Importantly, these utilities are generally not absolute: they are relative to the particular constraint satisfaction problem (CSP) in which the constraint is being applied. In relation to a particular solution, a given constraint may be satisfied or violated, and it is often useful to be able to represent and reason about which constraints are satisfied/violated by a given solution [5]. The ability to make statements about whether a constraint is satisfied or not in a given context is commonly called *constraint reification*.

The goal of the work described in this paper is to create an open, reusable commitment management service (CMS) based on Semantic Web standards. The chief requirement is that the CMS should be reusable in different domains, able to manage commitments over services described in a wide range of domain-specific service ontologies. This requirement motivates the Semantic Web approach: it is our expectation that the majority of service ontologies will be defined in a SW-based representation, currently OWL or RDFS.[2] By rooting our CMS in the Web and Semantic Web architectures, we also exploit existing XML-based interchange formats (including RDF syntax), transport protocols (HTTP, SOAP, etc) and logical foundations (including description logic and rules). Building on these foundations, the requirements for our CMS are:

1. an open format for expressing individual commitments as constraints over service descriptions;
2. an open format for capturing a set of commitments as a soft constraint satisfaction problem;
3. an open format for representing and communicating the solution to a soft CSP;
4. a reference implementation of a constraint solver able to operate on (1) and (2) to produce (3);
5. demonstrations of the CMS working in at least two distinct domains, to provide proof-of-concept of reusability.

In light of these requirements, this paper offers the following:

- We review our Semantic Web Constraint Interchange Format (CIF) [12], which builds on the proposed Semantic Web Rule Language (SWRL) [9]. This format (CIF/SWRL) provides an open representation for expressing individual commitments as quantified constraints over service descriptions defined in terms of OWL or RDFS ontologies.
- We present an ontology for representing soft CSPs and their solutions. The ontology — which is intended to complement CIF/SWRL but is also potentially usable with other constraint and rule representations — allows utility values to be associated with constraint expressions. The solution format allows constraints to be labelled to indicate whether they are satisfied or not in a particular solution.

---

[2] For example, OWL-S (http://www.daml.org/services) or WSML (http://www.wsmo.org).

- We describe our reference implementation of a constraint solver based on the Java Constraint Library (JCL)[3], and present two demonstration systems using the CMS, one in an e-commerce domain (multimedia service provisioning) and the other in an e-response domain (disaster management).

The paper is organised as follows: Section 2 presents an abstract scenario involving an agent reasoning about it's commitments using constraint solving, motivating the need to represent utility values and constraint reification; Section 3 describes our the CIF/SWRL constraint interchange format; Section 4 surveys approaches to handling soft and reified constraints in various CSP-solving frameworks, and describes our ontology for representing soft CSPs; Section 5 describes the two virtual organisation demonstrator implementations; Section 6 provides discussion and conclusion.

2 Managing Commitments as Constraints

To illustrate the use of soft constraints for modelling and managing commitments, we now present a detailed example. This example is a simplification of the type of problem that occurs in virtual organisation service-provisioning application domains.

Consider two service-providing agents, a1 and a2. Each agent can provide a certain amount of resource x (12 units from a1 and 10 from a2). The agents have existing commitments — c1, c2 and c3 on those resources, as shown in the first schedule in Figure 1:

- c1: 5x from time 0→5 on a1
- c2: 3x from time 6→10 on a1
- c3: 5x from time 0→7 on a2

Note that in this simple example we only look at a single type of resource (x). However, the solution to the commitment management problem presented here generalises to any number of resource types and combination [5]. We restrict ourselves to a single resource type here only for the sake of clarity.

If a new request, N is received by the agents to provide 15x from time 0→10, then the agent has four main choices:

- Reject N and satisfy existing commitments c1, c2 & c3 (Schedule 1 in Figure 1)
- Accept N and break c1 & c2 (Schedule 2)
- Accept N and break c3 (Schedule 3)
- Accept N and break c1 & c3 (Schedule 4)

(Note that there are many permutations of the exact amounts of the resource x, but in terms of commitments satisfied or broken these are the four main choices.)

As the number of agents and commitments increases the number of possible combinations of solutions that satisfy all the commitments (and solutions that break commitments) grows exponentially. Also the number of trivial solutions (i.e. solutions that vary in extremely small detail) increases (e.g. schedule 3 could take 7x from a1 and

---

[3] http://liawww.epfl.ch/JCL/

306

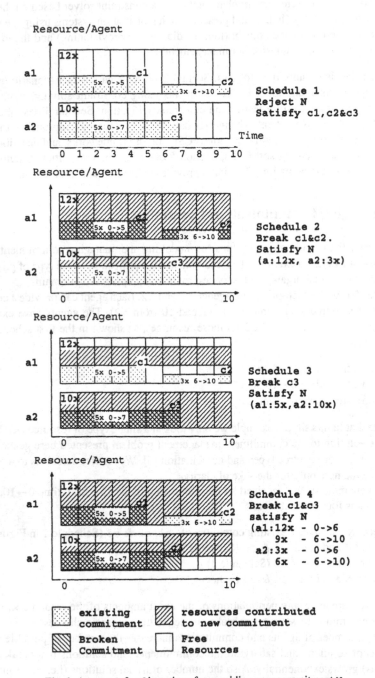

Fig. 1. Agent a1 & a2's options for providing new commitment N

8x from a2 rather than 5x and 10x which would not affect the commitments broken). The main emphasis behind the CSP-solving procedure is to find solutions that break commitments (i.e. solutions that are different enough in outcome that they break different commitments). As a result of this we need to equip the CSP solver with a method for differentiating between solutions. We also need a way to prioritise commitments so that we can rule out solutions that break commitments that have been specified *a priori* as 'must-complete' tasks.

This kind of commitment management mechanism can be implemented as a reification extension to a cumulative scheduling CSP solver that uses a combination of reification and constraint value labeling to provide the required commitment management and prioritisation — details are provided in [5], and further discussion of our virtual organisation demonstrator implementations appears in Section 5.

3   A Constraint Interchange Format Based on SWRL

Our Constraint Interchange Format (CIF) is derived from the Colan [1] constraint language, which is based on range restricted first order logic.[4] Earlier versions of the CIF language were aligned with RDF [11] and SWRL [12]. CIF constraints are essentially defined as quantified implications, for example:

$(\forall ?x \in X, ?y \in Y)$ p(?x,?y) $\land$ Q(?x) $\Rightarrow$
  $(\forall ?z \in Z)$ q(?x,?z) $\land$ R(?z) $\Rightarrow$
    $(\exists ?v \in V)$ s(?y,?v)

Commitment c2 from the example in Section 2 can be written in this syntax as follows:

$(\forall ?t \in Time)$?t$\geq$6 $\land$?t$\leq$10 $\Rightarrow$
  $(\exists ?c \in Commitment)$ hasService(?c,?s) $\land$
    hasServiceType(?s, 'x') $\land$ hasAmount(?s,3)

Unary predicates and named sets in these expressions (P, Q, X, Y, Commitment, Time, etc) are RDFS or OWL classes, while binary predicates (p, q, hasService, hasAmount, etc) are RDFS or OWL properties. When CIF is used to express commitments, most of these terms will come from domain-specific service ontologies — examples are given in Section 5. Due mainly to the addition of explicit universal and existential quantifiers, and nested implications, CIF constraints are not expressible in SWRL as it stands, so we have defined CIF/SWRL as an extension of SWRL: we reuse the implication structure from SWRL, but allow for nested quantified implications within the consequent of an implication. Compared to the SWRL syntax in [9], this simply adds the quantifiers and supports nested implications. Note that the innermost-nested implication has an empty body as it is always of the form "*true* $\Rightarrow$ ...". (In the above syntax this is implicit; the following abstract syntax, and the RDF syntax given in the appendix make this explicit.)

Figure 2 shows the CIF extensions to the abstract syntax given in SWRL and OWL documentation [9], using the same EBNF syntax. A constraint expression retains

---

[4] The term "constraint" is often used rather freely; in this paper we use the term for logical expressions within the scope of Colan — see [12] for broader discussion of the relationship between rules and constraints.

the URIreference and annotation syntax features from SWRL so as to allow statements to be made about the constraints themselves (see Section 4.1). Note that nesting is handled by extending the original SWRL grammar, allowing a constraint to appear recursively inside a consequent.

```
constraint   ::= 'Implies(' [ URIreference ] { annotation }
                 quantifiers antecedent consequent ')'
antecedent   ::= 'Antecedent(' { expr } ')'
consequent   ::= 'Consequent(' consexpr ')'
consexpr     ::= constraint | { atom }
expr         ::= atom | disjunct | conjunct | negation
disjunct     ::= 'Or(' { expr } ')'
conjunct     ::= 'And(' { expr } ')'
negation     ::= 'Not(' expr ')'
quantifiers  ::= 'Quantifiers(' { q-atom } ')'
q-atom       ::= quantifier '(' q-var q-set ')'
quantifier   ::= 'forall' | 'exists'
q-var        ::= I-variable
q-set        ::= description
```

Fig. 2. CIF/SWRL abstract syntax in EBNF

The definition of antecedent is extended from SWRL to allow combinations of disjunction, conjunction, and negation expressions. In the simplest case where an antecedent is a conjunction of atoms, the syntax allows omission of an explicit And structure — the "and" is implicit (as in the SWRL syntax). However, disjunctions and negations are always explicit, as are any conjunctions within them. It is worth noting that a consequent can be only a conjunction — CIF/SWRL does not allow disjunction or negation here.

As defined by the SWRL EBNF, an atom may be a unary predicate (for example, P(I-variable(x)) or a binary predicate (for example, q(I-variable(y) I-variable(z))). The only other notable additional syntax is the quantifiers structure, a list of individual quantifier expressions, each of which contains a reference to a SWRL I-variable and an OWL description. So, in the informal expression "?x ∈ X" x is an I-variable and X is an OWL/RDFS class identifier.

The example commitment c2 re-cast into the abstract syntax is shown in Figure 3. Note the empty antecedent in the innermost-nested implication.

The RDF syntax for CIF/SWRL is summarised in the appendix.

4 An Ontology for Representing Soft CSPs

Before presenting our soft CSP ontology, we examine common features of soft CSPs in the literature and in practical implementations, in order to identify the minimal features required of the ontology.

```
Implies(
    Quantifiers(forall(I-variable(t) Time))
    Antecedent(
        greaterThanOrEqual(I-variable(t) 6)
        lessThanOrEqual(I-variable(t) 10))
    Consequent(
        Implies(
            Quantifiers(exists(I-variable(c) Commitment))
            Antecedent()
            Consequent(
                hasService(I-variable(c) I-variable(s))
                hasService(I-variable(s) 'x')
                hasAmount(I-variable(s) 3))))))
```

Fig. 3. Example constraint shown in the CIF/SWRL abstract syntax

Soft constraints can be represented and implemented in a variety of ways, depending on language and system used. In this section we look at a number of CSP-solving frameworks (based on Prolog and Java), and describe ways in which we can model soft constraints using the features available in those frameworks. We then give a brief overview of some of the soft constraint literature.

Prolog Implementations In many Prolog implementations, the issue of soft constraints can be modelled with reification. Reification is the attachment of a boolean value to each constraint. If a constraint is satisfied, then the boolean value is set to true, otherwise it is set to false. This means that it is possible to reason about the constraints, by reasoning about these boolean values.

Given an unsatisfiable problem, the aim then is to find the best subset of simultaneously satisfiable constraints (i.e. true values), by utilising the attached boolean values.

These values themselves can then form the basis for a meta-level CSP, the solution to which is an assignment of reification values to constraints at the lower level. SICStus[5], GNU Prolog[6] and SWI Prolog[7] all provide a system of reification.

Java Implementations In Java, two dominant constraint libraries are Java Constraint Library (JCL)[8] and Choco[9].

The JCL attaches a floating point number to each tuple of a constraint rated from 0.0 (important) to 1.0 (not important), so each outcome pairing is given a value showing its preference as a solution. When solutions are returned from the solver they are given a 'score' dependent on what tuple has been chosen. These may be used to prioritise the solutions dependent on preferences.

---

[5] http://www.sics.se
[6] http://gnu-prolog.inria.fr/
[7] http://www.swi-prolog.org/
[8] http://liawww.epfl.ch/JCL/
[9] http://choco.sourceforge.net/

This method can easily model the reification described in the Prolog systems. If we add '0' to each domain of possible values for each variable, we can class this as a 'not applied' value for that variable (i.e. if the variable is assigned to 0, we take it to be not satisfied). We can mark a constraint tuple where an assigned value is 0 as 1.0 (i.e. not important), and other possible values as anywhere between 0.0 to 0.9; therefore the preference will to be find a value other than 0 for that constraint (i.e. satisfy the constraint). Obviously this requires some work-arounds when zero value assignments are required for specific values, but in the case of the commitment management examples we have been investigating, this method has proved satisfactory.

Choco is a system for solving constraints, also written in Java. It is a library for constraint satisfaction problems (CSPs), constraint programming (CP) and explanation-based constraint solving that is built upon an event-based propagation mechanism. The type of constraints that can be handled by Choco are arithmetic constraints (equality, difference, comparisons and linear combination), boolean and user-defined N-ary constraints. The propagation engine maintains arc-consistency for binary constraints throughout the solving process, while for n-ary constraints, it uses a weaker propagation mechanism with a forward checking algorithm. Choco uses a system of explanation based solving[10]. Using this method, a constraint program can describe why certain decision were taken (i.e. why variable x cannot take the value a) and so show why a problem fails. This information can then be used to find subsets of satisfiable constraints within the given set.

Soft Constraints in the Literature A number of people in the literature look at the scoring, or ordering, of constraints in CSP solving in two main ways [2]:

- Assigning values to each possible tuple in a constraint.
- Assigning a value to the actual constraint itself.

There are a number of ways that these two methods are modelled. Fuzzy CSPs [8] allow constraint tuples to have an associated preference (1 = best, 0 = worst). Again, as described in the Java Constraint Library section, we can still model (and have modelled) partial CSPs using this method, by adding a tuple with 0 values to the domain of possible values, and assigning this a '1.0' preference (i.e. worst outcome). Similarly weighted CSPs [4] assign preference, but the value given with each tuple is associated with a cost. The main factor in these types of CSP is that a value is associated with the individual tuples in a constraint, not the actual general constraint itself.

Freuder and Wallace [7] talk more in terms of the actual constraints themselves, and relaxing them. They talk about sets of solutions, rather than the actual individual solutions to each variable. They then talk about a partial ordering of solutions, where the solutions are ordered by a given distance metric.

4.1 The CSP Ontology

We were interested in developing a well formed means of representing a set of one (or more) constraints that, when combined, form a single (soft) CSP, the ultimate goal being to facilitate interchange of information between a CSP problem constructor and an

---

[10] http://www.e-constraints.net/

appropriate solver. The solver would process the problem and return to the constructor zero or more solutions, each solution identifying those constraints that are satisfied and those that are violated by that solution. This would then allow the CSP constructor to decide itself which solution to select.

As discussed in Section 4, soft CSP solvers typically allow each constraint to be assigned a *utility value*, defined as a floating point number with a value ranging from 0 to 1 inclusive. These values represent the significance, or importance, of that constraint with respect to the other constraints comprising the CSP. Essentially, this value represents the degree of softness of each constraint, with a higher number implying a lower softness, and therefore a greater desirability to satisfy that constraint. However, depending upon the strategy employed by the CSP solver, a constraint with a lower utility value may still be satisfied in preference to violating another constraint with a higher utility value.

From the preceding discussion, it is clear that a utility value is not an intrinsic part of a constraint itself, rather it can be viewed as a kind of annotation on a constraint, with respect to a particular CSP (set of constraints). Similarly, the status of a constraint in terms of whether it is satisfied or not can be seen as an annotation of that constraint with respect to a particular solution. Therefore, we decided to create a separate ontology to represent a CSPs, independent of the (CIF/SWRL) representation of the individual constraints themselves. While for our practical purposes the ontology would be mainly used to annotate CIF/SWRL constraints, in principle it should be usable with other constraint and rule representations.

Figure 4 is a graphical depiction of the OWL CSP ontology, which is expressed in OWL DL and SWRL (classes are drawn as ovals, primitive data types as rectangles, and properties are arcs going from the domain and pointing to the range of that property). Initially, a CSP constructor would create an instance of a `ConstraintProblem` with one, or more, instances of `ValuedConstraint`. Each `ValuedConstraint` is assigned a utility value (real number) with the actual constraint expressed using CIF/SWRL. At this point the constructor would have only a representation of the CSP itself; there would be no instances of the `Solution` class. Only once the CSP has been passed onto a solver will any instances of `Solution` be created (or not, if no solution can be found).

The properties `satisfies` and `violates` are used to represent the fact that a particular solution instance satisfies a particular constraint, or not. Clearly, the use of these properties must be disjoint between the same instances: a given constraint can only be satisfied or violated with respect to a given solution. OWL DL does not enable us to enforce this check[11], so we define a rule to enforce data integrity in this case.

The first two solutions from Figure 1 are represented in triple form as follows using the CSP ontology:

```
<ex:soln1> <csp:satisfies> <ex:c1>
<ex:soln1> <csp:satisfies> <ex:c2>
<ex:soln1> <csp:satisfies> <ex:c3>
<ex:soln1> <csp:violates>  <ex:N>
```

[11] Disjoint property axioms are expected to be available in OWL 1.1, which is still decidable: http://www-db.research.bell-labs.com/user/pfps/owl/overview.html

312

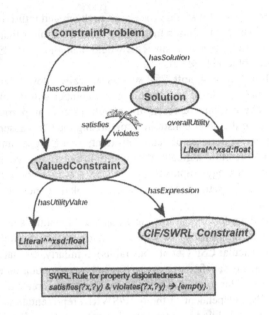

Fig. 4. Graph of the CSP ontology

```
<ex:soln2>  <csp:violates>  <ex:c1>
<ex:soln2>  <csp:violates>  <ex:c2>
<ex:soln2>  <csp:satisfies>  <ex:c3>
<ex:soln2>  <csp:satisfies>  <ex:N>
```

While adding SWRL rules to a DL knowledge base can make inference undecidable [10], this particular rule is within the DL-safe subset of SWRL (as the disjointness is imposed on named `ValueConstraints` rather than any possible ones). Therefore, it is still possible to have decidable reasoning support for our OWL DL + SWRL version of the CSP ontolgy.

5 Demonstrator Systems

To demonstrate reuse of the commitment management service it has been applied in two distinct domains: e-commerce and e-response. In the first domain, the CMS has been used in the context of a multimedia service provisioning demonstrator system developed as part of the Conoise-G project [14]. A customer wishes to subscribe to a package of multimedia services for their mobile device — a screenshot from the demonstrator, including a PDA simulator, is shown in Figure 5. A service ontology defines available service types and characteristics, from which the user can select their requirements via their user-agent. These requirements are then posted to the network of service-providing agents via a yellow pages, inviting agents to bid to provide the elements of the required package.

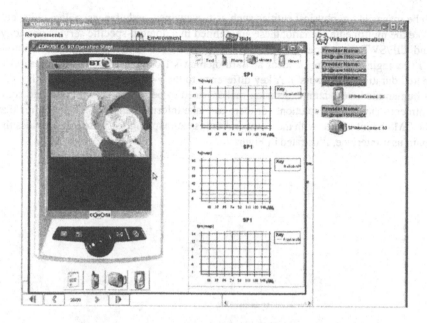

Fig. 5. The Conoise-G virtual organisation demonstrator system.

Here, a virtual organisation is entirely agent-mediated: in response to a call for bids, an agent reasons about its available resources and commitments on those resources, and decides whether and what to bid. If it is already representing a virtual organisation, the available resources and existing commitments are the combined resources and commitments of the organisation. In making its deliberations, the agent has the option to seek to recruit other service providers to extend the resources it can provide; it can also opt to free-up resources by breaking existing commitments as described in Section 2.

Commitments on resources are expressed as constraints on classes defined in a Conoise-G media ontology, which defines all application domain-specific terms for the multimedia service provisioning scenario. These include the service classes **MovieContent**, **HtmlContent**, **PhoneCalls**, and **TextMessaging**, all of which the ontology defines to be (indirect) sub-classes of the generic Conoise-G **ServiceProfile** class (based on DAML-S). The Conoise-G demonstrator is built on the FIPA standard agent platform[12]; the content of all inter-agent communication is RDF. The CMS is implemented using the Java Constraint Library; RDF processing is done using Jena2[13], by means of which the RDF transport format of the CSPs is converted into the JCL native CSP format for solving.

The scenario for our second application domain — e-response — is a fictitious disaster in the city of London, UK.[14] Here, the services upon which commitments need

---

[12] http://www.fipa.org/

[13] http://www.hpl.hp.com/semweb/jena2.htm

[14] Details are available at: http://e-response.org/

314

to be managed are physical entities such as fire engines, ambulances, police units, etc.
Like the multimedia scenario, these are defined in a domain-specific service ontology,
and CIF/SWRL constraints express commitments over them (for example, "commit
10 fire engines to a fire incident at Bartholemew's Hospital, from 10am, for an estimated duration of 5 hours"). A key difference to the e-commerce scenario is that this
is human-mediated: human decision-makers need to be presented with possible commitment management solutions for them to make informed choices. This requires that
the CMS be interfaced with the Compendium issue-mapping software that provides the
main user interface, illustrated in Figure 6.

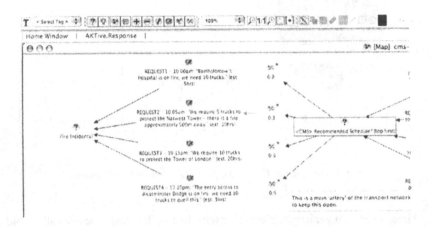

Fig. 6. The e-response virtual organisation demonstrator system.

Together, these two demonstrators illustrate a range of application dimensions for
the reuse of the CMS, in managing commitment knowledge in both autonomous, agent-
mediated virtual organisations, and human-mediated decision-making. In both cases,
commitments are expressed using CIF/SWRL against pre-existing service ontologies.

6 Discussion and Conclusion

In this paper we presented a set of components comprising a reusable commitment management service for agents operating in virtual organisations. The components build on
the Semantic Web architecture, so allowing the management of commitments over Semantic Web services (and indeed any service defined using OWL or RDFS). Some
of the components have more general applicability than commitment management:
CIF/SWRL and the soft CSP ontology are reusable for any application of CSP and
soft CSP-solving in a Semantic Web context (one such application is described in [12]).
While there exists an XML-based proposal for representing CSPs [3], to the best of our
knowledge our proposal is the first CSP interchange format founded on RDF and OWL.
Note that, while the CSP ontology is designed to work with CIF as the constraint
representation, it is conceivable that other constraint and rule representations could be

used as the values of the *expression* properties of `ValueConstraints`. As work continues on standardising Semantic Web rule and constraint languages[15], we will consider suitable extensions to the CSP ontology.

The SWRL FOL proposal to extend SWRL to full first-order logic[16] shares many of the features we earlier proposed for CIF/SWRL. While, at the time of writing, the SWRL FOL proposal lacks an RDF syntax, we anticipate it would not be hard to fully align CIF/SWRL with SWRL FOL. The main differences are in the syntactic form for the quantifier parts of expressions, a more expressive consequent (SWRL FOL allows disjunction and negation here), and a more complex syntax for simple conjunctions (SWRL FOL opts not to follow the SWRL "list format" for these).

Currently, work on the e-response scenario is ongoing, and our focus is moving onto effective integration of human-mediated and agent-mediated decision processes.

Acknowledgments This work is supported under the Advanced Knowledge Technologies (AKT) Interdisciplinary Research Collaboration (IRC), which is funded by the UK Engineering and Physical Sciences Research Council (EPSRC) under grant number GR/N15764/01. The AKT IRC comprises the Universities of Aberdeen, Edinburgh, Sheffeld, Southampton, and the Open University. See also: http://www.aktors.org

The commitment management service was developed in the context of the Conoise and Conoise-G projects, involving the Universities of Aberdeen, Cardiff, and Southampton, and British Telecom, and funded by the DTI/Welsh e-Science Centre, and BT. We are grateful to Gareth Shercliffe and Patrick Stockreisser for their work on the Conoise-G demonstrator user interface. See also: http://www.conoise.org

References

1. N. Bassiliades and P.M.D Gray. CoLan: a Functional Constraint Language and Its Implementation. *Data and Knowledge Engineering*, 14:203–249, 1994.
2. Stefano Bistarelli, Hélène Fargier, Ugo Montanari, Francesca Rossi, Thomas Schiex, and Gérard Verfaillie. Semiring-based CSPs and Valued CSPs: Basic properties and comparison. In Michael Jampel, Eugene Freuder, and Michael Maher, editors, *Over-Constrained Systems*, pages 111–150. Springer-Verlag LNCS 1106, August 1996.
3. F. Boussemart, F. Hemery, and C. Lecoutre. Description and representation of the problems selected for the first international constraint satisfaction solver competition. Technical report, CRIL, Université d'Artois, 2005.
4. Ken Brown. Soft consistencies for weighted csps. In *Proceedings of Soft'03: 5th International Workshop on Soft Constraints*, Kinsale, Ireland, September 2003.
5. S. Chalmers, A. D. Preece, T. J. Norman, and P. Gray. Commitment management through constraint reification. In *3rd International Joint Conference on Autonomous Agents and Multi Agent Systems (AAMAS 2004)*, pages 430–437, 2004.
6. I. Foster, N. R. Jennings, and C. Kesselman. Brain meets brawn: Why Grid and agents need each other. In *Proceedings of the Third International Joint Conference on Autonomous Agents and Multi-Agent Systems*, pages 8–15, 2004.

---

[15] http://www.w3.org/2005/rules/

[16] http://www.daml.org/2004/11/fol/

7. Eugene C. Freuder. Partial Constraint Satisfaction. In *Proceedings of the Eleventh International Joint Conference on Artificial Intelligence, IJCAI-89, Detroit, Michigan, USA*, pages 278–283, 1989.
8. Hans W. Guesgen and Anne Philpott. Heuristics for solving fuzzy constraint satisfaction problems. In *2nd New Zealand Two-Stream International Conference on Artificial Neural Networks and Expert Systems (ANNES '95), 1995.*, 1995.
9. I. Horrocks, P. F. Patel-Schneider, H. Boley, S. Tabet, B. Grosof, and M. Dean. SWRL: A Semantic Web rule language combining OWL and RuleML. Technical report, W3C, 2004. http://www.w3.org/Submission/SWRL/.
10. Ian Horrocks and Peter Patel-Schneider. A proposal for an OWL Rules Language. In *Thirteenth International World Wide Web Conference (WWW 2004)*. ACM, 2004.
11. K. Hui, S. Chalmers, P. Gray, and A. Preece. Experience in using RDF in agent-mediated knowledge architectures. In L. van Elst, V. Dignum, and A. Abecker, editors, *Agent-Mediated Knowledge Management (LNAI 2926)*, pages 177–192. Springer-Verlag, 2004.
12. C. McKenzie, P. Gray, and A. Preece. Expressing fully quantified constraints in CIF/SWRL. In G. Antoniou and H. Boley, editors, *Rules and Rule Markup Languages for the Semantic Web (RuleML 2004)*, pages 139–154. Springer-Verlag, 2004.
13. T. J. Norman, A. D. Preece, S. Chalmers, N. R. Jennings, M. M. Luck, V. D. Dang, T. D. Nguyen, V. Deora, J. Shao, W. A. Gray, and N. J. Fiddian. CONOISE: Agent-based formation of virtual organisations. *Knowledge-Based Systems*, 17:103–111, 2004.
14. J. Patel, L. Teacy, M. Luck, N. R. Jennings, S. Chalmers, N. Oren, T. J. Norman, A. Preece, P. M. D. Gray, P. J. Stockreisser, G. Shercliff, J. Shao, W. A. Gray, N. J. Fiddian, and S. Thompson. Agent-based virtual organisations for the grid. In *Proc 1st International Workshop on Smart Grid Technologies*, 2005.

Appendix: CIF/SWRL RDF Syntax

To support publishing and interchange of CIF constraints in the Semantic Web context, we provide an RDF/XML syntax as an extension to the one given for SWRL. The full RDF Schema for the CIF/SWRL syntax is available at the project website[17]; here we merely summarise the necessary extensions to the SWRL RDF syntax:

- We define a new rdfs:Class Constraint, with two associated properties: hasQuantifiers and hasImplication. The range of the former is an RDF list (of quantifier structures) and the range of the latter is a ruleml:Imp.
- We define the parent class Quantifier with sub-classes Forall and Exists. Two properties var and set complete the implementation of the q-atom from the abstract syntax. The range of both is an RDF resource: in the case of var this will be a URIref to a SWRL variable, while for set it will identify an OWL/RDFS class.
- Note that the SWRL RDF syntax allows the body of an implication to be any RDF list, so it already allows the nested inclusion of a Constraint.
- We define OrExpression and AndExpression as sub-classes of rdf:List, and a Negation class that has a swrl:argument1 property to point to the negated atom.

RDF/XML code samples are available on the project website.

---

[17] http://www.csd.abdn.ac.uk/research/akt/cif/

SESSION 5:

MODEL BASED SYSTEMS
AND SIMULATION

On-Line Monitoring of Plan Execution: a Distributed Approach

Roberto Micalizio   Pietro Torasso

Dipartimento di Informatica, Università di Torino

Torino, Italy

{micalizio,torasso}@di.unito.it

Abstract

The paper introduces and formalizes a distributed approach for the model-based monitoring of the execution of a plan, where concurrent actions are carried on by a team of mobile robots in a partially observable environment. Each robot is monitored on-line by an agent that has the task of tracking all the possible evolutions both under nominal and faulty behavior of the robot and to estimate the belief state at each time instant. The strategy for deriving local solutions which are globally consistent is formalized. The distributed monitoring provides on-line feedback to a system supervisor which has to decide whether building a new plan as consequence of actions failure. The feasibility of the approach and the gain in the performance are shown by comparing experimental results of the proposed approach with a centralized one.

1 Introduction

In the recent years, growing efforts have been spent for providing multi-agent systems with a *closed loop of control feedback* in order to complete the given task despite something has gone wrong (see e.g. [5]). In general these efforts advocate the presence of a system supervisor which synthesizes an initial plan, and possibly adapts on-line such a plan when unexpected events occur. Within the control loop a critical role is played by the activities of *monitoring* and *diagnosis*. In fact, monitoring on-line the progress of the task allows the detection of discrepancies between the expected nominal behavior of the system and the observed one. While the diagnosis is essential for singling out the root causes of the failure of the task carried on by the agent.

Monitoring the activity of software agents as well as robotic ones is a challenging problem, in particular when the actions of the plan are performed by a team of concurrent executors in a complex and dynamic environment where only some events are observable and the executors may fail.

Informally, the task of monitoring consists in tracking the evolutions of the system under consideration (i.e. maintaining a history of system states as accurate as possible) and detecting anomalies whenever they occur. In this paper, we have to monitor a plan with concurrent actions carried on by a team of plan executors. We will assume that plan executors are *robots*, however they are domain dependent, for example in the Air Traffic Control domain (see [9]) plan executors are the airplanes which execute their own flight plan.

As discussed in [1], the successful execution of a plan is threatened by unexpected events which may cause the failure of some actions (the anomalies the monitoring has to detect). In our approach, plan *threats* are faults in robot functionalities or robot competitions which may arise when a number of robots request the same resource simultaneously.

A planner coping with any particular class of domain dependent threats has a choice of either (1) attempting to prevent the threats, or (2) attempting to deal with threats individually as they arise ([1]). Some approaches to plan monitoring and diagnosis (see e.g. [11]) consider just atomic actions and require that the monitored plan must satisfy a *concurrency requirement* which prevents the occurrence of robots competition for accessing the resources.

We present a system supervisor able to deal with threats when they arise, in this way, given a high-level goal, a planner may synthesize a plan P without the (heavy) request that all the possible threats are prevented. We do not require that the actions are atomic and, as suggested in [1], each of them is associated with a nominal duration: when the actual duration of an action exceeds its nominal time the action is considered *failed*. Moreover, the actions may require some resources that typically can satisfy just a limited number of requests per time instant, thus the execution of the plan must, in general, satisfy a set of *resource constraints*.

While a centralized approach to the monitoring of the execution of plan P is discussed in [6, 7], the present paper present a distributed approach to the problem. In particular, the paper formalizes an approach where the plan is distributed among several plan executors (robots) and each executors is on-line monitored by an agent. In order to establish a control loop, our monitoring framework provides the supervisor not only with the status of the plan but also with the (possibly not nominal) *outcome* of the actions. As we will discuss, the actions outcome is a useful piece of information exploited by the supervisor for taking a decision on whether building a new plan in response to a failure. In general, however, the supervisor would need also to know the root causes of a failure (i.e. a failure explanation). For space limits, in this paper we do not discuss the diagnostic component responsible for fault identification or for singling out specific threats: a possible solution for this problem is reported in [6].

The paper is organized as follows, in section 2 basic concepts about the distributed plan monitoring are introduced, in section 3 a formalization of a multi-robot environment is presented, while in section 4 the distributed approach to the monitoring is discussed. In section 5 we present some experimental results we have gathered by using the simulated RoboCare environment (see [4]), and compare the centralized approach (described in [7]) vs. the decentralized one.

2   Characterizing the Problem

The problem we are interested in concerns the specification of a closed loop of control feedback established through the presence of *monitoring* and *diagnosis* services. In such a way the supervisor has the capabilities for looking after the progress of the plan and for dealing with unexpected threats. In [6] the services of monitoring and diagnosis are performed in a centralized way by the plan supervisor itself which collects all the available system observations and keeps track of the progress of the actions the robots are performing.

In the present paper we focus our attention on the on-line monitoring service and we describe how the monitoring of a given plan P can be distributed among a team Ags of software agents. The reason why we propose a distributed approach stems by the observation that a centralized one may result computationally expensive when the number of robots grows. In fact, a centralized approach has to build a global representation of the system status which takes into account all the possible combinations of the robots states. However, given partial observability of the environment, this representation may contain a huge number of alternatives and therefore it could become unmanageable.

We thus propose to decompose the task of monitoring the robot team T into a set of sub-problems; each sub-problem is assigned to an agent $i \in Ags$ and consists in monitoring just the robot rb_i. The only available observations for agent i are the messages sent by a set of sensors distributed in the environment in response to a detected event concerning rb_i, and messages volunteered by rb_i itself about its status (e.g. current position). It is worth noting that in most cases the observations are not sufficient for precisely inferring the status of each robot.

The partitioning described above does not guarantee that the sub-problems are completely independent of one another. In fact, since robot interactions may arise, the actual progress of the action carried on by rb_i depends on the rb_i's health status as well as on the occurrence of robot interactions which involve rb_i. Therefore agent i needs to cooperate with other agents in order to maintain a globally consistent representation of the status of the robot rb_i.

Effective cooperation among agents is reached by adopting two strategies which result to useful in the context of the distributed problem solving ([3]). First of all, we reduce as far as possible the number of cooperating agents, in particular, each agent $i \in Ags$ determines on-line (i.e. at each time instant) the subset of other agents (denoted as *dependency set*) it has to cooperate with by taking into consideration the actions currently executed by the team of robots. Clearly, since the actions change over time also the relations among the software agents need to change.

The second strategy concerns what sort of data the agents exchange for achieving cooperation. Instead of sending the rough data that each agent directly receives from the sensors and the robot, the agents exchange partial results which will be subsequently refined by integrating them with the partial results inferred by all the other agents in the same dependency set of agent i.

Whenever an agent detects the failure of an action it informs the supervisor by means of the *outcome* of that action. The outcome of a failed action represents a first kind of data the supervisor can rely on in order to take a decision for overcoming that particular failure. Of course, in case the supervisor revises the original plan P, the new plan needs to be redistributed among the software agents.

3 System Model Formalization

Global State and Local States The *global state* is expressed in terms of status of the robots $T = \{rb_1, \ldots, rb_n\}$ and of status of the resources $RES = \{res_1, \ldots, res_m\}$.

Dealing with global states may be computationally expensive in many domains, especially when the domain is naturally distributed, such as in a Telecommunication Network [8]; for this reason we partition the global state into a set of *partial states* and introduce the notion of *robot states*.

Robot States. A robot state s is a portion of the global state that is expressed in terms of the status variables of a single robot rb_i: $Var(rb_i) = \{v_{1_i}, \ldots, v_{k_i}, res_{1,i}, \ldots, res_{m,i}\}$. The variables v_{j_i} $(j : 1, \ldots, k)$ are status variables of rb_i and in particular they include the health state of robot rb_i. We represent the robot health state by variable $v_{health,i}$, whose domain is the set $\{ok, abn_1, \ldots, abn_h\}$ of behavioral modes: ok denotes the nominal mode, $abn_1, \ldots, abn_h$ denote not nominal modes. In general, when a robot has many functionalities its health status can be represented by means of a set of health variables, one for each sub-system, as discussed in [6].

Because of the partitioning of the global status, we duplicate each status variable of the resources by creating a private copy for each robot rb_i; we denote with $res_{j,i}$ the status of the resource res_j w.r.t. rb_i; $res_{j,i}$ can assume values in the domain: *free* (rb_i is not interested in res_j), *requested* (rb_i has requested res_j), *busy* (rb_i is using res_j) and *released*(rb_i has just relinquished res_j).

Partial States. A partial state σ represents the state of a subset O of robots; $Var(\sigma) = \bigcup_{rb \in O} Var(rb)$ indicates the status variables over which σ is defined, while $Rbts(\sigma)$ is used for denoting the set O of robots.

The value that the variable $v \in Var(\sigma)$ assumes in σ will be represented as $\sigma(v)$.

Belief State. As we will formalize in section 4, one of the results of the on-line monitoring task is a representation of the system status at each time instant. Since some status variables are not observable, the monitoring task cannot unambiguously determine the status of the system at each time t; actually, the monitoring process is able just to estimate a set of possible, alternative states where the system can be at t; this set is known in literature as *belief state* (at time t) and we will denote it with $\mathcal{B}_t$. Obviously, the accuracy in the system status representation directly depends on the system observability, the more observations are available the more the system representation is accurate (i.e. the belief states contain fewer alternative states).

Action Templates In some approaches to the monitoring of plan execution (e.g. [11]) each action is assumed to be atomic and is modeled by means of *pre-* and *post-* conditions which must be satisfied when the action starts and ends respectively. However, when the actions are not atomic the monitoring needs a more complex action model.

An *action template* α is a detailed model of an action; in particular, it specifies all the possible sequences of sub-steps that a robot can take for carrying on the action both under nominal behavior and abnormal behavior. Thus we explicitly model both normal and abnormal behavior of an action according to the health status of the robot performing it. Moreover, α specifies in which action sub-steps particular resources are required, used and released.

As usual in the discrete event systems ([8]), an action template is modeled as an automaton $\alpha = \langle S_\alpha, \Sigma_\alpha, \Delta_\alpha \rangle$.

S_α is the set of states in which a robot can be when it is executing α. S_α is partitioned into the sets:

- I_α all the possible initial states where preconditions of α are satisfied;
- G_α the final states where the action goal has been reached: each state in G_α sat-

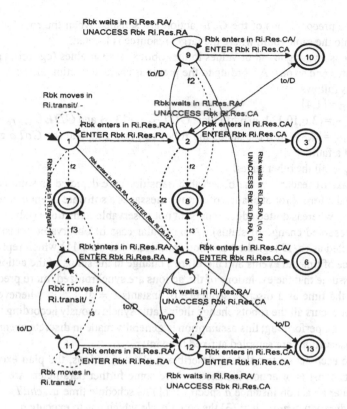

Figure 1: The GoTo action in the RoboCare environment.

isfies the post-conditions of α. The final states are further distinguished between the sets GOT_α of the final states achieved before the occurrence of the action timeout (i.e. on-time) and $GDEL_\alpha$ of the final states achieved after the occurrence of the action timeout;

- U_α the final states where the goal is unreachable (e.g. because of a fault in the robot performing α);

- N_α all the intermediate states.

Σ_α is the set of observable events regarding α; only the agent monitoring α can observe the events in Σ_α. We distinguish between:

-exogenous observations coming from the environment (robots + sensors); they capture a status change of the robot performing α;

-endogenous observations are a set of timeout events, that is, when the actual duration an action a (instance of α) exceeds its nominal duration the monitoring agent generates a corresponding timeout event *to*.

Finally, $\Delta_\alpha \subseteq (s \times 2^{\Sigma_\alpha} \times s')$ is the transition relation defined between two robot states $s, s' \in S_\alpha$. A transition $\tau \in \Delta_\alpha$ (denoted as $\tau : s \xrightarrow{E} s'$) is *observable* iff $E \neq \emptyset$.

Figure 1 shows a simplified example of the fine-grained model of the *GoTo* action defined in the RoboCare environment (see [6, 7] for details). The goal of a robot rb_k executing a *GoTo* consists in accessing a target resource *Res* moving in the environment. The preconditions of the *GoTo* action are satisfied when the robot is initially located into the same room where the target resource is located.

Each state is an assignment of values to the robot status variables (eg. robot position, health status and so on). According to the previous characterization the states are partitioned as follows:

- $I_{GoTo}=\{1,4\}$
- $G_{GoTo}=\{3,6,10,13\}$, in particular: $GOT_{GoTo}=\{3,6\}$ and $GDEL_{GoTo}=\{10,13\}$
- $U_{GoTo}=\{7,8\}$; in these states the robot can not complete the *GoTo* as consequence of a fault.
- N_{GoTo} all the other states.

For the sake of readability the observable transitions are depicted as solid edges (labels have the form ⟨ robot change of status / messages a software agent can receive as response⟩), whereas dotted edges represent not observable transitions (labels describe the not observed change of status). A particular case of observable transitions are those labeled as to/D (eg. the transition from state 4 to state 11) which represent the occurrence of timeout events and therefore a change in the status of the action.

We assume that the evolutions of the actions are synchronized; more precisely we consider the time as a discrete sequence of instants $t = 0, 1, \ldots$; whenever a time increment occurs all the robots change their status synchronously according to the actions they are performing; this assumption is generally made in discrete event systems where observations are sampled at fixed time intervals.

While each action template α describes a class of actions, the plan executed by the robots consists of action instances where some further parameters are specified; in particular an action instance a specifies: (1) its schedule time $a.schdTime$; (2) its nominal duration $a.nomDur$; (3) the robot $a.rbt$ which has to execute a; and finally, (4) $a.resources$, is the subset of system resources needed during the execution (e.g the resource Res in the GoTo example). Hereafter we will denote with $act(rb_i, t)$ the action instance that robot rb_i is executing at time t; however, when the robot identifier and the time instant are not needed, we will indicate an action by the letter a.

System Model The system model is a tuple $M = \langle RES, T, CONS, A \rangle$ where RES and T have been previously defined as the set of available resources and the set of mobile robots respectively; $CONS$ is a set of global constraints defined over the private copies of the variables $res_{j,i}$. In particular, for each resource res_j, there exists a global constraint $cons_j \in CONS$ representing (in a logical formula) which assignments to variables $res_{j,i}$ (for the robots $rb_i \in T$) represent a consistent access to resource res_j. Finally, A is the set of action templates, which represents the set of actions the robots can execute.

Plans and Sub-plans An instantiated plan is a tuple $P = \langle M, A, < \rangle$ where: M is the system model; A is a set of instances of actions; $(A, <)$ is a partial order relation between action instances in A: $a < a'$ implies that action a must finish before action a' starts i.e. $a.schdTime + a.nomDur < a'.schdTime$. The relation $(A, <)$ encodes a set of temporal constraints between action instances.

A sub-plan P_i of P is a tuple $\langle M, A_i, <_i \rangle$ where A_i is the subset of actions in A agent i is responsible for (i.e., $\forall a \in A_i$, $a.robot = rb_i$); $<_i$ is the precedence relation $<$ restricted to the actions in A_i. We assume that the relation $(A_i, <_i)$ is a total order relation.

4 On-line Monitoring of the Plan Execution

The monitoring of plan execution has to face some challenging issues. First of all, since we relax the concurrency requirement, we have to deal with competitions among robots for accessing the same resource. This is particularly challenging because given an action a, the resources in $a.resources$ can be used in different steps of a and these steps are not necessarily observable; it follows that the troublesome interactions among robots can not be completely anticipated. In addition to that, each agent i just observes events $e \in \Sigma_{act(rb_i, t)}$, so agent i has not a complete view of the world; with $obs_i(t)$ we denote the set of observations gathered by agent i at time t. In order to detect the completion/failure of $act(rb_i, t)$ the agent i needs to exchange information with other agents and to build a portion of the system state which is globally consistent and handles possible harmful interactions involving rb_i.

Besides the global plan P, the monitoring needs to know the initial belief state of the system $\mathcal{B}_0$, that is, the set of alternative system states at time 0 (when the actions are not dispatched yet). We consider $\mathcal{B}_0$ as a further input to the monitoring and require that the following assumption holds:

Assumption 4.1 *At time 0, the given initial belief state $\mathcal{B}_0$ satisfies all the global constraints.*

It is worth noticing that Assumption 4.1 does not require to know the actual status of the robots (e.g. at time 0 the health status of some robots may not be nominal).

The Plan Execution Monitoring Task. Under a centralized point of view, the problem of monitoring the execution of a plan can be formally defined as the tuple $PEM(t) = \langle P, \mathcal{B}_0, obs[0, t] \rangle$ where P is a global plan, $\mathcal{B}_0$ is the initial belief state of the system, $obs[0, t]$ is the set of all the system observations available in the interval $[0, t]$. As shown in [6], the solution to the centralized $PEM(t)$ is the belief state $\mathcal{B}_t$ where each state $\sigma \in \mathcal{B}_t$:

(1) is a possible system evolution at time t,

(2) is consistent with the observations $obs[0, t]$,

(3) is determined according to the actions of P scheduled in $[0, t]$ and to the initial belief state $\mathcal{B}_0$.

As argued in [6], the estimation of the belief state $\mathcal{B}_k$ at time k (k:1..t) can be computed by projecting the previous belief state $\mathcal{B}_{k-1}$ by means of a transition relation for the whole system Δ and filtering out all the projections which are not consistent with the available observations received at time k.

In the following we show how the problem $PEM(t)$ can be decomposed into a set of sub-problems $PEM_i(t)$ (for $i : 1..|\mathcal{T}|$) and how the global belief state $\mathcal{B}_t$ can be reconstructed from local belief states.

The sub-problem $PEM_i(t)$, assigned to agent i, is the tuple $\langle P_i, \mathcal{B}_0, obs_i[0, t] \rangle$ where: P_i is the sub-plan monitored by agent i and $obs_i[0, t]$ is the set of observations the agent i receives in the interval $[0, t]$.

Given the sub-problem PEM_i, agent i has to estimate the sequence of *robot belief states* $\mathcal{B}_1^i, \mathcal{B}_2^i, \ldots \mathcal{B}_t^i$ where each $\mathcal{B}_k^i$ ($k : 1..t$) is a set of possible states of robot rb_i at time k. In order to do that, agent i could behave similarly to the centralized case; in particular it should project the previous robot belief state $\mathcal{B}_{k-1}^i$ by means of the transition relation $\Delta_{act(i.k)}$ only. This strategy would be effective if the agents were able to observe any event concerning the monitored robot. However, since the agents have to deal with uncertainty, the agents get belief states which are not necessarily globally consistent. For example, at a given time instant k, some robot state $s \in B_k^i$ may be inconsistent with some robot state $s' \in B_k^j$ because, for a particular resource res_l, the values $s(res_{l,i})$ and $s'(res_{l,j})$ do not satisfy the constraint $cons_l$ associated with res_l. The possible global inconsistency of the robot belief states is a consequence of the partitioning of the $PEM(t)$ problem into a set of sub-problems which are not completely independent of one another. For this reason, we have to isolate the *set of dependencies* existing among the sub-problems. To do so we introduce the following *bound relation* $\mathcal{R}_t$.

Definition 4.1 *At time t, two concurrent actions* $act(rb_i, t) \in A_i$ *and* $act(rb_j, t) \in A_j$ *satisfy the bound relation iff:*

  i. $act(rb_i, t).resources \cap act(rb_j, t).resources \neq \emptyset$, *or*
  i.i. *there exists* $act(rb_k, t) \in A_k$ *such that:*
    $act(rb_i, t)\mathcal{R}_t act(rb_k, t)$ *and* $act(rb_k, t)\mathcal{R}_t act(rb_j, t)$

It is easy to see that the bound relation is an equivalence relation since it is reflexive, symmetric and transitive. Thus, denoting with $CrtAct(t)$ the set of the actions the robots are performing at time t, the transitive closure of $\mathcal{R}_t$ induces a partitioning of the set $CrtAct(t)$. Moreover, since there exists a one to one relation between monitored actions and agents, it follows that the bound relation induces a partitioning also of the set Ags of software agents; with $AQS(t)$ we denote the quotient set $Ags/\mathcal{R}_t$. The bound relation highlights the dependencies existing among the sub-problems in which $PEM(t)$ has been decomposed. In particular:

Definition 4.2 *The* dependency set *of agent i at time t is the equivalence class* $dep(t) \in AQS(t)$ *computed with reference to agent i.*

A dependency set $dep(t)$ individuates a subset of agents which need to cooperate since their sub-problems $PEM_i(t)$ ($i \in dep(t)$) may interact with one another. It is worth noticing that the notion of dependency set based on the bound relation $\mathcal{R}_t$ is *safe* in the sense that two concurrent actions $act(rb_i, t)$ and $act(rb_j, t)$ may be in the same dependency set even if robots rb_i and rb_j require the resources in $act(rb_i, t).resources \cap act(rb_j, t).resources$ at different time instants; but it can never happen that they are not in the same dependency set if rb_i and rb_j access a resource at the same time.

Distributed On-line Monitoring. For describing how the distributed monitoring is performed we have to define: (1) how the agents in the same $dep(t)$[1] cooperate and (2) what result they achieve from the cooperation. For the sake of exposition we consider first the second topic.

The common solution of the sub-problems $PEM_i(t)$ (for each agent $i \in dep(t)$) is a *dependency belief*:

Definition 4.3 *Given an agent dependency set* $dep(t)$ *at time t, a* dependency belief $\mathcal{B}_t^{dep(t)}$ *is a set of alternative, partial states* σ *such that:* $Rbts(\sigma) = dep(t)$ *and* σ *is consistent both with the observations* $obs(t)$ *and with* $CONS$.

---

[1] Each agent i can locally infer the $dep(t)$ by exploiting the current time instant t and the global plan P where the schedule time and the nominal duration of each action are defined.

$\mathcal{B}_t^{dep(t)}$ represents all the possible consistent states of a subset of robots whose actions are monitored by the agents in $dep(t)$.

Now we are in the position for describing how the agents in $dep(t)$ build $\mathcal{B}_t^{dep(t)}$. Since each agent $i \in dep(t)$ can compute the robot belief state $\mathcal{B}_t^i$; one could build the dependency belief $\mathcal{B}_t^{dep(t)}$ by composing these local belief states and by filtering out those states not satisfying the global constraints. Unfortunately, this strategy is not viable: even if the resulting dependency belief is globally consistent, it may maintain *unfeasible states* (i.e. impossible system states).

To point out this issue, let us consider the following example. At time t-1, the resource res is used either by robot rb_i or by robot rb_j, but given the partial observability we can not state which robot is using res; thereby in $\mathcal{B}_{t-1}^{dep(t-1)}$ there exist (at least) two alternative states $s1$ and $s2$ where $s1(res_{l,i})$=*busy* $\wedge$ $s1(res_{l,j})$=*requested* and $s2(res_{l,i})$=*requested* $\wedge$ $s2(res_{l,j})$=*busy* respectively. At time t agent i estimates the set $\mathcal{B}_t^i$ and according to state $s1 \in \mathcal{B}_{t-1}^{dep(t-1)}$ and to progress of $act(rb_i, t)$, $\mathcal{B}_t^i$ contains at least a state $s1' \in \mathcal{B}_t^i$ where $s1'(res_{l,i})$=*released*. Similarly, agent j estimates $\mathcal{B}_t^j$ where there exists a state $s2'$ such that $s2'(res_{l,j})$=*released*. If the dependency belief $\mathcal{B}_t^{dep(t)}$ were computed by composing $\mathcal{B}_t^i$ and $\mathcal{B}_t^j$, the composition would produce a (partial) state σ such that $\sigma(res_{l,i})$=*released* $\wedge$ $\sigma(res_{l,j})$=*released*; even if the state σ satisfies the global constraints, it is easy to see that σ is an *unfeasible state* since at previous time instant only one of the two robots was using res (thus only one robot could release res).

In order to build a dependency belief $\mathcal{B}_t^{dep(t)}$ which maintains only feasible states, the agents need to exchange and compose not just the estimated belief state $\mathcal{B}_t^i$ but the whole projection from $\mathcal{B}_{t-1}^{dep(t-1)}$ to $\mathcal{B}_t^i$. More precisely, the agents exchange one another the *set of transitions* $\mathcal{D}_t^i = \{\tau : \sigma \xrightarrow{E} s'\}$ such that: (1) $\sigma \in \mathcal{B}_{t-1}^{dep(t-1)}$, (2) $E \subseteq obs_i(t)$ and (3) s' results by projecting $\Delta_{act(rb_i,t)}$ from $\mathcal{B}_{t-1}^{dep(t-1)}$.

Since a transitions set $\mathcal{D}_t^i$ can be seen as a relation, the composition of the transitions sets $\mathcal{D}_t^i$ and $\mathcal{D}_t^j$ ($i \neq j; i, j \in dep(t)$) can be expressed by relational operators: $\mathcal{D}_t^i \otimes \mathcal{D}_t^j = \sigma_{CONS}(\mathcal{D}_t^i \bowtie \mathcal{D}_t^j)$.

The tuples resulting from the (natural) join $\bowtie$ represent projections and have the form $\sigma_{t-1} \xrightarrow{E} \sigma_t$ where σ_{t-1} and σ_t are partial states mentioning the robots rb_i and rb_j at times t-1 and t respectively. The selection σ_{CONS} filters out all those projections which do not satisfy the global constraints in σ_t. In the following we formalize the relation of $\mathcal{R}$derivability between dependency beliefs based on the composition of transitions sets.

Definition 4.4 *Let $dep(t-1)$ and $dep(t)$ be the dependency sets of agent i at time t-1 and t respectively. The dependency belief $\mathcal{B}_t^{dep(t)}$ is $\mathcal{R}$derivable from $\mathcal{B}_{t-1}^{dep(t-1)}$ if and only if $\mathcal{B}_t^{dep(t)}$ is built as follows:*

1. Each agent $i \in dep(t)$ locally builds the set of transitions $\mathcal{D}_t^i$
2. The agents exchange with one another the sets of transitions
3. Every agent $i \in dep(t)$ computes $\mathcal{D}_t^{dep(t)}$ by incrementally composing all the transitions sets, formally $\mathcal{D}_t^{dep(t)} = \otimes_{j \in dep(t)} \mathcal{D}_t^j$;

4. Finally, agent i gets the dependency belief $\mathcal{B}_t^{dep(t)} = \mathcal{\pi}_t(\mathcal{D}_t^{dep(t)})$; the projection $\mathcal{\pi}_t$ returns all the partial states at time t i.e., the states $\{\sigma_t \mid \exists \tau \in \mathcal{D}_t^{dep(t)}, \tau : \sigma_{t-1} \xrightarrow{E} \sigma_t\}$.

It is worth noticing that the definition of $\mathcal{R}derivability$ holds even when the dependency sets $dep(t-1)$ and $dep(t)$ are not identical.

Proposition 4.1 *Let* $\mathcal{B}_t^{dep(t)}$ *be* $\mathcal{R}derivable$ *from* $\mathcal{B}_{t-1}^{dep(t-1)}$.

If $\mathcal{B}_{t-1}^{dep(t-1)}$ *is globally consistent, then* $\mathcal{B}_t^{dep(t)}$ *is globally consistent too. Moreover, all the states in* $\mathcal{B}_t^{dep(t)}$ *are feasible states.*

On the basis of Proposition 4.1 we can state:

Proposition 4.2 *The global belief state* $\mathcal{B}_t$ *can be reconstructed as the Cartesian product of the globally consistent dependency beliefs; formally* $\mathcal{B}_t = \prod_{dep(t) \in AQS(t)} \mathcal{B}_t^{dep(t)}$.

The proofs are omitted for lack of space.

Action Outcome Once agent i has built the dependency belief $\mathcal{B}_t^{dep(t)}$, it has to check whether the action $act(rb_i, t)$ has been completed. The nominal or abnormal behavior of $act(rb_i, t)$ is summarized by the concept of *outcome* (i.e. the termination status of an action); it is analogous to the action health mode introduced in [11].

The nominal outcome of $act(rb_i, t)$ is *goal achieved*, it is determined by evaluating the predicate $IsIn(\mathcal{B}_t^{dep(t)}, GOT_{act(rb_i,t)})$ which holds iff $\forall \sigma \in \mathcal{B}_t^{dep(t)}, \sigma \vdash s$ where s is a state in $GOT_{act(rb_i,t)}$. We can determine all the other not nominal outcomes in a similar way: in particular, we say that the outcome of $act(rb_i, t)$ is *goal achieved with delay* when the predicate $IsIn(\mathcal{B}_t^{dep(t)}, GDEL_{act(rb_i,t)})$ holds. Finally we can conclude that the action outcome is *goal unachievable* in case the predicate $IsIn(\mathcal{B}_t^{dep(t)}, U_{act(rb_i,t)})$ holds.

Note that the Proposition 4.1 guarantees the global consistency of the dependency belief $\mathcal{B}_t^{dep(t)}$, so the outcome of action $act(rb_i, t)$ can be derived by inspecting the $\mathcal{B}_t^{dep(t)}$ only.

The Algorithm The on-line monitoring is carried out by the concurrent execution of the algorithm reported in Figure 2 by each agent $i \in Ags$. This algorithm summarizes the main steps in estimating the dependency belief state according to the above characterization.

At line 01 the initialization steps are performed. In lines 02 through 20 agent i keeps track of the progress of the action rb_i carries on. More precisely, every iteration of the while cycle corresponds to an instant t: in lines 04 through 06 agent i gathers the observations at time t, determines the current dependency set and gets the previous dependency belief. In lines 07 through 11 agent i builds the dependency belief $\mathcal{B}_t^{dep(t)}$ according to the definition of $\mathcal{R}derivable$ (Definition 4.4); in particular, at line 10, the composition of the transitions sets is performed. Once the dependency belief has been determined the algorithm checks whether the current action $act(rb_i, t)$ has been completed or it has failed; thereby the algorithm evaluates the predicate $IsIn$ w.r.t. the (possibly faulty) final states of $act(rb_i, t)$ (lines 13 through 29). In case the action fails an alarm message could be sent in order to draw the attention of the supervisor;

```
00  On-lineMonitoring (P, P_i, B_0, rb_i) {
01      t = 0; dep(0) =T; B_0^{dep(0)} = B_0; H_i={B_0^{dep(0)}};
02      while(true){
03          t = t + 1;
04          ⟨ gather observations obs_i(t)⟩;
05          dep(t) =dependencySet(P, t);
06          B_{t-1}^{dep(t-1)} = H_i.getBeliefAtTime(t - 1);
07          D_t^i = transitionsSet(Δ_{act(rb_i,t)}, obs_i(t), B_{t-1}^{dep(t-1)});
08          ⟨send D_t^i to each agent j ∈ dep(t) - {i}⟩;
09          D_t^{dep(t)} = D_t^i;
10          ⟨receive D_t^j from each agent j ∈ dep(t) - {i} and compose D_t^{dep(t)} = D_t^j ⊗ D_t^{dep(t)}⟩;
11          B_t^{dep(t)} = π_t(D_t^{dep(t)});
12          H_i.add(B_t^{dep(t)});
13          ifIsIn(B_t^{dep(t)}, U_{act(rb_i,t)})      act(rb_i, t).outcome="goal unachievable";
14          if IsIn(B_t^{dep(t)}, G_{act(rb_i,t)}){
15              if IsIn(B_t^{dep(t)}, GOT_{act(rb_i,t)})      act(rb_i, t).outcome="goal achieved";
16              else act(rb_i, t).outcome="goal achieved with delay";
17          assignNextAction(P_i, rb_i, t);}
18  } }
```

Figure 2: The On-Line Monitoring Algorithm

on the contrary, when the action has been completed the algorithm simply dispatches a new action to rb_i according to the plan P_i.

Exploiting Action Outcomes. The outcome of an action is an important piece of information exploited by the supervisor in order to properly adjust the plan in response to an action failure. Let us suppose that for a given action the not nominal *goal unachievable* has been detected. In this case the supervisor can determine the subset of actions in the plan that will not be executable as consequence of this failure[2]. In case the subset does not involve a large number of actions and the main goal of the plan can be achieved despite the action failure, the supervisor could avoid to repair the plan P; on the contrary, when the goal is no longer achievable, the supervisor can invoke the planner in order to build a new plan which achieves the same goal (if possible). Analogously, when the not nominal outcome *goal achieved with delay* is detected, the supervisor can assess whether this delay could cause the delay of some other actions and then violate some temporal constraints. Also in this case the supervisor invokes the planner to build a new plan.

Finally, we have to notice that, sometimes, knowing the outcome could not be sufficient for the supervisor in order to decide whether to re-plan. In fact, an outcome conveys the information that an action is failed, bit it does not single out the root causes of the failure. In other words, the supervisor needs a diagnosis explaining the failure. A detailed description how a diagnosis for an action failure can be inferred is out the scope of this paper, but [7] describes a way for inferring high-level diagnoses by means of abductive rules which relate the not nominal outcome with the occurrence of faults in some robot functionalities or of robot interactions.

---

[2]To this end the supervisor can exploit a simple set of causal links between actions as described in [2]

	Scn-1	Scn-2	Scn-3	Scn-4	Scn-5
#Robots	4	6	8	10	12
# Actions (avg.)	126.1 ± 24.6	167.3 ± 26.2	206.1 ± 29	275.6 ± 40	323.1 ± 45.6
Action lifetime (avg.)	26.4 ± 3	26.4 ± 3	26.4 ± 3	26.4 ± 3	26.4 ± 3
# Active robots per time (avg.)	3 ± 0.2	4.3 ± 0.3	5.2 ± 0.5	7.6 ± 0.3	9 ± 0.4
Plan duration (avg.)	1011 ± 186.1	1011 ± 186.1	1011 ± 186.1	1011 ± 186.1	957 ± 58.4
# Injected faults (avg.)	2 ± 0.5	2 ± 0.5	2 ± 0.5	2 ± 0.5	2 ± 0.5
# Harmful interactions per plan (avg.)	3 ± 0	4.2 ± 0.37	7.6 ± 0.4	9.4 ± 0.3	12.1 ± 0.5
# Robots involved per interaction (avg.)	2.84 ± 0.2	3.2 ± 0.2	3.85 ± 0.3	2.9 ± 0.2	2.7 ± 0.2

Table 1: The Characteristics of the five scenarios.

Relying on an action diagnosis, the supervisor can decide to re-plan just a (subset) of sub-plan(s) instead of building a new global plan. For example, if action $act(rb_i, t)$ of type *acttype* fails due to a fault in some functionalities of rb_i, it is possible that rb_i could be able to execute other types of action different from *acttype*. In this case the supervisor could re-plan P_i by taking into account the health status of rb_i and removing from P_i all the actions of type *acttype*. In some other situations the negative effects of an action failure can not be overcome by re-planning just a sub-plan and the supervisor has to build a new global plan.

5   Experimental Results

In order to prove the effectiveness of the distributed approach we compare it w.r.t. the centralized approach described in [6] in the context of the RoboCare Project [4]. In the RoboCare scenario, mobile robots provide services in a health-care institution where the critical resources are doors and beds. In such an environment we have modeled five different types of actions: the automata representing them have, on average, 14 states and 26 transitions where the number of observable transitions is just 6 (i.e. the environment is just partially observable).

For running the experiments we have simulated an environment with 10 rooms, 14 doors and 18 beds. In order to verify whether the decentralized approach scales up better than the centralized one, we have defined five scenarios involving an increasing number of robots (from 4 to 12). In each of these scenarios, the test set consists of 30 plans whose main characteristics are summarized in Table 1. The plans are very challenging since involve a large number of actions (i.e. the sub-plan of each robot is complex) and each action lasts for a long period (on average 26.4 istants). Moreover, each scenario is characterized by a high degree of parallelism as demonstrated by the number of active robots per time. Finally, during the simulation of these plans we have injected up to 3 faults (even simultaneous) and forced harmful interactions involving a significant number of robots. Both the centralized and the distributed approaches are implemented in JDK 1.4.2 SE and use the JavaBDD[3] package for symbolically encoding the belief states by means the Ordered Binary Decision Diagrams formalism (see [10]). The software agents of the distributed approach are threads running on the

---

[3]http:\\sourceforge.net\projects\javabdd.

		MT-Avg [msec]	MT-Max [msec]	#S-Avg	#S-AbsMax	#DepSet	#AgsDS
Scn-1	Centr.	3 ± 0.3	34	47.8 ± 3.5	144	1	4
	Decentr.	1.3 ± 0.2	46	13 ± 5.3	61	2.6 ± 0.2	1.53 ± 0.23
Scn-2	Centr.	8.6 ± 0.9	157	287 ± 56	1296	1	6
	Decentr.	3.3 ± 0.6	63	65 ± 9.2	805	4 ± 0.4	1.47 ± 0.38
Scn-3	Centr.	16.1 ± 2.2	5109	2116 ± 497	8748	1	8
	Decentr.	5 ± 1.1	110	306 ± 150	3633	5.3 ± 0.7	1.5 ± 0.54
Scn-4	Centr.	39.8 ± 3.4	15610	15008 ± 3911	78732	1	10
	Decentr.	9.6 ± 1.4	94	347 ± 208.7	2274	7.3 ± 0.6	1.37 ± 0.17
Scn-5	Centr.	97 ± 17.3	51578	-	>100,000	1	12
	Decentr.	7 ± 0.9	94	2548 ± 166	1405	9.5 ± 0.4	1.26 ± 0.07

Table 2: Centralized vs. Decentralized Approach.

same PC[4], which has been used for all the experiments.

Table 2 reports the main features used for the comparison between the centralized approach and the distributed one. More precisely, **MT-Avg** and **MT-Max** are the average and the absolute maximum time respectively, required by the monitoring at each time instant. In the scenarios involving a large number of robots it is apparent that the distributed approach out performs the centralized one even if we have to take into account that the centralized approach is more space consuming (because of the size of global belief states and the temporary OBDD structures) and therefore the garbage collector is invoked more often.

The distributed approach performs better than the centralized one as concerns the number of estimated states. In Table 2 we report the average (**#S-Avg**) and maximum (**#S-Max**) number of states belonging to the global belief B_t in the centralized approach. As concerns the distributed approach we report the average and maximum number of states maintained by the largest dependency belief $B_t^{dep(t)}$. It is easy to see that the distributed approach involves a number of states much smaller than centralized approach even if we compare the number of global states with the product of local states in the dependency belief times the number of dependency beliefs reported in column **#DepSet**. The improvement in the representation of the status of the system is more significant for more complex scenarios (*Scn-3* and *Scn-4*); in the *Scn-5* scenario the number of estimated states has always exceeded the threshold of 100,000 states in each plan simulation and direct confront is not possible.

Finally, if we consider the large value of **#DepSet** together with the small number of agents per dependency sets **AgsDS** we see that the monitoring task can actually benefit of the distribution among the team of software agents.

6 Discussion and Conclusion

In this paper we have formalized a distributed framework for the on-line monitoring of a plan. The framework takes into consideration that the plan is carried on by robots

---

[4] Intel Pentium 1.86 GHz, RAM 1 GB, Windows XP OS.

in a dynamic environment which is only partially observable. This is particularly challenging since the number of possible trajectories to be traced during the monitoring process grows dramatically (as the preliminary experimental results show).

A relevant contribute of the proposed approach consists in extending the framework discussed in [11] in fact: (1) we allow plans with not atomic actions; (2) the faulty behavior of each action type is explicitly modeled, therefore our monitoring can trace the system even after the occurrence of plan threats; and (3) we release the concurrency requirement which in many cases could be a very strong requirement; we thus allow that two concurrent actions may interfere each other for the use of the same resource. Moreover we have experimentally demonstrated how the solution of distributing the monitoring task by associating a software agent with each robot achieves better results than the centralized monitoring; in fact the decentralized approach is significantly more efficient when the plans to be monitored involve a large number of robots.

The monitoring on-line requirement has been met by adopting symbolic methods (in particular OBDDs) for computing and representing belief states.

References

[1] L. Birnbaum, G. Collins, M. Freed, and B. Krulwich, 'Model-based diagnosis of planning failures', in Proc. AAAI90, pp. 318-323, (1990).

[2] C. Boutilier and R. I. Brafman, 'Partial-order planning eith concurrent interacting actions', Journal of Artificial Intelligence Research, 14, pp. 105-136 (2001).

[3] N. Carver and Lesser V., 'Domain monotonicity and the performance of local solutions strategies for cdps-based distributed sensor interpretation and distributed diagnosis', AAMAS Journal, 6, 35-76, (2003).

[4] A. Cesta and F. Pecora, 'Planning and scheduling ingredients for a multi-agent system', in Proc. PlanSig02, pp. 135-148, (2002).

[5] T. Estlin, D. Gaines, F. Fisher, and R. Castano. 'Coordinating multiple rovers with interdependent science objectives'. In Proc. AAMAS05, pages 879-886, (2005).

[6] R. Micalizio, P. Torasso, and G. Torta, 'On-line monitoring and diagnosis of multi-agent systems: a model based approach', in Proc. ECAI04, pp. 848-852, (2004).

[7] R. Micalizio, P. Torasso, and G. Torta, 'On-line monitoring and diagnosis of a team of service robots: a model-based approach', AI Comm., to appear, (2006).

[8] Y. Pencole and M.O. Cordier, 'A formal framework for the decentralised diagnosis of large scale discrete event systems and its application to telecommunication networks', Art. Int., 164, 121-170, (2005).

[9] F. de Jonge, N. Roos, and J. van den Herik. 'How to keep plan execution Healthy'. In IJCAI Workshop on Agents in real-time and dynamic environments, (2005).

[10] P. Torasso and G. Torta, 'The role of OBDDs in controlling the complexity of model based diagnosis', in Proc. DX04, pp. 9-14, (2004).

[11] C.Wittenven, N. Roos, R. van der Krogt, and M. deWeerdt, 'Diagnosis of single and multi-agent plans', in Proc. AAMAS05, pp. 805-812, (2005).

Incremental Fault Isolation for Dynamic Processes

George M. Coghill

School of Engineering and Physical Sciences, University of Aberdeen
Aberdeen, Scotland

Guofu Wu

Icom Innovations Ltd., Shrewsbury, England.

Abstract

In this paper we present an extension to the HS tree method for fault isolation developed by Reiter. This tool is combined with an ITMS based on root antecedents and used to perform incremental state based diagnosis on dynamic process systems. The approach is demonstrated to work by application to an industrial process - an ammonia washer system.

1 Introduction

Model based diagnosis seeks to provide an account of observed errors in a system by utilising principled knowledge of a physical system's structure and behaviours. This knowledge is *explicitly* encoded as one or more *models* of the system, often in the form of a set of constraints or even *local* rules [3]. Knowledge on how the system behaves when there is an abnormality may also be used for pruning spurious diagnoses [10] Given the observation of the physical system, MBD systems are able to *generate*, *test* and *discriminate* diagnoses by reasoning about the model of the system. This *generate-test-discrimination* process is vital for incremental model based diagnosis; and the process can be an iterative one.

It is usually assumed that all information relevant to a diagnosis is readily available at the time when diagnosis is required. However, this is not always the case: for example, not all measurement may be available at the appropriate time, the cost of getting the additional information may be costly, or multiple faults may occur that develop at different rates. Under such circumstances the ability to perform diagnosis incrementally is desirable.

In the rest of this paper we present an outline of consistency based diagnosis and describe a means of calculating diagnoses. After this we present a novel extension to Reiter's Hitting Set Algorithm which enables Hitting Set Trees to be constructed incrementally. This is followed by an application of the metod to an industrial example, and finally we present some conclusions.

2 The basic principles of consistency-based MBD

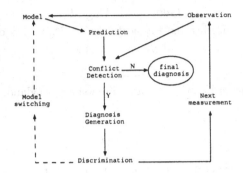

Figure 1: MBD process

The diagnostic process (depicted schematically in Figure 1[1]) starts when one or more faults are detected. *Fault detection* can be simplified by taking a simple model. For example, if a certain set of system variables have values outside the normal range, the diagnostic system will report that a fault has occurred in the plant, and at the same time the next task of the diagnostic process is invoked: *fault isolation*. This task requires the diagnostic process to isolate the fault to a set of localised entities or sub-systems. To perform this task, a structural model of the plant is required. Finally, the suspects obtained are pruned to enhance the quality of final diagnosis, or to obtain information about what kind of faults the suspects cause, what direction and how much the deviation is. This task is called *fault refinement/identification*. In this paper we focus on fault isolation.

In the consistency-based approach any difference between the *observations* from a physical system and the *predictions* by the system model are considered to be caused by one or more faults in the system (see Figure 1) .

Definition 1 (Observation (OBS) [9]) *An observation is a finite set of first-order sentences describing the measurements from the system. For example, the observation of a bath tub can be: level = +, outflow = +*

Definition 2 (System [9]) *A system can be represented as a pair (SD, COMPS) where SD, the system description, is a set of constraints; COMPS is a set of constants denoting the components of the system.*

Each entity [2] in COMPS has a localised constraint describing its correct behaviour without reference to the functioning of the whole system. The fact that every constraint in SD is assumed to be *local* implies that each constraint

---

[1] The dotted lines represent diagnostic tasks that are optional in any particular diagnostic process.

[2] Each entity can be a physical component or a logical element.

will not refer to more than one component. This requirement is helpful in isolating faults to individual components.

Each component in the system has one or more mutually exclusive *modes*, indicating the status of a component. For example, only two modes, $\neg AB(c)$ when component c is working as desired, and $AB(c)$ when c is not normal, are considered during *fault detection* and *fault isolation*. The system state is said to be *specified* when every component is assigned a mode.

Definition 3 (Mode assignment [5]) *Let* $\Delta \subseteq COMPS$, $OK \subseteq COMPS$ *and* $\Delta \cap OK = \emptyset$ *then a mode assignment* $D(\Delta, OK)$ *is:*

$$D(\Delta, OK) = \bigwedge_{x \in \Delta} AB(x) \wedge \bigwedge_{x \in OK} \neg AB(x)$$

The mode assignment is complete if $\Delta \cup OK = COMPS$.

During *fault refinement*, each component is either assigned $\neg AB$ mode or a specific fault mode rather than simply mode AB. For example, a tank may be assigned a "leaking" mode during fault refinement.

A diagnostic problem manifests itself when the assumption that all components are working as desired leads to a conflict, i.e.

$$SD \cup OBS \cup D(\emptyset, COMPS)$$

is inconsistent. To explain the inconsistency, a number of assumptions $\neg AB(c_i) \ldots \neg AB(c_x)$ where $c_i \ldots c_x \in COMPS$, must be identified and retracted, meaning that some components must be assigned fault modes.

Definition 4 (Diagnosis[4]) *A diagnosis for (SD, COMPS, OBS) is a set* Δ *such that the complete mode assignment* $D(\Delta, OK)$ *satisfies* $SD \cup OBS$, *that is,* $SD \cup OBS \cup D(\Delta, OK)$ *is consistent.*

Definition 5 (Minimal diagnosis [4]) *A diagnosis* Δ *is minimal iff no proper subset* $\Delta' \subset \Delta$ *such that* $SD \cup OBS \cup D(\Delta', OK)$ *is consistent.*

Calculating just the *minimal diagnoses* is one way to dramatically improve efficiency, Therefore, minimal diagnoses are of primary interest.

3 Calculating the diagnoses

The objective of this section is to describe how to determine all diagnoses of $(SD, COMPS, OBS)$. The method presented in this section is proposed by Reiter [9] based on the concept of a *conflict set* as described below. Suppose a variable x receives two contradictory values, say α from observation and β based on the assumption $\neg AB(c1) \wedge \neg AB(c2)$, where $c1, c2 \in COMPS$; as a consequence at least one of $c1$ or $c2$ is abnormal, $AB(c1) \vee AB(c2)$. When this occurs, $\{c1, c2\}$ is known as a conflict set.

Definition 6 (Conflict Set [9]) *A conflict set C for (SD, COMPS, OBS) is a set such that $C \subset OK$, and $SD \cup OBS \cup D(\Delta, OK)$ is inconsistent, where $D(\Delta, OK)$ is a complete mode assignment to COMPS. If no subset of C is a conflict set, then C is a minimal conflict set for (SD, COMPS, OBS).*

According to the definition of a conflict set, we can have the following proposition [9]:

Proposition 1 *$\Delta \subset COMPS$ is a diagnosis for $(SD, COMPS, OBS)$ iff Δ is a minimal set such that $COMPS - \Delta$ is not a conflict set.*

Thus conflict sets are a step towards determining the diagnoses. Reiter [9] proposed a way to compute the diagnoses without requiring that all the conflict sets are available at the same time. Reiter's algorithm combines conflict recognition with candidate generation to obtain the diagnoses, thus avoiding unnecessary computation. The idea is to construct the minimal *hitting sets* for the conflict sets of $(SD, COMPS, OBS)$. The algorithm for computing hitting sets relies on a theorem prover TP(SD, COMPS, OBS)[3] that is able to return a conflict set for (SD, COMPS, OBS) when requested and when $SD \cup COMPS \cup OBS$ is inconsistent.

Definition 7 (Hitting set) *Suppose C is a collection of sets, set H is a hitting set of C if*

- $\forall x \in H, x \in \bigcup_{S \in C} S$

- $\forall S \in C, H \cap S \neq \emptyset$

H is a minimal hitting set of C if no proper subset of H is a hitting set of C.

Reiter proposed and proved the following theorem which is the basis for calculating diagnostic candidates.

Theorem 1 (Theorem 4.4, [9]) *$\Delta \subset COMPS$ is a diagnosis for (SD, COMPS, OBS) iff Δ is a minimal hitting set for the collection of conflict sets for (SD, COMPS, OBS).*

As indicated by the definition of hitting set, the calculation of the hitting sets of a collection of sets can be implemented by choosing one member from each conflict set of (SD, COMPS, OBS). However it requires all conflict sets be available and it is inefficient. Reiter [9] suggested an improvement by constructing a *Hitting Set Tree*.

Definition 8 (Hitting set tree [9]) *A hitting set tree T of a collection of sets C is the smallest edge-labelled and node-labelled tree with the following properties:*

- *The root is labelled by $\sqrt{}$ if $C = \emptyset$, or an arbitrary set $\Sigma \in C$ otherwise.*

---

[3]Which in the current context will be a qualitative simulator.

- If node n is labelled by set Σ, where $\Sigma \neq \sqrt{}$, then for each $\sigma \in \Sigma$ a successor, n_σ, is created and joined to n by an edge labelled with σ.

- Let $H(n)$ be the set of edge labels on the path from node n to the root. If $\exists \, \Sigma \in C$ such that $\Sigma \cap H(n) = \emptyset$, then label n with Σ. Otherwise, label n with $\sqrt{}$.

Once a complete hitting set tree is obtained, a minimal hitting set for C is $H(n)$ if n is labelled $\sqrt{}$. For a diagnostic problem, each node n_i in the hitting set tree, except those labelled $\sqrt{}$, is labelled by a conflict set S returned by the theorem prover (simulation engine).

The computation of a conflict set must be seen as very expensive, because every access to a conflict set involves a call to the theorem prover. Therefore, the algorithm to create the hitting set tree must keep the tree as compact as possible: only the minimal hitting set is calculated and presented in the tree. Reiter [9] provided an algorithm to generate a pruned tree, and Greiner *et. al.* [6] improved it to guarantee completeness:

1. Generate the HS-tree in the *breadth-first* style: generate all the nodes at a certain level before progressing to generate nodes at the next level.

2. Reusing node labels:

   (a) If n and n' are nodes in a HS-tree T and $H(n') - H(n) = \sigma$, then link this σ-edge from n to n', instead of creating a new descendant for n. Hence a node may have two parents in the tree.

   (b) If no node n' is found such that $H(n') - H(n) = \sigma$, create new nodes for n as instructed by Reiter's algorithm on constructing the HS-tree.

3. Closing the node:
   If node n and n' are nodes in the HS-tree T, where n is labelled $\sqrt{}$, and if $H(n) \subset H(n')$, then close node n'. When a node is closed, a label is not computed for it and no successor for it is generated.

4. Pruning the tree:
   If $\Sigma \in C$ is used to label a node n for the first time, then attempt to prune T as indicated as below:

   (a) If there exists a node n' labelled by S in T and $\Sigma \subset S$, then relabel n' with Σ. For each $\alpha \in S - \Sigma$, the α-edge is not allowed. The node connected by an α-edge and its descendants are removed except those nodes with another ancestor.

   (b) Interchange the position of S and Σ in T.

The proof of this algorithm's correctness is in [6].

Once the complete pruned HS tree is obtained, the diagnoses of (SD, COMPS, OBS) are:

$$\bigvee_{label(n)=\checkmark} H(n)$$

Following the pruning rule one can see an advantage of the algorithm: it does not require that the conflict set determined by the theorem prover be minimal. This feature is essential for incremental MBD, where conflict sets may not be known in advance.

4   An Incremental Diagnosis Generator

The diagnosis generator uses a consistency based and state based approach [8] to propose candidates when faults occur in the system. It has utilised the concept of conflict sets to produce diagnoses. However, Reiter's algorithm cannot employ knowledge that has been obtained previously. Assume that a complete set of diagnoses have been obtained for (SD, OBS, COMP), if more measurements are postulated, or more knowledge about the system is now available, it is desirable to build upon the calculated result. To achieve this goal, one interesting question is asked: how can we reuse the previous result to calculate minimal hitting sets when one more conflict set is available? That is, if it is known that a collection of conflict sets C's minimal hitting sets are already available (ie $HittingSets(C) = T$), how can one resolve $HittingSets(C \cup \{c\})$ efficiently, where c is the newly discovered conflict set?

One obvious approach is to construct a new HS tree by applying Reiter's algorithm on $C \cup \{c\}$, as indicated in Figure 2. However, large amount of computation effort is wasted if T is already available, where T is the HS tree of C. A better idea is to build the HS tree T' of $C \cup \{c\}$ based on T.

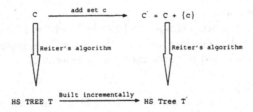

Figure 2: Building hitting set incrementally.

The rules for building T' incrementally are:

1. Open the nodes labelled by $\checkmark$ (checked nodes) and create descendants if necessary:
   A node n is checked (labelled $\checkmark$) because there $\neg\exists s \in C$ such that $H(n) \cap s = \emptyset$. Once a new set c is added to C, we must examine if the previously checked node in T is still qualified to keep its label $\checkmark$ in the new tree T'.

- If $H(n) \cap c = \emptyset$, relabel n by c and then build the subtree for n according to the revised hitting set algorithm proposed by [6].
- Otherwise, keep n's label and carry on to examine other checked nodes in T.

2. Keep all the previously closed node closed.

A node n is closed (labelled by $\times$ because there is a checked node n' such that $H(n) \supset H(n')$. When a new set c is added to C, if

- n' keeps its label $\sqrt{}$ in the new environment, according to node closing rule 3 in the revised algorithm [6], n is still closed;
- n' is relabelled by c, it can also be proved that n should be kept closed.

Proof:

Suppose $c = \{c_1, c_2, \ldots, c_\mu\}$, because n' is relabelled by c, μ descendants for n', $\{m'_1, m'_2, \ldots, m'_\mu\}$, are created according the definition of the HS tree, where c_x-edge points from n' to m'_x. Therefore $H(m'_x) = H(n') \cup \{c_x\}$, where, $0 < x < \mu + 1$. Because no set $s \in C \cup \{c\}$ satisfies $s \cap H(m'_x) = \emptyset$, all descendants of n' are labelled $\sqrt{}$.

Suppose n is open,

(a) if $H(n) \cap c = \emptyset$, then n is relabelled by c. Following the definition of the HS tree, μ descendants, $\{m_1, m_2, \ldots, m_\mu\}$, are created for n, where $H(m_x) = H(n) \cup \{c_x\}, 0 < x < \mu + 1$. Since $H(n) \supset H(n')$, we have $H(m_x) \supset H(m'_x)$. Because m'_x is checked, m_x is closed according to the rule of closing a node. This means all successors of n should be close, making no contribution to obtaining minimal hitting sets.

(b) if $H(n) \cap c \neq \emptyset$, we can always find node m'_x such that $H(m'_x) \subset H(n)$ based on the above analysis, and hence n is relabelled $\times$ according to the rules of closing a node. $\square$

3. Guarantee the breadth-first style by using a priority-queue as the agenda for creating subtrees.

When previously checked nodes are relabelled in T, the breadth-first style must be kept when creating subtrees for the relabelled nodes so that only minimal hitting sets are calculated. When a checked node n is open, if it is closer to the root than all other open nodes, it should be processed first. To guarantee this, the agenda is implemented as a priority queue. Given two nodes m and n, if $H(m)$ has fewer members than $H(n)$, m has a higher priority in the queue. If the sizes of $H(m)$ and $H(n)$ are equal, then the left node in the HS tree has higher priority.

A diagnosis filter refines the candidates obtained by the diagnosis generator. It also identifies the fault modes of the system in question. The diagnosis filter utilises multiple models for this purpose. Details of this task are outside the scope of this paper; see [12].

4.1 The QR inference engine and the ITMS

In addition to the diagnosis generation our MBD system required at least other modules: a qualitative reasoning (QR) engine (as noted previously) and a Truth Maintenance System (TMS) to enable switching of context as required during the diagnostic process (ie, after a discrepancy has been observed).

In the current version of the system we utilise a constraint based QR engine similar to QSIM [7] or Morven [2]. For this paper we restrict our attention to models in which variables take their values from the set of the signs: $\{+, 0, -, ?\}$[4] as do their rates of change. Constraint based qualitative models consist of conjunctions of constraints (e.g. ADD, MULT or the monotonic function relation - $M^{+/-}$). We also assume that the system models can be causally ordered to facilitate dependency recording.

Truth maintenance systems keep track of the dependencies between inferences and identify when inconsistencies occur. They also facilitate context switching which permits the deriving of the same conclusions in different ways. In our approach we utilise an incremental truth maintenance system (ITMS) based on the root antecedents of the propositions supported [11]. This ITMS enables fast and accurate context switching to be performed; which is essential for carrying out incremental fault isolation.

5 An Industrial example: the ammonia washer system

A simple but real industrial process will serve to illustrate the principles presented. Consider an ammonia washer system in a steel manufacturing by-product plant as shown schematically in Figure 3, where only the flow path of washing liquid is depicted. The system consists of a number of components:

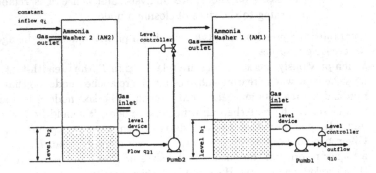

Figure 3: The liquid flow scheme in a ammonia washer system

---

[4]Here '?' refers to the ambiguous value that covers the whole real number line. It arises when one subtracts values of the same sign or add ones of opposite sign.

an inlet pipe, two washer tanks, two pumps, two controllers, two valves and a pipe connecting the tanks. The two washer tanks are identical in terms of design. Details of this system can be found in [1] and [12]

The ammonia washer system is decomposed into a finite set of system components. There are no quantitative models available for this sytem, therefore we utilse a constraint based qualitative model. One or more qualitative constraints governs the behaviours of each component. To construct the simplest model that is sufficient for the goal specified above, the outflow is considered to be monotonically related to the level of the fluid in the washer. The rate of change of levels are related to the *net* amount of fluid that is pumped out/in.

To summarise, the complete normal model is:

$$C1: \quad q_{21} = M^+(h_2) \tag{1}$$
$$C2: \quad h_2' = q_i - q_{21} \tag{2}$$
$$C3: \quad q_{10} = M^+(h_1) \tag{3}$$
$$C4: \quad h_1' = q_{21} - q_{10} \tag{4}$$

where q_i, q_{21} and q_{10} are inlet flow to AW2, flow from AW2 to AW1 and outlet flow of AW1 respectively. h_2 and h_1 are the levels in washer AW2 and AW1 respectively.

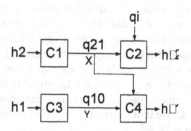

Figure 4: A constraint model of the ammonia washer system.

Each constraint of the model is associated with a unique name for the convenience of dependency recording and referencing. In addition, each constraint is related to only one component or one mechanism of the plant, because each constraint must be *local*. For example, $C1$ is related to the pump P730 Similarly, $C2$ is related to AW2, $C3$ to pump P731, and $C4$ to AW1. If some constraints are inconsistent with the observations, the components related to these constraints form a conflict set.

It is assumed that the ammonia washer system is continuously monitored. The fault data for the plant were collected by deliberately shutting down the appropriate components (in this case the pumps) for a certain period of time to simulate faults. There are two sensors giving numeric measurements of the levels in AW1 and AW2 respectively. It is assumed that the sensor signals are already processed and thus noise free. The numeric measurements are translated

	t_0	t_1
h_2	$[+\ 0]$	$[+\ +]$
h_1	$[+\ 0]$	$[+\ 0]$
h_2	$[0\ 0]$	$[+\ ?]$
h_1'	$[0\ 0]$	$[0\ ?]$

Table 1: Measurements and extension of measurements at time t_0 and t_1, where Pumps P730 and P731are observed to have failed at t_1

into qualitative values by means of pre-defined mapping rules. Based on the theory of state based diagnosis [8], the measurement can be extended by using continuous conditions. For example, the derivatives are estimated by calculating the qualitative changes between two consecutive but qualitatively distinctive time points.

The sampling rate is not required to be slow enough to allow fault trends to manifest themselves over time, because only qualitatively distinctive measurements are of interest. On the contrary, the sampling rate should be fast enough to provide *gapless* measurements (no qualitative state is missed)[8]. A simple way to translate numeric data into qualitative data is to define a normal range for each observed variable. When the detected value is out of bounds for a pre-defined duration, the measurements at this instant and the immediate previous qualitative state are passed to the diagnostic engine. If the measurements are within bounds, they are treated as unchanged no matter how fast they change over time within bounds. For example (for the process operating at steady state), if a variable is $[+\ 0]$ at time t_0, and if it is detected to be within bounds at time t_1, its value remains $[+\ 0]$. If it is detected to be lower than the normal range but still above 0, its value is $[+\ -]$; if it is detected to be above the normal range its value is $[+\ +]$.

5.1 Experimental results

One possible scenario is presented in this section to illustrate the method; further information is contained in [12]. In this scenario it is assumed that the plant is initially running normally at its operational steady state. The fault monitor reports a fault when any of the observed variables are out of their normal ranges. The measurements at the fault state (i.e. t_1) and the immediately previous qualitative state (i.e. t_0) are translated into qualitative data and passed to the fault isolation process, the diagnosis generator. The diagnoser takes the inputs and extends the measurements (e.g. by predicting derivatives of the measured variables). Table 1 shows the qualitative measurements and extension of measurements of the two consecutive states, where at state t_1 both pumps P730 and P731 fail. Also, the inflow is considered to be constant, i.e., $q_i = [+\ 0]$ and $q_i' = [0\ 0]$ at time t_0 and t_1. Next, the task of fault isolation is commenced using the qualitative model of the ammonia washer system. In this task, the qualitative inference engine propagates the values of the observed variables to the rest of the model, making judgements and passing them to the ITMS. The ITMS takes the judgements and builds the dependency networks. Once a conflict is detected, the ITMS can return the cause of the inconsistency in the format of a collection of conflict sets. Once the conflict sets are obtained, the candidates are calculated by building HS trees of the conflict sets. Details of how the conflict sets are generated can be found in [1].

With these inputs and the qualitative model, the conflict sets {C1, C2} and {C1, C3, C4} are found. Figure 5 shows the hitting set tree for the scenario when these conflict sets are provided. Edge labels from the root node to a check node are assembled into a minimal hitting set. A minimal hitting set is a diagnostic set.

Conflict sets: {C1, C2}, {C1, C3, C4}

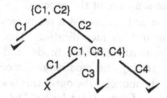

Figure 5: The HS tree for the scenario when the conflict sets {C1, C2} and {C1, C3, C4} are provided

It turns out [1] that the conflict sets generated at this stage are the same for both the failure of pump P730 and the failure of both pumps. This is reflected in the fact that C1 is returned as one of the diagnoses. It should be noted that this constitutes a partial diagnosis of the plant since C1 is the constraint associated with the failure of pump P730 (one of the two pumps which have failed). In order to obtain the final complete diagnosis more information is required. This can be obtained by switching context and re-comparing the predictions in the new context with the observations. The context switching is facilitated by the ITMS and in the present case there is a discrepancy in the new context and and new conflict {C2, C3, C4} is found. If the fault had in fact been the failure of P730 alone so such new discrepancy would have been occurred, and hence no new conflict set been found. This new conflict is then used to extend the HS tree in accordance with the incremental HS algorithm as shown in Figure 6. This gives the final set of proposed candidates for fault isolation as: {C1, C2}, {C1, C3}, {C1, C4}, {C2, C3} & {C2, C4}[5]. It may be observed that the final set of candidates after the complete fault isolation process only differs

---

[5]The same result could have been obtained by placing a sensor at location Y in Figure 4 but such measurements would have been expensive and were not available, and in this case turn out not to be necessary.

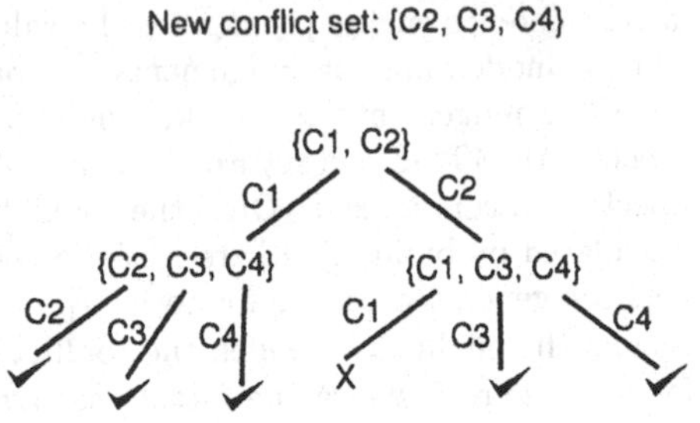

New conflict set: {C2, C3, C4}

Figure 6: The extended hitting set tree for the fault scenario when both pumps fail

from the partial diagnosis in that C1 is no longer a single fault diagnosis; which highlights the incremental nature of the process.

At this stage we have only proposed a set of possible candidates. This set can be refined by means of fault identification. This requires that fault modes be provided for each constituent of the model and searches through the set of proposed candidates testing the predictions generated by incorporating the relevant fault modes in the model. Obviously this is a smaller search space than that of every combination of component faults. Detailed discussion of the fault identification process is outside the scope of this paper, but some details may be found in [1, 12]. For the current fault situation fault identification selects {C1, C3} as the best candidate, which is correct.

6   Conclusions

In this paper we have presented a method for performing fault isolation which is an incremental extension to the HS tree algorithm developed by Reiter. This tool is combined with an ITMS based on root antecedents and used to perform state based diagnosis on dynamic process systems. This approach demonstrated to work on an industrial process - an ammonia washer system. The incremental HS algorithm makes use of the information available in any particular situation to generate diagnoses. These diagnoses may be partial, with the complete diagnosis only being made when more information becomes available. This method constitutes a novel approach to incremental diagnosis of dynamic processes that is also applicable to static systems

Acknowledgements

The authors gratefully acknowledge the support of the EPSRC under grant GR/M24881/01.

References

[1] George M. Coghill. A feasibility study on model-based diagnosis for an ammonia washer system. Technical report, Centre of Intelligent Systems, Department of Computer Science, University of Wales, Aberystwyth, 2000.

[2] George Macleod Coghill. *Mycroft: A framework for Constraint Based Fuzzy Qualitative Reasoning*. PhD thesis, Heriot-Watt University, 1996.

[3] Adnan Darwiche. Model-based diagnosis under real-world constraints. In *AI magazine*, volume 21.2, pages 57–73. AAAI, 2000.

[4] Johan de Kleer, Alan K. Mackworth, and Raymond Reiter. Characterizing diagnoses and systems. In Walter Hamscher, Luca Console, and Johan de Kleer, editors, *Readings in Model Based Diagnosis*, pages 54–65. Morgan Kaufmann Publishers, Inc., 1992.

[5] Oskar Dressler and Peter Struss. The consistency-based approach to automated diagnosis of devices. In U. Gnowho, editor, *A Greate Collection*. CSLI, 1996.

[6] Russel Greiner, Barbara A. Smith, and Ralph W. Wilkerson. A correction to the algorithm in Reiter's theory of diagnosis. In Walter Hamscher, Luca Console, and Johan de Kleer, editors, *Readings in Model Based Diagnosis*, pages 49–65. Morgan Kaufmann Publishers, Inc., 1992.

[7] Benjamin Kuipers. *Qualitative Reasoning: Modelling and Simulation with Incomplete knowledge*. MIT Press, Cambridge, MA, 1994.

[8] Andreas Malik and Peter Struss. Diagnosis of dynamic systems does not necessarily require simulation. *DX - 1996*, 1996.

[9] Raymond Reiter. A theory of diagnosis from first principles. *Artificial Intelligence*, 32:57–96, 1987.

[10] Peter Struss and Oskar Dressler. Physical negation: Integrating fault models into the general diagnostic engine. In Walter Hamscher, Luca Console, and Johan de Kleer, editors, *Readings in Model Based Diagnosis*, pages 153–158. Morgan Kaufmann Publishers, Inc., 1992.

[11] G. Wu and G. M. Coghill. A propositional root antecedent itms. *DX-2004 Carcasonne, France*, pages 185–190, 2004.

[12] Guofu Wu. *Incremental state based diagnosis of dynamic physical systems*. PhD thesis, University of Wales, Aberystwyth, 2003.

Qualitative Approaches to Semantic Scene Modelling and Retrieval

Zia Ul Qayyum, A. G. Cohn

School of Computing
University of Leeds, Leeds – UK
zia@comp.leeds.ac.uk , a.g.cohn@leeds.ac.uk

Abstract

This paper investigates the use of qualitative and spatially expressive semantic descriptions for image classification. In particular, it addresses the question of how a qualitative representation performs compared to a more quantitative one, using a semantic based symbolic approach. The approach is based on using different qualitative spatial representations applied to local semantic concepts such as grass, sky, water etc in a corpus of natural scenes images, to learn qualitative class descriptions and categorise them into one of six semantically meaningful classes such as coasts, forest etc. Three kinds of qualitative spatial relations, namely Allen's relations [1] applied on the vertical axis of images, chord representation [9] applied on segmented semantically labelled image regions, and relative size of semantic concepts in each image have been investigated. A number of well-known supervised learning techniques have been applied to determine their usefulness. It is shown that a purely qualitative representation can result into better image description and perform at the similar level or even slightly better, compared to an existing largely quantitative representation [20]. Such qualitative and spatially expressive descriptions may therefore have utility in semantic querying and image retrieval systems.

1.   Introduction

Large collections of digital images are being created and stored in various domains such as medical, astronomical, biological. With growing user interest to find useful and interesting patterns from these volumes of data, image classification is an area of active research in computer vision and pattern recognition.

Most of the work in this area has been based on describing the image using low level features like colour, texture etc whereas semantic image description is arguably a more natural way of describing image features and it may bridge the gap between a human's description and that of a computer. Moreover, humans would usually describe the scenes in terms such as "… having some snow patches in a small lake with high peaks of mountains and sky on top of image ….". A semantically rich and qualitative spatial representation, therefore, may enable such description in a natural way and provide an abstract representation of low level concepts for reasoning and knowledge extraction.

The existing techniques in image description and image classification are predominantly quantitative and based on describing and categorizing the images using their low level features like colour, texture etc [15,12,18,19,9]. Scene descriptions are thus not expressed in terms of underlying semantic knowledge and on qualitative and spatial relationships between attributes used for image description. The approach taken here addresses these issues by applying a variety of qualitative spatial theories onto semantically annotated image regions/patches and to the relative size (region occupied by each concept) of each of the semantic concept in an image. This abstracts away from dealing with low level image features and makes the descriptions more expressive, intuitive and spatial, and potentially useful for semantic querying and image retrieval. Several machine learning algorithms have been applied to these representations to investigate the usefulness and accuracy of such a representation. The proposed scheme does not rely on existing segmentation techniques as these techniques have their own respective limitations which affect overall categorisation accuracy of the classifier. Rather, it is based on segmenting the image into a grid of 10x10 resulting in 100 patches which have then been labelled with underlying semantic concepts extracted using low level features.

In the research reported here, a collection of 700 natural scenes images has been used. A variety of experiments have been carried out to investigate qualitative semantic-based image descriptions for classification/ categorization. A sample from the image data set used is displayed in Fig. 1[1], which illustrates the six classes/categories with which all 700 images are labelled.

Fig. 1 **Sample images of the six categories of natural scenes**

The work builds on work of Vogel [20]. She envisaged an image description which is semantic, descriptive; region based and may be evaluated quantitatively as well as through psychophysical experiments [21]. As described above, to obtain a region based semantic image description, she divided the image into a grid of 10x10 regions to extract local image regions. By analyzing these regions in images, nine local[2] and discriminating semantic concepts have been identified and used in her work, namely: sky, water, grass, foliage, flowers, field, mountain, snow, trunks and sand. Using these labels, 99.5% of the images were annotated [21]. A label "rest" is used for unidentified or other occurrences. Then, a model was built to

---

[1] In fact for copyright reasons, we have substituted similar images in this paper, and the percentages in Fig. 2 have been hand estimated.

[2] Vogel cites nine semantic concepts in her work [20], while the data set she provided and which has been used in experiments contains two extra ones (mountain and snow) – however these occur infrequently (about 0.5 %) and the basis for comparison will be largely unaffected.

categorize images into six semantically meaningful categories sky_clouds, coasts, landscapes_with_mountains (lwm), field, forests, waterscapes, cf Fig.1. Images were represented by frequency histograms of local semantic concepts such as grass, foliage, water etc. Based on this representation, the percentages of concept occurrences, concept occurrence vector (COV), were evaluated on 3-5 image regions (e.g. top/middle/ bottom) and based on a semantic typicality measure the images were categorized into one of the six classes as described above. The approach is partially spatial through its division of the image into horizontal bands (i.e. top/middle bottom) but is mainly based on the metric value of a discriminant semantic concept. The following figure describes this approach.

Fig.2   A segmented image with 9 local semantic concepts and COV

A supervised classification activity using the above described image description data was carried out with a support vector machine (SVM) classifier. A classifier accuracy of 74.1% was reported with classified image regions when applied on three image areas while 86.4% with annotated image regions applied on 5 image areas [21].

The rest of paper is organised as follows: section 2 provides an overview of some of related work in the area of image retrieval/categorization and other allied techniques. An extensive review of literature is not intended here, therefore, different approaches in the field of image understanding and categorisation have been briefly described to highlight major streams of research in this area and techniques used therein, experiments and methodology in the current work have been discussed in section 3, results of different experiments are presented in section 4, our results and conclusions are summarised in the last section.

2.   Related Work

In early research on image retrieval, image description and categorization has mainly been accomplished through low-level feature vectors like colour, texture and shape, whereas semantic scene description is arguably a natural way to describe image features and it may bridge the gap between a human's description and that of a computer. In most of the literature, semantics is only found in definitions of scene classes like indoor vs. outdoor, mountain vs. forest etc while classification itself is based on low level image features. These earlier research directions underline the basic assumption that the images with similar colour and texture features are semantically closer.

Szummer et al [15] used a k-nearest neighbour classifier to classify the scenes in two broad categories only "indoor" vs. "outdoor". They computed low-level image features - colour and texture (using the model of Mao et al [8]), on four sub blocks of the image and then combined the classification results on sub blocks using a multistage classification approach and have reported a good classification accuracy of 90.3%. Vailaya et al [18] also used colour and texture features to classify natural scenes in a hierarchical manner, using a K-NN classifier. The images at the first step have been classified into two categories namely city vs. landscape scenes with an accuracy of 93.9%, then the landscape scenes further categorized as sunrise/sunset vs. forest & mountains with 94.5% classification accuracy, and then at a 3rd stage, the latter category has classified into forest or mountain images with an accuracy of 91.7%. Semantic attributes were first used by Oliva et al [11] to classify images into three semantic axes. They used a data set of natural and artificial images and developed an approach to classify and organise real-world scenes in broad semantic axes: first artificial to natural, then 'open' to 'closed' in natural scenes, while the artificial scene axis was scaled from 'expanded' to 'enclosed'. The discriminant spectral template containing the spectral content for low level features of the image were computed which had the capability to differentiate between different semantic contents of an image and organises an image along only one semantic axis/class. Discriminant analysis has been used to maximise the intra class distance and minimise the inter class dispersion. The classification accuracy of 90% has been reported in categorizing images into "artificial" vs. "natural"; 88% in case of classifying natural scenes into open vs. closed and 82% in case of artificial ones to be divided into expanded vs. enclosed. Vailaya et al [19] have described a hierarchical scheme for classifying vacation images using colour and edge direction features. They classify at a first step images into city vs. landscapes with 95.3% accuracy, then the landscapes category is further classified into sunset, forest and mountain classes with an accuracy rate of 94.9% and finally an accuracy of 93.6% for forest vs. mountain classification. The probabilistic model of low level features required for the Bayesian framework was estimated using vector quantization. The work carried out by the Vailaya et al [18,19] and Oliva et al [11] is similar to that of Szummer but they have classified the images into different classes in a multistage classification framework. Gorkani et al [5] have proposed a scheme to categorize natural scenes into two semantic categories, city vs. landscapes. The scheme is based on a dominant orientation criterion, which is evaluated using multiscale steerable pyramid in 4x4 sub blocks of image. An image which has a dominant vertical orientation or even a mix of vertical and horizontal orientation had been categorized as a city/suburb scene and landscape otherwise. An accuracy of about 90% has been reported for classifying the city/suburb scenes using this technique.

All of the above techniques use low level image features and some have even used spatial content as well, by applying the schemes onto blocks of 4x4, and mainly categorise the image corpus into two classes in the first instance and then may hierarchically categorise the individual classes into further subclasses whereas none of the above has reported a classification scheme for classifying the images into more than two classes in one iteration. Secondly, while the rate of accuracy is quite high it is likely that there will be less variation of low level concepts along only two branches of categorization. Our approach and that of [20,21], on the other hand, provides a classification scheme for categorizing natural scene images into six semantically meaningful classes.

In an attempt to improve the image description and categorisation accuracy by using underlying semantic concepts, Serrano et al [16] have used two semantic attributes, namely sky and grass, and low level colour and wavelet texture features to classify images into indoor vs. outdoors using support vector machines (SVM) with an overall accuracy of 87.2%. The semantic scene attributes, sky and grass, were predicted using the same low level features and integrated into the classification scheme already learnt for an improved two step indoor/outdoor classification scheme using a Bayesian network which resulted in an improved classification rate of 90.7%. This shows that the use of low level semantic concepts in image description may improve expressiveness and classification accuracy, which supports our approach. Recently, Boutell et al [2] have suggested a primary reason for higher classification errors and presented a scheme for multi class classification. They have suggested that this error rate is due to the assumption that classes in the data and thus in the experiments are usually taken to be mutually exclusive but this is not the case often in practice. They have proposed a framework to deal with the situation of multi class problems where classes semantically overlap. They used a SVM on a feature vector of size 294 per image, (each image divided into a grid of 7x7) and a neural network with one output node for each class in their experiments. They have reported an accuracy rate from 78.3-79.5% in single label and 76.1-81.3% in multi-label classes data sets. Maron et al [6] have described a method for categorizing natural scenes into waterfall, mountain and fields. The images are modelled as bags of multiple instances (sub regions) and a bag is labelled as positive if at least one instance in the bag is positive and negative otherwise. The model learns scene templates for each class and then a probabilistic diversity density method (Maron et al [7]) is used to learn concepts from multiple instance examples. The classification results are evaluated based on the RGB colour features of an image that are closer to at least one positive instance in every positive labelled bag of instances for a class.

Segmentation of image regions for feature extraction is yet another important technique which is widely discussed in the literature and used in image retrieval and computer vision context. Pal et al [12] have written a survey on various image segmentation techniques. It has been observed that colour, texture and shape evaluated on segmented image regions results in relatively improved models for retrieval or classification purposes. But segmentation algorithms still tend to over or under segment the image, making the classification very difficult because overall categorization is constrained by the accuracy of segmented regions [21]. By contrast, the scheme in this paper is based on regular subdivision of images.

Image annotation has also been used to obtain a better image description and classification accuracy. Picard et al [13] introduced the idea of annotating image regions using texture. The framework selects a best model from a multitude of texture models to annotate the image regions with semantically meaningful labels. It first learns from the user's input and interaction and then propagates the learnt labels to other similar regions. Town et al [17] developed a system to classify segmented image regions into semantic labels using a neural network, segmenting the image using colour and texture features. This approach and the one presented in this paper are similar in using the semantic labels but labelling of image regions in our approach can be described as to be region based contrary of segmentation approach based on low level colour and texture features.

We have used Allen's interval calculus [1], chords patterns [9] and a third qualitative representation, namely relative size, to conduct different experiments with Vogel's data set. Although Allen's calculus was originally intended for temporal representations, it can also be used for representing 1D space [10,22]. These representations are discussed further in the following section.

3. A Qualitative Approach to Image Classification

Building on Vogel's work [20], we have carried out different experiments on the same data set and compared the intuitiveness of image description and the classification rate.

In extending Vogel's work, we have used the same annotated image regions and class information for each image as she did and have compared the results in terms of classification accuracy and image description intuitiveness. The proposed representation results in a more expressive and spatially rich scene description which arguably is more meaningful and comprehensible by the user. Moreover, user queries like " retrieve/find images with 'no' water", "return images with mountains 'above' forest" or "retrieve images with rocks 'meeting' water 'and' water relatively 'greater than' foliage .." etc may be processed by a retrieval system more easily.

We have investigated three main kinds of qualitative spatial relations

1) the relative size (measured in grid squares) of each of the concept occurrences in each image. The relative size is calculated for all possible pairwise combination of semantic labels. Since there are 11 labels and only one ordering needs to be considered, this gives 66 pairings. Each may be regarded as an attribute of the image with possible values of 'Greater than' (>), 'Less than' (<) and 'Almost Equal to' ($\approx$). These relations are defined as:

Let |P| denote the number of occurrences of a patch type 'P'. If 'P1' , 'P2' are two patch types, then:

- P1 > P2   iff $(0.9*|P1| > (|P2|)$
- P1 < P2   iff $(1.1*|P1| < |P2|)$
- P1 $\approx$ P2   otherwise

Note that we have used a tolerance of $\pm 10\%$ since it is relatively unlikely that two attributes/labels would ever have exactly equal size in similar images.

2) Allen relations [1] (measured on vertical axis between the intervals representing the maximum extent of each concept occurrence). Allen's calculus has been used to represent 1D spatial knowledge using thirteen

relations namely, 'before' (Bf), 'meets' (Mt), 'overlaps' (Ov), 'during' (Dg), 'starts' (St) and their inverses 'after' (Af), 'met-by' (Mb), 'overlapped-by' (Ob), 'contains' (Co), 'started-by' (Sb), 'finished-by' (Fb) respectively, and 'equal' (Eq). Since the learning algorithms we use require a fixed number of attributes, the dummy relation "No" has been added to this representation if either or both of the attributes being evaluated using Allen's relations are missing/ do not exist. This representation has been evaluated over all 66 possible pairs of semantic labels used for image description.

3) Chord patterns [9] of semantic concepts applied to each grid row. In this approach, each semantic feature is a 'tone' and the set of these in each row forms a 'chord'. Thus each image will have ten chords such as "foliage sky" or "grass sky sand water" etc. This representation thus generates set-valued attributes. An image is represented by attributes corresponding to each of these chords and by attributes recording the relationships between each pair of adjacent chords (9 in all). If 'C1' and 'C2' represent two adjacent chords, then relationships between these two may be one of the following five relations:

- C1 and C2 are equal/have same set of labels – '$\equiv$'
- C1 is contained in C2 – '$<$'
- C1 contains C2 - '$>$'
- C1 and C2 have some labels in common – 'C1 $\cap$ C2 $\neq \emptyset$'
- C1 and C2 are distinct chords - 'C1 $\cap$ C2 $= \emptyset$'

Figure 3 shows a segmented image described by the relative size and Allen relationships while Fig.4 illustrates an image described with the chord representation.

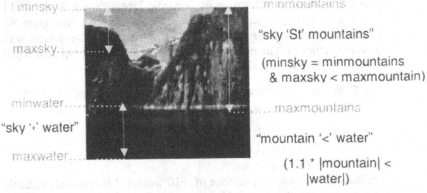

"sky 'St' mountains"

(minsky = minmountains
& maxsky < maxmountain)

"mountain '<' water"

(1.1 * |mountain| <
|water|)

Fig.3   Qualitative representation of an image using relative size and Allen's calculus

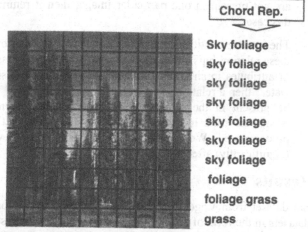

Fig.4   Qualitative representation of an image using Chords representation

In addition to these three basic kinds of spatial relations, several variants and representations were also investigated. Following Vogel's top/middle/bottom approach, Allen's relations have also been determined in three horizontal bands of each image namely, the top, middle and bottom. A coarser grained representation for chord patterns was also used where the top, middle and bottom form three chords and even coarser representation with just two chords for each half of image.

Since Allen's calculus might be viewed as too fine grained when applied to 10 rows per image and resulting in many of the Allen relations having zero count in a particular image, the data was pre-processed by grouping the 13 Allen relations into following six (by disjoining the respective relations with an 'OR') to have a linear ordering between the relations.

- BM   combining "Before" and "Meet"
- Ov   "Overlap" relation
- LG   combining   "Starts", "During", "Finishes",
            "Started by", "Contains", "Finished by" and
            "Equal"
- Ob   "Overlapped by" relation
- AM   combining   "After" and "Met by"
- No   if no Allen relation exists between two attributes of an
            image.

As with the full set of Allen relations, this representation was applied to the entire image and also on top/ middle/ bottom regions.

One aspect is worth mentioning here in regard to the Allen relations is that 'Bf', 'Mt', 'Ov', 'St', 'Dg', and 'No' occur with a much higher frequency than all the others. Similarly with the Allen grouped relations, 'BM', and 'No' have the highest frequency. The reason for this is two fold:

i.   The relationships are being evaluated amongst all possible
        combinations of concepts/attributes, so if one or both of the two

are not present in one particular image, then it returns 'No' in this case.

ii.   The inverse relations disappear from the representation because these relationships are being evaluated amongst all possible pairs of attributes in an upper triangular fashion... so if "sky is 'Bf' water" then a relation of the form "water is 'Af' sky" would not be present in the representation. The relations were ordered within the pairs in such a manner so that 'Bf', 'Mt' and 'St' predominated. We claim that a different ordering would not (significantly) affect our results.

4.   Results

The original dataset from Vogel [21] has been preprocessed to form fifteen new different datasets in the form of each of the above mentioned representations. Only a representative sample is presented here due to space limitations. These have been used to have a comparison amongst different machine learning algorithms/techniques and qualitative spatial representations of semantic concepts. The data mining tool WEKA 3.4 [23] has been used to carry out various experiments on the data. Naïve Bayes, J48, AdaBoostM1 and SOM have been applied, which are implementations of the well-known decision tree algorithm C4.5, boosting with base classifier as J48 – C4.5 decision tree learner and support vector machines respectively [14,4,3]. Support vector machines have been reported to be more accurate even in high dimensional feature space [3]. The experiments have been 10 fold cross-validated to improve the reliability of results and minimize the effect of over fitting.

The results of these experiments are as below in Table 1: (Note that the labels DS1 to DS15 will be used for the different datasets and the aliases S1 to S4 for the machine learning algorithms in the subsequent discussion below).

Experiments / Classifiers	Naïve Bayes (S1)	C4.5 (S2)	AdaBoostM1 with C4.5 – (S3)	SMO C=1.0, γ = 0.01 (S4)
Allens & Size Relations - - DS1	81.4%	83.0 %	82.71%	83.0%
Allens on T/M/B Regions along with Relative Size - - DS2	87.3%	85.3%	88.14%	86.7%
Allens Relations only -- DS3	81.3%	80.57%	80.43 %	81.0%
Relative Size Relation only – DS4	80.7%	81.14 %	82.29%	83.0%
Allens Relations only on T/M/B Regions -- DS5	81.14%	81.28%	83.57%	83.14%
Allens Grouped & Size Relations -- DS6	79.9%	82.6%	82.4%	81.7%

Allens Grouped Relations only – DS7	79.1%	77.7%	79.0 %	80.57%
Allens Grouped on T/M/B & Relative Size Relations – DS8	85.43%	83.43%	85.43%	86.29%
Allens Grouped on T/M/B Regions Relations – DS9	81.1%	81.3%	83.57 %	83.14%
Chord Rep. (1 chord per row) – DS10	83.14%	74.29%	79.29%	82.0%
Chord Rep. & Relative Size Relation – DS11	86.43%	82.14%	84.29%	85.14%
Chord Rep. on T/M/B Regions – DS12	79.14%	70.86%	77.57%	82.71%
Chord Rep. on T/M/B Regions & Relative Size Relation – DS13	84.57%	82.57%	85.43%	84.56%
Chord Rep. on T/B Regions – DS14	75.43%	71.29%	72.43%	76.86%
Chord Rep. on T/B & Relative Size Relation – DS15	83.71%	81.0%	81.71%	83.43&
Relative Size on T/M/B Regions – DS16	84.71	83.14	85.29	84.29

Table 1. Results of % accuracy on 15 data representations using four machine learning algorithms

First, it is noteworthy how well the size relation above (**DS4, DS16**) performs. This representation can be viewed as a purely abstracted form of Vogel's representation and performs surprisingly well compared to her more much more fine grained quantitative representation. The Allen representation alone relation (DS3) and its variant on top/ middle/ bottom regions (DS5) does almost as well and even better respectively than relative size alone, while the chord patterns representations do not do well (DS10, DS12, DS14). However, adding relative size representation to either Allen or chord representation produces a performance equal to, or even surpassing Vogel's results (DS2, DS8, DS11).

A perhaps surprising aspect of the results above is that the Allen relations already allow the representation, to some extent, "one region is above or below another"; but adding the top/middle/bottom regions gives a noticeable further improvement. Secondly, the boosting algorithm AdaBoostM1 with J48 as base classifier has given equal or even better classification rate in some cases as compared to well known and acclaimed support vector machines. The same effect has been observed in the case of chord representation. Vogel obtained her best classification rate with SVM.

Table 2 (results using Allen's representation along with its different variants and the relative size relation) and Table 3 (results using the chords representation and its variants) provide comparisons of results, rounded to one decimal point, of Vogel's classifier using support vector machine and our experiments. The results are presented as percentages of accuracy in each category. These results reveal that the misclassification rate is greater in classes like waterscapes/rivers, coasts and lwm. The confusion matrices, though not presented here for space reasons, also reveal that most of the confusion in almost all of the models is due to higher rate of misclassification in "waterscapes" and "coasts" classes and then in "lwm" and "fields", which is one factor in retarding the accuracy percentage of the classifier. The apparent reason is due to the fact the some images in these categories are less typical and can be classified into one of the two classes. The same aspect has also been reported in Vogel's work. Moreover, if we could minimise the effect of unlabelled instances or "rest" label, the classifier accuracy would be expected to increase significantly.

Classes	Vogel's Work	DS1		DS2		DS4		DS8	
		S3	S4	S3	S4	S3	S4	S3	S4
Sky_clouds	94.1	67.6	70.6	94.1	91.2	70.6	73.5	91.2	91.2
Rivers/ Lakes	73.1	75.4	77.2	81.6	81.6	66.7	75.4	76.3	80.7
Coasts	80.3	78.3	81.1	82.5	81.1	77.6	77.6	78.3	82.5
Forests	95.1	93.2	88.3	96.1	94.2	93.2	91.3	96.1	94.2
Plains	91.6	79.7	78.9	86.7	82.8	79.7	80.5	85.2	82.8
Lwm	89.4	93.8	90.4	92.1	92.1	93.8	91.0	89.9	89.9
Accuracy Rate	86.4	83.7	83.0	88.1	86.7	82.3	83.0	85.4	86.3

Table 2: Comparison of results using Allen's representation and relative size relation with Vogel

Classes	Vogel's Work	DS10		DS11		DS13		DS15	
		S3	S4	S3	S4	S3	S4	S3	S4
Sky_clouds	94.1	88.2	88.2	79.4	76.5	82.4	82.4	76.5	73.5
Rivers/ Lakes	73.1	64.9	67.5	70.2	76.3	71.9	74.6	65.8	72.8
Coasts	80.3	72.0	74.8	80.4	79.7	84.6	81.8	76.9	79.7
Forests	95.1	89.3	89.3	93.2	92.2	92.2	91.3	92.2	93.2
Plains	91.6	80.5	86.7	82.8	85.2	82.8	83.6	78.1	82
Lwm	89.4	86.0	88.2	93.3	92.7	93.3	91.6	93.3	90.4
Accuracy Rate	86.4	79.3	82.0	84.3	85.1	85.4	84.6	81.7	83.4

Table 3: Comparison of results using Chords representation and relative size relation with Vogel

The results (as with those of Vogel) may be improved by a better image regions annotation scheme, using different labels to annotate the image regions, using different machine learning algorithms or even considering different number of classes to categorize the images. For example, if the concept "rest" is removed from the data which corresponds to the unlabelled patches or any other label from the ones used in annotation scheme, the classification rates improve significantly to range between 91% to even 94% which implies that the classification rate is adversely affected by the misclassification of the annotated regions/patches.

The results of our experiments are not significantly better than the previous work by Vogel. The aspect, which differentiates the current work from her methodology, is the use of purely qualitative spatial representations, (the Allen relationship applied vertically and Chord representation along with the relative size relationships). This appears to allow slightly better classification overall (provided her top/middle/bottom separation is also maintained). Moreover, it can be argued that the qualitative representation is more intuitive in that the descriptions of classes do not rely on metric information. Another important aspect of this representation which is worth mentioning is the provision of qualitative spatial classification rules for image description and classification using semantic concepts. This has the potential for spatial and semantically meaningful querying and image retrieval. Below, we give examples of rules extracted from DS2, DS8 and DS13 using the algorithm PART [24].

In DS2

BwaterBsnowsize = AEQ   AND
MtrunksMrocks = Eq   AND
BskyBfield = Eq: **Fields**

In DS8

BwaterBsandsize = AEQ   AND
TfoliageTrocks = No   AND
BskyBfoliagesize = LTH   AND
TmountainTflowers = BM   AND
TgrassTfoliage = BM   AND
TflowersTsand = BM   AND

BfoliageBflowerssize = GTH AND
BfoliageBmountain = No: **Forest**

IN DS13

WaSnS = GTH   AND
ChR2 = rocks_water_: **Coasts**
RoSnS = GTH   AND
WaSnS = AEQ   AND
RoReS = GTH   AND
SaRoS = LTH   AND
GrRoS = LTH   AND
FiRoS = LTH: **lwm**

In these rules, semantic concepts have been used to define variables in learning schemes like watersnowsize represents the relative size of water region with respect to snow and 'T','M' or 'B' denote the respective variable calculated in top (top three rows), middle (rows 4 - 7) and bottom (rows 8 -10) regions of the image. The symbols "Bf", "Eq", "BM" etc represent Allen's relations "Before" and "Equal" and "Before or Meets" respectively, while "LTH", "GTH" and "AEQ" represent relative size of two concepts to be "Less than", "Greater than" or "Almost Equal". We present rules here in the raw form as extracted but these could easily be made more human-readable in an automatic way. e.g the rule for DS2 can be read as: "If water and snow are approximately equal in size in the bottom region AND trunks and rocks cover the same vertical portion of the middle of the image

AND sky and field cover the same vertical portion of the bottom of the image THEN image is categorised as 'fields'.

5. Conclusions

We have presented an approach to develop a qualitative and semantically meaningful approach for image categorization based on underlying semantic knowledge and on qualitative spatial image description. The approach does not rely either on segmentation techniques applied directly on low level image features for an image description. Moreover, image categorization is purely based on learning from a semantic qualitative representation contrary to most previous techniques which use quantitative metrics for determining the class memberships. It has also been observed that the classification accuracy can be significantly increased by deploying an improved image region labelling scheme or if two overlapping classes namely coasts and lwm are merged together.

We thank Julia Vogel for providing labelled data set and helpful discussions and acknowledge financial support provided by National University of Sciences & Technology, Rawalpindi – Pakistan, and EPSRC grant EP/DO61334/1 to Zia Ul Qayyum and A.G. Cohn, respectively.

References

1. Allen, J. F. "Maintaining knowledge about temporal intervals". In Communications of ACM, vol. 26, no. 11, November 1983.

2. Boutell, M., Luo, J., Shen, X., and Brown, C. "Learning multi-label scene classification". Pattern Recognition, vol. 37, no.9, pp. 1757-1771, September 2004.

3. Cristianini, N. and Shaw-Taylor, J. "An introduction to support vector machines and other kernel based methods". Cambridge University Press, 2000.

4. Freund, Y., and Schapire, E. R. "Experiments with a new boosting algorithm". Proceedings of Thirteenth International Conference on Machine Learning, pp. 148-156, 1996.

5. Gorkani,M.M., and Picard, W.R. "Texture orientation for sorting photos at a glance". In Proceedings of International Conference on Pattern Recognition, Vol.I, pp. 459-464, Jerusalem, Israel, October 1994.

6. Maron, O. and Lakshmi Ratan, A. "Multiple-instance learning for natural scene classification". In Proceedings of 15th International Conference on Machine Learning, PP 341-349, 1998.

7. Maron, O., and Lozano-Pe'rez, T. "A framework for multiple instance learning". Advances in Neural Information Processing Systems, 10,1998.

8. Mao, J., and Jain, A.K. "Texture classification and segmentation using multiresolution simultaneous autoregressive models". Pattern Recognition, Vol. 25, No. 2, Pp 173-188, 1992.

9. Mörchen, F., Ultsch, A.: Discovering Temporal Knowledge in Multivariate Time Series, Weihs, C., Gaul, W. (Eds), In Classification; The Ubiquitous Challenge, Proceedings 28th Annual Conference of the German Classification Society (GfKl 2004), Dortmund, Germany, Springer, Heidelberg, (2005), pp. 272-279.

10. Mukerjee, A., and Joe, G. "A Qualitative Model for Space". In Proceedings of AAAI-90, Morgan Kaufmann Publishers, pp 721-727, 1990.

11. Oliva, A., Torralba, A., Guerin-Dugue, A., and Herault, A. "Global semantic classification of scenes using power spectrum templates". In Challenges of Image Retrieval CIR. Newcastle UK, 1999.

12. Pal, N.R. and Pal, S.K. " A review of image segmentation techniques". Pattern Recognition, Vol. 26, Pp. 1277-1294, 1993.

13. Picard, R., and Minka, T. "Vision texture for annotation". ACM Journal of Multimedia Systems, 1995.

14. Quinlan, J.R. "C 4.5: Programs for machine learning". Morgan Kaufman Publishers, Inc. 1993.

15. Szummer, M., and Picard, R. "Indoor outdoor image classification". In Workshop on Content-based Access of Image and Video Databases. Bombay, India, January 1998.

16. Serrano, N., Savakis, A., and Luo, J. "Improved scene classification using efficient low level features and semantic cues". Pattern Recognition, vol. 37, no. 9, pp. 1773-1784, September 2004.

17. Town, C., and Sinclair, D. "Content-based image retrieval using semantic visual categories". Tech. Report 2000.14, AT&T Laboratories Cambridge, 2000.

18. Vailaya, A., Jain, A., and Zhang, H. "On image classification: cit vs landscape". Pattern Recognition, vol 31, no. 12, pp. 1921-1935, December 1998.

19. Vailaya, A., Figueiredo, M., Jain, A., and Zhang, H.J. "Bayesian Framework for Hierarchical Semantic Classification of Vacation Images". IEEE International Conference on Multimedia Computing and Systems, pp. 518 -523 vol.1, 1999.

20. Vogel, J., and Schiele, B. "A semantic typicality measure for natural scene categorization". In: Pattern Recognition Symposium DAGM 2004, Tubingen, Germany, September 2004.

21. Vogel, J. "Semantic scene modelling and retrieval". PhD Thesis of Julia Vogel, selected Readings in Vision and Graphics, Vol. 33, Hartung-Gorre Verlag Konstanz, 2004.

22. Walischewski, H. "Learning regions of interest in postal automation". In Proceedings of 5th International Conference on Document Analysis and Recognition (ICDAR'99), 1999,Bangalore, India.

23. Witten, I.H., and Frank, E. "Data Mining, Practical machine learning tools and techniques with JAVA implementations". Morgan Kaufman Publishers, 2000.

24. Frank, E. and Witten, I.H. "Generating Accurate Rule Sets Without Global Optimization." In Shavlik, J., ed., Machine Learning: Proceedings of the Fifteenth International Conference, Morgan Kaufmann Publishers, 1998.

A Platform for Simulating Language Evolution

Carl Vogel and Justin Woods*
Computational Linguistics Group
Trinity College Dublin
Dublin 2, Ireland
vogel@tcd.ie

Abstract

A platform for conducting experiments in the simulation of natural language evolution is presented. The system is paramaterized for independent specification of important features like: number of agents, communication attempt frequency, agent short term memory capacity, communicative urgency, etc. Representative experiments are demonstrated.

1   Background

A large and growing literature on natural language evolution argues specific claims (e.g. the bidrectional sign emerges as an optimal linguistic information structuring device (Hurford, 1989)), through construction of special purpose simulations, and demonstrating relevant emergent behavior within those systems. Any simulation of emergent behavior has to be scrutinized for the possibility that the behavior is actually determined by the way underlying assumptions are encoded in initial conditions of the system. If initial conditions, rather than parameters of influence, determine the emergent behavior, then it has not truly emerged. Equally, some of the encoded assumptions may not in fact determine the outcome, but may be nonetheless questionable and worthy setting as an input parameter rather than as a precondition. Many assumptions are innocuous, but others are fundamental to the sorts of results that can emerge in these tailored systems.[1] When these risks are attended to properly, a very interesting program of research can be pursued, as has been documented widely in the literature. An argument is presented here that a platform is necessary which is parameterized for as many of these assumptions as possible so that the interaction of values for the relevant parameters may be more comprehensively explored in a common setting. A system which meets some of these requirements is detailed in §2. The system has been under development for some time (Vogel & Woods, 2002). This article describes its present incarnation, and the results of experiments conducted within it in response to relevant questions that persist in the literature about language evolution.

---

*Now: European Patent Office, Gitschiner Strasse 103, D-10969 Berlin (jwoods@epo.org)

[1]Steels (1997), for example simulates a world in which only 10 objects exist.

The simplifying assumption of semantic transparency is surprisingly prevalent in research practice in simulating language evolution. For example, Hurford (1989) simulated populations of interlocutors associating concepts with symbols on the basis of different sampling strategies. The sampling is of how other agents map symbols to concepts when they produce utterances and when they interpret utterances. In his simulations, the Saussureans, the ones who use one sort of sampling to dictate their own utterances and interpretations, are the winners. A bidirectional sign emerges from the assumption that it is possible to ascertain what other language users mean by something at the very start of language development. Kirby (1998) considers the extent to which language development (its complexities and systematicities) can be explained without direct genetic factors. He measures the size of the grammar in relation to the number of expressible meanings over time. He models utterances as pairs of forms and meanings. "Each individual learns only from utterances (form-meaning pairs) produced by its neighbors" (Kirby, 1998, p. 7). Thus, here again learners of the language have direct access to intended meaning.

Here as well, the assumption is troubling. Other researchers have also noted this. Oliphant (1999) describes a social/cultural model with a consideration of genetic factors. Smith (2002) discusses research on either side of the assumption that language is a genetic or social construct. Oliphant comments on the fact that it is problematic to assume that hearers are presented with transparent access to intended meanings, with an example isomorphic to Quine's "Gavagai". However, in the simulations he constructs he nonetheless assumes that learners have simultaneous access to signals and meanings, leaving it as "an open question how learners extract the signal/meaning pairs that they associate" (Oliphant, 1999, p.g. 16). The intention here is to examine directly this association without assuming it as a given. If early agents originally had perfect communication of meaning as a means to make arbitrary linguistic associations with them, there is nothing to motivate making the mapping. The only apparent advantage of language as a transparent representation system for meanings is in recording meanings in the context of a broken chain of communicators (if one has a non-broken chain of communicators, then meanings can be passed from one directly to another) and in that case the language as a mapping between arbitrary sounds and meanings might serve as a means of communicating otherwise lost information. However, this would suggest either that writing systems would be much older than they are or that in the early days of language, parrots were more prolific and interwoven into human life than researchers have until now concluded from fossil evidence. There is, of course, a lot of advantage in having language available as a distinctly imperfect representation system with peace-keeping potential inherent in ambiguity and other individual advantages that might accrue from being able to lie. However, an imperfect representation system would have little need to assume prior perfect communication of meaning to accompany the bootstrapping.

Another assumption implicit in the evolution literature which requires close examination is the speed with which especially social models of linguistic development should proceed towards convergence. For example, the work mentioned by Oliphant (1999) includes experiments that reach a stable state after about 1000 rounds; similarly that of Steels (1997). However, particularly if language is a socially sustained construct, it would seem that for a language to come into existence at all, and to persist as a cultural artifact, it must prove quite useful quite quickly. Even assuming that it does make communication easier, thus enhancing adaptive value, one would want a situation in which without cheating by allowing interlocutors free access to meaning anyway roughly successful communication (or at least not obviously unsuccessful communication) emerges extremely quickly. It is extremely difficult to imagine the first users of language lasting more than a few dozen unsuccessful attempts at linguistic behavior, much less thousands.

Certain fundamental features of the simulation platform are still lacking, and arguably some will always be lacking: a simulation of natural language evolution will never count as the evolution of a natural language. However, the factors which impinge on the simulation may well be related to the real thing.

2 A Language Evolution Workbench

2.1 Design Issues

The experiments reported in §3 are based on a general architecture for simulating social models of language evolution.[2] The following set of parameters is provided within the system; these are named and outlined in §2.1.1–§2.1.6.

2.1.1 Number of agents

Steels (1997) reports on an experiment involving up to 50 agents, with ten active agents at any moment in time. There is an initial population, and gradual turnover not sensitive to communicative success (hence, this is a social model rather than a selectionist one). The experiments of Hurford (1989) involved a constant population size of 30 agents. Hurford (2000) supposes that at any one time there are four adults and one child language learner. The workbench presented here allows as an independent parameter the specification of an integer number of agents. Clearly, the capacity to experiment with a range of settings is desirable. Setting the value of the parameter at 1 essentially models the situation in which an agent evolves a language of thought in the Chomskyan sense, rather than an externally viable communicative tool.

Other agent-based features would be useful as parameters, given the sorts of experiments that have been conducted in the literature to date. Interaction constraints among agents are not modelled at present (for example, one might want to suppose that more than one agent can hear an utterance in a context at any one moment of time). Elimination of agents over time is not modeled.

---

[2]The system is implemented in sicstus-Prolog. It is available to other researchers to experiment with their own views on parameter settings, and for relevant enhancements that parallel our own development of the system.

2.1.2 Size of phoneme space

Human languages vary widely in the number of phonemes they make use of de Boer (1997) reports on a range of 11 to 141, with around 30 as a typical range for a human language. Clearly, there is an interaction between the number of discriminable sounds and the number of atomic signals available in a language, even if at a basic level, phonemes are meaningless, but give rise to the duality of patterning in which meaningful units may be formed (Carstairs-McCarthy, 1998a, 1998b). In the system described here, the total number of phonemes available to each agent may be specified, but constraints on potential co-occurrence of phonemes cannot be stipulated (cf. de Boer, 2000).

2.1.3 Semantic Space

One of the fundamental issues to be examined in simulating the emergence of natural language is in the estimating the space of possible meanings. Setting aside abstract entities and intensions, it is important when considering a simulation to know whether it assumes an open or closed semantic space in extensional terms: the number of objects that exist and the number of relations that they can stand in. Thus, there are two relevant dependant parameters: **Size of entity pool** and the **Size of relation pool**.

Note that the simulations of Hurford (1989) operate five objects and seven signals. Steels (1997) assumes 10 and Kirby (2000) assumes 100 possible meanings. While the results that they obtain are interesting, it seems that a richer semantic space is prerequisite to language: with a finite atomic space of meanings, compositional signals are unnecessary. Thus, in the system described here, any natural number of discriminable entity types may be named, and any number of instantiations of seven basic event types are possible.

Relation types are as follows: R^1(one animate argument); R^2(two animate args); R^3(one human arg, one unconstrained arg, one animate arg); R^4(two animate args and one inanimate); R^5(one human arg and one relation arg); R^6(one unconstrained arg); R^7(one human arg, one unconstrained, one relation). Thus, given the number specified as an input parameter, a corresponding number of events types are constructed by distributing the number over these seven sorts of event types. A third dependent parameter, **Zipfian vs. random distribution of events**, determines whether the sorts of event are randomly distributed, or exhibit a greater systematicity. That is, in a Zipfian world certain events happen a great deal more often than other events, with a Zipfian distribution to them. Such a world might appear more structured than a randomly distributed world, and that underlying structure may lead to correspondingly more structure to utterances about the world. Nonetheless, it is a parameter to explore in its interaction with other parameters of the system. That the meaning space is open ended is ensured by event types which conform to schema (R^5) and (R^7) which are recursively structured (e.g. like believing one is seeing someone see some other event.) If one were to allow fourteen event types, and if a random distribution resulted in an even distribution of those fourteen among the seven schema, then there would be four basic sorts of one place events that could happen, two constrained to have animate objects and two allowing inanimate arguments as well. Similarly, four event types would allow recursion. The discriminibiliy of an event type is distinct from its occurrence. Thus, any instance of a recursive event can involve arbitrarily much recursive event structure. Hence, the space of possible things to communicate about when events of the constructed types start to happen is unlimited: the meaning space is unbounded, even though extensional.

2.1.4 Number and length of epochs

The **number of epochs** is one of a number of dependent parameters which jointly determine the duration of a simulation. **Epoch length** can be thought of as a span of communication among agents in which events happen, one agent produces a comment on the event and another agent interprets that comment relative to its own perception of the event. Given that this is about the association of signals to meanings for the very first time, it is reasonable to imagine that one parameter should be a sort of **forgetting threshold**, such that if a symbol-meaning association is not frequent enough during a stretch of conversation, then it is forgotten. Thus, an **epoch length** as set here is the point at which new, under-utilized, associations are forgotten. The forgetting threshold can be seen as mimicking the effect of lexical self-propagation among groups of agents and the random turnover of agents provided in Oliphant's (1999) social model. Section 3 outlines results of simulations in which the parameter is set to 0, thus providing a purely social/cultural model. The **number of epochs** is then the total number of such conversations to model.

2.1.5 Communicative Success

It is implicit in the discussion so far that some research in the area pursues a genetic model of language evolution (e.g. Hurford, 1989) and others favor a social model (e.g. Kirby, 2000). Both of these instances of those approaches, and, in fact rather a lot of simulations in the literature, assume a semantic transparency in which during learning stages the simulated interlocutors have access to each other's signal and meaning pairs. The rest of the system dynamics bootstrap from telepathy. Separate from whether interlocutors can know that they are 'talking about the same thing', it is possible to model success of communication. The least assumption-laden approach to the onset of communication is apparently fairly pessimistic: events happen, but agents individuate events according to their own perspectives, and comment on them accordingly. Because this is about the ontogenesis of language there is no good reason to assume that there are shared ways of mapping symbols onto meanings (unless one makes the assumption that in fact, everyone share's one's own mappings). In such a pessimistic setting, interlocutors can have a measure of success if they see the world the same way, but describe it differently. Language may have emerged to satisfy the needs of gossip more than survival (cf. Power,

2000), but success in actual communication probably does matter some times. The examples provided by Cushing (1994) about miscommunications involving aircraft crashes are striking in part because such spectacular ramifications of miscommunications so rarely ensue. Thus, in the simulation platform discussed here, it is possible to set at a value between zero and one the **Probability that success matters**, and within that, if any particular coin toss determines that success does matter, **Level of necessary success** necessary.

2.1.6 *Sensitivity to recency vs. frequency*

A final parameter that we mention here relates to how an agent constructs an utterance in response to an event or how an agent comes to interpret an utterance. The system assumes that creative language use is also a possibility, but that there is a tendency for each agent to explore its memory of past associations between symbols and meanings during production and interpretation. Because of the preponderance of recency and frequency effects in human behavior, it seemed reasonable to include agent sensitivity to one or other of these as a parameter in exploring differential impact on emergent system dynamics. An agent who is sensitive to recency rather than frequency has access only to local coordination processes as only the most recent prior event can have an impact on the current one, while frequency based agents have additional access to global co-ordination (cf. Garrod & Doherty, 1994)

Of these parameters, phoneme space and semantic discrimination capacity are explored in detail in §3. In addition to issues named above in which the system does not provide a mechanism for providing relevant constraints on parameters, other parameters are under exploration.

2.2 Measurable Quantities

Before providing details about the representations and key algorithms involved, we mention some of the system behaviors that are interesting to measured as a way of assessing the state of convergence on a communicative system: Level of understanding achieved in a communication; Average understanding of last 10 utterances; Homonomy ratio; Synonymy ratio; utterance complexity.

While the interlocutors themselves cannot inspect each others' meanings, it is possible to externally monitor their degree of communicative success. Even with pessimistic assumptions about the amount of miscommunication that might persist in the world, actual communication can be successful, unbeknownst to the interlocutors. Convergence on use of terms can emerge even if individuals assume only that they share meanings without attending to evidence either way. Success in communication is computed as an average over all communications and in the ten most recent utterances.

However, other meaning-based assessments of linguistic innovation are also important. Evidently, natural language tolerates more homonomy than synonomy; 'synonomy' here refers to a state in which one meaning can be denoted by a larger number of *basic* expressions. Natural language supports a larger amount of synonymy at the phrasal level than lexical. If one were rationally designing a language one would prefer the alternative of more synonymy than homonymy to increase the likelihood of arriving at the same meaning from distinct signals rather than having the same signal yield many meainings. While we accept a point emphasized by Steels and Kaplan (1999) to the effect that homonomy is most acceptable when the intended meanings of homonym sets is maximally distinct, we nonetheless take it as an independent validation of linguistic properties within a simulation system for the number of synonyms to be smaller than the number of homonyms.

Any number of important measures of the system dynamics can be made, and here we have commented on measures we have been using to guide our understanding of the mutual impact of various parameter settings. Some of these measures could be calculated in different ways, and additional measures included.

2.3   Implementation Issues

The system does not assume that there is transparency of meaning, does assume that agents have the same space of possible meanings available to them, and the same range of basic concepts. However, agents need not segment events into constituent events in the same way, even though they decompose complex events into the same set of conceptual atoms. Entities, entity types and event types are represented as Prolog atoms, their numbers are determined by settings to input parameters. Events themselves are modeled as instances of Prolog lists pairing event types with arguments. Entities are classified as either human, animal or inanimate, with event types selecting arguments of type: human, animal, animate, inanimate, event type or without constraint.

Based on the numbers given as parameters, a corresponding number of event types and entities is created, assigning them to the possible categories as disscussed in §2.1.3. Random distinct Prolog atoms are constructed for each, varying in form for human readability. An example event is this:

(1)   [ihdixos,spmg,davr,fizg];

where ihdixos was an atom constructed to correspond to an event type with, it happens, an animate first argument, an inanimate second argument and an animate third argument. Animacy of the arguments actual arguments is randomly assigned, but relations are constructed to have expectations of which arguments can participate in its limited set of roles. Recall that some event types embed relations as arguments. Thus, although there are a finite number of events as provided by an input parameter, if one or more of those event types is of a sort that allows embedding, then during the course of simulation in which events happen and speakers comment on them, individual events may be arbitrarily complex. In the limit there is an infinite number of possible events even given finite specification of the number of event types. This is richer than boundless iterability of a finite set of events.

Perhaps more important is that the events do not themselves prejudice learning towards the context free grammar implicit in a predicate argument representation of an event with the functor providing the left-hand nonterminal and the arguments supplying the righ-hand side of a production. When an event happens (e.g. (2)) the speaker selects a random element of the set of all sublists of the event, where each list of sublists corresponds to a perspective on the event. For example, (3) and (4) are two distinct perspectives an agent might have with respect to the example event.

(2)   [ihdixos,spmg,davr,fizg]

(3)   [[ihdixos],[spmg],[davr],[fizg]]

(4)   [[ihdixos],[spmg,davr],[fizg]]

The speaker and hearer are not constrained to have the same perspective.

Phonemes are also arbitrary atoms. A speaker, upon witnessing some event, uses pairs of phonemes to refer to each element of the event. At the outset, this involves invented pairs for the association, but over time, past experience interacts. Thus, one element of constraining structure imposed on the model, is that speakers try to talk about the entirety of their perspective on an event placed before them. However, through iteration between being a speaker and a hearer, a speaker may come to prefer a more complicated way of referring:

(5)   Event: [jilufks,furk]
       Uttered: [[[jilufks],[[r,q],[r,v]]],[[furk],[[e,y]]]]
       Heard: [[[vmpk],[[r,q]]],[[furk],[[r,v],[e,y]]]]

Here an event occurred, and a speaker used a four-phoneme complex,

(6)   [[r,q],[r,v]]

to pick out the event type and a two phoneme complex to pick out the argument. Thus, words are modeled as lists of pairs of phonemes unrestricted in length. There is sufficient space for duality of patterning to emerge without being built-in. No model of articulatory constraints on possible phoneme pairings is made.

The hearer has unobscured access to the same event commented on by the speaker. This models the sharing of cognitive possibilities among communicating agents. However, perspectival divergence is also possible. The hearer can partition the event differently. The onus on the hearer is not to find a phoneme sequence for each part of the perspective on the event, but something in the conceptual space for each phoneme sequence to mean. Another assumption that is not parameterized is that there is no noise—while the hearer may segment the signal differently (as above), the hearer has perfect access to the stream of phonemes uttered, but not segmentation or denotation.

The asymmetry in responsibility between speaker and hearer does not contradict the Saussurean perspective. Speaker is required to comment on everything in its perspective on the event; hearer is required to ground every word it segments from the signal either in its perspective on the shared event or on past interpretations. Perspective is known to confound theoretical assumptions. Schober (1993) demonstrates the lack of speaker attention to hearer perspective in identifying use conditions for definites. The asymmetry we suggest here contradicts the Saussurean perspective only to the extent that those empirical findings do.

There is no initial grammar that constrains the system, neither explicitly, nor implicitly in the structure of semantic representations of events. There are only associations of meaning sequences with phoneme sequences.

2.3.1 Algorithms

The basic architecture of the system involves iterating through the following process based on the input parameters.[3]

1. Initialize:

   clear memory, etc.

   generate enough agents$^\pi$, phonemes$^\pi$, entities$^\pi$ and relations$^\pi$

2. If out of Epochs$^\pi$, show statistics & quit.

3. Forget any symbol/meaning pair from the last epoch that occurred no more often than the forgetting threshold$^\pi$

4. Run another epoch.

   (a) Some relation obtains at random

   (b) A speaker comments on that event, note taken

   (c) A hearer observes the event and interprets the utterance, note taken

   (d) Omniscients observe the degree of common understanding

   (e) If it's a situation falling under the probability that success matters$^\pi$, and if success is less than a threshold percentage$^\pi$,

   then ignore the utterance

   else, note the symbol/meaning association (updating frequencies), and go to 4a

5. Goto 2

This algorithm involves iterations of speakers commenting on events, and hearers interpreting utterances in the context of a jointly witnessed event. These subroutines are outlined below. Both speakers and hearers have the capacity to innovate. Both speakers and hearers are influenced by the history of communication (modulo that which is forgotten because it happened so infrequently). That influence of history may be frequency based (depending on all prior utterances) or recency based (depending on the most recent utterance). Because over time speakers and hearers will interchange roles and be equally influenced by their own past interpretations as by associations put forward through their utterances, there is a communal knowledge base of past interpretations. It is important to point out that in our idealization there is

---

[3] A superscript is supplied for each quantity that is parameterized.

only one knowledge base of past utterances, modeling the agents' dual roles as speakers on some occasions and hearers on others.[4] This is not a model of differential memories among the participants, nor is there a real model of information state beyond the immediate event. A richer extension of the system would include participant-indexed knowledge bases and information states, with updates, downdates, queries, disputes and acknowledgements.

Speaker comment on events

1. The event is modeled as the list of atoms given by a relation name and its arguments.

2. The speaker individuates that event.
   This is modeled by:

   (a) This list of possible partitions of the event list is formed.

   (b) A random partitioning is selected from that list.

3. The speaker associates a symbol/phoneme sequence with the structured perceived meaning.
   This is in partial relation to what has been uttered and construed before.
   For each meaning segment in the speaker's individuated meaning:

   (a) Identify all the phonemes associated with it in the past

   (b) If that list is nonempty:

      i. Choose a random element of it.[5]

      ii. If some chance event happens, whose probability diminishes with the number of words uttered (and remembered) so far, then just invent a new phoneme sequence to associate with the meaning.[6]
      Otherwise, the uttered phoneme sequence is the random choice among past events.

   Otherwise, that meaning hasn't been noted before, so make up a new phoneme pair to associate with the meaning unit.

Hearer interpretation of an event

1. The interpreter hears an event and segments the stream into units.

2. Interpretation associates meanings with the segments in relation to the event that occurred and the history of past associations

3. The interpreter is either frequency$^\pi$ or recency$^\pi$ sensitive.

---

[4] One could well argue that this idealization is at best of an individual communicating with itself. To the extent that it's a valid argument, one must also agree that communicating with oneself is a nontrivial ability to have emerged. Recall, for example, Jaynes's (1976) hypothesis that the origin of human consciousness is in the integration of the hemispheres, the end of interhemisphere intraindividual discrete communication; also recall the arguments of Fodor (1983) and Chomsky's minimalism that the role of language is not so much interpersonal communication as interfacing to the rest of cognitive architecture.

[5] This implements frequency effects: it is not the most frequent pairing that is necessarily selected, but frequent pairings have higher probability of selection from memory than infrequent pairings.

[6] Thus, innovation is possible at any stage, whether influenced by frequency$^\pi$ or recency$^\pi$.

(a) If there are no more "words" in the segmentation, association is done.

(b) Find all past associations of meanings with the next word.

    i. If frequency sensitive, select a random element of this list as the current interpretation of the word.

    ii. Otherwise, if recency sensitive, select the last interpretation of the word as the current.

    iii. If no past associations exist for the word, then on the basis of the hearer's own individuation of the event, associate a meaning-segment with the speech segment.

(c) Goto 3a

Notice that the model assumes that speakers have more opportunities for innovation than hearers, but that both have opportunity to innovate.

3 Sample Experiments & Results

Assume the following parameter settings: Number of agents: 100; Size of phoneme space: 41; Size of entity pool: 1000; Size of relation pool: 100; Number of epochs: 30; Attention span: 30; Forgetting threshold: 0; Probability that success matters: 25%; Level of necessary success: 75%; Sensitivity to frequency; Zipfian event distribution. A typical run of the simulation will have the behavior as graphed below on the left. The plot on the right holds all of the other parameters constant, but uses a random distribution of events types.

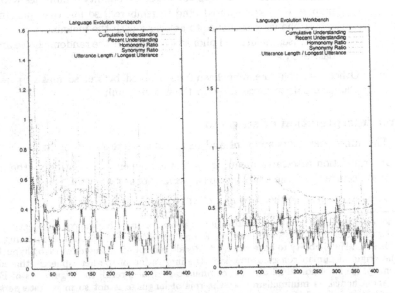

The two graphs both plot utterances on the x axis and an interpretation of the y axis as a percentage. The value exceeds 1 when an utterance exceeds the length of the longest utterance so far. In both cases, synonym and homonym ratios appear to cross path In both cases, average recent understanding, the amount of utterance signal and meaning pairs speakers and hearers agree upon, is relatively quickly in the 30% range, yet slightly better in the non-zipfian world. Note that these are not particularly demanding constraints on the likelihood that mutual understanding is important, or its level of importance when it is important. The following two are represenative runs just like the above pair, but with understanding set at the inverse level: 75% chance that an utterance's meaning matters, but when it does, a 25% level of sharing is necessary before the interlocutors move on to the next event.

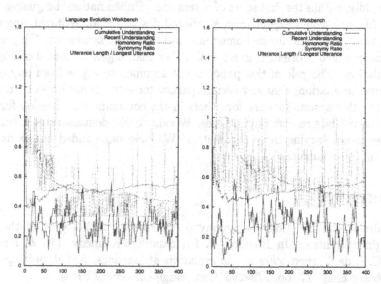

These outputs are intended to indicate the sorts of experiments that one might conduct using the simulation platform. Additionally, it would be possible to plot other relevant values, perhaps localizing the evaluations to individuals rather than summing over all of them as in the plots depicted.

4 General Discussion

In some other theoretical work and also some simulations it is assumed that language evolution begins with perfect mappings between primal utterances and associated meanings, those mappings available to the language learner from the start of learning, and even as language itself begins its evolution. We do not feel that it solves any problems to assume that initial communications are perfect (which is what one has if both utterance and meaning are available to both speaker and hearer) and that what evolves are complications in syntactic features. In our model, this is a parameter: although we can observe the degree to which understanding has taken place, it isn't necessarily the case that the interlocutors know both what was said and what was meant. A question we explore is whether under such pessimistic assumptions about interintelligiblity a systematic language can emerge with actually successful communication, success rated by external observers.

We have presented an implemented system which has been used to explore parameters in simulations of linguistic evolution which might serve among the preconditions for the first appearance of language. We have shown here the perhaps surprising result that external observers of communicators who do not know if they are communicating successfully, under a range of reasonable parameter settings, tend to observe better than chance success in linguistic communication between the agents. We also observe that convergence on successful communication under reasonable parameter settings tends to happen very rapidly, within the first score of utterances. Unlike natural languages, and rather like one would expect from a rational design for an artificial language, the system tends to minimize homonomy and maximize synonymy. We present the system which is oriented to a social rather than a genetic model of linguistic evolution. The role of this paper is not so much to argue from any other particular simulations that any certain parameter settings are important, as it is to offer this system forward for others in the community to develop further and cross-validate research hypotheses. Woods (2003) demonstrates a number of experiments varying those parameters. We have since added questions and reflection (metalanguage).[7]

References

Carstairs-McCarthy (1998a). Synonymy avoidance, phonology and the origin of syntax. In Hurford, J. R., Studdert-Kennedy, M., & Knight, C. (Eds.), *Approaches to the evolution of language. Social and cognitive bases*, chap. 17, pp. 279–296. Cambridge University Press.

Carstairs-McCarthy, A. (1998b). *The Origins of Complex Language: An Inquiry into the Evolutionary Beginnings of Sentences, Syllables and Truth.* Oxford: Oxford University Press.

Cushing, S. (1994). *Fatal Words: Communication Clashes and Aircraft Crashes.* University of Chicago Press.

de Boer, B. (1997). Self organisation in vowel systems through imitation. In Coleman, J. (Ed.), *Computational Phonology, Third Meeting of the ACL SIGPHON*, pp. 19–25.

de Boer, B. (2000). Emergence of sound systems through self-organization. In Knight, C., Studdert-Kennedy, M., & Hurford, J. (Eds.), *The Evolutionary Emergence of Language: Social Function and the Origins of Linguistic Form*, pp. 177–198. Cambridge University Press.

Fodor, J. A. (1983). *The Modularity of Mind.* Cambridge: MIT Press.

Garrod, S. & Doherty, G. (1994). Conversation, co-ordination and convention: an empirical investigation of how groups establish linguistic conventions. *Cognition, 53*, 181–215.

---

[7] Lucinda Longmore, MSc dissertation in preparation, TCD.

Hurford, J. (1989). Biological evolution of the saussurean sign as a component of the language acquisition device. *Lingua*, *77*, 187–222.

Hurford, J. (2000). Social transmission favours linguistic generalisation. In Knight, C., Studdert-Kennedy, M., & Hurford, J. (Eds.), *The Evolutionary Emergence of Language: Social Function and the Origins of Linguistic Form*, pp. 324–352. Cambridge University Press.

Jaynes, J. (1976). *The Origins of Consciousness in the Breakdown of the Bicameral Mind.* Princeton.

Kirby, S. (1998). Syntax without natural selection: how compositionality emerges from vocabulary in a population of learners. In Knight (Ed.), *Second International Conference on the Evolution of Language.* Oxford: Oxford University Press.

Kirby, S. (2000). Syntax without natural selection: how compositionality emerges from vocabulary in a population of learners. In Knight, C., Studdert-Kennedy, M., & Hurford, J. (Eds.), *The Evolutionary Emergence of Language*, pp. 303–323. Cambridge University Press.

Oliphant, M. (1999). The learning barrier: moving from innate to learned systems of communication. *Adaptive Behavior*, *7*(3-4), 371–384.

Power, C. (2000). Secret language use at female initiation: bounding gossiping communities. In Knight, C., Hurford, J. R., & Studdert-Kennedy, M. (Eds.), *The Evolutionary Emergence of Language*, chap. 5, pp. 80–97. Cambridge University Press.

Schober, M. F. (1993). Spatial perspective-taking in conversation. *Cognition*, *47*, 1–24.

Smith, K. (2002). Natural selection and cultural selection in the evolution of communication. *Adaptive Behavior*, *10*(1), 25–44.

Steels, L. & Kaplan, F. (1999). Bootstrapping grounded word semantics. In Briscoe, T. (Ed.), *Linguistic evolution through language acquisition: formal and computational models.* Cambridge University Press.

Steels, L. (1997). Synthesizing the origins of language and meaning using co-evolution, self-organization and level formation. In Hurford, J. (Ed.), *Evolution of Human Language.* Edinburgh University Press.

Vogel, C. & Woods, J. (2002). Simulation of evolving linguistic communication among fallible communicators. In Hurford, J. & Fitch, T. (Eds.), *Proceedings of the Fourth International Conference on the Evolution of Language*, p. 116. Harvard University, Cambrige, MA.

Woods, J. (2003). Declaratives, interrogatives, semantic space and the emergence of communication. Master's thesis, Computational Linguistics Lab, Trinity College, University of Dublin.

SHORT PAPERS

Improving the Interpretability of Classification Rules in Sparse Bioinformatics Datasets

James Smaldon and Alex A. Freitas

Computing Laboratory, University of Kent, Canterbury, CT2 7NF, UK

James.Smaldon@gmail.com, A.A.Freitas@kent.ac.uk

Abstract

This paper proposes a modification in rule induction algorithms aimed at improving the interpretability of the discovered rules. This modification is proposed in the context of sparse bioinformatics data sets where the presence of a feature is much less common than its absence, so that rule conditions with positive values of the feature tend to be more informative than rule conditions with negative values of that feature. The proposed modification consists of inducing only rules having positive values of the features, rather than rules using both positive and negative values of the features.

1. Introduction

The motivation for this paper came from a case study in bioinformatics reported in [6], where a biologist had difficulty in interpreting many rules discovered by a data mining algorithm. In that application the vast majority of the predictor attributes denoted whether or not a protein had a certain biological motif. For each motif (attribute), the value "present" was much less frequent in the data than the value "absent", i.e., the dataset was very sparse. Hence, a rule with conditions of the form "IF a protein has biological motif X" was easier to be interpreted by the biologist than a rule with conditions of the form "IF a protein does not have biological motif X", because the latter is much less informative.

The central idea of this paper is to modify two rule induction algorithms to discover rules having in their antecedent only conditions of the form "IF a protein has biological motif X", and not conditions of the form "IF a protein does not have biological motif X", in order to improve the interpretability of the discovered rules. Rule interpretability is often important in data mining [4], [8].

2. Rule Induction with Modified CN2 and Ant-Miner

The two rule induction algorithms modified in this work are CN2 and Ant-Miner. CN2 is a well-known rule induction algorithm [2]. Ant-Miner is based on the relatively new paradigm of ant colony optimisation [7]. Both CN2 and Ant-Miner are sequential covering algorithms, where a classification rule is discovered, examples covered by the discovered rule are removed from the training set and the process is repeated until (almost) all training examples are covered. Both algorithms construct a classification rule by adding one condition at a time to the rule, and they discover rules whose antecedent can include both conditions of the form "IF a protein *has* biological motif X" – called *present-motif* conditions – and conditions of the form "IF a protein *does not have* biological motif X" – called *absent-motif* conditions. In order to improve the rule interpretability, we modify these algorithms to discover rules having *present-motif-only* conditions.

In the original CN2 and Ant-Miner algorithms the set of candidate conditions is initialized with all conditions of the form $(A_i = V_{ij})$, where V_{ij} is the j-th value of the i-th attribute, $\forall i,j$. By contrast, in the proposed modification (for both algorithms) the set of candidate conditions is initialized only with *present-motif-only* conditions, i.e., conditions of the form $(A_i = $ "present"). Once a condition is added to a rule, the system removes just that condition from the set of candidate conditions to be considered in the next iteration of the rule construction procedure. By contrast, in the original algorithms, when a condition like $(A_i = $ "present") is added to a rule, the system has to remove both that condition and the condition $(A_i = $ "absent") from the set of candidate rules.

3. Datasets and Experimental Setup

Experiments were done with four bioinformatics datasets involving two protein function prediction problems. The first problem consists of predicting whether or not a protein has post-synaptic activity, based on the biological motifs found in the protein primary sequence [6]. Each example (record) corresponds to a protein. Each predictor attribute corresponds to a Prosite pattern (a biological motif). An attribute can take on the value "present" or "absent", indicating whether or not the Prosite pattern occurs in a protein. The class attribute is post-synaptic activity, which can take on "yes" or "no". The second problem is the classification of G-Protein Coupled Receptors (GPCRs). In the 3 GPCR datasets used in our experiments [5], each example (record) corresponds to a protein. However, different kinds of predictor attributes (motifs) were used in the 3 datasets, viz.: Interpro entries, Prints motifs, and Prosite patterns. All these attributes are binary, indicating whether or not a protein has a motif.

The datasets used in our experiments are somewhat modified versions of the datasets used in [6], [5], as follows. First, the post-synaptic dataset described in [6] included 2 continuous attributes (sequence length and molecular weight). In our experiments these 2 attributes were removed – only the Prosite pattern attributes were used. Second, in the GPCR datasets described in [5] the classes to be predicted are arranged in a four-level hierarchy. Our experiments involved only the prediction of classes at the first level of the hierarchy. Third, both the post-synaptic dataset [6] and the GPCR datasets [5] had a large number of attributes. In order to greatly reduce the time taken by the rule induction algorithms, we worked only with the set of the 50 best attributes for each dataset. To perform this attribute selection we used the attribute selection algorithm described in [3]. The reduced post-synaptic dataset had 2081 examples. The 3 reduced GPCR datasets (with Interpro, Prints and Prosite motifs) had 540, 323 and 177 examples, respectively.

We used the default parameters of CN2 [1], [2]. Ant-Miner was used with its default parameters [7], [9], with the exception that the parameter Max_uncovered_cases was set to 5 in the unordered rule set version. All the results reported in the paper were obtained by performing a well-known 10-fold cross-validation experiment.

4. Computational Results

The results concerning predictive accuracy are shown in Table 1. The numbers after "±" are standard deviations. Experiments were done with the ordered rule list [2] and unordered rule set [1] versions of CN2; as well as the ordered rule list [7] and unordered rule set [9] versions of Ant-Miner.

Table 1: Comparing predictive accuracy (%) using present motif only (Pres.) vs both present and absent (Pres/Abs) motifs

Algor.	Unordered vs. ordered rules	Pres/Abs vs. Pres. motifs	Dataset			
			Post-synapt.	GPCR Interp.	GPCR Prints	GPCR Prosite
CN2	Ordered	Pres/Abs	96.92 ±0.33	90.75 ±0.85	92.25 ±0.70	81.13 ±2.62
		Pres	96.88 ±0.36	90.71 ±0.90	92.56 ±0.51	80.75 ±3.30
	Unordered	Pres/Abs	96.83 ±0.37	90.20 ±0.87	93.20 ±0.59	84.48 ±2.48
		Pres	96.78 ±0.34	**85.75 ±0.70**	93.50 ±0.29	**63.20 ±1.49**
Ant-Miner	Ordered	Pres/Abs	96.73 ±0.36	87.98 ±0.52	87.60 ±1.73	66.13 ±3.03
		Pres	**88.23 ±0.17**	**78.89 ±0.45**	85.80 ±1.73	**49.52 ±2.69**
	Unordered	Pres/Abs	96.44 ±0.47	87.02 ±0.65	96.59 ±0.56	79.74 ±1.49
		Pres	96.73 ±0.31	86.30 ±0.54	**92.29 ±0.79**	**61.67 ±0.57**

Out of 16 cases (2 algorithms × 2 kinds of rule ordering × 4 datasets), there are 7 cases (in bold in Table 1) where the use of present motifs only led to a significant drop in accuracy, by comparison with the use of both present and absent motifs. A difference in two accuracy values was considered significant if the corresponding confidence intervals – taking into account the standard deviations – do not overlap. In the other 9 cases there was no significant difference between the accuracies with present motifs only and the accuracies with both present and absent motifs. Results concerning rule simplicity (measured by the total number of conditions in all rules) are shown in Table 2. In all 16 cases, the use of present motifs only led to a significant improvement in simplicity (reduction in rule set/list size).

Table 2: Comparing the total number of conditions in all discovered rules using Present motif only (Pres) vs. Present and Absent (Pres/Abs) motifs

Algor.	Unordered vs. ordered rules	Pres/Abs vs. Pres. motifs	Post-synapt.	GPCR Interp.	GPCR Prints	GPCR Prosite
				Dataset		
CN2	Ordered	Pres/Abs	50.90 ±0.40	31.80 ±0.70	39.00 ±0.60	58.90 ±0.99
		Pres	**45.80 ±0.33**	**24.80 ±0.59**	**28.10 ±0.46**	**44.20 ±0.79**
	Unordered	Pres/Abs	57.30 ±0.47	57.90 ±1.95	68.70 ±1.46	97.10 ±2.40
		Pres	**46.60 ±0.31**	**32.90 ±0.75**	**34.60 ±0.56**	**47.60 ±1.13**
Ant-Miner	Ordered	Pres/Abs	306.91 ±10.28	233.50 ±6.27	207.30 ±6.71	217.60 ±11.74
		Pres	**9.20 ±0.20**	**3.10 ±0.10**	**2.00 ±0.00**	**2.10 ±0.10**
	Unordered	Pres/Abs	355.60 ±19.20	245.80 ±1.11	188.00 ±0.00	229.70 ±5.05
		Pres	**32.00 ±0.00**	**6.0 ±0.00**	**4.00 ±0.00**	**5.00 ±0.00**

5. Conclusions

The central idea of the proposed method – aimed at improving the interpretability of discovered rules – is to modify rule induction algorithms to discover rules having in their antecedent *present-motif-only* conditions.

Concerning the simplicity of the discovered rule sets or lists, the use of *present-motif–only* conditions consistently reduced the size of the discovered rule set or list in all cases. In addition to this clear gain in *syntactical* simplicity, the use of present motifs only has the important advantage of improving the *semantic* comprehensibility of discovered rules to biologists, because in general it is easier for biologists to interpret specific conditions of the form "IF a protein has biological motif X" than to interpret much more generic conditions of the form "IF a protein does not have biological motif X".

Concerning predictive accuracy, unfortunately the use of present-motif-only conditions led to a significant drop in accuracy in 7 out of 16 cases. On the other hand, in the majority (9 out of 16) of the cases the significant gains in syntactical and semantic simplicity were obtained without any significant drop in accuracy. This is a promising result in applications where rule interpretability is very important. However, one should be careful with the potential significant drop in predictive accuracy in applications where accuracy is very important.

Although we focused on sparse bioinformatics datasets only, the basic idea of the proposed method is also potentially useful in sparse datasets from other application domains – a possible topic for future research.

References

1. P. Clark and R. Boswell. Rule induction with CN2: some recent improvements. Proc. 5th European Working Session on Learning. 1991.

2. P. Clark and T. Niblett. The CN2 induction algorithm. Machine Learning, 3(4), 261-284. 1989.

3. E.S. Correa, A.A. Freitas and C.G. Johnson. A new discrete particle swarm algorithm applied to attribute selection in a bioinformatics data set. Proc. 2006 Genetic and Evolutionary Computation Conf. (GECCO-2006), 35-42, ACM.

4. R.J. Henery. Classification. D. Michie, D.J. Spiegelhalter, C.C. Taylor. Machine Learning, Neural and Statistical Classification, 6-16. Ellis Horwood, 1994.

5. N. Holden and A.A. Freitas. Hierarchical classification of G-protein-coupled receptors with a PSO/ACO algorithm. Proc. IEEE Swarm Intelligence Symposium (SIS-06), 77-84. IEEE, 2006.

6. G.L. Pappa, A.J. Baines and A.A. Freitas. Predicting post-synaptic activity in proteins with data mining. Bioinformatics V. 21, Supp. 2, ii19-ii25, Sep. 2005.

7. R.S. Parpinelli, H.S. Lopes and A.A. Freitas. Data Mining with an Ant Colony Optimization Algorithm. IEEE Trans. on Evolutionary Computation, 6(4), 321-332, Aug. 2002.

8. M.J. Pazzani. Knowledge discovery from data? IEEE Intellig. Systems, Mar/Apr. 2000, 10-13.

9. J. Smaldon and A.A. Freitas. A new version of the Ant-Miner algorithm discovering unordered rule sets. Proc. 2006 Genetic and Evolutionary Computation Conf. (GECCO-2006), 43-50, ACM.

An Agent-Based Approach to Non-Distributed and Distributed Clustering

Ireneusz Czarnowski and Piotr Jędrzejowicz

Department of Information Systems, Gdynia Maritime University

Morska 83, 81-225 Gdynia, Poland

E-mail: {irek, pj}@am.gdynia.pl

Abstract

The paper proposes an agent-based approach to non-distributed and distributed clustering. To solve the clustering problem instances the authors have designed and implemented a specialized A-Team architecture using JABAT middleware. The paper includes a short overview of the JABAT and a description of the proposed architecture. To evaluate the approach a computational experiment involving several well known benchmark instances of the clustering problem has been carried.

1 Introduction

The paper proposes applying the A-Team concept to obtain solutions to the non-distributed and distributed clustering problems. Clustering is the partitioning of a data set into subsets (clusters), so that the data in each subset (ideally) share some common trait - often proximity according to some defined distance measure.

While „classic" data mining algorithms invariably operate on centralized data, in practice related information is often acquired and stored at physically distributed locations due to organizational or operational constraints. Centralization of such data before analysis may not be desirable because of computational or bandwidth costs. In this paper clustering of the centralized data is referred to as a non-distributed clustering problem as opposed to a distributed clustering where the relevant data is stored at distributed locations.

A middleware environment developed by the authors and referred to as JABAT (JADE-based A-Team) is used to implement the proposed approach. The paper contains a short overview of the functionality and structure of the JABAT as well as the formulation of non-distributed and distributed clustering problems. To validate the approach computational experiment results are shown and discussed. Conclusions focus on evaluation of the proposed approach.

2 Overview of the JABAT

The JADE-based A-Team environment (JABAT) described in a more detailed manner in [2] is a middleware supporting the construction of the dedicated A-Team architectures used for solving variety of computationally hard optimization problems. JADE is an enabling technology, for the development and run-time execution of peer-to-peer applications which are based on the agents paradigm [1]. JADE allows each agent to dynamically discover other agents and to communicate with them according to the peer-to-peer paradigm.

The JADE-A-Team produces solutions to combinatorial optimization problems using a set of agents, each representing an improvement algorithm. To escape getting trapped into a local optimum an initial population of solutions called individuals is generated or constructed. Individuals forming an initial population are, at the following computation stages, improved by independently acting agents, thus increasing chances for reaching a global optimum.

To perform the above two classes of agents are used. The first class includes *OptiAgents*, which are implementations of the improvement algorithms. The second class includes *SolutionManagers*, which are agents responsible for maintenance and updating of individuals in the common memory. All agents act in parallel. Each *OptiAgent* is representing a single improvement algorithm An *OptiAgent* has two basic behaviors defined. The first is sending around messages on readiness for action including the required number of individuals (solutions). The second is activated upon receiving a message from some *SolutionManager* containing the problem instance description and the required number of individuals. This behavior involves improving fitness of individuals and resending the improved ones to a sender. A *SolutionManager* is brought to life for each problem instance. Its behavior involves sending individuals to *OptiAgents* and updating the common memory.

Main assumption behind the proposed approach is its independence from a problem definition and solution algorithms. Hence, main classes *Task* and *Solution* upon which agents act, have been defined at a rather general level. Interfaces of both classes include function *ontology()*, which returns JADE's ontology designed for classes *Task* and *Solution*, respectively.

3 JABAT-Based Approach to Clustering Problem

The clustering problem (CP) can be defined as follows. Given a set of N data objects, partition the data set into K clusters, such that similar objects are grouped together and objects with different features belong to different groups.

In a traditional approach clustering algorithms and data mining algorithm are used basing on the assumption that all data can be pooled together in a centralized data repository. In the real life there are, however, more and more cases where the data have to be physically distributed due to some constraints. As a consequence the distributed clustering is, recently, attracting a lot of attention as there are many cases where pooling distributed data for clustering is not feasible. Applying the traditional clustering tools might not be possible [3]. Hence, clustering and also knowledge discovery from multi-databases has became an important research field and is considered to be more complex and difficult task than clustering and knowledge discovery from mono-databases [4].

In this paper we propose the JABAT-based architecture with a view to solving non-distributed and distributed clustering problems. All the required classes are defined and placed in the package called *CP*. The *CP* is represented by the following classes: *CP_Task* inheriting form the *Task* class and *CP_Solution* inheriting from the *Solution* class. *CP_Solution* role is to store and maintain solutions of the clustering problem instances. A solution of the problem is represented as a permutation of vector numbers allocated to each cluster. Such a representation includes also the number of elements in each cluster and a value of the objective function. The proposed approach is based on employing three kinds of optimization agents - random local search, hillclimbing local search and tabu search agents.

To assure proper communication between optimization agents and the solution manager the *CP_TaskOntology*, inheriting from the *TaskOntology*, has been defined. This class is used to sending basic task parameters including the number of clusters, attributes and instances, as well as the location of the respective dataset. An optimization agent, after having received the message, reads the data from, the file specified in the received message. Communication in the opposite direction - from optimization agents involves resending an improved solution.

The proposed JABAT architecture is used to determine both - the number of clusters and the allocation of objects to clusters. This is achieved through repeatedly searching for the best allocation of objects to clusters for different variants of the number of clusters. Allocation generated by JABAT for each variant of the cluster number is then evaluated using the overall average silhouette width [5].

JABAT agents, acting within the predefined time slot, attempt to solve, in parallel, k^* independent clustering problems, where k^* is the arbitrarily determined maximum number of clusters. After the allowed time has elapsed, solutions obtained for different number of clusters can be evaluated and compared with solutions produced by the k-means algorithm.

The JABAT has been extended to cover the distributed clustering case. The local clustering aims at finding the optimum solution at the local sites. Using JABAT allows for agent migration to locations where the distributed data is, physically, stored. While such a migration is not always necessary since URL addresses of distributed data sets are known at the problem definition stage, migrating agents may help to better use available computational resources. A solution of the distributed clustering problem at a local level is represented by the following data: number of clusters, for each cluster a set of object numbers, for each cluster the value of its representative (its centroid), for each cluster the value of its e-range (maximum distance between the centroid and an object belonging to the cluster), value of the clustering quality measure.

Table 1: Comparison of the results - JABAT versus k-means algorithm (value of the square error of the cluster dispersion)

K	Ruspini		Iris		Heart		Credit	
	k-means	JABAT	k-means	JABAT	k-means	JABAT	k-means	JABAT
2	89337.8	89337.8	152.4	152.4	343.0	338.2	548.8	528.6
3	51063.5	51155.4	78.9	74.4	316.7	311.2	480.9	468.7
4	12881.1	12881.1	57.3	52.4	297.4	287.5	449.0	420.8
5	12138.3	11425.2	49.7	46.8	275.4	245.4	366.5	326.1
6	9379.6	8530.8	41.8	33.9	256.0	226.0	333.8	313.9
7	7509.4	5022.0	31.6	25.4	230.9	198.7	302.6	278.5
9	6469.7	5194.0	29.3	28.1	201.2	186.2	296.0	275.8
10	5990.1	4813.5	28.0	23.2	185.1	175.2	289.0	268.9

Solutions from the local level are used to obtain the global solution. This is done through merging local level solutions. In each case when a cluster e-range calculated at the local level is fully covered by an e-range of another cluster from the local level and different location the former is absorbed by the latter. In all other cases the proposed procedure for the non-distributed clustering is run with all centroids, excluding the absorbed ones, being treated as objects which need to be allocated to clusters, the number of which is determined by using the average silhouette width technique.

4 Computational Experiment Results

To validate the proposed approach several benchmark instances have been solved. The proposed JABAT-based architecture has been used to solve four instances of four popular benchmark clustering, including Ruspini (75 objects; 2 attributes; natural dataset has originated from 4 clusters), Iris (150, 4, 3), Credit approval (690, 15, 2) and Cleveland heart disease (303, 13, 2) problems.

The results obtained by JABAT have been compared with the solutions produced by the k-means algorithm. In Table 1 values of the objective function for the non-distributed case and for different numbers of clusters are shown. It can be seen that the proposed agent based approach outperforms k-means algorithm.

Tables 2 shows the results for the non-distributed and distributed cases produced by JABAT and k-means algorithm. In Table 2 the clustering accuracy (CA), the number of clusters produced (NCP) and the square error of the cluster dispersion (SE) are compared. The distributed clustering instances have been produced by a random partition of each of the non-distributed instances into two datasets representing two locations. Clustering accuracy has been calculated through comparison with benchmark solutions.

Table 2: The clustering results as produced by the JABAT and the k-means

Algorithm	JABAT				k-means			
Attribute	Ruspini	Iris	Heart	Credit	Ruspini	Iris	Heart	Credit
	Non-distributed							
CA	100%	100%	100%	99%	100%	89%	93%	94%
NCP	4	3	2	2	4	3	2	2
SE	12881.1	74.4	338.2	528.6	12881.1	78.9	343.0	548.8
	Distributed							
CA	91%	83%	74%	82%	90%	71%	73%	78%
NCP	4	3	3	2	4	3	3	2
SE	29401.3	77.9	373.0	586.3	36164.6	142.6	461.2	802,6

5   Conclusion

Main contribution of the paper is seen as proposing an agent-based architecture which is scalable, interoperational, distributed and parallel, and which can produce good quality results when solving non-distributed and distributed instances of the clustering problem.

Agent-based clustering seems to be well suited to deal with the distributed clustering problems. Migration of JABAT agents is an easy and natural process and a local level clustering can be easily carried on sites where the data are stored. This would eliminate necessity of transferring data between sites and help in more effective use of the available computational resources.

Acknowledgements
The research has been supported by the KBN, grant no. 3T11C05928

References

[1] F. Bellifemine, G. Caire, A. Poggi, G. Rimassa. JADE. A White Paper, Exp, 2003, 3(3): 6-20.

[2] P. Jędrzejowicz & I. Wierzbowska. JADE-Based A-Team Environment, Lecture Notes in Computer Science, Springer Berlin/Heidelberg, 2006, 3993: 719-726.

[3] H. Kargupta, B.H. Park, D. Hershberger, E. Johnson. Collective Data Mining: A New Perspective Toward Distributed Data Analysis, Accepted in the Advances in Distributed Data Mining, H. Kargupta and P. Chan (Eds.), AAAI/MIT Press, 1999.

[4] Shichao Ahang, Xindong Wu, Chengqi Zhang: Multi-Database Mining, IEEE Computational Intelligence Bulletin, 2003, 2(1).

[5] A. Struyf, M. Hubert, P.J. Rousseeuw. Clustering in Object-Oriented Environment. Journal of Statistical Software, 1996, 1 (4): 1-30.

Transparency of Computational Intelligence Models

Peter Owotoki, and Friedrich Mayer-Lindenberg

Hamburg Harburg University of Technology (TUHH) Germany

{owotoki, mayer-lindenberg}@tu-harburg.de

Abstract

This paper introduces the behaviour of transparency of computational intelligence (CI) models. Transparency reveals to end users the underlying reasoning process of the agent embodying CI models. This is of great benefit in applications (e.g. data mining, entertainment and personal robotics) with humans as end users because it increases their trust in the decisions of the agent and their acceptance of its results. Our integrated approach, wherein rules are just one of other transparency factors (TF), differs from previous related efforts which have focused mostly on generation of comprehensible rules as explanations. Other TF include degree of confidence measure and visualization of principal features. The transparency quotient is introduced as a measure of the transparency of models based on these factors. The transparency enabled generalized exemplar model has been developed to demonstrate the TF and transparency concepts introduced in this paper.

1 Introduction

A recurring theme in popular culture is that of trust or the lack thereof for applications of artificial intelligence (AI). As depicted in films such as i,Robot, stealth, blade runner etc, intelligent agents (IA) may be nice to have and they may prove useful as personal/professional assistants or for other purposes, but one day they will turn around and behave in completely unpredictable ways with very dire and unforeseen consequences, hence they must be resisted. One reason for this lack of trust is because the decision making and reasoning processes of the IA are not transparent to end users. Among professionals it is not uncommon that AI systems are rejected for this same reason because many widely used computational intelligence (CI) models (e.g. artificial neural networks), which provide the cognitive abilities of IA, are notoriously opaque black box systems. They perform very well at intelligently approximating desired functions but provide to users little or no view into their underlying decision mechanisms and are opaque with regards to the employed reasoning processes.

This opacity of learning models is a major barrier that limits the widespread adoption of IAs both by professionals and in the general public. Because IAs will play a bigger role in managing the increasing complexity of our existence, it is imperative that existing and new CI models be made more transparent especially when embedded in applications where humans are the end users. To achieve this it is necessary to formalize the definition and description of the qualitative phenomenon of transparency; to identify the factors which constitute it; and to develop a metric for measuring this.

Our work provides a formal definition for transparency of CI models and presents the factors that determine it. The transparency enabled generalized exemplar (TEGE) model, which is a transparency constrained modification of Salzberg's NNGE method [1] has been realized to demonstrate these concepts of transparency.

2   Defining and Measuring Transparency

CI Models comprising the following computing paradigms – artificial neural networks or connectionist computing, fuzzy logic computing, evolutionary computing and machine learning methods [2] – enable agents to behave intelligently in a specified domain Λ defined as,

$$\Lambda \mapsto \{X^N, Y\}, X^N = \bigcup_i^N X_i, Y = M(X^N) \tag{1}$$

X^N is the input space defining the universal set of internal and environmental stimuli; Y is the output space and the universal set of responses from the IA. Function $M : X_i \rightarrow \{y_i\}$ is approximated by a CI model. Given new stimulus $X_i \in X^N$, the CI model M enables the IA to autonomously select the appropriate response y_i while taking existing constraints and biases into consideration. Normally the agent has been trained with a model of the domain consisting of varying degrees of domain knowledge and datasets of the stimuli/response pairs $\{(X_0, y_0), (X_1, y_1), \cdots (X_i, y_i)\}, \quad i < N$.

With regards to transparency, the decision process of an IA can be described as,

$$D = M(X_i), \quad D = \{y_{optimal}, T\} \tag{2}$$

Given the stimulus $X_i \in X^N$, use the CI model M to decide on the optimal response $y_{optimal}$ and give the tuple T of transparency factors which justify and explain the selection of $y_{optimal}$.

In opaque or black box systems T is the null tuple. There is neither any justification nor any form of explanation for the recommended action. The user is expected to take the decision of the agent in good faith. Typical black box systems perform very well on some metrics of accuracy during training and validation and based on this the user is expected to trust them to continue to perform well in real life and novel situations. In many domains users will demand and prefer more transparent systems to the opaque ones.

2.1 Transparency Quotient

The transparency of a CI model is determined by the elements of the transparency tuple T. We identify three transparency factors namely – comprehensible rules and explanations R, degree of confidence measure κ and visualization of the relationships between principal components or features V. In other words:

$$T = \{R, \kappa, V\} \tag{3}$$

A CI Model may implement some or all of these transparency features and the degree to which these features are implemented determine the transparency quotient $\sigma(M) \in [0,1]$ of the model which we define as:

$$\sigma(M) = \frac{|TFs\ implemented\ in\ CI\ Model|}{|T|} \tag{4}$$

CI Models with $\sigma(M) = 0$ are completely opaque models, whereas those with $\sigma(M) = 1$ are fully transparent based on the transparency factors in T (3).

3 Describing the Transparency Factors

Three transparency factors (TF) have been identified as shown in (3). It is expected that the number of TF will increase as more work is done on this interesting concept of transparency. Each of these factors is hereby discussed in more detail.

3.1 Comprehensible Rules and Explanations R

Production (IF–THEN) rules provide high level symbolic explanations of the decision process in a way that is comprehensible for humans. Modern AI systems use a multiplicity of CI models with diverse representations some of which easily map to rules and others which must be modified or hybridized before rules can be extracted from them. Examples of CI Models with representations from which rules can be extracted relatively easily include logic based systems; divide and conquer methods e.g. decision trees; instance based learning methods such as CBR and the nearest neighbor family of methods.

Other methods e.g. artificial neural networks have properties which make them desirable in many application scenarios but require substantial modifications before rules can be extracted from them. Three approaches can be used to achieve this:

The first approach involves post processing of a trained model in a process designed to simplify the extraction of rules from the weights or the properties of the trained model. An example of this approach for neural networks can be found in [3].

Another approach creates new transparency aware models whose representation can be mapped directly to production rules. One example is the Adaptive Resonance Theory (ART) [4][5], a neural network model with output that map easily to rules.

A final approach is to create a hybrid of the opaque model with another rules aware CI model e.g. a neurofuzzy system [6].

3.2 Degree of Confidence κ

This is a measure of confidence in the decision of the CI model that $y_{optimal}$ is the correct action chosen in response to the environmental stimuli X_i. It is a probabilistic value of accuracy for every decision process of the IA, i.e. $\kappa \in [0,1]$. As with rules, some CI models have representations that readily provide this degree of confidence measure e.g. Bayes based models and other probabilistic learning methods. Other models must use any of the three approaches described above for rules to generate κ. For example in evolutionary computing the degree of confidence measure can be derived by evaluation of the fitness of the individual chromosome.

In addition to increasing the transparency of a CI Model, the degree of confidence measure also improves the handling of uncertainties and the accuracy performance of the CI model due to the finer (fuzzier) degrees of its output.

3.3 Visualizations of Principal Features V

Visualization of data has been used to discover and understand underlying concepts, and to refine queries in data mining systems [7]. In scientific discovery to better understand complex phenomena, scientists routinely use visualization of datasets from the appropriate domain [8]. This ability to see the unseen [9] explains why visualization is one of the elements of our TF. Visualization can be achieved by visually representing the relationships between pairs of features or attributes of the input space X_i. In an n-dimensional feature space the number of visualizations is:

$$n \cdot (n-1)/2 \tag{5}$$

The implication of this in domains with large feature spaces is that the visualizations become cumbersome and incomprehensible leading to visual overload and defeating the concept of transparency. To avoid this, only important features of X_i are visualized. These relevant features can be selected by using some dimensionality reduction algorithm such as principal components analysis [10] or by weighting the relevance of the features to the learning process.

4   The Transparency Enabled Generalized Exemplars Model

The transparency enabled generalized exemplars (TEGE) Model has been developed to demonstrate the concept of transparency. It is based on a modification of the non nested implementation [11] of Salzberg's NNGE method. TEGE and NNGE classify new instances (examples or stimuli) according to the class of the nearest instance in memory or to the nearest exemplar which have been generalized and stored as axis parallel hyperrectangles in Euclidean n-space. The NNGE method has been shown [12] to perform comparably well to the k-nearest neighbor method widely used in many different applications. Stripped of its TF the TEGE model is equivalent to the NGE model. The TEGE model achieved maximum transparency quotient $\sigma(M) = 1$ by implementing all the TF in T (3).

Comprehensible Rules R : Rules were derived from the axis parallel hyperrectangles of the generalized exemplars as illustrated in figure 1.

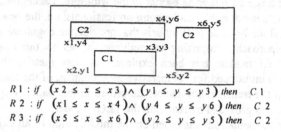

$R 1 : if \ (x 2 \leq x \leq x 3) \wedge (y 1 \leq y \leq y 3) \ then \quad C 1$

$R 2 : if \ (x 1 \leq x \leq x 4) \wedge (y 4 \leq y \leq y 6) \ then \quad C 2$

$R 3 : if \ (x 5 \leq x \leq x 6) \wedge (y 2 \leq y \leq y 5) \ then \quad C 2$

Figure 1 Boundaries of the Hyperrectangles of the input space with corresponding rules

Every exemplar corresponds to a rule with the antecedent part formed as a conjunction of n clauses, where n is the dimension of the hyperrectangle or the number of features. The class of the exemplar corresponds to the predicate of the rule.

Degree of Confidence κ : The degree of confidence was derived as a function of the distance of the stimulus X_i to the nearest instance or exemplar in memory.

$$\kappa = g(D_{EH}), \ D_{EH} = w_H \sqrt{\sum_{i=1}^{n} \left(w_i * df_i(E, H)\right)^2} \tag{6}$$

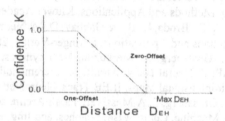

Figure 2 Trapezoid shaped confidence function

The confidence function g is a bounded regression over the distribution of the distance measures collected during training. The confidence function can also be realized with intelligent linear discrimination methods such as support vector machines, however in our experimentations, the trapezoid shaped function of figure 2 was found to provide acceptable results. In keeping with Ockham's razor we settled for this simpler function in our implementation.

Visualizations of Principal Features V : Ordering the weights of the features w_i (6) provides the basis for selecting the important features used for visualizations. The feature weights w_i were based on the mutual information between features and classes of the training dataset.

5 Conclusion

This paper addressed a lingering barrier to the widespread acceptance of intelligent agents (IA) in the general public and among professionals, i.e. the opacity of many of the computational intelligence (CI) models that provide the cognitive abilities of IAs. An integrated approach comprising of multiple factors to the novel concept of transparency of CI models has been explored. A new metric, the transparency quotient, has been introduced for comparative measurement of the transparency of CI models based on the transparency factors described in this paper. Implementation as proof of concept was provided by realizing the TEGE model.

The TEGE implementation was based on the modification of an existing CI model and making it transparency aware. Other implementations of transparency will require the creation of new hybrid models or the development of brand new transparency aware standalone CI models. The creation of these new models provides direction for further research on this exciting concept.

One current application area we are exploring is in the aircraft health monitoring domain. CI Models are used to monitor the health states of different cabin systems and the transparency features helps the maintenance crew to more easily accept the new technology, become familiar with it and also develop trust in its outputs.

References

1. Salzberg, S. A nearest hyperrectangle learning method. In Machine Learning 1991; 6(3): 251-276.
2. Zimmermann, H-J., Tselentis, G., Van Someren, M., & Dounias G. Advances in CI and Learning: Methods and Applications. Kluwer Academic Publishers, 2002
3. Garcez d'Avila, A. S., Broda, K. B., & Gabbay, D. M. Neural-Symbolic Learning Systems: Foundations and Applications. Springer-Verlag, 2002
4. Carpenter, G.A., Grossberg, S., Markuzon, N., Reynolds, J.H., & Rosen, D.B. Fuzzy ARTMAP: A Neural Netw. Archit. for Incremental Supervised Learning of Analog Multidimensional Maps. IEEE Trans. Neur. Netw. 1992; 3(5): 698-712
5. Carpenter, G. & Grossberg, S. A Massively Parall Archit. for a Self Orgnz. Neur. Pattern Recogn. Machine. Comp. Visn, Graphcs, and Img. Proc. 1987;37: 54-115
6. Tsakonas, A., Dounias, G., & Tselentis, G. Using Fuzzy Rules in Multilayer Percept. Neur. Netw. for Multiresolution Proc. Signals: A Real World Applic. in Stock Ex. Mark. In Proc. of Sym. on Comp. Intell., and Learning 2000; 154-170
7. Cooper, J.W. & Byrd, R.J.: Lexical Navigation: Visually Prompted Query Expans. and Refinem. In Proc. 2nd ACM Int'l Conf. Digit. Libr 1997; 237-246
8. Roussinov, D. & Ramsey, M. Inform. Forage through Adaptive Visualiz. In Proc. of the 3rd ACM Conference on Digital Libraries 303-304. Pittsburgh, PA. 1998
9. McCormick, B.H., DeFanti T.A. & Brown M.D. ed. Visualization in Scientific Computing, Computer Graphics 1987; 21:6
10. Joliffe, I.T. Principal Components Analysis. Springer-Verlag 1986
11. Martin, B. Instance-Based learning: Nearest Neighbor with Generalization. Master Thesis, University of Waikato, Hamilton, New Zealand 1995
12. Wettschereck, D. & Dietterich, T.G. An experimental comparison of the nearest-neighbour and nearest-hyperrect. algorithms. Machine Learning 1995; 19:5-27

Exploring Web Search Results Clustering

Xiaoxia Wang and Max Bramer
School of Computing, University of Portsmouth, UK
xiaoxia.wang@port.ac.uk, max.bramer@port.ac.uk

Abstract

As the number of documents on the web has proliferated, the low precision of conventional web search engines and the flat ranked search results presentation make it difficult for users to locate specific information of interest. Grouping web search results into a hierarchy of topics provides an alternative to the flat ranked list and facilitates searching and browsing. In this paper, we present a brief survey of previous work on web search results clustering and existing commercial search engines using this technique, discuss two key issues of web search results clustering: cluster summarisation and evaluation and propose some directions for future research.

1. Introduction

Traditional web search engines often return a long list of ranked links in response to user queries. Web users have to go through the long list to identify desired information. This problem gets worse as the web continues to grow. As pre-clustering of the entire corpus (e.g. Yahoo!) "would not be flexible enough to capture the themes of web search results" [5], there are many attempts using post-retrieval document clustering to bring the returned search results into order.

Clustering techniques can be used on search engines to organize retrieved results into a hierarchy of topics based on their similarities. This can help users both in locating desired information more easily and in getting an overview of the retrieved set [22]. The dynamic nature of search results introduces new challenges to document clustering technology. Zamir identified several key requirements of web search results clustering in [23]: Coherent clusters; Ease-of-browsing; Speed.

This paper is a brief survey of research trying to achieve the above key requirements. Section 2 gives an overview of work on web-based clustering techniques. Section 3 and 4 discuss two key issues of ephemeral clustering that have not been well addressed: search results clustering summarisation and evaluation. Section 5 points to future directions. An expanded version of this paper is available as [18].

2. Related work

Scatter/Gather [3] is the first to use clustering technique as a browsing tool in information retrieval. [22, 23] followed this paradigm and proposed the notion of search results clustering. They attempted to cluster "snippets" instead of full web documents. In their Grouper system, STC (Suffix Tree Clustering) treats a document as a string instead of a set of words. The two distinguishing features of STC are: linear time complexity; clustering documents according to shared phrases instead of word frequency. These make it "a substantial momentum" [20] of ephemeral clustering. The Carrot system [20] extended STC's application into Polish Language by using different stemming techniques. SHOC [25] is based on latent semantic indexing and designed to work in Chinese. Complete phrases and continuous cluster definition were introduced to overcome STC's limitations. LINGO [15] is a slightly modified version of SHOC. It identifies cluster labels first, and then assigns search results to different groups.

Other methods include combining links and content in a k-means framework [19]; using an N-gram based robust fuzzy relational algorithm in Retriever [9]. Microsoft [24] proposed a system to extract and rank salient phrases based on a regression model, which is trained by human labelled data, but the additional training phase is hard to adapt to the Web [6]. SnakeT [6] took advantage of two offline knowledge bases and attempted to extract sentences involving non-contiguous terms.

In addition to the above academic tools, there also has been a surge of commercial interest in implementing clustering techniques in (meta-) search engines: Vivisimo, Grokker, Clusty and Iboogie provide cluster hierarchies in addition to ranked list; Kartoo and Mooter use a network visualisation interface; Copernic and Dog-pile concentrate on supporting users on query formulation. Among the various clustering search engines, Vivisimo generates very well described thematic groups and can be considered a benchmark in current research [15], but this software is not publicly accessible. Much academic research attempts to address the search results clustering problem, but only SnakeT claims to achieve efficiency and efficacy performance close to Vivisimo.

3. Clusters summarisation

Within the field of IR, document clustering is also known as Automatic Taxonomy Generation (ATG). A key issue of ATG is how to generate appropriate labels for the hierarchical structure. ATG algorithms can be categorized into different types depending on if the taxonomies are generated by clustering words or documents, thus the process of generating clusters summarisation is also different.

3.1 Clusters-come-first approach

The traditional clustering methods such as K-means and AHC (agglomerative hierarchical clustering) fall into this category. The basic idea is representing documents as N-dimensional vectors of word frequencies, where N is the total number of distinct non-stop words in the whole document collection. Once the documents are converted into vectors, appropriate similarity measures and clustering algorithms can be chosen for clustering. Further details can be found in [4]. The set of top ranking words with high occurrence frequency within the cluster can be used as cluster summarisation. We briefly described STC algorithm in section 2. This algorithm is also based on clustering documents but captures shared phrases (contiguous terms) as labels of clusters instead of words with high frequency. The recently developed SnakeT system attempted using knowledge base to enrich the collection of words extracted from snippets to attain cluster labels. Approximate terms (involving non-contiguous terms) were extracted as hierarchy labels and attained a good performance.

From the above examples, we can see the approaches based on clustering documents form concept hierarchy by clustering documents first, then extracting terms from documents within the cluster as cluster summarisation. So it is a clusters-come-first approach and is also called polythetic clustering since the clusters are labelled by multiple concepts (terms).

3.2 Summarisation-come-first approach

The ATG algorithms based on clustering words focus on organizing words according to thesaural relationship [10]. Some are based on analysing the phrase in which a term occurs to infer the term relationships [7]. Some use phrasal analysis in addition to knowledge base to organize terms into a concept hierarchy [21]. A brief description of how they utilise different phrase analyse methods can be found in [16]. Some other methods using term co-occurrence to produce structure of related terms are surveyed in [10].

The approaches in this category first form a concept hierarchy by analysing the relationship between words, then assign documents to appropriate nodes (topics and subtopics). They are also called monothetic clustering as the cluster assignment is based on a single feature. Monothetic clustering is claimed to be well suited for generating hierarchies for search results because user can easily understand clusters described by a single feature [10]. But we believe there have been no formal experimental comparisons between monothetic and polythetic search results clustering, possibly due to the lack of standard evaluation measures in this application area.

There is another approach called co-clustering, which clusters words and documents simultaneously. The details of several examples (FCoDoK, FSKWIC, RPSA) are covered in [10].

4. Clustering evaluation

An important aspect of cluster analysis is the evaluation of clustering results. In this section we introduce the commonly used document clustering evaluation measures and briefly review ephemeral clustering evaluation in the literature.

Clustering results can be evaluated externally by comparing with pre-defined classes in several ways: purity, entropy and mutual information, which are defined in [2]. If a cluster is viewed as the result of a query for a particular category, the F-measure [17] can also be used to evaluate the document clustering results. Because the search results are generated dynamically, there are no predefined categories to compare with. One solution is to manually classify and assign labels to documents [14], or manually assign relevance judgement to each document [22] so that the effectiveness for information retrieval can be evaluated.

The second approach is based on internal criteria when ground truth is not available. Because the goal of clustering is to group a set of points into clusters so that points in the same cluster are more similar than points in different clusters [8], the clustering results can be evaluated by calculating the ratio of the average inter-cluster to intra-cluster distance. [1] proposed two criteria: compactness and separation, which reflect the inter-cluster and intra-cluster similarity. Additionally, how well the labels predict the cluster contents can be measured by Expected Mutual Information Measure (EMIM) [13].

There are also other methods involved in evaluating clustering hierarchy quality: [16] performed a user study to judge the quality of relationship between child and its parent nodes in the hierarchy. [12] also use parent-child pair in evaluation but they are only interested in how many common pairs are shared by two hierarchies. These are classified as relative evaluation measures because only similarity between two hierarchies is of interest in this scenario.

The research from IBM [11] combines the above measures to evaluate clustering hierarchy in terms of six desirable properties. They adopt *compactness* criteria from [1] and interpret separation as *sibling node distinctiveness*, which is more suitable for hierarchy evaluation. The idea of using *coverage* and *reach time* metrics was originally from [12, 13], but the first metric was called reachability in their work. The *reach time* metric measures how quickly a user can reach all relevant documents. *Node label predictiveness* and *general to specific* are difficult to quantify thus user study is used to rate the hierarchy.

5. Summary and future research

In this paper, we present an overview of web search results clustering approaches and discuss two important aspects: clusters summarisation and clustering evaluation. The dynamically generated search results introduce many challenges to clustering techniques. We propose some directions for future research. First, the goal of search results clustering is to provide an efficient searching and browsing tool for online use, thus necessitating accurate cluster summarization. SnakeT's performance makes us believe that using off-line information to aid clusters label extraction/generation is a promising research direction. Second, standard evaluation methods need to be developed so that the monothetic clustering and polythetic clustering algorithms can be compared under a general framework. How to choose suitable objective and subjective measures to make an effective combination in this application area remains an open question.

References

[1] Berry, A. and Linoff, G. (1997) Data Mining Techniques: For Marketing, Sales, and Customer Support, 1 ed., New York, USA, Wiley.

[2] Cover, T. M. and Thomas, J. A. (1991) Elements of Information Theory. Wiley-Interscience.

[3] Cutting, D. R., Karger, D. R., Pedersen, J. O. and Tukey, J. W. (1992) Scatter/Gather: a cluster-based approach to browsing large document collections. Proceedings of the 15th International ACM SIGIR Conference on research and development in information retrieval.

[4] Everitt, B. (1974) Cluster Analysis. London: Heinemann Educational (for) the Social Science Research Council.

[5] Ferragina, P. and Gulli, A. (2004) The Anatomy of a Hierarchical Clustering Engine for Web-page, News and Book Snippets. Technical report, RR04-04 Informatica, Pisa, Italy.

[6] Ferragina, P. and Gulli, A. (2005) A personalized Search Engine Based On Web-Snippet Hierarchical Clustering. Proceedings of the 14th International World Wide Web Conference.

[7] Grefenstette, G. (1994) Explorations in Automatic Thesaurus Discovery. Kluwer.

[8] Jain, A. K. and Dubes, R. C. (1988) Algorithms for Clustering Data. Prentice Hall, New Jersey.

[9] Jiang, Z. H., Joshi, A., Krishnapuram, R. and Yi, L. Y. (2002) Retriever: improving web search engine results using clustering. In Managing Business and Electronic Commerce.

[10] Krishnapuram, R. and Kummamuru, K. (2003) Automatic taxonomy generation: issues and possibilities. Proceedings of fuzzy sets and systems (IFSA), Volume 2715, pages 52-63. Springer-Verlag.

[11] Kummamuru, K., Lotlikar, R. and Roy, S. (2004) A Hierarchical Monothetic Document Clustering Algorithm for Summarization and Browsing Search Results. SIGIR'04.

[12] Lawrie, D. J. and Croft, W. B. (2000) Discovering and comparing topic hierarchies. Proceedings of RIAO conference, pages 314-330.

[13] Lawrie, D. J. and Croft, W. B. (2003) Generating Hierarchical Summaries for Web Searches. SIGIR'03, Toronto, Canada.

[14] Leouski, A. V. and Croft, W. B. (1996) An Evaluation of Techniques for Clustering Search Results. Technical report IR-76, Department of computer science, University of Massachusetts, Amherst.

[15] Osinski, S. (2003) An algorithm for clustering of web search results. Master Thesis. Poznan University of Technology, Poland.

[16] Sanderson, M. and Croft, W. B. (1999) Deriving concept hierarchies from text, Proceedings of SIGIR, pages 206-213.

[17] Van Rijsbergen, C. J. (1979) Information Retrieval. Butterworth-Heinemann Ltd

[18] Wang, X and Bramer, M. (2006), A review of web search results clustering. University of Portsmouth School of Computing Technical Report.

[19] Wang, Y. and Kitsuregawa, M. (2001) Link based clustering of web search results. Proceedings of the 2nd International Conference on Web-Age Information Management, Xi'An, P.R.China.

[20] Weiss, D. (2001). A clustering interface for web search results in Polish and English. Master Thesis, Poznan University of Technology.

[21] Woods, W. A. (1997) Conceptual Indexing: A better way to organize knowledge, a Sun Labs technical report: TR-97-61. Editor, Technical Reports, 901 San Antonio Road, Palo Alto, California 94303, USA.

[22] Zamir O. and Etzioni, O., (1998) Web document clustering: a feasibility demonstration. SIGIR 98, Melbourne, Australia.

[23] Zamir O. and Etzioni, O., (1999) Grouper: A dynamic clustering interface to web search results, Proceedings of the eighth international world wide web conference, Toronto, Canada.

[24] Zeng, H. J., He, Q. C., Chen, Z., Ma, W. Y. and Ma, J. W. (2004) Learning to Cluster Web Search Results. SIGIR'04, Sheffield, South Yorkshire, UK.

[25] Zhang, D. and Dong, Y. S. (2001). Semantic, Hierarchical, Online Clustering of Web Search Results. In ACM 3rd Workshop on Web Information and Data.

Case-based Intention Selection for Autonomous Agent that Acts in Structured Synthetic Worlds

Haris Supic

The University of Sarajevo, Bosnia and Herzegovina

haris.s@bih.net.ba

Abstract

This paper presents a new approach called stepwise case-based reasoning (SCBR) for intention selection. In this paper an agent that autonomously selects its intentions by using this approach is called an *SCBR agent*. An SCBR agent is an entity that selects the next intention based on previous interaction experience. An SCBR agent's interaction experience is represented in the form of two different types of cases: *plan cases and contextual cases*.

1. Introduction

Case-based reasoning (CBR) is a type of reasoning based on the reused past experiences called cases [1, 2]. In general, a case consists of *a problem*, *its solution* and *an outcome*. The basic idea of CBR is that the solution of successful cases should be reused as a basis for future similar problems [2]. A CBR system that continuously interacts with an environment must be able to autonomously create new situation cases based on its perception of the local environment in order to select the appropriate actions to achieve the current mission goal [3]. Laza and Corchado shows how to build deliberative BDI agents (*belief, desire, and intention*) using a case-based reasoning model [4]. Olivia et al. [5] also describe a framework that integrates CBR capabilities in a BDI architecture. The relationships between autonomous systems and CBR systems constitute the research reported in [6, 7, 8]. This paper describes a case-based approach to intention selection for an autonomous agent acting in 3D synthetic worlds. This approach is called stepwise case-based reasoning (SCBR).

Most synthetic worlds contain structures that remain static during the lifetime of an agent. These static structures represent local environments and each local environment represents a particular context. An SCBR agent that performs stepwise case-based reasoning is adequate for the synthetic worlds that contain identifiable configurations (structures) of the local environment. In this paper, types of identifiable local environments are called *contextual classes*. Furthermore, concrete examples of local environments are called *contextual instances*. Examples of contextual classes and contextual instances for the autonomous navigation tasks are illustrated in figure 1. An SCBR agent uses the two types of actions as follows: **internal actions for focusing of attention and external actions.**

Internal actions for focusing of attention. By applying this type of actions, an SCBR agent can autonomously create new contextual case that reflects changes in the environment. Formally, an action for focusing of attention f is an n-tuple

$f=(A_1, A_2, ...A_n)$ where A_i is a perception attribute, $i=1,2,...n$. A perception attribute is a relevant feature of the environment that is important for an SCBR agent's next intention selection. An action for focusing of attention is an abstract representation of an SCBR agent's internal action.

External actions. An external action a is an n-tuple $a= (v_1, v_2, ... v_p) \in R^p$ that represents manipulative actions selected by an SCBR agent that change state of the environment. For example, an SCBR autonomous navigation agent may have the defined an external action as three-tuple $a=(\Delta x, \Delta y, \Delta\theta)$ where Δx denotes the shift of an agent in X direction, Δy denotes the shift of an agent in Y direction and $\Delta\theta$ denotes the shift of an agent orientation.

2. Plan Cases and Contextual Cases

2.1 Intentions and Behavior Routines

The term intention denotes a determination to act in a certain way or to do a certain thing. In the model of the SCBR agent, there are two types of intentions: *plan intentions* and *contextual intentions*. Plan intentions are planned in advance at the beginning of the current mission due to the fact that the synthetic world contains certain static structures that do not change over time. This is an opposite of the contextual intentions. A contextual intention represents an SCBR agent's desire that is the most appropriate for the given contextual conditions. Contextual intentions will have to be left unspecified until the situation in which they are required arises and relevant perception attributes of the local environment can be determined by selecting an appropriate internal action for focusing of attention. Plan intentions and contextual intentions are in hierarchical relationships. An example of a plan intention for autonomous navigation tasks is *"exit-from-room"*. An example of a contextual intention is *"move-right-to-avoid-obstacle"*.

Behavior routines. Behavior routines are defined as n-tuples $b=(i_1, i_2, ...i_j, ...i_n)$, $1\le j \le n$, where the two types of n-tuples are possible. If all elements i_j, $1\le j\le$ n, in n-tuple denoted as b are *plan intentions*, then b is called *a plan behavior routine*. Furthermore, if all elements i_j, $1\le j\le$ n, in n-tuple b are *contextual intentions*, then b is called *a contextual behavior routine*.

2.2 Plan Cases

A plan case c_p is a *three*-tuple $c_p=(d_p, b_p, q_p)$ where: d_p is *a description component*, b_p is *a solution component*, and q_p is *an outcome component*. A description component d_p is an n-tuple $d_p = (c_1, c_2, ...,c_i,...c_n)$, $1 \le i \le n$, $c_i \in C$, where C denotes the set of all contextual instances. A solution component b_p is a plan behavior routine. An outcome component q_p is an n-tuple $q_p=(q_{p1}, q_{p2}, ...q_{pi}, ...q_{pn})$ where q_{pi} denotes a perception stimulus $q_{pi}=(v_1, v_2, ...v_j, ...v_k)$ that represents the distinctive states of the environment. An SCBR agent receives this perception stimulus as a consequence of a specific previously selected internal action for focusing of attention $f_{qp}=(A_{p1}, A_{p2}, ...A_{pi}...A_{pk})$, $i=1,2,...k$.

Here we show an example of a plan case $c_p=(d_p,b_p,q_p)$ from the autonomous navigation tasks in indoor environments. Figure 1 shows an indoor environment. An example of a plan case is $c_p=(d_p,b_p,q_p)$ where:

- $d_p=(R_1, H_1, L_1, H_2, L_2, R_2)$;
- $b_p=((exit\text{-}from\text{-}room,\ go\text{-}to\text{-}end\text{-}of\text{-}hallway,\ go\text{-}right,\ go\text{-}to\text{-}end\text{-}of\text{-}hallway,\ enter\text{-}to\text{-}room,\ go\text{-}straight)$;
- $q_p= (q_{p1}, q_{p2}, q_{p3}, q_{p4}, q_{p5}, q_{p6})$, where

  $q_{p1}=((8, 5.5, 1.57, 5.5),\ q_{p2}=(4,6,3.14,4.5),\ q_{p3}=(3,8,1.57,2.8),$
  $q_{p4}=(3,12,1.57,6),\ q_{p5}=(4,14,1.05,2),\ q_{p6}=(5,17,1.05,2).$

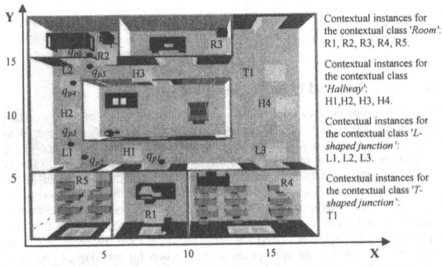

Figure 1: Example of an indoor environment. The figure shows contextual classes as follows: 'Hallway', 'Room', 'L-shaped junction', 'T-shaped junction'.

Here we assume that the internal action f_{qp} is defined as $f_{qp}=(X,Y,\ \theta,\ \Delta S)$ where:

- X,Y and θ denote perception attributes that represent x-coordinate, y-coordinate and the orientation of an SCBR agent relative to the X-axes, respectively;
- ΔS denotes the perception attribute that represents the distance an SCBR agent traversed from one contextual instance to other. For example, the interpretation of the perception stimulus $q_{p1}=((8, 5.5, 1.57, 5.5)$ is: $X=8$, $Y=5.5$, $\theta=1.57$, $\Delta S=5.5$.

2.3 Contextual Cases

A contextual case is a *three*-tuple $c_c=(d_c,b_c,q_c)$ where:

- d_c *is a description component of a contextual case* $d_c=(f, sp_f)$, *where f is an internal action for focusing of attention, and sp_f is a perception stimulus that an SCBR agent receives as a consequence of the previously selected action f;*
- b_c *is a contextualal behavior routine, and*
- q_c *is an outcome component of a contextual case.*

An outcome component of a contextual case is a perception stimulus that an SCBR agent receives as a consequence of a specific previously selected internal action for focusing of attention $f_{qc}=(A_{c1}, A_{c2}, ...A_{cn})$. Formally, an outcome component of a contextual case is $q_c=(v_1, v_2, ...v_i...v_n)$, $v_i \in D_{ci}$, $i=1,2,...n$, where D_{ci} is a domain of a perception attribute A_{ci}.

Here we show an example of a contextual case $c_c=(d_c, b_c, q_c)$. Formal specifications for the contextual case c_c are: $d_c=(f, sp_f)$, $f=(L,R,D,\theta R, \theta L)$, $sp_f=(1,2, 2, 0.5, 0.7)$, $b_c=(mrao, md)$, $q_c=(5,1)$. This example uses the following perception attributes: a distance from an obstacle to a left wall *(L)*, a distance from an obstacle to a right wall *(R)*, a distance from an obstacle *(D)*, an angle to a front-right corner of an obstacle *(θR)* and an angle to a front-left corner of an obstacle *(θL)*. The solution component b_c contains elements: *mrao (moving-right-to-avoid-obstacle)* and *md (moving-to-door)*. The meaning of the outcome component q_c is determined by internal actions for focusing of attention to the outcome of behavior routines. We will assume the following internal action for focusing of attention $f_{qs}=(\Delta S, \Delta T)$ where ΔS denotes the perception attribute that represents a distance, and ΔT denotes the perception attribute that represents a time interval. The outcome component $q_c=(5,1)$ of the contextual case c_c indicates the traveled distance $\Delta S=5$ by applying behavior routine b_c, and time interval $\Delta T=1$ it takes an SCBR agent to travel the distance ΔS.

Plan cases are used to support reasoning processes at plan abstraction level. As a result of reasoning processes at plan level an SCBR agent select an appropriate *plan behavior routine*. On the other side, contextual cases are used to support reasoning processes at contextual abstraction level. As a result of reasoning processes at contextual level, an SCBR agent selects appropriate contextual behavior routines.

3.   An Example of Navigation Task Execution

In order to evaluate the SCBR approach, we have developed a synthetic world for the autonomous navigation tasks in indoor environments. The synthetic world contains a model for synthetic vision similar to the one described in [9, 10].

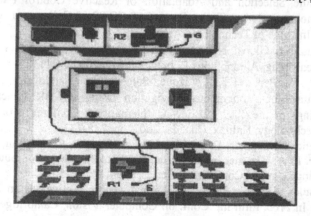

Figure 2: An example of navigation task execution.

402

Figure 2 illustrate an example of a navigation task execution. The SCBR agent is here commanded to go from the room R_1 to the room R_2. As the agent navigates this synthetic world, a line is drawn indicating the agent's progress from the start location (S) to the goal location (G). From the example it is obvious that the SCBR agent is successful in carrying out the navigational task.

4. Conclusion and Future Work

This paper describes an approach to the next intention selection based on case-based reasoning at the two abstraction levels: plan abstraction level and contextual abstraction level. This approach uses the two types of cases: plan cases and contextual cases. As an illustration of the SCBR intention selection approach, an example from autonomous navigation tasks in indoor environments is presented. From the behavior of the SCBR agent in the synthetic world it can be concluded that the SCBR approach can be an underlying approach for autonomous agent's intention selection. The next step in this line of research should concentrate on developing an appropriate indexing scheme for efficient case retrieval.

References

1. Aamodt, A., Plaza, E. Case-Based Reasoning: Foundational Issues, Methodological Variations and System Approaches. *AICOM,* 1994, 7(1):39-59
2. Kolodner, J.L. Case–Based Reasoning. Morgan Kaufmann Publishers, Inc., San Mateo, CA, 1993
3. Supic, H., Ribaric, S. Autonomous Creation of New Situation Cases in Structured Continuous Domains. Springer-Verlag, Heidelberg, 2005, pp. 537-551, (Lecture Notes in Computer Science no. 3620)
4. Laza R. and Corchado J. M. Creation of Deliberative Agents Using a CBR Model. Computing and Information Systems Journal, 2001, 8(2):33-39
5. Olivia, C., Chang, C.F., Enguis, C.F., Ghose ,A.K. Case-Based BDI Agents: An Effective Approach for Intelligent Search on the World Wide Web. AAAI Spring Symposium on Intelligent Agents in Cyberspace, CA: AAAI Press, 1999, pp. 20-27
6. Ram, A., Arkin, R.C. Case-Based Reactive Navigation: A Case-Based Method for On-line Selection and Adaptation of Reactive Control Parameters in Autonomous Systems. Tech. Rep. GIT-CC-92/57, College of Computing, Georgia Institute of Technology, Atlanta, USA, 1992
7. Kruusmaa, M. Global Navigation in Dynamic Environments Using Case-Based Reasoning. Autonomous Robots, Kluwer, 2003, 14(1):71 – 91
8. Urdiales, C., Perez, E.J., Vázquez-Salceda, J., Sandoval, F. A Hybrid Architecture for Autonomous Navigation Using a CBR Reactive Layer. Proceedings of the 2003 IEEE/WIC International Conference on Intelligent Agent Technology, Halifax, Canada, 2003, pp. 225-232
9. Tu, X. and Terzopouls, D. Artificial fishes: Physics, locomotion, perception, behavior. In A. Glassner, editor, Proc. SIGGRAPH 1994, Computer Graphics Proceedings, Annual Conferences Series, 1994, pp. 43-50
10. Terzopoulos, D and Rabie, T. Animat vision: Active vision in artificial animals. In Proc. Fifth Int. Conf. on Computer Vision, Cambridge, MA, 1995, pp. 801-808

On Clustering Attribute-oriented Induction

Maybin Muyeba[1]   M. Sulaiman Khan[1]   Zhiguo Gong[2]
[1]School of Computing, Liverpool Hope University, UK
[2]Faculty of Science and Technology, University of Macau, Macau, PRC
muyebam@hope.ac.uk, m_sulaiman78@yahoo.com , fstzgg@umac.mo

Abstract

Conceptual clustering forms groups of related data items using some distance metrics. Inductive techniques like attribute-oriented induction AOI) generate meta-level descriptions of attribute values without explicitly stated distance metrics and overall goodness functions required for a clustering algorithm. The generalisation process in AOI, per attribute basis, groups attribute values using concise descriptions of a tree hierarchy for that attribute. A conceptual clustering approach is considered for attribute-oriented induction where goodness functions for maintaining intra-cluster tightness within clusters, inter-cluster dissimilarity between clusters and cluster quality evaluation are defined. Attributes are partitioned into natural common parent concept clusters, their tightness, dissimilarity and quality computed for determining a cluster to generalise within the chosen attribute. This principle minimises over-generalisation and follows a natural clustering approach. Overall, AOI is presented as an agglomerative clustering algorithm, clusterAOI and comparative effectiveness with classical AOI analysed.

1. Introduction

Attribute-oriented induction (AOI) [1] is a data mining technique used to extract descriptive patterns from database data by generalisation. The generalisation consists of replacement of initial concepts (data in the database) with higher level tree hierarchy concepts for each attribute, dropping non-generalisable ones (tuple keys) and controlled y a user-supplied attribute threshold value. The highest value for any tree hierarchy is value "ANY". Interesting rules in AOI are reported in [2] as mainly those consisting of interior concepts. AOI can be viewed and presented as an agglomerative-hierarchical clustering technique [3]; and define some metrics for defining tightness and dissimilarity inside and between clusters respectively. In [3], several properties for solving any hierarchical clustering problem are addressed. We approach the problem by using a similar agglomerative-hierarchical approach, in section 2.

A basic distance metric based on a concept tree hierarchy is used in [3]. This assumes implicitly, similarity and dissimilarity metrics between concepts. Our approach utilises the same principle but enhances it explicitly by using heuristics as follows: Tightness T, for measuring concept similarity within clusters by natural groupings and evaluating distinct concepts in those clusters; distance D, where distinct concepts of any cluster are evaluated; interestingness F (cluster quality), where evaluation of interesting concepts in clusters uses a fuzzy membership function with defined concept tree metrics; goodness G, a function of T, D and F where T is implicit within D. Generally, interestingness of AOI is focused on complexity of concept trees by measuring depth and heights of nodes as a notion of distance but is not sufficient for our case. This paper provides a framework for clustering data using the AOI induction algorithm using some new metrics.

The paper is organised as follows: section 2 presents AOI as conceptual clustering; section 3 discusses experimental application; and section 4 concludes the paper.

2. AOI as Conceptual Clustering

Similar approaches for definitions and formulations for our problem are given in [4] but more clustering literature are given in [5][6]. One of the main differences is that we define our range set of all mappings as a version space. To evaluate cluster quality using tightness ($T_n(C)$) and distance ($D_n(C)$) of cluster C, we use an expression of goodness $G_n : (D_n(C), T_n(C)) \rightarrow \Re^+$. Tightness functions $\{T_n\}$ were defined as monotone non-increasing under generalisation i.e. for $c \leq c', T_n(c) \geq T_n(c')$, for a partial order on the set of all clusterings and so are inversely proportional to distinct values of concepts in the cluster. D_n was defined as the difference in attributes between clusters and decreases with every generalisation step. We argue that tightness functions are firstly monotone increasing and later decreasing at various points in the generalization process according to our redefined tightness functions. We propose to merge clusters based on concepts with nearest parent concepts (a natural grouping of concepts) rather than just a user threshold as in classical AOI.

Suppose a database D, expressed as leaf concepts $\phi^j{}_l$, with height l for each attribute j's concept hierarchy, where $\sum_{j=1}^{m} \phi^j{}_l = n = |D|$ has m attributes and n tuples. Assume also that a concept hierarchy H_j is defined for each attribute A_j, j=2,..,m, A_1 is a primary key attribute, and a prime relation contains p tuples after generalisation of v tuples. We shall use h clusters for attribute A_j as $\phi^j = \{\phi^j{}_0, \phi^j{}_1, ..., \phi^j{}_h\}$, where $\phi^j{}_i$ is a collection of common parent concepts within H_j, where for leaf concepts, h=n. We use the terms $\phi^j{}_i$ and $C^j{}_i$ interchangeably whenever convenient. So database values (known as *leaf concepts*) are the initial clusters $D = \{\phi^0{}_l, .., \phi^m{}_l\}$, where $H_j = \{\bigcup_{k=0}^{l} \phi^j{}_l\}$.

We have defined a mapping function $f()$ for mapping concepts to higher concept tree levels, distinct function counter $DIST()$, intra-cluster boolean function P for evaluating concept membership and boolean function I for evaluating if a concept is interior or not (all not shown in this paper due to lack of space). All other functions, for example intra-cluster and inter-cluster functions, derive from and use these functions. In AOI, a concept s of attribute A_j will be interesting if $s \notin \{\phi^j_i \cup \text{"ANY"}\}$, $1 \le j \le m$. The function for *intra-cluster tightness* is a boolean function $P(c,d)$ such that $\{\exists c, d \in \phi^j_i \mid P(c,d) = \{0,1\}, f(c) = f(d) \in \phi^j_{i-1}\}$. The function for inter-cluster dissimilarity also uses the function g above to qualify concepts belonging to a particular cluster (and thus disqualify them from others) and also uses the $DIST()$ function. The meaning of goodness is broken down into three categories: Intra-cluster (IntraC), inter-cluster (InterC) and cluster-quality (CQ) as :

$$Gn\,(C) = Gn\,(IntraC\,(C), InterC\,(C), CQ\,(C)) \tag{1}$$

$$IntraC(C) = \frac{\alpha}{\left| \bigcup_{i=1}^{k} C^j_i \right|}, \alpha = 1 \tag{2}$$

The tightness function T is accordingly $Tn\,(IntraC\,(C), InterC\,(C))$. Note that $\bigcup C^j_i$ is inversely proportional to the distinct values of a cluster and monotonically increases value. This union operator works well for generalisation as the smaller items (lower level) are included in the larger concept abstractions.

$$InterC\,(U) = \sum_{i=1}^{k} |C^j_i| - \left| \bigcup_{i=1}^{k} C^j_i \right| \tag{3}$$

Equation 3 gives the difference between clusters in $U = \{\bigcup C^j_i, 1 \le i \le k\}$ for attribute A_j. Note that InterC (U) value decreases as generalization proceeds. The fewer clusters we have the better the value for inter-cluster function, but this affects cluster quality up to some optimal value (see figure 1). Equation 4, which uses the distance metric of equation (5), determines the quality of cluster C^j ; and value "ANY" evaluates to 0. The higher the level of a concept, the more generalized it will be and its quality is high by equation (4).

$$CQ(C^j_i) = F_i(A, C^j_i) = \sum_{i=1}^{\left| \bigcup C^j_i \right|} (1 - \frac{d(c,\text{"ANY"})}{Level(\text{"ANY"})}), c \ne \text{"ANY"} \tag{4}$$

The interestingness value for clusters of concepts can not be predetermined by simply moving to the level just before "ANY" for each concept because of the diversity of parent clusters and combination of database attributes.

$$d(x, y) = | Level(x) - Level(y) | \qquad (5)$$

$$HM = \frac{n}{\sum\limits_{i=1}^{n} 1/x_i} \qquad (6)$$

To aggregate IntraC, InterC and CQ values, the harmonic mean (equation (6)), usually used in information retrieval, is used. Each x_i is a value calculated from functions 2, 3 and 4.

3. Experimental Application

In order to depict the frameworks usability, classical AOI and cluster AOI algorithms are compared. Consider table 1 and some predefined concept hierarchies for attributes "Colour" and "Diameter" of a Ball. The first generalization process determines common parent clusters for attribute 1 "Colour".

Table 1. Ball database

Colour	Diameter
Red	16
Red	2
Orange	7
Yellow	34
Green	25
Blue	28
Violet	8

Table 2. Classical AOI

Clusters ϕ^j_k	Cluster Quality	HM
$k=1$ Attrib 1	0.00	0.228
Attrib 2	0.00	
$k=2$ Attrib 1	0.99	0.76
Attrib 2	1.00	
$k=3$ Attrib 1	1.33	1.60
Attrib 2	0.0	
$k=4$ Attrib 1	0.00	0.00
Attrib 2	0.00	

Table 3. Cluster AOI

Clusters ϕ^j_k	Cluster Quality	HM
$K=1$ Attrib 1	0.00	0.88
Attrib 2	0.00	
$K=2$ Attrib 1	0.99	2.40
Attrib 2	1.00	
$K=3$ Attrib 1	1.32	2.46
Attrib 2	1.32	
$K=4$ Attrib 1	1.33	1.60
Attrib 2	0.00	
$K=5$ Attrib 1	0.00	0.00
Attrib 2	0.00	

For cluster $C^1_1 = \{red, red, orange\}$, $| \bigcup C^1_1 | = 2, | \bigcup C^2_1 | = 2$ and so on. To generalize attribute 1, traditional AOI replaces all cluster values with parent concepts but cluster AOI generalizes the largest cluster size to prevent unnecessary generalization. For InterC, low values are recorded as database concepts are not yet grouped into different parent clusters to start with. In table 2 and considering cluster 1 ϕ^j_1, cluster quality CQ will be zero as shown because there is no interestingness value derived from primitive values, similarly the value "ANY" is evaluated to "?" or zero. Note that in table 3, clusters ϕ^j_1 and ϕ^j_5 are less important than ϕ^j_2, ϕ^j_3 and ϕ^j_4, which have more interior concepts. Thus cluster values (figure 1(a) or table 3, column 3) are more relevant (not falling far below 1) for cluster AOI as compared to classical AOI (table 2, column 3). Also, for cluster quality evaluation (figure 1 (b) using equation (4)), cluster AOI can give better clusters but takes a few more generalisation steps. The results seem to suggest some notion of interestingness by our approach where classical AOI gives less interesting clusters. Performance of both methods needs to be tested with large data and concept hierarchies.

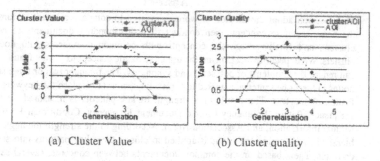

(a) Cluster Value   (b) Cluster quality

Fig. 1. Cluster Value and Cluster quality of clusterAOI and classical AOI

4. Conclusion

The paper has presented a framework for clustering attribute-oriented induction (AOI) algorithm by explicitly defining goodness functions, namely inter-cluster, intra-cluster and cluster quality. We conclude that because classical AOI works by generalizing values without cautiously determining interesting concepts (by clustering them), the new clustering approach can be more effective in overcoming the problem of overgeneralization and thus improves cluster quality and overall cluster value. Further experiments will consider generalisation order of attributes and use of larger data with more complex concept hierarchies. Other heuristic measures of interestingness will be investigated and compared with our approach.

References

1. Han, J., Cercone, N. & Cai, Y. Attribute-Oriented Induction in Relational Databases. G. Piatetsky-Shapiro & W. J. Frawley (eds), Knowledge Discovery in Databases, 1991, 213-228.
2. Fudger, D. R & Hamilton, J. A Heuristic for Evaluating Databases for Knowledge Discovery with DBLEARN, International Workshop on Rough Sets and Knowledge Discovery, Banff, Canada, October, 1993, 29-39.
3. Pitt, L. and Reinke, R. E. Criteria for polynomial-time (conceptual) clustering, Machine Learning", 1988, 2(4):371-396.
4. Heinonen, O. & Mannila, H. Attribute-Oriented Induction and Conceptual Clustering, Technical Report Report C-1996-2, University of Helsinki, 1996.
5. Jain, A., M. Murty, and P. Flynn. Data clustering: A review. ACM Computing Surveys, 1999, 31 (3), 264-323.
6. P. Berkhin. Survey of Clustering Data Mining Techniques, Accrue Software, 2002, [http://www.accrue.com/products/rp cluster review.pdf]

Chinese Text Clustering for Topic Detection Based on Word Pattern Relation

[1]Yen-Ju Yang, [2]Su-Hsin Yu,

Department of Information Management, Tatung University, Taiwan

{[1]yjyang@ttu.edu.tw, [2]g9312005@ms2.ttu.edu.tw}

Abstract

This research adopt the method of word expansion to compose relevant features into the same semantic concept, then conduct the corresponding documents to concept clusters, and finally merge the concepts with common documents into document clusters. We expect the mechanism, the use of semantic concept to form a feature index, can reduce the problems of polysemy and synonymy. The frequent two or three sequent nouns in the same sentence are used to form a key pattern to replace the keyword as the feature of the text. The distributive strength of key patterns is measured by Pattern Frequency, Pattern Frequency-Inverse Document Frequency, Conditional Probability, Mutual Information, and Association Norm. According to the strength the agglomerate hierarchical clustering technique is applied to cluster these key patterns into semantic concepts. Then, based on the common documents between concepts, several semantic concepts are merged to a group, in which the corresponding text will be considered as topic-related. The experimental results show that our proposed text clustering based on five strength measures of key patterns are all better than the traditional VSM clustering. PFIDF is the best in average F-measure, 97.5%.

1. Introduction

Information searching and news & magazines reading are the most common activities when people are surfing Internet nowadays. However, if the information responded by Internet does not assemble according to the topics, then the user needs to spend more time on distinguishing the topic of every search result. The problems of assembling the topic can be solved by clustering techniques[6][9] and vector space model[8] is a kind of document representation method before clustering. The weakness of this model applied to document clustering is its assumption, which states that there is no relation between features[2]; however, the words in natural language are not independent and irrelevant, some of the words always appear at the same time[2]. Therefore, this model using only word index to proceed with the matching to the text may result in the problem of word matching errors, since the polysemy[10] in the word relation will cause too much information retrieved; but synonymy[10] will cause too little information on retrieval.

In order to solve the above problem to promote the outcomes of text-topic clustering, we try to discover the co-occurrence relation between words by the method of word expansion, by which to extract the enhanced text features to reduce the problems of collocation, polysemy and synonymy. After the related features are clustered and viewed as semantic concepts, the corresponding documents will be found out.

2. Research Methodology

2.1 Algorithms

The words of Chinese nouns, Arabic numerals, and English are filtered through as the basic elements to further composed to text feature, and the frequent two or three sequent words are formed a key pattern, *2NP: Patterns formed by two sequent words (the words only include Chinese nouns, numbers, English)* and *3NP: Patterns formed by three sequent words (the words only include Chinese nouns, numbers, English).*

The research algorithm is as follow stages:

1. Input each document, then after word segmentation and tagging, 3NPs are selected.
2. If the frequency of 3NPs in document collection higher than the threshold value α will become Key 3NPs.
3. Use 3NPs as filtering elements, if the document does not contain any Key 3NP, then this document is considered as an independent cluster, which means that the topic only has one related document.

4. After documents are filtered by 3NP, the 2NPs will be extracted from these documents. If the frequency of 2NPs higher than the threshold value β will become Key 2NPs.
5. Calculate the strength of each Key 2NP in the text.
6. Use the strength to calculate the association between Key 2NPs.
7. Based on the Ward's method as clustering criterion, perform agglomerate hierarchical clustering technique on all Key 2NPs, and every formed pattern cluster will be considered as a semantic concept.
8. Each semantic concept corresponds to the documents that contain Key 2NPs.
9. Merge several semantic concepts into an identical cluster, each document cluster will be considered as a topic, and its documents are directly related to the topic.

Based on the algorithms, the system framework is divided into four modules that we describe them from section 3.2 to 3.5:

2.2 Key Patterns Extraction

The processes of Key Patterns Extraction include the Stage 1 to Stage 4, and the main function of this module is to extract the distinctive 2NP and 3NP. We use AutoTag 1.0 of CKIP to handle with the Chinese text segmentation. For example, "台灣捷安特躍居第二", it becomes "台灣(Nc) 捷安特(Nb) 躍居(VG) 第二(Neu)" after segmentation, "台灣,捷安特", and "捷安特,第二" are 2NPs, "台灣,捷安特,第二" is 3NP.

Filtering is needed after composing of Pattern in order to reduce the dimension of the feature, the threshold values that used in this research are $\alpha>=2$, $\beta>=2$, which means that the Key Pattern at least has to appear in two documents.

2.3 Key Patterns Relation Analysis

Key Patterns Relation Analysis mainly handles Stage 5 to Stage 6. The main function is analyzing the relation between Patterns, calculation of Pattern strength and indication of the relation between Patterns are the two major works.

2.3.1 Pattern Strength

Before proceeding with relation analysis, the distribution of each Key Pattern in each document is evaluated, and 5 measures are used.

❖ Pattern Frequency, PF

This frequency that Pattern appears in the text is considered as one kind of the strength. The more the Pattern appears, the higher the degree of repeat, and the stronger the strength[4].

❖ Pattern Frequency Inverse Document Frequency, PFIDF

Higher frequency words are not necessarily important, if one word has the highest numbers of appearance in all documents, then its ability on differentiating document category is lower, and weighted lesser. But if the numbers of appearance in a particular document is high, but appears very less in other documents, then its ability on differentiating document category is stronger, weighted greater[2]. We change the original words into Pattern in weighting Formula (2-1), where N is the number of documents in corpus; n_i is the number of documents that Pattern i appears; and $freq_{i,j}$ is the frequency of Pattern i appearing in the document j.

$$w_{i,j} = \frac{freq_{i,j}}{\max_m freq_{m,j}} \times \log \frac{N}{n_i} \qquad (2\text{-}1)$$

❖ Conditional Probability, CP

Pattern that is composed of same words will have different usage because of the context sequences and has different probability. This research also uses this kind of concept to calculate every Pattern's strength, the stronger the value, the stronger the co-occurrence of the two words in a Pattern. The formula is shown in (2-2).

$$\Pr ob_j(i_2 \mid i_1) = \frac{(\frac{freq_j(i_1,i_2)}{N_j})}{(\frac{freq_j(i_1)}{N_j})} = \frac{freq_j(i_1,i_2)}{freq_j(i_1)} \qquad (2\text{-}2)$$

i_1 and i_2 are the components of ith 2NP and j means jth document.

❖ **Mutual Information, MI**

Formula (2-3) calculates the mutual appearing frequency of two words i_1 and i_2 in the Pattern, if the value of MI is very high, represents that the chance of the pattern appear mutually is more than the chance of the pattern appear separately[3].

$$MI_j(i_1,i_2) = \frac{\operatorname{Prob}_j(i_1,i_2)}{\operatorname{Prob}_j(i_1) \times \operatorname{Prob}_j(i_2)} = \frac{\frac{freq_j(i_1,i_2)}{N_j}}{\frac{freq_j(i_1)}{N_i} \times \frac{freq_j(i_2)}{N_i}} = \frac{N_j \times freq_j(i_1,i_2)}{freq_j(i_1) \times freq_j(i_2)} \tag{2-3}$$

❖ **Association Norm, AN**

Lee[5] thought that using Mutual Information would be influenced by the length of the document, since different document lengths would bring unstable word frequency problem, which means that when the document has more words, the outcome of retrieval will be better; and vice versa. Association Norm can avoid this problem, so we also adopted. Its formula is shown in (2-4).

$$AN_j(i_1,i_2) = \frac{\operatorname{Prob}_j(i_1,i_2)}{\operatorname{Prob}_j(i_1) + \operatorname{Prob}_j(i_2) - \operatorname{Prob}_j(i_1,i_2)} = \frac{(\frac{freq_j(i_1,i_2)}{N_j})}{(\frac{freq_j(i_1) + freq_j(i_2) - freq_j(i_1,i_2)}{N_j})} \tag{2-4}$$

2.3.2 Patterns Association

Attar et al. [1] used the association method in English word stems, here this method is developed to calculation of the association between Pattern(Key 2NP) and Pattern(Key 2NP). The main concept of using this method is originated that two Patterns with similar neighborhood should possess with certain synonymity relationship.

First, a Pattern Vector Space Model is constructed for the Key 2NP in document collection; this vector space is represented by a matrix with Row K and Column T, which means that in this document collection there are K number of Patterns and T number of documents in total. Each element $m_{i,j}$ in matrix M, is the strength of Pattern in each document referred to the five evaluation in sub section 2.3.1.

Next, the association matrix C between Patterns is further generated, the idea of this association matrix is from the Association cluster of Attar et al. [1][2]. The Matrix C is Matrix M times its transpose matrix, $C=MM^T$ in Formula (2-5), where $c_{u,v}$ is the association factor of Pattern u and Pattern v; $m_{pu,j}$ is the strength of Pattern u in Document j ; $m_{pv,j}$ is the strength of Pattern v in Document j.

$$c_{u,v} = \sum_{d_j \in D_l} m_{p_u,j} \times m_{p_v,j} \tag{2-5}$$

Association factor $c_{u,v}$ quantifies the degree of association between Patterns, but without normalization, so Formula (2-6) is used to normalize association factor $c_{u,v}$ into [0, 1]

$$A_{u,v} = \frac{c_{u,v}}{c_{u,u} + c_{v,v} - c_{u,v}} \tag{2-6}$$

Finally, in order to compare the neighborhood relationship between two Patterns, another Matrix S is constructed. Extract all the association values in Vector Pu, and Vector Pv, use of cosine coefficient of angle between two vectors to proceed with similarity measure as shown in Formula (2-7). Therefore the synonymity relationship between two Patterns is conducted by neighborhood,

$$s_{u,v} = \frac{P_u \bullet P_v}{|P_u| \times |P_v|} \tag{2-7}$$

$P_u = (A_{u,1}, A_{u,2}, ..., A_{u,K})$ = The Association Vector Value of Pattern u

$P_v = (A_{v,1}, A_{v,2}, ..., A_{v,K})$ = The Association Vector Value of Pattern v

2.4 Key Patterns Clustering

The process of Key Pattern Clustering includes the Stage 7, after obtaining the synonymity relation matrix of patterns; this module is responsible to group Patterns into different clusters. Punj and

Stewart[7] have pointed out that Ward's method is the methods with better outcomes in hierarchical clustering; therefore this research chooses Ward's method to group the Patterns.

The main spirit of Ward's Method lies in the fact that the variation in the clusters can become the smallest [7], for example, at the beginning there are five Patterns and need to be partition into four clusters, then there will be ten combinations, these ten combinations each uses the sum of the square of the distance to average in Formula (2-8), and each gets the variation value in total clusters, the composition with smallest variation value is the best result.

$$ss = \sum_{i=1}^{n} \sum_{j=1}^{m} (x_{ij} - \overline{x_i})^2 \tag{2-8}$$

x_{ij} is the value of Pattern j in cluster i, $\overline{x_i}$ is the mean of all patterns in cluster i, $\sum_{j=1}^{m}(x_{ij} - \overline{x_i})^2$ means the variation in cluster i, m is the number of Patterns in cluster i, and n is the number of clusters.

As to the number of clusters n at this stage, we set to $n = N\text{-}Cs$, the number of documents in original corpus N subtracting the number of documents that has already been separated as single cluster Cs. This means the highest number that Patterns being clustered, since each document will at least be allocated to one cluster in the future, so this number of clusters is the most largest possible topic number in clustering documents, and the agglomerated process can end earlier.

2.5 Texts Clustering

The process of texts clustering is included in the Stage 8 to 9, the main purpose is to combine several semantic concepts into one topic. After the semantic concepts clustered in Stage 7, Stage 8 conducts each semantic concept to its corresponding document, the corresponding principles are as follows: (1)*The document belongs to a particular semantic concept:* If one certain document contains two or more Key Patterns belonged to the same concept, then the concept includes this document. This method is similar to document classification; it uses Key Patterns as attributes to classify the documents. **Under this situation one document may be fall into several concepts.** (2) *The document does not belong to any semantic concept:* If the Key Patterns of document unable to appear two or more Key Patterns in any clusters, and result in this document unable to allocate to any cluster, then this document becomes independent and forms a new cluster by itself, which means that the only document in a new topic.

Since one topic may contain several semantic concepts, then in Stage 9 based on common documents to proceed with concept merging [11]. In our early experiment shows that the limitation in [11] is stricter, which leads to concept clusters cannot be combined, and then influences the documents in same topic scattered into different clusters and decrease the recall rate, so in the follow-up experiment changes the r value in Formula (2-9). When the ratios of the intersection to the two clusters are both greater than r, then the similarity will be 1 and merging is granted.

$$similarity(B_1, B_2) = \begin{cases} 1, & iff(|B_1 \cap B_2|/|B_1|) > \gamma \quad and \quad (|B_1 \cap B_2|/|B_2|) > \gamma \\ 0, & otherwise \end{cases} \tag{2-9}$$

$|B_1|$ and $|B_2|$ are the number of documents in cluster B_1 and B_2. $|B_1 \cap B_2|$ means the number of intersection of documents between two clusters. r is reduced to 0.4.

3. Experiments and Results

About the experimental corpus, we use *Spider* to randomly collect the online news from Google News Taiwan BETA (http://news.google.com.tw) from February 20 to March 30, 2006, which includes Taiwan, business, technology/science, sports, blend1 and blend2. The blend1 includes four types of news – Taiwan, business, technology/science, and sports. The blend2 includes five types of news – Taiwan, business, technology/science, and international. In order to understand the text clustering quality of our presented methodology, the comparison of experimental results and the related news with same topic from Google News is performed, and the evaluation standard is the use of Recall and Precision in IR domain. Average Recall, Average Precision and Average F-measure are calculated among all data topics in Google News.

The number of documents and topics for each news category are listed in Table1. The traditional document clustering by Vector Space Model is the baseline in Table 2. The average F-measure for the five measures of pattern strength in each category can reach 91.2% or more, especially in business news, the five methods can all make average F-measure reach 100%. For the average of total categories, the average F-measures for the five methods can all reach 95.5% or more, the best situation is PFIDF that reaches 97.5%, while the VSM only have 87.89%, that is the increasing rate of our method achieves 11%. The worst cases are occurred in blend1 and blend2, since the documents are non-homogeneous. Figure1 is the result of average Recall, Precision and F-measure.

Table 1: The Number of Documents and Topics for Each News Category

Number \ Category	Business	Tech/Sci	Sports
# document	7	17	20
# topic	3	3	6
Number \ Category	Taiwan	Blend1	Blend2
# document	101	157	251
# topic	31	46	57

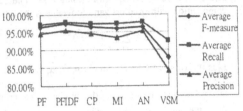

Figure 1: Performance of the experiment

Table 2: The Average F-measure

Strength \ Category	Business	Tech/Sci	Sports	Taiwan	Blend1	Blend2	Average
PF	100.00%	95.65%	99.07%	94.28%	94.60%	95.59%	96.53%
PFIDF	100.00%	100.00%	100.00%	93.77%	96.11%	95.10%	97.50%
CP	100.00%	95.65%	99.07%	93.92%	95.99%	94.27%	96.48%
MI	100.00%	95.65%	100.00%	94.99%	93.85%	91.20%	95.95%
AN	100.00%	95.65%	100.00%	94.23%	95.36%	94.05%	96.55%
VSM	100.00%	100.00%	86.18%	81.41%	81.20%	78.55%	87.89%

4. Conclusion

In this paper the feature based on word pattern replaces the traditional keyword is addressed, and make use of PF, PFIDF, CP, MI, AN to evaluate the relationship between Patterns, and then hierarchical clustering is used to group patterns with synonymity relationship to reach the purpose of semantic concept clustering. At last merging several concepts with common documents into the same topic so as to achieve topical text clustering. The experimental result shows that all five measures of pattern strength are all better than the traditional VSM clustering method.

In viewing the topic that is wrongly clustered, the first and the most serious problem is because some 2NPs involve in several topics, therefore when it comes to the final concept merging stage, several topics may easily merge into one topic and then affect Precision. The second factor that affects recall and precision is because some subjects in the classification of Google News are ambiguous. Integration of the above conclusion, the prospective direction is to find out conscientious, careful, and suitable merging rule. We also hope increasing testing documents and different forms of testing collections such as English corpus, which is one of the important jobs to verify our presented research method is reliable and robust, but in the mean time the other faster and suitable clustering methods for large corpus should be tried as well.

Reference

1. Attar, R.; Fraenkel, A.S. Local Feedback in Full-Text Retrieval Systems. Journal of the ACM 1977, 24 (3), 397--417.

2. Baeza-Yates, R.; Ribeiro-Neto, B. Modern Information Retrieval; Addison Wesley, 1999.

3. Church, K.W.; Hanks, P. Word Association Norms, Mutual Information, and Lexicography. Computational Linguistics 1990, 16 (1), 22-29.

4. Fragos, K.; Maistros, Y.; Skourlas:, C. Discovering Collocations in Modern Greek Language. In Proceedings of 1st International Conference on Natural Language Understanding and Cognitive Science: Porto, Portugal, 2004, 151-158.

5. Lee, C.-M. Vector Information Retrieval Technique with Word Bigram Relation Model. Master Thesis, Department of Information Management, Tatung University, 2004.

6. Lin, S.-C. Topic Extraction Based on Techniques of Term Extraction and Term Clustering. Computational Linguistics & Chinese Language Processing 2004, 9, 97-111.

7. Punj, G.; Stewart, D.W. Cluster Analysis in Marketing Research: Review and Suggestions for Application. Journal of Marketing Research 1983, 20 (2), 134-148.

8. Salton, G.; Wong, A.; Yang, C.S. A Vector Space Model for Automatic Indexing Commun. ACM 1975, 18 (11), 613-620.

9. Seo, Y.-W.; Sycara, K. Text Clustering for Topic Detection, CMU-RI-TR-04-03; Robotics Institute, Carnegie Mellon University, 2004;

10. Steels, L.; Kaplan, F.; McIntyre, A.; Looveren, J.V. Crucial Factors in the Origins of Word-Meaning; Oxford University Press: Oxford, 2002.

11. Zamir, O.; Etzioni, O. Web Document Clustering: A Feasibility Demonstration. In Proceedings of the 21st annual international ACM SIGIR conference on Research and development in information retrieval: Melbourne, Australia 1998;Vol. 6. 46-54.

Text Classification using Language-independent Pre-processing

Yanbo J. Wang, Frans Coenen, Paul Leng, Robert Sanderson
Department of Computer Science, The University of Liverpool
Liverpool L69 3BX, United Kingdom
{jwang, frans, phl, azaroth} @ csc.liv.ac.uk

Abstract

A number of language-independent text pre-processing techniques, to support multi-class single-label text classification, are described and compared. A simple but effective statistical keyword identification approach is proposed, coupled with a number of phrase identification mechanisms. Experimental results are presented.

Keywords: Text Mining, Multi-class Single-label Text Classification, Text Pre-processing.

1. Introduction

In this paper we present and compare a number of approaches to text pre-processing for multi-class single-label text classification that operate in a language-independent manner. Rule-based classification systems operate, in general, by deriving a set of classification rules from a training set of previously-classified data: in this case, text documents. In the work described here, we apply a Classification Association Rule Mining (CARM) algorithm to derive these rules. CARM methods require each record in the training set to be expressed in the form of a set of binary-valued attributes, from which predicates for classification rules are formed.

The aim of the work described is to examine ways in which these textual attributes can be defined. We consider both single-word attributes (keywords) and phrases, defined in several ways. We wish to identify strategies that can be applied statistically, without deep analysis of the linguistic structure of the documents, and so will be essentially language-independent.

The following section describes some related works in text pre-processing for text classification. In section 3 we introduce a number of approaches we have considered for the identification of keywords and phases. In section 4 we present experimental results obtained using the TFPC (Total From Partial Classification) CARM algorithm [1], and in section 5 discuss our conclusions from this analysis.

2. Related Work

In theory, the textual attributes of a document could include every word / phrase which might be expected to occur in a given document set. However, this is computationally unrealistic, so we require some method of pre-processing documents to identify the *key* words and phrases that will be useful for classification. Various techniques have been proposed to identify keywords within document sets such as Hidden Markov Models [2], Naïve Bayes [8] and Support Vector Machines [4]; however these all tend to make use of specific language-dependent meta-knowledge. Other methods use statistical information, such as word frequency. A well-known technique is the TF-IDF weighting (Term Frequency - Inverse Document Frequency) where TF is the number of occurrences of a given term in a given document and IDF is a measure of the total number of documents in a document set compared to the number of documents containing a given word [9]. Related techniques which include other statistical information derived from the document set have also been proposed in recent years (i.e., information gain [10], odds ratio [7], CORI [3], etc.) which improve the effectiveness of the approach.

3. Keyword and Phrase Extraction

The approach described here commences by processing each document (d) in the document base (D) to identify the "words" in it. The resulting collection of words is stored in a binary tree, in which each word is stored together with the identifiers of the documents in which it appears and its support value (S), i.e. the number of documents that contain the given word. Four types of word are identified:

1. **Stop marks:** Not actual words, but the punctuation marks ('!', ',', '.', ':', ';' and '?'),
2. **Noise words**: Words whose support is above / below user defined Upper / Lower Noise Thresholds (*UNT / LNT*) and which are therefore unlikely to prove significant. Noise words are thus either very common words that appear frequently across the document base or very rare words that appear in very few documents.
3. **Ordinary words (non-significant words)**: Non-noise words that do not serve to distinguish between classes.
4. **Significant words**: Keywords that do serve to distinguish between classes.

To identify significant words, we calculate, for each word (w) and class (C), the *contribution* made by w to C, defined as (proportion of documents in C that include w) / (proportion of all documents that include w). *Contributions* greater than 1 indicate that w may be a significant word for classifying C. We identify significant words as those whose *contribution* exceeds a significance threshold value (G) for at least one class.

Key phrases are then sequences of words that include at least one significant word. A number of different schemes for defining phrases can be identified depending on: (i) what are used as *delimiters* and (ii) what the *contents* of the phrase should be made up of:

1. **Delimiters: stop marks and noise words, Contents: significant and ordinary words (DelSN-contGO).** Phrases are made up of sequences of one

or more significant words and ordinary words, including at least one significant word.

2. **Delimiters: stop marks and ordinary words, Contents: significant and noise words (DelSO-contGN).** The rationale here is that there are many noise words which are used to link important words into a short, significant phrase, and so should not be treated as delimiters.

3. **Delimiters: stop marks and noise words, Contents: significant and "wildcard" words (DelSN-contGW).** As 1 but replacing ordinary words in phrases by wild card symbols that can be matched to any single word.

4. **Delimiters: stop marks and ordinary words, Contents: significant and "wildcard" words (DelSO-contGW).** As 2 but replacing noise words in phrases by wild card characters.

4.   Experimental Results

For our experiments three document sets were used:

- The Reuters-21578 set[1] of 21,578 news documents. Following the practice of many researchers (for example [6]), we use only the 10 most popular classes, and considered only those documents uniquely placed in one of these. As a consequence two classes were dropped as they had very few documents associated with them, leaving 6,643 documents. We refer to this data set as Reuters.D6643.C8.

- The USENET (20 NEWSGROUP) set[2] [5]. There are exactly 1,000 documents per group (class) with the exception of one class that contains only 997. Due to efficiency issue, we randomly split this data into two document sets, each of 10 classes: NG.D10000.C10 and NG.D9997.C10.

A chosen document set is divided into a training set and a test set. The training set is processed to identify words and phrases, which are then used to recast all documents in the set as bags of words / phrases. From this, a text classifier is generated using TFPC, although in principle any general classification algorithm could be used. The accuracy of the resulting classifier is determined using tenfold cross-validation.

Initial experiments examined the four methods outlined above for defining key phrases; the selection of values for the *UNT*, *LNT* and *G* thresholds; and variations in the support and confidence thresholds used in the application of the CARM algorithm. In these experiments, the Del-SN algorithms (using stop marks and noise words as delimiters) performed significantly better than the alternatives. In general, and consistent with general Association Rule Mining (ARM) experience, we found a low support threshold (0.05-0.15%) worked best, and also a relatively low confidence threshold of around 35%. It was also found that a low *LNT* (of about

---

[1]   http://www.daviddlewis.com/resources/testcollections/reuters21578/
[2]   http://www.cs.cmu.edu/afs/cs/project/theo-11/www/native-bayes/20_newsgroups.tar.gz

0.2%) was also beneficial to ensure that potentially significant words were not omitted.

Varying the other parameters was more problematic, partly because, for implementational reasons, it was necessary to limit the number of attributes (phrases) to 2^{15}. Because the three threshold parameters all influence the number of phrases generated, this limit was sometimes reached without identifying words and phrases that are significant in some classes. For this reason, a final set of experiments was conducted that refined the approach for identifying significant words. These experiments, focussed on the **DelSN-contGO** algorithm, began by identifying significant words for each class, placing these in order of their *contribution* to that class. The final selection of significant words was then made so that each class has an equal number n, i.e. the n words with the highest *contribution* to the class. Some results using the NG.D10000.C10 document set are given in Figure 1. Best accuracy is obtained with an *UNT* of 7% and a support of 0.05%.

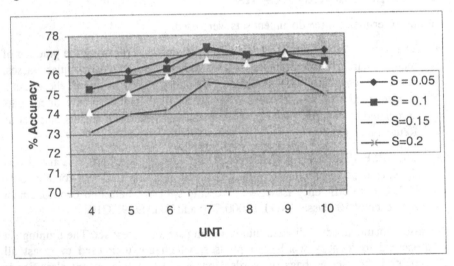

Figure 1 Accuracy obtained for a range of support and *UNT* values (confidence= 35%, *LNT*=0.2%, *G*=3, max # significant words=1500) for NG.D10000.C10

5.   Conclusions

We have described here an approach to text classification that is based on a pre-processing of documents to identify significant words and phrases to be used as attributes in the classification algorithm. The methods we describe use simple numerical measures to identify these attributes, without the need for any deep linguistic analysis. Preliminary experiments have indicated values required for the threshold parameters to give best results. In future work, we intend to use the framework described to investigate other ways of defining phrases, and to determine optimal parameter values.

References

1. Coenen, F., Leng, P. & Zhang, L. Threshold tuning for improved classification association rule mining. In: Ho, T.B., Cheung, D. & Liu, H. (ed) Proceedings of the 9th Pacific-Asia Conference on Knowledge Discovery and Data Mining (PAKDD 2005), Hanoi, Vietnam, 2005 (LNAI 3518, Springer, pp. 216-225)
2. Collier, N., Nobata, C. & Tsujii, J. Extracting the names of genes and gene products with a hidden markov model. In: Proceedings of the 18th International Conference on Computational Linguistics (COLING 2000), Saarbrücken, Germany, 2000 (pp. 201-207)
3. French, J.C., Powell, A.L., Callan, J., Viles, C.L., Emmitt, T., Prey, K.J. & Mou, Y. Comparing the performance of database selection algorithms. Technical report CS-99-03, Department of Computer Science, University of Virginia, January 1999
4. Kazama, J., Makino, T., Ohta, Y. & Tsujii, J. Tuning support vector machines for biomedical named entity recognition. In: Proceedings of the ACL (Association for Computational Linguistics) Workshop on Natural Language Processing in the Biomedical Domain (ACL 2002), Philadelphia, PA, USA, 2002 (pp. 1-8)
5. Lang, K. Newsweeder: learning to filter netnews. In: Proceedings of the 12th International Conference on Machine Learning (ICML 1995), Tahoe City, California, USA, 1995 (pp. 331-339)
6. Li, X. & Liu, B. Learning to classify texts using positive and unlabeled data. In: Proceedings of the 18th International Joint Conference on Artificial Intelligence (IJCAI-03), Acapulco, Mexico, 2003 (pp. 587-594)
7. Mladenic, D. & Grobelnik, M. Word sequences as features in text-learning. In: Proceedings of the 7th Electrotechnical and Computer Security Conference (ERK 1998), IEEE Region 8, Slovenia Section IEEE, Ljubligana, Slovenia, 1998 (pp. 145-148)
8. Nobata, C., Collier, N. & Tsujii, J. Automatic term identification and classification in biological texts. In: Proceedings of the 5th Natural Language Pacific Rim Symposium (NLPRS 1999), Beijing, China, 1999 (pp. 369-375)
9. Spärck Jones, K. Exhaustivity and specificity. Journal of Documentation 1972; 28:11-21 (reprinted in 2004; 60:493-502)
10. Yang, Y. & Pedersen, J.O. A comparative study on feature set selection in text categorization. In: Proceedings of the 14th International Conference on Machine Learning (ICML 1997), Nashville, TN, USA, 1997 (pp. 412-420)

AUTHOR INDEX